A HISTORY OF
THE WORLD

Andrew Marr

A HISTORY OF
THE WORLD

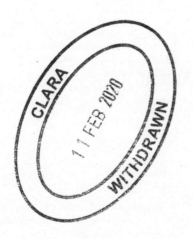

MACMILLAN

First published 2012 by Macmillan
an imprint of Pan Macmillan, a division of Macmillan Publishers Limited
Pan Macmillan, 20 New Wharf Road, London N1 9RR
Basingstoke and Oxford
Associated companies throughout the world
www.panmacmillan.com

ISBN 978-0-2307-5595-6 HB
ISBN 978-0-230-76430-9 TPB

Typeset by Ellipsis Digital Limited, Glasgow
Printed and bound by CPI Group (UK) Ltd, Croydon, CR0 4YY

Visit www.panmacmillan.com to read more about all our books
and to buy them. You will also find features, author interviews and
news of any author events, and you can sign up for e-newsletters
so that you're always first to hear about our new releases.

For Harry, Isabel and Emily

Russia

Finland

Poland

Ukraine

Kazakhstan

Mongolia

Turkey

Georgia

Uzbekistan
Kyrgyzstan

Turkmenistan
Tajikistan

China

North
Korea

South
Korea

Japan

Greece

Syria
Lebanon
Israel

Iraq

Iran

Afghan.

Pakistan

Nepal

Bh.

Bang.

Burma

Taiwan

Egypt

Saudi
Arabia

Oman

Yemen

India

Laos

Thailand

Cam. Vietnam

Philippines

Chad

Sudan

Eritrea

Dj.

Sri
Lanka

Brunei

Malaysia

C. A. R.

South
Sudan

Ethiopia

Uganda

Kenya

Somalia

Indonesia

Papua New Guinea

Solomon
Islands

Democratic
Republic
of Congo

Rw.
Bu.

Tanzania

Angola

Zambia

Malawi

Vanuatu

New
Caledonia

Fiji

Namibia

Botswana

Zimb.

Mozambique

Madagascar

Mauritius
Réunion

Australia

South
Africa

Sw.

New
Zealand

SAUDI ARABIA   BAHRAIN
Egypt   QATAR
Libia   SOUTH Yemen
Algeria   UAE
Tunisia   OMAN
Morocco   DJIBOUTI
Mauritania
WESTERN SAHARA
MALI
NIGER
CHAD
SUDAN
ERITREA
ETHIOPIA
Somalia

KAZAKH
KRGY
TAJIK
AFGH
UZBEK
TURKMEN
IRAN
Turkey
IRAQ
Syria
Kuwait
UAE
OMAN
YEMEN
JORDAN

PAKISTAN
BAGLADESH
INDONESIA

Contents

Acknowledgements xi

Introduction xiii

Part One
OUT OF THE HEAT, TOWARDS THE ICE
1

Part Two
THE CASE FOR WAR
51

Part Three
THE SWORD AND THE WORD
109

Part Four
BEYOND THE MUDDY MELTING POT
183

Part Five
THE WORLD BLOWS OPEN
249

Part Six
DREAMS OF FREEDOM
307

Part Seven

CAPITALISM AND ITS ENEMIES

385

Part Eight

1918–2012: OUR TIMES

467

Notes 567

Bibliography 581

Index 591

Picture Acknowledgements 613

Acknowledgements

I would like to thank the following people. My long-suffering family, from my wife Jackie to my children Harry, Isabel and Emily, have put up with an abstracted, often absent apology for a human being for a long time. But this project has also meant I have been a less good friend to my friends; and so apologies to them too. I will now reform, and start drinking at lunchtime again.

This book would not have happened without the excellent Ed Victor, who has looked after me, and sometimes askance at me, for many years now; nor without the superb team at Macmillan, Jon Butler, Georgina Morley, Tania Wilde and Jacqueline Graham – another relationship that has been sustained for years. Mary Greenham, who runs most of my life, struggled hard to stop me going insane. As to whether she succeeded, the verdict remains open. Among the many historians who have kindly given their advice, read parts of the manuscript or helped me find information, are Mary Beard, and the Open University team associated with the filming project. Kate Sleight did a wonderful job of combing out some of my particularly embarrassing errors, while Sue Phillpott was a superb copy-editor: in thanking both, I of course wish to underline that mistakes remaining are all my own work.

The project itself, beginning with the BBC, was the brainchild of Chris Granlund, friend and comrade, with whom I have now made twenty-two hours of documentary television. As before, I could not have worked at all effectively without the wonderful London Library. Though I do not use researchers for my writing, many of the BBC team contributed very useful thoughts, objections and advice and are mentioned below. The BBC team was led by Kathryn Taylor, who had to juggle documentary and drama, the latter filmed in South Africa. The director-producers who did the work in the field, and with whom I have spent many hours in jolting vans, airports, dodgy hotels and dusty locations, were Robin Dashwood, Guy Smith, Renny Bartlett, Neil Rawles and Mark

Radice, who suffered from a horrible bike crash but is now on the mend. The man in charge of the camera, who spent many happy months telling me to move to my left, or back a bit, was Neil Harvey, who is the best director of photography in the business, and the sound genius was Simon Parmenter. Chris O'Donnell was a particularly enthusiastic and shrewd member of the team, and I would also like to thank Alison Mills, Julie Wilkinson, Katherine Wooton and Michaela Goncalves for organizing one of the biggest projects that BBC documentaries have had to grapple with in many years.

Finally this book also depended on the friendly help of local historians and archaeologists, and our fixers in Russia, the Ukraine, Germany, France, the Netherlands, Switzerland, Spain, Italy, Greece, Turkey, Israel, Egypt, India, China, Mongolia, Australia, Japan, Mali, South Africa, Peru, Brazil, the United States and Shropshire.

Introduction

... what men have made, other men can understand.

Isaiah Berlin, quoting Giovanni Battista Vico

... history ... is boredom interrupted by war.

Derek Walcott in *The Bounty*

Writing a history of the world is a ridiculous thing to do. The amount of information is too vast for any individual to absorb, the reading limitless and the likelihood of error immense. The only case for doing it, and for reading it, is that not having a sense of world history is even more ridiculous. Looking back can make us better at looking about us. The better we understand how rulers lose touch with reality, or why revolutions produce dictators more often than they produce happiness, or why some parts of the world are richer than others, the easier it is to understand our own times. The size of the subject brings obvious risks: dull abstraction on the one side; a bewildering hubbub of vivid tales on the other. I have selected subjects and moments, which seem to me usefully representative, and attempted to link them with a broader narrative. But I could have written another book with an almost entirely different selection; and no doubt another after that.

My overall theme is straightforward. In our ability to understand and shape the world around us, we humans have been a tumbling, bounding biological acceleration of skill and thinking, which has led to a recent acceleration in our numbers and our power. We now understand quite a lot about how life began on this planet, about the structure of what is around us, and the planet's place in the cosmos. We are even beginning to explore our own self-consciousness, that bright star in 'the awakening of the world', as one philosopher has put it. Our population today is probably too large for the planet to sustain for very long – though that depends on how we choose to live – but our technical abilities give us at least a chance of getting through, just as we have survived other challenges. On the other hand, this technical and scientific brilliance has not been matched by much in politics to give us a similar sense of pride.

Imagine being able to summon up, and talk to, a peasant woman from Jesus's time, or an Aztec warrior. If you showed them your mobile phone, and tried to explain how it worked (assuming you know), you would have no chance of making them understand. A world of unfamiliar concepts would have to be described to them first – almost a history book's worth. But if you wanted to tell them about Stalin, or corrupt politicians, or the struggles between dictators and people in the Arab world today, they would get the picture immediately. We have made advances. Most places are far less violent than earlier societies. A world under the United Nations festers with poverty and splutters with wars, but it is better than a world of competing empires. Yet when it comes to our appetites, our anger, our relationship with power, there has been nothing like the advance we have seen in our scientific and technical culture. The more one knows about our early history as hunter-gatherers and our long history as farmers, and then about the dizzying acceleration of world trade and industry that has taken us into modern times, the less mysterious today's world seems. In the end, I hope most of what follows will make the reader think not only of long-dead empires and far-off places, but of the here and now.

History, meanwhile, keeps changing. This has been a golden age for history buffs, with fresh and detailed work in a vast number of fields pouring from the presses every year – everything from histories of money to forgotten European realms, from comparisons between the Roman and Chinese empires to new insights into Stalin and the Second World War. Nobody could hope to read all of it, but this book has been fuelled by manic reading for years, across many different fields. I have confined the endnotes to essential reference points only because of the endless profusion of 'additional reading' that would otherwise result; I calculate that around two thousand books, never mind pamphlets and journals, have been read for what follows.

I have also been hugely lucky to have made a series of eight films for the BBC on world history, a project which allowed me to visit around sixty sites, everywhere from the Peruvian deserts to the Ukraine. Seeing where things happened – Tolstoy's estate, or the workers' village for Egypt's Valley of the Kings – does affect how one understands particular stories. Certainly, the television project has changed my own approach. Television storytelling insists on zooming in on *this* person doing or saying *this*, *then* with *that* result. Television abhors abstraction. It wants character, dates, actions. As a result much of what follows is, unapologetically, an example of a kind of history-writing that is currently very unfashionable, the 'great man/great woman' school of history, albeit twisted into new shapes by environmental, economic and social histories.

For there are no abstract forces in history. Everything that brings change is natural. Some of it has been non-human – the climatic shifts, volcanoes, diseases, currents, winds, and the distribution of the plants and animals that have shaped humanity. But most of human history has been made by human choice and human muscle. That is, it has been made by individuals, acting inside their societies. Some of them have had a much greater impact than others, hence the 'great'. Because we live in a slightly hysterical democratic culture, which yelps loudly about equality in order to dodge talking about its huge gaps in wealth and power, there is a certain nervousness about this. Isn't the history of small changes to the domestic practices of farming families, or the role of women in mercantile early-modern networks, more 'real' than what emperors or inventors did?

In short, no. History is about change, and it makes sense to concentrate on the biggest change-makers. Yes, all people are equal in their dignity and their potential value. Yes, most of us live our lives in the lulls. Yes, everyone should have equal status in law. But to suggest that therefore everyone's story or achievement is equal, and of equal interest, is ludicrous. The Burgundian peasant who followed the oxen, fed his family, lived blamelessly, and who died, mourned by his village, at the ripe old age of forty-two, is not as important a historical figure as Charles V of Spain, or Siddhartha, the Buddha. It is interesting to read about the sailors of coastal Europe who found new fishing grounds and made small but useful improvements to their vessels as they searched further and further away for cod. Christopher Columbus depended on their accumulated knowledge. But as an individual life, his story matters more.

No 'great' people are anything other than firmly embedded in their societies or time, giving them a limited range of possible actions and thoughts. Apart from religious leaders, it is almost impossible to find a historic character of whom we can unequivocally say that, without him, or her, such-and-such would *never* have happened. James Watt could not have invented his steam engine a hundred years earlier or if he had been living in Siberia; he was standing on the shoulders of many other inventors, mechanics, educationalists and merchants. He was in the right place at the right time. If he had not invented the separate condenser, somebody else would have done. But he *did* invent his new kind of steam engine; and the hows and whys of that moment matter. The peoples of the Mongolian steppe, pushed by hunger and realizing how important a weapon their horses were, would always have attacked the settled societies around them – and often did so. But had Genghis Khan not united warring clans and provided ruthless, inspirational leadership, the story of much of Asia would have been different.

So what follows is inevitably an elitist history, since the people who had the power, money or leisure to change societies were disproportionately drawn from those who were already privileged. This sometimes does mean 'kings and queens'. Only a member of the privileged Mughal ruling family could have become emperor when Aurangzeb did. But the fact that it was Aurangzeb, and not one of his brothers, had important consequences, because he was a religious zealot who bankrupted Mughal India and inadvertently opened the door for the British. Cleopatra was a pure-bred member of the Greek ruling house of Egypt (not that they were very pure) but the fact that she, and not her brother, ruled at the time of Julius Caesar and Mark Antony had consequences for the classical world.

Later, as the churn of more educated societies throws up a wider range of characters, the class background of the change-makers widens. But the great men or great women are the ones with the brains, courage or luck to make breakthroughs that others do not. Robert Oppenheimer, father of the atomic bomb, matters more than the very clever physicists of his time who were never at Los Alamos. Hitler was a lower-middle-class drifter who became a brilliant demagogue. Germany without Hitler would have been different, and his story is vastly more important than the story of the many ultranationalist beer-hall orators whose parties shrivelled and vanished. So it is clear, I hope, that when I say this is a 'great man' way of telling history, I am not suggesting that anyone stands outside the coincidence of their time and place – the social moment which empowers them or neuters them. Nor am I using 'great' in a way that implies moral admiration. Some of the greatest of great men have also been the biggest bastards alive.

As this story advances I hope readers will enjoy the nit and grit of little facts that switch on the lights, all of which are plundered from real historians. In a recent book on Italy we learn that at the start of Italian unification, in 1861, a grand total of 2.5 per cent of Italians spoke what we would recognize as Italian.[1] From another, that to pass their exams, Chinese bureaucrats in the fifteenth and sixteenth centuries had to memorize 431,286 different characters.[2] The first throws light on Italy's struggle to be a modern nation. The second reminds us why China took so long to develop a large literate middle class. Had it done so – had Chinese depended on twenty-odd phonetic letters – then China's history would have been different.

The shape of human history can be told through numbers, the rising number of people on the planet, from perhaps a few thousand pairs at our last moment of near-extinction to today's leap towards seven billion now and nine billion before long. If we put these numbers on a graph, with a timeline as our horizontal, then the story would still be a simple but dramatic acceleration leap.

To begin with, the long flat acres of time when the human population barely seemed to move. There are up to seventy thousand years of hunter-gatherer family groups spreading slowly from Africa. There are around ten thousand years during the invention of agriculture, the development of tribal societies and small towns, when the population curve only slowly starts to stretch its neck upwards.

Next come the beginnings of civilizations, around 5,500 years ago, with the next great invention after farming, which is writing. Then follows the rest of human history, starring trade and the industrial revolution. In our own times the people-line rockets skywards, mainly thanks to cleaner water and medicine. Why has the acceleration happened? Why such a slow burn, followed by a rocketing population? It originates in the ability to alter the rest of the natural world shown by *Homo sapiens sapiens* (and what an exuberantly boastful tag we have chosen – two 'wises', not one). Other creatures adapt to the environment around them, evolving characteristics and behaviour which give them a niche, a biological cranny, in which they can survive and even thrive. Merely by living, they may change that environment, as anyone who has seen termite nests, or watched the impact of beavers on a river, can confirm. All life changes the world, which is in a constant process of flux.

Humans, however, with their superior mental and communications skills, have taken this ability to shape the world to a different level. We have hunted and driven other mammals to extinction. We have tethered and changed animals beyond recognition – look at the ancestors of the modern cow, or the Highland terrier. We have done the same to plants – taking a corn-cob all the way from a fingerbone-sized piece of starch to a swollen barrel of nourishment, for instance. Now, with fish farms we are altering even the size, shape and musculature of fish. This has given us a surplus of energy no mere predator could hope for. Using it, we have grown from family groups to tribes to villages to cities to nations, allowing us to change much more of our original environment. We have altered the courses of rivers and dug into the mineral covering of the planet, pulling out coal, oil and gas to give ourselves more power, exploiting ancient vegetable reserves that lived and died long before we arrived. In very recent times our understanding has allowed us to develop medicines and technologies that have extended our lifespans dramatically.

Again, none of this has come about because of impersonal forces. It has been done by the accumulated acts of millions of individual humans, working away in our own immediate interest like the tiny creatures who make up vast coral reefs – except, of course, with self-consciousness, and so able to give a running commentary on it all. One survey of human history concludes simply: 'What drives history is the human ambition to alter one's condition to match one's hopes.'[3] A better chewy root; a fatter goat; safety in the trees from the raiders; a livelier tune; a more interesting story; a new flavour; more children for one's old age; a way to avoid the taxman; a watch; a mangle; a bicycle; an air-ticket to the sun – these are the modest lures and small whips that drive us forward until the next leader of some kind makes another leap.

There is no evidence that we have changed biologically or in our instincts during the time covered by this book. There have been small evolutionary changes. The way our upper and lower teeth meet has altered as our diet has changed; the 'overbite' caused by more grinding of grain came quite late on. Human groups who kept cows so as to drink their milk developed digestive systems to cope, while Asians who never did this did not. The different human populations that scattered out of Africa in different directions, and eventually squatted down in fertile spots, became separated from one another. They developed cosmetic differences: skin colour, eye shape and subtle variations in skull design, which produced a certain mutual suspicion after those geographical distances were closed again. But in our rough size and strength, our abilities to imagine, reason, communicate, employ delicate hand strength, plan and sweat, we have stayed the same. We know more. We have not got smarter.

If we have not got cleverer, how have we increased so many times over, and often improved our individual material lives so successfully? The answer is that we are a collaborative and learning creature, gathering up the work and successes of the past and building on them. We stand not on the shoulders of giants, but on the shoulders of our grandparents and of our great-great-great-grandparents too. The point was made recently by a clever researcher who tried to build a simple electric pop-up toaster completely from scratch. It was almost impossible. You need the history of oil exploration, plastics and so on first, and the industrial specialization that followed.

Left to itself (undisrupted by war, natural catastrophe or famine) this process produces, quite necessarily, that acceleration in human population. Writing was invented in Mesopotamia – and independently in China and America and India. But once it was moving around the Mediterranean, it was quickly adapted and advanced. It did not have to be reinvented by the French, the Ottomans or the Danes. Farming was invented up to seven times in different parts of the world between twelve thousand and five thousand years ago; but as has been pointed out, the steam engine did not need to be invented seven times to spread around the world.[4]

There is another consequence of this, which may make us flinch. Farming was created by millions of people learning independently about the shapes of grasses, how to tend them, where to make water flow, and so on. It was a change embodied in human family experience, and therefore a cautious one, even if its consequences were momentous and unexpected. The industrial revolution was different. Steam power needed coalminers and metallurgists, lawyers and financiers; but few people who travelled on trains or wore the clothes produced by steam-driven machines needed to understand the technology. Specialization means that, overall, the advances are no longer embodied in individual lives; most of us need only take them on trust. As human civilization becomes more complex, individuals necessarily understand less about how it actually works. The personal ability of most of us to affect the course of our society (never strong) may seem, therefore, to vanish. Of the billions of us today who depend on digital technology or modern medicine, very few have the faintest clue about how it all happens. Individually, we have almost no control over anything. This is why politics, our only wobbly lever, continues to matter so much.

And history is also the story of the bumps and setbacks that occur when more people, using more energy, build larger societies. Throughout early history, many big setbacks were caused by nature – by volcanic eruptions, sometimes big enough to destroy crops, summers and even ecosystems; by changes in weather systems big enough to destroy whole human cultures; and by lesser events such as floods, earthquakes and rivers changing their course. Much of early human religion is devoted to a worried and puzzled attempt to ask the rains to keep coming and the underground rumbling to stop. The story becomes more interesting as soon as humans are able to do more than react – build dams, irrigate, or move.

Later on, the disruptions to human development may still be caused by natural events, but the likelier culprits are human. Once we settle we can quickly become victims of our own laziness and ignorance, killing off handy animal species, or deforesting land for farming, which then blows the topsoil away. The inhabitants of Easter Island made this mistake; but so did the ancient Greeks and the Japanese, who both nevertheless found ways to cope. Once we trade across large areas, we spread diseases to which some bodies are less hardened than others. This set back human development in the late Roman and Chinese world. It had even more awesome consequences when, after thirteen thousand years of separation, the peoples of Europe arrived in the Americas.

Then we come to the rueful reflection of the Caribbean poet Derek Walcott, quoted above, who thought history was boredom interrupted by war. There has certainly been a lot of war. New research has shown that early hunter-gatherer societies were frantically warlike: kingdoms and empires just meant more people and better weapons, so bigger fights.

But war often has an ambiguous effect. It is horrible, obviously. But conflict drives new inventions, makes people think more deeply about their societies, and by destroying some realms, allows new ones to emerge. Adversity makes the survivors stronger. The disappearance of easy-to-catch fish or deer forces people to develop new ways of fishing and hunting. Floods make people devise flood defences and new irrigation; and by requiring villages to combine together, they have set them on the road to creating states. Plagues depopulate regions but can also, as in Europe in the fifteenth century, free the survivors to lead different and more adventurous lives. Wars spread terror and destruction – but also technologies, languages and ideas.

Amid so much bold assertion, it is worth remembering that history amounts to the fragments that survive from a vaster buried story. Some of the most wonderful moments of advance have happened to people (and in places) about whom (and which) we are almost completely ignorant. Who was the first to realize that squiggles could be made to stand for sounds of parts of words, and not only as mini-pictures of something else? Who first understood that it was possible to read without speaking the words out loud? Who fermented grain and drank the results? From southern China to Arabia, wet soils and shifting deserts have hidden civilizations which were once mighty and which collapsed for reasons we may never understand.

There is so much we do not know. We do not know why the great palaces of the Greek Bronze Age were deserted and how those people lost the art of writing. For most of history, all we have left are the accidental remains, the things that could not rot or that somehow survived the sandpapering of time. In most places the wood and earth buildings, colourful textiles, languages, paintings, songs, music and stories have gone for ever; the cultures that were mostly made of wood and wool, tunes and stories, are the ones hardest to retrieve.

What follows will be very disproportionate. Not only the endless savannahs of prehistory but the long periods of quiet social stability, the lulls, will be passed over in a paragraph or two. Convulsions that take place in a few decades in small places, such as in Greece around 400–300 BC or in Europe around 1500, will be pored over. For change is increasing – but also discontinuous and sometimes sudden. The conditions for a revolutionary break can be searched out, back through earlier centuries or decades, but the moment of breakthrough is still the nub of the story.

However, before we start, let us pause and admire the 99 per cent; the forgotten heroes of the quieter years, busy with the hard graft of just getting on, keeping going and surviving – that peasant who followed his oxen, the farmers who worked and fed families and paid taxes without ending up being killed by Mongol raiders or recruited by Napoleon, the women who dug and birthed and taught in ten thousand vanished villages. This is a book about great change-makers and their times, but all of it takes place surrounded by the rest of us who kept the show on the road.

Vasily Grossman, the great Russian novelist of the Soviet era, who appears later in this book, wrote in his masterpiece *Life and Fate*:

> Man never understands that the cities he has built are not an integral part of nature. If he wants to defend his culture from wolves and snowstorms, if he wants to save it from being strangled by weeds, he must keep his broom, spade and rifle always at hand. If he goes to sleep, if he thinks about something else for a year or two, everything's lost. The wolves come out of the forest, the thistles spread and everything is buried under dust and snow. Just think how many great capitals have succumbed to dust, snow and couch-grass.

Wise words from a non-professional historian which, during the writing of this book, have been ringing in my head.

Part One

OUT OF THE HEAT, TOWARDS THE ICE

From Seventy Thousand Years Ago to the Early Mediterranean Civilizations

So where should we start? Physics and biology push back so far that our brains struggle. There is the Big Bang, 13.7 billion years ago (perhaps only one of many) and its consequences – the coming of the elements and the galaxies and the planets. This is deep time, parts of it still visible in the night sky every day of our lives, through which flow mysteries even today's cleverest humans do not understand, such as dark energy and matter.

We could start more locally, with the early history of Earth, beginning some 4.5 billion years ago and following the growth of life in a thin, fragile membrane wrapped round a whizzing ball of iron and rock. We could begin with carbon capture, and the fifth of Earth's atmosphere being composed of oxygen, without which this would be just another dead, hot lump of wrinkled geology. This is the Creation story of modern mankind – no feathered serpents, giant turtles or six-day creative explosion by a moral experimenter, but something just as awe-inspiring in its scale and mystery.

We could fast-forward through the first half-billion years of the living rock, when it was water-shrouded (a little over 70 per cent of it still is), and talk about the evolution of life on dry earth.[1] We could rehearse our Charles Darwin, telling the story of the first tiny mammals, our ancestors, and how they took advantage of the disappearance of the great lizards, or dinosaurs. More conventionally, we could chart what we know of the complex and delicate family tree of early apes and hominids from which we spring.

Any one of these starting-points would be informative and useful. Our human history, as it is told today, is only a final page after a vast preface of intense astrophysical events, chemical reactions and evolutionary changes. It does not start with a creator moulding men and women from mud or blood with his own hands, nor in the Garden of Eden. What follows here is a history of the social, global human, how-

3

ever: so let's begin with a woman, and a birth; to put it poetically, an African Eve.

Mother

She had a different name. No one has known it for around seventy thousand years. She had one; for she lived among talkative and highly social people. 'Mother', for reasons that will become obvious, will do. She was probably young, tough, stocky and dark-skinned. She was a traveller, part of a people always on the move. She was also heavily pregnant. Her tribespeople were hunters and expert gleaners of berries, shellfish, roots and herbs. They carried tools and hides and a couple of babies with them, tied with sinews and skins around adult backs, but there were surprisingly few children in the group. Those who didn't learn early to walk, keep quiet and keep up tended to die, picked off by predators following the group.

In their own way the travellers were, however, formidable, armed with spears and razor-sharp chipped-stone cutting edges that had been developed over around a hundred thousand years of hunting, and (if they were anything like later hunter-gatherers) while fighting rival tribes. Their average age was relatively young, something that would remain true of all human societies until very recent history. But there would have been people in their fifties or sixties. It is now thought that the female menopause may have been a useful evolutionary adaptation to provide grandmothers, who could care for the young while younger women were breeding: tribes with grandmothers would be able to support more children to adulthood, and therefore would grow at the expense of tribes without older women.

The men would have been marked by hunting scars but would be vocal and thoughtful tacticians, experienced in tracking game and exploiting their understanding of other animals. The oldest, the father of this clan, might be in his sixties. Hunters in their thirties or forties may have been the most effective food-gatherers. This group had been moving for years, slowly north through what are now called Kenya and Somalia, towards a strip of water that looked possible to cross. The flow of water was lower than it used to be, leaving dry patches of land. Wading between them would have been a risk worth taking, because the game and the vegetation around them was getting harder to find. Life would be easier on the other side.

The group would have had no idea they were about to leave one continent where all humans originated; nor any notion of just how far their descendants would walk, working their way along beaches, a mile or two every year, clearing out the shellfish and the crabs in rock pools, gorging on a beached whale, spearing ridiculously incurious goats. All life was a journey. Always, a new track must be made. Ahead of them and behind them, once they had moved on, the easier prey would return, but to stay put in a single place would be unnatural and dangerous. Declare anywhere 'home', and you would die of hunger. So though the water was a challenge, and everyone was watching everyone else as they waded – for the group had a language and talked about their plans – this was just another day.

They were probably clothed, in some way: a study of body-lice DNA suggests that they were infesting clothing around a hundred thousand years ago and it is thought humans lost most of their own fur millions of years ago. This group, much larger than a single family, would be accustomed to sharing out tasks; and this was directly related to the problems that started again with Mother's labour pains. Like all women, she knew the birth would be painful. Ever since anyone could recall, human babies had been born with surprisingly large heads, so big that to force them out through the vagina was agonizing. Mother would give birth standing up, surrounded by her sisters. Her baby would be helpless, a wobbling, vulnerable thing, for far longer than the children of other animals.

It was a puzzle, about which many things would be said during the long nights of storytelling. But the vulnerability of the modern human child was a long-term strength because it forced families and tribal groups to share out work and to cooperate. Today's hunter-gatherer societies generally have a clear division of labour between male hunters and females gathering plants, and it is likely this was already happening by Mother's time. It would be many tens of thousands of years before people realized that the big head, the relative helplessness and the consequently painful birth added up to an evolutionary triumph, producing animals able to tell stories.

Historians of human evolution also suspect that our warlike, xenophobic and mutually hostile character likewise evolved in Africa, and for the same reasons. Tribes, extending beyond family groups, are at an advantage if everyone works together, 'for the good of the tribe', even if what they do is dangerous or unpleasant for them at the time. This means that tribal bonding is very important; without a sense of belonging and mutual dependence, the tribe falls apart. The other side of this is that, in a world where human tribes are moving around, searching for game, the tribal bonding is likely to be reinforced by hostility to other tribes. This obviously continues to matter.

Everywhere on the planet, early human societies seem to have worked hard to differentiate themselves from their neighbours, wearing different headdresses, jewellery, clothing and, above all, speaking different languages. The British zoologist Mark Pagel points out that, even today after so much cultural homogenization, there are seven thousand different languages spoken by humans, almost all of which are mutually unintelligible. Why? Other animals are not like this. He argues that our good qualities – our capacity to be kind, generous and friendly, allowing us to evolve cooperative and bigger groups, to 'get along with each other' – have to be set against bad qualities, 'our tendencies to form competing societies often not far from conflict'. In hunter-gathering groups competing for land, conflict is common and tribal war often a fact of life.

We have been hunter-gatherers, we humans, for far, far longer than we have been farmers – at least ten to fifteen times as long. We are only now becoming a species that mainly lives in cities; but if we say we have been dominated by cities for a century or two, then our hunter-gathering trail is a thousand times longer. So it would be literally unnatural if much of our behaviour did not relate in some way to that inheritance; above all in our combination of sociability and mutual suspicion. And so back to Mother.

For she was the mother of almost all of us. (There is another earlier, even mistier, figure: 'Mitochondrial Eve', who would be the mother of everyone, Africans included, far earlier in the human story, perhaps some 200,000 years ago; but her story is less well understood.) Our character's maternal achievement is to be understood literally, rather than as a parable. There are arguments about this, as there are about every aspect of early society, but the balance of probabilities is that she is your super-Mother. If you are a New York lawyer, she is where you came from. If you are an aboriginal Pacific Islander in a cancer hospital, or a German farmer or a Japanese office-cleaner or a Pakistani Londoner at university – you come from our Eve. Stephen Oppenheimer of Oxford University, a specialist in DNA studies, says: 'Every non-African in Australia, America, Siberia, Iceland, Europe, China, and India can trace their genetic inheritance back to just one line coming out of Africa.'[2] That is, one group. One journey.

This seems now to be the consensus view. At first sight, it also seems impossible. How can one woman giving birth to one child be the mother of most of the human race? The answer goes by the name of 'matrilineal drift', and works like this. In each generation, some families do not reproduce successfully. It may be because of disease, a hunting accident, incompatibility – but some maternal lines die out. Over very long periods of time, therefore, almost all do. They have gone, and gone for ever. Imagine the process as a huge scythe, sweeping backwards through thousands of generations, gathering up a dark harvest of never-made-its. As the Darwinian writer Richard Dawkins reminds us, we are the children of survivors.

The seeming paradox is that alongside this scythe there is an ever-widening delta of humans being born and actually surviving. Why? Because for those who do survive long enough to procreate, if they can have child-survivors at just a little above the two-for-two natural replacement rate (and the same applies to those child-survivors, in turn), mathematics decrees a surprisingly fast upwards line of population growth – all of which must therefore be children of the earliest survivors. (There were patrilineal ancestors too, of course; it is just that nobody has yet found a DNA trace that helps us pursue them this far back.) Though hard to grasp and feeling like an optical illusion in heredity, 'drift' makes better sense when we recall that this is a period when the overall human population is barely increasing, and when life expectancy is very short. Eve is our universal mother because tigers, snakes, landslides and microbes got the others.

Eve's tribal group was already a remarkable achievement in survival against the odds, part of a human population of several hundreds of thousands in Africa, which had emerged in competition with other varieties of clever ape. Human history, properly understood, starts when we move from being just another form of prey in the cycle of eat-and-be-eaten, a creature blown about by the natural world, to a creature beginning to shape the world. We move from happens-to, to makes-happen.

But *Homo sapiens* was only one branch of a tree of hominids who were learning how to alter their environment, if only in a minor way. There are almost no historical arguments as complex and heated as those about modern man's origins. The reason is straightforward: scientific advances in the study of human DNA and in the dating of bone fragments and other material keep challenging, and sometimes overturning, earlier theories. It may be the furthest-back part of human history but it is changing faster than the history of, say, the Second World War. Amateurs must step delicately across an exciting minefield.

One thing that is now widely agreed, however, is that this is a story in which climate plays a pivotal role, more so than we used to realize. The cooling and warming of the planet because of solar activity, meteorite strikes, eruptions or tiny changes in its angle of spin affect the advance and retreat of deserts, the opening or closure of bridges for migration, and thus the story of our storytelling ape. In general, the more complicated the changes in the climate, even when they produce the extinction of other animals, the faster the advance of hominids seems to have been.

Adversity favours the versatile. The first attempts by tree-living African hominids to live on two feet came after cold, dry weather attacked their forests two million years ago. The open grasslands that resulted made it imperative to be able to run and hunt and see into the distance, and scientists believe this eventually resulted in *Homo erectus*, an important early version of humanity, with a brain around two-thirds the size of ours.

There were further changes in brains, as the warm Pliocene epoch gave way to the ice ages of the Pleistocene and to new challenges. Inside Africa, it now seems, a great complexity of hominids evolved. But *Homo erectus*, which ranged far out of Africa, evolved first into the bigger-brained *Homo heidelbergensis* – people who were hunting and making axes in England half a million years ago, and had a brain not so much smaller than ours, around 1,200 grams compared with our 1,500. Modern 'us-sized brains', had evolved in Africa around 150–100,000 years ago. This gives modern humans the largest brain for body size of any known animal, about seven times bigger than you might expect for our heft.[3]

This picture of human development is a brutal simplification. There are intimidating-sounding lists of pre-modern human species, varying greatly in height, shape of skull, leg bones and weight. Though scientists name and slot them into seemingly neat divisions, as evolutionary trees are assembled, the truth must have been messier. Chris Stringer of London's Natural History Museum usefully reminds us that species 'are, after all, humanly created approximations of reality in the natural world'.[4] Skulls of similar age, which are alike but not identical, hide subtler variations between early humans lost to us, so we should not get too scared by the thicket of scientific names.

What most needs to be grasped is that modern humans were not just a single super-bright, planet-conquering ape, who leapt as if by magic from an earlier world belonging to dim ape-men. Those earlier species, including the famous Neanderthals, and in Asia the 'Denisovans' (both coming after *Homo heidelbergensis*), also survived dramatic changes in climate and pushed into new territories as pioneers, equipped with cutting- and killing-tools. They probably decorated themselves, may have had some form of language, and may even, at the edges, have interbred with the newcomers, *Homo sapiens*. More interesting to us, though, is what they lacked.

So let us now return to Mother and her tribal migration. Did it really happen that way? Everyone agrees that Africa retains a genetic diversity of humans not found anywhere else, and that all humans began there at some point. But there has been a major argument about whether all non-African modern humans originated in a single (or nearly single) movement out of the continent, spreading round the world from around seventy thousand years ago. The alternative idea is that these other species, which had left Africa and colonized Europe and Asia much earlier, in fact survived. Could they have evolved into, and in places also bred with, *Homo sapiens*?

Between the two extremes there are shades of grey, but these offer two radically different views of today's humanity. One says that, in essence, all non-Africans are close relatives, 'Mother's' children. The other argues that different human populations emerged more slowly and separately in different parts of the world. This, it is claimed, may explain why many of us look and even behave so differently. The latter view has been more popular among academics outside the Western tradition, and our ideas about contemporary humanity barely need spelling out. This is not a dry argument. Are we family, or rivals?

Scientific opinion is now heavily tilted to the 'out of Africa' or 'recent African origin' model, mainly because of advances in tracing one particular form of DNA marker, mitochondrial DNA, leading back to Africa, where modern humanity, *Homo sapiens*, did not begin to appear until about two hundred thousand years ago. But the old picture of apes simply getting cleverer and cleverer until 'our lot' walked out of Africa and began populating an empty Europe and the Middle East seems to be wrong. Just like other animals, earlier hominids had been on the march long before. Recent archaeological discoveries in South Africa suggest that fire, and cooking, were being used nearly two million years ago by *Homo erectus*, though this is a highly controversial issue. It would help explain the growth in brain size, since cooking greatly increases the quantity of calories that can be ingested; and brains are very energy-hungry.

At any rate, before our migration the world was already inhabited by other kinds of people. What happened to them? It is likely that they were victims of changing climate conditions, destroyed by cold and hunger when temperatures fell again, or possibly by modern humans who were better organized and able to adapt. Nor, it seems, did modern humans leave Africa through Egypt, breaking first into the Mediterranean and European worlds, as Europeans once thought. We first went south, heading down along the coast of India and South-East Asia, foraging for shellfish as we went, and eventually somehow made it to Australia across the sea. Again, scientists argue about this, but it seems possible that aboriginal Australians arrived in their land many thousands of years before aboriginal French or Spanish got to theirs. And tracing back through the DNA trail suggests that the Cro-Magnon Europeans were descended from people who, before turning north, lived in today's India. History is the story of migration, as much as settlement, long before Columbus or the Irish arrived in America.

What caused the *Homo sapiens* push out of Africa? Again, there are rival theories.

Around 73,500 years ago a massive volcano erupted in what is today called Sumatra. This was by far the biggest such disaster of the past two million years,[5] and some scientists suggest that modern humans nearly did not make it through at all when the eruption misted the skies and radically cooled the planet. Some argue that the human population fell back to only a few thousand individuals in southern Africa, causing a bottleneck in evolution for thousands of years. This may have produced a radical pruning-back and regrowth of a more ruthless and organized humanity, better able to migrate round the world when conditions improved – Mother's well organized tribe. Others think this has been exaggerated and that, bad though the conditions were, many species survived them.

Once that human migration from Africa had happened, however, it is clear that further episodes of chilling and heating shaped their later movements and ultimate success. It took a long time for the routes to open up across today's Middle East and into Europe. But once humans arrived there, a later volcanic eruption in Italy, some thirty-nine thousand years ago, and sporadic 'Heinrich events' – when icebergs broke off into the Atlantic producing severe periods of cooling – kept the climate unpredictable. The northern ice cover retreated and then came back again several times. The migration patterns of deer, bison and other animals shifted. Comfortable refuges became grim; and then grim wastelands bloomed. Repeatedly, humans had to alter their habits and behaviour to survive. Again: adversity favours the versatile.

It seems that after the African migration, small numbers of *Homo sapiens* were better adapted to manage these shifts in climate than earlier versions of human had been. If so, this happened not because of classic Darwinian evolution (there wasn't time) but because of the accelerated development caused by culture – language, learning, copying, remembering. We became more skilled with our fingers. In bigger groups, we were able to allow specialization – the best trackers to track, rope-weavers to weave, arrowhead-makers to chip. Working together we were better, more lethal, hunters. Human groups struggling to cope with a cold, drier world had to learn new things, including the ability to make more complex language, empathize with prey (about which more soon) – and both fight with, and learn from, rival groups.

Chris Stringer says that this allowed the acceleration that replaced the 'two million years of boredom': 'Through imitation and peer-group feedback, populations could adapt well beyond the abilities of an isolated genius, whose ideas might never get beyond his or her cave, or might be lost through a sudden death.'[6] It may very well be that other *Homo* groups were also able to speak, plan ahead, and so on, but not so well, and were therefore destroyed by the rate of change in the world around them; or were wiped out (and possibly eaten) by us. Another historian of early people, Brian Fagan, has argued that this new cooperation involved the invention not simply of speech but of abstract thought, 'a new realm of symbolic meanings, which thrived in a world of partnerships between humans and their sur-roundings' and which included, for the first time, art and perhaps religion.

Carrying all this with us, we spread first into Asia and then Europe. We reached the far east of Asia around 40,000 years ago and arrived in the Americas, across the 'Beringia' land bridge (long gone), around 20,000 years ago. By 12,000 years ago we had reached the southern areas of South America, and the final areas of human habi-tation were the islands of the mid-Pacific. Hawaii and New Zealand were reached only a thousand years ago, by people whose culture was still essentially that of the Stone Age yet who had developed impres-sive star navigation and boat-building. This spread of *Homo sapiens* is very fast compared with the 1.4 million years or so for the develop-ment of our previous ancestor, *Homo erectus*, into us.[7] In biological time, it is like an explosion. Everywhere we arrived, there is evidence of the extinction of other large mammals.

We should rid ourselves of any comfortable or complacent sense that contemporary humans, sitting in coffee bars or driving cars, are superior in intellect to the hunter-gatherers who emerged from those hard African aeons. Hunter-gatherers had to be able to do many more different things than today's urban people, and it has been estimated that men have lost around a tenth of their brain size compared with the people of the last ice age, and women 14 per cent. The Australian scientist Tim Flannery points out that the same is true of domesti-cated animals compared with their wild forebears, and for the same reasons: 'Overall, life for all members of our domesticated mixed feed-ing flock is made so much more accommodating that its members can invest less of their energy in brains . . . If you doubt how far our civi-lization has turned us into helpless, self-domesticated livestock, just look at the world around you.'[8] This may seem harsh, but it is a useful corrective to our modern condescension. Early humans, driving out of Africa, were extraordinary, rather terrifying creatures.

Caves of Genius

We know more about the first European settlers, the Cro-Magnons, than we do about the first Asians and Australians, but this is more to do with the history of archaeology, and European self-satisfaction, than with anything else. Predictions are dangerous when it comes to early history, but it seems safe to say that the big new discoveries are likely to come in China and other parts of East Asia. Meanwhile, the Europeans enjoy the odd bits of poetry awarded to early cultures by the accident of where their bones were found. They are 'Aurignacians', 'Magdalenians' or 'Gravettians', which is confusing, though better than the preferred modern academic term 'European Early Modern Humans', or EEMHs.

So, who were they?

Most people living then would have known only small local groups. It has been estimated that throughout this long period there was rarely a gathering of humans on the planet numbering more than three hundred or so. There must have been breeding across different groups, or the genetic cost would have been horrendous, so there must also have been contact between tribes at the edge of their range. We are sure they had language, but what kind? Settled people in Celtic or Chinese cultures had different dialects in different valleys, altering every few score miles. The same is true in Papua New Guinea, Australia, pre-European North America and the Amazon Basin.

The languages that emerged in different parts of the world are very different from each other, though hints of some original or 'Ur-languages' can be traced through common-sounding words. But over larger distances, there are big differences in the way sounds are formed – where in the mouth and throat, how the lips and tongue are used – and the way grammar works. It seems likely that the Cro-Magnon people, like aboriginal Australians, had a kaleidoscope of local dialects and languages with enough familiar words and sounds to allow communication across the edges of rival tribal groups.

We also know that later agricultural societies worshipped deities associated with their survival – gods for water, rain, sun, corn. So it seems likely that hunter-gatherer societies gave a special place to the aspects of nature they relied on most heavily – the animals they killed and used. Today's hunter-gatherers tend to show reverence for, and close observatory interest in, the birds and animals they live off. African hunters are known to mimic animals they intend to pursue, to try to get inside their thinking. Surely the cave paintings of aurochs and bison have a similar origin? Modern hunter-gatherers also have creation myths, stories about where they came from. It seems unlikely that the darker-skinned earlier versions of ourselves did not have those too.

And indeed, the three hundred or so painted cave sites in Spain and France discovered so far imply a belief system based on animals and the natural world. Looking, drawing, copying – using the hand, eye and memory – seem to constitute a very early human characteristic, and it is always possible that the cave paintings are 'art for art's sake' rather than having a spiritual purpose. Yet the use of cave art by people in Africa and Australia, and the intensely repeated images, suggest some kind of religious system. We have very early bone flutes; and the paintings would have been made in the semi-darkness.

There must have been stories, too. It is not a fantastic leap to imagine music-driven underground rituals intended to ensure that the deer and horses keep migrating, or to honour the giant creatures brought down by spear-throwing hunters. The association of darkness, bulls and mystery is deeply embedded in the European imagination. Similar art may have been made elsewhere, and lost. It may yet emerge in many other places: 6,000-year-old paintings were found recently in a cave in Inner Mongolia, northern China. But what we have in south-western Europe is a wonderful trumpet-blast for the arrival of fully modern humans, art already quite as accomplished and moving as the later drawings of a Rubens or a Van Gogh.

Our relationship with a closer contemporary relative, the beetle-browed humans we call Neanderthal, is a darker story. These people can be defined as a separate species or a subgroup of our own, and were physically distinct: heavier-boned, with differently shaped skulls and perhaps without full speech. They appear fully developed only around 130,000 years ago and survived in Europe until between 30,000 and 24,000 years ago – though they disappeared earlier in Asia. So as an 'unsuccessful' species, an all-round failure much mocked by cartoonists, they survived, roughly speaking, for 100,000 years – much longer than has *Homo sapiens* outside Africa so far, and indeed fifty times longer than the period that separates you, reading this, and Christ.

What happened to them? There was no cataclysmic event. Modern humans lived alongside their near-relatives for around thirty thousand years. Scattered archaeological evidence suggests Neanderthals may have copied the new super-hunters, altering their own tools. Biologists fiercely disagree about whether the two groups interbred, and the latest thinking is that probably they did – a little; there is (a little) DNA evidence from some scattered communities. The 'new people' clearly enjoyed advantages. The Neanderthals may have used a form of humming or singing communication rather than full-scale language; it has been suggested that because they lived in small groups they did not need to convey complex information, but only emotion.[9] So far as we know, though they buried their dead and may even have used makeup, they made no art and did not invent bows, harpoons, needles or jewellery.

They survived well in climatic conditions that we can barely comprehend; the 'old stone age' was a time of ice sheets arriving and retreating, testing the flexibility of humans to the utmost. Neanderthals had to rely on the skins of the animals they killed to protect them from the cold, but modern humans had a secret weapon, more important even than their better cutting edges, their spear-throwers or the bows that would allow them to kill from a distance: they had sewing. Many beautifully formed needles have been found, as well as the awls to cut the holes needed for the thread to pass through. As with today's Inuit people, Cro-Magnon man could dress in clothes that fitted closely and were worn in layers, giving much greater protection and flexibility than bear-hides. Brian Fagan says: 'The needle allowed women to tailor garments from the fur and skin of different animals, such as wolves, reindeer, and arctic foxes, taking full advantage of each hide or pelt's unique abilities to reduce the dangers of frostbite and hypothermia in environments of rapidly changing extremes.'

The needle plus the better weaponry, and the group-planning allowed by full language, made Cro-Magnons unbeatable. The Neanderthals may simply have been driven to extinction by competition. Or worse: there is unsettling evidence from Les Rois in France of butchery marks on a Neanderthal skull, suggesting that modern humans may have eaten the contents. The Neanderthals were probably canni-

bals, at least some of the time, but it is possible that any interaction we
had with them back then was far removed from mere social observa-
tion, still less regular interbreeding: 'Neanderthals? Mmm. . . . Far too
tasty to flirt with.'

Of course, we have only the bony, stony splinters of lives lived in
wood and colour, and enriched by music, stories and ideas about the
cosmos lost to us. But such vast stretches of time have left their marks
on us. Some anthropologists believe that our preferred, normal size of
family and friendship groups – the people we really know and interact
with, not our Facebook friends – reflects the size of prehistoric hunting groups. Then, there was even more need for a division of labour.
The skinning, curing, cutting, stitching and cooking had to happen
alongside the hunting and foraging. Sexual division of labour was
already a fact. It has been argued that such seemingly subtle differences between the sexes today as men's greater enthusiasm for
strongly tasting food and drink (curries, pickles, whisky) are dim
reflections of the hunter-gatherer past, when men foraged further and
had constantly to test the edibility of dead flesh and berries.

The way our brains process visual information, ruthlessly focusing
on movement, is certainly an early hunting (and running-away) adaptation. Is our readiness to close the curtains and huddle in front of a
television set when winter arrives a memory of the safety felt in
underground caves? Knowing for sure so little about our early society
can make us drily cautious when we try to imagine this lost vast
stretch of human history. Probably, the more boldly we let our imaginations range, the more realistic we are being.

But what lessons can safely be drawn from prehistoric hunter-
gatherer societies?

First, that we were, from early on, the pawns of climate. Human
civilization emerged during a warm, wet phase of Earth's oscillation.
Our earlier close-squeak moments came as a result of global cooling,
and there is no reason to suppose the cycles of warming and cooling
have been for ever suspended. We may be heating the planet up dangerously fast again and we may disappear as a result. But our history
reminds us that we are versatile. We are here because we are good
adapters.

Second, we are both extraordinarily creative and extraordinarily
violent. Indeed, the two seem worryingly inseparable. A range of

modern historians and archaeologists have effectively debunked the myth of the noble savage, which infected European thinkers – reacting against their own leaders' war-making – from the Enlightenment of the 1700s to Communism and into our own times. There is a history of lethal raiding and occasional massacres that has been uncovered from Stone Age Europe to the New Guinea Highlands, from Alaska and the Americas to the Asian steppe, which clearly pre-dates war-making states.[10] As we shall see, it was certainly not universal. But hand-axe-shaped holes in the skulls of murdered Europeans suggest prehistoric man was doing more than making art.

The archaeologists Stephen LeBlanc and Katherine Register, after contemplating the evidence of war and massacre among the Anasazi people of New Mexico long before Europeans arrived, have made a long study of prehistoric warfare, which they conclude was regular and very brutal. They say this about those famous, glorious caves:

> Even more evidence of warfare is found among the paintings at Lascaux and other caves in France and Spain. These earliest known human artworks feature magnificent renditions of bison, mammoth, and deer but also include sticklike human figures with spears projecting into their bodies. Somehow, descriptions of these less-than-harmonious sides of the world's wonders don't often make it into the travel brochures. There is a failure to look for or see evidence of warfare because of a myth and the pre-occupation with the idea that the past was peaceful.[11]

As I have argued earlier, this was probably linked with our strong group-bonding, which allowed us to populate the world in the first place, to celebrate 'us' and, by extension, to demonize 'them'. We probably wiped out other human types, we certainly wiped out other mammals; and throughout our history we have, in the intervals between making art and love, tried very hard to wipe out each other. We began, and we remain, agents of instability.

The Farming Puzzle

In the Introduction, I warned that this would be a 'great man' and 'great woman' version of human history, and that kings mostly mattered more than peasant farmers. But this is only so *because* of those farmers. Because of agriculture, the human population of the world rose hugely. Because people stopped moving around in bands of hunter-gatherers and settled down to look after crops and animals, they developed villages, then towns, then civilizations. Thicker versions of primitive maize, the heavy seeds of Asian grasses, the collected-and-replanted wild rice in China, are the tiny items upon which the Aztecs, Sumerians, Egyptians and early dynasties stand. And us too. Without farming – no class divisions, no surplus to elevate kings and priests, no armies, no French Revolution, no moon-landing.

So what is the puzzle? It is that people would choose to farm in the first place; because it did not make for an easy life. The chances are that, if you are reading this, then of the seven billion people alive right now you are among the one billion living in the rich world and within that one billion you have lived your life in a town or city. We have lost touch with the importance of farming, its perils, its hopes and timescales. Farming has become something most people who read books like this have never had to bother about. Famines happened in recent European history only because of wars or political incompetence. Our abundance is so great, no disaster-movie producer has even contemplated famine as a Western plot line.

Yet farming, which was mostly back-breaking, boring work, is coming back to haunt us, the victims of its very success. Farming made the human population take-off possible. It took nearly ten thousand years from the first attempts at agriculture for the world's population to reach a billion. Now we are adding extra people at a billion every dozen years. World food stocks, held for emergencies, are tiny. This means that to avoid famine every person needs to be fed by a far smaller patch of land than ever before. This will not be easy. According to the US National Academy of Sciences, measured by weight humans make up less than 0.5 per cent of the planet's animals but consume a quarter of its plants' production. It is time to remember how interesting and important mere farming really is.

And to salute those who began it. For the archaeological record is clear. Early farmers had in general worse health and lived shorter lives than their hunter-gatherer predecessors and rivals. Fused and mis-shapen vertebrae, bad knees and bad teeth tell a story repeated in cultures all around the world. In a study by the anthropologist J. Lawrence Angel in 1984, it was shown that human lifespans actually fell between the hunter-gatherers of the Palaeolithic period some twenty-five thousand years ago, when men lived for around thirty-five and a half years, and the height of the agricultural revolution five thousand years ago, when men lived on average to thirty-three. Men lost about six inches in height by becoming farmers; women shrank by about five inches. Later jokes about farmers always protesting about the weather, or being naturally glum, are rooted in a basic truth. It is a hard life, hedged about with worry. For early farmers the basic toil of cutting down trees, irrigating fields, hand-ploughing with branches and harvesting with slate and stone sickles was compounded by the fear of the crop being eaten by wild animals or stolen by better-armed and more aggressive hunters.

So again, why – why in a world of leaping salmon and herds of antelope, a world relatively empty of humans but filled with berries and game, would people choose to stick in the mud? Ancient myths of Gardens of Eden, of a golden age and of carefree people living in the forests are reminders that farming – shaping nature rather than pluck-ing it – has never seemed an obviously attractive bargain. It is no accident that later on, when rulers emerged, they so often had them-selves portrayed as hunters, and that even in the modern world hunting is a sport of kings. No monarch has had himself portrayed ploughing, or digging potatoes. The world of the hunter seems some-how nobler, grander and more exciting than that of the farmer, bowed over his furrows or uneasily patrolling the walls of the sheepfold.

One answer to the question of the rise of agriculture is that it simply allows far more humans to be alive. It has been estimated that a hunter-gatherer needs about ten square miles of game and berry-filled land to live on, whereas agriculture can produce enough calories in a tenth of that space to keep fifty people alive. More humans and therefore less available hunting land suggests that agriculture was the only answer. Yet this is to put the question the wrong way round. The increase in population came after agriculture started, not before. Across the planet, throughout this period, vastly more land was inhab-ited by hunters than by farmers: this is the unrecorded narrative of the Indian forests, the Eurasian steppes, the jungled islands of East Asia and the migrations of the Americas. Most people found ways of *not*

farming. And yet farming was repeatedly invented in completely separate parts of the world.

It happened first in the Fertile Crescent, which curves from today's
Jordan and Israel, up to Anatolia in today's Turkey, and then like a
sickle back east into Iraq. It happened in northern China next. Then in
Mexico; and independently in the Andes; then in what is now the eastern United States. It may have developed independently in Africa too,
and in New Guinea. Thousands of years separate these 'origins of
farming' breakthroughs, but they are clearly more than a coincidence.
And once farming is firmly established, it often spreads, as it did from
the Fertile Crescent into Europe some four thousand years after its
invention, and into the Indus valley in today's Pakistan, and Egypt.[12]

Though historians argue about the reasons, they mostly agree
that, again, climate change was very important. There was no single
'ice age': as we have already hinted. But around fifteen thousand years
ago the coldest part of the last ice age was coming to an end, and the
climate of the key landmasses north of the equator began to improve.
Without the greater fecundity of plants there could have been no
farming. In the milder, wetter climate there was an early abundance of
animal life too, which provided hunters with an easy living. But from
the Americas to Australia, there is enough evidence of mankind's
arrival being followed by extinctions of large mammals to suggest that
we simply became too good at hunting for our own long-term survival. The game got harder to find. Migrations of deer, horses,
antelopes and others shrivelled and changed course. Animal bones
found near human settlements actually get smaller over time, as the
bigger adults are killed off.

By around eleven thousand years ago, some groups of humans
realized that by keeping some animals near by – to begin with, the
ancestors of today's sheep, goats and pigs – they could ensure for
themselves meat and hides. People had probably been gathering edible
seeds for centuries before they started to plant stands of them, then
returned to the same place for the annual harvest of seed-heavy
grasses or nutrition-rich peas. Most plants and animals are, of course,
useless to humans – the indigestible foliage, the poisonous roots, the
thin-fleshed, hard-to-catch birds and insects – so careful selection of
those species that would repay care and attention was crucial. We have
to imagine an individual discovery, repeated again and again – those

grasses, with those slightly heavier grains swaying on that particular incline where the stream turns course, gathered and returned to, and eventually helped along, helped to multiply. In societies where men would be expected to hunt further from their settlements, this was probably a breakthrough made by women.

In this, the people living in the Near East were especially fortunate. There are fifty-six edible grasses growing wild in the world – cereals like wheat, barley, corn and rice. Of those, no fewer than thirty-two grew on the hills and plains of the Fertile Crescent of today's southern Turkey, Syria, Jordan, Israel and Iraq, compared with just four varieties apiece in Africa and America, and only one native variety, oats, in Western Europe. Furthermore, the peoples living in the Fertile Crescent had access to the wild originals of emmer wheat, barley, chickpeas, peas, lentils and flax, as well as more animals suitable for domestication. Over the course of later history, invaded by everyone from Egyptians and Persians to Arabs and Crusaders, this has not been a blessed slice of the world; but it began very lucky indeed.

The Americans had llamas, the Chinese, pigs. But these people of the Fertile Crescent had at their disposal a disproportionate number of the thirteen large animals that can be domesticated. They had not only pigs and nearby wild horses, but also cows, goats and sheep, plus those thirty-two grasses. Jared Diamond has pointed out that, by contrast, the most benign part of Chile had only two of the fifty-six prized grasses, 'California and southern Africa just one each, and south-western Australia none at all. That fact alone goes a long way toward explaining the course of human history.'[13]

So in the Fertile Crescent, people called Natufians were gathering grain around thirteen thousand years ago; and early on – presumably in order to stay close to the precious grain – they settled down in villages rather than moving around as hunter-gatherers. They were not quite alone in this: at around the same time, it is now thought, groups of hunters living near the Yangtze River in China were also gathering and eating wild rice.

But then the climate changed again. The cooling was not as dramatic as during the ice ages proper, nor permanent, but it was dramatic enough. This brief period is known, after a plant whose advance and retreat are used to measure it, as the 'Younger Dryas'. The Natufians found the grain they had been enjoying began to die out in the colder, drier plains. Higher ground attracts more water and keeps more species alive in hard times, so it was growing in the hills, but they had to go further to find and collect it. Elk and mammoth disappeared at the same time.[14] Something similar must have happened in China too. Never underestimate the power of laziness: under this pressure people seem to have made the next logical step. Instead of going to the bother of migrating and building new villages, following the changing patterns of the wild grains, they started to collect surplus grains, carry them home and plant them. It seems an almost insignificant shift, a labour-saving way of avoiding long walks. But it was a huge one for humanity. In the Fertile Crescent, and in China, where a similar shift happened with rice and millet, agriculture had begun.

This may also explain why the first villages appeared where they did. There is most biodiversity in the hills and mountains, but people prefer to live in sheltered valleys. It was here that they found 'just right' places, not too exposed to wind, but near enough to the wild plants that they could gather and try to grow – from the corn, beans, squash, avocados and tomatoes of the Mexican mountains to the scores of grasses and beans in the Atlas mountains. No doubt plants were regularly brought down and tried out, and only the most promising were kept – those that were most nourishing, those that were hardiest and those that changed pleasingly fast into fatter versions of themselves when selected. To start with, and for a long time, this planting of crops and tethering or tending of animals was accompanied by hunting. The antelope would be culled as they migrated; deer and fish would be brought home.

But farming humanity had walked into a trap. Not for the last time, we had taken a decisive step whose consequences could never have been imagined, and from which there was no pulling back.

The trap was that settled farming communities swiftly produced bigger populations. Even with Late Stone Age technology, each acre of farmed land could support more than ten times as many people as each acre of hunted land. It was not simply about food, either. As we have seen, hunting tribes, always on the move, have to carry their children. That limits how many babies a woman can have. Once people settled down, the birth rate could rise, and it did. Larger families mean more mouths to feed, which means that farming and herding become

ever more important. Once broken, the fields can never be safely abandoned. The herds can never be untethered and returned to the wild.
The farming men and women may be shorter in stature, more prone
to disease – because parasites and pests settle down as well – and they
may die earlier. Their days may be longer and their worries greater.
They may have lost the freedom to roam through the wild and magic-
al places. But they are feeding more children – nephews, nieces, even
grandchildren.

They cannot stop. Before, they were shaping and taming the plants
and animals; now the plants and animals are shaping and taming them,
too.

They also had to develop other skills. They had to grind and sift
their grain, and store it. Their precious domesticated animals, which
had to be protected from wild beasts and allowed to wander for food –
but not too far – must be exploited in every possible way. Wool could
be sheared and carded and woven. Blood could be drawn off and used
to enrich meal. Some farmers developed the odd habit of drinking the
milk of lactating goats and cows – and most of their European descendants remain lactose-tolerant to this day. The preparation of hides, the
weaving of ropes to help with ploughing, and making baskets and pottery for storing or cooking grain – a whole new world of domestic
jobs and skills emerged.

Farming was the most important human revolution of all. It produced
not only an immense political change, as hierarchies grew from the
sweat and success of farmers, but also less easily tracked changes in
human consciousness. Presumably, the settled communities lost touch
with the wider geography that their hunting forebears had known;
and, with the 'other', the unknown, surrounding them. Villagers
turned a little in on themselves and away from the lands of the wild
beasts and passing hunter groups. Farming would eventually allow
food surpluses for leaders and full-time priests; people able to live
without actually ploughing or herding themselves.

But the arrival of farming also meant the emergence of the home,
or homeland. And as the archaeology shows, settling down produced
people who could pay in grain or hides for 'luxury' materials such as
salt, sharp cutting stones, pretty shells and herbs. So quite early on,
traders must have been carrying their packs along newly worn tracks.

It turned out to be a rather more complex bargain than the first handful of fatter seeds might have suggested.

The rise of farming does indeed shape all of later history. The relative paucity of animals to domesticate, and the later start at farming that was the fate of the people who had arrived in Mesoamerica, meant that the civilizations established there were about three thousand years behind those of Europe and Asia and so would be very vulnerable to conquest. The degradation of the soil in the Mesopotamian delta led to the fall of the Sumerian civilization, and the overuse of agricultural land in the classical world led eventually to the desertification of North Africa. Both of these farming failures created political vacuums – relatively thinly populated stretches of land – which in due course would accelerate the spread of Islam.

Thin soil propelled both Vikings and Mongols. But first came towns.

Gentle Anarchists

One day, Tokyo and London, LA and Moscow, will be gone and forgotten. One day far in the future – let us hope – undulating mounds of stone, weirdly shaped green cover and buried walls, motorways and metal objects, will lie quietly, as planetary scars. If this is hard to imagine, reflect that the first towns are already long gone. Some are buried deep below today's towns. Long before the walls of Jericho fell to Joshua's priests' trumpets, it had been an ancient settlement, one of the oldest in the world, with a fresh spring, mud-brick dwellings and even a wall and a tower, though these are thought to have been to protect its people against floods rather than attackers.

North of Jericho, on the Anatolian plains of today's Turkey, are scores of odd-looking mounds, roughly symmetrical hills, gently rising above the modern fields of wheat, barley and maize. Quite probably, most of them are the remains of Neolithic towns, each once home to thousands of people: a lost, noisy world of early farmers and their families who had settled down and worked together for many centuries, worshipping leopard-gods, saving up for goods from far away, making jokes, marrying and burying their dead.

All this is a reasonable guess because one of these mounds has been opened up, initially by British archaeologists. It has proved to be a revelation, a treasure trove of knowledge about what happened after the shift to agriculture. Today Catalhoyuk is a small area of excavated earth under metal canopies, with a modest collection of archaeologists' housing near by. It looks a little like a film director's set for a movie set in the trenches. It is rather less well known than Rome or Angkor Wat, but in human history it is almost as significant.

Its buildings were lived in from around 9,500 to 7,700 years ago. It has no defensive walls. Nor does it have any buildings much grander than the others, or standing apart. There are no signs of rulers, priests, warrior quarters, lesser workers' huts – it is just one egalitarian hive. In some ways the homes feel remarkably modern. With a hearth and a living room, a pantry close by, and other rooms which seem to have been bedrooms, the typical home was kept scrupulously clean with regular whitewashing of the walls and floor. When you walk around, the strangeness vanishes and these dwellings, about the size of a modern city apartment or a cottage, feel familiar – modest, but big enough.

Yet the sense of familiarity is only skin-deep. This is not a town as we know towns. Catalhoyuk had no streets, no squares or public buildings. Its people entered their honeycomb of homes through door-openings in the roofs, with ladders leading down, almost as if they were entering man-made caves. They socialized, we must assume, on the roofs which, connected together, would have made a large, safe, flat space for craft work or gathering and talking, and probably had canopies to keep off the sun. (In this area of Turkey, with its broiling summers, people still often sit out on the rooftop under a shade, and sleep overnight there too.)

The houses were renovated or rebuilt by partially knocking down the original, then building upwards on the ruins, so that they grew almost like a human coral, structure on structure. In places, there are eighteen separate layers of homes. Rooms were ornately decorated with plastered bulls' heads, paintings of leopards and of hunts, and with stone and clay figures of women and animals. Unlike Jericho and other early urban centres, here everything seems to happen in the home. The current lead archaeologist for the site, Ian Hodder of Stanford University, says: 'In a modern town we would expect to identify different functional areas and buildings such as the industrial and residential zones, the church or mosque or temple, and the cemetery. At

Catalhoyuk all these separate functions occur in one place, in the house.'[15]

In these houses people stored their food, enough for a single family, in large carved wooden containers, and wove baskets and mats; they made daggers and belt buckles from flint and bone, polished obsidian mirrors, created bracelets and other jewellery; made curious stamp-seals, perhaps for marking property or their own skin; and they cooked and cleaned. All about was excellent farming land, streams and ponds with fish and birds; and the population grew to around seven thousand, perhaps ten thousand – which made it one of the largest human settlements on earth at the time. From the rubbish tips outside the town we can tell they lived well, on wild pigs, ducks, geese, sheep, fish, barley and oats.

The most striking thing about Catalhoyuk is where the bodies were buried. The dead were carefully curled up – 'lovingly' seems a reasonable description – and then interred under the floors of the houses, under the stoves, or under the platforms where the living slept. Some think they were first exposed to be picked clean by vultures; the current view is that this was not so, and people simply got used to the smell of decomposition. Some of the dead had their heads removed after death, and these were then plastered and painted and kept. Presumably they were the heads of significant people, perhaps the one-time heads of households. They seem to have been dug up, replastered and buried again, a kind of family memento that would be recycled through generations. One house had more than sixty corpses in it.

There are more mysteries in Catalhoyuk: in the houses, the bulls' heads and paintings of leopards suggest a worship of natural power and aggression in the world outside. The inhabitants did not need David Attenborough to bring a sense of the danger of the sunlit outside world into the dark, cave-like womb of the home. But the practice of building home after home on the same site, and burying family members there and preserving heads, all point to ancestor worship, common throughout China and Japan, and indeed in the Mediterranean world up to Roman times.

These are people living in nuclear families, or at least nuclear homes, and identifying themselves with their parents, grandparents and back through the generations. They are saying, 'We *are* this ground, this place, this footprint on the soil; a strong assertion of set-tlement after the thousands of years of nomadic roving. Does that sound odd? If so, it is only because most of us are now real city-dwellers who have lost any direct connection with a specific patch of earth, one that belonged to our ancestors. But for most of human history this identification of lineage and land was normal (even if burying granny under the stove was not).

The second part of the Catalhoyuk message is about equality. As time goes on, and layers grow upon layers, there are some houses that are larger, more decorated and with more burials than others – which suggests the slow emergence of dominant or more powerful families. But there is still nothing like a ruling or priestly class. Catalhoyuk offers a glimpse of an alternative society before the rise of class divi-sions, the warriors, chiefs and kings of later towns. It is a more peaceful society, poised somewhere between the early farming villages and the fighting empires ahead. Catalhoyuk enthusiasts see it as an egalitarian Eden, where women were venerated, there was no war, and families with only small amounts of personal property lived peaceably and cooperatively together.

We are told this simple anarchism is inherently unstable. Perhaps it is, but the people of Catalhoyuk seem to have managed pretty well for at least fourteen hundred years. There was enough surplus wealth for paintings, pottery and weaving, and a good diet; but not enough for swords or taxes. Lucky them.

The Child-people of Stonehenge

Our prejudices about early mankind are so smeared with blood and glinting with warriors that we have to ask whether the Catalhoyuk story of – relative – peace and love was rare, even unique. One way of trying to answer this is to travel forward in time, but to a more primi-tive part of the world that offers interesting comparisons.

What is now called Britain developed more slowly than the Fertile Crescent, and had a harsher climate. While Catalhoyuk was rising, nine thousand years ago, the ice sheet was only just finally leaving the British highlands, and the lowlands there were thinly populated by hunters and gatherers. As the ice went, Britain became mostly covered with thick forests of oak, elm, alder and lime, plus birch and willow in the north. A squirrel could have crossed from one side of it to the other without ever setting foot on the ground. Or so it is said.

Two thousand years further on, after Catalhoyuk had risen and was on the way down again, Britain was still a tough place for farmers but they were already changing the landscape. They had started on small strips of coastal land and were now hacking back the forest and planting clearings with wheat. This slash-and-burn agriculture is only a short-term proposition. The soil gets quickly exhausted and more clearing must follow, with the previous 'fields' left to revert to woodland. A thousand years later – for we are still at the stage where change happens slowly – the clearings were bigger. Something like regular farmland was appearing, particularly in the south of what is now England, ploughed and no doubt fertilized and weeded.

The people were growing primitive varieties of wheat and barley and maybe flax. They seem to have grown no vegetables, but added berries and nuts to their diets. They ploughed with oxen, reared cattle, pigs and some sheep, and from very early on had domesticated dogs – the bones of some dogs looking like those of modern Labradors and some like terriers' have been found. Dogs, among the first domesticated animals, contributed vital help for guarding and hunting. But the historian Rodney Castleden has noted that from their bones it is clear that 'some dogs lived to be old, beyond their useful working lives, so their owners kept them out of affection'.[16]

The doggy people themselves did not live to be old. An analysis of bones from one community in Orkney, which was then an advanced part of the British Isles, shows that 70 per cent were either teenagers or in their twenties. Just 1 per cent were over fifty. This was a young society, evidently. The skulls suggest they were delicate, fine-featured people, nothing like the heavy, glowering early Britons of popular legend. We do not have their clothes, of course: a culture existing in a warm, moist Britain that mostly built and carved out of wood, and wore woven wool, leather and possibly flax capes, hats and tunics, leaves very little behind. But by looking at the tiny remnants of similar cultures on mainland Europe, and studying buckles, pins and tools that have survived, it is possible to plausibly posit the kinds of tightly sewn and comfortable clothes the British wore.

Though we call this the Neolithic or 'new stone' age, we might as accurately call it the age of wood and leather. People started by living in rectangular wooden homes wearing leather clothes (made supple and smooth using disgusting techniques apparently involving copious amounts of urine, cow dung and raw animal brains). They went on to wear woven clothes and to live in larger, communal houses and in villages centred on cleverly built roundhouses, where hundreds could sleep under the same roof.

Speaking of the people living at Skara Brae, the beautifully made stone village started around five thousand years ago on a curving bay in Orkney and uncovered by a storm in 1850, Castleden says the overall impression is of a high level of domestic comfort: 'Living conditions for ordinary people were apparently at least as good as they were in medieval Britain over four thousand years later: at Skara Brae probably rather better.'[17] Walking through some of the homes and passages of Skara Brae today vividly recalls the domestic cosiness of Catalhoyuk – the same family rooms with dressers and places to sleep and corridors, all made in stone, rather than mud and plaster. There may or may not have been chieftains and priests, but this was not a war-torn culture.

In the Middle and Late Stone Age, the Orkneys and Shetlands were, far from being marginal archipelagos, advanced places. Their pottery circulated around Britain, and their stone circles, burial places and villages were unusually large and complex. They were way ahead, for instance, of the damp southern bog now known as London.

For centuries historians have found it impossible to believe that early British culture could have developed so impressively, leading up to the great monument of Stonehenge itself, just by gentle evolution. There must, surely, have been a warrior or priestly elite directing things, and perhaps having arrived as invaders from the continent? Yet there is no evidence of any such elite, nor of a cultural migration. There seems no reason not to believe that the British developed more like the people of Catalhoyuk had, in communities of a rough equality, scattered in their hundreds across the agricultural land and connected by trade links. For all the vivid modern legends of human sacrifice (there may have been some) and violent death, Neolithic Britain has left remarkably little evidence of war or organized violence, and none at all of castles or palaces.

But if so, how were so many people mobilized to create Stonehenge, or the awesome 'hill' at Silbury – which involved shifting as much earth as the average Egyptian pyramid being built at the same time – or the stone villages and monuments of the Orkney and Shetland islands themselves?

These were astonishing achievements. We are talking of people with no metal, no towns, nothing we would recognize as writing. But they lived on islands traversed by roadways connecting thousands of village settlements – the 'Sweet Track' in the Somerset wetlands, three miles of split oak, needing ten thousand pegs and made six thousand years ago, is Europe's oldest built road – and must have produced the essential tools, including flint blades and axes, on a virtually industrial scale. The flint mines were deep enough to require miners working with little lamps. The boats carrying produce around the coasts must have been comparatively big – either dugout canoes tied together or even animal-skin vessels on a skeleton of wood. There is evidence of windlasses, of sophisticated joinery and immaculately made stonework. This is a sophisticated and patient culture.

Above all, there was time and there was cooperation. Stonehenge grew over a thousand years, more or less, starting with an earthwork, before it became a vast structure including eighty-two bluestones dragged 150 miles from Wales, and the sandstone, or sarsen, blocks weighing up to 53 tons each, taken from around twenty miles away. These were shaped, smoothed, raised and then topped with more, as lintels. How was it done? Various overground and water-borne routes have been proposed. Wheels were known, but it is thought the stones would have been too heavy, and the ground too rough, for wooden axles to cope. They could have been rolled on logs, but that would have been a very long job indeed. Sledges are thought more likely, drawn by oxen or teams of men, after the Welsh stones had been unloaded from boats.

As to shaping and raising them, there are several possible and plausible techniques, including using wedges and fire to crack the stones, digging wood-lined pits to raise them, and building slowly raised platforms to put the huge lintels in place. It is an awesome achievement but it did not require giants – or tyrants. The large tribal communities of the area, by working together and allowing themselves as much time as it took (rather as the later builders of cathedrals worked in generations of time), could have managed the various evolutions of

Stonehenge, and the other great Neolithic sites, even the supremely impressive ziggurat-cum-hill at Silbury.

Hardly anybody disagrees about what Stonehenge was used for. Its alignments to the rays of the rising midsummer sun show that it was a temple of some kind. It was not an accurate stone calendar, as some have claimed, but complex markers for moonrise show a detailed interest in lunar cycles. Some new carbon-dating of post holes, where the measurements were taken, suggests this began incredibly early, around ten thousand years ago – so before Catalhoyuk. We cannot know the details of British beliefs so far back, except that they were associated with the sun, bringer of warmth and fertility, and with the moon, and so must have involved the seasonal celebrations and prayers typical of farming people everywhere. The huge barrow graves, with bones broken and burned before burial, suggest a reverence for ancestors and tribal or family continuity, which is certainly echoed in the white-plastered rooms of Anatolia. Darkness and death, a close interest in the seasons and the awesome power of the sun, family and memory; the rest is detail.

So we must think of an ingenious, patient, skilled and youthful culture, not one of white-bearded Druids or terrifying, blood-soaked chieftains. They come later, in the Bronze Age. The henges and the huge roundhouses were eventually abandoned. We cannot tell why. It may have been because of rising population pressures which caused conflict over scarce and degraded agricultural land. At any rate, a bloodier age lay ahead, as it did for the Fertile Crescent and for Neolithic China too. Yet we should remember that the age of peaceful farming communities, worshipping the sun and moon, tending their animals and crops, trading at their borders with others and eventually building remarkable monuments, lasted in Britain for thousands of years, much longer than empires, dynasties or democracy. It never happened again – in Britain, or in Europe.

The last word on this ought to go to Rodney Castleden:

> With something approaching ecological balance and communities as a matter of routine living peacefully within their means, it is possible to see within the Neolithic culture an object lesson for modern industrial economies and societies in the west. They show few signs of outlasting the Industrial Revolution by more

than two or three centuries, whilst the Neolithic subsistence economy lasted ten times as long.

This is a strong warning, but there are simply far too many of us now, depending on too much consumption, to really be able to heed it. And anyway, even as the British henge-builders were coming to their mysterious end, humanity was about to make the next stride towards recorded history – into the city.

The Cities of the Plain

South-east of Catalhoyuk two mighty rivers run south towards the sea. The Fertile Crescent saw the first farmers and the first large set-tlements, and so it is not surprising that it also gave birth to the first cities and the first empires. 'Mesopotamia' simply means the land between these two rivers, the Tigris and the Euphrates. As they get nearer the sea, they slow and sprawl, curling into tangled deltas. A wonderfully rich farming area of dark, moist soil became available just before the start of the marshes. It offered similar advantages to the watery land around Catalhoyuk, but on a much bigger scale, and it attracted people from all over the region. They settled down in homes built first of reeds and later of mud bricks, coalescing into villages. What is probably the first city, Eridu, emerged about seven thousand years ago, not so long after Catalhoyuk was abandoned. Within a few hundred years there were many more towns in the area. Eridu was a brick-built settlement with layer upon layer of temple buildings, and may have started as a communal site at which different villages could worship the gods. These were altogether bigger places. There would be no gentle anarchism here.

The villages had had to come together, to create and then to main-tain, the complicated system of waterways and dykes needed for agriculture. Workers had to be organized to do this; the excellent farming produced surpluses of grain and these allowed the introduc-tion of rulers and priests, who developed temples and employed servants to tend them. Because the Mesopotamian world was a muddy, watery, sun-baked flatland it is not surprising that its most characteristic major buildings would be ziggurats, raised pyramid-platforms where gods could be worshipped. All around the world people have associated gods with height, and in this land of no mountains the only way to reach up was to build. Eridu itself was built on a low mound by a freshwater lagoon, with the desert on one side, the marshes on another and the farming land on another.

It was the perfect meeting-point of different geographies and its gods were headed by the male Apsu, who represented sweet water, and the female Tiamat, representing salt water. But the water gods did not pay enough attention: Eridu probably lost its dominance around four thousand years ago when, it seems, there was a major flood. The next great city, Uruk, had begun at around the same time, and at its height had a population of around eighty thousand, which would have made it the world's largest settlement, with ten times as many people as Catalhoyuk. Its king Gilgamesh is the subject of the first work of literature with a named hero – the first name in history. Gilgamesh may or may not have been a real king but his story, which incorporates a biblical-scale Flood, is a very human one of sex and betrayal, friendship and failure, journeying and death.

We know this because eventually it was written down. At Uruk and other towns of the Mesopotamian plain, the symbols scratched on clay tablets, which represented quantities and ownership of corn, beer and other goods that were traded, developed so far that they became writing. Over many centuries a system of notation and recording evolved into a system that could record stories and ideas. The reason was identical to the one that created Uruk in the first place. Climate changes, in this case leading to an even hotter, drier environment, compelled the farmers to build much larger and more sophisticated waterways to keep their land productive. Individual families or villages were far too small, and had too little spare time, to achieve what was needed. Only by combining in large numbers, organized by managers, could they survive. The managers seem to have been priests, or at least to have been based in the temples, from where they oversaw vast irrigation projects.

Once the system of manpower and specialized skills was in place, the managers had the brawn to build ever greater temples. The feedback from successful irrigation to the power of those who directed it is obvious: over time, the managers were able to claim they spoke for, with, and to, the gods. They were responsible for the settlement's very survival. The original ruling class, high on their platforms, ears tilted to the heavens, had arrived. Below them, totting up the deliveries of grain, beer, meat and metals they required from the toilers, were the scribes or middle management. You cannot have a hierarchically organized society without the paperwork – or in this case, the clay-work.

Feedback is an essential idea. It explains why, once people are organized and crammed together inside a city wall, the rate of development accelerates. For the Sumerians and after them the other people of ancient Mesopotamia, the Akkadians and Babylonians, experienced a speed of change completely unlike anything humans had known before. Priests demand their special places – intimidating, nearer the gods. This required huge numbers of workers and full-time craftsmen, as well as measuring and planning. That in turn meant detailed note-taking, indeed writing. Then, large tributes of food, beer and raw materials were called for, to keep the building workers alive.

Making people pay what were in effect taxes would not have been pleasant; force would have been needed. At the same time, all the accumulating wealth would be a temptation to robbers and ultimately to rival cities. So walls were built and some men given the job of full-time protectors. A warrior class emerged. Nothing, sad to say, has advanced technical progress faster than war. The invention of bronze, replacing flint or bone as the cutting-edge technology, gave the Sumerians a brief advantage. Then came chariots, first slow and four-wheeled, later two-wheeled. (They may have developed first for that next novelty, leisure time, which the upper classes used for hunting.)

Priests of religion. Large-scale building projects. Writing. Taxes. Soldiers. Kings. The ability to make war. All arrive in human history alongside one another, based on the first cities, which are really the first concentrations of stored wealth, themselves based on riverside farming cultures that needed to work together to tame nature. This is the shift that is more powerful than the old ties of clan, kin and lineage, and marks the next important moment in human development after farming itself. Rivalry between cities and peoples will start to accelerate change, unless and until full-scale war brings catastrophe; which from time to time it does. The rise of trained bureaucrats, with their cuneiform writing implements, permits different people with different languages to communicate; Sumerian becomes the lingua franca for Mesopotamia, and scribes become bilingual. A momentum is under way, which may be lost here or there but which has never stopped since.

The first cities also nurtured a flowering of abstract thought. The ruling class of kings and priests had time to speculate, not least about the mysterious world of winking lights and movements overhead that had also obsessed the builders of Stonehenge. So it is no surprise that Mesopotamia gave us mathematics, both the simple sums to tally trade and taxes and the more complicated ones used to try to track the stars. Looking up, the Sumerians and Babylonians wondered about this nightly message, with its shapes and regular patterns. If the gods were able to send messages back to them, were these the divine writing? Was there a pattern, which could then be imposed on the hazier rhythms of human life?

Reading the stars required measurement of angles. The Sumerians plotted the movements of the five planets they could see – Mercury, Venus, Mars, Jupiter and Saturn – and named a day after each. They then named one day after the Moon and another after the Sun, giving them a seven-day week. Seven was regarded as a perfect number; and the Sumerian week is of course our week, its days still named in the Sumerian fashion, though with Roman or Old English words. Saturn becomes Saturday, Sol ('the sun' in Latin) becomes Sunday. Luna, the moon, becomes *lundi* in French, or our Monday (Moon-day). Mars is *mardi*, though in English, thanks to a Norse god, Tuesday. Similarly, Wednesday is Wodin's day, but Wodin was the god associated with the planet Mercury. Jupiter is *jeudi*; or in English, Thursday, Thor being the northern god associated with Jupiter. Venus is *vendredi*, or Friday. The Sumerians also developed a counting system based on the number sixty, which is divisible by eleven other numbers and so particularly handy for Bronze Age accountancy. From this we get our 60-second minutes, 60-minute hours, 360-day years and 360-degree circles. By Babylonian times, scribes had to be fast and accurate: one examination tablet from their city of Nippur asks, 'Do you know multiplication, reciprocals, coefficients, balancing of accounts, administrative accounting, how to make all kinds of pay allotments, divide property and delimit shares of fields?'[18]

All of this is remarkable enough, but the first cities also bring a flowering of art and design, with gorgeously made alabaster carvings and mosaics and graceful (as well as useful) stamp-seals for parcels of goods from Uruk, plus inlaid gaming-boards, musical instruments and delicate gold jewellery from Ur – even before we get to the amazing carved reliefs of the Assyrians and Babylonians. Today, thanks to the habits of nineteenth-century archaeologists, the loveliest of these things can be found in Berlin and (to a lesser extent) London, not in Iraq. Each Mesopotamian city had its own gods, culture and reputation. Uruk was famous not only for its huge ziggurat and sky-god but for its sexy female deity Inanna, who was associated with all kinds of fertility and whose rites shocked one Babylonian writer: 'Uruk . . . city of prostitutes, courtesans and call-girls . . . the party-boys and festival people who changed masculinity to femininity'.[19] (And it took a lot to shock a Babylonian.)

So these first cities are among the most important sites in the human story. Successive floods have reduced many of them to gritty stumps, and obliterated others. Neglect, war and the lack of interest of later cultures followed by aggressive, treasure-hunting Victorian archaeology has meant that while some of their greatest carvings and other artefacts are in European museums, the sites themselves are often dusty disappointments. This is tragic, since the achievements of the Sumerians, Akkadians and early Babylonians were huge, and in some ways much more impressive than those of the better-known Egyptians. Their city culture was bureaucratic and clearly in some ways oppressive, weighing heavily on farmers, requiring payment in return for the canals and wells that kept their fields so fertile. It allowed the emergence of kings with enough muscle to go to war against one another, and to carve out the first empires, along with the misery that early mass-killers such as Sargon of Akkad brought to the land. But these first cities were also places of beauty, intellectual advance, wonder and – quite clearly – a great deal of not very innocent fun.

Da Yu to You

You might imagine that the earliest named Chinese hero was a warrior-ruler like Gilgamesh, or some bearded sage; but you would be wrong. He is a public servant, an engineer and only latterly a king. Da Yu, or 'the Great Yu', a figure who stands just on the wrong side of the line between myth and history, was the man who tamed the Yellow River, that life-giving but capricious core of early Chinese culture. Da Yu's father, so the story goes, was a man called Gun who had been given the job by the local ruler of dealing with devastating river floods. Most early cultures, particularly across Asia and Europe, have flood stories, suggesting that there was a time of flooding so bad that it remained in the consciousness of peoples for millennia.

In China's case, Gun tried to cope by building dykes, presumably using the same rammed-earth technique found in early Chinese towns. But more floods came and simply washed the earth walls away. The king who had commissioned Gun punished him by cutting him into many pieces. Gun's son, the presumably rather anxious Da Yu, then took on the job in his scattered father's place.

Da Yu, it is said, worked ferociously hard – but he did not build dykes. First, he travelled up and down the river talking to the local tribes and persuading people that they would have to work together and accept central authority if the problem was to be coped with. The parallels with the rise of the Mesopotamian cities are obvious. Next, he had channels dug to send the water to other rivers, and irrigation systems built to spread it across the farmland. Instead of confronting his enemy head-on, Da Yu confused the river by dividing it. For thirteen years he worked fanatically, reducing his hands and feet to callused pads. It is said that during that time he passed by his home on three occasions. The first time he heard his wife in labour, but did not stop or go in. The second time, his son was old enough to call out his name. He did not stop, because the floods were in full spate. The third time, his son was over ten years old. Again, Da Yu ignored him, and kept working. Today he would be pursued by the Child Support Agency and condemned by newspaper columnists. Things were different then.

The king was so impressed by his diligence and dedication that he passed the throne to him. Da Yu reigned for forty-five years, and then by passing the throne to his son founded the Xia dynasty.

Later, copious amounts of nonsense were glued onto the story, ranging from Da Yu cutting through a mountain with a magic battle-axe, to his having engaged the services of a yellow dragon and a black turtle to help him. But the first key point is that, according to the earliest Chinese historians, the first Chinese dynasty began with attempts to control flooding. And that is at the very least a good guess on their part. About four thousand years ago there seems to have been a collapse in Chinese settlements, at just the time when the same was happening in the Middle East and Egypt. Going back to those flood stories, Noah and the rest, the historian Ian Morris asks, 'Could climate change have brought on an Old World-crisis?'[20] The same annals that describe Da Yu speak of rain continuing for nine years, causing catastrophic flooding.

But there is no Noah, no Ark: China starts with a public-servant hero, an organizer working for the state. There is something here that feels very unWestern.

From almost the beginning, Chinese culture looks, as well as feels, distinctively Chinese. Put a reasonably educated person from anywhere in the world in front of certain late-Neolithic pottery, or very early bronze vessels, or show them the first symbols being used for writing – and even if they have never seen such things before, they will probably instantly declare: 'Chinese.' The origins of the Chinese are shrouded in archaeological uncertainty and political argument. Many Chinese insist they did not emerge, like the rest of the world's human population, out of Africa, but evolved separately from an earlier ape migration, that of *Homo erectus*, in China. Thus they are biologically distinct from foreigners – satisfying to the Chinese world view, even if the scientific consensus outside China is that they are wrong.

Overall, human development in China followed along similar lines to that of the Fertile Crescent, but around two thousand years later – though in some things, like pottery, it was more advanced. The breakthroughs in the taming of plants and animals, the appearance of villages, graves suggesting ancestor worship, are all relatively similar. Yet by the time myth first begins to edge into history, Chinese objects are already different-looking. Today's archaeologists tend to emphasize the variation and complexity of ancient China – many cultures, many different kinds of pottery and building, scattered over a wide area. Recent finds have upended the old idea of there being one central Chinese civilization, in the north, which spread to the rest and has carried on more or less intact. But what is very different from the European experience is the emotional grip of a continuity with earliest times on the Chinese imagination.

For instance, the culture known as Longshan lasted for around a thousand years, from roughly 5,000 to 4,000 years ago, about the same time as the various phases of the Neolithic cultures of Britain. But while Europeans have lost any record or memory of the Stonehenge people, Chinese history claims a link with the first kings and cultures. There were five mythical emperors, primordial godly rulers who gave mankind the key inventions of civilization such as cooking, farming, fire, medicine, marriage, the domestication of animals. The last of these mythic rulers is said to have introduced writing, pottery and the calendar – the very inventions which indeed mark out the Longshan culture from earlier settlements.[21] (In claiming that humans began as parasites or worms on the body of the creator, Pan Gu, there may be an element of early human self-criticism too.)

After the five emperors come the dynasties that are considered the beginning of historic China – the Xia, the Shang and the Zhou. In the almost two thousand years they cover, we have the names of kings, increasingly complicated and beautiful artefacts, evidence of cities, temples and fortresses, and writing that is clearly the predecessor of modern Chinese. In short, we have China.

Right at the beginning of this, however, we are still in the dim and misty place where there is more myth than evidence. Of around 300 BC, the *Shang-Shu*, or 'Book of History', is the first written text about what is called China's first dynasty, the Xia. The same account talks of ten thousand states coexisting at the same time, so clearly the Xia were hardly China-straddling. Archaeology suggests numerous rival chiefdoms. The Xia are said to have been founded in 2205 BC by our remarkable tamer of rivers and floods, Da Yu. All early Chinese history is the history of dynasties, one succeeding another like the succession of kings and queens that British schoolchildren once memorized. Even if he was plucked from half-remembered oral traditions by later writers keen to proclaim one China, Da Yu is in at the start of all this. He was supposed to have divided central China into a neat series of parallel box-like zones. The centre of the nine *zhou*, or provinces, was the province of the king, leading eventually to a zone for foreigners and then to the wilderness beyond – all of which sounds like the Chinese version of the Middle Kingdom and therefore suspiciously like propaganda.

So did the Xia kings even exist, never mind Da Yu himself? Until recently the general view was that this was an entirely mythic story –

with, after all, a gap of almost two thousand years before it was written down. But the discovery of what seems to be a Longshan-culture
capital city, at Erlitou, has changed minds. The Xia may not have been
a big dynasty but they probably did exist on the banks of the Yellow
River, and emerged from the Longshan culture itself. Erlitou, discovered in 1959 in Henan Province, has produced examples of beautiful
bronze-cast wine vessels, or *jue*, which have the spindly delicacy of
modernist designs. The city was centred on a large palace complex of
rammed-down earth walls, a way of building that was very labour-
intensive but produced rock-hard structures which still exist across
China.[22]

Chinese archaeology is very exciting just now, because so much
remains to be discovered: recent excavations of tombs have found
beautiful vases, jade ornaments, bronze weapons, very early writing,
evidence of the cultivation of silk and the worship of ancestors. Unlike
Catalhoyuk, this was a hierarchical civilization, run by kings, or priest-
kings, and able to mobilize large numbers of workers.

We know that Chinese farming was heavily based on the rich allu-
vial plains of the Yellow River and its tributaries. In this, the early
growth of human settlement was no different here than around the
Tigris, the Euphrates, the Nile or the Indus – all of which produced
cities, kings and complex religions. Rivers make rich soil, but they also
bring danger. As we have seen, they flood, and their waters need to be
unravelled and spread about for maximum farming success. As much
as wild plants or wild animals, they need to be tamed. But the necessary work calls for leadership and organization, which in turn means
hierarchy and rulers. Farming villages do not need to combine in large
numbers simply to grow crops or tend animals. But they do if they
want to divert rivers, create networks of irrigation channels and flood-
protection systems. The role of civil engineering in human history is
often overlooked.

So Da Yu's story is a kind of explanation for the growth of political authority. He becomes king of the Xia because he has earned it by
organizing the people for their own good. It is hardly a radical proposition that, in general, kings and emperors bring oppression; they may
start small with labour-gangs building dykes, but they progress to
fortress walls and armies and tax-collectors. The underlying message
of the Da Yu tale is that this imposition of authority is still better than

disorder – in this case, the chaos unleashed by rivers that change their direction, or floods that wipe away the livelihoods of millions. In other words, rulers are better than the alternative. It is a message that would have pharaohs and Babylonian priests nodding in agreement.

But the fact that the story of Da Yu, and then the ups and downs of the dynasties that followed the Xia, were written down and made part of a national narrative matters almost as much. Authority, imposed early on because of the need to mobilize the masses to control nature, is then passed down, generation by generation. And as in the West, the Chinese rulers claim their authority not simply because they are good at organizing, or able to scare their subjects, but because they have a special link with the gods. They can have a quiet word and help end the famine, or stop the rains. So the great leaps forward in Chinese art and technology are closely related to religious rites. Ever more ingeniously cast and elaborately carved bronze vessels, musical instruments and animal bones, baked then broken to read the future, turn up in Chinese archaeological sites. Great squat tripods and bronze drinking vessels whose sides are as mazed and rippled as coral reefs may seem strange things for early cultures to invest so much energy in. In fact they are ruthlessly political: they are about power.

Nile Nightmares

Ancient Egypt, our third river civilization, often seems a culture to gape at, not to love. It touches the modern world hardly at all. Sphinxes and pyramids have become globalized visual kitsch. Museum audiences queue around the world to stare at gold or painted relics. Cultural tourists descend by the planeload to see the temples and funeral complexes of the Valley of the Kings. But for such a long-lasting and successful culture, the Egyptians have left relatively few marks on later ways of thinking. The religion of Horus and Osiris enjoyed a brief revival of interest during the twentieth century among occult dabblers and circus-tent crooks. Pharaonic mysteries have briefly enthused the makers of movie mystery capers. But compared with the deep influence of Judaism and its later developments, or the power of Greek thought, or Roman politics – or even, across Asia, the continuing influence of early Chinese and Indian thinkers – ancient

Egypt has little left alive. The Mesopotamians' stumpy relics of pow-
dered brick are pathetic compared with the physical remains of the
Egyptians, but they produced more in the way of science, mathematics and technology to pass on than the creators of this great death cult
on the edge of the desert.

Egyptologists (not to mention Egyptians) would say that this
impression is ignorant and unfair. The people of ancient Egypt were
formidable artists and builders, and they developed a complex religion,
sustaining them for millennia. Many humbler grave-sites than those of
the rulers show evidence of a colourful culture that had more respect
for women than had its rivals and whose people loved life, revelling in
the natural world, enjoying beer, food, sex and gossip. Their obsession
with the afterlife came about because they liked this one so much,
believing that with proper preparation they could have more of the
same.

And yet we are left with those forbidding bird- or dog-headed
deities, the scarabs and the blank stares of superkings whose vast
monuments still insist on awe, but nothing more. Why is this? The
culture's lack of portability through time and space seems to be linked
with its relative absence of physical movement in its own time – it was
just remarkably self-sufficient. Ancient Egypt proper lasted for more
than three thousand years, from the pre-dynastic kingdoms to the final
disappearance of the Greek pharaohs in Roman times. Very early art
from the Nile has an earthy directness that sets it apart; some of the
simple clay models of farmers and animals are similar to the attractively human early art of Mesoamerican people. But quite soon an
Egyptian style becomes fixed and hardened, and although a practised
eye can distinguish between dynasties and even reigns, it barely evolves
for two millennia.

There is a well made sculpture of a king (Khasakhemwy) from
2675 BC which would not look out of place among those of his successors fifteen hundred years later.[23] In the great temple of Luxor is a
little inner temple built to celebrate Alexander the Great being
declared pharaoh in 332 BC. The artwork on one wall faces images
from the early so-called New Kingdom of more than a thousand years
before; and the two look very similar, though there has been a certain
falling-off in subtlety. One obvious reason is that, for the ancient Egyptians, there was no art for art's sake. Art was an expression of religion

and of earthly power. Its job was to describe the hidden world of powerful gods; to record man's relationship with them; and to intimidate
travellers or rebels through the power of its kings. This required an art
of repetition and sometimes gigantism, not of humanism or realism.

The culprit is also the hero of the Egyptian story, the Nile. The
world's longest river, it is unusual in flowing from south to north.
Since its prevailing winds blow from north to south, people with
simple sailboats found it an excellent two-way conveyor belt. Better
still, it not only provided its people with ample fish and wildfowl, but
(before Nasser's Aswan Dam in modern times) it flooded regularly
every year, bringing fresh water and silt to produce remarkably rich
soil. The floods were not entirely regular. If they came late, or too
early, or if they were too strong or too weak, they could disrupt the
planting and cause hunger.

Ancient Egyptian history is marked by periodic disruptions, revolts
and fallings-back; and these seem to have to do with times when the
flooding Nile misbehaved. Yet compared with the civilizations on the
Tigris, Euphrates, Yellow River and the Indus, in today's Pakistan, the
Egyptians were blessed. Not only did they enjoy a four-thousand-mile
streak of remarkable fecundity, culminating in a great flood-plain delta
on the shores of the Mediterranean. But they were also well protected
by deserts and mountains to east and west and by a relatively unpopu-
lated African hinterland in the south. Egypt was invaded, by Libyans
and Persians and the mysterious 'sea peoples'; but this happened relatively rarely. The flatter plains of Mesopotamia, or the land highway of
Palestine, were much easier prey for armies of chariots and horsemen.

Egypt was a hard place to attack and almost impossible to hold for
long; and so, in the ancient world, it always recovered.

The Nile had a political effect too. Though we speak of 'Egypt'
there were really two Egypts. The two-way transit system knitted
together people along a huge expanse, bringing black African Nubians
and Mediterranean dwellers together in a single state. We cannot get a
full sense of how ancient Egyptians saw their geography without
understanding that for most of the time Upper Egypt, the more
African south, dominated Lower Egypt, the more Mediterranean
north. Egyptians today are still quick to note the difference, marked in
the shape and colour of bodies. Egypt was a late starter compared
with the Mesopotamians, partly because the land around it stayed so

rich in plants and wildlife for so long that peoples were not forced to settle. Then the desert encroached further and the first unifying kings arrived from the south, bearing wonderful names such as Narmer, or 'Baleful Catfish'.[24]

As with the story of Da Yu and the Xia, only centralized royal power could have made a single nation of such a strung-out series of settlements. To use the river's bounty effectively, people here too needed a complex network of canals and irrigation systems, which had to be carefully cleaned, dug out and restored every year. So the habit of communal working, people's readiness to dig and build together away from their fields, was set early on.

This would later become very useful when it came to the Pharaonic temples. The Egyptians believed the Nile flowed from the underworld. They spent a lot of time – quite reasonably – worrying about the annual flood. Nile gods featured early in their belief system, so when their kings associated themselves with the flow of the river they acquired huge symbolic power. Geography isn't everything. Often in human history the power of an individual or of an idea turns upside down what we might have expected from the position of rivers, or the shape of a coastline. But if geographical determinism works anywhere, it works for this land made by the Nile, protected by the Nile, serving the Nile's rulers – and eventually limited by the Nile.

Of the monuments of ancient Egypt few are as moving as Deir el-Medina, just round the mountainous corner from the Valley of the Kings and across the river from Luxor. All about are vast monuments. There is the awesome Temple of Karnak at Thebes; then the intimidating one of Rameses III at Medinet Habu, which celebrates that pharaoh's military victories with a manic sense of scale that would leave any twentieth-century dictator jealously gaping. There are the 'Colossi of Memnon', a pair of faceless monsters commemorating King Amenhotep III; and the stage-set remains of Queen Hatshepsut's mortuary temple. All embody everything we have come to expect of the ancient Egyptians; all are intimidating places, impressive in a Nazi or Stalinist way.

Deir el-Medina is very different, a grey maze of stone and mud-brick walls now only a few feet high, looking rather like a very large sheep-pen, or an abandoned village from Gaelic Scotland, somehow lost in the baking desert hills. Above it, on higher ground and cut into the face of a reddish cliff, are numerous holes, some with tiny brick pyramids near by. Compared to the other sites in the vicinity, Deir-el-Medina has very few visitors. This, though, was where the craftsmen who worked for the priests and the pharaohs lived with their families. They were not slaves.[25] They worked hard, often labouring underground as they struggled to finish a tomb before its patron died. They were paid in wheat, clothes and honey-flavoured beer. They had the weekends off (an Egyptian week lasted ten days, so the break was less frequent). They worked for two four-hour shifts and could call on the work of poorer peasants and slaves to make their lives easier. Organized under two overseers, who lived in the village, they celebrated the death of a pharaoh because it meant more work for them in the years to come. They enjoyed feast days, when there was drunkenness and the occasional orgy, and they passed down their skills from one generation to the next. The Egyptian skill in mummifying corpses, too, was the domain of these artisan workers.

Most remarkably, they found time to build their own funeral temples to take them to the afterlife. The day job meant raising great structures and tunnelling deep into the rock to prepare a final resting place for the great ones of the New Dynasty. But meanwhile they were building their own versions, complete with small pyramids and beautiful painted chambers twenty or thirty feet below ground. Their surfaces, still astonishingly brightly coloured, celebrate the love of a man and wife; the families of the workmen; the surrounding natural world of waving corn, ducks and monkeys; and food in plenty. Here ordinary people were buried and, remote from the grand 'come and get me' monuments that lured grave-robbers to the pharaohs even in ancient times, many of them rested untouched until excavations began in the modern era.

This would be interesting enough. But these people also recorded many of their thoughts on small pieces of limestone, often the waste from all that digging, and on broken pieces of pot, and on papyrus. Written in simplified popular script, then thrown away three thousand years ago, a lot of it has survived. These ostraca record popular stories, legal complaints, love poems, books of dreams, gossip, feuds, wise sayings, the angry disinheriting of children by a woman who feels they did not look after her well enough in her old age, laundry lists, problems with defective donkeys, and even a cure for piles (flour, goose fat, salt, honey and green beans: mix into a paste and apply to the backside for four days).

One particular bad character, a foreman called Paneb, seems to have been constantly making murderous threats to other workers, stealing from royal tombs, harassing other women into making clothes for him, and having illicit sex with another man's wife, a lady called Tuy, and other married women. He was eventually tried by the pharaoh's vizier and removed from his job, though we do not know what eventually happened to him. This may have been the result of a village feud, but it shows there was a trusted and effective system of justice at work.

The story of this village is not only a refreshing and unusual instance of the voices of ordinary workers – skilled and valued people, but manual workers nevertheless – and their families emerging from distant history. It also shows that they shared the religious convictions of their rulers and, as soon as it was possible, aspired to share their underworld too. Indeed, when we consider the lives of such people – proud of their skills as stonemasons, painters, carpenters, makers of clothing and cooks, who ate reasonably well, mixing fish and meat with a basic diet of vegetables, bread and beer; who had a rich spiritual life that made sense of their world; and who trusted in a system of fair law – the idea of a downtrodden semi-enslaved world of ancient toilers falls away. Were the lives of these villagers not better in most ways than the lives of millions of poorer-paid or unemployed people in tower blocks today?

Back to the Bull

The Minoans were the first European civilization (from around 3600 to 1160 BC, though only just, since their island of Crete lies in the far south of the jagged Greek peninsula. They were trading and seafaring people, whose pottery turns up in Egypt and whose art was influenced by the Egyptians. They were literate, though their form of writing has never been deciphered. They seem to have been relatively unwarlike. Their art and architecture are instantly attractive, giving an initial impression of an airy, tranquil, female-dominated society whose palace walls ripple with dancing dolphins. Amid the fat red columns and excellent sewerage systems are images of a little bull-dancing here, a moment of saffron-gathering there. But the Minoans are particularly useful as a warning not from history – but about history and how we romanticize it.

The great Minoan palace of Knossos is one of the most popular tourism sites in the eastern Mediterranean, and has been for a century. Sightseers already half in love with this hot, rosemary-scented island idyll learn that it was destroyed in the aftermath of a terrible earthquake at Santorini. The words 'lost civilization of Atlantis' are muttered. This is how many modern Europeans like to think of their earlier selves – peaceable, artistic, liberated and romantically doomed – a story that is half-Eden and half the *Titanic*. But it is almost all bull.

Knossos is an old building, at least by our standards. It dates back to between 1905 and 1930 – AD – and has been described by one archaeologist as one of the first reinforced concrete buildings ever erected on Crete, bearing unsettling echoes of Lenin's mausoleum in Red Square and the modernist architecture of Le Corbusier. Cathy Gere found it suited to the urban sprawl now encroaching on the site: 'today all of Greece is liberally studded with half-built, low-rise, skeletal modernist ruins, stairs climbing to nowhere'.[26]

The dubious reconstruction of a Bronze Age palace, filled with faked-up pictures, was the lifetime achievement of a British archaeologist, Sir Arthur Evans. Knossos had been discovered by a local Greek antiquarian, who had started to dig in the 1870s. But with an excellent classical education and wealthy from the family's paper-mill business, Evans bought the entire site when Crete became independent of the Ottoman Empire. Like his friend the German archaeologist Heinrich Schliemann who had discovered (and accidentally partly destroyed) Troy in 1871, Evans saw himself as reconnecting the modern and ancient worlds and cleansing the dirty industrial mess of modern Europe through the revived memory of simpler, nobler times. As Gere puts it, Evans was infused and animated by spiritual hunger and he wanted nothing less than 'the pagan re-enchantment' of the modern world.

To achieve this, in his hunger, Evans first supported the ruined buildings he was excavating with wood and plaster, and then slowly began to 'improve' them with the flexible and useful recent invention of reinforced concrete. The extent to which his re-imagining of the

Knossos complex is an accurate and reasonable guess, or merely a modernist fantasy, divides even the experts. Evans was searching for a pacific, sexually relaxed paradise and, in Crete, avoiding any evidence of military fortification; later on, he commissioned modern artists to 'touch up' ancient wall paintings so comprehensively that they produced new ones. The Swiss–French father-and-son team, both called Émile Gilliéron, produced reconstructions that go far beyond the evidence, yet are now reproduced around the world, and they probably went on to make full-scale fakes.

The reconstructions included images of black African warriors used by the Minoans, according to Evans's fantasy, to invade the mainland Greeks, whom he associated with Germanic militarism. Shrewd observers noticed something odd. The English novelist Evelyn Waugh, visiting the Heraklion museum where the paintings were on show, wrote of his suspicion that 'their painters have tempered their zeal for accurate reconstruction with a somewhat inappropriate predilection for the covers of *Vogue*'.[27] Even the name 'Minoan' came from Evans's belief that he had discovered the original site of King Minos's famous labyrinth, where according to classical myth the hero Theseus killed the half-bull and half-man Minotaur. The myth placed King Minos on Crete and had it that the Minotaur devoured fresh Athenian children; there is something sadistic about the story. And what the Minoans really called themselves, we cannot say.

So from this rubble, what can we know for sure about the people we call Minoans? Their civilization lasted for around thirteen hundred years and survived not one but a series of natural disasters including a hugely destructive earthquake and two volcanic eruptions, and a tsunami which devastated coastal settlements and their all-important shipping. Recent archaeology, influenced by the huge destructive power of the 2004 tsunami in Asia, suggests similar devastation in Crete. The Minoan 'palaces' that scatter the island, linked by stone roads, are probably urban, religious and trading centres. They traded in tin, very well made and painted (and unfaked) pottery, as well as a wide range of foods, oils and other staples. Their agriculture was sophisticated and it does seem that their religion was dominated by priestesses and by some form of bull-worship. A game or ritual involving leaping over bulls, grasping them by their horns – which must have been far more dangerous than modern bull-fighting – is seen on genuine images. Even if their art was not quite as sexily exuberant as that of the reconstructors, it was sinuous and immediately attractive.

But there is a darker side to the culture. It is now thought that they did go to war and did protect their citadels with defensive walls. At Anemospilia, a temple near Knossos, as stark and unadorned an excavation as the other is rebuilt and imagined, three skeletons were found by a Greek-led team in 1979. They had apparently all died in the immediate aftermath of the later volcanic eruption. One is thought to be of a twenty-eight-year-old priestess and another of a priest; the third is the skeleton of an eighteen-year-old boy, tethered in a foetal position and with an ornate knife sticking through him. The arrangement of blackened and white bones suggests he was still bleeding to death when the final disaster struck, and the obvious conclusion is that he was a human sacrifice designed to appease the volcano.

Far from being a society of peace and love, wafting about in gossamer garments and admiring the dolphins, the Minoans seem to have been as bloody as anyone else. Just as the first Cro-Magnons were able to combine beautiful art and cannibalism, so the first civilization in Europe combined beauty and human sacrifice. The hunter-gatherers had struggled with the natural challenges produced by an erratic and difficult climate; their Minoan descendants were still struggling with natural threats big enough to overwhelm their way of life. In between, man had begun to learn how to reshape nature; but outside a few specially favoured river valleys this remained a precarious and uncertain victory.

The end of the Minoan story is messy; most scholars now believe they were not wiped out by a single cataclysm as the tourist guides say, but were sufficiently weakened by eruptions and earthquakes to make them relatively easy meat for invading Mycenaean Greeks from the mainland. Certainly, Greek-speakers replaced the late Minoan elites not very long before their civilization, too, mysteriously disappeared. As we shall see later, the end of a lively and sophisticated Bronze Age Mediterranean world is one of history's more tantalizing puzzles.

By this point, Eve's children have already laid the foundations of the modern world. Most of the spadework has been done over a span of fifty thousand years by people whose names we will never know and most of whose languages remain a mystery. They have cleared forests, invented agriculture, raised the first towns and cities, and advanced enough in learning to use mathematics and writing, preserving their names and stories. They have also begun to develop a class system and fighting elites. They have invented war.

Part Two

THE CASE FOR WAR

The First Great Age of Empire, from the Assyrians to Alexander, and How Civil Conflict Produced Radical Advances in Religion, Writing and Philosophy

War, and more war: a dreary chronicle of swollen-headed butcher kings, charcoaled cities, and flies buzzing on silent flesh? It is true that the early Mediterranean, Indian and Asian worlds saw almost incessant warfare, a great churning of empires and armies which, you might have thought, would push civilization back to a dark age. And indeed, around three thousand years ago there *was* a dark age, a mysterious collapse across what had been a cradle of civilization. Everywhere archaeologists report depopulation, palaces abandoned, and the widespread loss of skills, including writing.

But out of the disaster arose new empires, now with iron weapons, about to write down their own history and chronicle their own wars. And however terrible war may be, the awkward truth is that war has been a huge driver of change in human history. When we reach into a purse or pocket for coins, when we argue about dangerous extremists in our democracies, or about the mingling of cultures; when we write our thoughts down using the alphabet or read headlines about threats to the traditional family, we are using tools and thoughts given to us by this apparently remote age of empires, thinkers and warrior-kings.

So here, from Greece to India and China, is the case for war.

Greek Glory and the First Empires

> murderous, doomed . . .
> hurling down to the House of Death so many sturdy souls,
> great fighters' souls, but made their bodies carrion
> feasts for the dogs and birds
>
> Homer, *Iliad*

Into written history strides a story we still read today. It begins in the middle of a war, with the rage of the warrior Achilles, and it comprises just two weeks' worth of bickering, sand, heat and very bloody death in front of the walls of a city. The action takes place near the end of a decade-long siege, a pointless stalemate. This is the *Iliad* of Homer. With that and his other great poem of journeying and heartache, the *Odyssey*, Homer began to make Greece. For the classical Greeks, these books were the Bible and Shakespeare combined, a source of cultural identity, a vast storehouse of expressions and a treasury for orators.

Educated Greeks of the fifth century BC prided themselves on knowing these huge poems by heart. Since then, Homer's tales and the surrounding myths of Helen's abduction and the Trojan Horse have dug their way into the world's imagination, their influence extending from Roman generals to the poets of Shakespeare's England and modern film-makers. Here is one place where a true world culture begins; and it is the earliest known work of Western literature. Not only is the *Iliad* a war story, but it is an unusually convincing one, about an army whose leaders are petty and sometimes mutinous, where disease stalks the camp and wounds are frightful and the enemy is to be admired, not merely hated. And in which the good guys die. It glories in violence, this poem, yet it was written by someone who found the human lust for war silly and bitter. He was deeply conflicted about conflict, and thus a deathless poet of the human condition.

These are the centuries when mankind's core civilizations moved from bronze weapons to iron ones, and from oral tales to stories written down. The role of war as a dark driver of change is unavoidable. Advances in metalworking, wheels, horsemanship, sailing, mathematics and counting, architecture and religion, are driven by confrontation – in China, India and the Mediterranean. This is, obviously, an ambiguous story. Greece is a good place to start it, both because of what will happen there and what had happened just before the Iron Age, when we get a tantalizing glimpse of a better future that would be snuffed out. Across the Mycenaean Greek world of Homer's heroes a dark shadow would soon fall, scattering the people, destroying the palaces and cities, until even the ability to write was lost. The Greeks who followed, using Homer to recall their identity, blamed war for their predicament.

We do not know quite what happened. Around 1000 BC some great disaster or string of disasters hit the eastern Mediterranean, causing a dramatic depopulation. If the Greeks coming later, in early classical times, thought this was somehow connected with the Trojan conflict, then perhaps war was part of the story. Historians think invasions of Dorian tribes from the north, coming upon Greek statelets weakened by local conflicts, and wiping them out, may have been responsible. Alternatively, this collapse might have been driven by natural disasters – climate change or a series of terrible earthquakes, provoking local wars of mere survival. One single cause seems unlikely.

We do know that before this great and mysterious disaster, the Bronze Age world of the Mediterranean was booming. Excavations and written inscriptions are filling in some of our knowledge. Few finds have been as outstanding as that of a merchant ship, cruising off the Turkish coast a century or so before the Trojan war. It was discovered by a local diver and then recovered by underwater archaeologists during 1984–94. Known as the Uluburun shipwreck, the boat has been dated (from the analysis of firewood it carried) to around 1310 BC. Built of cedar and oak from Lebanon, it was probably travelling from Cyprus or Palestine, perhaps to Rhodes or to the Hittite empire, when it suddenly went down close to shore. Bones from the meal the sailors were eating when it happened have been recovered.[1]

More amazing, though, was its cargo. There was a huge haul of carefully made copper ingots from the mines on Cyprus, shaped to be easily carried on pack-animal saddles, and tin ingots too, for the manufacture of the bronze used for armour, weapons and tools. There were sacks of cobalt, turquoise and lavender-coloured glass, many musical instruments, jars of beads, olives and dye from Canaan, hard black wood from Africa, exquisite gold jewellery from Egypt, elephant tusks and hippopotamus teeth, ostrich-egg shells and turtle shells, swords from Italy, Palestine and Greece as well as other weapons thought to have come from Bulgaria and the Alps. The many tools included axes, drill-bits, tongs and saws. There was food too, including pine nuts, figs, coriander, almonds and pomegranates, as well as amber from the Baltic, the seal of the Egyptian queen Nefertiti, and even two writing-books made of boxwood, ivory and beeswax, with a stylus for writing – a kind of notebook described by Homer.

This was the find from just one ship, quite small and miraculously preserved for 3,300 years. Its hold was like a knot with threads reaching out to Italy and the Balkans, sub-Saharan Africa, the Baltic, the Assyrian world, Mycenae and Egypt. It is vivid evidence of the relative wealth, sophistication and cosmopolitan culture that disappeared. The chance discovery of a single boat overturned many old ideas about the Bronze Age, and makes one wonder about the civilizations that might have emerged out of centuries of commercial rivalry rather than military confrontation.

It was not to be. In the Iron Age, war rather than trade would be the repeated trigger for change. The wars dimly remembered by Homer's listeners would eventually give way to a time of conflict that gave today's human civilizations the alphabets of the West, the sophisticated writing of the East; the great philosophies of classical Greece and Confucian China; architectural styles we still use and religious ideas that inspire billions of modern people.

Democracy was an idea forced on phalanxes of fighting men, all on the same level, protecting one another against richer men on horses. Monotheism emerged from the brutal invasion and enslavement of a small tribal people caught between empires. Chinese ideas about order and duty came only after the hideous experience of interminable disorder between states. By contrast, the cultures least directly affected by the pressures of war or invasion, like that of Egypt, changed least and gave less back to the common human story. So we have to ask: would a peaceful Mediterranean, trading raw materials and luxuries but mainly tending goats and fishing, have produced a Sophocles or a Pericles? Few collective human experiences are as bad as war, with its train of rape, starvation, mutilation and physical destruction. Yet war brings change, including sometimes, change for the better.

Uncertainty about war is knotted through Homer's poetry. His Greek and Trojan heroes are larger than life – young, magnificent animals, brimmingly alive. Looking back to the age of heroes, many of his listeners believed that the Greeks who landed on the sandy shore of the Troad had literally been giants. The bones of prehistoric beasts were claimed as relics of dead superheroes, whose doings interrupted the never-ending afternoon tea of the gods on Olympus. Yet Homer shows these men as all too human, when they sulk, bitch, boast and have petty quarrels about status. And in the end when they die they go not to a glorious southern Valhalla, or to be comforted by teams of virgins, but fade away into a grim, spectral underworld and pithless semi-existence.[2]

To understand this brilliant combination of excitement and grief-stricken wisdom we need to remember Homer's audience, and what had happened to the Greeks of his own time, who lived between the Bronze Age heroics of Mycenae and the beginnings of the classical Greece of city-states. About Homer himself we know next to nothing. He was said to have been blind. Some scholars think he did not even exist – that 'Homer' is a neat shorthand for an anonymous group or tradition of storytellers – though others rebut them by pointing to the crafty shaping and coherence of the poems. Whoever he was, or they were (and I will use the singular for simplicity), Homer used a particular dialect of Greek called Ionic, from what is now the western coast of Turkey, where Troy stands too.

Building on hints embedded in the poems, historians now think he lived around 750 BC, which is some five hundred years after the war he purports to describe. Yet there are parts of the *Iliad* that seem much older, above all the famous 'Catalogue of the Ships', which lists the city-states and the peoples making up the Greek force and which describes a Bronze Age political world, not one from Homer's time. Homer could have written the poems, rather than composed them in his head to be spoken, since around fifty years earlier the Greeks had begun to use an adapted alphabet to note down their own words.

Troy was real. The series of ancient settlements and fortresses uncovered first by the already mentioned German adventurer Heinrich Schliemann in 1871–3 match the geography and setting of the siege that Homer describes. Unfortunately, as an inexperienced archaeologist, Schliemann dug so deeply and so quickly he probably destroyed most of the Trojan city, which formed one of the layers of excavations (and there are still arguments about exactly which). Walls made of big limestone blocks protected 'Troy VI' of around 1350 BC, though, and it had seven-metre-high towers, a grand inner citadel and a deep well. The site's amazing gold treasures, including what Schliemann thought was the crown of Helen of Troy, date from much earlier. But this was certainly a powerful, important place, perfectly situated for trade and for extorting tribute from passing ships.

Troy, or Ilium, was a city of the Hittite world, under the protection of the great empire that ruled all of Anatolia. The Hittites themselves, early users of iron, and chariot-imperialists, have only recently, after major archaeological finds, fully reappeared in history. Troy to them was a vassal state on the extreme western edge of their world. They were literate: Hittite tablets, mainly diplomatic and other records, unearthed at their capital city of Hattusa make clear that Troy was part of a wealthy, complicated network of military and trading links – the Hittites called it Wilusa.

We also know about the Greeks who besieged Troy because they have left towns; and they too were literate, using a primitive script called Linear B. They are often known as the Mycenaeans, after Mycenae, the impressive citadel with lion-decorated gates that Homer tells us was King Agamemnon's capital. It was one of these early Greeks' main fortified bases – though recent scholarship suggests Thebes may have been at least as important. The Greeks? They had swept down into the valleys and islands named after them around five hundred years before the Trojan conflict. They were warriors based on a clan system who built defensive hilltop forts across the mainland. They swiftly became effective sailors and raiders, and would help to destroy the Minoans.

The Mycenaean Greeks seized defeated people as slaves and were probably some of the mysterious 'sea peoples' who so terrified ancient Egyptians. They developed colonies and traded – their pottery turns up across the eastern Mediterranean. Hittite records treat them as a single people and complain about their poor behaviour, including the transportation of seven thousand people from Anatolia to Mycenae.[3] Greek records there also refer to lists of loot and slaves: 'Twenty-one women from Cnidus with their twelve girls and ten boys, captives. Women of Miletus. To-ro-ja – Women of Troy.'[4]

Did a great alliance of Mycenae-era Greeks go to war with the Trojans? It is likely. Troy was close and rich. Historians today suggest it was a war over trade levies rather than the abduction of a beautiful Spartan queen called Helen. Yet women had high status and were often taken captive in Bronze Age fighting, and there was a Helen cult in Sparta well into classical times, so that part of the story might have some distant factual basis. Sadly, only a couple of generations after the war Homer describes, that great black curtain fell across the Mediterranean world. The palaces are abandoned. The superb gold-working skills of the Mycenaean Greeks disappear. Written words vanish.

Homer's first audience was a migrant and impoverished one, a scattering of refugees remembering the good old days and asking repeatedly, What went wrong? The *Iliad* was part of a longer cycle of at least six epic poems, which have now been lost, telling of the origins of the war and how it ended – with the taking and destroying of Troy.[5] Homer's 15,700-line poem could not have been recited or heard at one sitting; perhaps it was meant for festivals of several days, or perhaps it was delivered like modern television dramas, in episodes.

However it was heard, though, it demonstrates the great irony that war gives as well as taking away. No Trojan war, no Homer. No Homer, no (or at least much less) familiar classical Greek culture. For by the time these people re-emerge in history, reciting their tales of Achilles and Hector, Paris and Helen, they will be forming the most impressive civilization of ancient times.

Concerning Knowledge – Be Humble

And they will be doing it with a new invention, something simple, clever and which shaped the Western world. It has no single inventor we know of, and appeared quite mysteriously among a people who have left the world little else.

'Concerning knowledge: here and now be humble (you yourself!) in this basement!' Thus the short, peppery order halfway down a tunnel leading to the tomb of a king. His sarcophagus was discovered in 1925 in the Lebanese port city of Byblos. King Ahiram is shown sitting on a throne, being offered a lotus flower by a priestess – just another day in the life of just another king. Around him are sphinxes. There is a longer inscription, which seems to suggest a father-and-son burial and warns in rather obscure terms against grave-robbery: 'One should cancel his registration concerning the libation tube of the memorial sacrifice.' Perhaps, when it was carved, this was a terrifying threat. Another translation suggests more directly that the son buried the father and is warning off anyone who digs him up: 'may the sceptre of his rule be torn away, may the throne of his kingdom be overturned.'

What makes Ahiram's sarcophagus remarkable, however, is not the art or the words, but how the words are written. For this is the earliest example known of the Phoenician alphabet, written in Byblos about three thousand years ago. From this script of twenty-two stark letters, simple and memorable, all of them consonants, derived the writing of the ancient Greeks, and Aramaic, and the script of the Etruscans of Italy, and thus Latin, and every European language. Many scholars believe Indic and Brahmi scripts come from Aramaic too, which would mean the Phoenicians' invention has covered almost every part of the world except China and the Far East. It is not quite a coincidence that 'Byblos' gives us the word 'Bible': the city was a trading city for papyrus to write on, and the Greek word for papyrus became the name for book, hence Bible.

Who were the Phoenicians? This is again a Greek name, for the trading and coastal people originally from Canaan. Living around modern Lebanon, Syria and Israel, they had been driven to the coast, probably by the relentlessly unpleasant Assyrian war machine, the great people-stirrers of the age. The coastal Canaanites were great shipbuilders and sailors, turning their ports of Tyre and Byblos, and later the great colony of Carthage, into hubs for Mediterranean trade. The old Egyptian word for a vessel that could venture out into deep sea was 'Byblos boat', and there were stories that by 600 BC the Phoenicians had sailed around Africa – a tall tale made more credible by the strange fact that they claimed they had eventually found the midday sun coming up on the right-hand side of their vessel. We know a little about their gods, and what they looked like – they wore conical caps, simple cotton gowns, adored gold jewellery, and the men had combed, oiled beards. The women, according to carvings and inscriptions, seem to have had more power and freedom than was common in the ancient world.

The most famous, though probably mythical, Phoenician was Dido of Tyre, also known as Elissa, who founded Carthage in 813 BC after tricking the North African locals. They had said she could have as much land as she could fit into an ox-hide, so she cut it into such a thin single strip that she had a sizeable area for a settlement. Dido also fell in love with Aeneas, making his way from the Trojan disaster to Italy, and when he insisted on leaving her, killed herself on a funeral pyre. That, at any rate, is what the Romans said. The ox-hide story may refer to a Bronze Age view of the Phoenicians as wily double-crossers, the fate of traders throughout time. Later, the Phoenicians would be used by the Persians and even the Macedonians to provide ships from which their armies could fight. They were useful go-betweens who needed, therefore, easy ways of keeping track of sales and bartering.

Their alphabet used very simplified versions of hieroglyphs, pictures-standing-for-the-thing, and turned them into sounds, one sign for each sound. The names of their letters (such as *gimel, dalet, sin*) came from the original images (here, camel, door, tooth). They sound vaguely familiar even now; the Phoenician alphabet starts *aleph, beth, gimel, daleth*. The letters look odder to us, though a little more like Greek or Hebrew. Once the marks' correspondence with tongue and lip sounds was established, they could be arranged to mimic real speech. This may sound obvious, but it was a huge leap of logic.

Once you knew the sounds of the letters you could work out the sounds of words, and thus read messages without having to know the meaning of thousands of little drawings. The messages could be carved quite quickly because the alphabet was simple, and they could also be written on wax tablets, like the one discovered on the trading vessel – they were surely for commercial messages and record-keeping by busy traders with no time to waste. And, of course, the sounds could be used for different languages, just as German and Portuguese, for instance, are written with the same letters. So the Phoenician experiment could spread around the Mediterranean world and be quickly adapted. We believe the Greeks took it up by about 800 BC, just before Homer was at work, and they quickly improved it by adding vowel sounds.

The Samaritans had their version, derived from a joint and even older script; and Hebrew writing came from that same source. So not only Homer, but the Bible too, pay tribute to these little-known people. Here is perhaps the greatest case in world history of an invention devised for humdrum purposes, traders' notations in a multilingual market, outstripping its origins and altering human life. In a similar way, the development of a US military communications system into the World Wide Web is a parallel – but it is a *smaller* achievement than alphabetic writing. Poignantly, the Phoenicians themselves have left us very little writing of interest – some rather dull religious verses, lists, and cross injunctions from long-dead kings.

The Hebrew Idea

The Hebrews would be rather marginal to world history, just another Middle Eastern people of somewhat obscure origins, were it not for their great idea, monotheism. They came to believe in a single universal god who has a personal relationship with everyone who believes in him. This developed in written texts, and was transmitted through writing; and it so outleaped its origins, detonating around the world like a series of mental explosions, that it has come to seem normal. Monotheism changed the world far more than any mere emperor, technology or scientific discovery.

Belief in a universal god who lives not in one particular temple, or by one gurgling stream or atop a particular misty mountain, and who listens to the believer, seems to respond to a deep human need, even though when the Hebrews developed the idea it seemed very odd. Britain's Chief Rabbi, Jonathan Sacks, argues that the shift is from religions rooted in the world, towards a source of meaning lying outside any world that can be seen or touched: 'The gods of polytheism, in all their buzzing, boisterous confusion, were within the universe. They were subject to nature. They did not create it.' The Jewish god, by contrast, gave life meaning from outside, and also allowed a new politics of the Covenant, 'of a people pledging themselves to one another and to the common good, a politics of "we, the people"'.[6] This new way of understanding would bind people together with a new intensity. Sadly, it would divide them with a fresh ferocity, too.

Historians argue fiercely about how the Hebrew people discovered one-godism. We do not even know quite where they themselves first came from. According to their tales the man named as their original prophet, Abraham, who may really have existed, was born in Ur, that decaying imperial river city of baked-brick terraces and Mesopotamian gods. The religion of the Mesopotamians has pre-echoes of Judaism. It is possible that the Jews did spend around four hundred years in captivity in Egypt before breaking free under a leader with an Egyptian name, Moses, and trekking to the Promised Land where they ousted local tribes and settled down. But there are no Egyptian records to show this, nor any archaeological evidence, and the Old Testament story seems to have been written down seven centuries later.

We do know that a people called 'Israel' were living in the hills and valleys of present-day Israel around 1200 BC, thanks to a boastful inscription by the pharaoh Merneptah listing the peoples of the area who have just been crushed. Among them, 'Israel is laid waste: his seed is not!'[7] (This probably means that the farmers' crops, rather than all the males, have been destroyed.) Archaeologists find the culture of these people to be very similar to that of the coastal dwellers near by in the land generally called Canaan. They had the same kinds of utensils, houses and writing. More to the point, they seem to have had similar gods. The northern group of Hebrews did not call their god Yahweh but El, which was the name of the chief god of the Canaanites. There were a dozen of these Hebrew tribes living in the area. Some might have arrived recently, but they probably originated in Arabia and had been a desert people, pushing towards slightly more fertile land. The word 'Hebrew' means 'someone from the other side' of the Euphrates river, hence 'immigrant' or perhaps just 'wanderer', and from early on they distinguished themselves from their neighbours.

To start with, the Hebrew god was not alone in his universe. El (as in Isra-el) was the father god, the Zeus, of a divine family. His wife was Asherah, his children were the storm-god Baal, who also brought fertility, and his sister Anat. Baal in particular continued to be worshipped for a long time as, slowly, the tribes of Israel began to differentiate themselves from their neighbours. Yahweh replaced El. The idea of 'god' as a Greek-style being walking on the earth, speaking and intervening personally in human life – the bickering deities that we find in Homer following human affairs like football spectators – faded in favour of a more transcendent, obscure and alarming presence. This took centuries, and is traced by scholars of the oldest parts of Jewish writing in what Christians now call the Old Testament.

The strip of coastal land which is now Israel, Palestine and Lebanon was as bitterly fought over in ancient times as it is today. Then, it had the misfortune to find itself between the two great river peoples, the Egyptians and the Mesopotamians, including the Assyrians of the River Tigris. We have seen with the Phoenicians how trade can spur invention. The wider theme of this section, as noted earlier, is that war does too, and of this the Israelites are a prime example. Conflict pushed them on the next step to full-blown monotheism.

Around three thousand years ago a kingdom was established, with a royal house that included such famous figures as Saul, David and Solomon. It had fought off another advanced coastal people, the Philistines. This kingdom is remembered as the high point of ancient independent Israel. There, an elite of teacher-preachers, the prophets, developed a new way of thinking about religion and ethics. Isaiah, Jeremiah and others spoke of justice and of the equality of men under the unchanging laws of a universal god, which were more important than the laws of kings or empires.

By the 700s BC, however, the kingdom had broken into two, a northern state called Israel, with its capital city of Samaria, and a southern one, Judah, based at Jerusalem. At the time, a favoured by-product of war was the deportation of defeated elites. Instead of simply being slaughtered, kings, teachers, craftsmen and their families were carried off to the victors' city to work. This left the defeated territory leaderless and in a sense de-civilized. In 722 BC this happened to the northern kingdom, effectively wiping out ten of the twelve tribes of Israel and deporting around twenty-five thousand people. The Assyrian empire, with its huge capital at Nineveh, produced a series of hugely successful warrior kings, who carved out most of the Middle East as their fiefdom through a mixture of intimidation and raw terror-tactics. Their army was by far the most professional and well-equipped of the age and their punishments for anyone who stood against them included decapitation, flaying alive, impaling and deportation. We know the details of their brutal behaviour because they boasted about it on clay tablets and memorialised it with stone-slab carvings. These manage to be both beautifully made and entirely horrible, war propaganda intended to intimidate visitors to Nineveh.

Twenty years after the fall of Israel, Judah rebelled against the Assyrians, and faced another massive army. The city of Lachish was wiped out and Jerusalem was saved only by huge bribes to the conquerors and, perhaps, by an outbreak of disease among the besiegers. Then the high priest Hilkiah announced he had discovered a scroll of the laws given by Yahweh to Moses, in a corner of the Temple. Under the king Josiah a fresh period of religious development began, based on written documents, as the priests were set the task of telling the complete story of the Jews. The tone was more aggressive, more strident.[8] Idols of the old Canaanite gods Baal and Astarte were destroyed. Male prostitutes were expelled from the Temple. But Judah was still a small, soft nut between the pincers of rival empires, and Josiah was defeated by the Egyptians, not long before the next empire arrived.

These conquerors were the formidable Babylonians, led by their king Nebuchadnezzar. There were two phases to their attack. In the first, the Jewish king and ten thousand of his people were taken into captivity. But this did not finish Judah off. There was a revolt, led in part by the prophet Jeremiah. The Babylonian army came back in 586 BC for a fearful siege of Jerusalem. After many months of being driven to starvation and perhaps even cannibalism, the inhabitants were overrun and the city almost completely destroyed. A further twenty thousand people were taken off, not to Nineveh this time, but to Babylon. The Temple, where Yahweh had resided, was almost obliterated.[9] The famous 'Babylonian exile' during which, by the waters, the captives lay down and wept, remembering Zion, had begun.

For the people of Jerusalem, led east from their small dusty city, Babylon must have been an awesome spectacle. It was one of the world's great centres, a melting-pot of Middle Eastern peoples, mingling under its huge gates, by its ziggurats, in its temples and hanging gardens. It was a glittering spectacle of blue- and yellow-glazed tiles, statues of bulls and lions and dragons, and great processional roads. Here, sensible exiles would adapt and conform. The Jews, however, refused. Their scribes and priests consulted written scrolls and decided that Yahweh had not, after all, been destroyed with his Temple. Instead, he had followed his people like a giant shadow and was with them in their exile. He was with them, however, for only so long as they observed purity laws, which had originally been just for the priests. They must keep themselves apart from heathens.

Circumcision, refraining from pork, regular prayers, and a further refining of the holy texts, all helped give the exiled Jews a stronger sense of group identity. They were in the melting-pot, but they did not melt. The Jews were influenced by Babylon, of course. Biblical stories including the Flood, which echoes a famous Mesopotamian myth, and the multilingual building project of the Tower of Babel, are surely echoes of stories they picked up there. Meanwhile, the horror of what had happened to Jerusalem darkened the religion, bringing a stronger sense of divine wrath and final judgements.

All this is central to the history of world religion. Under the influence of war and exile, the Hebrews evolved a notion of God which was based on written scripts, which treated all believers equally – while dividing them from the rest of unbelieving humanity – and which was mobile. Religion involved a text, an idea of equality and oneness in faith, and had a claim to universality. There had been other monotheistic cults and full religions, such as Persian Zoroastrianism, but there had been nothing remotely like this before. Later Judaism, Christianity and Islam would follow this pattern. For the post-exile Jews, Yahweh had his Temple with its empty room, its holy-of-holies, whence he would return and again be worshipped. But he was not, like other gods, rooted to one spot, or one land. He did not need to communicate through a single holy place.

Modern monotheism had arrived. The Babylonian captivity did not last so very long. After just forty-five years (compared with the four hundred of the fabled Egyptian exile), as soon as Persia's King Cyrus had defeated Babylon, he sent the Hebrews home. They carried with them something new.

Cyrus, Cross-dresser

One man, and one man alone, was responsible for the Jews returning to Judah and thus for the development of their faith, and the faiths of Christianity and Islam that grew from it. He is the only Gentile given the honorific title of 'Messiah'. On a pillar at the dusty remnants of his once great capital of Pasargadae in today's Iran is carved what is believed to be his image. A bearded man with a bizarre crown and four wings stands dressed in a flowing gown. The inscription once above it read simply: 'I, Cyrus the King, an Achaemenian'.

But he is clearly a cultural cross-dresser. His gown is one of those worn by the Elamites, a people dwelling in the highlands of south-western Iran. His crown is an Egyptian one, but with Assyrian and Phoenician twists. His wings are Persian.[10] What message is he trying to send? A rather wordier message from Cyrus helps us out. It comes on the side-drum-shaped clay 'Cyrus cylinder' found at Babylon and now in the British Museum in London. It was made after he had captured Babylon (peacefully, he insists) and released the Jews from exile. Like the winged relief, this is propaganda. It is how Cyrus II wanted to be seen. It begins with the conventional 'look at me', top-dog rhetoric: 'I am Cyrus, King of the globe, great king, mighty king, King of Babylon, king of the land of Sumer and Akad . . . king of the four quarters of the earth . . .'

So far, so standard. But the next thing Cyrus wants us to know is that this champion of the god of the Jews also favours the Babylonians' god Marduk – 'and I sought daily to worship him'. Along with freeing slaves and rebuilding houses he had restored sanctuaries, and not only for Marduk but for many other lesser gods across his new empire 'beyond the Tigris river, whose sanctuaries had been in ruins over a long period[;] the gods whose abode is in the midst of them, I returned to their places and housed them in lasting abodes'.

The Greeks, who were fascinated by Cyrus and his descendants, believed that the Persians were simply more open than other people to foreign influences. There are suggestions that, because they were originally nomadic barbarians, they advanced in civilization by taking in and digesting the architecture, clothes, war technologies and gods of longer-settled people. But history offers plenty of examples of barbarian invaders who simply burn, oppress, and move on. The Greeks were trying to understand one of the mysteries of Iron Age history – how it was that an obscure tribal people suddenly erupted across Asia and built, and sustained, the greatest empire yet known. However, unlike the Jews, the Greeks misunderstood Cyrus.

Well aware that his Persians were a small minority taking power over many ancient and once-powerful civilizations, Cyrus had found a new way of governing. Under him, so long as you did not rebel, you had freedom of worship and custom. This was the first multicultural empire. But that did not make it less warlike or ruthless in repressing its enemies. Cyrus II was almost constantly at war with someone, and though he built a famously lovely capital, with huge, carefully planted gardens called *paradeiza* (hence our 'paradise'), most accounts say he died as he had lived, fighting. The most colourful account says he was fighting a fierce tribe led by a female ruler called Tomyris, in today's Kazakhstan; he had won one battle by tricking them into getting drunk on unfamiliar alcohol, but Tomyris had her revenge, leading her troops for a second attack in one of the fiercest fights of ancient times, after which Cyrus was decapitated. His body was returned to Pasargadae, where his impressively stark limestone tomb still stands.

This story comes from the 'father of history', also labelled 'the father of lies' by later jealous rivals, Herodotus. He probably visited Babylon, searching for information about his life's work, the history of the struggle between the Greeks and the Persians. A gripping writer and a great storyteller, Herodotus tried his best to get first-hand information, and certainly travelled widely in the ancient world, but he also had the fatal journalist's enthusiasm for a ripping yarn. He never even tried to be drily factual. He lived in a world which was god-haunted, superstitious and credulous – even more so than ours – at a time of oracles and vengeful deities. He may not tell us what really happened, and he is famously useless on causation; but Herodotus does tell us what the people on the street, and in the villages, thought had happened, and why.

Herodotus says Cyrus was the grandson of the King of the Medes, Astyages, which is probably true. He also says that Grandpa Astyages had a dream in which his daughter 'made water in such enormous quantities that it filled his city and swamped the whole of Asia'.[11] This somewhat indecorous behaviour was interpreted to mean that there was trouble ahead, so Astyages married her off to a quiet, dull man called Cambyses. She became pregnant. Old Astyages had another dream, this time that a huge vine grew out of his daughter's vagina and spread across Asia. Dr Freud being unavailable, the Magi interpreted this as meaning that Astyages' grandson would usurp the throne. So orders were given to have the baby boy taken away and killed.

The servant could not face doing this, and passed the job to a poor herdsman and his wife, who brought the boy up as their own. When he was ten, Cyrus was playing a game called 'kings' in a village street with other boys, and his behaviour was so noble that the trick was suspected. The servant who had failed to kill off the baby was rewarded by having his own son casseroled and served up to him. On the advice of the Magi, Astyages spared Cyrus; Cyrus then led a revolt by Persian soldiers against the king, and though Astyages impaled the Magi for getting things so wrong (quite rightly, it has to be said), he was duly overthrown.

Cyrus treated his murderous grandfather with great consideration and allowed him to stay at court until he died. Though clearly a mixture of prurient gossip and traditional mythic storytelling, Herodotus' account points to a truth about the historical Cyrus, or at least how he was perceived in the markets and byways where the historian listened and took notes. Cyrus was a strange mix of the ruthless and the tolerant, who came from an old line of warrior-rulers and for whom both lineage and authority were problematical. As a fighter, he combined troops from different peoples, introducing tactical innovations from across Asia to win spectacular victories.

One of the most famous was over King Croesus of Lydia, in what is today western Turkey. The Lydians were well known to the Greeks; Herodotus says they invented gold and silver coinage. It was certainly reliable. In Lydia, the river that contained substantial amounts of ore still runs past the archaeological remains of a very early mint, where the metal was refined and the coins stamped. Lydian-style coins, whose great merit was that their weight, purity and therefore value were accepted far beyond the small state itself, provided a monetary system imported by Cyrus into his empire. Currency became current in Asia thanks to Cyrus's war.

Herodotus also says that Solon, who composed the first unified law system for classical Athens, visited Lydia and warned Croesus that he could not be called happy until he was dead, because one never knew what might happen next. When Croesus was waiting to be executed on a pyre of wood, he told the Persian king about Solon's words. Cyrus thought of his own case, and relented, keeping Croesus as a prisoner and adviser. When he asked the defeated Lydian whether he had actively wanted war, Croesus replied with perhaps the most famous sentence Herodotus ever scratched down: 'No one is fool enough to choose war instead of peace – in peace sons bury their fathers, but in war fathers bury their sons.'

Herodotus' interest in Persian culture, shared by other Greek writers, was practical and urgent. Had Cyrus, and the great kings who followed him, solved the problem of how to rule well? They had created an empire linked by fast, straight roads and governed by local administrators, or satraps; their tolerance of local religious customs allowed them to rule without an oppressively large force, and they seemed remarkably open to other people's ideas. Their armies were huge and composed of many different peoples; their main cities were impressive.

Herodotus notes that the people kiss when they meet in the street, rather than speaking, and he admires the custom whereby even the king refrains from putting someone to death for a single offence. They abhor lies and debt. They never pollute rivers 'with urine or spittle', or even wash their hands in the water they use to drink. They have an interesting way of taking decisions:

> If any important decision is to be made, they discuss the question when they are drunk, and the following day the master of the house . . . submits their decision for reconsideration when they are sober. If they still approve it, it is adopted; if not, it is abandoned. Conversely, any decision they make when they are sober, is reconsidered afterwards when they are drunk.

This system too has lasted: it is widely practised in the British democracy at Westminster. The Persians were clearly an impressive people, to be learned from as well as feared.

The Greek Miracle

We last left the Greek world itself scattered and emigrant, settlers amid the ruins of their first civilization, listening to Homeric tales of the age of heroes. Between about 800 and 550 BC the Greek story was one of gradual revival, based on their distinctive communities called *poleis* (singular: *polis*, which we normally translate as city-state). These varied greatly in size. Athens was a rare example of a survival from the Bronze Age, which had lost her hegemony over the surrounding area but regained it to become the largest of these city-states. Most examples of the *polis* tended to involve one easily defended high point, or acropolis, with a town around it and then villages and agricultural land around that. Other rural Greeks remained in their *ethnos*, or clan.

The earliest towns were hardly defended; later, stone walls and fortified gates appeared, to protect them not against Persians but against other Greeks. Up to nine in ten ancient Greeks were farmers, working relatively poor soil and struggling with the early effects of deforestation. They relied on wood and charcoal for fuel, and timber for

house-beams and ships, but from early on, having hacked back the relatively sparse forests climbing the mountains of their archipelago, they
had to import from the Black Sea and Asia. They ate little meat, keeping goats and sheep mainly for clothing and milk, and depended
heavily on barley, wheat, olives, grapes and figs: beer-drinkers, like the
Egyptians, were regarded as rather odd. The Mediterranean diet was
established early.

The geography of Greece was crucial to the development of this
civilization. Lots of sharp-ridged ranges running down to the sea created separate city-states growing independent of one another, likely to
experiment in different ways of running their affairs. These early states
were not egalitarian, like the first Anatolian towns. Most had developed from semi-tribal groups run by warrior-aristocrats, who owned
most of the land and wealth. This continued even when the Greeks
became more urban and republican in their government; as late as the
golden age of Athens, the state was riven by deep class conflicts,
wealthy nobles being resented by the rest.

However – to simplify a much more complicated story – the aristocrats steadily lost political ground as urban life became more
important. They lost out first to 'tyrants', an Asian word which really
meant 'usurpers', taking over sole control of a state. Then they started
to lose ground to group decisions made by ordinary citizens, often
meeting as families or tribes. By the seventh–sixth century BC, the
Greeks had a complicated religious pantheon comprising both the
'family' of Olympian gods that had probably been brought down by
the first Aryan invaders, and local cults. They shared a language,
though found it hard to understand some of the rival dialects. They
were also divided by culture, the Greeks who lived on the Asian coast
being richer and perhaps softer than the western Greeks of the Pelo-
ponnese.

The most important early development came about through their
method of fighting. In the seventh century BC the Greeks had mas-
tered the skill of fighting on foot in tightly organized phalanxes of
soldiers, each carrying a large shield to protect the man to his left, and
charging with spears, switching to swords for close fighting. From this
two things followed. First, it required general discipline and mutual
trust, virtues developed in the *polis*. Second, it meant that anyone who
could afford the basic equipment – a bronze helmet, greaves, shield

and spear – was a useful fighter. This included small-time farmers as well as craftsmen and tradesmen. The old dominance of small numbers of aristocratic cavalry, all set to protect their patch, was trumped by common men fighting together. The political implications hardly need to be spelled out: one historian says that, without this development, 'nobody would have dared kill off their community's main fighting force, the nobility'.[12]

Why did it happen? Greek terrain, with its narrow valleys and mountainous gorges, was not particularly suited to horse warfare, and certainly not to the fleets of chariots favoured in Asia. You could hardly even start a charge across Attica without instantly tumbling head over heels or losing your wheels. It was not a landscape made for emperors, any more than is Switzerland or Afghanistan. Later, a similar extension of people-power would emerge at sea, as the Greek states developed navies of war galleys that needed to be rowed by disciplined and experienced men working in perfect unison. This time the recruits came from those too poor to kit themselves out as hoplite warriors on land. So a common feeling stemming from a shared head-quarters and familiar geography was fortified by the act of fighting together – and, soon, by a common enemy. Solidarity started in warfare.

Apart from religious ideas and languages, not to mention the Homeric stories, the Greeks shared an enthusiasm for athletics, prepared for naked in gymnasiums. All-Greece games, contests in music and fighting as well as racing, were an early way of binding Greeks together. Since each city-state had a different calendar including different start times for each year, the games became a crucial way of measuring dates and timespans: the names of the winners of every Olympic Games since (allegedly) 776 BC became their version of our numerical counting of '2012' or '1945'. The gymnasia, where men went oiled and naked, produced a strong culture of homosexual admiration, and love affairs between boys and older men.

These are the early distinctive signs of Greek culture, but they emphatically did not lead to all these city-states developing a single answer to ruling and to the problem of power. Political competition turned the Greeks into historians and philosophers. One of the more extreme political systems, and a challenge to other states, was that of the Spartans. Though Pheidon of Argos is supposed to have introduced the tactic of phalanx fighting around 670 BC, it did not become a Spartan obsession until they had been beaten in battle by the men of Argos. The Spartans were already a warrior people, who had subdued a semi-enslaved landscape of farmers and helots (or serfs), as well as subsidiary villages who produced the food that allowed them to concentrate on their overriding hobby and interest – war.

The Spartans developed a state, with pre-echoes of Samurai Japan, or Facism, which self-consciously rejected the nurturing of the gentler arts being enjoyed in other Greek states. Babies judged weak-looking were left out to die. Boys and girls were separated at the age of seven. Boys were brought up in military-style training camps and later sent out to steal and kill food for themselves. Girls, too, were made to run and wrestle naked; later on, any one of them might provide a wife to be shared by several Spartan-citizen brothers. Spartans who fought and lost often killed themselves. The Spartans had two kings at any one time and a senior council of men aged sixty and over, who would put their proposals to all-male meetings of citizens.

Alongside this 'balance of powers' constitution, which allowed the city-state to avoid tyranny while giving its fighters an equal say, the Spartans shunned modernizations such as money, or walling their villages, and relied on their terrifyingly well organized semi-permanent army. The result was a dominant military state, which made other Greek states nervous but which could be engaged by them to topple tyrants or confront enemies.

Sparta rose to its greatest fame when it led the federated Greeks against the Persians. When Cyrus defeated Croesus in 546 BC it was the Spartans who sent a message ordering him to back off, and who forty-seven years later would rally the western Greeks against Persia in the Ionian revolt. And in the twenty-five years that followed, it was the Spartans above all who kept the epic fight going. Yet other Greeks, particularly the Athenians, laughed at the Spartans for their uncouth ways, seeing them as long-haired, unwashed, uncultured killers.

Athens, Sparta's great rival, was also a slave state, which gave extensive voting and other rights to its male citizens. Its original tyranny had been toppled with Spartan help in 510 BC. Two years later, Athens's ruler Cleisthenes proposed a radical new system of voting and representation, based on local parish- or village-level elections and on larger 'demes'. The deme was a territorial division, which could be as large as a small town and which would now replace the family name as the main badge of belonging. This was an important shift. Himself the grandson of an Athenian tyrant, Cleisthenes believed that the rivalry and power struggles between families had led inexorably to breakdown and tyranny. Only by ending the obsession with family or 'gene' could order be restored.

Crucially, his complex plan led to a single assembly of citizens, all men aged over thirty, who would take the biggest decisions. This was too large to be practical, since there were around twenty-five thousand such people, but these elected a council of five hundred who ruled Athens day by day. The full assembly would meet too, generally around six thousand Athenians traipsing into the city most weeks to listen and vote. This was 'democracy' in action, the one thing almost everyone knows about ancient Athens. It proved surprisingly robust because of its relative moderation. Instead of being executed, those who threatened the system could be 'ostracised', or sent packing after a vote – conducted with pieces of broken pottery – of the assembly. Many were allowed back from exile after doing their time.

Democracy as a system survived in Athens for nearly two hundred years, on and off, though it never caught on widely in the ancient world. To work, it demanded an educated citizenry, though only perhaps a tenth of them could actually read, as well as people who had learned how to speak publicly, to reason and to follow complicated arguments. This development of what we might call civil society was as important as the results of the voting.

Athenian 'democracy' did not include women, younger men or slaves, however. As Athens developed her gorgeous architecture and sculpture, her theatre and music and philosophy, she relied on slaves just as much as unsmiling Sparta did. And as Athens came to depend ever more on her silver mines to buy the corn she could not grow herself, huge numbers of slave miners were imported: one account suggests 150,000 at one time.[13] But slaves were used heavily on farms as well – the historian Xenophon refers to twenty thousand absconding from Athenian farms during a Spartan invasion – and as paid craftsmen, including for the great public buildings. It has been estimated that for every free male Athenian citizen there were two slaves. Without the slaves, captured in wars, the Greek farmers could not possibly have spared the time to learn to speak and vote, or to serve as active citizens; nor could the Greek aristocrats have enjoyed the wealth and leisure to study philosophy. Again, it was war that underpinned the 'Greek miracle' – and rather more substantially than many of its admirers like to admit.

The fighting against the armies of the Persians went on by land and sea. It had begun with the Ionian revolt of 499 BC, a rebellion by Greeks in Asia against their masters, which ended in Persian victory. But then Cyrus's successor Darius, taking over after an interlude dominated by less-than-great Kings of Kings, determined to punish Athens for supporting the rebels. The campaign began well for the Persians, who mopped up small Greek island states and destroyed the rebel *polis* of Eretria before landing on Attica to make for Athens. There, at Marathon in 490 BC, the Athenians won a surprising and remarkable victory. They were heavily outnumbered. Even modern historians accept that the Persian army was anything from twice to ten times as large, and had both cavalry and archers, which the Athenians lacked. But these citizen soldiers did a most surprising thing: they charged the Persian enemy at the run, with a deliberately weak centre but strong wings, and rolled them up, producing a great slaughter.

The robustly partisan Herodotus says the Greeks

> closed with the enemy all along the line, and fought in a way not to be forgotten. They were the first Greeks, so far as I know, to charge at a run, and the first who dared to look without flinching at Persian dress and the men who wore it; for until that day came no Greek could hear even the word Persian without terror.

The Persians got back to their ships and tried to sail round to Athens for another attack; but the Athenian army had beaten them to it. The story of this extraordinary run in armour back to the city is believed to have produced the 26-mile marathon race of modern times. Another legend has it that the Athenian courier Pheidippides ran the twenty-six miles back to his city to tell them of the victory and stiffen their determination to resist, dying after he delivered the message. Unfortunately there seems no historical evidence for this.

After Darius's death and a ten-year hiatus, his son Xerxes mounted a much larger invasion, intended to finish the Greeks off. By now the federation led by Athens and Sparta embraced more than seventy other Greek states, though even more were standing on the sidelines or supporting the enemy. Herodotus calculated the Persian army at 5.2 million men, a ludicrous figure; but it was certainly a huge force, brought across the Hellespont by rope bridge and barges, including special horse-barges. Herodotus gives a vividly exciting account of the famous fight at the narrow pass of Thermopylae, where King Leonidas and three hundred Spartans whom he had selected himself – 'all men in middle life and all fathers of living sons' – held back the Persians for days, until they were betrayed and all died.

Xerxes' army then poured down towards Attica and the Athenians had to evacuate their city, which was burned behind them. Eventually, in the narrow straits of Salamis, the combined Greek fleet won a crucial victory over the Persians. Two further major battles, at Plataea on land and Mycale by sea, were also Greek victories, ending the invasion. Historians have argued since that these fights were crucial to Western civilization because it relied so heavily for its development on the thought, art and politics of the Greeks, which would otherwise have been snuffed out by Persian despotism. Like other historic military turning-points, the imbalance of forces was probably exaggerated, but these Greek victories were the prototype of 'the war to save civilization', a trope used by the Russians before Borodino, by the British in 1940, and by scores of other forces.

The Greek victory did lead to a golden age for Athens, since rather oddly Sparta did not seize the leadership of Greece that her achievement in battle suggested she deserved. The eighty years from around 450 BC embrace the rise of the great statesman Pericles, the writing of the first historians – including, of course, Herodotus – and the rebuilding of the Athenian Parthenon under the sculptor Phidias. Athenian drama had emerged, exuberantly, from its origins in the performance of sacred song. And alongside the tragedies of Sophocles, Aeschylus and Euripides flourished a riotous and very rude tradition of comedies, most of them now lost, which acted as a constant criticism and heckle of Athenian life.

These performances became ever more showy and expensive, as rich Athenians competed to fund them (rather like later Roman emperors competed to show the best games). They were originally staged with full musical accompaniment for the chorus, the main players in exotic masks and intoning in rhythmic speech – bright, open-air celebrations of urban life at festivals attended by tens of thousands of people, enjoying the food stalls, the wine and the gossip. Having just the words of some of the dramas is a little like knowing the operas of Handel or Verdi only from their librettos. In a similar way, seeing the superbly crafted statues of Athenian heroes and gods in galleries, in cool white stone, hardly reflects the vividly painted public presences they would originally have been. And above all, of course, towered the philosophers, arguing about the nature of reality, what might constitute the good life, and how best to organize human societies.

This wealth and confidence came from the great conflict. It originated in decisive military victory over the Asian superpower of the day. The crackle of criticism and laughter came from democratic winners, sure enough of themselves to laugh at themselves. The intense search to *understand* – to understand the constitutions of the 158 Greek states studied by Aristotle, and the differences between Asian and Greek societies, as Herodotus sought to do; to understand the causes of civil war as Thucydides tried to, or the nature of the good society, as Socrates and Plato attempted – all this curiosity was not idle, and certainly not simple: it was the rich fruit of war.

Aborigines and Aryans

Among the forces in the Persian army marching under Xerxes towards the Spartans, Herodotus tells us, were a group dressed in cotton, armed with iron-tipped cane bows, and in chariots pulled by horses or wild asses. These were from India. The early history of that vast triangular protrusion from Eurasia is one of the most lively, still-developing subjects of study. As described earlier, it is now thought that the world-changing migration out of Africa brought people to India much earlier than to the Mediterranean, Europe or China. The indigenous forest-dwellers of southern India still look more like the aboriginal Australians and East Asian islanders who were part of humanity's first southern march than like northern Aryan Indians, who came much later.

For almost as soon as the early history of India was opened up by British scholar-explorers in the nineteenth century, it was assumed that India's great civilizations came from outside, rather than being cooked and shaped at home. And it is true that waves of migrants and

conquerors, from tribal Asian herders to Greeks, Persians and Mongols, pushed their way into India through the north-west gap between
the Himalayas and the sea. Each of them radically changed the subcontinent. The British were different only in that they, like the
Portuguese and French, arrived by sea. Yet it may well be that India's
earliest-known civilization, the mysterious urban centre of the Indus
valley, or Mohenjo-Daro, was indeed home-grown. At the start of the
new Indian republic in 1947, one leading politician, Jaipal Singh, a representative of the tribal (or forest) people, claimed to speak for the
ancient Indus valley tradition, labelling other Indians newcomers: 'The
whole history of my people is one of continuous exploitation by the
non-aboriginals of India.'[14]

So what was this, perhaps aboriginal, civilization? The baked-brick
cities of the Indus River plain had excellent water systems and plumb-
ing, writing that has not been decoded, and some interesting art. This
includes a small figure who could be practising yoga, and another
which could be a very early version of the later Hindu deity Siva.
There are many finely cut seals showing the bulls, elephants and tigers
so important to later Indian religion and art. And there is a very sexy
nude dancing-girl, whose challenging pose and bangles prefigure the
erotic sculpture of much younger Hindu temples but whose face is
that of an aborigine. So it is possible – no more than that – that the
very first human migrants from the Horn of Africa who had stayed in
India created the essentials of Indian religion and art long before
invaders arrived from the north.

By the time these Indians were marshalled under Persian banners
against the Greeks, however, they were ethnic cousins of the people
they were fighting. Connected by the tips of their empires, the Indians
of the fifth and fourth centuries BC certainly knew of the Greeks, calling them 'Yona', a word derived via the Persian for 'Ionians'. These
northern Indians, like the Persians, spoke a language that had the same
origins as Greek, Latin and every major European language of today.
This is old news, thanks to a discovery made in 1785 by a brilliant English lover of India, who had been sent to Calcutta as a High Court
judge, Sir William Jones.[15]

Jones, a superb linguist, had become one of the first Europeans
to learn Sanskrit, the academic language of Hindu scholarship.
Spotting clues in key words and in the grammatical structure, he

saw that it was part of what would be called the 'Indo-European' family of languages. This was originally the language of the Aryans, ancestors of so many later noisy tribes. They had been pastoral people, depending on cattle and horses, who had migrated in waves from their original homeland, which was probably around the Caspian Sea or the Ukraine. 'Aryan' is a word whose implication of racial superiority, after the Europe of the Nazis, can make modern ears twitch. But it is just a useful label. We could as well say that Indians, Mediterranean people and Europeans are 'all Caspians' or 'all Ukrainians' (though we don't).

Because ancient peoples can be tracked by words as well as by stones, it is generally accepted that the Aryans moved to the west, driving into Turkey, Greece and the Balkans, as well as into what is now Iran, and into India too. They had probably crossed into today's Pakistan at around the time of the Trojan war, and were reaching the great Ganges plain a couple of hundred years after that. It is possible that the Dorians were another branch of the Aryan migration, displacing the Mycenaean Greeks at roughly the same time – in which case, at the battle of Marathon distant cousins had confronted one another on the battlefield without knowing it.

The ancient hymns, or 'vedas', of the Indian Aryans, orally transmitted with great care, show them to be warlike and horse-obsessed. On the other hand, they had no words for 'plough', 'writing' or 'elephant',[16] so they may indeed have had to learn from the indigenous people they merged with, defeated or displaced. We do not know what happened, though these Aryan incomers had a culture of animal sacrifice and cattle-stealing, which fits with herders turning into raiders. They had clearly been part of the wider Near Eastern family. Stories such as those included in the Puranas show similarities with the tales of Mesopotamia and the Bible, including a great flood in which a god, Vishnu, warns the lawgiver Manu to build a boat, then takes him to a mountain peak to save him.

The Aryans had followed a familiar historical path. They had moved from roaming with animals to settling. The Rig Vedas, the oldest Sanskrit stories, paint a picture of a tribal culture with chieftains, priests, orgiastic sacrifice parties, and cattle as the common currency. The historian John Keay has memorably compared it to the clan system of the Scottish highlands before the arrival of sheep cleared the glens: 'All . . . whether Indian or Scots, shared a language (Gaelic/Sanskrit), a social system in which precedence was dictated by birth, and a way of life in which both wealth and prestige were computed in cattle. In Scotland as in India, the rustling of other clans' herds constituted both pastime and ritual.'[17]

But in India as in Scotland, farming eventually won. By the time of the Scottish clans, Scotland's original forests had long gone, cleared for fuel and farmland and leaving behind a thin ecology that could sustain few people. The Indian Aryans were luckier. Northern India then was very different from the heavily populated and intensively farmed khaki plains of today. As the ancient texts make clear, once the invaders left the Punjab and migrated eastwards, they found a lushly forested terrain, rich in wildlife and game, spreading slowly to the waterlogged Ganges delta itself. The land was inhabited by forest people, hunter-gatherers whose way of life was comparable to that of the people of the Amazon or the highlands of New Guinea. Even in twentieth-century India there were forest-dwellers excluded by, and suspicious of, the urban and farming culture all around them.

The Iron Age was the age of the iron plough as much as of the iron sword. Mile by mile, the forests were burned for farmland, the soil broken by ploughing, and crops of barley were sown. The game retreated, and villages became small towns. The Aryans settled. Eventually rice paddies would be carved out of the watery land where the forests ended. This was a long-lasting and stable change. Parts of today's India, for instance in Bihar towards the border with Nepal, contain villages built of wood and woven reeds, whose farmers plough with oxen and tend rice and vegetable fields, burning cow-dung for fuel, as they have done ever since the Iron Age. Yet soon the great Indian rivers were being used for trade and transport, and a network of roads began to link the north. Thus, under the great white ridges and the blue arms of the Himalayas, in the valleys and plains, a northern Indian civilization was evolving.

As with ancient Greek, Semitic, Nordic and Mesopotamian cultures, the Vedic-age Indians had a family of gods and goddesses who required endless and complicated sacrifices. These gods were the responsibility of the Brahmin priests, who occupied the top rung of a developing caste system.

Caste is a complicated and much argued-about issue. To begin with it was no more than a rough and ready division of people by their role, such as happened in Europe and Russia too. In the Indian formulation, after the priest-teachers, the Brahmins, came the warriors and administrators (*kshatriyas*); then the farmers and traders (*vaisyas*), and finally the workers and servants (*shudras*). This is not, of itself, surprising. Agricultural societies and early urban ones maintained skills and knowledge by passing it down within families. Before mass education, know-how was too precious to squander by allowing everyone choice. It was hoarded. Potters shaped potters and charioteers gave their sons the reins.

Evidence from early scriptures suggests that, nevertheless, some people could move between these groups. On the other hand, some DNA evidence (much contested) suggests that today's higher-caste Indians have closer genetic links to Europeans than lower-caste people have. In which case, the Brahmins, *kshatriyas* and *vaisyas* may be the children of Indo-European invaders, while the lower castes, doing the rougher, dirtier and more routine work, are more likely to be descended from the earlier people of India. If true, this would be a remarkable example of cultural persistence. But we also have to remember that, in terms of biology, 'ancient history' is hardly even yesterday; if we think of modern lifespans, say seventy years, then the Greeks of Marathon and the ancient Aryans of India are only around forty spans away.

What is unarguable is that this early Vedic system of caste became steadily more rule-bound and hard to evade. As the towns and trade grew, there was more specialization, so that functions were defined and slotted into a more complex structure, like drawers added to a giant chest. As in other cultures, the growth of towns and states led to more complicated and overbearing hierarchies of power and wealth, and made what we would call social mobility harder, too. At the bottom of the scale, the worker-families with the nastiest duties were turned into a subclass of exploited helots, the 'untouchables'. But then, after all, the Greeks had their slaves.

The Rebel at the Tree-root

There were other parallels between northern India and the Greek world. As the clans settled down, many of them came under the rule of kings, some hereditary and others elected. Other clans developed a system that has been translated as 'clan organization' or 'government-by-discussion'. More simply, it was a form of republic in which most men had a say, at regular meetings. The term *rajah* could mean something close to 'elector-citizen' as well as 'ruler'. Thus a political map of northern India at around the time of the birth of classical Greece shows a patchwork of rival states not so very different from the states of the Greek world, which also had government-by-discussion, contending with tyrannies.

By 600 BC in northern India there were sixteen *mahajanapadas*, or 'great states', from the Indus in the west to the Ganges and its tributaries. Magadha, Licchavi, Kosala, Kura and Panchala were names possessing something of the resonance there of Athens, Sparta, Corinth and Thebes in south-eastern Europe. Kingdoms challenged republics. How best to rule, how best to live, were issues as live in India as in Athens. Here too there were leagues and alliances, wars and fallings-out; and great interest in the best balance of power and in the duties of citizens. There were cruder quarrels too. One particularly long war was fought between King Bimbisara of the powerful Magadha state and the republican 'knights' of Licchavi. A courtesan at the Licchavi capital of Vaishali, called Amrapali, who was seduced by Bimbisara and bore him a child, was at the centre of the affair – a Helen of the Ganges. Such are the old stories, still told in modern India. This same woman, Amrapali, later became a follower of an individual who was certainly more than a legend.

The first biographies of the Siddhartha Gautama, the Buddha, appear around six hundred years after he lived. They give place names, dates and a plausible life story. But the pause is a long one, making him the least historically visible of the major ethical revolutionaries of the age of the great empires. Confucius did not get a biography until some four hundred years after he died, the work of the Chinese historian Sima Qian; but Mengzi, or Mencius, who lived a century after

Confucius, did write about him; and his own reported conversations fill in gaps. (Compared with Buddha and Confucius, Christ is a much clearer historical figure. St Mark is reckoned to have written his account only forty years or so after the death of Jesus, in the year 70 when Jerusalem fell. There are good reasons to think he may have had the stories directly from St Peter, the historical Christ's companion. In addition, there is supporting evidence from non-Christian sources, such as the Jewish historian Josephus and mainstream Roman writers, about large numbers of followers of 'Chrestus' less than a century after his death.)

Yet archaeology and ancient texts do explain a lot about the society the Buddha emerged from, as well as his teaching. By his time, the Brahmin system with its priestly hierarchy and sacrifices was very strongly entrenched, but it was also being challenged by dissident travelling teachers and sects. This probably reflected the severe social disruption being experienced by north India at the time, which was undergoing a major increase in population and fast changes to many people's lives. The villages and local markets had been added to, with sizeable towns and even cities of around thirty-five thousand people springing up, accompanied by a money culture, shops, cart paths, moats and fortified walls.

Unlike stone-built Greece or Persia, we have almost no architectural remains of a people who built with pounded earth, mud bricks and wood. Their words, repeated in scriptures and poems long enough to make Homer look terse, have lasted better than their buildings – or anything they made that was much larger than pottery and ironwork. In the so-called republics or *gana-sanghas*,[18] Brahmin authority seems to have been more questioned than in the kingdoms. Siddhartha Gautama came from one of the former, the small clan-republic of Sakya, inside today's Nepal, which elected its own chief. Academic arguments persist about just when Siddhartha was born; recent scholarship is shifting his dates forward by about eighty years, from around 566 BC to nearer the middle of the following century. But the often quoted description of him as a prince, living a life of royal luxury, hardly squares with what is known of the Sakya clan and seems an embellishment.[19] He was more likely to have been a reasonably well-off leading clan member.

Siddhartha married his cousin, had a son and lived a comfortable

life until, aged twenty-nine, he rebelled and set off to seek enlightenment, leaving his family behind with the briefest of farewells and no
apparent remorse. Some traditions say this happened after his refusal
to take part in another bloody bout of inter-clan warfare. Walking off
would not have seemed such a strange thing to do in the India of Siddhartha's time. There was a tradition of men leaving their villages and
families and going to seek spiritual truth in the forests, or begging by
the roads. Shaven-headed 'seekers' in ragged robes seem to have been
widely respected, even if their views differed wildly. The tradition can
be likened to the wilderness treks of Israelite prophets, or those of the
later Christian saints and mendicants moving from village to village.

At a time of social change and civil warfare, the appetite for new
thinking is famously keen. In 1949 the German philosopher Karl
Jaspers called the period from 800 to 200 BC 'the axial age' because the
revolution in spiritual thought was so powerful that the rest of human
history rotates around it. It seems an essential product of the greater
leisure and wealth created by the rise of town- and city-based civilizations, and the disturbing effect of the wars between them. As a phrase,
the 'axial age' has fallen from fashion, but there was clearly a rethink-
ing of old beliefs going on from Greece to China. The conflict
between small Indian states in the Buddha's time is a perfect example
of it.

We are told that Siddhartha tried some of the techniques used by
other seekers, beginning with ascetic renunciation and begging in a
nearby city. He gave this up to wander, study under hermit monks,
and meditate. He rejected extreme mortification, the practice of starving until one was almost a living skeleton, for a 'middle way' between
that and worldly indulgence (attractively, rice pudding seems to have
helped do the trick). After meditating under a sacred fig (or Bodhi) tree
for forty-nine days and nights at a small village in northern India, he
achieved enlightenment at the age of thirty-five, finally understanding
the source of human suffering. What did he conclude? That the pains
of birth, illness, ageing and death were caused by a lust for sensual
pleasure and renewed life, which repeats itself in the cycle of death
and rebirth until overcome by mental and moral willpower. At this
moment, the seeker breaks the tragic cycle. He achieves a state beyond
the physical world, of pure mind and serenity, or nirvana.

The Buddha or 'enlightened one', as Siddhartha was now known, started to gather disciples, who became monks. With them he travelled around the Ganges flood plain, preaching to anyone who would listen. The former courtesan Amrapali, who (as noted earlier) had provoked a war, became a devoted follower; her son became a Buddhist monk. The Buddha founded monasteries, including some for female monks. He rejected both animal sacrifices and the caste system, and survived assassination attempts by supporters of Brahminism, to live on to the age of eighty. Or so it is said – and, again, how can we know? Stories of the Buddha's life and his sayings were transmitted by methodical mass chanting, rather like rote-learning in traditional schoolrooms. This allowed them to be passed on, generation by generation, with the minimum of error, though corruptions will always appear. But much early history starts as oral history, and it is confirmed surprisingly often by archaeology. We cannot brush it away.

In this story there are obvious similarities with the stories of Christ and Muhammad: the leaving-behind of ordinary family life to seek enlightenment in natural solitude (under a tree, in a cave, or in the desert); then there is the gathering of disciples; preaching through stories to everyone, not just an elite; and the rejection of earlier religious systems. Unlike the founders of the great monotheisms, however, the Buddha never claimed divinity for himself, or his system. Many would argue that strictly speaking Buddhism is not a religion but a system of self-control, which allows its followers to escape the limitations and pains of everyday life.

But it involved a pacifist and tolerant attitude, which made it a public matter, not simply a private practice; and it was open to everyone, of whatever past creed or social position or race. In the centuries after the Buddha's death his followers tapped into attitudes already present in Indian thinking – the renunciation of wealth and power, vegetarianism, pacificism – and extended them into a 'do unto others' creed. By contrast, Christianity would become intertwined with the very worldly and aggressive power of the later Roman Empire, and Islam would arm itself even more dramatically.

Buddhism was indeed different. In essence, it was a radical rejection of everything that goes to make up what we call history – earthly empires, developing technological skill, changing political systems and ideas. The Buddha says, Walk away from all that, and instead look inside yourself. So it is hardly surprising that, with one exception we shall come to later, Buddhism rarely features as a history-shaping system of belief. This does not mean it was not hugely influential. It spread to the countries of South-East Asia, where superbly elaborate Buddhist temples and courts would emerge, under the patronage of Buddhist kings. The influence of Buddhist monks and art in China was huge, and it spread from there to Korea and to Japan, where the story of its early art seems at times almost completely a Buddhist one. Buddhism would be persecuted in most of these places. It did not, however, produce a political or imperial system of its own; the Buddha would have been aghast if it had.

In India itself, Buddhism would later be almost exterminated until modern times, and it was only under the Victorian British Raj that the Buddha's existence as a real, historical figure came to be acknowledged. All the same, it remains a very important belief system. Bodhgaya, where the haggard former aristocrat meditated his way to enlightenment under the fig tree, is today perhaps the most attractive of the pilgrimage sites of the world's great religions. Calm, smiling, saffron- and plum-shrouded monks and nuns from Thailand, Burma and Sri Lanka chant under the shadow of an ancient temple. There is a refreshing air of cheerfulness, and the religious tat is more meagre, cheaper and less obtrusive than in Rome, Jerusalem or (I suspect) Mecca.

What, meanwhile, of the even greater contemporary civilization to the east of India?

Kongzi's Mid-life Crisis

Aged fifty-four, a middle-ranking bureaucrat in a failing, riven state had had enough. He resigned as minister for law and order, said goodbye to most of his friends and went off on a thirteen-year ramble. This was not a Buddhist search for solitude and enlightenment, but a political journey. After visiting many rival states and finding little employment, the civil servant came home again, amused and rueful at his relative failure. By the time he died, he had attracted a small group of friends and followers. The career of Kong Fuzi, or Kongzi, or 'Confucius' (in the Latinized version of his name made appealing to faltering Western lips by Jesuit missionaries two thousand years later), was hardly stellar.

Yet his influence was huge. For good or ill, Confucius was treated as a kind of god by scores of Chinese emperors, and had a huge effect on Chinese life. Reviled by Mao Zedong and the original Communists, in the year 2012 his influence is growing again as new generations of Chinese search for values beyond threadbare Communism or materialism. A state-sponsored and fairly dreadful film has been made about his life. In the central Confucian temple in Beijing – one of around three thousand such temples – where emperors once worshipped the thinker, small children, sent by parents anxious to impart something more than mere facts, are again being taught his ideas.

Depending on one's view of the row about Buddha's dates, the two men were alive at roughly the same time. The Chinese were more careful with records, and we believe Kongzi lived from 551 to 479 BC. Like Siddhartha, he was born in a marginal state and at a time of civil strife and war, in which the old order was being challenged. If India had her yellow-robed forest 'seekers', China had her wandering philosophers, by tradition hundreds of them. Like the Buddha, Kongzi communed with rulers without coming under anyone else's sway; like the Buddha he preached the importance of doing unto others as you would like them to do to you; like the Buddha he never came close to asserting his own divinity. But he too would later become the focus of a semi-religion that elevated him into mythical status.

Kongzi's China was divided, like the Buddha's India and golden-age Greece, into rival states. After his death it too would plunge into vicious local wars. Instead of Athens, Corinth, Sparta, Panchala, Maghada, Sakla and the rest, China had the states of Wei, Zhou, Song, Han and Chu. But politically, China was if anything even more chaotic. The chronicles for the time list more than 140 states, whose rulers and priests behaved in ways that contemporary Greeks, Persians or Indians would have understood. They tried to divine the future by reading the cracks on the burned shoulder-bones of cows, or the undershells of turtles, which was no sillier than the Greek habit of listening to the ramblings of women who had inhaled poisonous vapours, or the Roman penchant for fingering chicken entrails.

What made China different was that it had been united. This was the source of Kongzi's deep conservative romanticism about a lost past. The states of Kongzi's time were themselves the shattered shell fragments of a much greater China, that of the Zhou dynasty which had lasted for more than seven centuries, following the fall of the Shang. Chinese imperial history can sound impenetrable to outsiders, but at this stage the story is pretty straightforward. The Shang were the first historically certain dynasty, following the cloudy story of the Xia and Da Yu.

Shang China was, like early India, a much wilder place than it later became, with extensive forests and impassable marshes, not yet drained for rice. Where Chinese civilization probably first took root, along the Yellow River, roaming animals included tigers, bears, elephants, rhinos and panthers; the climate was fierce, with cold winters and very hot summers, as well as the regular flooding. Shang society was, again, in some ways like early Aryan India, an aristocratic and warrior hierarchy setting much store by raiding and hunting, living off the backs of an impoverished peasantry.

Like the Assyrians and Persians, the Shang fought from chariots and used powerful bows. A cascade of subkings, dukes, local rulers and fighters derived their position from the emperor. Their cities and fortresses were built with walls which, when dug up today, are still sharp-edged and hard. They had wooden buildings in the same long-eaved and rectangular pattern of later Chinese architecture. (The wood eventually gave way to brick and the thatched roofs were mimicked in yellow and green glazed tiles, but the essentials remained for a remarkably long time, China being untouched by the imported styles and hybrids that gave European architecture such diversity.) After lives spent in their square, pillared country homes, the Shang nobility were given lavish burials, with superb bronze vessels, silks and lacquered coffins. They were addicted to human sacrifice, and huge numbers of servants and prisoners seem to have been murdered and partly dismembered to keep Shang aristocrats company on the way to the afterlife.

It was not all dark. Under the Shang, extensive terraces were built for agriculture, land was cleared and more canals were dug. Remarkably, a script of at least four thousand characters, found written on diviners' animal bones, bears enough resemblance to modern Chinese for archaeologists to be able to read some of it straight off. Shang culture looks in many respects like the world of the Aztecs, with their human sacrifices and complex, gnarled art. Just as in central America, an attractive human-scale 'folk art' had given way to ever more complex, severe, encrusted ritual designs, which seem to mirror the more forbidding society developing in cities and palaces.[20] Shang bronzes are particularly famous, quite extraordinary achievements in casting. But they inspire only admiration; they are not appealing.

The Shang were ousted by the long-lasting Zhou, and it is to them that Kongzi looked back with dazzled admiration. One historian says that the Shang deserved to go: 'Drunkenness, incest, cannibalism, pornographic songs and sadistic punishments enliven the catalogue of liturgical improprieties.'[21] The man who more than any other put an end to such poor behaviour was the headmasterly Duke of Zhou. His older brother won a great victory over the Shang around 150 years after the siege of Troy, at a site called Muye, but had then retired home and died. Since the king's son was too young to take over, the duke led a regency council, which eventually overwhelmed the earlier dynasty and established the Zhou as its replacement under 'the Mandate of Heaven'.

This is an important concept in Chinese history. As a new ruling family from the edge of Shang China, the Zhou had to tread carefully. They needed continuity to keep the loyalty of the followers of the ousted dynasty. Later dynasties would have the same problem. So the Duke of Zhou declared that the Zhou were merely the tools used by a just Heaven to punish the Shang. Given this job by Heaven, the deal required that the new king must be reverent and kind. The duke said: 'As he functions as king, let him not, because the common people stray and do what is wrong, then presume to govern them by harsh punishments . . . In being king, let him take his position in the primacy of virtue. The little people will then pattern themselves on him throughout the world.'[22]

This was a crucial doctrine for Kongzi. A virtuous king produces a virtuous people. Thus begins a chain of obligation and mutual service. If everyone acts according to their role, trying to be whatever they are – mother, baker, teacher, soldier – as well as they can, then the good life and the good society emerge. 'Knowing your place' is a positive social virtue, not merely submissiveness. This is a family-based and profoundly anti-individualistic way of thinking; but if we, in our extremely (and excessively) individualistic culture do not try to under-

stand it, we have no chance of understanding Kongzi, or Chinese history, or indeed today's China either.

After explaining the Mandate of Heaven to the people, the Duke
of Zhou stood down and handed back control to the rightful king, his
nephew – a modest gesture rare in the Chinese story. Kongzi spoke a
lot about the duke. The heyday of the Zhou dynasty was for him and
his generation a little like the age of lost heroes was for the Greeks of
the same time. But by his day the system devised by the Zhou, which
had parcelled out the Chinese heartland into subsidiary principalities,
had completely broken down. The principalities, with their own cities,
became effectively hereditary, then started to harden into rival independent states. One historian puts it beautifully: the House of Zhou
'now burned only as a wraithlike source of ultimate authority in a
world where all the states and principalities had freely entered into a
struggle for survival . . . bonds of lineage and loyalty were losing their
hold'.[23] The time in short, was out of joint. Kongzi would come to
think that he was born to set it right.

He was born, apparently, in Chanping village in the Lu kingdom.
Lu's connections with the failing dynasty were particularly poignant;
the Duke of Zhou himself had returned to run Lu after handing back
control of China. So Lu was a rare, loyal vassal of the Zhou, or meant
to be. It is said that Kongzi's father was a famous warrior and strongman called Zou He, who married a 'woman of the Yan clan' and made
love to her 'in the wilds', or by some accounts on a sacred mound in
the forest. The boy was born with a deformed head, either a lump on
the skull or a depression, and a strangely sunken face.[24] He grew up to
be notably tall. In the China of the time, he might well have been
abandoned to die. That he was not may explain Kongzi's lifelong devotion to his mother. His father died early, and though he could claim
the status of gentleman, just about, Kongzi seems to have had a tough
start.

In the *Analects*, or collected sayings, which provide the most
authentic-sounding record of Kongzi himself, he says: 'I was poor and
from a lowly station; that is why I am skilful in many menial things.'
He was educated, however, and managed to make a career working
for the struggling and divided Lu state. He was a keeper of livestock
and grain for the family of Lu's chief counsellor, then became minister of public works, then minister of crime (or law and order). Kongzi

married, though little is known of his wife, and he may have divorced her. Since he robustly mocked writers who made up things they did not know, we had better watch our step. The later Chinese historian Sima Qian says Kongzi was actually quite a successful civil servant. Under his regime, 'lamb and pork sellers stopped charging inflated prices, men and women walked on opposite sides of the street and no one picked up things left on the road'.[25]

At this point, we need to confront what is the biggest obstacle to a modern appreciation of Kongzi – his obsession with ritual and the correct performance of rites. The rites governed funerals, celebrations, daily meals and meetings between people of different stations: it has been estimated that a properly educated gentleman had to obey some 3,300 rules. What we know of this period comes from a sparely written history of Lu, mainly diplomatic, called *The Spring and Autumn Annals*, which may have been written by Kongzi himself; and from the *Zuo Commentary* on them.

'Spring and Autumn' was merely a contemporary poetic way of saying 'a year', or 'annual', but it is now the way this entire period of Chinese history is named. The chronicles are heavily concerned with proper authority, status, procedure and rites; and for Kongzi getting the rites right was of paramount importance, as already mentioned. It was probably a failure to apportion the ritually correct amount of meat after a sacrifice that led to him storming out of his job and taking to the road; and when his mother died he insisted on the full set of rites, old-fashioned and expensive as they were. He mourned her for three years.

Why were rites so important?

The answer, in one word, is family. Kongzi mentioned the deity very little and may have been agnostic himself. The sincere and proper performance of traditional rituals was a way of achieving self-control and of maintaining social order in a network of family and clan ties. In traditional China the well ordered family (in contrast to the Greek *polis*) was the fundamental unit. It was held together and got its sense of identity through rites for mourning the dead, celebrating festivals, remembering one's forebears, conducting family meals, honouring local gods, and so on. When one state or clan destroyed another, the victors would try to eradicate the losers' rites; by doing so they were wiping out their collective memory, traditions and identity. Rites were what made you who you were; without rites, conducted seriously, you were nothing.

The bonds of extended families spread into the early Chinese mini-states, which functioned almost like well ordered, formal tribes. But in the good society, the bonds (marked and policed by rites) also went further than blood-kinship. The bonds between landowner and peasant, buyer and seller, ruler and ruled, subsidiary state and greater kingdom, spread out beyond the family but were covered by similar traditional acts of ritual. However, in Kongzi's time this ancient way of being (of knowing who you were, and what your life should be) was being challenged and overthrown by an alternative – the state. It is still too early to talk of an absolutist or totalitarian state, but these rising Chinese states demanded obedience and ruled by fear, through a bureaucracy which had nothing to do with family. It is not ridiculous to detect here faint echoes of the impact of Communist or Fascist states' hostility to family ties.

In Kongzi's ideal world, just as the good father exercised authority with kindness, so the good ruler had to be merciful. In the *Analects* we read: 'The Master said, Govern the people by regulations, keep order amongst them by chastisements, and they will flee from you, and lose all self-respect. Govern them by moral force, keep order among them by ritual, and they will keep their self respect and come to you of their own accord.'[26] *Ren*, which means something like 'virtue', led to the 'way' or *dao*, which can be compared to the Bible's 'path of right-eousness'. Ritual means treating everyone with respect, and Kongzi's version of 'the golden rule' sounds very much like Christ's: 'Deal with the common people as though you were officiating at an important sacrifice. Do not do to others what you would not like done to your-self.'

If this is a conservative or even a reactionary message, as is often said, then Kongzi's conservatism is a kindly alternative to violent and abusive power; it is the conservatism of a Shakespeare who thinks the world is better when kings behave like kings, fathers are just, and so on. In China, ritual also allows the individual to control himself, even master himself. In one passage in the *Analects*, a follower who has been reminded about the importance of ritual quotes back at Kongzi a poem:

As thing cut, as thing filed,
As thing chiselled, as thing polished.

The writer Karen Armstrong elaborates: a gentleman 'was not born but crafted. He had to work on himself in the same way as a sculptor shaped a rough stone and made it a thing of beauty.'[27] This shows that 'correct ritual', which can seem an eerie and meaningless echo of an ancient civilization, is not so different from meditation, prayer or any programme of rigorous self-improvement. It is about mastery and order of the self and of society.

These seemed an urgent matter in Kongzi's China of warring states, increasing luxury and disorder, where even Lu was disrupted by usurpers, leaving the rightful duke broke and powerless. On the borders, barbarians were waiting. In China itself, a much worse civil war was brewing, which would bring horrors then undreamt-of. Later Chinese thinkers would develop alternative readings. Monzi, for instance, thought Confucian thinking was elitist and argued for a less elaborate, stripped-down system of social justice. But just as Siddhartha was provoked by the turbulence of northern India, and the Jewish prophets were stirred by the experience of war and exile, without the violence and the feuding Kongzi would never have been driven to become a teacher.

The rival state of Qi was worried that, schooled by Kongzi, his master the Duke of Lu was becoming too successful and might invade. So Qi's ruler sent the duke presents and concubines to corrupt him, and according to legend it worked. The duke revelled in his luxury and failed to perform the proper rites. Furious, Kongzi decided to find a better master to serve. He can be made to sound a rather forbidding character. Whereas the Buddha was turned into a moon-faced, gilded god figure encrusted in scripture, Kongzi would be elevated into an intimidating-looking, court-costumed old wizard with a sinister beard.

But he can hardly be blamed for that. Nor can the real Kongzi be held accountable for the rigidly imposed and humourless doctrine of imperial Confucianism that developed later, and which ruled by outlawing any deviation from tradition, however minor. Kongzi was exalted first into a cult figure and then into a state religion, to be worshipped as a god. But great thinkers are often fated to be known only in translation. We know Christ only through his disciples. To use the Christian parallel again is not entirely outlandish, either: in Kongzi's temples other philosophers who picked up his thinking and tested it are arrayed as four evangelists, while the next tier of Confucian thinkers are lined up as twelve apostles. Though the West has nobody quite like Kongzi – a conservative moralist regarded as worthy of worship, yet not quite the founder of a religion – it takes only a little effort to make him seem familiar.

It is noticeable that the worst excesses in Chinese history, the great repressions and slaughters, have come from the anti-Confucian side. They came from the lineage- and clan-crushing Chinese emperors who used terror and savage punishments to build their states, right down to Mao Zedong, whose Communist revolution in the mid-twentieth century attempted to tear up and destroy the powerful and still-persisting Chinese tradition of the family. Confucian sayings were hacked off the walls of villages where they had guided and comforted peasants for centuries. Mao understood that if people no longer knew, never mind honoured, their ancestors – if their identity was stripped away – they would be softer putty in the hands of the state. In his own day, Kongzi understood the wickedness as well as the futility of this.

In life, Kongzi never found his ideal state. He tramped the lanes and roads of ancient China, gathering followers who repeated his stories and arguments, and picking up odd pieces of work but never landing another court position. By the time he died, he good-humouredly regarded himself as a somewhat laughable failure. The *Analects* and other reminiscences paint a vivid picture of Kongzi as a man ready to mock himself, who loved food (but could manage with plain fare) and was proud of his ability to hold his drink. Unlike the great Greek teacher Socrates, his conversations with his followers aimed to get at useful truths rather than to entangle them in their own logic, or display his own argumentative brilliance. Like Socrates, though, he was well served by those followers who spread his ideas across all of thinking, arguing and literate China, at just the time when civil war was forcing men to debate exactly what a good society meant, and how to get it.

Dying Well

Socrates, too, could hold his drink, especially his last drink.

The greatest tragic scene in the story of democracy was written not by a playwright but by a philosopher – though Plato, the pupil of ugly, snub-nosed, infuriating and yet somehow lovable Socrates, had had ambitions to write for the stage. Plato's account of his master's death remains awe-inspiring. Socrates had been found guilty, quite narrowly, on charges of corrupting the youth of Athens and failing to respect her gods. Most historians regard them as trumped-up charges and the trial as unfair, even hysterical. It is unclear exactly what 'corrupting' meant, except that Socrates was a disdainful enemy of democracy and would never keep his mouth shut. He was a famous figure who had been mocked by the city's comic poets for years, and whose circle included some of the more sinister aristocrats of the age.

When found guilty, Socrates gently derided the court over the question of his penalty, and this may have encouraged them to sentence him to death rather than exile. But once sentenced, he refused to scurry off and escape, as he could easily have done. The Athenians may have expected him to make it easier for everyone by doing exactly that, but Socrates felt it would expose him to ridicule. He accepted the verdict, telling the court that it was time to be going, 'I to die and you to live; but which of us has the happier prospect is unknown to anyone but God.'

His followers were with him in prison on the day appointed for the execution, which was to be effected by his taking a drink containing an infusion of hemlock. Hemlock, modern biologists tell us, paralyses the muscle system and eventually causes death by asphyxiation, which cannot be pleasant. Socrates had a bath, said goodbye to his wife and three sons, before sending them away (because he did not want any hysterical grief). He teased one grieving follower, Crito, for being upset at the thought of burying him – what would be buried, he explained, would not be Socrates, just a body. Socrates was some kind of agnostic. He did not know whether death was the end, oblivion, or whether it was a transition to another world, the Hades of the Greek imagination, peopled with spirits of the dead. But if it was oblivion, there was nothing to be frightened of, since he would not know. If it was Hades, he said, he would meet some old heroes and talk to them.

It was the day appointed for the execution. Sunset approached, and the jailer arrived to tell him the time had come. Socrates found this man, who was also grieving, to be 'charming', and ordered the poison to be brought. Crito pointed out that the sun was still visible on the hills: Socrates could wait a while longer, as so many others had, and enjoy some more life with his friends. Socrates declined. Again, it would make him seem ridiculous in his own eyes. The jailer returned with the poison. Socrates asked whether he could spill some as an offering to the gods to help him on his journey. No, said the man, there was just enough to kill him.

In his *Phaedo*, Plato says Socrates then raised the cup to his lips and 'quite readily and cheerfully he drank off the poison. And hitherto most of us had been able to control our sorrow; but now when we saw him drinking, and saw too that he had finished the draught, we could no longer forbear, and in spite of myself my own tears were flowing fast.' Socrates had asked the jailer what would happen, and he had been told to walk around until his legs felt heavy, then to lie down. Socrates did so, and

> then he lay on his back, according to the directions, and the man who gave him the poison now and then looked at his feet and legs; and after a while he pressed his foot hard, and asked him if he could feel; and he said, 'No'; and then his leg, and so upwards and upwards, and showed us that he was cold and stiff. And he felt them himself, and said: 'When the poison reaches the heart, that will be the end.'[28]

His final words to Crito were to tell him to sacrifice a cock to the god of healing – for he saw death as a kind of healing – and then he covered his face, fell silent and died.

How should we read this story? The background is, yet again, war. After the heroic defeats of the Persian armies by Athens and Sparta working together, Athens had grown swollen with power. It took a long time, twenty years or so, to mop up the Persian forces still holding Greek towns in Asia. The Athenians had formed an alliance, the Delian League, to help their navy complete the job. Lesser Greek states contributed ships, and soon, because it was easier, money instead. They slid from being allies of Athens to being subjects of Athens. Athens went from defiant city-state to mini-empire. Her democratic institutions remained, but the old spirit of the city changed. Greater wealth and more incomers meant wider gaps between the classes as well as more citizens who were far removed from the farmer-soldiers of before. The sense of a single community waned.

Her old rival Sparta began to shift uneasily, and eventually, when Athenian power and ambition became too much for commercial rivals such as Corinth, the Greek world went to war with itself. Sparta and her allies dominated the fighting on land; Athens ruled the waves. Year after year, the Spartans would invade and the Athenians would simply retreat behind their awesome long walls, which connected the city to its port in a bone-shaped defensive structure which allowed them to bring in plenty of food by sea, sitting out the besiegers. Peace treaties were agreed, and lapsed, during a long and murderous stalemate. Then Athens made a huge mistake. Egged on by a glamorous soldier, Alcibiades, her people agreed to attack Syracuse, in what is now Sicily, a rich ally of Sparta's ally Corinth. Greed was part of it, since the capture of Sicily and even eventually Italy would have made Athens so strong she could have hoped to dominate all Greece.

But the attacks proved disastrous. The people of Syracuse, aided by Spartans, beat back two Athenian fleets and trounced the Athenians on land until the once dominant state was virtually bankrupt. The war went on for long enough, even after that. The Spartans made deals with the old common enemy Persia, as a result of which many of the Greek Ionian states, freed during the old wars, went back to the Persians. And after a naval battle in which Athens lost her main source of food and could easily have been starved into submission, Sparta finally won. The walls of Athens were torn down and she became subject to Spartan control. The golden age had sunk, bloodily, into the sea.

All this was bad enough. But the story of the Syracuse disaster and what came after is intertwined with that of one of the most attractive and yet wicked figures of classical Greek history, Alcibiades. An aristocrat related to Pericles, and good-looking enough to win many lovers of both sexes, Alcibiades was one of Socrates' favourite pupils. Plato says that Socrates had saved his life in battle and the two were inextricably linked in the minds of the Athenians – even though Socrates seems to have resisted Alcibiades' sexual charms, famously spending a chaste night under a blanket with him.

As we have seen, Alcibiades had been a prime mover in the catastrophic mission against Syracuse. He had persuaded Athens to increase her fleet, upping the stakes disastrously. But before the ships left he was accused of being involved, perhaps as a drunken aristocratic joke, in the mutilation of some sacred statues – the *Hermai*, which featured phalluses and stood at intervals around the city. Though he left with the fleet, under joint command, Alcibiades was then summoned back to stand trial for blasphemy. He defected to Sparta, and fought successfully against Athens before falling out with the Spartans too and selling his services to the Persians.

Later on, allies of his in Athens (where he had been condemned to death in his absence) rather remarkably managed to have him recalled: the charges against him were lifted and he was again put in command of the Athenian forces. This time, luck seemed to have deserted him, and after some defeats at the hands of the Spartans he was dismissed from Athens yet again. He died in exile, apparently surprised by Spartan assassins while at his mistress's house, running at them naked with a dagger in each hand, then felled by a shower of arrows. Plutarch claims that the assassination had been fixed by another of Socrates' old pupils and a one-time friend of Alcibiades, Critias. The American journalist I.F. Stone has rightly said that the story was made to order for that Plutarch-reading lover of a great plot, William Shakespeare.[29] It is the play Shakespeare ought to have got round to but somehow never did; and it reminds us how small the ancient Greek world really was.

Alcibiades and Critias were certainly dangerous men. After the defeat at Syracuse, Athenian democracy had been briefly knocked to one side by the so-called Four Hundred, a group of aristocrats who in 411 BC overthrew the government and briefly took power, a move that led to killings and a climate of fear. Alcibiades was thought to have been involved, and the coup foundered when the plotters fell out. Middle-class and poorer Athenians made common cause, and restored democracy. Then in 404 when Athens was finally defeated by Sparta, democracy fell again, this time under the rule of the Thirty Tyrants, a rich oligarchy led by Critias which suspended the right to vote or have a jury trial for all but a tiny aristocratic minority. This was an altogether bloodier business. They ruled with a Spartan army, Vichy-like collaborators, using gangs of whip-wielding thugs to keep order,[30] exiling and executing popular leaders.

Socrates stayed in Athens under the tyrants' rule, even though many other eminent citizens left for a relatively comfortable exile. He excused himself later by saying he had been ordered by the Thirty to arrest a man for execution, but in fact he slipped away and left the job to others – hardly the action of a heroic resister. Once more, middle-class hostility triumphed, the Thirty were ousted, and democracy returned. But by the time of Socrates' trial, a mere four years later, the Athenian regime must still have seemed to be teetering, and Socrates was not its friend.

His death was a tragedy, not because he had the answers to the key philosophic conundrums of the ancient world, but because it showed that even in this relatively open society the greatest minds could not always express themselves freely or follow their thoughts wherever they led. The most pressing problems for would-be democracies and open societies – and Athens was really more the latter than the former – have never been about the minutiae of voting systems, or even about the right balance of powers, hard though these are to achieve. They have been about how to deal with critics who seem genuinely threatening, as Socrates, old though he was, seemed in 399 BC. This would be the case for French revolutionaries of the Enlightenment, for the US during the McCarthy era, and is so for today's Western democracies struggling with Islamist preachers of hate.

For how long can you hang on to your principles of free speech and free thought, before giving way to fear?

As a philosopher, Socrates was a dissolver of certainties, a sceptic and a mocker. He did the minimum possible service in the Athens *polis*, was about as inactive a citizen as he could manage to be. He had fought as a soldier, but he chose not to use his great skills in open political argument at the great assemblies; he preferred private teaching. His critics dismissed him as a 'sophist', by which they meant a cynical teacher of the arts of argument – a purveyor of logic to suit every occasion. This was unfair. His radical doubt and self-questioning could never have produced a handbook for good living, still less a constitution, but he remains an essential contributor to the maturing of the human mind.

Learning to question is more important, even, than learning to believe. Socrates' fluidity is shown by the very different paths taken by his followers, and their followers – Plato's darkly authoritarian republic is a world away from Aristotle's sophisticated defence of the city-state. As in China, where the supporters and foes of Kongzi would lock horns for centuries, Socrates' death began an argument that has never ended.

Alexander the . . . Quite Good

We have spent much time with the Greeks, Chinese, Indians, Hebrews and Persians, observing how, over hundreds of years, social change and ideas that have lasted to our own time were provoked and given focus by war. Technical change was happening too, with the spread of sophisticated metalworking, chariots, and writing, and with ships able to make long sea voyages, though the pace of change was gentler here.

There were many other peoples for whom these centuries were important ones. Humanity's advance guard was still pushing down through the Americas, clearing land and starting to farm; the first coastal American civilizations date from this time. In the Pacific, seafarers were finding and colonizing the last major unpeopled islands, an epic of courage and navigation that nobody recorded. In Europe, the Celts – who will make an appearance in the next section – were thrusting earlier settlers aside. In Japan, Burma, Thailand and Korea the first dynasties were establishing themselves. Elsewhere, including Russia and Africa, we know very little beyond the probable movements and settlements of nomad tribes.

All of these are interesting and much studied stories, but are less important than the development of the four essential hubs of advancing humanity, those to be found on the plains of China, across northern India, in Persia and the Near East, and around the Mediterranean. The conundrum there is that war, at this stage even more than trade, had clearly driven change; yet these local wars had been destructive (as wars always are), resulting as they did in the collapse of cultures and cities that might well have flowered.

We must go back one last time to the Greek world, for if there is one man who embodies the tragic ambiguity of these messages it is Alexander III of Macedon, better known as Alexander the Great.

This is the man under whom the Greeks broke the boundaries of their archipelago, and flung out east and south across central Asia in a fury of war-making. Alexander, though he came from the rougher northern state of Macedon, was a product of Greece's golden age. Schooled in hoplite fighting, he carried a copy of Homer's poems with him, allegedly using it as his pillow. He was taught by the great Aristotle, a follower of the Socratic tradition, and himself a Macedonian by birth. Alexander's father Philip had hired the philosopher to teach the prince and his companions from the ages of thirteen to sixteen. Their school, a leafy hideaway in the hills, has been rediscovered. There, Alexander was taught about the Persians, including Cyrus – the information culled from Herodotus – as well as a sweep of subjects including natural history, botany, geography and mathematics. Aristotle's later writings on education imply that Alexander may not have been the very best of pupils; or perhaps he was merely saying that teenagers are headstrong and don't listen. From early on, Alexander dreamed of uniting West and East, bringing together the thinking warriors of Greece and the ease, wealth and customs of Asia. Yet for true admirers of the Greek golden age, Alexander would be a fatal messenger.

The Greek message for the world had been that the town was where humankind expresses itself best. There, a rough political equality between citizens, speaking freely and listening attentively, living under clear, agreed laws, could produce a better way of life – more artistic, philosophical, even proto-scientific. Law, a settled and codified system of fairness, allows people to live successfully in larger groups than families or tribes. So Greek city-states were proud of their laws and revered their ancient law-makers. Greek philosophy spent much thought on the question of law. Greek cities had been places where, slaves apart, the gaps between rich and poor were not so wide as to destroy any sense of communality.

These city-states also demonstrated the power of competition. Laws, constitutions, political systems, artisan skills, fighting styles – all improved when constantly tested against one another. Greek competition flung out questions and answers that still reverberate around the world. Is it possible to be a true republic and an empire at the same time? No. Can democracy survive vast disparities of wealth? No. Does success produce decadence? Yes.

But then, after the horrors of the Peloponnesian war, this vigorously competitive world collapsed. Democracies did become empires. Athens, then Sparta, then Thebes, became dominant over lesser city-states and over one another.

The hoplite citizen armies, undermined by mistrust and defeat, began to give way to hired forces, mercenaries. As one historian puts it, 'Poor, disenfranchised citizens, landless men, refugees, foreigners, and slaves became more numerous . . . Single and separate cities, where the citizens' voices could perhaps still be heard, had lost control of their own fates.'[31] And when eventually the largest city-states were conquered by the Macedonians in 338 BC, the true age of the city-state ended. For the Macedonians brought the leader cult, the rule of kings over subject peoples, across most of the Greek world – and Alexander, for all his love of Homer, was just a very glamorous tyrant.

History offers many examples of marginal-seeming peoples suddenly erupting over their borders to overwhelm or dominate the richer civilizations near by. The Persians had seemed to come from almost nowhere to overturn the great war culture of Assyria. In China, the frontier state of Ch'in would soon leap on, and bring down, her richer, softer rivals. Macedon too was a frontier territory in the Greek world, beyond which there were only barbarians. The Macedonians spoke Greek, though it sounded a little strange. With forests and marshes to deal with, and a tough climate – it snows heavily and can be bitterly cold even in the springtime – they were anything but decadent.

They were tribal people, not town-dwellers. Hard to govern and loyal to their nobility, they had only relatively recently come under the full control of their kings, based near the coast. These kings, great hunters of bears and lions, had imported some of the culture of the Greek golden age, including flamboyant palaces. Their new capital, Pella, had a huge central open area, or Agora, where pottery, metalwork, glasswork and statuary were manufactured, excellent wine was sold, and goods from around the Mediterranean were displayed. The palaces were richly decorated with bright frescos and elaborate mosaics; their gold jewellery was delicate and lovely. There are hints of a slight inferiority complex: they imported a lot from the more fully evolved states to the south. More practically, they had developed and advanced Greek phalanx fighting to supplement their royal cavalry. The more southerly Greeks, though, had not taken them terribly seriously. Macedon was the place to which it had been suggested Socrates might flee to escape his death penalty. Tellingly, he had laughed off the idea as absurd.

The first great King of Macedon was Philip II, Alexander's father, who had exploited the wars of the Greek city-states to build a powerful military position. He had conquered his nearby rivals Illyria and Thrace in a sequence of campaigns, leading his army in person and losing both an eye and much blood in the process. His cavalry fought in V-formation, without stirrups, and his infantry used extraordinarily long spears, some nineteen feet long, so they presented the appearance and effect of an infuriated giant hedgehog running at speed. Bribing, menacing, fighting and outsmarting, Philip brought the city-states (including Athens), already in disarray, under his control. It was a huge achievement. Only Sparta had held out against him. Philip had warned the Spartans that if he brought his armies successfully into their territory he would destroy their cities and kill all their people. They replied, rather magnificently, with the single word 'If'. Next, he planned to invade Asia. But as he was preparing for the invasion, Philip's domestic circumstances took a turn for the worse.

He had taken several wives, and in 336 BC he did something to provoke his senior divorced wife. We do not know precisely what the feud was about, though Philip had also taken a younger wife, but this senior wife was not a woman to be trifled with. She was Olympias, a Lydian princess and the mother of Alexander. She was also a worshipper of the god Dionysus, and was reputed to sleep with snakes in her bed, though this was probably a reference to the snake-handling rites of the Dionysiacs. It was later suggested she had actually conceived Alexander while bedding the Persian king – who had then sent her back home because her breath was smelly.

For whatever reason, Philip was hostile to Olympias, and in order to isolate her he decided to marry his daughter (by another wife) to Olympias' older brother, the King of Lydia. Dynastically, this would cut Alexander out of the succession. But it is rarely a good idea to infuriate a Greek wife, or ex-wife. As he was preparing for his daughter's wedding, Philip was murdered by one of his own bodyguard. Many thought Olympias was behind it, avenging herself on her husband and helping ensure her son's succession.[32] After a bloodthirsty family struggle Alexander did succeed, inheriting a superb army and a feud with a Persian empire, already racked by its own dynastic troubles.

He was only twenty years old when he came to the throne, long-haired, clean-shaven and with a mesmeric gaze, but apparently rather short. He had been helping his father rule, and fighting in battles, since he was sixteen. Aged thirteen, he had been given his famous black horse Bucephalus, after mastering the seemingly untamable stallion. As a teenager he fell in love with his male lover Hephaestion, who like Bucephalus would remain with him for most of his short life. His father's entourage was usefully mixed. With Greece at Philip's feet, the Macedonian court attracted great writers and artists, including the playwright Euripides and the painter Apelles, as well as musicians and philosophers. But Alexander also grew up with the sons of the rougher Macedonian nobility, who were living at his father's court as pages and hostages.

His obsession with the East started then, among exiled Persians and travel stories. Herodotus taught him, amongst other things, about the interesting habits of the Medes, Persians and Egyptians. Homer taught him the cult of single combat and glory-searching and shared with him his belief that the Trojans, those wily old Asians, were admirable in their way. As already noted, Alexander was tutored by Aristotle himself, who was well paid to educate the prince in natural philosophy, politics and government. All this adds up to the most impressive education of any prince we know of in the ancient world – laid out before him were the martial inspiration of Homer, the tough world of Macedon, the best of Greek thought and curiosity and a ready openness to Asia. It made of Alexander a man ready to reach from one world deep into another, taking those territories in his hands in a mighty effort to bring them all together.

His father's army lived off the land, eschewed luxury, could cover thirty miles in a day, and was supported by siege engines, archers and javelin-throwers. These were the men who would power across Asia and into India, some of them, tough as old buzzards, fighting well into their sixties. Alexander's conquests offer us one of the ancient world's most jaw-dropping epics. After putting down local rebellions in Greece – once-mighty Athens did not even try to fight, but immediately sued for peace – he took his forces to war against the last of the Persian empire's Kings of Kings, Darius III, who initially ignored this impudent boy's invasion.

Winning his first victories in what is now Turkey, near Troy, Alexander found many cities coming over to him; and copying the old Persian habit, he left them effectively to run themselves, so long as tribute was paid. At Issus in 333 BC he defeated a Persian army led by Darius in person, who fled leaving both his crown and his wife on the battlefield. Sieges of the great trading cities Tyre and Acre followed, before Alexander was welcomed as a liberator by the Egyptians, who made him pharaoh and named him an incarnation of their gods Ra and Osiris. He swept on into Mesopotamia for his greatest victory, at the battle of Gaugamela, where he shattered the much larger army of Darius, after which he pursued the Persian emperor, who in the end was assassinated by his own soldiers.

Alexander declared himself King of Kings and ruler of Persia. He went on to seize Babylon and, after a rare reverse in a Persian ambush, took the great city of Persepolis, which was badly burned in the process.

Cleitus, a general who had saved Alexander's life in an earlier battle, hacking off the arm of a Persian about to kill the king, in 328 became embroiled in a drunken argument with him during a conference of generals at Samarkand. (The Macedonians drank their wine undiluted, everyone present at the conference was intoxicated, and probably frustrated by a slow campaign.) Cleitus told Alexander to his face that his father Philip had been the greater king, and in the ensuing scuffle an enraged Alexander killed him with a spear. Alexander is said to have been distraught. Later writers portrayed Cleitus as a man speaking truth to power, an honest old fighter who realized his king's head had become impossibly swollen. Certainly, by now there were clear signs that Alexander, never modest, had become drunk not only on his unwatered wine but on his astonishing succession of victories. Declared master of the world by the Egyptians, he took to claiming that his real father had been a godlike mix of the Greek Zeus and the Egyptian Ammon.

But he had a problem. He had been *too* successful. His Macedonians were a small minority of the combined forces he now commanded, and a tiny minority of the people he had conquered. He

needed the respect of his new Asian subjects, even if it meant offending Greek sensibilities. So he adopted Persian dress, and allowed the
custom of being greeted with a kiss of obeisance, which was considered respectful by Persians and Medes but hopelessly decadent by
Greeks. Alexander was now claiming to be a god, they murmured. He
chose a wife, Roxana, from among the Sogdian people, east Iranians in
what is now part of Afghanistan and Uzbekistan, marrying her at a
grand ceremony. This may have been shrewd politics, or lust, or even
love. Alexander certainly began to try to meld the Macedonian Greeks
and Asians together, in the manner of a true world emperor. He
ordered thirty thousand Asian boys to be trained as Greek-style fighters, and gave his lover Hephaestion a Persian title and position.

According to the Greek-Roman historian Arrian, who wrote the
most complete surviving life of Alexander, he also organized a remarkable mass wedding between Greeks and Persians at the old capital of
Susa. He himself now also married the eldest daughter of Darius and
gave her sister to Hephaestion, so their children would be cousins; to
another eighty of his crack Macedonian 'companions' he gave wives
from the Persian and Median nobility in a group ceremony that
sounds like a multiple wedding of the kind later favoured by the
Moonie Unification Church. Arrian says:

> The weddings were celebrated after the Persian manner, seats
> being placed in a row for the bridegrooms; and after the banquet
> the brides came in and seated themselves, each one near her own
> husband. The bridegrooms took them by the right hand and
> kissed them . . . This appeared the most popular thing which
> Alexander ever did . . . Each man took his own bride and led
> her away; and on all without exception Alexander bestowed
> dowries.[33]

He also ordered that the names of another ten thousand Macedonians who had married Asiatic women should be registered. It was an
astonishing experiment in cultural mixing – as if Queen Victoria had
ordered her English, Irish and Scottish troops to take Hindu and
Muslim brides, or as if General Custer instead of fighting at Big Horn
had tried to mate the US Cavalry with Sioux squaws. Sadly, it seems,
few of the marriages lasted very long, though Alexander's successors
after the break-up of his empire did put down roots across parts of

Asia, allowing a new form of Greekness to spread far beyond the Mediterranean.

Further battles had preceded this, as Alexander led his armies into what is now Pakistan and India, where they fought their first war elephants. His horse Bucephalus was killed east of the Indus, and his lover Hephaestion died soon afterwards; grief, wounds and the effects of heavy drinking began to wear Alexander down. His troops, on the far side of the known world, had had enough, and they eventually mutinied at the prospect of further advances against Indian rulers. They demanded to return home. Even Alexander could not resist. He pulled back, returning eventually to Babylon, where he raised a funeral pyre to Hephaestion. Now in charge of a vast spread of the world's surface, stretching from the Himalayas to the Balkans, he planned new campaigns, into Arabia, then along the African coast and into Italy. Had he lived, he might even have snuffed out an obscure but stroppy and ambitious city called Rome. Some say he was poisoned. More likely he caught a bug, perhaps typhoid fever; but in June 323, aged thirty-three, Alexander died in Nebuchadnezzar's palace.

His astonishing life makes the case for war, and the case against it. Inspired by Greek culture and greedily curious about the world of the Persians and Indians, he acted as a kind of giant bloody cultural whisk. The Greek world would now have huge influence in Asia Minor, Egypt, and deep into Mesopotamia. A rash of new Greek-style cities were founded, even though Alexander's empire had lasted for a hummingbird's wingbeat. His generals divided most of the classical world between them, and a new period of Greek, or Hellenistic, culture flowered. Philosophers opened new schools, sculptors and painters found work in new places, and something like a common language began to spread.

Yet the slaughters, the mass deportations and burnings that Alexander was also responsible for did not produce a stable or attractive political system. He had spread the look of classical Greece, but not its essence. He could never have done so, because its essence was independent-minded and civic. It was bottom-up, not top-down. Democracy cannot be imposed with spears (or guns). Alexander's was an imperial vision spanning many cultures, but his huge military success merely pushed the Mediterranean back to a world of kings and emperors, local tyrants and neighbourhood dynasties. It is possible that the reader may think of later parallels. Alexander smoothed the ground for the Roman invaders – at least, the Roman emperors thought so. Inspired by Homer's heroes, and irresistibly heroic himself, he showed the limits of what heroes can do. Alexander was the gravedigger of the great Greek experiment, never its champion.

Part Three

THE SWORD
AND THE WORD

*From 300 BC to around AD 600: Classical Empires
in China, India and Europe and Their Confrontation
with New Religions*

By the time of Jesus's birth, around half the human beings alive on the planet lived under one of two great empires. Even if many of them were barely aware of the fact – for the peasants and farmers far from great cities heard about the outside world rarely and only in garbled form – this was a new thing in world history. It would never happen again. Rome and Han China emerged at roughly the same time and ruled over roughly the same number of people – 45 million in the case of Rome at its imperial peak, 57.6 million according to a Han tax census. Both covered roughly the same amount of territory, some four million square kilometres, though one was based on the edges of an inland sea, and the other on vast plains intersected by rivers. Their armies, marching in disciplined formations with uniform armour and weapons, chariots and cavalry, looked similar too.

Romans revered their household gods and their ancestors; so did the Chinese. But they were both practical, down-to-earth cultures. Each regarded themselves as more serious, disciplined and civilized than any possible rival. The Roman emperors claimed to rule *orbis terrarum*, 'the whole world'. Their Chinese rivals ruled the empire of 'all under heaven'. Roman emperors claimed divinity, posing as gods answerable only to Jupiter. Chinese emperors claimed a similar semi-divine status. The Romans built awe-inspiring walls to keep out the barbarians, and so did the Chinese. The Romans had their arrow-straight roads, the Chinese their long straight canals. Their empires were even divided into around the same number of administrative units. Their troops were urged on with very practical benefits – the Chinese won money and extra status for every severed enemy head they presented after battle, while valorous Romans could win land at home.

The Roman Empire had been made possible by one rising power on the edge of the Mediterranean world defeating its squabbling rivals; Han ascendancy was based on the final resolution of war between seven states, imposed by one from the margins. They knew little of each other, these Romans and Chinese. They were some 4,500 miles apart, separated by baking deserts and mountain ranges; the sea route was two thousand miles longer than that.[1] Yet their empires almost touched fingers. There seems to have been a confused Chinese notion of an alternative, possibly mythical, other China somewhere in the far west, while the Roman word *Seres* may refer to the Chinese.

In AD 97 a Chinese general, Ban Chao, tried to send an envoy to Rome to suggest a joint pincer movement against the Parthians, who with their brilliant cavalry were causing equal pain to both empires. The envoy never made it through to the emperor Trajan. It was just too far. He gave up and turned back. Thus, one of the great 'what ifs' was lost at some dusty way-station east of Egypt.[2] The envoy, Gan Ying, did, however, pick up rumours about the Romans, reporting back that they had more than four hundred walled towns and a capital city near the mouth of a river; that they were 'tall and honest' and that they selected kings from the worthiest men who, if calamity came, would accept demotion without getting angry.[3] Gan Ying said the Roman 'king' had thirty-six leaders with whom he discussed events of the day, and that he took petitions from the common people. This was true; there is some vague impression of the Senate conveyed here, and it is clear that the notion of politics, involving losers and winners, was unfamiliar and interesting to the Chinese.

And that was not the only fascinating thing about the Romans. Gan Ying was particularly excited to report that they were amazing conjurors who could produce fire from their mouths and juggle twelve balls at a time.

Seventy years later, according to Chinese records, a Roman delegation arrived by sea in Vietnam, then part of the Chinese empire, possibly sent by the great philosopher-emperor Marcus Aurelius. They were sent away; the only links remained distant trading ones. Around the time of Christ, Roman women were wearing scandalously semi-transparent silk dresses, which caused much head-shaking amongst Roman moralists. This silk came from China, via long sea voyages from Vietnam to what is now Sri Lanka and then on to Egypt. Roman glassware and coins have been found in China. There is even a faint possibility that Roman legionaries and Han soldiers fought one another in Kyrgyzstan, the Romans in 'fish-scale formation', after being captured by Parthians in 54 BC.

The empires lasted a similar length of time. The Romans, who had started as unimportant town-dwellers in central Italy, grew partly by attracting migrants and partly thanks to their astonishingly successful and very violent military campaigns. Their rise to hegemony began with the fall of the Greek kingdoms established after Alexander's career, and with the destruction of their North African rival, Carthage, in 149–6 BC. Some seventy years earlier, China's first emperor had united the former warring states there. The Roman world would fall apart into two empires: the Western, which dissolved after AD 400, and the Eastern (or Byzantine), which lasted until the fall of Constantinople in 1453 to the Ottoman Turks. The Han empire was gone by AD 220, though united China only really disintegrated in 317. (Even then, the southern half, less damaged by invasion and culturally more conservative, bears comparison with the long survival of the Eastern Roman Empire.)

So each of these great empires lasted for around half a millennium, not such a long time compared with the earlier civilizations of Mesopotamia and Egypt, but impressive by modern democratic standards. A question that is being increasingly asked by historians, as today's China rises, is whether our world, with a single united China but a fragmented Europe, derives in any way from the Roman and Han foundational experiences. After all, China remained broadly politically united for around half the time after the rise of its first emperor, while the Mediterranean and European west was never again united after the fall of Rome. Why?

Geography, say some. China is divided by river valleys and mountains but is also surrounded and cut off from the rest of the world by deserts and seas. Achieving political unity was no easy job. It has been calculated that between 656 and 221 BC there were no fewer than 256 separate wars in China. But once that phase had passed there was a strong topographical logic to this single area, with its long belly-shaped coast. As soon as roads, canals and walls had drawn the lines of communication and defence, they tended to stay put. Invasions from outside would keep challenging the country, but they failed to wipe away the cultural map of the One China.

The Mediterranean and European world is very different. True, the 'middle sea' made it easier to move around the classical Roman Empire, but there were fewer natural barriers to halt invaders, while Europe was divided by innumerable rivers, flowing in all directions, and by mountain ranges. Geographically it was an awkward, rumpled, riven peninsula, and therefore always less likely to hold together politically.

While instantly satisfying, this explanation seems a little too slick. For centuries China was divided. Her people in the north and south pursued very different lives, spoke different languages and at times were ruled by different empires. China very nearly pushed out into the world with great ocean-going fleets. That she did not was a political decision. Meanwhile in the West, for a time it seemed as if the Eastern Roman Empire might eventually reunite the Mediterranean. Much later, rulers such as the Habsburg Charles V and the Corsican adventurer Napoleon Bonaparte came close to uniting Europe, despite those rivers and mountain ranges.

What other forces are relevant? The role played by outsiders was certainly important. The nomadic and herding people of central Asia, armed and militant, produced waves of forced migration that washed across Europe. Many settled, before being pushed to move again by another wave. In China, the steppe peoples were kept out more effectively until, with the Mongols, they utterly overwhelmed the empire. But they did so so swiftly and comprehensively that they could replace it with their own imperial rule, and therefore could maintain its unity.

Though both the Chinese and European worlds would be shaken by the arrival of challenging religions, the effect of monotheism – both Christianity and Islam – was more dramatic in the West than was the impact of Buddhism on China, where emperors were able to repress it. This meant there was an edge, a desperation, to Europe's wars of religion which China did not experience. Monotheism would divide Western mankind into believers and outsiders, again and again, though following different patterns. Nothing quite like this happened in China where, as we shall see, law and conservative social thinking had more impact than religion. Then there are cultural differences, such as the greater difficulty of learning written Chinese, which kept a bureaucratic elite self-contained and powerful in ways not experienced in the West. These are all issues we will come back to.

The story in both China and the Roman world is, however, similarly bloody and brutal, replete with tales of cynical rulers, state terror and the persecution of dissenters. Attractively humane thinkers emerge in both worlds, and some gloriously beautiful buildings (though Han China was built mostly in wood and pounded earth, materials which, as mentioned earlier, do not survive). Yet these were also power structures erected by force and fear, able to express their beauty and philosophy only on the sweating backs of the vast majority, who were farmworkers. The Roman imperial achievement relied on the incorporation of local elites and the reputation of the legions; the Chinese more on pure force. But whether the educated elites studied the sayings of Confucius or of Christ, whether they kowtowed to an emperor or read the proclamations of a senate, armies marching under central control slaughtered rebel peoples and proclaimed their authority by means of public and deliberately repellent punishments. If might was right, centrally organized and mobilized might was righter still.

Ashoka

Before either Rome or Han China rose to its zenith, there existed another great empire, with a very different story. The third empire, which embraced perhaps a quarter of the world's people, was that of Mauryan India. It covered almost all of modern India, excepting the far south, plus what is now Pakistan and much of Afghanistan too. Its population in the second century BC is guessed at fifty million and it began in 322 AD, when the Romans were still struggling to get to grips with central Italy and the Chinese were enduring a vicious and seemingly endless war between rival states. Yet this third empire had collapsed again by 185 BC, despite the brilliance of its greatest ruler, Ashoka. After the Mauryas, who took on the classical world and defeated it, India was never able to reach out and dominate anywhere else. Much of the political and religious shape of the modern world was first settled two thousand years ago, by historical figures whose names we know.

The Mauryan rulers are on the edge of visible history, however. Ashoka was only properly identified, as a historical rather than a mythical figure, by an eighteenth-century amateur philologist called James

Prinsep whose day job was running the British mint at Calcutta. Ashoka's empire is less known and less documented than those of the Romans and Chinese, and always will be. There are three main sources. One was a Greek historian, Megasthenes, who worked for Seleucus Nicator, Alexander the Great's general who carved his own mini-empire, centred on Persia and what is now Pakistan. Megasthenes probably visited the great Mauryan capital city Pataliputra, which is now buried somewhere under modern Patna, undoubtedly one of the most chaotic and polluted metropolises in the world. Unfortunately, his own book has long disappeared and is known only from what later historians lifted from it. The second source is an Indian manual on how to rule, which may have been written, at least in part, by one of the advisers to the Mauryan court. And the third source is Ashoka's own words, carved in stone and on pillars across much of India.

Ashoka's grandfather, Chandragupta, is now believed to be the same Indian ruler identified by Megasthenes as 'Sandrokottos', who had met Alexander the Great. Chandragupta rose up against the previous dynasty of north India, the Nanda. With the help of an apparently wily and ruthless adviser he defeated them, and founded his own dynasty in 321 BC. His strategy had been to wear the enemy down from the outlying areas before moving towards the centre, in a long war of attrition as the former empire gradually shrank. The legend has it that he did this after hearing a woman tell her child not to eat from the middle of a dish because the centre was bound to be hotter than the edges.

Chandragupta now turned on the Greeks, so recently unbeatable, and about 303 BC defeated Seleucus. It clearly was no wipe-out, because in return for the new territories he won, Chandragupta gave Seleucus five hundred of the many thousands of war elephants he owned.[4] Alexander's had been the first Western army to face the awesome sight of Indian war elephants, and he had brought some back to Baghdad as his personal guard. For the Greeks, such a gift to Seleucus was like being given several regiments of Tiger tanks or attack-helicopters. The elephants were traded, borrowed and gifted by Greek kings: the Egyptian kings, for instance, used Indian war elephants against the Jews during their revolt, and later on they would be used against the rising power of Rome.

If the ancient texts concerning government are to be believed, Chandragupta's empire was not only warlike but highly interventionist, bureaucratic and paranoid, as he spread it across most of the Indian subcontinent. Yet we know very little about the ruler described as an Indian Julius Caesar; and less about his son, who took over after Chandragupta abdicated in 297 BC and reputedly starved himself to death as an act of pious self-denial. It is, rather, his grandson Ashoka who concerns us. He ruled from around 268 BC to 233, and was known from Buddhist writings well before a breakthrough translation of the mysterious written rock and pillar 'edicts' scattered across India gave him a voice in the modern world. Quite who he really was, was less clear. But these edicts, decoded in 1837 by the British mint supervisor, revealed a surprising story.

Ashoka, whose name can be translated as 'without remorse', began by living up to it. First there was the bloody succession battle. He may not have actually killed ninety-nine rival brothers, as the scriptures say, but the gap between his father's death and his enthronement as king suggests a hard tussle. He then turned on one of the few parts of India not under his direct control, Kalinga, and after a terrible battle reconquered it. According to his own inscriptions, 100,000 soldiers were killed in the fight and many more people died, either from wounds or from the aftermath of the slaughter; a further 150,000 were deported.

A Caesar would have boasted of the death-toll; so would a Chinese warlord or indeed Chandragupta. Ashoka, however, seems to have had a dramatic change of heart, including a conversion to full Buddhism, perhaps at the instigation of his wife. In one of his inscriptions Ashoka said he felt remorse for this war, 'for when an independent country is conquered, the slaughter, death and deportation of the people [are] extremely grievous . . . Today, if a hundredth or a thousandth part of those people who were killed or died or deported . . . were to suffer similarly, it would weigh heavily on the mind of the Beloved of the Gods [meaning himself].' Ashoka went on, in this thirteenth rock edict, to warn his own descendants against new conquests, and called on them to impose only 'light punishments'.

Had Ashoka gone no further, this would have been a remarkable moment in human history, the first and last recorded instance of a remorseful conqueror apologizing for his victories. It is as if Napoleon, after the battle of Austerlitz, had announced he was disgusted by his politically incontinent behaviour and was going to become a Quaker. But Ashoka then went on to try to create an empire based on the Buddhist notion of *dhamma*, which means something like virtue, good conduct and decency. It implied kindly behaviour towards underlings and relatives, the avoidance of killing – not only human animals, but all animals – and religious toleration. In carved edicts ranging from the frozen mountains of the north to the hot forests of the south, Ashoka urged vegetarianism, a ban on sacrifices, respect for different religious sects; and described all mankind as his children.

These sayings were inscribed in various languages, including forms of Aramaic in the north-west, on the edge of the Greek world, as well as versions of Sanskrit and local dialects, in a script known as Brahmi. The first edicts were carved on rock faces and boulders where travellers might gather, sit down and listen to whoever could read them out. Later on, at Pataliputra Ashoka set up a factory of sorts to manufacture huge pillars, topped with lions, to be floated down the Ganges and other rivers so they could be erected all over central India. It was as near as an early king could get to broadcasting, through loudspeakers of polished sandstone. Ashoka, no more modest than most emperors, boasts in these edicts of planting shade trees by the sides of roads, setting up regular rest-houses and digging wells. He abjures war and violence, he says. Later still he spread the word yet further, sending out Buddhist monks to take his message of peace to Burma, Sri Lanka, Egypt and even Greece.

If this all sounds too good to be true, it may be: India had so many competing religions and was so riven by differences of caste and language that any dynasty hoping to last for long would have needed some kind of unifying idea. Almost certainly, Ashoka was self-consciously creating what modern rulers would call an ideology. Even if it was a notably gentle one, the actual administration of his empire may well have been rather less liberal. He retained capital punishment to a limited degree, and in his edicts growled from time to time at the forest-dwellers, who seem to have been both untamed and unimpressed by this Buddhist liberal. Even his vegetarianism was not absolute: he excepted venison and peacock, apparently, which he found particularly tasty. Above all, we have to rely on his word. If all we knew of Stalin were his blandly humanitarian speeches, we might remember him as an avuncular softie. But because Ashoka so berates himself for his earlier bloody wars, it is likely that he was a genuine Buddhist convert who tried his best to establish an 'empire of goodness'.

This seems all the more plausible because, very quickly, he failed. In his last days he is supposed to have given away all his property, ending his life as the proud possessor of half a mango. The huge range of Indian communities did not stay loyal or united for long, after his death. Little is known of his successors as Mauryan rulers, except that the last one was assassinated, and the empire broke up to be followed by half a century of chaos. Eventually it would be followed by a silver or even a golden age under the Gupta dynasty, who began to rule in AD 320 and under whom Sanskrit writing, decimal mathematics and other advances flourished. When the Muslims poured into northern India, they began to force the Buddhists out. Facing Hindu hostility too, Ashoka's creed virtually vanished from India.

Yet he is rather more than a footnote in history. Modern India, with its jagged fissures between different religious and ethnic groups, rediscovering year by year just how hard tolerance is, has adopted Ashoka as an intellectual hero. Ashoka's three-headed lion is one of the republic's most familiar symbols, appearing for instance on its banknotes. And in 1956 there was an eloquent protest against religious intolerance, showing that Ashokan political Buddhism was not quite dead.

B.R. Ambedkar was one of the great figures of early Indian democracy, a brilliant lawyer from the 'untouchable' caste. He rose to chair the committee that wrote the new republic's constitution,[5] which abolished untouchable status and gave special voting rights to this outgroup of labourers, cobblers, cleaners and dirty-work specialists. But Ambedkar remained deeply frustrated and angered by India's failure to do more for his people. To him, whatever the letter of the law, Hindu caste prejudice – religious prejudice – was still a fact of Indian life. So in 1956, shortly before he died, at a ceremony attended by vast numbers he publicly converted to Buddhism. A million people attended his funeral and many of his lower-caste followers also became Buddhists, contributing to a revival of the belief system in today's India. Clearly, some of the moral message of Ashoka's pillars was still crackling through the airwaves.

The First Emperor

China's First Emperor is about as radical a departure from the benign if naive figure of Ashoka as it is possible to imagine. Qin Shi Huang Zheng, who ruled at roughly the same time, also erected stone pillars on hilltops to proclaim his works. But Zheng was not to be remembered in his own words. His reputation for paranoia, cruelty and ruthlessness came from a scandalous later history. It has been bolstered in recent times by the discovery of part of the awesome death city he had constructed for himself, featuring the world-famous 'terracotta army'. If Ashoka was seeking the annihilation of all appetites and of selfhood, Zheng wanted to be protected for ever by a bureaucracy and a military machine made of mud and bronze, all painted and ready to repel demons.

His was an earthly vision, born of conquest and fear, which would have made more sense to Romans and even Egyptians than Ashoka's Buddhist withdrawal. Zheng is more potent in today's China and around today's world than is Ashoka. Though, like the Indian ruler's, his dynasty disappeared quickly, Zheng's was just as quickly replaced by the Han dynasty, which picked up his political achievements, minus some of the savage paranoia. He may have been an unpleasant character but he unified Chinese scripts, built great public works, finally ended centuries of civil war and enlarged the idea of China itself. His message for humanity may be a sour-faced one, but it has stuck.

One of the biggest problems concerning Zheng is the written history available to us. It is by Sima Qian, whom we met earlier as the first biographer of Confucius. He is one of the great literary figures of Chinese history-writing, an Asian Plutarch, whose own life was marked by tragedy. Like his contemporary Latin historians, he knew very well that overstepping the mark in criticizing rulers could result in exile or death – or in his case, castration. Again like other historians, Sima Qian seems to have realized that he could make coded criticisms of his own rulers by attacking their predecessors, particularly if they had been defeated. So he passes on the worst scuttlebutt about Zheng. His chronicle the *Shi Ji*, a history of the Chinese dynasties, tells us that Zheng was probably the son of a barrow-boy merchant, an immigrant to the state of Ch'in, called Lu Buwei. This merchant had a beautiful lover who caught the eye of the crown prince. He handed her over. The courtesan, however, was already pregnant. She passed off the child as the prince's. The prince became king and the courtesan his queen. A baby was born.

The child was Zheng, and thus a bastard and a fraud. Yet, aged thirteen, he rose to the throne of the state of Ch'in when his 'father' died. Bad enough – but at this point the story becomes really racy. The merchant Lu Buwei returned to the arms of his lover, now the dowager queen, but became tired of her. So he . . . But at this point it is probably best to quote directly from our historian: 'He therefore searched about in secret until he found a man named Lao Ai who had an unusually large penis . . . when an occasion arose, he had suggestive music performed and, instructing Lao Ai to stick his penis through the centre of a wheel made of paulownia wood, had him walk about with it, making certain that the report of this reached the ears of the queen dowager so as to excite her interest.'[6]

And excited it was. In an attempt to hush the gossip, Lu Buwei first had the well hung Lao Ai convicted of some minor charge and sentenced to castration. The operation was faked, however, and with some extra-careful shaving of the face to suggest he had become a eunuch, Lao Ai was left to enjoy a happy life in private with the queen, now an empress. She gave him gifts and two children. Sadly for them both, however, Zheng, by now surrounded by a strangely behaving mother, dodgy 'adviser' – who was also his rumoured real father – a fake eunuch and two half-brothers who were potential successors, decided the time had come to assert himself. He exiled his mother (though she eventually came back). He exiled Lu Buwei, who later on decided to poison himself rather than face a further banishment. He had the half-brothers killed. And he had Lao Ai, the erotic wheel-spinner, torn into four by chariots attached to his limbs. Their supporters were beheaded or banished – but mainly beheaded. Had the film-maker Quentin Tarantino turned his hand to Shakespeare's *Hamlet* the effects could hardly have been more satisfactorily splattered.

But of course, none of this may be true. We have Sima Qian's words to take on trust, or perhaps those of later anonymous mudslinger historians who added to the record. These were all working for the Han empire, which replaced the Ch'in, and had no reason to boost Zheng's reputation. Yet Sima Qian, at least, seems to have been a painstakingly serious writer. He fell out with a later emperor when he defended a friend, a general who had lost his army. For this misdemeanour Sima Qian chose the humiliation of castration as his punishment, so that living on as a half-man he could at least finish his book.

Meanwhile, at the cost of various relatives and the sniggering of chroniclers, Zheng had been left in full control of the biggest and most aggressive of the Chinese kingdoms, just as it completed a series of takeovers that would make it the hub of a unified empire. Zheng's Chi'in forebears had done most of the work already. They had fooled the people of Shu, living in what is now Sichuan beyond the near-impassable Qinling mountains. The story goes that the earliest Ch'in king, Hui, presented the Shu king with some beautifully made stone cows whose nether quarters were painted with gobbets of gold. The credulous royal neighbour asked for these gold-excreting marvels as presents, and allowed King Hui to build a road with wooden bridges and galleries through the mountains so they could be moved to Shu. Behind them, of course, came the Ch'in army, surprising and overwhelming their rivals, and seized a vast new territory.

One by one, the other rival states of old China were outfought and outflanked by the Ch'in forces, until late in the First Emperor's reign, driving deep into the south, he finished the job of uniting all the main regions. These were bloody enough wars, fought mainly with infantry and crossbows, but probably not as destructive of agriculture and towns as had been the earlier depredations of the warring states. What the ordinary 'black-haired people' of the Chinese plains, struggling to bring in their crops and avoid being conscripted by one of the passing armies, really thought of their First Emperor, we can never know.

Other areas of the world at this time were being shaped by religion, as well as by the rise and fall of kings: China was different. As noted earlier, there was a long tradition of worship of ancestor spirits and local gods. The complicated set of customary beliefs known as Daoism could at different times be used to support or to challenge imperial power. Buddhism would spread across China from Ashoka's India with monasteries and monks who, again, were sometimes tolerated or supported and at other times persecuted. But there were no people-shaking or dynasty-rocking new religions of the kind that would upend the Mediterranean world. The educated Chinese had philosophy as their unifier. By the time of the First Emperor, though, the humane, conservative social vision of Kongzi – Confucius – had been challenged by a new school of political thought, normally known as Legalism.

The Legalists put the need for order and submission above everything else. It was a creed based on fear of social anarchy and designed to appeal above all to rulers. Law, severe but impartial and certain, was the overriding social good. Legalists taught that the state should organize the people, irrigate the land, standardize weights and measures and allow its servants and soldiers promotion on strictly practical grounds – how many enemies they had killed, for instance. In return, the state organized families and villages into groups to spy on one another. The fearsome arsenal of state punishments included being torn apart, boiled alive, beheaded and sawn in two. For the lucky ones, there might be merely a bit of finger-slicing or kneecap removal. On the other hand, recent evidence suggests that the law was at least applied carefully and impartially and may not have been, in practice, quite as cruel as it sounds.[7]

Thanks to the silver tongue of the sinister Legalist sage known as Lord Shang, the Ch'in state took this doctrine to its heart. Situated on the north-western edge of the Chinese plains, Ch'in was already regarded by its rivals as mildly barbarous, too close to the edge of the known world to be properly civilized. Legalism had made it even grimmer, even tougher and more repressive. Its war philosophy now involved the mass slaughter of the enemy when possible, and terror tactics. Ch'in has been persuasively compared to that other ruthless militarized state, Sparta, and to modern dictatorships too. By the time of the First Emperor, Lord Shang was long gone (himself executed, one is glad to report, having been caught by his own system of spies), but his influence was as strong as ever.

He would have greatly approved of one of Zheng's more notorious actions, when on the advice of his Legalist grand councillor Li Si he ordered the rounding-up and burning of most of China's bamboo books of poetry, history and philosophy. According to Sima Qian, his purpose was to spread ignorance: by destroying records of the past, the court would wipe out people's ability to challenge new laws by appealing to tradition and history. This makes Zheng's move sound like a Maoist 'Year Zero' attempt to obliterate memory. In fact, as historians have recently pointed out, many works of history as well as most books of practical instruction were spared; and it was comparatively easy to hide bamboo books, even if the penalties for doing so included tattooing and being buried alive. Chinese tradition is insistent that Zheng did bury many Confucian scholars alive. Mao would praise him for this, but said he should have killed more. It is possible that Sima Qian was exaggerating to make his profession seem even more martyred and heroic than it was. Certainly, the Chinese passion for historical records and poetry was barely interrupted.

Zheng's wars against the last rival states were not his final legacy to China. He survived an extraordinary assassination attempt, when the killer gained access to him by bringing him maps of enemy territory and the severed head of a rebel general (the general had been in on the plot, and had magnanimously cut his own throat, to help). But rolled up in the map was a dagger and, according to Sima Qian, the assassin and the emperor fought hand to hand before Zheng won, his courtiers simply looking on, horror-struck. Not surprisingly, Zheng grew ever more paranoid, building covered walkways between his palaces so nobody could be sure where he was.

Grandiose building projects, including huge canals and waterways, became steadily more important to him. Famously, he ordered the extension and patching-up of earth and stone walls to keep out the barbarians – part of what would become the Great Wall of China – and established packed-earth roads to connect the many parts of the empire. The anarchic rivalry between the states concerning such things as coin values, measurements, axle lengths and scripts at last came to an end. In particular, without Zheng, it has been argued, China would have no single system of writing, and therefore no coherent cultural identity.

He travelled his new realms, showing himself and his army to the subjects of the new empire, and raising triumphal columns. His self-aggrandizement led to him 'punishing' a hill that had been struck by lightning, cutting down its trees and painting it red; and to a fruitless search for immortality that involved hunting large and probably mythical sea creatures with a crossbow. He may have contributed to his own death by swallowing mercury pills that a doctor had suggested as a short cut to immortality.

Which, in a way, they were, for Zheng is known today outside China mainly for his huge funeral monument with its estimated eight thousand warriors – the 'terracotta army' – its horses, chariots and administrators, buried under a vast mound near Xian. We have to go back, one final time, to our historian, who tells us that at the centre lies the man himself, surrounded by a model of the Chinese world, with rivers made of mercury and a constellation of stars above him. It is possible that this is all true. There is indeed evidence of abnormal quantities of mercury under a nearby hill, suspiciously regular in shape and about the right size for the funeral palace itself. Perhaps, over the next few decades, the greatest archaeological excavation in world history will reveal Zheng himself.

Zheng, like other Chinese, believed in a shadow world after death, similar to this world and which had to be carefully prepared for. Under earlier local dynasties many other Chinese kings and nobles had been buried with specially killed servants and specially made replica goods. Nor would Zheng's beliefs have seemed outlandish to Egyptians, Greeks, Vikings and other ancient peoples who believed in sending off mortal bodies well geared up for a life to come. Religious ideas involving human equality before a god, or a moral judgement awaiting the living, would have seemed ridiculous to him – as ridiculous as a clay army to protect you from devils seems to us.

Yet Zheng also had a second and subtler idea about immortality. He called himself 'the First Emperor' because he intended to be followed by the second emperor, the third, and so on, for thousands of generations. He did not expect his Ch'in dynasty to collapse as rapidly as it did, and the numbering stopped almost immediately. But the notion of an unbroken succession of emperors held the Chinese imagination right up to the Nationalist and Communist insurrections of the twentieth century; and the idea kept Zheng's memory as its originator for ever alive, in itself a kind of life-in-death. With a common script and a common language, secure communications, and a sense of themselves as one people under one ruler, the Chinese would produce the longest-lasting and most unified of the ancient civilizations. The price they paid for this was that they were not exposed to the liberating, unsettling, destabilizing idea of monotheism – those personal, universal, mobile religions that would rip apart the only real rival the Ch'in and Han empires had, far away to the West.

The Maccabees' Sting

Of all the nations to the west of the Chinese, none would have puzzled them more than the people of Judah. We last met the Israelites after their Babylonian exile, while they were refining their unusual religion. Judah, a small blob of a country centred on Jerusalem and Jericho, was squeezed between two of the Greek states that Alexander had spawned, that of the Ptolemies in Egypt and the Seleucids in Syria. By around 200 BC Judah had fallen under the control of the Seleucid Greeks, and a culture war now began between the Greeks, with their sophisticated, pleasure-loving, philosophical traditions, and the intense, inward-looking Israelites under their high priests.

Greek, or Hellenistic, culture was by now the common property of much of the Western world, providing access to a single set of stories, heroes, ways of thinking, eating and behaving. In cities all over the eastern Mediterranean, statues, paintings and buildings – including theatres and gymnasia – gave Greek culture great allure. It can be fairly compared to the magnetism of the film, the music and the food of twentieth-century America. To reject it required great strength of purpose. Inevitably many Jews, particularly richer ones, 'Greeked' themselves, competing in athletic games, dressing like Hellenes and even – apparently – managing to reverse their circumcisions. The Greek Seleucid kings wanted Jerusalem's high priest to serve as their colonial governor. An unseemly series of dodges, bribes and even a murder degraded the holy office, as the Greeks tried to turn Judah into a normal Greek society. From 167 BC the Seleucid king Antiochus IV banned many Jewish rites, outlawing circumcision, Jewish feasts and sacrifices. Worst of all, Zeus was brought, in statue form, into the Temple itself.

At this point one of the books of the Old Testament that Protestant Christians are rarely familiar with, that of the Maccabees, continues the heroic story of the Israelites' resistance to the would-be modernizers. The accounts start with Alexander the Great, whom the Israelites rightly saw as the initial cause of the trouble: 'And he subdued countries of nations and princes, and they became tributaries to him. And after these things, he fell down upon his bed, and knew that he should die.' A long line of horrors committed by Antiochus is then enumerated, including the slaughter of mothers who circumcised their children (the children too were hanged). But then a priest, Mattathias, appeared who refused to bow to the Greeks. When 'a certain Jew' who had clearly become semi-Greek arrived in the Temple to sacrifice to a pagan idol, as Antiochus had ordered, Mattathias killed him – and the king's messenger too – then fled into the mountains.

There, a resistance army was formed. To start with, religion trumped military common sense and a thousand Jews died because they had refused to fight on the Sabbath. The no-fighting-on-the-Sabbath rule was quickly suspended. When old Mattathias died at the ripe old age (apparently) of 146, his son Judas Maccabeus took over as commander. Much of the rest of the narrative, written soon after the event, recounted the guerrilla war waged by the Jews against the Greek armies, which, armed with their elephants, seemed terrifyingly powerful. Jewish militants seized and forcibly circumcised children, pagan altars were overthrown; and eventually Jerusalem itself was recaptured by the Jewish insurgency. Compared with many parts of the conventional Bible, it is an exciting war story.

Mattathias's other sons, Jonathan and Simon, became kings in their new – Hasmonean – kingdom. They expanded Judah's territory, smiting unfortunate and weaker neighbours in their path, and made a powerful if dangerous friend by allying with a rising city of which they knew little, Rome. The Maccabees' war of independence had been a new thing for the Jews, a great political triumph. It had, however, come at a fearful price in terms of deaths. It seems to be around now that Jewish theology started to grapple properly with the notion of an afterlife, something earlier Judaism had said little about. Presumably there was a feeling that these martyrs must have died for something.[8] The Book of Daniel, written at around this time, says that 'many who sleep in the dust of the earth will awaken – these for eternal life, and those for disgrace, for eternal abhorrence'. This was a new idea that would leave a heavy imprint on two thousand years of Christian teaching; and it seems to have emerged out of a guerrilla war.

Strikingly, though, the success of the revolt did not push back Greek influence. Under the Hasmonean kings the Greek language became widely used, alongside Hebrew and Aramaic. Jewish communities began to trade and spread throughout the Greek world, until it was said that there were around a million Jews living in Alexandria alone. This must be an exaggeration, but it shows how large Jewish communities loomed. Damascus became another big Jewish centre. Most large ports had Jewish communities, with their meeting-houses known by the Greek word 'synagogue', in which their sacred books were edited and codified and taught. The books were translated into Greek, and many believers seem to have spoken languages other than Hebrew and Aramaic. Non-Jews who supported synagogues and adopted the religion had a special name of their own, 'God-fearers'.

The short life of the independent Jewish kingdom came to an end in 63 BC thanks to Gnaeus Pompeius Magnus ('Magnus' in homage to Alexander the Great), a bull-faced superstar general whose glitter was blinding the late Roman republic. Pompey, as we know him, was a charismatic career soldier with a brutal edge. He could be sentimental, not least about Julia, Julius Caesar's daughter, but he notched up five wives, and a mistress who boasted that he liked to bite her, leaving marks, when they made love. He had won his first big victories in North Africa as a young man, and had put down first a Spanish rebellion, then pirates in the Mediterranean. In his latest campaign he had swept through Pontus and Asia Minor, almost reached the Caspian Sea and then turned on Syria, where he had snuffed out the kingdom of Antiochus XIII, descendant of the man who had provoked the Maccabee revolt.

Unfortunately for the Jews, they were busily engaged in a civil war of their own between two brothers, the princely sons of Queen Salome, each supported by one of the main sects, the Sadducees and the Pharisees. One brother, Aristobulus, bribed the Romans for help while he was being besieged in the Temple at Jerusalem, which was by now a massive fortified structure. Pompey's general arrived, and took large amounts of gold and silver. Pompey himself now became suspicious of his new ally: arriving in Jerusalem, he sided with the other brother, Hyrcanus, and besieged the Temple himself. His troops used catapults, siege towers and battering rams to break their way through. They then marched into the 'holy of holies', the sanctuary in the centre of the Temple restricted to the high priest, and sacked it. Some of the Jewish defenders were so appalled that they killed themselves. As part of his vast train of loot, Pompey took many Jewish prisoners back to Rome, where some were freed and settled, living near what is now St Peter's Basilica.

Judah was now merely another Roman possession, which would soon have a puppet king called Herod imposed on it. Oddly, though, Jewish influence on other people continued to grow. De-kinged, pushed out of their own little world, Jews continued to thrive elsewhere in the Mediterranean. An argument rages between Jewish historians about the extent to which Jews now went out to convert others. The conventional wisdom is that they do not, and never did, proselytize – but if so, how can one account for the huge expansion of Judaism in this period? The great Jewish historian Salo Baron points out that, having been a people of around only 150,000 in the fifth century BC, they accounted for around 10 per cent of the Roman Empire by the first century AD. Norman Cantor, another US-based Jewish historian, reckons: 'At the time Jesus of Nazareth lived and died and Herod's Temple was destroyed, some six million Jews lived in the Roman empire . . . Of these, two-thirds were living in the Diaspora.'[9] This seems too large a proportion to be accounted for by birth rate or journeys made.

Because Jews themselves were later on the sharp end of Christian and Muslim missions, there is a reluctance to accept that Judaism was itself a missionary religion. Yet as early as 139 BC, Jews were being expelled from Rome for trying to convert Roman citizens. A little later the great lawyer-politician Cicero complained about proselytizing Jews. Two emperors, Tiberius and Claudius, transported Jews from Rome for the crime of trying to convert Romans.[10] Roman writers such as Horace, Seneca, Juvenal and Tacitus all discuss the issue. Later, the emperor Theodosius published ferocious decrees in the Christian era against anyone who attempted to make converts to Judaism.

Judaism, and then Christianity (initially seen by Romans as a version of the same), were disruptive creeds because of their emphasis on equality before God, and their denial of the divinity of emperors. They argued for a reality outside the reality of daily life in the empire. They became popular beliefs among the literate middle classes of the Roman world, the traders and small landowners remote from real power; Jews (though not, to start with, Christians) served as soldiers too. They represented a restless, ceaseless force. The Jewish historian Shlomo Sand makes the point that 'every monotheism contains a potential element of mission. Unlike the tolerant polytheisms, which accept the existence of other deities, the very belief in the existence of

a single god . . . impels the believers to spread the idea of divine singularity . . . The acceptance by others of the worship of the single god
proves his might and his power over the world.'[11]

This is such an important story to the West, and such a complicated one, that it is worth trying to summarize it so far.

The Hebrew people had first separated themselves from what had
been common in the Mediterranean, the worship of many gods. Very
slowly and with much argument they had narrowed their focus to a
single god, Yahweh. Many Jews had disagreed over this, but with time
their one-god prophets won the argument. When their first kingdoms
were destroyed and their leaders exiled to Babylon, the priests developed this thinking further. God was both the only god and the
potentially universal god, unconfined to a single area. Instead of walking only his own land, he was everywhere and nowhere. This god had
a relationship with every believer, and his laws were written down;
they could be carried around and easily disseminated.

The later Judean kingdom fought a vicious war of liberation, as
we have seen, and in contemplating its many martyrs it developed
another powerful idea, that there might be an individual, personal life
after death. Because of the military politics of the ancient world –
Greek conquest, then Roman Empire – the people who held these
beliefs became widely scattered around the Mediterranean, as traders
and merchants with their own communities and buildings. Believing
themselves to be in possession of a vital truth, they spread the word
and tried to convert others. Conventional Jews were later elbowed
aside as the main monotheistic influence, by radical breakaways who
believed everyone should convert to their faith – the followers of Jesus
of Nazareth, of whom more later.

This is a story of the endless human search for meaning, belonging and consolation. And it came about because of the geography of
the Middle East, its ancient wars and trade routes, and finally the awesome power of Rome. Christianity, then Islam, would destroy any
chance the classical world might have had to develop a single, unified
civilization on the Chinese model. But without its imperial conquerors, those materialistic, this-worldly generals, monotheism would
not have got going; nor have spread until it conquered the conqueror.

The Rise and Fall of the Romans

The conquerors of the Jews had been polytheists. Like the early Jewish kingdoms, early Rome was an obscure place on the fringes of the Greek world. It has also been compared to the kingdom of Ch'in, another austere, ruthless state on the edges, which had to toughen up to survive. At about the same time as Judah was defeated by the Babylonians, the small kingdom of Rome was defeated by its neighbouring power, the Etruscans. Like the Jews, the Romans told stories about their earliest origins. Instead of the exile in Egypt, they had the tale of Aeneas leading them from Troy to their promised land, a group of small hills by a marsh. Or – another story – they had been founded by a wanderer called Romulus, who had been suckled by a wolf and later murdered his brother.

So, from the first, Roman stories involved swagger (Troy was about as good an origin as the ancient world could imagine), migration and violence. Rome turned out to be well placed. It was far enough from the centre of the Greek world to be mostly left alone. It was on a river, the Tiber, which sea-going ships could navigate at least part of the way, yet its fortified hilltops offered protection from seaborne raiders. Finally, it was on the southern edge of a part of Italy that was under the domination of the Etruscans. The Etruscans were traders as well as warriors, with a Phoenician-derived alphabet and strong links with the Greek states. They would give the Romans many of their customs, including the grouping of citizens by hundreds, or 'centuries', and would ensure that this small city was connected from early on with the wider Mediterranean culture. For a period the Romans were ruled directly by Etruscan kings, though they eventually rebelled and threw them out.

The essence of the Roman story is politics and war, not religion. Traditional Roman religion involved a complicated array of gods, which they would later try to align with the famous Greek pantheon; the Romans were always incorporators, or as the historian Mary Beard puts it, 'intellectual sponges'. Their priests tried to read the future by watching how birds flew, or how sacred chickens ate.[12] Offerings of slaughtered animals, omens, libations poured on the ground, naked men leaping around whipping passers-by – this is all the fairly routine business of primitive worship, characterized by its practitioners' credulity and in no way charming. Paying homage to local gods and worshipping, or merely revering, one's ancestors were common in China or Japan. But societies that allow ideas to immigrate change faster. And not even the Vestal Virgins were as interesting as they sound. It is no great surprise that later on, the Romans did indeed become the ultimate soakers-up of everything from Greek philosophy to African cults, Egyptian rites to Judaism. Religion, Roman-style, only becomes properly interesting when Roman emperors declare themselves to be gods; and that was about politics, not really about religion at all.

And the politics was always interesting. One of the last Roman kings, an Etruscan warrior said to be the son of a slave, introduced a code of laws and organized regular meetings of all citizens. Once the kings had been deposed, Rome had aristocratic rulers, as did most Greek communities; but the Roman *plebs*, the poor, managed to establish basic rights of their own, defended by tribunes. From very early on, there was a rough balance of power in a city which – unlike most others – positively welcomed all comers. The Romulus story suggested the city had been founded by runaways: migrants and freed slaves could become Roman citizens and eventually work and fight for the republic. This was a hierarchical and macho society, however, in which fathers wielded almost untrammelled power over the family and women were excluded from public life. And because Rome was hemmed around by hostile rivals, jostling for space in a fertile part of Italy, it was a military society.

At the top of republican Roman society were the aristocratic families who traced their influence back to the time of the kings and who formed the Senate. Relatively early, this immigrant society also developed elections for key posts. In 367 BC a major change took place when it was agreed that all classes, not only patricians, could be elected as consuls, so long as they were wealthy enough. A complicated, lengthy system of elections plus experience accumulated in office resulted in the Senate evolving into a tough and effective ruling body. Serving as its executives was a double-act of consuls, with a kind of super-magistrate elected each year. Then came the rest, the ordinary citizens organized into tribes and able, in their own assembly, to vote for new laws by simple majority.

If this sounds remarkably democratic, it was not. A Roman form of jerrymandering, involving block votes and the intimidation of voters, kept the well off, mostly, in control. A republic meant a ruling system without kings, not a representative one. But the Senate was able to draw in a constant supply of new talent and to balance factions among the richer citizens. The voting system and the tension between different bodies kept absolute power, the folk memory of tyrant kings, at bay. Most impressively, the Senate was able to balance its own traditional authority with rights for incomers and poorer citizens, both those living inside the walls and those farming beyond.

There was always tension, and later on, at times of food shortage or military failure, an almost revolutionary spirit could flare up. When it came to arguments about land and justice, Roman citizens had louder voices than their counterparts in most other regions of the Mediterranean world. They may have been more Philistine and more provincial than the Athenians, but the Romans had evolved a clever political equilibrium, which generally warded off any possibility of internal chaos. Their system threw up a regular supply of good administrators and law-makers, and they managed to absorb large numbers of new 'citizens' from far outside the city itself. Priding themselves on their austerity and plainness, the Romans of the early republic developed no literature or philosophy of their own that we know of. Their buildings were mere mimicry. But they went to war like nobody else.

Many military leaders have known that striking terror into your enemies' hearts is half the road to victory. Roman practice, as the city extended its influence through central Italy, was straightforward. It was terroristic, or at least terror-based. If a city surrendered, it would become a vassal. If any resistance at all was offered, it was to be completely destroyed and every living thing in it slaughtered – right down to children, domestic pets, even the rats. Roman citizens were conscripted for army service and, as with the free Greek hoplites, citizenship and war-making, solidarity and attack, became intertwined ideas. Fighting in tight phalanxes with long spears and short, stabbing swords, the ancestors of the imperial legions were a fearsome force by the early 200s BC.

Success bred success. Cities intimidated into surrendering could provide new citizens, and therefore new soldiers; slaves poured in to take on other work. The Romans did not have the huge military might needed to destroy and take over the rest of Italy in a flash. It was the propaganda of their terrorism – surrender fast or you will regret it – combined with their ability to put an arm around the shoulders of the local elites, reassure them, and rule through them – that did the trick. So almost every victory produced more manpower to fuel the next one. After defeating the invading Gauls, who had once managed to sack Rome itself, the Romans were able to subdue their old foes to the north, and then the Greek colonies further south.

In the end, the Greek world could no longer ignore the upstart bully-boy city in the west. And they had, it seemed, a terror weapon to terrify even the Romans. War elephants, as we have seen, had arrived in the Greek world from India. For a while they seemed a transforming military force. One of the Greek rulers who deployed them was Pyrrhus, King of Epirus, who borrowed them from the Greek rulers of Egypt. A dashing, silver-armoured leader, Pyrrhus was asked for help against the Romans by one of the Greek states in Italy under attack. He brought his elephants to Italy, the first time they had been seen there, and won two victories against Rome.

What is extraordinary, however, is that the Romans, though awed by the creatures – and not believing they were mortal until one had its trunk severed – did not break. They held these inheritors of Alexander's power to such bloody draws that Pyrrhus famously declared: 'Another such victory, and we shall be lost.' Later, the Romans tried to frighten the elephants by covering pigs in fat, then setting them on fire and driving the screaming animals at them. Nasty – but it seems to have worked because Pyrrhus eventually withdrew back to Greece, where he continued to use elephants to fight, until killed when an angry woman threw a roof-tile at him.[13]

For the Romans, this all turned out to be good preparation. They were about to go to war with Carthage and would soon confront more of the beasts, this time led by the man synonymous with elephant war, Hannibal.

Carthage, a Lost Future?

Among the great speculations of classical history has been the thought that Carthage, not Rome, might have won the Punic wars. Its greatest general Hannibal came within a whisker of success. After the horrendous battle of Cannae in 216 BC, which left between 50,000 and 70,000 Romans dead, the road to Rome lay almost undefended. Roman allies defected. Romans panicked. Hannibal was urged by his cavalry commander to march south and finish the city off. He did not, but for a short time he had a huge advantage. Had he taken Rome, our world might have been very different.

Carthage, which had survived for six centuries on the North African coast protected by huge harbour walls, was essentially a sea power, whose navy at the time was as large by tonnage as those of Britain, Spain or France in the 1700s. Its merchant ships traded with the Canary Islands, sailed down the Atlantic coast of Africa, picked up tin from Britain and criss-crossed the Mediterranean. Perhaps a Carthaginian West would have sailed to America centuries before the Europeans actually did. Carthage was a great manufacturing power too, producing the fabulously expensive purple dye that coloured so distinctively Roman senators' togas, plus strong wine, ceramics and metalwork of all kinds, and many sorts of cloth. Its fleet was mass-produced and then assembled at speed, like modern flat-pack furniture, a trick that would be forgotten until the rise of Venice – and which allowed the Romans to reverse-engineer Carthaginian vessels and make themselves seafarers too.

Carthage had her theatres, her famous orators, and a constitution which, although run first by kings and later by oligarchs, gave a strong voice to the ordinary citizens. Many of them emigrated and set up colonies themselves. In his *Politics* Aristotle, writing nearly two hundred years before Carthage finally fell to the Romans, warmly praises Carthaginian institutions: 'The superiority of their constitution is proved by the fact that the common people remain loyal to [it]. The Carthaginians have never had any rebellion worth speaking of, and have never been under the rule of a tyrant.'[14] By the time of its destruction Carthage was certainly one of the greatest cities on the planet; its population was much larger than Rome's at the time. And of course, it was in Africa. A classical Mediterranean world whose dominant power was in North Africa, not on the Italian peninsula, would have felt different in ways we can barely imagine.

There were darker sides to Carthaginian life. Roman critics claimed the Carthaginians engaged in child sacrifice, as did their

Phoenician forebears, though modern historians are sceptical and after Cannae, the Romans resorted to it too. The Carthaginian army, unlike the Roman, was mainly composed of mercenaries, from Spain, Numidia, Libya and the Balearic islands.[15] Only around three thousand Carthaginians fought as infantry, in the so-called Sacred Band. It seems to have been a suspicious society, to the point of paranoia about would-be tyrants. Unlike Roman generals enjoying their triumphs, Carthaginian generals had to risk being plotted against and even executed when they returned from their victories. Yet with all that said, the utter destruction of Carthage when the Romans finally won the third Punic war leaves a terrible gap in the historical record of the Mediterranean. We have no detailed idea of what their buildings looked like – just some foundations and pillars to go on.

We have none of their writing, poetry, plays, art, histories, family stories or hopes. It is as if, after the Second World War, nothing written in German – no German poetry – nor any German music, or buildings, survived. Had the fortunes of war gone slightly differently, of course, there would have been no imperial Rome, either. Would schoolchildren now be brushing up on their Punic verbs, studying the epic sea voyages of Carthaginian heroes to the Caribbean, listing jokes made about Hamilcar by Carthaginian orators? Sometimes, seeking deep causes, we create the illusion of inevitability. It is possible that Carthage ultimately fell because it lacked the flexible and open attitude to citizenship and the sinewy political system of the Roman republic. It is equally possible that it fell because of a few bad decisions on battlefields. Apparently insignificant causes can trigger momentous changes.

At any rate, after long years of bloodbath and struggle across Italy, Sicily and North Africa, Carthage finally fell. After his epic crossing of the Alps, when it was his cavalry rather than his elephants that mattered most, and his bloody victories over the legions, Hannibal's ravaging of Italy eventually ended when he was defeated by Scipio 'Africanus' and sent into exile by his own people. Carthage would finally be annihilated in 146 BC, wiped out in an orgy of Roman killing, rape and destruction.

Once Carthage had gone, Rome could turn on the Greek states that had inherited Alexander's world, on Macedonia, and the Seleucid empire, which ran from present-day Turkey to the steppes. As a system of powerful military empires, the Greek world was starting to collapse. In its ideas about beauty, philosophy, the arts and mathematics it would have a very long half-life, almost as the conscience of the Roman world. Some of its greatest thinkers and inventions were yet to be born. But it is from the fall of Carthage and the Greek kingdoms to the Roman legions that we can date the real beginning of the imperial Roman world.

Money and Politics

Why? Because the Roman republic, with its boasted austerity and virtue, its all-in-this-together patriotism, could not survive its own success. The plunder that began to pour in, and would arrive in ever greater quantities, corrupted its political system. A sudden new source of wealth tends to corrupt any political settlement. The Roman system of taxation and spending was rackety, to say the least. The wars allowed massive personal fortunes to be accumulated over which the state had virtually no control. It is estimated that rich Romans were, for instance, about twice as rich as the wealthiest Han Chinese aristocrats. To start with, the poor were bought off with subsidized food and public entertainment. By 167 BC, direct taxes on Roman citizens went altogether, replaced by 'tribute' from Sicily, Greece, Spain and Africa.

Roman magistrates sent out to govern the equivalent in acreage of New South Wales were allowed to enrich themselves, returning wealthy enough to bribe and organize their way to greater power at home. Corruption became endemic in the politics of the city. Yet the poor, still paying indirect taxes, had a hard time of it. As the super-rich bought up farms and ran them with slaves, the peasants who had once been seen as the backbone of Roman virtue were displaced and sent jobless to the city. In this period we learn of a new disease, *luxuria*, or decadence, or simply 'too much'. The long decades of constant fighting, and the arrival of ever more captives, cowed allies and slaves, resulted in the Roman armies ceasing to be militias of citizens serving their time and becoming semi-independent and dangerous bodies.

Class war began to brew. On the one hand, the new decadence was horrifying Roman moralists. Greek homosexuality seems to have become more acceptable and the price of boy lovers rocketed. Gladiatorial fights had always been popular in Rome – they went back to Etruscan models – but now the 'games' became ever more lavish, featuring exotic animals and fighters, as rich office-seekers tried to buy popularity. Yet at the same time, hordes of displaced peasants and city workers struggling to live, the easily mobilized mobs of Roman politics, crowded the streets. Radical orators, most famously the brothers Tiberius and Gaius Gracchus, called for land reform and the cleaning-up of the political scene. Both were murdered in an orgy of violence, which started to sweep through Rome. Members of the aristocratic Senate seethed at the possibility of reform, though they were divided on the issue; eventually a military hard man, Sulla, took Rome to the edge of civil war before making himself dictator and increasing the powers of the senators and the army.

It is a sequence familiar in the capitals of other great empires: the extreme inequality created as loot from abroad pours in; the corruption of voting systems and of representative institutions; hoarse cries for change from the streets; the undertow of violence; the mailed fist as the army strides in to 'clean things up'. The imbalance of power created by empire, unbalances the empire itself. Roman life spun out of order, out of all control. Senators continued to act as if they were living in the old republic, speechifying and plotting. But the armies could no longer be trusted and social unrest worsened. The huge slave revolt begun by the gladiator Spartacus in the shadow of Mount Vesuvius shook this slave society to its core. His 70,000-strong force of former gladiators and farmers defeated two armies in the year 71 BC. (They would finally be crushed by the combined forces of most of Rome's available military power.) There was a rebel consul loose in Spain, and more trouble in Asia. But worse than all of this were the measures that had to be taken to restore order.

Returned from the east, Pompey was back in town – or rather, just outside Rome, waiting with his legions. The old Roman custom had been to award victorious generals a 'triumph', a processional parade through the city. The victor would ride in his chariot, a slave behind him reminding him that he was mortal. In front would be led his captives in chains, and perhaps some booty from the war. As Rome's reach and appetite had grown, these triumphs had become more lavish and extreme, days of riotous civic partying. Pompey was

Right. Sumerian fertility goddess: until the evolution of single-God monotheism among the Hebrews, families of gods, usually including a female fertility goddess, were near-universal.

Below. Inscription from Ugarit, in today's Syria. Modern alphabetic writing – what you are reading now – developed among the trading and sea-going people of Canaan, called Phoenicians by the Greeks.

Right. Shang axe-head: the Shang were China's first historically certain dynasty, a chariot-riding and warrior culture accused by later Chinese of incest, cannibalism and a liking for pornographic songs.

Left. In the hero Gilgamesh, we have the first named character in world literature.

Right. Hugging couple found at Catalhoyuk, in Turkey: this was among the first towns in the world, where people lived in a state of relative equality for thousands of years.

The Minoan civilization of Crete practiced bull-jumping and made beautiful art but was much bloodier and more violent than its first archaeologists thought.

Around 3000 BC, Orkney was one of the most advanced societies in Britain: the uncovered stone homes at Skara Brae are clean, cosy and seem ready to move back into today.

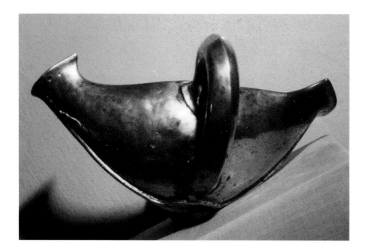

Above. A gold drinking cup from Troy:
this was not really owned by Homer's
King Priam but Troy was a real city, and
the Trojan war was almost certainly
an historical event.

Right. A head-dress from Ur, 2600 BC:
the Mesopotamian cultures produced
famous cities, empires and religions; but
too much of their art has disappeared.

Below. Dice from Mohenjo-Daro
in today's Pakistan: an ancient river
civilization on the Indus which may be
the origin of much of today's
Indian culture.

Painting from the workers' village near Egypt's Valley of the Kings. Craftsmen as well as Pharaohs had their own decorated tombs; and we know their gossip too.

Below left. Siddhartha, who renamed himself the Buddha, was among the most radical thinkers in history; the product of India going through a time of tumultuous change.

Below right. Erlitou wine cup: the earliest Chinese objects already look like nothing that could have been made in the West.

Left. Babylon, with its glorious enameled buildings and hanging gardens, must have awed as well as terrified the Hebrews taken there in captivity.

Right. A gold necklace belonging to King Croesus from Lydia: his royal mint produced reliable, pure coinage that spread across Asia, which is why we say 'rich as Croesus' today.

Below. The Cyrus cylinder: not quite the first international declaration of human rights, but Cyrus the Great was an empire builder of a new kind.

Socrates died by drinking poison – a martyr to free speech but also a genuine threat to Athenian democracy. We still have not untangled the challenge he laid down to open societies.

Confucius, or Kongzi, was the most influential conservative thinker in world history: his influence on Chinese political culture is as great as that of Ancient Greece on the West's.

The Assyrian capital Persepolis was decorated with vast stone murals, some recording ordinary life, others disgustingly sadistic.

A gold coin of Alexander III, 'Alexander the Great', who turned himself into a bloody cultural whisk, whirling together Greeks and Asians.

awarded an unheard-of three triumphs, the last of which featured a jaw-dropping caravan of strange animals, glistening loot, defeated kings and priests, soldiers and money.

As it turned out, Pompey did not prove an adroit enough politician to seize power in quite the way his critics had feared. But there were now two other military aristocrats and super-rich rivals at large. Crassus, a thuggish soldier, was now a plutocrat, who in a hideous display of revenge after the Spartacus war had crucified on the main road north to Rome some six thousand captured rebels. The other was Julius Caesar.

Caesar is the most famous Roman, who gave us our calendars – indeed, our modern way of measuring time – and whose assassination is the climactic scene of Roman political life. Though hindsight is blinding and we must rely on Caesar-struck historians, it seems that he was extraordinary from an early age. A top-notch aristocratic youth allied to the wrong side, he had survived the murderous dictatorship of Sulla, when lists of those to be judicially murdered had been pasted up in the Forum. He became a soldier while still in his teens and made a name for himself, not least by taking revenge on pirates who had kidnapped him and then foolishly let him go. He zigzagged, double-crossed and bought his way upwards through the dangerous world of Roman politics, taking one position after another and paying for lavish games, until he finally reached what should have been the top, the consulship, in 59 BC. Caesar then plotted to bypass the Senate, using the money and connections of Crassus and Pompey to help fix a lucrative military command for himself afterwards. The greatest Roman orator, Cicero, who had thought he was playing Caesar along, was entirely outsmarted. Caesar got his way, evaded his many enemies, and began years of fighting beyond the Alps, slaughtering Gaulish and German tribes and reaching Britain, though not staying there very long.

Caesar knew that the route to power in Rome came from a combination of fame, of a kind only won on the battlefield, and great wealth, also best won by conquest. His campaigns abroad were also campaigns for power at home. As he fought – and he was a brilliant general – he wrote crisply propagandistic accounts of his campaigns so as to burnish his image. In them he reveals clear military thinking, an ability to bounce back from reverses, a close, if cold, attention to the habits and foibles of the enemy tribes, and an acute sense of his own mythology. What Caesar's *Gallic Wars* do not properly explain is that he was engaged in destroying another civilization in order to improve his own position. This was not genocide, since he was prepared to do deals with tribes that knuckled under, and was interested in gathering slaves as well as mounds of corpses; but it *was* culturecide.

The Celts built mainly with wood. They had an oral culture, not a written one. Archaeological surveys during the latter part of the twentieth century suggest they were far more successful than once thought. They built roads, and possibly earlier than the Romans had. Celtic roads were often built across boggy land and forests, and were of oak bound together, so they have mostly vanished, except for fragments found in Ireland, Wales and Germany. Caesar would devote himself to reforming his calendar, but the Celtic calendar is argued by some to have been more accurate: the bronze find known as the Coligny Calendar is certainly sophisticated. Some Celtic historians argue that they had considerable urban centres, which we tend to call 'tribal forts' rather than 'towns' because we have swallowed Roman propaganda. Roman historians disagree, considering this an exaggeration. Some Celtic towns were round, while others in the south had long stone walls. Gaulish houses were certainly more than huts: they could have two storeys, and even courtyards. The Gauls seem to have had a system of counting populations.[16]

The Gauls mined gold and silver, produced their own worked gold ornaments, as complicated and heart-wrenchingly beautiful as any object made by Roman hands. They fought with sophisticated tactics – their chariots and large shields particularly impressed the Romans – and used iron ploughs and threshing-machines that were better than those most Roman farmers had. True, they were organized into archaic tribal groupings – but then so had the Latins been, until fairly recently. The Romans made much of their Druids' dreadful habit of burning people alive in wicker baskets to appease the gods, and their head-hunting, and these practices were regrettable; but the rebel-crucifying Romans, addicted as they were to blood-soaked arenas, were hardly in a position of high moral authority.

Some Gauls, at least, were well travelled, serving in Greek and Egyptian armies and settling in those lands, too. Their women had greater freedoms than Roman women, including complex divorce rights if they were ill-treated. Unlike Roman women, some may have risen to become leaders, and the revolt of Queen Boudicca certainly suggests this; there are also richly ornate female graves in France and Germany. Rather like native Americans, they showed a deep thirst for booze sold to them by Greeks and Romans, though this was wine rather than whisky: it appears to have been a welcome novelty for drinkers of wheat beer. Of their poems and music we know next to nothing. Unlike the Carthaginians, however, they were always likely to be defeated. What they lacked was the civic system, the sheer organizational reach, of the Roman world. In a fight between a nation and tribes, the nation will win.

Caesar's destruction of Gaulish culture involved not only the deaths in battle of more than a million people – 1.2 million according to his own bland accountancy – but also the starvation or taking into slavery of roughly the same number. This suggests that up to one in three people in Gaul disappeared, a slaughter rate that rivals the worst butchers of the twentieth century. To put it another way, Caesar had proportionately a similar effect to the Black Death, which killed between 30 per cent of people in the Middle East and anywhere between 30 and 60 per cent of Europeans. Unlike the bacterium *Yersinia pestis*, however, or the rat fleas that carried it, Caesar was mainly concerned with his own political career. The victories and his accounts of them, followed by processions of slaves and loot, built him an ever-growing popular reputation in Rome, while his personal wealth grew fatter. In effect, he had made himself warlord over a huge slab of Europe.[17] When the time came for renewing his position he struck a cynical deal with Pompey and Crassus, sharing the spoils in return for a further extension of his murderous but highly profitable rule. When he responded to the deaths of seventy Romans in an attack by German tribesmen by killing some 430,000 men, women and children, even some Romans, such as Cato, were disgusted.

By the time Caesar was ready to return, he had the money, the army and the popular reputation to permit him to do almost anything. His frightened enemies saw him as the enemy of the Senate, of the old order and indeed of the Roman republican constitution. Against that constitution he was forming an alliance of people ready to be bribed and entertained, individuals who saw him as an essential and successful new leader; and he was readying his legions. Caesar's only problem now was that, if he returned after his command was formally over, he could be prosecuted for his behaviour as consul so many years before. He could not be sure that he would not be found guilty and killed.

So he crossed the small river that separated his command from Roman territory, the Rubicon, and marched on Rome itself. If the constitution threatened him, he would destroy the constitution. Pompey, slow to grasp quite what a threat Caesar had become, declared himself a defender of the Senate. Then, along with many senators, he fled Rome to fight elsewhere. Caesar arrived in the city to claim his stolen inheritance; the people were well primed for the mass bribery that followed, and his relatives arguing his case. It was touch-and-go – paying off the legions was more difficult than expected – but enough of his enemies had fled into exile with Pompey and others to allow him to impose himself on the city. On the corpses of Celts and on the silence of empty villages Caesar had now raised as his political monument the death of Rome's once proud republican tradition.

'Caesarism' has become a bad word in politics, and for the best of reasons.

Cleopatra and Caesar: A Story of Failure

To try to see Cleopatra plainly we have to squint and shade our eyes – to squint past the splash of poetry and the flash of movies, past the Shakespeare and the Hollywood, past the lip-smacking Roman rumours and the erotic Victorian paintings. She was no vamp, no saucy baggage. She was a brilliant politician. She was a tough and wily Greek ruler trying to manipulate power as the Roman republic collapsed, not a pleasure-seeker with alluring eyeliner. Her life was a constant struggle to reverse the collapsing fortunes of one of the Mediterranean's great powers, Ptolemaic Egypt. And she was one of classical history's great losers. With her death, an empire dating back to Alexander the Great vanished, as did the rule of the pharaohs.

This is a story of civil war as much as it is a love story. After Alexander's death in Babylon in 323 BC, aged only thirty-three, his generals had fought over the many scraps that remained of his conquests. Hopes of a great Greek empire – greater than the Roman one that succeeded it – finally died with Antigonus the One-eyed, who had served

Alexander's father in their little Balkan state of Macedon, and whose fight to preserve his son's legacy ended when he was killed in battle at the age of eighty. Among the kingdoms that emerged was Egypt, ruled by Cleopatra's ancestor, Ptolemy Soter.

This Ptolemy had been a close companion and leading general of Alexander's, and had watched the great king found a new city, Alexandria, in Egypt. He moved quickly to claim control of it, and as part of his claim he managed to grab Alexander's body as it was being taken back to Greece for burial. In Alexandria, the corpse was encased in a great shrine. Ptolemy had to fight off rivals to keep it there, where it had a totemic power like the relics of later saints would have for Europeans. (Indeed, the bones of St Mark were stolen from Egypt by Venetians to give their young republic a similar legitimacy.) Ptolemy I, as he now was, buttressed Egypt by seizing what are now Israel and Lebanon, and the island of Cyprus.

The Ptolemies would rule Egypt for three hundred years – longer than the Bourbons in France or the Plantagenets in England. They were never a conventional family. Ptolemy II married his sister Arsinoë; incest and the confusing recycling of names would be features of the dynasty. In its first period, much of its energy was taken up successfully repelling rival Greek successors, particularly the Seleucids, whose capital was Syria's Antioch but whose empire stretched deep into Asia. The Ptolemies also invaded south, into modern Sudan, to acquire elephants of their own to match the Indian war elephants the Mauryas had handed over to the Seleucids. The dispatching of an ambassador to India resulted in Ashoka sending Buddhist missionaries to Alexandria in return.

The victories went on under Ptolemy III, but these Greek rulers of Egypt were a tiny elite, sitting uneasily on top of a much bigger people of traditional and alien views. Like the Normans when they conquered England, the Ptolemies did not bother to learn the local language. This was a wonderful boon for later historians, since it brought with it double- and triple-language proclamations – famously, in the shape of the Rosetta stone – which later allowed Egyptian hieroglyphics to be deciphered. It was less of a boon for the Ptolemies, who had to struggle against local revolts, led by would-be pharaohs who actually were Egyptian.

The kingdom, therefore, was a strange mix of ancient Egyptian and modern Greek. Most people held to the beliefs and cults of old Egypt, with its priests and temples, its sacred animals and complicated rites. Many hoped for a true Egyptian saviour king to reclaim the throne, rather as the Jews had hoped for a messiah. Over time, new gods were invented, part-Greek and part-Egyptian, as needed. Egyptian deities like Isis became a little Greek, while the Greeks incorporated the Egyptian gods Osiris and Horus into their pantheon. Before the advent of monotheism, a little mingling was no big problem. Still, the Ptolemaic rulers had to tread carefully: Cleopatra bought herself some much needed popular support by accompanying an auspiciously coloured sacred bull on his way to a temple. She was also the first of her dynasty to speak Egyptian as well as Greek.

Her land was still fabulously rich in resources. One of the early Roman plans for annexing Egypt proposed that it would be settled with Roman farmers and used as a new source of cheap food. As under the ancient pharaohs, most land was the property of the state, and the temples had huge estates to support them. Like the British in India, the administration of the country under the Ptolemies used the old system of scribes and village headmen to collect information and taxes. Some titles were changed from Egyptian to Greek, but essentially this was as it had always been. The Ptolemies did, however, try to introduce some Greek rigour into Egypt. They brought in a coin-based economy and a register listing all their subjects. They fixed the price of commodities and turned the temple priests into state officials, helping the dynasty to raise cash to fund its armies and fleets.

But some bad harvests and defeats, followed by the bad luck of a child-king ascending to the throne, caused them to start to lose ground to their rivals. One loss followed another. Like the smaller kingdom of Judah, which also needed allies, they looked for an ally to protect them, and plumped for that far-off but famously warlike city, Rome. This bought time for what had become a struggling dynasty – but at the inevitable price. As Rome grew stronger, pushing aside Carthaginians and Greeks, it slowly became more of a menace and less of a shield. The Roman Senate intervened more in Egyptian life. They began to regard this huge territory with its accumulated wealth, swarming populace and weak rulers as a dependant, not an ally. Ptolemaic Alexandria was being squeezed, very gently, to death.

This may have been inevitable. The kingdom of the Ptolemies had no effective way of debating policy or elevating good administrators. In practice, modern scholars now believe, the Ptolemaic state was far less efficient than its neat Greek system suggests. Farmworkers, for instance, regularly abandoned their fields as a way of threatening the tax-gatherers; corruption was rife; and many officials were untrained. By Cleopatra's time, between a seventh and a sixth of the population are thought to have been Greeks or Jews, a huge migration caused by the state's reliance on 'reliable' non-Egyptians to fight, administer and organize. Like the feeling of Anglo-Indians for Hampshire or Wales, the Greeks in Egypt retained a strong sense of their origins in Macedonia or Athens. Unlike Rome, Greek Egypt enjoyed nothing we would recognize as political participation. It remained a royal autocracy. And unlike Rome, or indeed British India, its principal city was not even officially part of its territory.

The story of Cleopatra is incomprehensible without some understanding of that unique and captivating place, Alexandria. The city itself was the dynasty's greatest achievement. Founded, of course, by Alexander, it was a city-state in its own right – inside Egypt, or 'by' Egypt but not quite part of Egypt. Again, later British parallels such as Hong Kong, or today's Singapore, come to mind. Like them, Alexandria was a melting-pot city of immigrants and merchants, which had soon swollen to half a million people, the same size as the capital of the Chinese empire of the time and, in the West, rivalled only by Rome itself. Even the Chinese had heard of its extraordinary Pharos lighthouse, one of the seven wonders of the ancient world, rising three hundred feet, and with a statue of Zeus and a blazing beacon to guide vessels into port. Alexandria boasted proper town-planning, grand buildings in the Greek style and above all its museum and library.

The word 'museum' derives from the worship of the Muses, and has caught on all over. The original museum in Alexandria was, however, less a collection of objects than an academic study centre, with living-quarters, restaurants and full-time researchers. The library, founded by the first Ptolemy and perhaps assembled by one of Aristotle's pupils, was not open to the public. It was an expression of state cultural pride, intended to contain a copy of every book written in Greek, which in classical times meant almost every book outside

China. It is supposed to have had between half a million and seven hundred thousand carefully filed papyrus rolls, organized in a 120-book catalogue. The librarians' obsession with their collection prompted them to pay a huge fee to Athens for borrowing the complete works of Aeschylus, Euripides and Sophocles so that they could be copied (rumour had it that the originals were kept and the copies returned), while ships arriving in Alexandria had to hand over any books for copying.

Thus a huge store of the literature, mathematics, philosophy and history of the ancient world, much of it now lost to us, was accumulated in Alexandria. There, the Old Testament was translated into Greek, which would be very important when Christianity began to spread. Much work was done on editing the two great poems we know as 'Homer'.

It is hardly surprising that with its patronage and its concentration of knowledge, Alexandria also became a centre of literary and scientific progress in its own right. Its poems were less famous than its inventions and practical discoveries. Euclid, who invented modern geometry, doing seminal work on prime numbers, conic sections and perspective, may have studied at Plato's Academy before he moved to Alexandria. Among his Alexandrian pupils is said to have been Archimedes, the mathematician and engineer who, legend relates, was killed by a Roman soldier after the siege of Syracuse because he would not leave a problem he was studying – 'Do not disturb my circles,' he is reported as saying. These are world-famous names today.

But what of Eratosthenes, the first man we know of to have accurately measured the circumference of the earth and produced the first reasonably accurate map of the ancient world? Or Hero, who apparently made a model steam engine? (Sadly, the Alexandrians did not have the skills in metalworking that could have led to Greek or Roman motor-cars.) More immediately useful was the mule-powered waterwheel, still in use, and Herophilos' discoveries about human anatomy, including the digestive and circulatory systems, which would not be matched until the European Enlightenment. Herophilos could apparently measure the pulse with a water clock. Others worked on quick-firing crossbows, the solar system and the use of compressed air to power engines. The Faiyum mummy portraits, which give us the most realistic and moving 'real faces' from classical days, were executed immediately after Cleopatra's time, but they most likely derive from a painting tradition which, as the extant sculptures would also suggest, reflects a fabulously skilled people. If this is decadence, the world needs more of it.

Ptolemaic Alexandria was, in short, a cauldron of creativity and invention, matching Enlightenment Scotland and the English Midlands at the beginning of the industrial revolution, or China under the Song empire, or early Muslim Spain. In only one of these cases, the first, did the inventiveness and scientific research lead to a transforming economic revolution. The reason has nothing to do with human intelligence and everything to do with the rare and 'just right' coming-together of curiosity, technologies, law, materials and motivation. By Cleopatra's time Ptolemaic Egypt was in military and economic decline. It may have been in intellectual decline too, for most of the inventions described above came early in the dynasty's history. On the other hand, it may not have been. We cannot tell where its future might have led.

What must have been clear to Cleopatra, however, was that the prize she was trying to defend against the Romans and other rivals was intellectual and cultural, not merely about territory and power. Why might we think that? There are no records of her early years. But the dynasty used scholars from the museum to tutor its children, and Cleopatra was said not only to speak eight languages but to have written books herself, including on weights and measures; she employed a philosopher as teacher for her own sons.

Her father's dependence on Rome and his naive attempt to play the competing leaders of the late republic had involved huge bribes, mostly to Pompey. This led him to borrow heavily. Taxation levied to pay for this, and the loss of Cyprus, which became a Roman colony, caused a popular revolt and he fled to Rome. His wife and eldest daughters were made rulers, but when Ptolemy was finally restored, with Roman help, he took a terrible revenge. His wife being dead by then, he had his daughter Berenice beheaded, put the Romans in charge of Egypt's revenue-gathering, and allowed a reign of terror to rip through the country. He named the Romans the guardians of his eldest surviving children, Cleopatra and her ten-year-old brother, yet another Ptolemy.

In the family tradition, the siblings were married. In the family tradition, too, they fought like sacred cats in a sack. When Ptolemy XII died the eighteen-year-old Cleopatra had no intention of sharing power with her brother, even though Egypt had no tradition of queens ruling on their own. She moved fast, won allies, declared herself 'a goddess who loves her father' – another family tradition was taking notably hypocritical titles – and had her face stamped on coins. For a while she seemed to have won, but a combination of political conservatism and famine allowed her brother and his supporters to oust her. She fled into exile, hoping to raise an army: even as a young woman, she had spunk.

At this point, luckily for her, her brother Ptolemy XIII made a terrible mistake. Pompey, whom we last met having fallen out with Caesar in the never-ending power struggle of these two military tycoons, had finally proved himself the worse commander as well as the lesser politician. Despite having much of the Roman Senate on his side and a considerably larger army, Pompey was finally defeated by Caesar (and his acolyte Mark Antony) at Pharsalus in central Greece, a battle Caesar believed to be his greatest victory. Pompey had few places left to run to, but Egypt was one. He had, after all, accepted the elder Ptolemy's bribes and been guardian to his children.

But Pompey had not realized that news of his humiliating defeat had travelled even faster than his fleet. To ingratiate himself with the victorious Caesar, the young king and his advisers decided to murder Pompey as soon as he waded ashore. He was stabbed by a former officer of his, then beheaded, while his wife and children looked on. The head was embalmed, placed in a box, and sent as a present to Caesar.

If Pompey had miscalculated, though, so had Ptolemy XIII and his advisers. They simply did not understand the rules of Rome's civil war, fought among men who respected one another and were connected by family ties. Pompey had been married to Caesar's only daughter Julia (though she had long since died). As far as Caesar was concerned, he was an honourable and powerful antagonist as well as a son-in-law, deserving of better treatment than beachside decapitation by a foreign child-king. Caesar headed for Alexandria. Ptolemy's throne was suddenly shaking again.

Much of Cleopatra's story is semi-legend, retold by Roman and Greek historians after the event. But Plutarch, in his biography of Caesar, is vivid and direct. He says that after Caesar arrived in Alexandria (with a dangerously small force) he did not think much of Ptolemy's welcome, and sent for Cleopatra. She would have been stopped in her tracks, even perhaps assassinated, if her brother's men had seen her. Over to Plutarch:

> So Cleopatra, taking only Apollodorus the Sicilian from among her friends, embarked in a little skiff and landed at the palace when it was already getting dark; and as it was impossible to escape notice otherwise, she stretched herself at full length inside a bed-sack, while Apollodorus tied the bed-sack up with a cord and carried it indoors to Caesar. It was by this device of Cleopatra's, it is said, that Caesar was first captivated, for she showed herself to be a bold coquette.

Caesar duly 'succumbed to the charm of further intercourse with her', and when brother Ptolemy arrived the next morning he discovered to his chagrin that his twenty-one-year-old sister had given Caesar something he couldn't.

The romantic legend has the soldier falling helplessly in love with the Egyptian seductress. Yet we don't know that Cleopatra had any earlier affairs, nor any later romance until her famous final one with Mark Antony. Cleopatra's kingdom was on the verge of final collapse. It contained some of the greatest treasures of human culture, but was virtually bankrupt and at the mercy of that efficient killing-machine known as Rome. Was there any future for Ptolemaic Egypt, except under the protection of the superpower of the age? Julius Caesar, with his clipped propaganda-prose, his million-plus victims, his utter cynicism about the religion of his own people, could hardly have been a less likely saviour. This was a country that had sided with his enemy, that was temptingly valuable and whose elite (those scented, Dionysus-worshipping, pleasure-loving Greeks) all true Romans had been brought up to regard as decadent and worthless.

Something had to be done. Cleopatra did it. Now, having made her bed, she lay on it. A vicious local war broke out in Alexandria, where Caesar had too few troops to control the uprising and street fighting. He came close to death. Part of the famous library was destroyed. Cleopatra stuck with him until Roman legions arrived to free them. In return she became effective ruler, and enjoyed a Nile boat cruise before bearing Caesar his only son. He, far from being infatuated to distraction, was busy studying his long-planned reform of the calendar. It was an Alexandrine who suggested to him the solution of a 365-day year, with an extra day every fourth year. Meanwhile, Cleopatra provided her own protection. In case anyone missed the point, she named the boy Caesarion.

How overwhelmed by love was the conqueror? Not entirely, perhaps. When Caesar marched off to continue the civil war against his enemies, now including Pompey's vengeful son and old political foes like Cato, he left some troops behind, just to keep an eye on Cleopatra.

She built a temple dedicated to his worship. In their different ways, both Caesar and Cleopatra were aspiring to the status of god-people. She was associating herself with the ancient cult of Isis, and her son with Horus. As Caesar piled victory upon victory, Rome capitulated and voted him ever more lavish honours. The pagan city, so brilliant by now in its literature and architecture, treated him as a man to be worshipped, and declared him dictator for a decade to come. A triumph even greater than Pompey's was declared, and another grandiose programme of rebuilding was begun as the spoils of Caesar's murderous civil wars poured in. The Roman abasement before him knew no limits. Caesar introduced some reforms, but made no attempt to stop what had become Caesar-worship. His house was decked out like a temple. His chariot was erected opposite Jupiter's. Cleopatra was there to watch both the bloodthirsty games put on in his honour and the growing Caesar cult; and to make sure that Caesar did not repudiate their child.

For her there was the chance, at least, of a radically remade politics in which these two god-people, she and Caesar, would jointly rule the known world. Caesar may have had the same dream, though he was not a dreamy type. He put her statue in the temple of his alleged goddess ancestress, Venus Genetrix. The Roman mob started to mutter that he intended to marry Cleopatra and shift his capital to decadent Alexandria. He had to keep working to manipulate and manoeuvre through the highways and byways of the politics of Rome, of course, but Caesar's attitude to religion seems always to have been cynical. It was a prop to power, a useful lever, taking many forms.

In different ways both Caesar and Cleopatra were harking back to a familiar old Hellenistic world in which successful rulers, such as Alexander, claimed divinity. Religion and worldly power had always stood together, priests and kings side by side, since the known world came into being. Caesar in triumph painted his face divine red, like Jupiter's statue, and was again declared dictator, this time for life. In fact, he turned out to have antagonized a lethal coalition of offended aristocrats and pro-republican conservatives, who would assassinate him in 44 BC, perhaps to make sure yet another planned war against the Parthians did not make him invulnerable.

The time came. After Caesar, arriving for a meeting of the Senate, had been set upon by half a dozen plotters, then stabbed to death, twenty-three wounds were found on his body. His last act had been to cover his face so that his death agony could not be seen. With perfect dramatic placing, he was left lying in blood near the statue of his great ally and then his enemy, Pompey.

Caesar had helped finish off a republic which, for all its faults, had lasted more than four hundred years. Its notions of citizenship and its rejection of monarchy had given the world something important. Caesar had not found a way of ruling this heterogeneous and sophisticated society, but his republican assassins had underestimated the popularity of a rich, god-mimicking strongman. They too were soon dead, while the association of divinity and worldly rule grew ever stronger in the Roman world. Its first true emperor, Caesar Augustus, was deified on his death by the Senate. Hardy soldier-farmers, in a tough republic, had mutated into rich imperial politicians, and now into servants to emperors.

Soon Cleopatra would be dead too, the last of the pharaohs. Caesar's death had eventually spawned another round of civil war, which by then must have seemed interminable to the citizens of Rome, but it was in fact about to end. Octavian, who had been declared Caesar's adopted son, fought Mark Antony, his beloved general, for the ultimate prize. There was little to choose between them in their view of the dying republican dream, or in their absolute appetite for power. If Octavian, later Augustus, would be declared a god, Mark Antony apparently believed he was descended from Hercules. Cleopatra struggled to avoid taking sides until she felt sure she could tell who would win, but was eventually summoned by Mark Antony to Tarsus to explain herself. In the tightest of tight spots once again, she replayed an old tune, appearing not swathed in a rug this time, but in a golden barge.

Shakespeare's devastatingly beautiful description – the best known – follows, quite closely, that of Plutarch, who elsewhere emphasizes that he knew people who knew people in Cleopatra's world. The queen, he says, sailed

> up the river Cydnus in a barge with gilded poop, its sails spread purple, its rowers urging it on with silver oars to the sound of the flute blended with pipes and lutes. She herself reclined beneath a canopy spangled with gold, adorned like Venus in a painting, while boys like Loves in paintings stood on either side and fanned her . . . Wondrous odours from countless incense-offerings diffused themselves along the river-banks.

Who would say no? Not Mark Antony, possessing divine blood himself, and at this time the seeming winner of the Roman world's struggle for supremacy.

The pair returned to winter in Egypt, allegedly for a feast of love-making and self-indulgence, during which Cleopatra usefully became pregnant again, this time with twins. She would call them after the sun and moon, Alexander-Helios or *Alexander Sun* and Cleopatra-Selene or *Cleopatra Moon*, infant gods who might also rule the world. Mark Antony then began a political reorganization of the Middle East, giving his lover back old territories, though not Judah, which remained with Herod. He next turned to destroy a new irritant for the Romans, the fast-riding, sharp-shooting interlopers on the Asian plains called Parthians, whom Caesar had also intended to attack. An Iranian tribal people who had developed their own empire and who traded with both the Mediterranean and the Han Chinese, the Parthians had developed more powerful bows and a form of mobile warfare against which the Roman legions seemed powerless.

Mark Antony was not the first great general to set off and then have to retreat, leaving behind tens of thousands of casualties. But his defeat by the Parthians weakened him at a time when his rival Octavian was on the rise in the West. It ended the dream of a new and even bigger 'Asian Roman Empire', or indeed any prospect of a neat division of the Mediterranean between the rival warlords. Few things in history happen neatly. Antony was to win a later great victory over the

Armenians, which was celebrated with Cleopatra in Alexandria. Antony was declared the living god Dionysus; and Cleopatra, 'Queen of Kings' and 'the youngest goddess'.

Octavian was quick to whip up Roman hostility to this threatening swagger: he read Antony's will to the Senate, in which he confirmed his preference for Alexandria over Rome. War was declared. Senators divided their loyalties. Legions prepared to march.

It ended with one of ancient history's least dramatic, if most important, battles. It was a sea battle, at Actium off the west coast of Greece, in 31 BC. Cleopatra commanded her own fleet in person, but when she and Mark Antony were faced with trying to break through Octavian's blockade, she panicked and led her warships into the open sea and home to Egypt. Antony was perhaps already likely to lose. His men had been weakened by malaria, his huge five-rank oared ships could not gain enough speed to ram effectively, and one of his generals had gone over to Octavian with his secret battle plans. At any rate, this last major sea battle of classical times ended almost before it had begun, when Mark Antony, seeing Cleopatra leave, followed her with just a few of his own ships.

After this, their cause was doomed. Octavian marched on Alexandria as the lovers enjoyed a final orgy. Mark Antony stabbed himself and died at Cleopatra's feet. She tried to negotiate with Octavian on her son Caesarion's behalf, but when it became clear that Octavian intended to parade her in his Roman triumph, she too decided to kill herself to avoid such ignominy. (Her sister had been paraded by Caesar at his triumph, but the mob had taken pity on her and Caesar had spared her. Later, Cleopatra had her murdered anyway; this was not the death of a romantic martyr.) Thanks to an image carried at Octavian's celebrations, showing Cleopatra killed by a cobra, the legend is that she committed suicide by placing an asp – a smaller, more credible serpent – on her breast, having had it smuggled to her in a basket of figs. Perhaps. Or maybe she simply used a reliable poison. She was not quite forty years old. Her death did not save Caesarion, who was caught and executed.

The Roman Peace

So ended not only Cleopatra's strategy vis-à-vis Mark Antony, but her original dream of uniting the worlds of Egypt, Greece and Rome in the person of an ultimate god-king. Octavian declared himself Caesar Augustus, and with Rome exhausted from civil war he was able to initiate a long spell of imperial peace. Edward Gibbon, the great English historian, famously described what followed as a happy period in human history, when the Roman Empire

> comprehended the fairest part of the earth, and the most civilised portion of mankind . . . The gentle but powerful influence of laws and manners had gradually cemented the union of the provinces. Their peaceful inhabitants enjoyed and abused the advantages of wealth and luxury. The image of a free constitution was preserved with decent reverence: the Roman Senate appeared to possess the sovereign authority

His book (published between 1776 and 1788), which opens with this analysis, was concerned with why such an era of human happiness should have ended; he called it *The Decline and Fall of the Roman Empire*.

His answer was the rise of Christianity, which we will come to. Most modern historians would shrink from blaming the followers of Jesus for the collapse of the Roman world. Another part of the answer was given in Gibbon's opening words, where he spoke of 'the *image* of a free constitution' and the Senate *appearing* to have authority. After his final victory, in 27 BC, Octavian restored the outward form of republican government, while reserving for himself the powers Julius Caesar had claimed, becoming warlord, dictator and head of the official religion. Yet he was a shrewd ruler as well as a lucky one. After some early campaigns, pushing upwards into central Europe and down towards Arabia, he more or less halted the Roman lust for expansion to concentrate on a programme of civic revival. Much of what we think of today as the glories of Rome – the grand buildings, the immaculately kept roads, the conquerors' peace and the lavish materialism of city life – derives from the peace established by Augustus. His rule was really a monarchy, with the trappings of republicanism, and it would soon harden into full-fig imperialism.

The weakness of such a system is the possibility of mad or bad kings. Rome would suffer from plenty of those, notably in Augustus' family, after he handed over power to one of his daughter's husbands, Tiberius. They included such horrors as Caligula, who was mad, and Nero, who was certainly bad. There followed 'the year of the four emperors', after which a rough tax collector's son, Vespasian, grabbed power. His son was killed, and a senator called Nerva returned to the old practice of adopting the best-seeming candidate as the emperor-designate – a good Roman compromise between politics and kingship that produced a run of strong emperors, first Trajan, of Arch and Column fame, whose conquests reached the Persian Gulf; and then Hadrian, of the famous Wall.

Life seemed so secure that the next emperor, Antoninus Pius, could rule for nearly a quarter of a century without leaving Italy, or going within hundreds of miles of the legions. He did, however, experience the problems of 'too much' in this early display-and-consumer society, when one of his circus festivals featuring giraffes, elephants, rhinoceroses, crocodiles and tigers cost so much he had to debase the currency to fund it. Then came Marcus Aurelius, another fighting emperor better known today for his fine meditations on life and duty, from the Stoic viewpoint. His son was a weak and unpopular figure who was killed young, ushering in another period of strife and uncertainty.

Yet this experiment in empire had been a considerable political achievement. As with so many later regimes, ultimate power was with the army, which was why so many Roman legions were permanently stationed far from Rome, on the new frontiers in Germany, Britain and North Africa. Roman administrators spread the rule of law through elites who might have started out as British, Gaulish, Dacian or Jewish, but who came to think of themselves as at least partly Roman.

Inside the long walls of Roman imperial power, new ways of living thrived. Something akin to a Mediterranean-wide middle class emerged, city-dwellers who as craftsmen, traders, shopkeepers, legal experts, teachers and builders accumulated enough wealth to enjoy exotic foods, public entertainments and well appointed private homes. Below them, but above the huge slave class, were the workers whose lives, though precarious, were also enlivened by the fast-food stalls of Roman towns, cheap wine and distractions including lotteries, gambling and circuses – lifestyles not so unlike those of millions of today's city-dwellers. Even if most people, herding goats or ploughing clay in distant villages, would have known little of all this, Roman imperialism brought obvious material benefits.

What it did *not* bring was a coherent system of beliefs that bound people tightly together, or that provided them with satisfying ways of explaining their fate. Had it done so, then Gibbon's bugbear, Christianity, could hardly have taken off with such vigour. Julius Caesar and Cleopatra had seen religion and politics as pretty nearly the same thing, as ways of veiling their power so as to obtain the fealty of the masses. Like the emperors who followed him, Caesar could offer booty and favours to a few, and hand-outs to appease the plebs. But he could not inspire faith. The world Caesar had been born into was already a fallen republic, cynical and greedy, which had already experienced the rule of a part-time military dictator, Sulla. Yet it still thought of itself as having a virtuous and stable republican future. Hitherto, reason, order and political compromise had been possible. After Caesar, they were not.

The Chinese Parallel

China's first emperor and his warrior state of Ch'in had engulfed the central area of that part of the world in a succession of terrible wars. Like Caesar, Zheng had had a megalomaniac vision of personal power. And paralleling Julius Caesar's fall, Zheng's death catapulted his empire into civil war, as would-be successors fought for control. China's civil war was worse even than Rome's. Yet in both cases, from the horror emerged a centralized empire with a better chance of peace. Perhaps sheer exhaustion, the bloodletting cure, was part of the explanation. Though none of the Han Chinese rulers has the world-wide fame of Augustus, their achievements were on a similar level.

They reduced military service, partially dismantled their huge armies and got rid of the most vicious of the Ch'in laws. They created the first truly meritocratic and efficient bureaucracy that we know about, based on competitive examinations. Indeed, this was one of their great inventions, ahead of anything in the Roman world. So too were the Han troops' semi-mechanized crossbows, fired by disciplined ranks moving forward then loading, like later European musket-based armies. Had it ever come to a fight between the Roman legions and the Han armies, the Chinese would surely have won. Like the Romans, the Han recruited tribes from the borders of their empire into their own armies – thus 'using barbarians to fight barbarians' – and as with the Romans, this eventually proved a problem.

Because Han China's buildings were mostly of carved and painted wood, and its art was painted on silk, very little of its physical glory survives – much less than of Rome's. In general its writings are more clerkish than the most gossipy and scandalous of the writers of the great Roman imperial age, but it was a highly sophisticated society.

The historian Ian Morris has devised ingenious scales of human energy consumption to chart the rise and fall of societies, and on that basis the Roman and Han empires did similarly well, their people using up seven or eight times as much energy as their ice-age ancestors. The Han suffered from plagues passed along trade routes between themselves and the Mediterranean (so, at just the same time, did the Roman world, presumably catching Chinese bugs). They suffered droughts and barbarian invasions too; but because of Zheng's centralization, the Chinese made progress. They had the peace and space to build new canals and roads, to spread fresh ideas about irrigation, to develop weights and measures, laws and money, that were all widely understood. With the Han empire they emerged into a world that would have been unimaginable during the long slaughter of the 'warring states period'.

In a similar way, the grandeur and relative prosperity of the Roman Empire at its height remains awesome, and it might have been hoped that a perpetual new Western order had been established. From southern Scotland to North Africa and from Portugal to Syria, a network of superbly engineered and maintained roads allowed Roman citizens to travel faster overland than any previous people – and as fast as any to come, until the arrival of the railways. Aqueducts, sewers, bathhouses and hypocaust heating literally underpinned the Pax Romana. Adminstrators could be trusted, even if they were never as effective as their Chinese rivals. The legions became foreign legions, as outlying tribes were brought in and tamed.

Many others would follow Edward Gibbon in calling this the greatest period of civilized peace the world had known to that point, despite the disappearance of anything like democracy, the slave revolts and the distant clash of war on the tribal margins. Yet as Gibbon's work tried to explain, this disciplined world would fragment and collapse. Many theories have been offered as to why. One that was *not* discussed in the eighteenth century can be added: climate change. Now, our better knowledge of Chinese history of the time makes the argument for it more persuasive. The world grew considerably colder between AD 200 and 500, after the so-called Roman warm period that had spread farming north and east through Europe and increased food production.

This climatic shift not only hit farmers and produced periodic famines, it forced the tribes of central Asia to move, or else die. They were highly mobile, and so they moved, shoving earlier migrants west until they broke into the empire. As noted, migration and trade spread unfamiliar viruses, and appalling plagues broke out across the Roman world, attacking every generation after the 180s. At the worst times, in the 250s, thousands were dying in Rome every day.[18] Hunger, disease and the challenge of armed and desperate migrants were factors that Roman Europe struggled to cope with. Han China suffered from the same perils – poor harvests, plagues and the consequent pressure of nomad tribes, in their case the Xiongnu. And although the Han had nothing like the disruptive impact of Christian zealots to cope with, they faced huge peasant rebellions and began to lose ground faster than did the Roman emperors.

Their empire would break apart, and a period of semi-anarchy and ferocious disputes between rival claimants for the Mandate of Heaven would ensue. Both the Western and the Chinese empires suffered severe inflation and a shrinkage of agriculture, and both suffered invasion and revolt. In China, the Han state broke into three kingdoms, those of the Wei, the Wu and the Shu Han. But this was only the beginning: the north collapsed, and small, unstable invader states replaced Chinese rule. The Jin dynasty, still claiming the Mandate of Heaven, retreated to the south and clung on, rather as the Byzantines clung on to Roman ways. The original promise of Zheng, the First Emperor, of an unchanging central state, which had been pursued with skill by the Han, now remained only a dream, an aspiration, as was the Holy Roman Empire. But unlike in the West, it was a dream Chinese rulers would re-establish.

Climate, living standards, economic development and politics cannot ultimately be disentangled. Measurements of historic pollution (and therefore of human activity) in ice cores and lake sediments show a sharp decline after AD 200, as both the Mediterranean and the Chinese civilizations shrivelled. Ian Morris writes that in the Roman world 'bones from cattle, pigs and sheep become smaller and scarcer after 200, suggesting declining standards of living, and by the 220s wealthy city-dwellers were putting up fewer grand buildings and inscriptions'.[19]

In the West, the decline of the old gods of classical times led Roman citizens to turn to Egyptian cults, beliefs going back to Zoroaster in Persia and extreme versions of Greek philosophies, mixed with new faiths arriving from the Middle East. Augustan stability, all those roads and ports, spread these belief systems faster. Some seem to have mingled ancient beliefs with Buddhist and Hindu thinking – the 'New Age' faiths of two millennia ago. Public culture had become cold and brittle, empty of deep human meaning. In China, there had been uprisings by Daoist religious groups, such as the 'Five Pecks of Rice' movement, which declared that a deep corruption had infected the court. It called for equal distribution of land, and proclaimed the need for personal moral reformation.

That too may sound familiar. The urge to find a personal meaning produced an urge for confrontation and martyrdom in China, as well as the West. But ideas in the West and East were different enough to take them in different directions. One idea, above all others, was to shake the Roman world, leaving the Chinese world untouched.

We return to monotheism. Cleopatra, on her way home from visiting Antony, had stopped en route to meet a local king. He later boasted that she had tried it on with him. The king was Herod, whose rule would become notorious around the world, thanks to the story of a thinker about to be born in Judah.

The Agitator Triumphant

Not even great conquerors can always foresee the results of their actions. One of the Greek cities taken under Roman rule by Pompey was the bustling Asian settlement called Tarsus, now in Turkey. This was where Antony had summoned Cleopatra and had been awed by her golden barge. Its people had been granted Roman citizenship; among them was a thriving industry of tent-makers, including Greek-speaking Jews, and to one of these families, of the tribe of Benjamin, a boy called Saul was born. Saul would become St Paul, declared by many theologians to be the real founder of Christianity as a world religion, and the transmitter of that religion to people all around the western Mediterranean, Jew and Gentile both.

Few have had as much influence on mankind as the Tarsus tent-maker, who was alive at the same time as Christ but who never met him. Paul had been, as he freely admits in one of his famous epistles, an outstandingly pious Jew, frequently in Jerusalem to study the Law of Moses. He tells the Galatians, who had just founded a church, how much damage he had done to early Christians and 'how I stood out among other Jews of my generation, and how enthusiastic I was for the traditions of my ancestors'. He may have been present for the first Christian martyrdom, of Stephen, stoned to death for declaring Jesus to have been the Messiah, a few years after the Crucifixion.

A man with more than a touch of fanaticism, Paul was a member of the populist Pharisee sect, and had done his best to round up and crush this small but irritating local heresy. Partly because he was a Roman citizen, free to move around the imperial world, and a Greek-speaker who could easily converse with its educated people, Paul would do more than anyone else to turn the little local problem into a global faith, a global movement, one that would help bring an end to the old Roman world and transform the West.

His letters to the various Christian communities that he helped found are the earliest Christian writings to have survived; the seven epistles generally considered certainly to be by him date from no more than twenty years after Christ's death. They tell us about Paul himself only in asides; much of our biographical knowledge comes from his friend Luke in The Acts of the Apostles, compiled perhaps fifty years later. Paul and Luke were both admirers of Rome, and writing in the aftermath of the tragic Jewish revolt against its rule. Though they were Jews, the thrust of their work was to take what had been Jesus's message to fellow Jews and pass it out into the rest of the world – to Greeks, Romans, Egyptians and anyone else who would listen, a light to lighten the Gentiles. One biblical scholar argues that without Paul, the Nazarenes – as the early Christians were called – would have remained 'a Jewish sect which sought only to remain within Judaism and did not intend to found a new religion'.[20]

Famously, Paul was travelling to Damascus from Jerusalem to root out Nazarenes when 'there came a light from heaven all round him. He fell to the ground and then he heard a voice saying, "Saul. Saul, Why are you persecuting me?" He asked who the voice was: "I am Jesus . . ."'[21] Blinded, he was led into the city to await further instructions. Albeit reluctantly, a member of the Nazarene church in Damascus, Ananias, restored his sight and baptized him into the new faith. Paul says that then, chosen by God, he hurried off to Arabia to consider his new life. Luke, on the other hand, says that he stayed in Damascus and learned about Christianity from the believers there.

It has often been said that Saul suffered some kind of epileptic fit or hallucination, and that his moral extremism simply flipped sides from Judaism to Christ. Believers, of course, would say that Christ did appear to him. But the tent-maker and former persecutor was shaken enough to change his life and his name – to the Roman, Paul – and to spend twelve to fifteen years criss-crossing the Middle East in a furious eruption of energy that would only end when he was executed in Rome during one of Nero's crackdowns on religious troublemakers. By his own account, he was at various times whipped nearly to death, stoned, shipwrecked; starving, thirsty, chilled to the bone; in danger from pagans and Jews, brigands and wild animals, 'so-called brothers' and natural perils. He had some mysterious but apparently disgusting illness and was frequently imprisoned.

Paul tried all the time to keep friendly connections with his old Jewish faith, and engaged in confrontations with Jews as he attempted to explain why Christ's message superseded their beliefs. He baptized uncircumcised Greeks and Romans, including a centurion. The single, mobile and class-blind God of the Jews, whose worship had already been spread, although thinly, throughout the classical world, would now have another attribute: he would become everybody's God.

The timing was almost perfect. Two years after the fires in Rome and Paul's death, reputedly by beheading (since he was a Roman citizen, he was spared crucifixion), the Jewish revolt against Rome began, with riots in Caesarea. It had been sparked by religious arguments and protests over taxes, but as the legions converged on the mutinous cities it became a full-scale rebellion that would be put down with exemplary Roman savagery. After a long and heroic siege Jerusalem fell to the legions in the year 70, and its inhabitants were either killed or sold as slaves. Herod's famed Second Temple was destroyed, and the Jews were to remain scattered until modern times. Had the Nazarenes been at that point still a Jewish sect based in Jerusalem, their religion would probably have been snuffed out and never heard of again, except by religious scholars. The faction of Christ-worship that was exclusively Jewish, originally led by Jesus's brother James, was indeed scattered in the ruins of the revolt, and soon disappeared from history.

Gentile 'Christianity' (the word appeared first in Antioch, used by Latin-speakers as an insult) was smuggled into the wider Mediterranean just in time. Its infancy was that of a rebel child of Judaism, but as Paul's writings show again and again, it was forced to define itself against traditional Jewish thought. Though he ended up on a Roman executioner's block, Paul admired the Roman state. He deliberately chose important Roman centres like Corinth, Antioch and Philippi to spread his message, and may well have hoped to win substantial support in Rome itself when sent there as a prisoner. Christians would be persecuted and exiled for a long time to come, but the possibility of an eventual deal between secular Roman power and the new religion could be glimpsed from early on. Unlike the rebellious Jewish leaders calling themselves Zealots, or the leaders of the revolt of 66–71, Jesus had shunned politics and spoke of giving Caesar what was Caesar's. Paul, a good Roman citizen, agreed.

Because Paul's reshaping of the Nazarene message was so influential, he has been blamed for much that followed – for Christian sucking-up to worldly power, for misogyny, fear of sex, intolerance. He was capable of great humane poetry: 'Love is always patient and kind; it is never jealous. Love is never boastful or conceited; it is never rude or selfish; it does not take offence, and is not resentful.' He was trying to get his message across to traditional communities at a time of huge turbulence, almost hysteria. Like his fellow believers, he thought the Messiah would return in glory, very soon, almost certainly in his own lifetime, to save believers and condemn the rest. Having faith, and concentrating hard on it at the expense of almost everything else, was an urgent necessity that could not be put off.

In the same letter to the Corinthians that contains his hymn to quiet love, he also warns Christians that 'our time is growing short. Those who have wives should live as though they had none . . . those who are enjoying life should live as though they had nothing to laugh about; those whose life is buying things should live as though they had nothing of their own . . . I say this because the world as we know it is passing away.' His words show him to be a control freak, a man with a temper and an authoritarian streak, and convinced that there is little time to waste; yet he can also be kindly, self-critical and thoughtful. He can sound like a twentieth-century revolutionary, darting between cells and factions, trying to hold them to the 'correct' ideological line and deploying a mixture of threat and flattery – fire and brimstone with a dash of charismatic charm. It is hardly unknown for the convert to become the most zealous hardliner, or the revolutionary leader to show a weakness for self-dramatization.

After Paul's death in Rome, and probably after the execution of St Peter there too – who is said to have requested upside-down crucifixion so that his death could not be compared to that of Jesus – a Christian community began to grow in the imperial capital. It was a time of great religious confusion. Judaism was reorganizing itself and different versions of Christianity were competing around the classical world. The scholar Diarmaid MacCulloch has pointed out how odd it is that Rome, the centre of anti-Christian persecution, became the great Christian city, rather than Baghdad. Indeed, Christianity could easily have become an eastern rather than a western religion. Over the next centuries Christian communities saw robust growth in Egypt, in Syrian and Judean cities such as Antioch, Gaza and Caesarea, in Anatolia in what is now Turkey, and in Rome itself, where the Christians were largely migrants. But Christianity did not take root easily in North Africa or Greece: despite the help Paul gave to the Ephesians, Corinthians and Thessalonians, it is possible that all three Christian communities failed to survive.[22] The well rooted Jewish communities and the common language of Greek had a lot to with the spread of the new religion; so too did the unifying effect of persecution. This seems a paradox, but many movements have been strengthened in their early stages by repression. From European Jews to Protestants to Islamists, the experience of repression, as the etymology of the word suggests, has meant a pressing-back, but also a pressing-together; it has intensified belonging and commitment.

Lines and Spirals: The Other Quarter

These stories have referred to, very roughly, three-quarters of the world's human population at any one time – the quarter in the Roman world, the quarter ruled by the Chinese Han, and the quarter living in India under the Guptas and their successors. What of the rest?

In the Americas, civilizations were emerging that were several thousand years behind Eurasia in their development, but impressive in their own right. The city of Teotihuacán, in Mexico, possessed an array of pyramids and temples that the Egyptians would have admired; and the great Mayan civilization of Yucatán and Guatemala produced sophisticated writing and a superb calendar system based on the stars, which divided the world into very long periods of time. Its nearest equivalents had been produced in Mesopotamia, more than two millennia earlier.

But lacking wheels and many of the animals of Eurasia, the Mesoamericans would, in general, pass on few fresh ideas to world culture. They had talented builders and sculptors, but their religions were mainly darker, more blood-soaked and more pessimistic than those of the cultures across the Atlantic. When the Spanish eventually arrived, they were horrified by the Aztec cult of mass human sacrifice, so extensive that it had forged a new war-making style, based on capturing enemies in order for them to have their hearts torn out on Aztec altars. There was no moral or spiritual equivalent to a Kongzi or a Jesus native to the American cultures – an absence that is worth pondering on.

One theory has already been discussed: the different distribution of animals and plants, which made agriculture slower and left Mesoamerican cultures far behind their European rivals. Another, often cited, difference is in the geographical shape of the two human-colonized landmasses. Eurasia, curling around the globe from east to west, has fewer climatic differences than the north-to-south stretch of America, which would allow for easier transmission of cultures. Yet these reasons are clearly not enough on their own. The Mesopotamians and Egyptians certainly had a dark side to their imaginations, but grew nothing like the pessimistic, gore-splattered religions to the west of the Atlantic. And even if the American cultures were one to two millennia 'behind' the European and Chinese, by the 1400s you might have expected something to match the Greek golden age, or the Jewish religious revolution. But there is nothing remotely similar.

Recently, there has been a surge of interest in two other differences, which go a long way to explain the gap. One is geological, rather than merely geographical: the world's tectonic plates are responsible for much greater instability in the Americas, including earthquakes and volcanoes. This may well have produced a darker human imagination, as people struggled to deal with a greater number of natural disasters (including the climatic cycles of the Pacific). These may have seemed inexplicable, other than as the massively punitive swipes of angry gods requiring to be placated. All through mankind's story human sacrifice has been the ultimate gift to a truly scary deity. As recently and trenchantly argued by the Cambridge historian Peter Watson, this may have combined with the greater proportion of mind-altering or psychoactive drugs in the Americas to create a bleak, ecstatic theatre of pain and death, rather than religions in the European, or Indian, sense.[23]

The greatest contribution the American cultures would bring to the world would be mainly through the new plants they domesticated, the corn, tomatoes, cacao, potatoes and squash which would be so eagerly adopted by others, radically changing populations, as well as tastes, in Europe and Africa. The mostly lost culture of the pre-Roman Celts is in some ways more typical of the people living at the edges of the advanced empires. Whether in south Indian forests, Africa, the Russian steppe or the plains of northern America, the little evidence we have points to tribal groups retaining ancient shaman- and nature-centred beliefs, combined with some sophisticated farming technologies and, in some areas, creating small urban centres.

Some of the lost kingdoms may well have been more interesting and surprising than the civilizations that had the luck to build in stone, to write, and thus be remembered. Hundreds of languages, ideas, systems of art and belief, have gone for ever. In a few areas, archaeologists are still turning up remarkable evidence of forgotten peoples. We could choose to look more closely at any of many examples of peoples at the edge of history during the age of the Romans and the Han, but one of the most intriguing was a people living on the Pacific coast of South America – the Nazca.

As the Chinese were struggling with their anti-barbarian walls and the Romans were enduring a spate of incompetent emperors, the Nazca were building a holy city of pyramids and plazas called Cahuachi. Today much of it looks simply like a series of small hills in the desert, a wilderness of grit and stone. There is an excavated central pyramid that has been unpleasantly 'restored' with strips of concrete and plaster. But as you tramp around the area, you notice small holes everywhere, then human bones, scraps of beautifully woven clothing and splinters of brick-red pottery. These are the leavings of grave-robbers. Lying exposed to the air, they date back to roughly the time when the Romans left Britain. Not far away are graves still containing huddled Nazcan figures, who look as if they died a week or two ago.

The deserts on the coastal plains of Peru are among the driest in the world. Hardly anything rots. But among the corpses and the skulls have been found some that look hardly human at all. Priests the world over have favoured odd-looking hats or headdresses to distinguish themselves from the rest. Nazca priests went one step further. From childhood their skulls were tightly wrapped between boards to push the bones upwards, producing elongated craniums – the original egg-heads. These skulls are eerie enough, looking more like space aliens or the originals of Munch's painting of a scream. In life, they must have inspired awe, if not downright terror.[24]

Like other early cultures, the Nazca were created by the special advantages provided by an unusual landscape. For though the desert is very dry, there are river valleys, and underground water is surprisingly close to the surface. Even today the transition between bone-dry, lunar desert and lush green is as dramatic as can be found anywhere on earth. It is reminiscent of the Nile valley, and of parts of southern Iraq; and indeed, like the ancient Egyptians and Mesopotamians, the Nazca were a river civilization. Like them, the Nazca had to learn to control the river flow and use it with maximum efficiency for irrigation. In their case the key was not canals, as in Egypt, or fields with sluice-gates and raised borders as in Mesopotamia, but underground water channels and filtration galleries, connected to the surface by beautifully made spiralling holes known now as *ojos*, or 'eyes'. These allowed people to keep the underground channels clean and the water flowing, for drinking, bathing, washing and farming.

As in the river cultures elsewhere, this system depended on large numbers of people working together under direction, and on the development of special stoneworking skills. As in Egypt, this helped shift a farming culture towards a more centralized and hierarchical one. As in Egypt, this led to towns and the rule of a priestly caste – who even practised mummification and built pyramids. So it is hard not to see the Nazca as later, littler, American Egyptians. And for a long time for them, life was good. In these lush crinkles in the desert modern farmers grow cotton, avocados, asparagus and much else for the world market. The Nazca people lived off maize, sweet potatoes, peanuts, beans, manioc, llama and guinea-pig meat, and squash.

They also fished at sea with nets and inflatable skin boats and used llamas as pack animals. The Nazca produced beautiful cotton and wool textiles and kept themselves working hard with the help of coca leaves, the chewing stimulant still popular in South America today. For wilder times, they used hallucinogenic drugs from a cactus plant. They made sophisticated pottery pan-pipes and trumpets based on a common frequency and standardized pitch, and, for personal decoration or trade, they particularly valued the shell of a thorny oyster, coloured a startling red. Their clothing included tunics, mantles, turbans and sandals. And according to the pottery record, these people survived and thrived for some seven hundred years – about the same time as elapsed between the rise of the Roman republic in its early encounters with Carthage and the death of the Western Empire, when Rome fell to the Vandals. They may not have developed (or needed) the great engineering skills of the Romans, but their system of aqueducts and *ojos* was a considerable achievement; some of it still works today.

In some ways they were an attractive culture. Their pottery was sensational, beautifully coloured and increasingly complex as their society developed. Some idea of the fantastical gods and creatures of their pantheon can be grasped by modern scholars' names for them – Spotted Cat, Mythical Harvester, Horrible Bird and Fan-headed Mythical Killer Whale. (Pottery figures suggest Nazca women had killer whales tattooed around their genitals – a formidable warning sign, presumably.) Their famous desert drawings show a high level of artistic skill. Some of their mummified bodies, found in local museums, are quite poignant, almost calling out to the visitor.

In other ways, however, they seem fearsome. Like the Celts and many other ancient people, the Nazca practised human sacrifice. Clearly, they regarded severed human heads as a source of power. Victims were decapitated, then their skulls were drilled through and roped together, cactus thorns often being stuck through the lips. The heads still abound in the area, with their braided hair and features hardly touched by time. Recent research by American university teams suggests that these heads were of the Nazca themselves, and therefore unlikely to be war trophies. The head-severing habit is fiercely debated by scholars, who are mostly stabbing in the dark. Towards the end of the Nazca period it seems to have become a kind of mania, until around a tenth of people, according to recent estimates, were decapitated. Why?

Other changes came, around the same time, in the mysterious drawings and lines that were created by removing red stones lying on the desert floor, revealing the brighter, whiter soil below. Earlier, Nazca drawings had been patterned and sometimes representational – such as birds, monkeys and fish, a hummingbird and a mysterious goggle-eyed humanoid. Later the lines evolved into long, straight strips pointing for miles in different directions, so like a modern airport that some have suggested they must have been created by aliens to guide UFOs. When you study them from nearby hilltops, they look as if they have been drawn with an engineer's metal ruler and pencil; and they cover an area of over 190 square miles. What were they for? How were they drawn? They can best be viewed from the air, which is why they were not much noticed until the 1930s. It was proposed earlier that the Nazca had some kind of smoke-filled air balloon, but this theory has now crashed to earth.

It has now been shown that the lines and images could have been created by scaling up drawings, using coloured twine and sticks, which seems far likelier.[25] The academic consensus today is that the lines probably had something to do with the presence of water under ground, those all-important aquifers, and the religious rituals practised to preserve them. But this is a consensus based on some heroic assumptions. What does seem to be the case is that later in their story the Nazca both increased the number of head sacrifices and drew longer and longer lines.

Something was changing their world.

It all coincides with big shifts in the weather. The year AD 535–6 was known around the world as the 'year without sunshine', when crops failed and the skies stayed dark. Probably a volcano or a meteor impact was the reason, but the effect was devastating, and it was followed by decades of heavy rain. In 500 there had been an El Niño weather event which dramatically worsened the coastal Pacific climate and also caused flooding and crop failure. Periodically, there are natural catastrophes – the earth's plates grinding, and causing earthquakes and tsunamis; the eruption of super-volcanoes or meteorite hits – for which no society has found a remedy. About how to deal with them, history has little advice.

Yet the El Niño, the events of 535 and the long rains, destructive as they were, ought not to have destroyed the Nazca. Even though there was a subsequent drought, the rains would have helped refill the all-important underground water supplies. Research by a Cambridge University team now suggests that the reason the Nazca failed was at least partly because they had cut down forests of huarango trees.[26] These had not only provided shade, fuel and building materials but had also underpinned the flood plain with their huge root systems – the largest by far in the Americas. Fixing nitrogen and helping fertilize the soil, these trees have been described as the 'ecological keystone species' for the area. Once the trees were cut down, perhaps to free up more land for cotton and maize, these unusual lush valleys were left to the mercy of the floods the Pacific brought – floods so bad, they washed away not only villages and fields but many centuries of painstaking human cultural development.

The Nazca religion with its stuffed human heads, its pointy-skulled priests, its hummingbirds, monkeys and arrow-straight lines, had told its people nothing useful about their deadly mistake. They were martyrs to their limited understanding – a far cry from the comfortable notion that 'indigenous people' always understand nature best. They had the wrong information and they made the wrong choices; instead of busying themselves with cutting off more heads they should have been worrying about cutting down their trees. They can stand for many other earlier civilizations which, far from living in harmony with nature, destroyed their own environment, and never made it.

The Triumph of the Christians

Christians had picked up the idea of martyrdom from Jewish thinking, but they extended it much further. There are numerous accounts of early Christians actively seeking death, urging uncertain Roman governors to insist on the penalty, which in the Roman Empire meant a painful and humiliating exit. The images of Christians being torn apart by wild beasts for the amusement of crowds are not simply products of the overheated imaginations of later painters or film-makers; early lives of the saints contain extremely detailed accounts of such horrible deaths, as well as roastings, flayings, disembowellings and burnings. Roman law was juster than many, but its punishments were designed to be public and to serve as deterrents: there is no reason to doubt that Christian martyrs experienced such terrible ends, alongside criminals and military renegades.

A rare record of the actual words of an early martyr comes in a 'passion' found in Greek and Latin, purporting to be the account of Perpetua, a twenty-two-year-old woman from a well-off family in Carthage who was killed in 203, with her pregnant slave Felicitas. They had been arrested for taking instruction in the new religion, and refused to recant, even though Perpetua was suckling her baby boy when they were imprisoned, alongside several male converts. The ancient text has a ring of truth, perhaps either having been written by Perpetua herself or dictated to one of the free Christians allowed to visit her. It was preserved in Greek monasteries throughout classical times and is therefore probably the earliest first-hand account of a Christian woman.

Dragged to the dungeon, Perpetua says, 'I was very much afraid, because I had never felt such darkness. O terrible day! O the fierce heat of the shock of the soldiery, because of the crowds! I was very unusually distressed by my anxiety for my infant.' Her father repeatedly tried to persuade her to recant, but failed. Her husband seems to have deserted her earlier on. She has visions in prison, of paradise and of a golden ladder, and of her brother who had died of cancer of the face but who was now, in the vision, healed.[27] She dreamed of fighting with a serpent and with an enraged Egyptian, whom she associated with the Devil. Her maid Felicitas so wants to be martyred that she prays that her baby be delivered before the execution date, because pregnant women were not killed.

Their martyrdom was delayed until the emperor's birthday and her prayer was answered. Felicitas's baby was born early and taken for adoption. Still with milk dripping from her breasts, the maid and her lady Perpetua were stripped, whipped, wrapped in nets and led into the arena. The male martyrs were attacked by panthers, bears and wild boar, the women by an enraged cow, before being killed by gladiators. Perpetua, says an anonymous observer who watched the slaughter, insisted on feeling the pain of a sword-thrust and then, helping the nervous young swordsman whose job it was to finish her off, 'she herself placed the wavering right hand of the gladiator to her throat' and so died. Among those watching, we must suppose, would have been her distraught pagan father and other relatives, as well as Christian supporters.

Martyrs seem to have volunteered for death and supported themselves as they made their way through the Roman legal system, gaining fame in the Christian communities while trusting that their inspirational stories would be passed around by the leaders later known as bishops. The Roman persecutions happened in spasms, with long intervals between them, and with variations of severity in different parts of the empire. In some areas, the people themselves so hated the Christians that they demanded their execution. There is some evidence from Gaul, for instance, that the Christians were mainly immigrants, craftsmen who had come to find work and were resented, and that this contributed to their deaths. In other places, they were largely left alone. When an empire-wide persecution was ordered, they might lose their jobs, or have their holy texts burned, but no worse.

The persecutions did not work. Christian communities continued to grow, though it has been estimated that by the year 300 only around one in ten people had converted. Most hung on to the old religions, but this made the Christian challenge no easier. Christians did not fit easily into the Roman world because they were determined not to. Their refusal to pay even formal homage to the cult of emperors and old Roman beliefs made it almost impossible for them to serve in the army, or take any state posts. They refused to attend the public baths, an unattractive decision for those around them. They kept knowledge

of their practices, notably the Eucharist, secret, which spread lurid
rumours about what they really got up to. They confronted Jews with
their message, sometimes in synagogues, provoking fights and riots.
So it is hardly surprising that they became occasional scapegoats for a
fearful urban fire or a protest.

Christianity offered a moral law but it also offered personal salvation, a one-to-one relationship with a universal god available to anyone
who wanted it, free of ethnic, racial, tribal or class barriers. Since the
ancient world was familiar with the notion of sacrifice, both human
and animal, Christ's self-sacrifice on the horrific execution rack of the
Cross was not so outlandish. In a world plagued by maniac and squabbling emperors and occasional famines, and with a class divide
between the plutocrats and the masses, the idea of an imminent cataclysm, and the end of time, may have been almost appealing. The era
when the Christians began to win over large numbers of converts
despite persecution was precisely the time of strife and hunger already
referred to, when new walls were being hurriedly raised in Roman
cities, often to protect the rich, and farmland was being abandoned.

The emperors likely to persecute Christians were not mere sadists,
but those who wanted to revive the old glories of the Augustinian age.
They were trying to turn back the water clock. For men like Diocletian, possibly the son of a slave himself, the profusion of cults and
unpatriotic, dissident religions was a prime example of the disorder
that had to be stemmed. He was a notorious persecutor whose name
was particularly damned by later Christian writers, but he was also a
great political reformer: it was he who, in 285, divided the rule of
Rome between two senior emperors (of which he was one), each
called Augustus, and two junior ones, Caesars, and he greatly
improved the tax-collecting system. He pushed back invasions and did
indeed restore law and order. But it was out of his persecutions and
the breakdown of his new imperial regime that the oddest character in
Christianity's early story emerges – the emperor who was proclaimed
not in Rome, but at York.

Constantine the Great is remembered as the emperor who converted
to Christianity and who, by protecting it and advancing it, turned it
into the state religion of the Roman Empire. From that turning-point
emerges the Christian Church as an institution of worldly power,

based in the old imperial capital, its popes joining hands with later would-be 'holy emperors'. The Christians changed Rome, and Rome changed Christianity; and the man at the centre of the deal was Constantine. For centuries the Church lauded his name: the greatest of leaders, a paragon of virtue and, in the Eastern Church at least, a saint. Some Christians today, however, revile him as the man who by making their faith a buttress to imperial power, politicized it and drained it of its revolutionary and redemptive message.

What would Perpetua have thought?

Constantine was undoubtedly a very strange kind of saint – indeed, a strange kind of Christian. He seized power on the back of his army, quartered at York, after his soldier-father Constantius suddenly died in 306. Declaring himself emperor of that part of Diocletian's quartet covering Britain, Gaul and Spain, he built his court at Trier on the Moselle River in what is now Germany before invading Italy and finally seizing Rome from a rival, one Maxentius, after a bloody battle. He later told the propagandist Church writer Eusebius that he defeated Maxentius after seeing a vision of the Cross in the sky, accompanied by the words 'By this sign shall ye conquer', and ordering his troops to place a sign of Christ – a Greek monogram – on their shields and flags. It was the first time that the Christ of peace and of a heavenly kingdom had associated himself with the outcome of a battle. And there are good reasons to be suspicious of the story. Constantine had previously associated himself with Apollo, the 'unconquered sun god' (Sol Invictus), whom his troops followed; his victory arch in Rome refers to the sun god, rather than to Christ.

Constantine with his co-emperor in the East, Licinius, went on to declare, at Milan in 313, an Edict of Toleration, ending persecutions; but even this did not refer to Christianity specifically, just to 'cults' in general. He seems to have believed in the general notion of one god, but to have kept his options open. When he finally turned on Licinius and the Eastern Empire in 324–5, and defeated him in battle – when again Constantine used Christian symbols – he indulged in an orgy of political killing. He murdered Licinius and his son, who was only ten and was also his own nephew. After dark rumours of an affair between his own illegitimate son Crispus – who had risen to the rank of consul – and his wife Fausta, both of them died too. There are arguments about precisely what happened, but all the original sources agree that

Crispus died by poison and Fausta by being suffocated or boiled to death in her bath.

One historian argues that, in fact, Crispus killed himself, and that Fausta, pregnant by him, was trying to abort her unborn child in the scalding water;[28] others insist these were political executions, cold for Crispus, hot for Fausta, ordered by Constantine. Either way, they are events more evocative of life in the Ch'in court than of the behaviour of a model Christian ruler. And when, in 330, Constantine fixed up a new capital for the reunited empire, away from Rome, he chose a small pagan city in Greece called Byzantium – and decorated it with statues of pagan gods.

Yet Constantine clearly valued the Church, and in particular the bishops, who throughout the eastern Mediterranean had become authority figures. They could be used to impose order in towns where the imperial bureaucracy was almost absent. And it was a ferocious and violent dispute inside the Church itself about the nature of Christ, setting bishops against bishops – the so-called Arian Heresy – that put Constantine at the centre of Church affairs. To resolve the argument and put an end to the disruption, in 325 he summoned the rival camps to a meeting, the Council of Nicaea, and enforced a compromise which resulted in the famous Nicene creed ('We believe in one God . . . And in one Lord Jesus Christ, the Son of God . . . And in the Holy Spirit . . .').

As emperor, Constantine saw himself as a bringer of order – if need be, to the Christian Church too, which should be as united and single as the empire. He began a huge programme of building, including a church on the presumed burial site of St Peter in Rome, and over the cave where Jesus was supposed to have been buried in Jerusalem. In return Eusebius, his biographer, told Constantine to his face in 336 that he had a semblance of 'heavenly sovereignty', and that his government conformed to the 'Divine original' and 'the monarchy of God'. Constantine had received from Jesus not a message of humility and love, but of power; he was 'the only Conqueror among the Emperors of all time to remain Irresistible and Unconquered'.[29]

It sounds remarkably like the kind of tribute that the pagan Julius Caesar, or Augustus, would have graciously accepted. Had Perpetua and the hundreds of others died for this? Perhaps it was the deal that Constantine always aimed for. The 'unconquered sun god', or Jesus

Christ? It hardly mattered, so long as imperial authority and the unity of the empire were achieved. Constantine may have felt that he had solved the conundrum presented to the West by emperors and martyrs, by Christ and Paul and Caesar and Pompey; that he had achieved a final resolution of the competing tugs of spiritual yearning and earthly power.

Of course, he had not. Even as the numbers of Christians soared, now that it was safe, even advantageous, to convert, and as churches were being raised all around the Mediterranean, the Church itself was starting to behave like an earthly power. It would divide, fight within itself, require kings and emperors to go to battle, and persecute its enemies with Roman ferocity. And after all that, it would face an even greater peril – a new religion, also built on the stories of the Jews, which came thundering out of the desert at the point of a sword.

Religious Blitzkrieg

The image is remembered throughout the world, and it is unforgettable; tens of thousands of wild Bedouin warriors on their camels, erupting out of the empty wastes of the Arabian desert, scimitars flashing as they fall upon the unsuspecting prosperous towns of late Roman and Persian times. The victories thunder like trumpet blasts as proud cities collapse – Cairo, Alexandria, Jerusalem, Ctesiphon, Acre. Had the armies of Islam not failed to take Constantinople, despite its tremendous fortress walls, in 717, all Europe might have been studded with mosques and minarets rather than cathedrals and bell-towers. As it was, Muslim influence would break the Persians, change China; and, by cutting off Western Christianity from the more mystical Christian traditions of Asia, dramatically change the West too. That all this could be attributed to a middle-aged trader on the edge of the desert, hearing divine words in a cave, does indeed seem little short of miraculous.

Yet much about the story is inaccurate. To start with, old Arabia, whence Islam erupted, was emphatically not an empty wasteland. In prehistoric times, from around 8000 to 4000 BC, it had been lush and fertile, if the bones found there are anything to go by – rhinoceros, giraffe, wild pigs and crocodile – and a happy hunting ground for

African tribes who left behind rock art. The dry period created the vast deserts of the north, the 'empty quarter' reaching into Syria, but around the coasts, particularly in the south, were fertile areas where complex civilizations had evolved long before Islamic times. In the east, in the area we know today as the Gulf states and Oman, then the country of Dilmun, good ports linked Mesopotamia and the Indus valley civilization with the Mediterranean, trading wool, copper and cereals.

Felix (happy, or fortunate) Arabia was known in the ancient world as a remarkably prosperous area, which later fell under the sway of the Assyrian, Babylonian and Persian empires. Alexander the Great was keen on seizing these Arab lands, lured by stories of their wealth and in particular the hugely valuable myrrh, frankincense and cinnamon they offered; he died too soon to benefit from them. In the south of the huge peninsula there had been a series of powerful kingdoms, some tracing their origins back to Noah's son, Shem. Of these, thanks to the Bible, the best-known is Saba (as in the Queen of Sheba), itself conquered by the kingdom of Himyar. These realms may have been marginal to a Mediterranean-fixated view of history, but they were rich and long-lived. The Sabaeans lasted for around a thousand years; a Roman military force sent by Augustus could not defeat them. They had had to develop sophisticated systems of water management including large underground aqueducts, some of which still work. In addition, they had created a great dam, the Marib dam, to trap monsoon waters and allow the irrigation of their fields.

For centuries it worked well until under the Himyar kingdom, about 570, it collapsed, causing a mass migration from the south of the Arabian peninsula to the north. Before that, the Sabaeans' trade in spices and oils was famous, and their agriculture was described as a 'garden paradise'. The biblical tale of the Queen of Sheba (this, pre-Islam, was an area with a tradition of female rulers) travelling to Solomon with a great caravan of gold, spices and precious stones may be a folk memory of the great wealth of the area. Sheba's biblical queen is supposed to have reigned around 950 BC, but hard information is negligible. There is, however, a vast 'temple of the moon god'. Mahram Bilqis in present-day Yemen is 'The Sacred Precinct of Bilqis', an alternative name for the Queen of Sheba, and is some 12,000 square yards in size. Though only partially excavated, it has revealed a tantalizing fragment of fresco, an alabaster head of a woman and some beautiful limestone carvings, as well as monumental pillars and meticulous stonework. It was still being visited by pilgrims until around AD 600.

These powerful but fallen civilizations were crucial to the Arabia in which Muhammad grew up. The migrations caused by lack of water had produced seething, densely populated oasis towns, as well as the trading and fishing towns on the coastline where he would live and begin to preach. The urban, trading and farming Arabs of the coasts and the south were very different from the desert tribes who managed to survive by grazing camels, goats and sheep further north. Their use of camels (evolved from the smaller camelids, which had migrated from prehistoric America into Asia) allowed them to move from oasis to oasis in ways no other people could. Both the Romans, in their Eastern Empire phase, and the Persians had found themselves forced to try to hem in the Arab raiders with buffer states, composed of Christian Arabs, who helped keep the peace. The Bedouin of the true desert were famous for their tight tribal ties, essential to their survival. Some of their war poetry bears a passing resemblance to passages of Homer.

There is little direct information about the life of Muhammad from his own time. Little seems to have been written down, and the scholar Tom Holland has argued recently that much was probably censored. Some two centuries on, collections of stories about him and sayings attributed to him were circulating – the Hadiths – but virtually nothing survives from the early 600s when the great events took place. Holland says:

> Of written evidence composed before 800, the only traces we possess are either the barest shreds of shreds, or else the delusory shimmering of mirages . . . The voices of the Arab warriors who dismembered the ancient empires of Persia and Rome, and of their sons, and of their sons in turn – let alone of their daughters and granddaughters – have all been silenced, utterly and for ever. Neither letters nor speeches nor journals . . .[30]

There are fragmentary references to this Arab leader in Christian writing from around the Prophet's time, and few doubt he really existed; but we must tread carefully.

So far as is known, therefore, in 622, after falling out with elders of his own tribe, the Quraysh, at Mecca, who objected to his claim to having received new messages from a *single* god, Muhammad led his followers on a trek north to the friendlier oasis town of Yathrib, later renamed Medina. There he continued to recite words he said God had dictated to him, initially while he was sitting alone in a cave; when written down, this speech direct from Allah would become the Koran. In Medina, apparently, Muhammad also began to deliver rules by which his followers should live. These included rules about the role of women, about honesty in trade (Muhammad had been a merchant), the correct attitude to war-making, and much else. It seems he retained much of traditional Arab tribal custom, perhaps in order to win over as many people as possible; if so, it was this very flexibility that produced the array of Muslim domestic and dress rules that are so controversial now. From Medina, at this stage friendly to Jews and Christians, those other people of the Book, Muhammad began to expand his influence up and down the caravan routes of the Arab world.

One of the secrets of the explosive spread of Islam is that, for the first time, Muhammad and his circle were able to yoke together the wealthier Arabs of the coastal areas and the Bedouin. There seems to have been a population explosion at around this time, and once the raiding, feuding Arab tribes of the desert had accepted the authority of the Prophet, there was little alternative but to send them out, towards the unbelievers. Across much of central Asia, where the speed of Islam's advance seemed almost miraculous, the Arab armies – usefully for them – were entering sparsely populated territory. Any other course but expansion would perhaps have led to breakdown and civil war in Arabia itself.[31] But this was not a case of a purely marginal, nomadic people suddenly transformed and then turning their attention to the civilized world; the people of Arabia had considered themselves cultured and important long before Islam.

The second misconception is that the Arabs fell upon a peaceable and united Christian world. The first waves of fighting merely spread Islam across the Arab world, and the most dramatic early victim was the Sassanid kingdom of Persia. The Sassanids, who had coexisted with the Romans for four hundred years, whose empire harboured Zoroastrians as well as various sects of Christians and Jews and who had been in close touch with China and India, had represented a golden age in Persian culture. But their endless wars with the Byzan-tines had exhausted them, and by the time the Arabs attacked in 632 they were poorly led by a boy-king and in severe economic decline. Syria and the 'Holy Land' were only just recovering from plague and war. They had suffered a catastrophic epidemic which had depopu-lated towns and villages and left fields untilled. The Byzantine Roman emperor Heraclius had just achieved a massive victory over the Sas-sanids, driving them out of Palestine and Syria after twenty years and restoring the 'true cross' to Jerusalem. He had then set about trying to impose Byzantine Christian orthodoxy on an area that had had strong rival traditions.

So when the armies of Islam arrived, they attacked lands still struggling to recover from disease and war, and with nothing of the self-confidence of the Christian Roman world or of the Persian one of just a few decades earlier. And though the armies of the Prophet would use camels, their horses were more important in battle; they fought with conventional straight swords, often imported from India, not with scimitars.

Does this explain the shocking military success of early Islam? No: these are only some useful corrections to the most simplistic version of what happened. Even then, it remains an astonishing story. Within a single generation after Muhammad's death, the Arabs had destroyed the Sassanid empire; taken the whole of the North African coast including the ancient civilization of Egypt; seized Palestine, Syria and what is now Turkey, and come almost to the gates of Constantinople itself. The dates tell the story better than words can: in 637, Syria is gone; in 638, Jerusalem falls; in 639, Mesopotamia and in 642 Egypt; at the same time raids and then invasions assault Cyprus and Carthage. In the east, the Arabs take Kabul in 664 and northern India around 710. By then they have crossed into Spain, ended the Christian Visi-gothic kingdom there. In 732 they touch the limit of the possible, reaching into central France, before they turn back. After this, the Mediterranean regions, the Middle East and Europe can never be united as the Romans had hoped. It can never be a Western version of China, because it will always be divided by religion.

This would, no doubt, have disappointed the Prophet, who believed his message was for all people of all races and previous faiths. Few ideas have had as much physical impact. The simple, austere creed of submission by all to One God and to the teachings of his Prophet drove these astonishing conquests. It was not a question of superior military technology or new tactics, nor access to special wealth or manpower. The 'hordes' of Muslim conquerors were modest in size compared with the established armies of the late classical age. Here was monotheism stripped of its Jewish particularism and its Christian humility, armed from the first against unbelievers. It gave invasion and expansion a religious meaning. It was an empire, this time, of individual believers, not the imposition of the beliefs of an emperor. It was a mass movement, not a landmass, directed by religious leaders and generals but driven by a new sense of belonging.

Hazy as he may seem to historians, Muhammad must have been a great leader. As with most religious pioneers, it is now hard to envisage how he was originally seen, but he is one of the best examples of the difference a single man can make. The change he imposed on the world easily outstrips the impact of Alexander or Julius Caesar – it is rivalled so far only by Zheng, China's First Emperor, and by St Paul. As a religious figure, Jesus has claimed more support – perhaps around a third of the world's believers today as against a fifth to a quarter who are Muslim. At the time when the people of Asia and North Africa were being converted to Islam, Christian missionaries were pushing north into today's Germany, France and Britain. But as we have seen, Christianity was the work of many leaders. And Jesus was preaching to Jews, not Rome or the West.

Like Christianity, Islam would suffer splits and would be compromised by having to deal with the earthly problems of power and politics. It would take on different shades in different conquered areas; like Christianity, it would have its eras of intellectual advance and of sleepy decay. It began proudly declaring itself open to all people equally, and indeed the first voice to call Muslims to prayer was that of a black former slave, Bilal. Yet soon Islam would be a slave-owning and slave-trading society too. Proclaiming itself simple and united, it would split into warring factions, at first centring on who had the better claim to inherit leadership. The majority Sunni Muslims supported Abu Bakr, one of Muhammad's close companions and his wife's father; while Shias supported the claim of Ali, his cousin and son-in-law. Even today, the two traditions of Islam are not particularly fond of each other, as we know.

The change Islam brought to the world provides a fitting conclusion to this section. From the rise of Rome and the unification of the Chinese states, the great conundrum had been about how earthly power and new, mass religions would be able to coexist. The imperial powers, better organized than ever before, and over larger areas, had nothing to offer beyond force and security. All suffered the humdrum erosions caused by leadership crises, changes in climate, economic downturns and lost battles. No leaders, not even Caesar or Augustus, had been able to transform themselves into the focus for a successful religious movement. For most of the masses, loyalty and adherence were a practical, not an emotional, matter.

Instead, the new ethical and spiritual ideas that gave people something they felt they needed had all come from the margins: from the quarrelsome provincial Jews, the northern Indian idealists who followed the Buddha, the Christians at the edges of the Roman empire, the Arab people of the southern desert. Some rulers simply tried to repress any inconvenient religious movement; this became a habit in China, as we have seen. Others, such as Constantine, tried for full-scale takeover.

But only Islam determined that earthly power and religious belief ought to become, in effect, the same thing. The sword was strong – an old thought. The word was strong – a newer thought. But for a century of dramatic collapse and change, the word, armed with the sword, proved unstoppable.

Part Four

BEYOND THE MUDDY
MELTING POT

*From AD 700 to 1480: The Great Age of Islam,
the Nomads Who Built Empires, and Europe's Awakening*

In the year 800, the world was led by two great cultures, the Chinese and the Muslim. From then until the Renaissance, a span of some six centuries, Europe was a comparative backwater. There, tribal groups who had migrated from Asia, and scattered people once ruled by the Romans, slowly came together, first into feudal kingdoms ruled by families, then into nations with fixed territories and (usually) languages. They believed there had been a time of Paradise, of natural abundance, but that the sin of the original people had plunged the world into a 'fallen', miserable condition, to be ended when Christ returned and when judgement was passed on human behaviour. After this, time would cease. Meanwhile, though they were excellent builders in stone and increasingly interesting thinkers, their civilization lagged behind others.

To today's educated European this may seem a grotesque idea. After all, these centuries include the rise of the papacy, the creation of Charlemagne's empire of now misty magnificence, the Crusades, and the emergence of many nations still clearly visible in today's world. This is the time of the unification and rise of England, France and Spain, not to mention the hammering-out of smaller nations such as Scotland and Portugal. It marks the beginnings of modern Russia and Poland. These are also the centuries of the first great Gothic cathedrals and of Christian monasticism at its peak; of the flowering of the chivalric tradition and the rule of the armoured knights. Given what we know about the explosion of European influence soon to take place worldwide, Europe's 'Middle Ages' and even what used to be called 'the Dark Ages' are essential groundwork.

For most of this period, however, Europe would have seemed backward to Islamic scholars or Chinese administrators. Compared with the sophisticated science and architecture of the Muslim world, which embraced today's Spain and parts of southern France while

stretching deep into central Asia, the tribes of Europe were comparatively unlettered and deeply divided. They had no city to rival Baghdad
or Cairo, never mind the greater-still Chinese metropolises of
Chang'an and Kaifeng. The Europeans had no properly maintained
system of roads or canals; little security in towns or for rural travellers;
a paucity of libraries; few places where the law was fair and sure; and
boundaries more fought-over than accepted.

Their understanding of the calendar and their ability to measure
time were rudimentary, and they produced few luxuries of their own.
The greatest cities of the Mediterranean world were not properly
European, in the later sense. Constantinople was only on the edge of
the Latin European consciousness and was becoming increasingly
'eastern' during this period, while Córdoba, its closest rival in size for
centuries, was the centre of Islamic culture until the 'Christian reconquest'. Paris, London and Rome did not compete. Only towards the
end of the period, when the Italian city-states of Florence, Venice,
Milan and Siena reach their most vigorous period, does European culture seriously start to rival that of the great Muslim cities or Tang and
Song China.

Part of the explanation is natural: problems of plague and climate.
A population of around fifty-five million people in the later Roman
Empire (about AD 400) is thought to have been halved by the 'plague
of Justinian', which arrived in 541 and was followed by waves of
bubonic death until the early 700s. This, combined with shrinking
agriculture, would have made a quick European recovery after classical
Roman times hard, in any case.

Justinian had been a visionary emperor, based in the Eastern
Roman capital of Constantinople, whose generals Belisarius and
Narses won back North Africa and Italy and briefly re-established a
single empire. His wife, Theodora, was a brilliantly scandalous figure,
allegedly a former circus performer and prostitute with as insatiable an
appetite for men as Justinian had for land: she is said to have bitterly
complained that God had given her only three orifices. At the Church
of San Vitale in Ravenna, their famous mosaic portraits set them
among ranked officials, glaring down, knowing and hardened. Justinian's was an astonishing achievement, but he had nothing like the
military manpower, nor the taxable resources, to truly rebuild the
glory that was Rome. Europe was simply too etiolated to recreate the

legions, the law, the roads and the aqueducts she had once relied on. Justinian could fight barbarian kings, but he could not fight plague and famine.

Across the Mediterranean, the Roman east and the Greek west were in any case diverging. Justinian worked hard to reconnect the broken links between the Roman popes and the patriarchs of the Orthodox Church, but the arguments were too bitter. It had taken centuries for the Roman Catholic leaders – originally local leaders of the sect – who clung on in the decaying former imperial capital, to emerge as 'popes' claiming authority over all Christians. They were able to do so because they enjoyed the prestige conferred on them by the fact that Rome contained the presumed graves of St Peter, referred to by Christ as the 'rock' on which the universal Church would stand, and of St Paul. Rome itself, for all the sad disintegration of the imperial palaces, and the sheep and cattle roaming in the Forum, had a unique history, and the early Christian community in the city was a comparatively large one. Though there were weak and even wicked early popes, there were also some gigantic figures, easily able to dispute with their Byzantine rivals and to engage in the violent power-politics necessary for survival in war-torn Italy.

Occasionally in the centuries that followed it seemed that a Roman pope allied with a powerful temporal leader might reunite the West. Had the huge Ostrogothic warrior-king Theodoric, who ruled Italy from 493 to 526, not been a heretic, it might have happened even before Justinian's wars. Because of the complex settlements of migrant people gradually rewriting the political map of Europe, popes mostly had to ally themselves with Frankish or Germanic warlords. The most obvious example is that of Charlemagne, the Frankish king who briefly created an empire stretching from northern Spain and the French Atlantic coast to western Germany, Switzerland and Bavaria. His father, Pepin, had protected the papacy already, and he gave the pope the territories that would remain – anachronistically, and thus infuriating Italian nationalists – well into the nineteenth century as the Papal States.[1]

Charlemagne came to Rome in 800 when, as it happened, an empress, Irene, was ruling in Byzantium. The Romans and the Franks had infinite male contempt for female rule, and therefore regarded the post of Roman Emperor as vacant. Pope Leo III accordingly crowned a possibly surprised Charlemagne as Holy Roman Emperor. But after Charlemagne's death, the Frankish empire soon broke up, and the papacy was reminded of its own weakness when Muslim Arabs invaded Italy from North Africa, reaching and sacking Rome itself in 846. Across Europe, from the Scottish midlands to northern Spain, Roman walls crumbled and Roman roads were abandoned for ancient pedestrian tracks and pack-animal pathways.

In the east these were not Dark Ages, however, and certainly not in China. At roughly the same time as Justinian's generals were trying to tie the Roman Mediterranean back together, the Sui emperor Wendi was successfully overthrowing the decadent Chen dynasty in the south, using massive fleets of five-deck floating fortresses. After the invasions of the northern nomads, Chinese reunification under a single efficient government allowed the rich rice-growing economy of the south to integrate once more with the more advanced north.

Above all, the 1,550-mile network of canals, rivers and locks known as the Grand Canal bound Chinese civilization together more tightly than Europeans could have envisaged. The canal system was more important in Chinese history than the Great Wall. Completed between 605 and 611, it joined the Yangtze delta to the busy northern heartlands around the city that is now called Beijing. It carried grain, salt, vegetables and luxury goods. Traders, armies and tax-collectors moved up and down it; great cities mushroomed along it. One historian likens it to 'the first transcontinental railroads in North America. It made China's economic integration feasible.'[2] Another says that it 'functioned like a man-made Mediterranean Sea, changing Eastern geography by finally giving China the kind of waterway ancient Rome had enjoyed. Cheap southern rice fed a northern urban explosion.'[3]

The great Muslim empires seem to have escaped the toll of plague more successfully than did the tightly packed Christian cities, and they were able, through most of this period, to use a transport system hardly less effective than the Grand Canal. Their camel and horse caravans made their way, knotted together, along great desert trading routes between fortresses such as Bokhara and Samarkand, producing a military system that united Persians, Arabs, North Africans, Indians and the tribes at the edges of China in a single faith. Cities such as

Baghdad and Cairo sat on key river systems. Sailors using dhows and new rigs of sail, as well as new instruments, spread both Islam and world trade much further than most Europeans could dream of.

'European' was not a word they would have recognized, anyway. The Europeans were part of 'Christendom', and for much of this period easterners were struggling to work out what that might mean. Europe was a geographically hemmed-in space, cut off from much of the Mediterranean by the Muslims and constantly pressed upon by the tribal migrations from the north and east – caught between salt water and the Saracens. (The word 'Saracen', though it became perjorative, derives from 'Sarah', Abraham's wife, from whom Muhammed was supposed to have descended.)

In practical terms, Christendom did not exist as a single entity. It was fought over by the rival Greek and Latin Churches. Yet inside Europe it was a crucial idea because it constantly ate away at alternative bonds of ethnic, geographical or tribal identity. The drive to convert the heathen, and bring them into the Christian family, created alliances between old Roman families and Frankish warlords; sent Irish monks to Scotland and England, and English missionaries to Germany; and allowed former tribal leaders from the forests and swamps of the east to join a bigger idea. Rival European peoples, speaking bastardized variants of sub-Latin strengthened with thickets of words from Celtic and Germanic tongues, would compete, and their rulers would fight, but at some level (unless they were heretics, pagans or Jews) they felt they were united under Christ.

And this had a certain urgency. Overshadowing any folk memory of the lost classical world was an expectation that Christ's second coming would not be long delayed. Paul's warning had stuck. After food and shelter, the most pressing imperative of human life was to prepare for this event, which would mark the end of human history; building earthly civilizations came a distant second.

Europeans' greatest monuments were religious ones, the monasteries and the cathedrals built by generations who were patiently awaiting their end times. The biggest potential political project, the 'Holy Roman Empire', never lived up to its nostalgic billing, either under the Franks or later under Germanic rulers. It was a long Gothic fantasy finally terminated by Napoleon. At a more practical level, however, there was a dogged knotting-together of European religious life.

Greek may have been mostly lost, but clerical vulgate Latin was everywhere. In the early 500s St Benedict brought the monastic tradition
from the Greek east into Italy, and his 'Rule of Benedict', obliging
monks to be chaste, poor and obey their abbot, spread a rare message
of peace and hope, drawing many young men from noble families
away from careers of plunder and war.

The secrets of Europe's later success can be found in three things,
which at the time seemed far from good news.

First, there were the successive waves of tribal migration. These
were caused by hunger on the huge grasslands of central Asia, where
small changes in human numbers could not be sustained by the herding culture; and by similar pressures in agriculturally meagre areas
such as Scandinavia. One tribal group would push the next further
west, and so on, until they found themselves crossing the Danube or
the Rhine and entering the old Roman world. In 376 the first rumbles
of this movement began as Ostrogoths arrived in what are today
Serbia and Bulgaria. They were followed by another tribe, the Alans,
and then by the Visigoths, who settled in central France before heading for Spain. In 406 more tribes poured into Gaul over the Rhine,
which had frozen. The Huns arrived in 441. The Vandals reached Spain
and North Africa in short order, and later sacked Rome.

Broadly, the Germanic tribes have been classed as, first, the Scandinavians; second, the North Sea peoples including Jutes, Angles and
Saxons who migrated to England, Scotland, parts of France and the
Low Countries; and third, the Lombards, Burgundians, Vandals, Goths
and others who poured through France and into Spain and Italy.[4] And
behind the Germans would come the next migrant invaders, the Slavs.

This brought with it the destruction of towns and churches, constant raiding and much misery for the settled farmers of the
post-Roman continent. It created new kingdoms, carved out by warlords, who would themselves soon disappear, a fast-moving pattern of
parasitic and squatter realms. The retreat of Roman rule had left
behind a landscape of walled towns, cultivated fields and large estates
that were still there when the marauders arrived. Neither the wine-
growing landowners of southern France, nor the city fathers of
Toulouse or Milan, nor the villa estates in the river valleys had any
idea their world was ending. Outside Britain, the invaders met with
little organized resistance as they grabbed for themselves landscapes

more fertile and forgiving than any they had seen before. Farmers battened down the hatches.

The sensible thing in dangerous times was to get protection. The migrations led to many peasants becoming voluntary serfs, accepting the control of a local armoured landowner, or knight, in return for a certain number of days' work on his land and a payment in grain or livestock. This new departure resulted in the feudal system, which would in turn produce new political identities. For many people, perhaps most, these identities were more clearly defined by landowners than by kings – such dynasties as the Percys, Sforzas, Douglases and Brandenburgs. The Germanic tribal migrants added hugely to Europe's already varied linguistic and cultural mix, since Celts, Latins, Iberians, Jews and Greeks remained in large numbers.

In essence, the next centuries of European history were the story of how these invaders were digested and accommodated. But how could this story be any kind of good news?

The answer is that competition works. It may have taken a few centuries of chopping and slashing, but the settlement and agglomeration of tribes produced a Europe of vigorously competing cultures, which would in turn become the dynastic and territorial states of later times. Lombards, Normans, eastern Franks and western Franks would evolve into Italians, French and Germans. The long-lasting conflict between Britons and Nordic invaders would eventually forge England and Scotland; and the Norman Conquest of 1066 would produce one of the strangest and most successful bastard nations of the region. Instead of living under a single emperor and a single theological authority, Europe would advance through competition and conflict, a buzzingly restless and sharp-elbowed culture. Dealing with centuries of inward migration made this change in direction inevitable.

The second well disguised blessing has already been mentioned: the fact that the Northern Europeans were cut off from the rest of the world. The mighty Islamic caliphates, stretching from north of the Pyrenees through North Africa to the Middle East and central Asia, acted as a religious and military cordon, and one that few Christians would venture into. Inventions from other parts of the world, from algebra to paper, gunpowder to porcelain, would take a long time to reach Europe. The loss of power in what had been the Roman ocean, the Mediterranean, meant 'Christendom' had to look north. This forced the development of former Roman provinces which would become France, Burgundy and Britain, now brought fully into the Christian world.

Across the European plains, with their thick soils of clay and loam, forests were torn down and heavy ploughs prepared for a landscape of barley and wheat. Popes turned to Frankish and Germanic rulers for protection because they had nowhere else to go; these Franks, Lombards and Goths were tamed in turn by southern influences. Towns in the north of Italy grew in importance. Genoa and Venice made themselves independent trading republics. The independent cities and guilds of Germany and the Netherlands developed technologies and skills of their own. The trading cities of the Hanseatic League formed a close network. The English wool trade spread across the continent. The English, Irish and Scots, who had been marginal to Europe since the retreat of the Roman legions, rejoined the mainstream as missionaries, fighters and traders. Dynastic kingdoms such as those of Burgundy, the Habsburgs, the Jagiellons in Poland and the Plantagenets created super-sized feudal realms following little geographical logic.

There was one significant exception to this relative isolation: the great Islamic civilization of al-Andalus in today's Spain and Portugal, which we shall come to next. But pressed up against the Muslim world, whether in the north Spanish kingdoms of Aragón, Castile and León, or those of the Balkans such as Serbia and Wallachia, Christians defined themselves collectively as a fighting, front-line culture. The most famous example of this, the four main Crusades that aimed to recapture Jerusalem and the 'Holy Land' of Palestine from the Muslim Arabs, began as an attempt by the papacy to rally Europeans and bolster the authority of Rome. Though some Middle Eastern land was captured and held for generations, and though the call to war against the Heathen inspired mass devotion, their brutality and the resulting death-toll rendered the Crusades a failure. They poisoned the atmosphere fatally and semi-permanently between the two biggest Abrahamic faiths, and conclusively demonstrated that Constantine's embracing of Jesus of Nazareth had corrupted his message: the Cross of suffering, pity and forgiveness emblazoned on the pennants of invading knights made no sense.

The Crusades brought their military ethos back to the heart of

Europe itself. The Teutonic knights carved out their own state in Prussia and Livonia, evolving from a pilgrim-warrior brotherhood dedicated to overthrowing the pagan people of the north to become a mini-empire of their own. Savage religious wars against Cathar heretics in the French Languedoc were made more brutal by the participation of battle-hardened knights-militant. Nor should we forget those who, with increasing unease, shared the continent and its islands without sharing its main linguistic roots or its political ideas at all – people such as the Irish Celts and followers of Scandinavian shamans. In Scotland a novel idea of kingship – kingship not of territory but of people voluntarily acknowledging a leader – emerged. Parts of Germany were ruled not by conventional feudal overlords but by bishops. Not only was Europe teeming with competing peoples – it was left with a far greater variety of political structures than anywhere else on the planet. Like a chemical reaction, the elements were mixed and compressed.

Eventually, even the division of Christendom into those two halves – Latin-Roman-papal in the west and Greek-Byzantine-Orthodox in the east – proved a strength, not a weakness. Byzantium, whose story comes later, stood for centuries against attackers both from the Germanic and Slavic north-west and the Tatar and Muslim east. After Justinian, it was unable to exert real influence in Italy. That left Christian Rome free to develop its own theology and continent-wide system of bishoprics, monasteries and alliances on the rubble of the Roman world. In its religious art and culture, as well as its feudal system of landholding, and its free cities, Western Europe went its own way. When eventually city-states and local rulers were sufficiently wealthy and secure to turn again to the lost learning and techniques of the classical world – learning preserved by both Islam and Byzantium – they would exploit it with a vigour all their own.

At the time, nobody could have foreseen this. While Saxons were chanting their war poems, the sophisticated Japanese Murasaki Shikibu was writing her epic novel, *The Tale of Genji*. When warlords such as Offa on the Welsh-British border decided to mint coins, he made rough and awkward copies of Muslim dinars. And later, when the first big Sicilian, German and French cathedrals were rising, in other parts of the world equally extraordinary stonework was being crafted by Toltecs and Maya. Before Europeans had seen paper, the Chinese were using it as currency. In the 1100s, while Englishmen were hacking each other to death in the conflict over the rise of the Plantagenets, and Germans and Italians were wading in gore during their wars of succession, Angkor Wat – which would be the world's largest religious building – was being created, first as a Hindu, later a Buddhist, centre by the Khmer civilization of Cambodia. Europe seemed, in short, nowhere particularly exciting.

Islam's Golden Age

The year 711 is not much remembered today, but the Muslim invasion of Spain shook Christendom and terrified rulers far to the north. For the best part of seven centuries, castles, mosques and cities ruled by Islamic rulers challenged the idea that 'Europe' and 'Christian' meant the same thing. The Visigothic kingdom of Spain, which quickly collapsed after Arab armies made the short crossing to Gibraltar, was a not an untypical model of post-Roman Europe. Its Germanic rulers, though frequently feuding amongst themselves and holding to an anti-Catholic version of Christianity, nevertheless managed to run a relatively well organized society, farming and living simply in the grand ruins of the Roman age and speaking a decayed version of Latin. The Visigoths were not so different from the Carolingians in France, the Saxons in England or the Ostrogoths in Italy. Yet within nine years of the first probing Arab advance, the Visigoths had lost almost all of the peninsula. The Arab armies were halted only at Poitiers in France, and then merely because their lines were already so far extended.

These 'Arabs' advancing through Spain were in fact a vivid mix of peoples. Some were from today's Arabia and Yemen, others were Syrians, and others still were Berber people of North Africa, who had only recently converted to Islam. Frightened Europeans called them 'Moors', even as they learned from them. (English Morris dancing, for instance, is really 'Moorish' dancing, originating with African Muslims.) What the watching Europeans did not know was that this Moorish eruption into Spain had only happened because of a cataclysmic event at the other end of the Mediterranean.

In 750 the Umayyad dynasty, whose empire extended for five

thousand miles and who had been the undisputed successors of the Prophet, were toppled, in a bloody revolt, by the Abbasids. The caliphate, that core expression of political Islam, had become hugely important. Many Arabs resented the former Byzantine and Persian officials who seemed to have taken over, and the Syrians who formed a phalanx around the ruler. So they rose up. The new Abbasid caliphate would survive for hundreds of years, moving the capital of the Muslim world from Damascus inland to a new great city, Baghdad – with momentous consequences, since this in itself made Islam more eastern. But the new caliphate would not include al-Andalus. The grandson of one of the defeated Umayyad caliphs escaped to Spain, where he and his successors would rule an independent state, the Mild West of the Muslim world.

Unlike the Baghdad-centred caliphate, this one was wedged, provocatively, deep into what had been Christian territory. Al-Andalus would alter Christendom irrevocably, mainly because of the remarkable intellectual and trading achievements of its Baghdad rival, with whom it kept closely in touch. The Abbasids saw themselves as inheritors of the learning of the ancient Greeks, but also of the Persians and the Hindu Indians. Part of their claim against the Christians of Byzantium was that they had forgotten, or had shunned, the great classical heritage. They were right; and in Western Christendom too there had been a deliberate turning-away from the knowledge of the classical age in favour of a fervent, God-soaked, symbol-drenched view of the world.

This made the Franks, Germans, English and others quite spiritual, but not very well informed about the material world around them. They could not accurately tell the time of day, and struggled along with a defective, slipping calendar. Their maths was primary-school primitive and their geography little better. The shape of the world outside Europe and the Near East was a mystery; but it was probably flat, and if you travelled too far, you would fall off. The Abbasids, by contrast, prided themselves on their curiosity and hard science, in a world that they mapped and whose circumference they measured. This was an almost perfect mirror image of the Mediterranean of the 1700s, by which time the Christians had fallen in love with science and technology and the Muslim world had become conservatively God-soaked and hostile to intellectual enquiry.

This must have something to do with territorial ambition. Just as the later saltwater Europeans were touching other continents and labouring to understand the Indian and Chinese civilizations, so the Abbasids stretched on land for some four thousand miles, from the Atlantic to the edges of India. Europeans needed new instruments to find their way across the oceans; Abbasid Muslims needed them to chart their way across deserts and mountain ranges, as well as across the sea. Europeans found new landscapes, plants and animals, which tested (and later overthrew) their ideas about how the world was made. Much earlier, Muslim thinkers had been confronted by ideas from many different sources, in an empire brimming with Jews, Greeks, Zoroastrian Persians and unorthodox Christians, and had struggled to make those ideas cohere.

They had nothing but contempt for the Christian Europeans. The geographer al-Masudi explained that because of their cold, dark climate 'their bodies are large; their natures gross, their manners harsh, their understandings dull, and their tongues heavy'.[5] Mathematics is the most obvious example of these Muslim thinkers' success. In 762 Caliph al-Mansur had laid out his new capital at Baghdad in a perfect circle, his gracious compliment to the Greek mathematician Euclid. Al-Mansur was a ruler with the self-confidence to encourage a revival of Persian learning, and to reach out to help the Chinese, sending thousands of mercenaries to help in their local wars. At Baghdad, the House of Wisdom, which was something like a combined research centre, library and college, fizzed with arguments about law, astrology, medicine, geography and many other subjects. There, mathematics was particularly prized.

Why was this? One underlying reason was to do with astrology, the reading of the stars, which Muslims, like Christians, believed could foretell the future, but which required 'the utmost precision in instrumentation and timekeeping, preparing star tables accurate not just to minutes of degrees but to seconds and beyond'.[6] Another was that with accurate measurements they could produce proper maps of their vast domains. Furthermore, by understanding the rotation and curvature of the earth they could calculate Mecca's exact direction when praying. Add to these mystical, imperial and religious concerns a love of numbers and patterns for their own sake, and the Abbasid fascination with maths makes perfect sense.

Trying to establish accurate figures for the circumference of the Earth, Caliph al-Mamun sent his surveyors into the desert to take readings of the sun's altitude, dividing the men into two groups marching in opposite directions, measuring as they went, until their sun calculations showed they had travelled one degree on the meridian. In the 820s Europeans would not have understood what he was doing, never mind why – any more than South American natives understood sextants and telescopes when Captain Cook arrived. But Muslim mathematicians were not working in isolation. Some years before, in 771, a group of Hindu scholars had arrived at Baghdad from India with scientific texts, including an explanation of the sine function, which, developed by Islamic thinkers, would produce modern algebra.

The greatest mathematician of the age, Muhammad al-Khwarizmi, who was probably an Uzbek, perfected mathematical tables to show the exact positions of the sun, moon and five major planets and thus to show the precise time. Indian number systems, today's 'Arabic numerals', the use of zero and decimal fractions, were all crucial to al-Khwarizmi's new world. His work on algebra, called *The Book of Restoring and Balancing*, uses his tables for proofs in the older science of geometry. His particular specialities included quadratic equations, essential to modern computer science.

Add to al-Khwarizmi's maths the comprehensive translation and study of Greek and Sanskrit sources, discoveries in astronomy, medicine, the natural sciences, engineering, water management and map-making, and you start to get a sense of how far ahead the Abbasid empire was. This was young Islam, open-eyed Islam, out and exploring new worlds, devout but fiercely practical and intellectually ambitious. Its perspective included sub-Saharan Africa, the coasts of India and the Red Sea, and even Russia. As the Abbasid achievement grew and matured a few Westerners, such as the Norman King of Sicily Roger II, were ready to learn from it. But the rising power of the papacy, casting around for a unifying cause, saw the Muslim caliphate as unspeakable polygamist heathens. It is hard to crusade against someone and learn from them at the same time. Had the rival Muslim world of al-Andalus not existed, much of this precious knowledge might not have arrived in Europe for centuries to come.

Though the overthrow of Spain's Visigothic noblemen was lightning-fast, leaving Christian rulers penned into a tiny, wet, mountainous corner of the north of the peninsula, the Muslim conquerors had never felt completely secure. The political history of al-Andalus, from the 700s through to the final defeat of Granada, the last toehold of Moorish Spain, in 1492, is as riven by dynastic quarrels, rebellions, invasions and spectacular overthrowings as any other part of Europe. From early on, threats from religious zealots from North Africa and from Viking raiders were often more serious than the challenges from the Christians in the north. And the tough Berber tribesmen who had made up much of the Arab-led army of conquest periodically rebelled, with some success.

The escapee Umayyad prince who founded the kingdom of al-Andalus, Abd al-Rahman, had arrived from North Africa with a small army to seize power. At Córdoba in 756 he declared himself 'Amir', or civil ruler. He dealt with rebel Abbasids by pickling their heads in salt and sending them back to Baghdad, which was apparently an effective declaration of independence. Abd al-Rahman I would rule for thirty-three years, dividing up the peninsula into manageable portions, forging a formidable army composed of slaves, many of them Christian, and establishing a gloriously beautiful capital at Córdoba. There his great mosque can still be seen, albeit with a Catholic wedding-cake-Gothic cathedral painfully inserted through its middle. Its world-famous forest of slim, cream- and pink-striped arches is a perfect stone metaphor for al-Andalus itself. The double arches mimic Roman building, particularly the aqueducts found all over Spain, but the effect is a memory of palm trees shimmering in a distant desert; oasis-classical. The mosque was built on top of a church, but Christians were given other sites for churches. And though the architecture is obviously 'Muslim' the mosaic decorations are by Byzantine craftsmen. A complicated conversation between rival faiths had begun.

For this exotic kingdom was the reverse of pure-bred. Much of the population remained Christian – though, because they had to pay a special poll-tax unless they converted, many did. Christians living peaceably under Muslim rule were called 'Mozarabs'; those who converted, 'Muwallads'. Some of the latter, feeling themselves disdainfully treated by Arabs, were prone to rebel, and there was a ferocious and very long-running Muwallad revolt under the charismatic bandit-king Ibn Marwan, who later converted back to Christianity. Jews were generally far better treated than in any Christian kingdom. Slaves could rise through the grand royal bureaucracy of Córdoba and female Christians were taken as concubines so that, to make things more complicated still, some of the most powerful amirs looked more European than Arab, with reddish-fair hair and blue eyes.

This was a land of mingle and double-cross. Christian kingdoms would seek support from Muslim rulers in their own local feuds; and Muslims would ally with Christians. Even El Cid, the great Christian warrior-hero, fought for Muslim rulers from time to time, if the pay was good enough. The landscape of central and southern Spain, littered with Christian and Moorish castles, fortified walls and ruined keeps, demonstrates just what a wild frontier country this was; but it was a lot more complicated than just Catholics fighting against Islam.

At its finest, al-Andalus was a glittering rebuke to the meagre, muddy kingdoms of northern Europe. Córdoba became one of the largest cities in the world, with a vast library of more than four hundred thousand books at a time when even substantial Christian monasteries could boast only a few score. Under its greatest ruler, Abd al-Rahman III, it had hundreds of public bathhouses and excellent running-water facilities, while even the grandest Christians kings still stank. Under al-Hakam II it openly proposed itself as an intellectual rival to Abbasid Baghdad, importing experts, particularly in the use of the astrolabe, that beautiful and ingenious device used to read the angle of the sun, moon and visible stars and thus determine one's position in longtitude. Invented by the Greeks, the astrolabe became a kind of simple universal computer for the Muslims, deployed for everything from astrology to architecture. When Muslim learning reached northern Europe, the astrolabe also became a symbol for the new natural science: Chaucer was among those who celebrated it in print.

Although al-Andalus was an independent kingdom, Muslim duties of Hajj and the eternal business of trade kept the two ends of the Mediterranean closely connected, and ensured Córdoba's fame. Al-Rahman's huge palaces and fortresses brought awed sightseeing embassies both from the Christian world – Paris, Rome and Constantinople – and from Cairo, Baghdad and Damascus. Córdoba's streets were clean, stone-paved and lit at night, and its libraries contained some of the sharpest minds known at the time, there honing their mathematics, astrology, grammar and astronomy.

Later, when the caliphate fell and Muslim Spain broke into many rival mini-states, or *taifas*, the learning and the expertise remained. Though the most obvious remains today are the fortified walls and spectacular castle ruins which testify to centuries of shifting frontier and religious warfare, the greatest Arab imports included a proper understanding of aquaculture, drainage and waterwheels; and new crops from the Near East and India that made southern Spain bloom with aubergines, peaches, apricots, oranges, lemons, melons, pears, cotton, rice and even vineyards. Later still, at the time of the more austere Almohad dynasty which ended the chaotic *taifa* period after invading from the mountains of Berber Spain, al-Andalus could still boast some of the greatest thinkers in Europe. They included Ibn Rushd, or Averroës as the Christians called him, who was a judge and lawyer at Córdoba, the most important of the Muslim thinkers, and a specialist in Aristotle; and Moses Maimonides, a Jewish physician and philosopher and author of *Guide for the Perplexed*.

The great philosophical debate of the time, which shook the Muslim world, pitted radical thinkers against the religiously orthodox. It was spearheaded by the Persian Avicenna, who tried to reconcile faith with the rationalist Greek philosophy of Aristotle. Writing from the 1020s onward, he distinguished between a remote, eternal Creator on the one hand and a complex day-to-day world of cause and effect, which he felt could be investigated and understood on its own terms. He suggested that God had simply set up the world, then had largely left it to follow its course, under rules that mankind could discover.

This was an invitation to the curious and determined, but it depended upon a passive and remote version of God which was not that of orthodox Muslim thinkers: their God was deeply and busily engaged in the world. The most famous of these orthodox thinkers, al-Ghazali, writing in the later part of the eleventh century, lashed Avicenna in a book splendidly titled *The Incoherence of the Philosophers*. But he in turn was attacked by Averroës, who also distinguished between the world of eternity, outside time, which was where God existed, and the week-by-week, colourful, smelly world of cause and effect explained by Aristotle. Like Avicenna, he was creating a space for human reason and investigation – a bubble in which enlightenment could thrive inside a universe made by God. There could hardly be a more all-encompassing proposition for the world of the time. Only by doing so could the probing, philosophizing inheritance of the Greeks, from that first age of reason, be revived in the Asia and Europe of Jewish, Christian and Muslim faiths. It was an invitation to think again, a battle-cry against passively leaving everything to God's will. Averroës felt this as a personal challenge. It was a hot argument. One of his key works, hitting back at al-Ghazali, has an even better title: *The Incoherence of Incoherence*.

Averroës, though commissioned to think radically by an Andalusian caliph, pushed things so far that he was banished from Córdoba in 1195 and his writings were burned. But translated into Latin, and discovered later by Christians as they seized Muslim strongholds, they would hugely influence the West. The historian Jonathan Lyons says that he gave Europe 'a thoroughly rationalist approach to philosophy that changed for ever the landscape of Western thought. This put Averroës almost five centuries ahead of Descartes . . . the West's traditional candidate for founder of modern philosophy.'[7] Alongside him were ranked Avicenna but also Moses Maimonides, the Jewish Andalusian who took a similarly radical and challenging view of the bubble space in which man could reason and argue. These are men who deserve to be as well known as Voltaire, Hume or Montesquieu.

The flow of Arab and Andalusian philosophy into the Christian world had been unleashed by the capture of Toledo from al-Andalus in 1085, revealing a hoard of books and manuscripts from Córdoba and Baghdad. Monks and translators followed. Scholars such as Oxford's Duns Scotus brought Averroës and therefore Aristotle to a Christian audience. In Paris and Naples, the great Christian thinker Thomas Aquinas absorbed his style of argument and, while disagreeing about aspects of Aristotle, found the Andalusian a vital inspiration, one transmitted to Dante in Florence. These early Christian Aristotelians encountered just the same kind of resistance from popes and bishops as had Averroës and Maimonides from caliphs and imams. Islamic arguments about the nature of God and the scope for human reason to unlock nature were mirrored very closely, in early European universities, in debates between teachers and students at Paris, Bologna and Rome.

Europe was waking up. A parallel transfer of knowledge in astronomy and mathematics now took place, influencing such later European thinkers as Copernicus and Fibonacci. This is where the

long European road towards the Renaissance and, later, the Enlightenment begins. It could not have started so early and so determinedly
without al-Andalus. Muslim Spain would fall back and eventually collapse not because of exotic Moorish decadence – too many baths, too
much sherbet – but for a more down-to-earth and familiar reason,
political division. The Arabs had originally been able to topple the
Visigoths because one Visigothic ruler could hardly glimpse another
without spurring his horse and charging; and the same thing happened
to al-Andalus. The religious and moral authority of the amirs was
undermined by the vagaries of lineage and by revolts. Waves of new
invaders, proclaiming more austere visions of Islam, would arrive
from North Africa and restore order, only to be challenged and check-
mated themselves. And by the beginning of the new millennium every
Muslim division, every period of instability, represented another
opportunity for the rising Christian kingdoms in the north.

Viking River

The political history of Russia starts with a trade route, and a frightened people. The Slavs were farmers and cattle-herders who lived in
what is now southern Russia, in parts of Eastern Europe and the
Ukraine, north of the Black Sea and west of the Caspian. The first
mentions of them by Byzantine historians in the mid-500s refer to
poor villages and primitive warriors, who spoke an uncouth, incomprehensible language. But the Slavs were not just another nomadic
people sliding westwards across Eurasia. Archaeology reveals hill forts,
iron ploughs and pottery. They were farming rich black soil, hunting
abundant game and fishing lakes and rivers, and able to survive formidably harsh winters. But despite the efforts of nationalistic modern
historians, they remain comparatively mysterious.

Often fighting among themselves, the Slavs were vulnerable to
the regular arrival of new nomadic peoples, such as the Huns and
Bulgars, pushing west across Asia. The most impressive of the cultures
of the area in this period was the Khazar empire, a feudal state in
which many Slavs lived with comparative safety. The Khazars have
world-historical importance, since, often allied with Byzantium, they
defeated the northward march of Arab Islam through the Caucasus in

the 600s and 700s, stopping the Muslim conquest of modern Russia and Eastern Europe. Had the Khazar state not existed, Russia would probably not have developed as a nation later on. The Khazar leadership, looking for a more forward-looking religion to replace their old beliefs (which included ritually killing failed rulers), converted to Judaism. They lasted for six centuries on the edge of the literate world, and at least one of their great military leaders was a woman. But intriguing, unusual and important as they were, they would be brought low before their literature and culture could be properly preserved or understood by modern humanity, and so remain one of the most tantalizing of the lost civilizations.

The people who defeated the Khazars claimed they had been invited in to protect the Slavs, both from their own tribal wars and from outsiders. It sounds like ancient propaganda, but it may even be true. Either way, the frightened people, if we can call them that, found themselves under the rule of strangers from the north.

They had been living with one asset of huge value, a river system so extensive it could connect the lush, wealthy world of Byzantium and the Near East with the agricultural and hunting peoples of Scandinavia and northern Europe. Northwards up those rivers went grain, wine, gold and silver and luxury cloths. Southwards came furs, slaves, amber, wood and honey. This called for urban centres. Trading posts, fortified towns and later cities began to appear along the Dnieper and the Volga and their tributaries, in much the same way that towns in the central states of the USA are clustered around autoroutes and railroads. Russia began with her rivers.

The incomers were called the Rus or, in Byzantium, the Varangians. They are better known today as Vikings, the eastern splatter of the explosion of warrior-sailors and farmers flinging themselves out from today's Norway, Sweden and Denmark from the 700s onwards. The Viking explorers, traders and raiders constituted the first major eruption of Europeans into other parts of the world. They would reach faraway places where they would try to settle but fail, including 'Vinland' in North America, and Greenland. In other places, such as parts of eastern Britain, Iceland and northern France, they settled successfully. Their descendants, the Normans, would carve out kingdoms in Sicily and conquer Anglo-Saxon England. These Scandinavians can claim a key role in the creation of that mongrel nation,

Britain, and they were also vital to the creation of mongrel Russia. Though other raiders, notably the Mongols, would have a huge influence here, nobody else would prove effective state-builders.

Vikings had been taking their flat-bottomed trading vessels south downriver for a long time before they finally reached the Black Sea itself. The same superb boat-building skills shown in their famous ocean-straddling longships, which allowed them to raid coastal monasteries and townships without warning, also enabled them to travel further on rivers than anyone else could.

The major Russian river systems presented obstacles – falls, rapids, underwater rocks – which meant boats had to be carried, or rolled, from one section of free-flowing water to the next. The hardest barriers were the cataracts south of Kiev, where for forty miles knife-sharp rock walls broke the water flow: the Vikings had names for them such as Impassable, Ever Fierce, Seether and Wave Force.[8] But the eastern Vikings, from today's Sweden and its major islands, had already learned while raiding and trading in Finland that their boats were light enough to be carried across land barriers. They could go where others could not. From the great Lake Ladoga in the north they moved steadily south and east downriver, establishing settlements from the 850s onwards.

To the far south-east, in today's Afghanistan, there was a wealthy Muslim settlement with huge silver-mines, ready to trade; and for the Vikings, Byzantium itself was simply Miklagard, 'the Great City', source of innumerable good things. Its story will be told later, but it is relevant now to note that in the narrative of Russia what mattered was that exploring Vikings reached this golden city early on, in 838. They later tried twice to raid it, only to be repulsed by Byzantine fleets with their secret 'Greek fire', but they eventually settled into an amicable trading arrangement. They would be allowed inside the city walls to trade, but never in groups of more than fifty, and always unarmed. Later, because of their fighting prowess, the Byzantine emperors would recruit Vikings as a personal fighting force, the famous Varangian Guard whose runic graffiti can be found to this day scattered around the eastern Mediterranean.

Meanwhile, far to the north, the Vikings were slowly forming a kind of imported ruling class along the Dnieper and the Volga. According to their own legends, around the year 862 three Swedish brothers were asked by the Slavs to stay and to institute a new kind of rule. The Rus *Chronicle of Past Times* (also known as *The Russian Primary Chronicle*), composed by monks at Kiev's beautiful labyrinthine Monastery of the Caves some two hundred years later, and presumably based on stories carried down, claimed that because 'there was no law amongst them, but tribe rose against tribe', the local people had told the Rus: 'Our whole land is great and rich, but there is no order in it. Come to rule over us.'⁹

But why had the Vikings ventured so far from their homeland in the first place? And what possible credentials did they have as state-builders? For Western Europeans these were, after all, terrifying pagan marauders, without law or mercy, ravening sea-beasts: 'Lord, preserve us from the fury of the Northmen,' prayed the English. Many modern historians argue that the key to Viking expansion was the familiar trigger of overpopulation. In the warm period towards the end of the Roman Empire, agriculture in the tougher northerly parts of Europe, as we saw earlier, had been more successful. Success of the kind experienced then tends to create a future population bottleneck. Farming and fishing communities that had lived in today's Denmark, Norway and Sweden since the end of the last ice age found that more boys were surviving than could be found land to farm. Viking culture favoured the first-born son, so there was soon a surplus of young men with no obvious future at home.

Centuries of fishing and of local trading, and an abundance of forest wood, had already produced sailing skills that inevitably prompted the thought of venturing further out across the apparently limitless 'whale road'. The Vikings were formidable fighters, cruel and ruthless, but in the 700s these were hardly unique qualities, particularly among all-male warrior-bands far away from their families. These men were not even all Scandinavians, but included Finns, Scots, Germans and Welsh.¹⁰ They have been remembered as worse than Saxons, Franks or Burgundians only because they were slightly more effective raiders. In fact, these warrior-bands were quick to settle down, take local wives and learn local customs – otherwise, they could not have established themselves so quickly in northern England and France and the Mediterranean. These 'berserkers', with their bloody myths and dragon-prowed ships, could turn domestic. Some turned up as Dukes of Normandy and then Kings of England.

The eastern branch, however, became Russians. Rurik, the eldest of those three brothers who arrived to rule over the local Slavs, may be a semi-mythic figure, but he founded a dynasty that lasted for five hundred years. The early chronology does not quite stack up, but Rurik's son Igor certainly was a historical figure. With a thousand ships he unsuccessfully raided Byzantium in 941, and his wife Olga was the first prominent Christian convert among the Rus. After her husband's death, she ruled in her own right and came to Byzantium to be baptized. Her capital Kiev slowly changed from being a large trading camp of log-cabins, workshops and storehouses into a royal Christian fortress, mingling Swedish warrior customs with new ideas learned from the Khazars and the Byzantines.[11]

Slaves were a major part of the trade south, along with hunting-birds and furs. Muslim silver coinage turned up early on in trading towns in Sweden, above all on the island of Gotland. But the exhaustion of the Muslims' Afghan silver mines led to an economic collapse in Kiev, and Olga's son – who refused Christian baptism – lashed out against the Khazars, and then, disastrously, against Byzantium. This is central to early Russian history because one of *his* sons, Vladimir, a bastard who had fled to Sweden, now came to his father's aid, returning with a huge following. After basing himself in the northerly trading town of Novgorod, he journeyed south down the Dnieper, seized Kiev, killed a half-brother and became the leader of the Rus.

Though sanctified with a huge, smug statue overlooking his city, Vladimir was an idol-worshipping pagan with unChristian attitudes to marriage (one chronicler described him as a *fornicator immensus*). His early success was based on raids against tribes and townships, bringing in tribute money to Kiev. But after failing to win against the Muslim Bulgars, in the 980s Vladimir seems to have decided to convert. He was not, however, sure which variety of monotheism to convert to. So, it is said, he summoned representatives of Western, Catholic Christianity, of Eastern, Orthodox Christianity, of Judaism and of Islam, to explain and debate their faiths in front of him. The story that the Swedish warrior-king ruled out Islam because he was horrified at its insistence on banning alcohol may be apocryphal, but Vladimir's decision to opt for Orthodox Christianity was momentous. The chroniclers say that his envoys influenced him by reporting back on the magnificence of the Hagia Sophia church in Constantinople: 'We no longer knew whether we were in heaven or earth.'[12]

Byzantium was rich, but politically embattled. Its then emperor Basil II, hard-pressed by Bulgar revolts, needed Viking help. Part of the agreement was that Basil's sister, the twenty-five-year-old Anna Porphyrogenita, would be packed off to distant Kiev to become Vladimir's (latest) bride. If this must have seemed a hideous fate for a sophisticated princess, it nonetheless did the trick: six thousand Viking warriors duly helped the Byzantine army to fight off its enemies. Anna was sent across the Black Sea and up the Dnieper to Kiev, where she married Vladimir. He was baptized and took the name Basil in honour of his new friend and brother-in-law, the emperor. Then, the leading idol in pagan Kiev was pulled down, tied to a horse's tail, dragged along, symbolically beaten with sticks, and thrown into the river. The other idols were smashed, saints' images set up in their place, and churches built where they had stood.

There had long been Christians in the land of the Rus, but it was now that a campaign of conversion began.

Vladimir brought in craftsmen and masons from Byzantium to build a lavishly decorated stone church, where he and his wife would later be buried; he imported monks and literacy, and he built huge ramparts around Kiev. Extraordinary multi-towered, onion-domed wooden monasteries and churches were erected, copying the most exuberant flights of fancy of Greek and Byzantine architecture but pushing them even further. The 'look' of Russian cities, with their painted wooden structures, walled kremlin-fortresses and gilded domes, begins with Vladimir and Christian Kiev. From now on, the settlements of the Rus began to spread outwards into the untamed tribal lands beyond the big rivers, and the long process of building a nation started. Swedes, interbreeding with Slavs and other groups, became Russians. Pagans became Christians. The people of the Dnieper and the Volga took to Orthodox Christianity, its scented, mesmeric services and its sad-eyed Virgin icons. Under a single ruling family, who would one day mimic the Caesar fantasies of Byzantium and call themselves 'Czars', the Russian system of aristocratic functionaries, or boyars, began to take shape.

This was all going on at much the same time as Norman England was being founded, in a similar process of military domination

followed by assimilation. Both Saxons and Slavs would change Norsemen into something different. In both places the bloody politics of
dynastic succession would grind on for centuries, but meanwhile
towns and traders were growing slowly bigger and richer, so that both
England and Russia hugely outpaced the Vikings' original homeland.
Like their old gods, the Norsemen had become shape-shifters.

Mali and Musa

The history of Africa would be almost as strongly marked by the successes and failures of the Muslim expansion as Russia had been.
Muslim traders and adventurers have given us much of what we know
of the African civilizations – and they can be called that, being town-
based – of sub-Saharan West Africa and the eastern seaboard.

At the time when Byzantium was hard-pressed by the Muslims and
the world of the Rus was still expanding, West Africa was dominated
by one Mansa ('King') Musa. He was fabulously wealthy. When he visited Cairo in 1324 on his way to Mecca for the Muslim pilgrimage, or
Hajj, he handed out so much gold in gifts that the price collapsed.
Musa would become known in Europe too, portrayed on a Catalan
atlas like a European king, sitting on his throne, with gold crown, orb
and sceptre. His empire of Mali was famous at a time when Europeans
had relatively little gold of their own. Though there were many myths
about Africa, this was not a myth. A modern African historian has
argued that Musa's empire 'was far stronger, far better organized and
even more literate than any Christian power in Europe'.[13] Even if this
is an exaggeration, it is not much of one.

And it provokes big questions. What was really happening in
Africa south of the Sahara at this time? Were there other empires we
know less of? And why, if Mansa Musa was a monarch to rival Christian princes and Arab caliphs, did Africa not go on to develop more
powerful and sophisticated home-grown civilizations to rival Europe?

To begin to answer this we have to jump far back in time, because
the African narrative concerns climate, minerals and luck. In prehistoric times the Sahara was not a desert but a damp, rich savannah. It
was home to game and to great rivers. Cave paintings show giraffes
and crocodiles: for thousands of years, this was rich terrain for human

hunters. Not until about five thousand years ago did it start seriously to dry out. This vast desiccation, across an area as big as the modern United States, had momentous effects for many societies. It divided the peoples of the Mediterranean and Near East from those of sub-Saharan Africa. An ocean of baking-hot grit proved almost as effective a barrier as the cold saltwater oceans. To the north of the Sahara, history was being written. To the south, in terms of writing, a stony silence prevailed.

There were fewer plants or animals that could be easily domesticated, as well as an abundance of game and berries that would have delayed the urge to farm. Archaeology can help fill in some gaps, and it is clear that human societies were developing quite fast in Africa too. By around 2000 BC, it is likely that the farming revolution had reached the then wetter lands of West Africa on the edge of the Sahara, around Lake Chad, and the Senegal and Niger rivers. Ironwork and sculpture were being made from around 800 BC, so although this part of the world moved from hunter-gathering later than Eurasia did, the familiar developmental steps were as clear here as in, say, France or Turkey. Knowledge of the new skills may have come from the Nubians, on the edge of the Egyptian territories; or from Mediterranean cities, such as Carthage. Though they left no written record, farmers were moving herds across the desert and small numbers of traders continued to risk the heat and aridity, using caravans of horses from around 1500 BC.

There are ancient Greek accounts of chariot-using warriors from West Africa, and desert drawings of chariots pulled by horses. Hanno the Carthaginian may even have tried to establish African coastal seaports so as to make trade easier; but with oared galleys, rather than the later European sailing ships, it would have been difficult to get very far south. The Romans did not try to; but they heard stories of gold-rich people living down there.[14] The earliest evidence of city life in Africa south of Egypt comes from the upper reaches of the Nile, in today's Sudan and Ethiopia. There, a series of half-remembered kingdoms and empires – including Kush, then the Christian Aksum – flourished between ancient times and the mid-900s. The use of iron had spread across the continent within two hundred years of Aksum's fall, reaching everywhere except deep forests where the pygmy people lived without metal, and the more arid savannahs of the Bushmen in the south-west.

After this, most African farming did not advance very far compared with Europe and Asia. Why not? One theory is the lack of strong draught animals to pull ploughs. The climate and the diseases were too much, it is argued, for horses or oxen to cope with – though today they seem to survive, perhaps better protected by man against microbes and carnivore predators. Most of Africa was left to herding, grazing and small-scale farming of root crops, which rarely produced enough surplus wealth for large societies. There were exceptions. One was Zimbabwe, an East African civilization using huge dry-stone walls for its palaces and towns, at its zenith between 1250 and 1450. These people had probably come from Mapungubwe, a kingdom of cattle-herders and gold and ivory merchants in today's South Africa, who were already living in stone-walled townships. The Zimbabwean kingdom was built on a far greater scale, so great, indeed, that later European explorers refused to believe mere Africans could have been responsible.

Zimbabwe had been a participant in a thriving coastal trade, dominated by Islam, the religion and culture that most influenced pre-colonial Africa. There is evidence of a network along the East African coast going back earlier, to classical times: Greek, Byzantine and Persian coins have turned up in Zanzibar and Tanzania.[15] The Africans with whom outsiders traded may have been Kushites who had moved south. But it was really Muslims who first opened up (and exploited) the wealth of sub-Saharan Africa. From the 700s Arabs had been raiding and trading south through the Sahara and down along the Indian Ocean coast of the continent, setting up enclaves and taking away with them the three things the Europeans would also later come after – slaves, gold and ivory. The written history of sub-Saharan Africa begins only when Arab traders start to record it; and it is thanks to them that we know about the other great exceptions, the empires in the sub-Saharan west.

There, the breakthrough had been the domestication of camels. Like horses, they had come originally from America, though there they died out. In Asia they had grown in size, and were probably first domesticated in Arabia around 2000 BC. Archaeological evidence suggests they had arrived in Egypt by 700 BC. Camels were being used by armies in classical times for transport, and by the Tuareg people to cross the Sahara by around the year AD 200. Excellent carriers of both men and cargo across desert, camels are also hard to tame and to manage. Though they mate all the year round, in the wild they reproduce slowly. A key breakthrough for early camel-using humans was learning how to artificially inseminate the beasts, to boost the size of their herds. Assisted in their reproductive duties, camels became the vital transport system that opened up the Sahara. Able to travel for up to nine days without water and to carry twice as much as an ox, they were soon bringing huge quantities of metal and cloth to the African peoples of the south.

The caravans were also bringing something humdrum, but rare in the south and essential to life – salt. Hunter-gatherers can get enough salt in the flesh of their kill, but once humans settled down to agriculture they needed extra salt, both for themselves and for their cattle. Salt was found in underground deposits in the Sahara, where it was mined in horrific conditions, often by slaves. By the AD 700s, the town of Timbuktu had emerged as a seasonal centre for the trade, where the salt was loaded onto large river canoes (of a kind still being used) and taken deeper into Africa. In return, the Muslims of North Africa were bringing back gold, as either ingots or gold-dust. The gold came from an empire now called Ghana (though this was almost certainly not its original name) and from smaller, more mysterious kingdoms to its south. It is only thanks to this gold-for-salt exchange that the Muslim world came to notice West Africa, and recorded what happened there.

Ghana collapsed as a political entity when it dared to confront the Berber traders and herders of North Africa. The Berbers produced a formidable empire of their own, the Almoravids, whom we have already come across in Spain. In around 1076 they turned south and moved against Ghana. Though they could not hold onto the area for long, they brought their religion into West Africa and created an opening for a new empire, built by Mande-speaking Africans who would call their kingdom 'Mali', or 'Mallel'. It would turn out to be the most formidable kingdom of sub-Saharan Africa so far. Even now, the area is agriculturally blessed compared with much of the rest of the continent. It lacks the near-impenetrable forests of further south. The great River Niger and its tributaries provide a lush belt of irrigated soil, where farming flourishes. The rivers were always an excellent transport and fishing resource. On the edge of Mali are rich goldfields, and across much of the terrain mounted cavalry could police and extend the empire. By the end of the 1200s an African kingdom of Muslim converts was well established. Its influence reached far west, towards the coastal Africans in one direction, and deep into the heart of the continent, where today's Nigeria is, in the other.

The former oasis trading camp of Timbuktu now rose to become a royal city; so did riverside Djenne to the south, which today possesses the world's largest mud structure, its formidable mosque. In the 1260s one king, Mansa Uli, made a pilgrimage to Mecca, and in 1324 the famous Mansa Musa did the same. It took him and his baggage train a year to cross the desert to Egypt. As soon as he arrived in Cairo with his royal standards, his parasols, his wealth, his open-handedness and his tall stories, he attracted the admiring attention of Arab writers. King Musa had apparently brought with him to Egypt eight thousand servants, many of them slaves. His army is said to have been 100,000-strong. Apart from being a religious duty, pilgrimage was a way of broadcasting the glory of the pilgrim and his country; and this certainly worked for Mansa Musa, whose fame reverberated very quickly.

Among the many Arab writers who described him, al-Umari from Damascus leaves a vivid portrait. 'This man,' he says, 'flooded Cairo with his benefactions . . . The Cairenes made incalculable profits out of him and his suite in buying and selling and giving and taking. They exchanged gold until they depressed its value in Egypt and caused its price to fall.' Musa was not averse to telling tall tales of his own. He told his host in Cairo that he had conquered twenty-four cities and that he ruled a country rich in cattle, sheep, goats, horses, mules, geese, doves and chickens – which may well have been true. But he also claimed his gold came from a 'gold plant', which blossomed in springtime after the rain, and had gold roots. It is possible Musa was ignorant about the origins of his wealth, since he added that another kind of gold plant left its roots in holes by the river where they could be gathered up like stones or gravel. Musa confided to his host that anyone in his kingdom who had a beautiful daughter would offer her to him, 'and he possessed her without a marriage ceremony, as slaves are possessed'. His host protested that this was not acceptable behaviour for a Muslim: 'And he said: "Not even for kings?" and I replied, "No! Not even for kings! Ask the scholars!" He said: "By God, I did not know that. I hereby leave it and abandon it utterly!"'[16]

Whether he really reformed we do not know, but during his reign (from around 1312 to 1337) Mansa Musa certainly reached out to the rest of the Muslim world in other ways, importing scholars and architects, and building mosques at home. After his death, in 1352/3, the greatest of the Arab travel-writers, Ibn Battuta from Tangier, visited Mali and recorded his impressions. He found it a place of reliable justice, safe and welcoming to travellers. Battuta had arrived after a long desert journey which even this hardened world-traveller remembered as particularly gruelling. Once, he recalled, he came upon a man who had lost his way and died of thirst, lying 'with his clothes on him and a whip in hand, under a little tree . . . There was water a mile or so away from him.'[17] Another time he had gone to defecate ('to accomplish a need') by the river and was offended by a local man coming to stand near by and observe him: it turned out that the man was worried that a crocodile he had spotted was likely to attack, and had nobly placed himself between them.

While in Mali, he was again offended. (Arabs seem to have found African customs as uncouth as European explorers would, a few centuries later.) As what would have been a welcome gift Ibn Battuta had been hoping for fine robes and money, but instead was presented by the new king with three loaves of bread and a piece of fried beef, plus some yoghurt. He soon cheered up, though, and goggled at the magnificence of the 'Sultan's' court, with its gorgeously dressed and armed bodyguard, musicians, acrobats and dancers.

Like Christian missionaries, Ibn Battuta could not come to terms with the nakedness of African women – 'their female servants and slave girls and little girls appear before men naked, with their privy parts uncovered' – nor with the African habit of eating carrion, dogs and donkeys. But he was pleased to find a national obsession with the Koran, and that Malian citizens dressed in clean white clothes for Friday prayers. He noted a general lack of 'oppression' and found the country remarkably safe – though slaves and women might have disagreed. In the words of a later historian, 'The general picture . . . is of a rich, prosperous, peaceful and well-ordered empire, in which effective government and organised communications and trade ran all the way from the Atlantic in the west to the borders of modern Nigeria in the east, and from the fringes of the forests in the south northwards into the desert.'[18]

Inside that empire most people were still farmers, growing millet and rice, breeding cattle and fishing. Trade in copper, salt and other goods brought in taxes for the government, and there was a currency of cowrie shells. Ibn Battuta recorded problems with locusts, while wild animals were a perpetual danger – he noted beasts like huge horses which lived in the river – presumably, hippopotami. But Mali is portrayed as a haven. Beyond its borders were cannibals who devoured slave-girls, horrific salt- and copper-mines, and many great dangers. Overall his verdict is positive, but we must take it cautiously. It is impossible to verify the accounts of Muslim travellers and historians, who often plagiarized one another.[19]

It may be that Ghana did not really 'fall' to Mali, nor Mali to the next empire-on-the-block, Songhai. Perhaps each of them simply expanded its population beyond their ability to feed them, then collapsed. It does, however, seem likely that among Mali's problems was one familiar to royal houses everywhere – the problem of succession. African tradition deployed a council of elders, or sometimes a matriarch, to decide succession. This might seem an advantage over automatic lineage succession, since it excluded the most stupid and weakest contenders. But it also produced feuds, which proved impossible to resolve over the large territory of an empire. Nor, according to another Arab historian, Ibn Khaldun, did it always result in good kings. One of Musa's predecessors 'was weak-minded and used to shoot arrows at his people and to kill them for sport. So they rose against him and killed him.'[20] (This seems fair enough.) After Mansa Musa came a series of usurpers, and rebellions too, so that Mali began to lose territory to the desert Tuaregs and to the Songhai of the River Niger.

Despite their pilgrimages and their grand mosques, the rulers of Mali had never been able to create the kind of united Islamic society the Arabs had forged and had then exported to North Africa and Spain. This was partly because of the powerful hold of native religion in Africa. Nature worship, and animism, still so popular today, were too strongly rooted to be overthrown, particularly outside the main towns. To his great irritation Ibn Battuta found that, even at court, alongside Muslim prayers figured mask dancers and the reciting of tribal stories (which he found tedious). Women still had to appear naked before the king, and all subjects had to sprinkle ash on their heads when they met him,[21] none of which was very Muslim. The

Songhai, who came next, were outright animists. According to the Arab chroniclers, they, in turn, were defeated by a Muslim warrior, Muhammad Toure, who was re-establishing aspects of the original Mali empire at much the same time as Christopher Columbus was setting sail for 'the Indies'.

A long period of feuding and division weakened this empire, too, and it fell in 1590 to a Moroccan army, supplemented by Christian mercenaries under a Spanish captain, who had carried cannon on the backs of camels all the way across the desert. This was a land adventure comparable to any voyage across the Atlantic; and, like the Spanish in America, the Moroccans set up a colony of around twenty thousand settlers.[22] Their influence persists today in Malian architecture. But the Moroccans could not occupy this huge swathe of West Africa for very long. Their invasion contributed to mounting political disintegration, during which many far smaller states were vying with each other for supremacy, including some states ruled by peoples of more mysterious origin such as the Hausa – whose language is not West African – and the taller, lighter-skinned, cattle-herding Fulani. Again as in the Americas, invasion triggered further disruptions and convulsions among local nations. By then, a complicated profusion of mini-states had evolved – and plenty of European ocean-going ships were prowling the coast.

This takes us leaping ahead towards the history of the European trade in African slaves. But it is important to remember how large and vigorous the slave trade was in Africa long before the Portuguese and their fellow Christians arrived. The Arab writers already quoted took slavery for granted, and bought their own slaves as they needed them while they travelled. Black Africans were taken north to perform menial jobs for the Muslim world, then imported later in large numbers as agricultural labourers when sugar cultivation began, in plantations in Morocco and Iraq. When Mansa Musa returned from his famous pilgrimage, one historian points out, there was 'a great demand of the Mali people for Turkish, Ethiopian and other slave-girls, and also for eunuchs and Turkish slave-boys. The slave trade thus went in both directions.'[23] Slaves were taken in raids, in countless small wars, and sold on. The Atlantic slave trade could not have happened without a strong previous tradition of slavery, as much part of Muslim history as the slave ships are of Christian history.

Though Ghana, Mali, the Songhai and the Zimbabwean kingdoms
are the most remembered of the pre-colonial African societies, there
were other kingdoms that have left no written record. They have often
left superb art behind them, hinting at rich cultures, now forgotten.
The Ife culture of today's Nigeria dates back to the 700s, when it
emerged out of the earlier Nok culture, which had produced stunning
pottery sculptures. The Ife, a Yoruba people, are most celebrated for
their sculpted bronze heads; they in turn were replaced by the Benin
empire, which survived from the 1100s until the very end of the nineteenth century. During what Europeans call the Renaissance, superb
brass panels were being created for the court of the Oba, the king of
Benin. Of a workmanship that the great Italian and German craftsmen
would have envied, these carved scenes were made from brass
imported from Europe in return for the inevitable gold and ivory.

The court of Benin allowed carved ivory scenes to be sent abroad,
but kept their greatest brass treasures at home. When hundreds of
these reached the outside world after a British military takeover of
Benin in 1897, Europeans and Americans struggled to take in their skill
and beauty. The then curator of the British Museum wrote that, at
first sight, 'we were at once astounded at such an unexpected find, and
puzzled to account for so highly developed an art among a race so
entirely barbarous'.[24] But anyone who looks at the tiny quantities of
wood-carving from African societies that have survived from before
the age of European colonization can see that the skill and flair were
not confined to the parts of West Africa where these empires rose and
fell.

Around the year 1400, there existed powerful African states on
both sides of the continent, as well as in Christian Ethiopia; plus a
multitude of smaller kingdoms where agriculture and trade were less
well developed. It was clearly a land of migrations, wars and politics
long before outsiders arrived. The more challenging African climate is
part of the reason that city-based civilizations did not make more
headway, and the bad luck of possessing gold, ivory and a slaving tradition made Africa dangerously tempting for Muslim and Christian
adventurers in possession of better metallurgy and sailing-ships. Yet
had Europeans not learned how to protect themselves against Africa's
formidable diseases so that they could invade it, and divide it up, then
a different Africa would surely have evolved, one more closely tailored

to that continent's own traditions and history. Mansa Musa might have been just one of many well known leaders, an African Charlemagne or a Henry VIII, rather than a fleeting glimpse of a lost tomorrow caught briefly in a passing mirror.

Genghis

A slight boy with reddish hair, almost naked and clutching a bow, was inching his way on his belly towards a small deer. He slipped out an arrow with a curious hole in its point and sent it flying. The cunningly designed arrow made a distinctive whine, causing the deer to look up, startled – at exactly the right moment to take the arrowhead through its throat. The boy, a fatherless and banished nomad, was living in the forest with his mother. Fearless and brutal, he was also exceptionally clever, with a talent for seeing into others' minds. He would soon kill one of his half-brothers in an argument about hunting. Though this happened in one of the most remote corners of the inhabited earth, a place of never-ending green plains, no buildings, and a vast sky, this boy would shake and reshape half the world. His name was Temujin. He would be known as Genghis Khan.

It is rare enough to be able to link, with one individual, history-shaping events across more than a single country. It is unique to be able to do it across such a range of countries as Genghis's career would touch. But without this fatherless boy who grew up living wild, it is most unlikely that the Mongol explosion would have happened with quite the force and direction it did. We know a surprising amount about Genghis's origins because, just a year after his death, the first Mongolian book – using a language his illiterate nomads had adopted and adapted – was written about his rise. It is called *The Secret History of the Mongols* and was composed, it says, 'at the time of the Great Assembly [which happened in Central Mongolia in 1228] in the Year of the Rat and the Month of the Roebuck, when the palaces were being set up at Seven Hills'.[25]

'Pastoralism' is the historians' dull word for the undull life of herders and nomads who for thousands of years moved through the vast green and brown oceans of the steppes and plains. These people lived in those large parts of the earth that were neither mountain nor desert, but not suitable for agriculture either. They were more than hunter-gatherers, though they did hunt and they did gather; they stand to one side of the easy, straight-line version of human development that moves from hunter-gathering to agriculture and thus to towns.

The people of the Asian steppes were the first, some six thousand years ago, to tame horses, initially so that they could eat them. (Across the other great steppe-like territory, the plains of America, where horses originated, they had been hunted to extinction early in the human story; so that nothing quite like the Asian herder culture developed among native Americans.) By about four thousand years ago the Asian steppe people were riding horses. This allowed them to move huge distances with their other animals, sheep, goats, cows, camels and yaks, to exploit the grasslands, carrying their homes – wood-and-felt tents – with them on carts. They never stopped anywhere long enough to become farmers, so they built no villages of stone or wood, and they never made a town. In many ways they have stepped lightly across the earth's surface, leaving behind very little compared with the rest of mankind.

Apart from the Mongols' own book, written history has given nomads a bad reputation. This is unsurprising: history was recorded by settled people, who feared nomads – and often rightly so. Whenever overpopulation or hunger on the steppe grasslands provoked a migration, these highly mobile people would end up raiding or invading the settled world.

The most famous early examples are the Huns, who by defeating Germanic tribes began 'the great migration' that destroyed the Western Roman Empire. By the time the Huns came riding in, they were feared as a bestial 'other', the antithesis of all that human settlement and civilization had achieved. Writing in the 550s, a Gothic chronicler called Jordanes said the Huns had been formed by the sexual union of witches and unclean spirits, who 'begat this savage race, which dwelt at first in the swamps . . . a stunted, foul and puny tribe, scarcely human, and having no language save one which bore but slight resemblance to human speech . . . they had, if I may call it so, a sort of shapeless lump, not a head, with pin-holes rather than eyes'. In China, where the attacks came from the Xiongnu, who may have been the same people as the Huns, they felt the same way, calling them wolves, flocks of marauding birds and 'furious slaves'.

But the nomadic invaders might leave behind more than carcasses and burning crops. In 2003 researchers published a paper in the *American Journal of Human Genetics* suggesting that the genetic material of a single male from around nine hundred years ago was shared by one in two hundred of all men alive, some sixteen million men scattered across Eurasia.[26] It is hardly unknown for powerful rulers to leave behind a substantial genetic spoor; examples can be found from Ireland to Africa. This, however, was on a different scale. The researchers concluded that the likeliest explanation was that the super-successful progenitor was Genghis Khan. The clusters of Y-chromosome markers fitted too well with the timing and spread of his Mongol empire to suggest any other explanation. The great invader took women from his vanquished foes wherever he went, never mind his legitimate children and the children of his concubines. However remarkable this may be, it is only one expression of the potency of this illiterate child of the steppes.

The Mongols, having swept up the other nomadic tribes of the area, would rule China as the Yuan dynasty. They would annihilate some of the most advanced Muslim cities and societies of central Asia. They would subdue the Rus, taking almost every major town and reducing its princes to tax-paying subordinates. They would enter Europe as far as Hungary, smashing Germany's Teutonic knights and reaching the outskirts of Vienna, spreading waves of panic and terror that have reverberated down through time. In just twenty-five years Genghis Khan conquered more of the earth's surface than the Romans managed in four centuries, creating (however briefly) the biggest land empire in history. China would never be the same again, influenced as it was by the reign of the great Kublai Khan, whose first capital of Shangdu (spelt by the poet Coleridge as 'Xanadu') so captivated Marco Polo. Kublai then moved to what would become Beijing and completely recast it, becoming the first emperor to rule China from that city.[27] Later, the Mongols, or Mughals, would turn south into India too.

The Chinese eventually absorbed their new Mongol rulers, and the Yuan dynasty did not last very long by Chinese standards, though they reunified China. But the Mongol arrival in Russia had a huge effect on that country's development – its words, its names, its clothing, its food, its tax system and its propensity to throw up 'Asiatic' rulers. Among

Mongol-descended Russians were the novelist Turgenev, the poet Anna Akhmatova and the composer Rimsky-Korsakov. Among the nomad tribes of the 'Golden Horde' were the Kalmyks. Lenin was a Kalmyk, as his Mongolian-shaped face shows.[28] In India, the great Babur, the first Mughal emperor, was descended from Genghis Khan; so without Genghis, no great Mughal flowering, no Taj Mahal, and no Pakistan.

But even with that record – establishing a military empire that changed the course of Chinese, Persian, Indian and Russian history – there is yet more to be said for Genghis as a unique shaper of world events. For despite their extreme brutality – of which more later – the Mongol hordes created a single space that linked east and west, China and the Mediterranean, as never before. Once the Mongol empire was established, Genghis and his successors provided a safe and well run route for silk, silver and other goods to pass between the emerging civilizations of Europe and China. The historian Ian Morris goes further. Because, he argues, the Mongols so devastated the great Muslim cities and cultures of Baghdad, Merv, Samarkand and Bukhara (which before the Mongols arrived were beautiful, advanced and teeming centres of culture and learning), they allowed the Mediterranean to leap ahead: 'Because they did not sack Cairo, it remained the West's biggest and richest city, and because they did not invade Western Europe, Venice and Genoa remained the West's greatest commercial centres. Development tumbled in the old Muslim core . . . by the 1270s, when Marco Polo set off for China, the Western core had shifted decisively into the Mediterranean lands that the Mongols had spared.'[29]

Genghis was born to a Mongol chieftain but given a name belonging to one of the rival tribes, the Tatars, because his father had just returned home with a Tatar captive. So the boy was called Temujin. He was probably born in 1162, into a world of interminable rivalries between tribes and of frequent wars with the Chinese to the south. He was said to be afraid of dogs; at eight he was betrothed and taken, as was the custom, to the girl's clan. But on his way home again his father was poisoned by hostile Tatars. Temujin boldly tried to claim leadership, as his father's successor, but the Mongol tribe were not about to be told what to do by a nine-year-old boy. They cast the family off. Temujin, his widowed mother Hoelun and six other young children, two of them half-brothers, were left homeless. They lived by foraging in the forest, gathering wild onions, seeds and herbs, eating the carcasses of dead animals and hunting small game. In a telling story, it is said that his mother gave Temujin and his brothers an arrow each and told them to break it. They did. Then she tied five arrows into a bundle and told them to break that. They could not. From unity, strength – a potent message for a banished boy.

At ten, it's said, Temujin killed one of his half-brothers. Later, when captured by enemies of his father, he managed to escape despite being shackled in a huge wooden collar. This was (and is) the Wild East, and Temujin's story resounds with further tales of horse thieves and famous feats until at last he rises in his clan, by force of personality, to a position of leadership. When he marries the young girl he had originally been betrothed to, and she is kidnapped (and probably raped), he and a childhood friend gather thousands of supporters and win her back – Temujin's first military victory. He and the bride, Borte, would stay close throughout their lives, despite his concubines and slave girls.

So far, this is the exhilarating but small-time story of a local warlord on the rise. But Temujin had just begun.

The people of the Mongolian steppe were divided into rival groups, including Tatars, Uyghurs and Keraits, as well as Mongols. There is a clear parallel here with the development of lineage groups among the native American people of the Atlantic seaboard – hugely extended families, connected through cousinhood, and then further extended by alliance. Genghis Khan's achievement was to find a way to meld the steppe tribes into a single people as they lived, rode and fought together – a bundle of arrows, not just one. He did this first by making shrewd alliances. By 1190 he had united all the Mongols, no small feat. Next, he turned his attention to the rival tribes, offering those he had defeated a share in future war spoils; and he also offered them brotherhood rather than exile or disgrace, thereby converting traditional enemies into new recruits.

Even so, a long and complicated steppe war followed, during which Temujin was nearly defeated, nearly shot dead with an arrow, and suffered reverses as well as victories. But his power steadily spread. One sorrow on the way was that a childhood friend with whom he had made a vow of everlasting blood-brotherhood had become a key rival. Defeated, the friend refused to join Temujin. He said, according to the *Secret History*, 'I would be the louse in your collar, I would become the splinter in your coat-lining.' Temujin, about to become Genghis Khan, the great ruler, sadly acceded to his request and granted him death by strangulation. By 1206, Genghis had subdued and united the steppe peoples and was ready to amaze the world.

As a military leader, he relied not simply on awesome brutality towards those who refused to surrender. He also brought in a new system of law (and later, writing), and was quick to learn from others. He used networks of spies, Chinese siege machines and huge mechanical bows, and even gunpowder-based bombs in ways the nomads never had before. His first victims were the Tangut, or western Xia (or sometimes, 'White Mongol'), a people whose empire was about twice the size of France and sat on the northern border of China proper, a sophisticated and advanced culture with good printing technology and a fine tradition of painting. Genghis more or less wiped it off the face of the map in what one of his modern biographers suggests may be 'the first ever recorded example of attempted genocide'.[30]

He moved on to destroy the military power of the much bigger Chinese Jin dynasty, seizing the city that is today Beijing and forcing the Jin to retreat south, where Genghis's successors would eventually hunt them down and end their dynasty entirely. His next victim was a khanate to the west of China, followed by the huge Khwarezmid empire with its gorgeous fortified trading cities of Samarkand, Bukhara, Urgench and Merv, already mentioned. These became scenes of some of the most horrific massacres in history. With a force of more than a hundred thousand men, each with two or three horses in tow, and now carrying a long train of Chinese siege engines and slaves, Genghis and his generals rumbled across the mountains to these oasis citadels, which boasted underground canals and glittering domes and had grown rich on silk and slaves. And there he unleashed hell.

It has been estimated that his armies killed 1.25 million people, over two years, out of the Khwarezmid empire's total population of around three million. This, as the historian John Man puts it, makes it perhaps the biggest proportional mass killing in history, 'an equivalent of the 25–30 per cent population cut meted out by Europe's greatest catastrophe, the Black Death'. The killings were done in batches after the cities had been taken, by soldiers working methodically, with swords and axes, through the old and the young, fighters and non-fighters. Pyramids of skulls were left in the sand, and lagoons of blood. All manner of special cruelties were reserved for those who had resisted particularly bravely. Samarkand, which surrendered pretty promptly, still lost three-quarters of its people.

After this, Genghis's armies divided. He turned south into Afghanistan and northern India, while his generals turned further north into the Christian kingdom of Georgia, destroying in 1221 the golden age it had enjoyed under its famous queen Tamara; and then further north still, towards Russia and Bulgaria. Major battles ensued, then a notable defeat of the Russian princes – after which they were crushed to death under a platform on which the Mongol generals were feasting. This probing attack revealed to the Mongols that there was plenty of rich grassland to allow them to drive much deeper into Europe. Under the rule of Genghis Khan's son, they would be back.

On their return they destroyed the first great Kiev-based Russian Christian civilization, shattering its towns and scattering its people, so that when Russia began to re-emerge as a Slavic state it would be situated much further north, in Moscow and Novgorod, giving Russia even today a different character. Everywhere, the Mongols brought terror; everywhere, slaughter. From China to Europe they were soon being described in ways that echo the terrified and disgusted reactions to the Huns, seven hundred years earlier. The English chronicler Matthew Paris wrote that the Mongols were 'inhuman and of the nature of beasts, rather to be called monsters than men, thirsting after drinking blood and tearing and devouring the flesh of dogs and human beings'.

In his later years Genghis Khan showed increasing interest in spiritual matters, summoning a Dao sage from central China to instruct him in longevity and good living. It sounds unlikely, and may have been more about prolonging his life than any real interest in ethics: if so the sage failed to help, because Genghis died in his early sixties after defeating the Xia again – they had failed to support him in his central Asian campaign, and paid the price. He died with his eyes set on new victories in China.

There are numerous stories about his death, variously ascribed to illness, a fall from his horse or even murder by a concubine who had hidden a pair of pliers inside herself and partially castrated him. He was buried in secret, and although another story relates that everyone involved was then killed to protect the sanctity of his resting place, this is probably as apocryphal as the pliers. Today, archaeologists believe they are homing in on the valleys where Genghis was buried, and it is quite possible that modern Mongolia will be the site of a spectacular discovery within a few years.

Genghis Khan's successors spread the Mongol empire to its furthest extent, taking all of China and Korea and, in the West, defeating the Poles and the Hungarians, whose army included French and Germans too. The same methods of slaughter so well known in Asia were repeated in Europe. The Mongols were by now using gunpowder and bombs fired by catapult, which horrified and perplexed the backward Europeans. They could almost certainly have overrun Germany, France and Italy had they chosen to, but internal fissures were beginning to break up their empire and the Mongol armies turned back. By now they had, however, taken effective control of Russia, requiring the princes and cities still standing to pay regular tribute.

It is true that Mongol power brought a period of peace to central Asia, allowing merchants and explorers to travel safely from the Mediterranean to the Pacific. Genghis, himself illiterate, oversaw the establishment of Mongol literacy. He showed complete religious tolerance, allowing Christians, Muslims, Buddhists and others to worship as they wished. Yet his was the peace that follows devastation and the tolerance of the all-conquering and irreligious. The smooth path now ready for Marco Polo and others had been achieved at the price of destroying the great Islamic civilization of central Asia, as well as many Chinese and European centres. Though they now had their own capital – Karakorum, a poor place, by all accounts – the Mongols were uninterested in building anything more than pyramids of skulls (and they were certainly proficient at that). They left no interesting thought or literature beyond their own history, created little of beauty; and across much of the world that they conquered they did little with their winnings.

But Genghis changed the world. He unintentionally helped Christian Europe to rise over the Muslim empire, and brought an end to a time of Chinese division. Some have tried to make of him an early apostle of globalism and free trade. In his own land, Mongolia, he is a formidable national hero: his equestrian statue, the world's biggest, gleams across the steppes, and his face glares from banknotes, hillsides and hoardings. But the truth is that, though the world would have been very different without the rise of the banished boy, it would probably have been much better off, too.

Marco the Mouth

Around some individuals, stories gather like flies. It is said that when Marco Polo, the traveller and tale-spinner, returned at last to Venice after a twenty-four-year journey into China and the Far East, he and his companions were dressed in greasy silk robes, shaggy fur and Tatar rags. They could hardly remember their Venetian – indeed, they were barely taken for Italians – but when they slit the seams of their clothes, a cascade of rubies and emeralds fell out. This story first emerges nearly two centuries after Polo returned, in 1295. Long before that, though, the man himself was mocked for his exaggerations. In his old age he was known to the Venetians as Marco il Milione, or Marco Millions. This was probably a reference not to his wealth, but to his enthusiasm for overstatement: 'millions' of this, 'millions' of that. It is also said that on his deathbed, his friends urged him to admit his exaggerations so as not to meet his maker with lies on his tongue. He replied: 'I never told the half of what I saw.'[31] He would have made a good British tabloid journalist.

Or a successful one, anyway: for Marco Polo's world-famous accounts of his journey to Mongolia and China, which transfixed medieval Europe, are hardly a model of good reporting. They include patent nonsense about the mythical Christian king Prester John, stories of miracles and fantastic hearsay met with during a journey that nobody trying to travel in his footsteps has ever been able to make proper sense of. There seems to be wild boasting about his important role in the Mongol Chinese court, none of it confirmed by the detailed Chinese records of the time. Many things that would strike most foreign travellers as noteworthy about the China of Marco's time – the Great Wall, chopsticks, tea, the foot-binding of women, the Chinese way of writing – he does not even mention. One careful study by a British academic who studied in Beijing and delved deeply into the sources concluded that Marco had probably never been to China at all, and had combined hearsay with plagiarism from other accounts.[32]

Yet his book, dictated in a Genoese prison to a French-speaking writer of romantic chronicles, became a huge hit, and has stayed popular precisely because Marco Polo could tell a good tale. It gives us even today a vivid glimpse into the world left behind after the Mongol eruption. Many of the strange facts he related, such as the Chinese use of pieces of stamped paper as money and their habit of burning pieces of black stone for fuel, turned out to be true. Moving beyond China, Polo told of Indian customs that would have seemed extremely bizarre, such as the worship of sacred cows and the self-immolation of wives on funeral pyres, and of places where a strange viscous substance oozed from the ground and could be burned to produce heat. He brought the first news to Europeans of islands such as Java and the Spice Islands, and of Burma – a new world of marvels, somewhere over the horizon. So it is hardly surprising that the *Description of the World*, written in 1298, probably in French, and then hastily translated into Italian dialects, Latin, Spanish, Portuguese, English, Irish and many more languages, set the European imagination on fire.

The Mongol invasions had by now carved out their roads of safe passage between the Mediterranean and China, reconnecting routes that had long been dominated by Muslim traders. From the seventh century onwards, sailors and merchants from Persia, Egypt and Mesopotamia had learned to use the Monsoon winds to get to India. By the 720s Muslim seafarers had arrived as far as coastal China, worrying the local Buddhists. After 750, when the Abbasids moved the capital of the Islamic world to Baghdad, which was connected by river to the Gulf, these trade links grew busier. Under one of the greatest of its dynasties, the Tang, China was unusually open to outside influence. Persian and Arab influence becomes noticeable in Chinese art, and thus in Japanese art too. Meanwhile, the traditional overland Silk Road continued to be used, though this was now complicated by a fresh central Asian rivalry between Islam and Tang China.

As so often, war and trade jolted along together. After the defeat of Chinese soldiers by the Arab armies at the battle of Talas River in today's Kyrgyzstan in 751, Chinese prisoners taught the Muslims the art of paper-making, at Samarkand, and the technology eventually passed to Europe. (Very slowly, however: the first paper mill there opened, in France, in 1189.[33]) The Tang would fall in 907, and political chaos would disrupt the trading system for the next fifty years, but the next dynasty, the Song, continued to participate in the Muslim market. Indian cotton and dyes went to China. Silk, spices and porcelain went further east. The Chinese wanted gold, slaves and horses as well as ivory and incense from the Arab traders. As one history of world trade colourfully puts it: 'Within a few centuries of the Prophet's death, his followers had knitted almost the entirety of the known world into a vast emporium in which African gold, ivory and ostrich feathers could be exchanged for Scandinavian furs, Baltic amber, Chinese silks, Indian pepper, and Persian metal crafts.'[34]

During the Song era, which lasted from 960 until the final victory of the Mongol Yuan over the south in 1279, the 'China-ness' of China became much clearer: a millet- and wine-consuming culture became a rice-eating, tea-drinking one. Under the Song, the highest achievements of Chinese porcelain manufacture, painting and book-making coincided with a busy ocean-going export trade. It was a golden age for Chinese culture, a time of intellectual curiosity and superb writing. The gunpowder-bombs, fire-throwers and giant catapults acquired by Genghis Khan had been Song inventions. This period saw some of the finest scholar-poets and some galloping technological inventiveness, while the celebrated Chinese bureaucracy hummed along busily in the background. But the Song were confronted by a series of more war-like invaders from the north, and in 1127 retreated to re-establish their capital in the south, where they thrived for a century and a half, beating back armies until they finally succumbed to Marco Polo's patron Kublai Khan. For the Europeans, this titanic battle between civilizations had been well hidden behind the mighty and hostile barrier of Islam, against which Crusaders continued to fling themselves in their unsuccessful holy war. So when the Mongol khanates gave central Asia a century or so of peace, they opened up a window into a centuries-long wall of mutual ignorance between China and the Mediterranean. To the Italians of Marco Polo's time the Chinese were as mysterious as they had been to the Romans. This other world brought smooth, soft clothing made by some unknown technique, and thin plates and bowls, far finer than anything the Europeans could make, as well as strange tales of mighty kings. But who were these people? It must have been a little like discovering life on the moon, and educated Europeans grew ever more curious and impatient. Marco the storyteller had acquired an insatiable market for information.

Whatever the truth about Marco's own itinerary, nobody doubts that some years earlier his father and uncle had travelled to the now vanished Mongol capital of Karakorum. They had been trading in the Crimea but had been forced east by a war being waged between two of Genghis's grandsons, and were among the first Westerners to arrive willingly at the Mongol headquarters. The Venetians had been enticed there by yet another of Genghis's grandchildren, the greatest of them all, Kublai Khan. He had won a war of succession and was now ruler of what we might call the Chinese end of the family firm. From the 1250s he had been digging deeper into Chinese territory, building his first capital at Shangdu, and from 1266 creating a huge new court complex at Beijing.

Kublai Khan is in many ways even more interesting than his grandfather Genghis, because he turned his back on the political and military tradition of nomad life and instead took over the more impressive Chinese traditions of government. Like Genghis, Kublai was refreshingly open-minded about other men's religions. He was far more interested in the outside world than later, complacent Chinese rulers. At Karakorum, alongside Persian Muslims were clergymen of the Nestorian and Catholic Christian faiths, a Greek doctor, a Frenchwoman, a Parisian goldsmith, the son of an Englishman called Basil, and many more.[35] At Shangdu and Beijing he used many Muslim technicians and advisers as well as native Chinese. Before long, Beijing even had a Catholic cathedral. When Kublai's armies pushed south to finish off the Song, he certainly used foreigners to design and operate siege machines and giant catapults – though Marco Polo's claim that he himself helped Kublai as a military adviser is widely disbelieved, not least because the dates do not fit. Kublai's victory over the Song was helped by generous attitudes to defectors and captives, too.

Kublai, we are told, had been interested enough in foreign religions to want Marco's father and uncle to take a letter to the pope, asking him to send the Mongol court up to a hundred learned Christians to make the case for conversion, as well as some sacred oil from Jerusalem. The merchants were given safe passage back, with special tablets of gold that operated as Mongol imperial passports. When they reached the Mediterranean, after a three-year journey, however, they found there was a papal vacancy. Clement IV had just died and there would be a long delay before Gregory X was elected to succeed, in

1271. Back in Venice, Polo senior was united with his son, who was then about seventeen. Eventually, the two of them set off for China, without the hundred theologians but carrying expressions of goodwill and presents from Pope Gregory. Marco would be away for virtually a quarter of a century. By his account, after extraordinary journeys, he lived at Kublai Khan's court as a favoured adviser, and travelled on behalf of the Mongol emperor throughout China and beyond, returning by sea via India, where he had been charged with transporting a princess to a local Mongol ruler. He travelled in a fleet of huge Chinese ships and brought back to Europe, among much other news, the first stories about the wealth of Japan, and about the Buddha, who Marco Polo thought would be considered a great Christian saint at home

Marco Polo's eventual return was followed by yet another outbreak of war between the Venetian republic and its arch-rival, Genoa. He was captured during a sea battle and imprisoned with the writer Rustichello da Pisa, to whom he recounted his extraordinary stories. Rustichello wrote them down and the rest is – well, not exactly history, but certainly a rattling good read. The book was translated early on, added to, messed about with, mistranslated; then it evolved in different versions for more than two centuries: 143 versions have been identified.[36] It was hugely influential, a pre-printing press bestseller of its time. Europe, for all its dynastic wars and greating cathedral-building, felt itself on the edge of alternative civilizations, and this book offered a door to a different future.

Meanwhile, the question nags away. Had Marco Polo really been to China? The case against is quite strong. Yet, if he had *not* been there, where had he been for those twenty-four years? And how did he accumulate so much information, some of it accurate? He could have heard other travellers' tales, or read now-lost books by Muslim merchants. On the other hand, many of us might fail to notice things later historians might find significant. Our memories falter. We embroider stories until we can no longer remember what is real, and what is invention.

Polo's book is filled with just the kind of commercial and earthy details a greedy Venetian merchant would be interested in – he was very much a man of his city. Venice, which had started as a loose collection of muddy islands used as sanctuaries by refugees during the late Roman wars, had developed into a vigorous, aggressive republic whose galleys and sailboats were intimately connected with the Muslim-dominated trading world, taking spices, slaves, salt, fur, iron and timber between the Christian kingdoms and the caliphates. From a family of merchants, who traded on the optimism and credulity of investors at home, it is not surprising that Marco Millions was prone to exaggerate his importance, to boast; nor that he failed to notice things that would fascinate later social historians. The news he was bringing was, in essence, very simple: There is a world beyond Europe, of wealth and opportunity, for those brave enough to seize it. This was the message Europeans would devour so greedily through all those translations and editions; and Polo's book would be followed by other travellers' tales, with a similar mix of apparent reportage and wild invention. A copy of Polo's tale was carried by Christopher Columbus on his epic voyage to the Americas: Columbus was particularly entranced by the prospect of 'Chipangu' or Japan.

There was, however, a final irony about Marco Polo's timing. For the wealthy, sophisticated China he described, with its beautiful cities (and it had about six million city-dwellers at the time, far in advance of Europe), its inventions, its luxuries and its superb organization, was actually on the wane. The Song, who had achieved so much, were already vanishing after wars of terrible slaughter and destruction, to the same Kublai Khan that the Polo family so much admired.

Why were the Europeans not quicker to follow in Marco's footsteps? Was this not the first great opportunity to spread beyond the Mediterranean again, overland towards China? They had long hoped that the Mongol world would be a useful ally against the common Muslim enemy; hence the pope's enthusiasm for converting Kublai (an aim unfulfilled partly because the Italians failed to demonstrate any exciting miracles to the sceptical Chinese).

Yet the opportunity was not grasped. Europeans continued to enjoy the luxuries and spices – vital for keeping food palatable – that came to them along the Silk Road. But within two years of Marco Polo's death in 1329, something occurred on the steppes where he had travelled, and in China's Yangtze valley, that changed everything.

A strange epidemic was killing people in huge numbers. By 1345 it was on the Chinese coast. By 1346 it had arrived in the Crimea, where

Marco's father and uncle had traded and begun their epic journey. The following year the Black Death, carried on ships and probably by rats, spread into the Mediterranean. By March 1348 Venetians were dying at the rate of six hundred a day. Boatloads of corpses were being ferried to outlying islands for burial. The doctors were mostly already dead. That same interchange of goods, people and stories that had allowed the ruthless maritime republic to rise was now wreaking its revenge. It is estimated that three-fifths of all Venetians died and fifty of her noble families vanished for ever.[37]

The Black Death is estimated to have killed between a third and a half of Europeans, and it had a similar impact on China. For both civilizations it marked a sudden and savage end to a time of growth and progress, exacerbated by a change in the climate that brought much colder winters and devastated crops.[38] In Europe it would have some surprising effects. Famously, because so many of the essential land-working peasantry in western countries like France and England were killed, those who were left were able to negotiate better wages and free themselves a little from the demands of landowners; the beginnings of a more mobile society, no longer quite so tied to noble families' landownership, emerged from the bacterial slaughter.

Oddly, in Eastern Europe the effect was almost the opposite. Landowners actually increased their power and range, and gradually forced the surviving peasantry into a tighter bondage, known to historians as 'the second serfdom'. This was possible because the landowners of eastern Europe, which had come to feudalism later, had been slightly more powerful and entrenched before the plague arrived. The cities of today's Poland, eastern Germany and Hungary were less populous and powerful than the wool-trading, wine-trading mercantile towns of northern Italy and England. The advances in legal rights and the power of the guilds in Western Europe may not have been dramatic by modern standards, but they were enough to tilt the advantage against the nobility when labour was scarce. In the east, the aristocracy was more ruthless and faced less resistance from the scattered peasantry. So a modest difference in the balance of power, suddenly exaggerated by the social disruption of the Black Death, caused wildly divergent changes that would result for centuries in Western Europe being more advanced and socially complicated than the similar-looking land directly to the east.[39]

France and Holland would influence the entire world; Poland and the Czech lands would influence only the world immediately around them.

These effects were, of course, invisible to those who lived through the ravages of the plague, which would return at intervals for centuries to come. In the first and particularly horrific visitation, cities became ghostly spectres of their once lively selves. Entire villages emptied, leaving their fields to return to weed and woodland. Religious mania and extremism flourished, and a dark view of the end times for Christian people became deeply engrained. Authorities tottered. Crafts and skills declined. The papacy shook. On the other side of Eurasia, the glory of Song China crumbled, and the peasants, there too, revolted. Marco's message of hope echoed in vain among peoples who were not yet strong enough to reach out and join hands.

Sailing from Byzantium

Here is how it finished. There were fourteen miles of wall protecting Constantinople, said to be the greatest city in Christendom. But inside the walls, among the multicoloured churches, the ancient Roman monuments and spacious squares, there were now so few people living that parts of the city had been turned back into farmland. In the 500s, this had been the largest city in the Western world, with half a million inhabitants. By the 1200s there were still four hundred thousand people there, and its wealth awed observers. The French Crusader Geoffroi de Villehardouin spoke of 'those high ramparts and the strong towers . . . the splendid palaces and the soaring churches'. The Crusaders, he said, 'never thought that there could be so rich and powerful a place on earth'. Not long afterwards, a Muslim merchant called Abdullah reported that it took a whole morning to cross Constantinople from side to side, and that it had almost one hundred thousand churches.[40] Yet by 1453, for Constantinople's last stand, to man those walls the last emperor Constantine XI Palaeologus had only around seven thousand able-bodied men left.

Confronting him was a vast army under the command of a sharp-nosed, cruel and brilliant young Turkish sultan, Mehmet II. He had already confounded the defenders by dragging his ships overland on rollers so that the city, encircled on two sides by water and on one side by land – where its famous walls were strongest – was effectively throttled. Mehmet had about a hundred thousand battle-hardened troops and excellent cannon, designed for him by a German engineer. He had already taken all the surrounding towns and forts, impaling any survivors in full view of Constantinople's defenders. Every desperate appeal for help from the Christian rulers of Europe had gone unanswered. A lunar eclipse, the slipping of the most precious icon as it was being carried through the streets, a violent thunderstorm, a thick fog and a strange red glow in the sky had already convinced many that God had deserted what had once been the greatest Christian city in the world. The tolling of bells and the processing of icons continued, however, as the desperate Byzantines called for help.

Now, the eleventh Emperor Constantine told his commanders they must be ready to die for faith, country, king and family. He reminded them that they were the descendants of Greek and Roman heroes. Into the vast Church of the Holy Wisdom, or Hagia Sophia, hundreds of priests and monks, nuns and ordinary people, gathered to celebrate vespers for the very last time.

In the early hours of Tuesday 29 May 1453, Turkish trumpets and drums sounded, and the attack began. Wave after wave of soldiers flung themselves at the cannon-damaged walls. Eventually, moving in perfect formation, the Christian-born slaves who had been transformed into janissaries, the faithful crack troops of Mehmet's army, began to overwhelm the desperate defenders. The Turks poured through the gaps, calmly killing as they came. In Hagia Sophia, priests continued celebrating mass even as the attackers forced their way through its great doors, stabbing and spearing the worshippers until they reached the altar, and the priests themselves, who died worshipping as the last service ended. Constantine, determined not to be taken prisoner, is said to have stripped off all his imperial insignia, the purple and the eagles, and thrown himself with his sword into the middle of the fiercest fighting, where he was quickly hacked to death.

The Byzantine, or Eastern Roman, Empire was one of the great success stories of the Mediterranean world; but it is remembered mostly for how it ended. It was long considered a large and impressive failure, to one side of the main thrust of European history.

What do most of us know of Byzantium? We have a vague impression of glitter and decadence; as the twentieth-century Irish poet W.B. Yeats had it,

> Of hammered gold, and gold enamelling
> To keep a drowsy Emperor awake . . .

We may be aware of the titanic walls, parts of which still stand, around the centre of today's bustling Istanbul, and of the strange art the Byzantines produced. It is a culture of mosaics and carved ivory, of heavy-eyed emperors and saints and solemn angels. Art historians tell us it led to the better-known altarpieces of the Renaissance, and its connection with the Christian Orthodox icons of Russia and Bulgaria is clear: the first great icon-painting of Russian history, still revered today in Moscow, was actually executed in Constantinople. But it seems somehow outside the mainstream of European art, a ghostly figure half-hidden in theological thickets and historical tangles. And that is true of Byzantium itself.

Even the naming is slippery. 'Byzantion' was the name of the old Greek city that Constantine took over and planned as the new centre of the Roman Empire. Following a Graeco-Roman tradition of rulers naming cities after themselves (as with Alexandria), he called it Constantinople. Its citizens called themselves Byzantines to distinguish themselves from Western Romans, but also sometimes *Romani* ('Romans' in Latin) because they also claimed to inherit the best of old Rome. We tend to talk about the Byzantine Empire. As noted earlier, awestruck Norsemen called the place Miklagard, 'Great City'; it was also known in Greek as the City of God. Today it is Istanbul. But whatever we call it, this was, as its modern chronicler John Julius Norwich reminds us, a remarkably long-lived human society. Founded by Constantine in May 330 and falling to the Ottomans in May 1453, it lasted for 1,123 years and eighteen days. That is, roughly the same timespan as distances today's British from the England of Alfred the Great, the Saxons and the Danes. If Byzantium was a 'failure' or 'outside the mainstream', it was a remarkably persistent failure.

The Victorian historians' contempt for it cast a long shadow. Norwich quotes W.E.H. Lecky, writing in 1869, who considered the

Byzantine Empire 'without a single exception, the most thoroughly base and despicable form that civilization has yet assumed . . . a monotonous story of the intrigues of priests, eunuchs and women, of poisonings, of conspiracies, of uniform ingratitude, of perpetual fratricides'.[41] Why such anger about Byzantium? Perhaps it is the historian's love of tidiness. Byzantium does not slot neatly into the narrative of a steady Western march to enlightenment. It has not endowed modern mankind with useful science or much original literature – though it had some wonderfully vivid and scandalous historians of its own. And of course, it ended badly.

But the main reason for the blanketing of Byzantium under layers of condescension and neglect is the centrality of religion to its civilization. For this was a culture more saturated in religious fervour and theological argument than any other in the history of the Mediterranean world. Though founded by a Roman emperor who wanted to impose Christianity on his subjects, it was only gradually that it became a real hub of the Christian world. Even as its jaw-droppingly beautiful and radical Church of the Holy Wisdom, Hagia Sophia, was being created under the emperor Justinian – it was consecrated in 537, and its world-famous dome now protects a mosque – the city housed many pagan shrines and statues to Roman gods. In law, military and engineering know-how, entertainments, learning and finance, Byzantium was the hinge between the classical and the Christian medieval worlds. But it was a creaky, slow-moving hinge.

The Byzantines were almost always fighting – the waves of nomad warriors arriving from the east, then the Muslim conquerors pressing through their rich eastern flanks; and, often, rival Christian kingdoms to the west and north as well. At its greatest extent, the empire embraced southern Italy, the Balkans, most of modern Bulgaria, Greece and Turkey, as well as the Crimea at the northern edge of the Black Sea. At its peak it attracted immigrants from across Europe and Asia to work and fight on its behalf, including Italians, the Vikings who became the Varangian Guard, and dispossessed Anglo-Saxons who had lost their homes after the Norman conquest of 1066. Long before the great walls fell, Constantinople had shrunk to little more than a city-state, with tiny patches of land outside.

But Byzantium's real conflict, which also never stopped, was about the true nature of God, Christ and the Holy Spirit, and the correct way to worship. Different beliefs about Christ's nature, the authority of the pope and the bishops, and many lesser matters radically, and tragically, divided the Byzantines and their Christian enemies.

We often find it hard to take such arguments seriously. But the problem may be ours; for Christians of the time, these were urgent and personal questions. When Constantine summoned all the Christian bishops to that great summit at Nicaea in 325 to discuss the views of Arius, the debate was about whether Christ shared the same divine substance as God or (as Arius and followers thought) was a lesser entity than God. This was no mere squabble, since if the Arians were right, then Christ's offer of salvation through faith in him was seriously questionable. It was a matter of life and death, no less. Arianism was condemned, though it survived and spread in popularity among many northern peoples. After this came other fierce arguments. Many were about the rituals and words used in church services, and later on about whether the pope in Rome or the Patriarch in Constantinople was the true leader of all Christians. Throughout, brilliant theologians, monks living in monasteries or as hermits, and bullish bishops from outlying churches would test one another and attract substantial popular followings.

The spirituality of Byzantium was transmitted through long music-accompanied services, the air laden with incense, in splendid golden churches that must have stunned and awed the worshippers. Western churches learned from them about how to delight – even drench – the senses. Today, the best way of getting some idea of what they must have been like is to attend a Russian service in one of the Orthodox churches in Moscow or Kiev. But Byzantine spirituality brought with it a fatal political consequence, because it cut off this Eastern, Greek-speaking Christian centre from the Rome-led, Latin and Western European world. The rise and sudden expansion of Islam sliced off Byzantium's eastern provinces – today's Turkey – and turned the city into an outpost of Christianity. Italians, French, Germans and Spaniards tended to regard Byzantium's version of Christianity as outlandish and heretical; and so long as the Byzantines abhorred papal authority, 'Christendom' did not really exist there.

At times this led Western Christians to attack their Eastern rivals directly. Most infamously, in 1202–4, the so-called Fourth Crusade went veering wildly off course, and under its Venetian leadership sacked Constantinople itself.

The pope had ordered yet another attempt to seize back Jerusalem from the Saracens. The Crusaders, under French leadership, had decided upon a novel plan. Influenced by the ambitious plans of Richard Coeur-de-Lion, who had recently died, in 1199, they decided to attack via Egypt. To do that, they needed a great fleet to transport them there; only Venice, with its ship factory at the Arsenale, could provide one. The Venetians were led at the time by a blind doge in his eighties, Enrico Dandolo, who drove a very hard bargain, and then announced he would join the crusade himself. But when the time came, far fewer Frankish Crusaders turned up than expected, and without the money to pay for their Venetian ships. Dandolo again drove a hard bargain: they must stop en route and take back a Balkan town that the Venetians had lost. This they did. But there they came across a deposed young Byzantine emperor, who asked for their help, in return for a reward, in getting his throne back from his uncle. At this point, the story gets murky. The Venetians had never wanted to attack Egypt anyway, since they had good trading relations there. But as trading rivals and Latin Christians, they loathed the Byzantines. (It may have been after a fight in Constantinople many years before that Dandolo lost his sight.) So yet again, they postponed fighting the Saracens and turned towards Byzantium instead. It would prove an awesome decision.

It was not particularly difficult for the combined Venetian and Frankish forces to defeat the Byzantine usurper and place his nephew in power, though it involved a bold attack on the famous walls from the unexpected, seaward side. But it proved much harder to get the money the young emperor had promised. He had also offered to place the Byzantine Church under the pope's authority. This rash promise, the aggressive behaviour of the Crusaders, the huge cost of paying off the Venetians, then a series of disastrous fires, all made the new emperor very unpopular in his city. He was duly murdered by another usurper, and the only way the Franks and Venetians could recoup their money was by means of a second attack. Dandolo, by now quite likely in his nineties, had heroically led his troops from the front in the first attack. Now, as the Venetians tied the masts of their boats together to create platforms from which to assault the walls, he decided to go for broke. Rather than simply looting the place, he would oust the Byzantine rulers entirely and make the city a puppet state under Venetian control.

The attack was successful, but what followed was horrific: a three-day orgy of burning, rape and looting which destroyed much of the classical inheritance of Constantinople. One Byzantine observer described the sacking of the great church itself as both a physical rape and a spiritual one: 'A common harlot was enthroned in the Patriarch's chair, to hurl insults at Jesus Christ; and she sang bawdy songs, and danced immodestly in the holy place . . . nor was there any mercy shown to virtuous matrons, innocent maids or even virgins consecrated to God.' John Julius Norwich argues that this sack of Constantinople, which saw all its accumulated learning go up in flames and its treasures taken back to Europe, may have been the single biggest such loss in history: 'Western civilization suffered a loss greater than the sack of Rome by the barbarians in the fifth century or the burning of the library of Alexandria by the soldiers of the Prophet in the seventh.'[42]

The cynical and brutal story of the Fourth Crusade had slow-burning consequences. The Byzantines had known bad times before. At the battle of Manzikert in 1071, they had been humiliated by 'Turks', nomads from the Far East. But nothing had been as bad as this. Though the puppet Latin state in Constantinople did not last very long, and though Byzantium recovered some of its power and self-confidence under later emperors, it would never again be the same. Its awesome system of walls, created in 412, had repelled every invader for nearly eight hundred years, but now they had been shown to be vulnerable. Stripped of much of its wealth, of much of its classical heritage and of its honour, with its old territory now carved up into mini-empires, subsidiary kingdoms, sultanates and duchies, Byzantium was no longer the mighty fist of the Christians, armed against all comers. In due course it would fall to the Muslim invaders. The Venetians, who took home statues of lions, horses and angels and vast amounts of precious objects, had accidentally aided the rise of Islam inside Europe. And the power of Venice would steadily grow.

So it is grossly unfair to dismiss Byzantium, with its passionate Christian faith and its inherited Roman and Greek ideas, as merely a sequence of unpleasant tyrannies. Yet to modern eyes it must seem an alien civilization. Certainly, it was highly conservative, slow-moving and anything but democratic.

For Europeans brought up to revere the classical Greek world, with its lucidity, its belief in reason and its political experimentation, Byzantium's stately hierarchy and its mysticism can be difficult to swallow. A better way to understand it might be to compare it with other dynastic empires such as the Ottomans' or the Chinese. Like the courts of the Song, Tang or Ming emperors, the Byzantines relied on a highly efficient and literate civil service, charged with taxing and administering many different peoples fairly. Again like the Chinese, the Byzantines made use of a large class of eunuchs, castrated either in childhood, or in adulthood as a precondition for serving at court. Barbaric as the practice might seem to us, eunuchs were very useful to many early empires. Unable to have children, lacking an independent family base, they were more dependable. They could also safely serve in the women's quarters, where they might hear the most secret of secrets. In China, Byzantium and under the Ottomans too, eunuchs rose to positions of great power and wealth, sometimes commanding armies and fleets.

The detailed court procedures and rituals of Byzantium, carried out in huge court complexes, were not so different from life in Beijing's Forbidden City. Just as those entering the presence of a Chinese emperor had to kowtow, banging their foreheads on the floor, so those in the presence of a Byzantine emperor had to commit *proskynesis* – a similar routine, but touching rather than banging. In Byzantium the powerful positions held by religious leaders as advisers and counsellors were analogous to those of the Confucian mandarins. The Chinese Mandate of Heaven, under which emperors had divine authority but had to act morally in order to retain it, would have been recognized in Constantinople, where any emperor found guilty of offending God would be killed or ousted. Sometimes, as in China, natural disasters were taken as signs of divine displeasure. Moreover, both empires made a fetish of their ancient origins, the Chinese harking back to mythical times and the Byzantines insisting on their continuity with ancient Greek and Roman culture.

Both empires retained their power through highly advanced engineering and technologies, secrets they tried to keep to themselves. The

Great Wall of China remains one of the world's most impressive works of civil engineering, designed as it was to keep out 'barbarian' nomads. The huge ramparts of Constantinople, similarly, to keep out wild people from the steppes, were in their way the Great Wall of Europe.

Another first was gunpowder. Once they had discovered that mixing together saltpetre, sulphur and charcoal produced this useful addition to their armoury, the Chinese could more easily keep their enemies at bay. They had discovered this during the Tang dynasty (618–907), and by 1132 under the Song had made an early kind of bomb, followed in 1259 by a bamboo-barrelled 'fire-spitting lance', a cross between a flame-thrower and a primitive gun.[43] The Byzantines, meanwhile, had been using 'Greek fire', that terrifying mix of sulphur, pitch, crude oil and nitre discovered in the 660s by a chemist called Callinicus. It was sprayed on enemy ships and soldiers – with devastating effects – using a sort of pump. In the 940s it was listed as an official Byzantine state secret by Constantine VII,[44] and was still one of Constantinople's secret weapons at the time of its fall in 1453.[45]

There are other parallels, including a similar skill in hydraulics and water clocks, a similar emphasis on public processions to impose royal authority, and a firm belief that their capital city was the centre (or navel) of the world. Most significantly, conservative empires, founded with a strong sense of their own past, worked in similar ways, deploying similar hierarchies of civil servants. Byzantium was not a particularly cynical culture, but dynastic despotism always leads to feuds between generations and between siblings, sometimes ending in treachery, murder and the plotting of palace coups. The great female intriguers of Constantinople, and their eunuchs, were cousins-under-the-skin of the dowager empresses of China, and theirs. The dynasties survived as long as they had technical superiority over their enemies, a strong peasant base from which to levy taxes, and an efficient bureaucracy. For some of the time, at least, Byzantium had all three.

It collapsed, as we have seen, partly because the Christian West was not prepared to come to its help; and, indeed, led by the Venetians, had done its best to fatally weaken it. It should be remembered that some Venetians and Genoese, as well as Spaniards (and perhaps a single Scot), rallied to Byzantium's cause in its final struggle, and died there. A Venetian ship had managed to slip past the Turkish blockade and sail through the Aegean, looking for a relief expedition, but had found nothing. The captain had asked his crew to have a vote about what to do – sail home to Venice, giving up Constantinople as doomed, or return to give the emperor the bad news and die alongside him. Only a single sailor voted to go home, and was shouted down: they returned, and died too.[46]

Yet the odd thing is that the fall of Constantinople, though a hugely symbolic event for Christian and Muslim civilizations alike, did not itself have world-shaking consequences. Very soon after they had absorbed the news, the Venetians and the Genoese were back again to negotiate new trading deals. Business never sleeps.

The Ottomans seized the Balkans, getting as far as Vienna, but they failed to overwhelm Western Europe and establish Islam across Christendom, as they had hoped to do. Quite soon, with its varied population and grand court, its eunuchs and stately rituals, Ottoman Constantinople seemed not so very different from what had preceded it. Even turned into a mosque, the magnificent church remained oddly familiar. Byzantium's artistic and literary influence, which had arrived in Italy, France and Germany as loot, increased with the revival of interest in classical Greece, which in turn would play a part in the Renaissance.

Leonardo

'The Moor', they called him, perhaps for his dark looks: Ludovico Sforza, Duke of Milan. One day, the duke received a remarkably boast-ful letter from a would-be military engineer. This young adventurer was offering to come and build light, portable bridges that would allow troops to chase the enemy, or flee from them, as he put it. 'Also I will make covered cars, safe and unassailable, which will enter among the enemy with their artillery, and there is no company of men at arms so great that they will not break it'; and he could make cannon, mortars, catapults, fireproof ships, underground explosions – you name it. The letter-writer, who was from the south, from a workshop in Florence, added that 'in time of peace' he could design buildings and aqueducts. 'I can carry out sculpture in marble, bronze or clay, and also I can do in painting whatever can be done, as well as any other.'

Ludovico knew his art, and he wanted a giant bronze horse made in memory of his father; he also knew his warfare, and must have been intrigued by this arms-dealer in ideas. Ludovico was not exactly old aristocracy. His father, Francesco, had been a mercenary warlord, who changed sides so many times he must have been perpetually dizzy. Need to fight the next city along the river? Francesco was willing. Take on the French? The pope? Simple.

The Italian Renaissance, apart from being a great age of devotional painting and Church architecture (not to mention slavery, riot and assassination), was an age of warlords. The civic-minded, peaceable citizenry of the towns of Lombardy and Tuscany were not natural fighters, yet they were often in conflict; so they hired warrior-leaders, the condottieri. Francesco Sforza had been typical of the breed. This thick-necked, heavy-eyed fighter, the illegitimate son of a mercenary and famous for being able to bend metal bars with his bare hands, had a knack of ending up on the winning side. He had fought almost everyone, including his own brother, a son, a son-in-law, and most of the possible enemies to be found in northern Italy.

When the Duke of Milan died without an heir, the city briefly returned to a form of republic, but factional fighting and famine brought a further crisis; the burly old soldier had moved in and taken over. To general surprise, he proved to be a shrewd and popular ruler, but when Francesco died and his oldest son Galeazzo Maria Sforza took the reins, he proved to be a different proposition altogether. A sadist and a rampant womanizer, he was said to have had a poacher executed by forcing a hare, fur and all, down his throat; to have nailed another man alive into his coffin; and to spend his leisure hours inventing tortures for his enemies. Pleasingly, he was assassinated. His son, aged seven, inherited; but Uncle Ludovico became regent, the son mysteriously died, and Ludovico found himself Duke of Milan.

Ludovico's story was not so surprising in the Italy of the time. English playwrights would soon be scouring histories of the ruling Italian families for the plots of their bloodthirsty tragedies. Nor was Ludovico uncultured. He had been taught by one of the great humanist scholars of the day – the 'humanists' being those who studied the Latin and Greek literature and philosophy emerging from al-Andalus and elsewhere, bringing old truths to young cities. He needed clever men around him, and to turn Milan into a truly brilliant court he needed culture – sculpture, music and painting.

So in October 1481, a strong, good-looking young man of thirty, wearing a short pink tunic and a curly beard arranged in ringlets, presented himself to the Sforza court. He was carrying a specially made lyre, because the effective ruler of Florence, Lorenzo the Magnificent, had sent him in the first instance as a musician and singer, as a kind of present to his Milanese ally.[47] With him was a sixteen-year-old youth who would later become a musician and actor. Tongues may have wagged: the Florentines were famous throughout Italy as sodomites. And in this case, tongues were almost certainly right, for the boastful singer and military engineer, who could also turn the odd picture, was history's famous homosexual artist, Leonardo da Vinci.

Leonardo, like Sforza's father, was illegitimate, the son of a multiply married Florentine pen-pusher and a peasant girl born in a small village. But his father had spotted the boy's precocious talents and had him apprenticed in the workshop of one of Florence's star sculptors and metalworkers, Andrea del Verrocchio. By the 1460s the great days of the small, independent-minded Italian city-republics were mostly long gone, but the tradition of guilds and workshops that had underpinned them lived on. The communes they then formed, in famous towns such as Pisa, Lucca, Mantua, Siena, Bologna, Verona, Padua, Genoa and Perugia, as well as Florence and Venice, had begun to emerge in the late eleventh century as the old imperial powers lost their grip.[48] Competing amongst themselves and specializing in particular skills and products, these cities had complex systems of election and justice, which generally shared power between local landowners and the tradesmen and craftsmen.[49]

For a while, particularly in Tuscany and Lombardy, it had seemed a hugely successful and novel system, more vigorous than the larger enclaves such as the Papal States, and Naples to the south. But factionalism, revolts by poorer, excluded citizens, as well as fighting among the richer families, reduced their influence, until one by one most of the city-state republics succumbed to the rule of local grandees, dukes and princes. Venice mostly managed to stick with its old, intricate republican system, but powerful, swaggering Florence was more typical of the contemporary trend. After bitter disputes between rival parties and factions, it eventually fell under the spell of a family of hugely rich bankers, the Medicis. In the same year that Leonardo joined Verrochio's workshop, Lorenzo de' Medici, 'the Magnificent' and grandson of Cosimo, the first Medici ruler, had just taken over.

Leonardo would do his apprenticeship in the busy, communal and relatively democratic worlds of the guild and the workshop, two building blocks of the Italian city-state. For tradesmen and professionals – doctors and sculptors, leather-workers and goldsmiths – the guilds were the key institutions that allowed them to play a full part in the life of the city. The guilds established and policed standards, organized religious processions, funded hospitals, and acted as mutual-aid and political networks. The workshops were mini-factories and at the same time offered a system of higher education, which gave young men the chance to learn directly from leading masters until they qualified to set up in business themselves.

In the 1470s, Verrocchio's was one of the leading artistic workshops in Florence. According to the art historian and biographer Giorgio Vasari, he had studied the sciences, particularly geometry, and worked as a goldsmith. He had then visited Rome and encountered the craze for sculpture based on works from classical times, which 'were being unearthed every day' there.[50] He had turned to sculpture, and afterwards to painting. As a brilliant, radical and intensely curious man he was the perfect teacher for Leonardo. In these studios a lot of collaboration took place; when Leonardo one day painted an angel into a work of Verrocchio's, Vasari tells us, and did it better than his master, Verrocchio simply gave up the brush and stopped painting. He had already been outmatched.

Leonardo had to leave the comradely world of the workshop and join the search for grand patrons. The old days of working for the whole community, in a spirit of city pride, were over. Artists and engineers needed rich dukes, bankers and bishops if they were to survive. Leonardo did well enough in Florence under the patronage of Lorenzo de' Medici; but clearly, he was not considered essential there, given that he was sent off to Milan to present himself as the ultimate all-rounder. In Vasari's biography there is already a faint note of warning. Although a genius, brilliant with pen and brush, interested in everything and a great model-maker, 'Leonardo started so many things without finishing them; for he was perfectly convinced that his hands, for all their skill, could never perfectly express the subtle and wonderful ideas of his imagination.'

In Milan, Leonardo would prove the truth of this. He made some beautiful pictures, decorated a chamber of the palace and bombarded the duke with drawings and plans for ingenious war machines. He designed pageants and helped with architectural rebuilding.[51] But his grand plan for a huge equestrian monument for the first Sforza came to nothing. It was too ambitious. The bronze collected for it was eventually used for cannon to be deployed against an invading French army. Then, when it came to the most famous commission of Leonardo's Milanese years, one of the most celebrated paintings ever, the phenomenally inventive artist-inventor overreached himself.

The Last Supper, painted during 1495–7 in the refectory of the Santa Maria delle Grazie convent in Milan, was in many ways the perfect challenge for an ambitious student of Verrocchio's, fascinated as he was, in particular, by lighting and perspective. The commission required Leonardo to make a massive painting extending to well above head height, which would allow the viewer to see Christ and his disciples clearly and appear to be a natural part of the chosen room, rather than simply attached to a wall. Leonardo solved the problems of lighting and perspective brilliantly, producing such strong effects that Christ's head seems to attract the viewer towards him.

Leonardo scoured the streets, and his notebooks, to find models for the disciples. When the prior complained about his habit of merely coming in on some days and staring at his work-in-progress, Leonardo was called before the duke. He explained that he needed to look and think before he could know what to do with his hands; and suggested that since he had not yet found a face with the malevolence and cruelty of a Judas, he could always use the prior's. The duke, apparently, roared with laughter.

Unfortunately, Leonardo was also experimenting with the paint itself. The traditional method of painting on walls was fresco, which involved putting wet plaster on the section to be painted, then applying watercolour quickly, before it set. This produces bright, fresh colours but allows for no second thoughts, and it did not suit Leonardo's slow, deliberate brushwork. So he tried something new. He coated the wall of the refectory with a mixture of pitch, gum and chalk and then painted on it dry, using tempera, the egg-bound paint

that normally lasts very well. It did not, however, last well on the prepared wall that Leonardo was working on. Less than twenty years
after he had finished, the painting was starting to flake, and forty years
after that it was described as 'ruined'. The cultured nouveau-riche
duke would never have known this, however, because long before the
painting had begun to deteriorate he was captured by the French, and
died in 1508 in an underground dungeon.

Leonardo may have been mortified – but perhaps not: he was a
compulsive dabbler and experimenter, and with his fizzing butterfly
mind, easily bored. He used other new (and unsuccessful) painting
techniques later, infuriated a pope who claimed he never finished anything, and produced hundreds of designs for hundreds of objects –
which, given the relatively primitive technology of his day, would
never have actually flown, attacked soldiers, flooded enemy cities or
blown up castles – the list is very long indeed. He produced gloriously
beautiful drawings and a few of the most exquisite and enigmatic
paintings ever executed.

But at the centre of his lifelong search was his dream of uncover-
ing a small number of underlying principles and patterns that would
explain all of nature. His notebooks are crammed with pictures and
speculations about the structure of vortexes, heart valves, cloud
shapes; the designs of leaves, human veins, bones and levers; about
how character is expressed in the shape of faces. Everywhere, he is
looking for correspondences. Are flowing human locks like rivulets of
water? Are human arms like birds' wings? Are there perfect proportions for the human body, and do they relate to the proportions of
horses' legs and muscles? What are the symmetries in plant forms, and
what are the rules that guide them? In Leonardo's world there is not
yet a clear divide between 'science' and 'art'. They are the same thing.
The artist coldly analyses form, perspective and the effect of distance
on colours, which will give his pictures their impact. The artist uses
lenses, learns how to cast metals, and works on his equations so he
knows how to support the dome of a new church.

For Verrocchio and Leonardo, 'science' simply means learning and
understanding; it is the practical preparation that allows buildings,
sculptures and paintings to be properly made.

This hunger for knowledge, not least his interest in forces and
engineering and such things as levers, has led Leonardo to be called

the original 'Renaissance man'. The image that blurs into our idea of Leonardo himself is that of his perfectly proportioned nude standing inside a square and circle, *Vitruvian Man*, the complete human, executed about 1487.

But what does this have to do with the Renaissance, if strictly defined as the rebirth of classical learning, as the humanists taught? Leonardo was not educated in – or apparently much interested in – Roman and Greek writers. He was looking for patterns and symmetries around him in a way that is much closer to the concerns of modern biologists and physicists than to Aristotle or Cicero. Yes, the Renaissance was inspired by all those statues dug up in Rome, and by the translation of old texts. This was the decoration, the trimming, of the age. Beefy cardinals, meanwhile, were enjoying the violent, sexually explicit stories of old Rome, and decorating their family palaces with soft porn lightly covered in a classical gauze. But Leonardo, like the best artists, remains alive because he was about looking – looking harder, looking afresh – looking ahead – and not about looking back.

Leonardo benefited from learning transmitted through the Muslim world – for instance on optics – and from the wealth brought to southern Europe by the new trade routes. Christian Europe had advanced not simply through her own exertions, but because of changes beyond her borders, from Genghis's annihilation of the core of Asian Islam, to inventions made in China under the Song and new thinking about God and the world that emerged in al-Andalus. Leonardo has become not simply the archetype of the Renaissance man, but of the European spirit at its boldest and most optimistic. But the West had moved beyond her old status as muddy melting pot long before he first picked up a brush. Now she was ready to explode outwards.

Part Five

THE WORLD BLOWS OPEN

*1492–1640: Europe Erupts in All Directions,
While the Rest of the World Struggles On*

It is said – rightly – that the two most significant changes in human history were the invention of agriculture, upon which everything else depended, and the industrial revolution, which shaped today's world. Some think the latest advances in digital technology and brain science add up to a third leap; others disagree. But if farming and capitalism were the first and second leaps, perhaps we need to add one more stage, a kind of half-leap forward, or just a purposeful stride.

This stage is global trade, which emerged out of the age of discovery. It was driven by the unequal distribution of plants, minerals and animals around the world, creating flows of sugar, tobacco, spices, and money. Without it, we would never have had capitalism and so we would never have had the industrial revolution – at least, not in anything like the way it actually happened.

We have seen plenty of examples of local trading systems extending huge distances. The achievement of the Arab sailors in linking India and the Mediterranean, and thus connecting with the sailing traders of the Far East, was one. The caravan traffic across the Sahara was another; the river system exploited by the Vikings, leading to the creation of Russia, a third. But it was only when Western European sailors, exploiting new ocean-going sailing ships, forged their way from continent to continent, that the real global trading system began. They were demonstrating a classic instance of incremental technology. A wooden bucket made of ropes, new keel and rudder developments and new ways of rigging sailcloth suddenly becomes a galleon, guided by compasses and star-reading instruments, and soon armed with cannon. These vessels had evolved over centuries from the galleys of the ancient world and from the old rounder, sea-going cargo boats.

Their effect was shattering. Scholars argue about this, but at the time of the arrival of these new boats, the Americas may have had a population of around fifty million people, roughly on a par with

Europe. These people were mostly concentrated in today's Brazil, Mexico, Peru and along the Mississippi River. Soon afterwards, population figures plunged. In the more advanced central and southern American regions, Spanish and Portuguese colonists reimposed a form of forced labour and slavery, leading to centuries of slow development and political stagnation. In the emptier north, different kinds of colonists eventually settled, learned to farm there, and built a democratic culture.

These changes left their mark on the balance of power and prosperity in today's world. The flow of gold and silver back to Europe, then to China, caused political turmoil in both these areas. In Europe, the old religious hierarchy found itself challenged, and the continent became radically divided: the needs of global traders brought about the invention of financial systems which, again, mark today's world. In the East, societies such as Japan and China struggled to find a way to respond to the new seaborne arrivals, who began to build empires wherever they could.

This part of the book will look at how, when Europe flung herself out around the rest of the world, using relatively primitive technology – most of it learned from others – some of the key building-blocks of modernity started to fall into place. This phase was once recounted as a self-admiring, heroic tale of explorers and conquerors, bringing religion and enlightenment to the natives; of exotic items arriving in European cities; of admirably self-reliant farmers ploughing virgin soil. It now reads like a much more brutal story, with Europeans trampling across much of the planet rather like the Four Horsemen of the Apocalypse. When we ask why certain parts of the world are so much richer than others – what has worked and what has not – we see that this is a key period.

And we shall also see that the real story was odder than any summary can convey; it takes in Europe's terror of coastal pirates, her admiration for national defenders such as Vlad the Impaler; the importance of staying cosy to the greatness of Russia; and the role of anti-smoking campaigners in England and Japan.

Trouble in Paradise

If the Spanish 'discovered' America in the 1490s, then Napoleon 'discovered' Russia in 1812. It was an invasion. The European invasion of America was one in which wooden ships, using the Chinese inventions of the compass and gunpowder, Muslim navigational mathematics and European Atlantic sailing skills, acted the part that horses and chariots played on land. It is remembered by Europeans and their modern American cousins as 'the discovery' only because the invaded peoples were so militarily weak and succumbed so quickly to disease. Also, after centuries of deforesting and draining, mass hunting and overfishing, Europe was so relatively barren in natural resources that the Americas seemed to many Europeans a rich, ripe, unplucked wilderness, another paradise. Preachers, sailors, entrepreneurs and writers announced the discovery of a land of empty forests and friendly heathens just waiting for the bounties of proper farming, property rights and the Gospel.

In fact, America's forests and prairies had been extensively hunted for millennia, after bands of Asiatics reached it across a land bridge perhaps around twenty thousand years ago.. The history of native Americans between then and the arrival of Europeans is a complex story of many different civilizations and of a continent which, far from being unpeopled, probably supported more humans than did Europe at the time of Columbus. In the 1490s, there were perhaps around seven to eight million 'Indians' in North America, many of them very effective farmers, which, added to the heavily populated Mexican and southern areas, suggests a population of 75–100 million, as compared with 70 million in Europe.[1]

American societies ranged from Inuit hunters to pueblo-dwellers, from sophisticated farming cultures and bands of federated tribes to empires. The first European descriptions of savages along the North American Atlantic coast, and the popular lore telling of fierce tent-dwelling hunters constantly at war with one another, are mere propaganda. Most people there were farmers, living in villages and small towns, or pueblos, growing a mix of crops, even if much of their agriculture was based on a slash-and-burn system, the farmers moving on every few years and allowing the land to regenerate – very similar to early farming in Britain, France and Germany. Their tribal systems were often characterized by a balance of power that included a place for leading women, who chose the male chiefs, as well as complex arrangements and alliances intended to avoid conflict. Above all, this was a very varied continent socially. It has been estimated that in North America alone there were over six hundred different societies and around a dozen unrelated language groups, 'in some cases more dissimilar than English and Chinese'.[2]

Though Columbus is credited as the 'discoverer' for Europeans, the Vikings had already reached America's northern Atlantic shore and had settled for a short time, while Basque sailors had long known the rich cod-fishing grounds off Newfoundland. After Columbus reached the south, the first northerly connections were French, Spanish, Dutch and, later, English fur-traders, followed by settlements many of which survived only thanks to native American food aid. But the impact of the Europeans resulted in a multi-faceted catastrophe, which is only recently being properly understood. From their first arrival in the 1520s up until 1900, it has been estimated that there were almost a hundred American epidemics, virtually wiping out entire peoples. Aside from those who died of disease, many died of hunger, the result of fields being left untended and crops unsown. The 'virgin' and empty paradise proclaimed by European settlers was in many areas, in fact, an open-air disaster zone.

The effect on native peoples did not stop with disease, of course. The desperate desire of Europeans for fur, particularly beaver pelts for hats, brought tribes into conflict as they hunted the animals to local extinction, and radically altered their traditional ways of living. The introduction of guns and alcohol had a similar impact. Further south, the Spanish had reintroduced horses, which had been wiped out by the first Americans. By the early 1700s escaped horses running wild, and others that had been bartered or stolen, underlay a huge change in the lifestyle of the Plains Indians, who had always hunted their bison on foot. Now, mounted, they became a much more effective – and war-like – nomadic people.

Finally, the invasive acts of colonization itself destroyed the native empires of Mesoamerica and the coastal cultures of North America, and caused waves of migration. Far from being 'timeless' and 'untamed', as was the claim, America had been a well populated continent. The arrival of Europeans, from the viewpoint of its original inhabitants, was one of the greatest disasters in history.

Christopher Gets Lost

Christopher Columbus, or Cristóbal Colón (Spanish), or Cristoforo Colombo (Italian) or Christofferus de Colombo, or Colom, or whichever name we choose from the medley by which this red-faced, white-haired seadog was known, can be thought of as a scout, the advance party. All invasions have men riding on ahead, then reporting back; in this case, they were riding three small ships, known by their crew by slang words for 'prostitute'. Columbus's flagship, the *Santa Maria*, was known to her sailors as 'the Dirty Mary'. When they left a little Spanish port village in 1492, these men had no fear of falling off the end of the world. They thought they would find Far Eastern lands, perhaps Japan, perhaps India, perhaps China with its 'Great Khan' (though that empire had gone a hundred years earlier – news travelled slowly). Columbus went to his deathbed convinced he had found 'the Indies', but his behaviour suggests that he was confused: he had claimed the Caribbean for the Spanish Crown, which he was hardly likely to do if he really thought this was part of the mighty Chinese empire.

Quite what he thought he was doing is a mystery. On his first voyage he carried nothing much to trade, just a few baubles, and no soldiers or priests, nor anybody to record in drawings what he would find. He cannot, of course, have had any idea that his little expedition would be the vanguard buzz before the huge swarm of European shipping going west – or the first few drops of water before the storm. His later explanations are so various and contradictory that it may well be that he did not know quite what he was looking for, though he wrote obsessively about gold. Columbus did carry great titles – Admiral of the Ocean and Viceroy – and the right to a tenth of everything he discovered. He had been granted all this by the Spanish monarchs Ferdinand and Isabella, who had just destroyed the last Muslim foothold in Europe, the little kingdom of Granada.

Columbus was a brave sailor, though he was perhaps an even better confidence-artist. He was certainly responsible for the most significant mistake in human history.

Perhaps we should say 'self-confidence-artist', for he had a formidable belief in his own destiny. His had been a long struggle to raise the funds for what was essentially a financial speculation. As we have seen, this was a time of intense competition in the western Mediterranean. The Portuguese, the real pioneer sailors, had reached the tip of Africa and were poised to establish reliable routes to India. They hoped to get to the African goldfields owned by Mali and Songhai, and to attack the Muslim bloc from the south. The Spanish had competed with them, and with French adventurers, for Europe's first Atlantic colonies, the scatterings of islands off the African coast. Of these, the Portuguese had Madeira and the Cape Verde islands, while between 1404 and 1493 the Spanish had secured the Canary Islands.

What had happened in the Canaries was small in scale, but an almost perfect test-run for the colonization of America. The local people, possibly of Berber origin, were tall and not particularly dark-skinned. They lived in tribal groups, and though they fought back against the Spanish, they lacked the advantage of both horses and guns, of which they had no knowledge. They were also vulnerable to European diseases. Many were taken back to Europe as slaves. Their culture has now completely vanished. In their place, the Spanish established sugar plantations and dreamed of gold, in this case the African gold not so far away across the ocean.

But what *was* beyond the Canaries, further west? Columbus was not alone in assuming that Japan and China could be as little as four weeks' sailing. Educated Europeans now accepted the world was round. As noted earlier, Christian sailors had Muslim astrolabes and Chinese compasses as well as classical maps. Among those who told Columbus that China was reachable was Paolo Toscanelli, a sage of Florence who knew Leonardo da Vinci and probably Amerigo Vespucci, who would later give his name to the continent.[3] On the other hand, other eminent geographers disagreed. They thought the voyage must be far longer than Columbus hoped, and too far for the boats of the time, carrying limited fresh water, to survive. Columbus failed to get Portuguese backing for his venture because its king's number-crunchers, the Junta dos Matematicos, did not agree with his distance calculations; and to start with, he had just the same trouble in Spain.

But Ferdinand and Isabella, swollen by their military triumph over the Moors, did eventually help. Their motives were a mix of greed, pride, piety and fear. They were greedy for gold, and also for the Eastern spices which had made so many merchants and cities rich along the long land route. Their conquest of Granada had been glorious, but also expensive. They were proud of their great Christian triumph, however, which had echoed around Europe, and they clearly had a sense of destiny to which Columbus's gamble appealed. Like other contemporary Christians, they believed Christ would return before long, and that their duty included finding as many souls as possible to bring into the Christian fold. Above all, they were afraid of being beaten to new discoveries. Columbus had already tried Portugal. He had sent a brother (who was delayed, after being caught by pirates) to talk to the English. And when the Spanish finally agreed to fund Columbus, he was on his way to sell his idea to the French.

Columbus was not Spanish himself, but Genoese. It was the aristocracy, Church and merchants of Spain, however, who stumped up, and they would do so again when he returned with enslaved natives, some interesting vegetables, parrots, and only a rather meagre tray of gold pieces – suggesting, in effect, that they play 'double or quits'. He had said he could reach Japan in four weeks' sailing from the Canary Islands, a journey he claimed was around 2,400 miles. But those Portuguese mathematicians were right: the real distance was about twelve thousand miles, and thus completely impossible for a ship of the time without landfall and fresh supplies en route.

He may well have known he was exaggerating, which makes the courage of simply setting off into the unknown even more remarkable. At least one other well organized exploratory fleet had sailed west and simply vanished. We should not forget, though, the sheer exhilaration and excitement that must also have been felt in just taking these new machines, ocean-going ships, and seeing how far they might go. Ferdinand and Isabella had offered a huge reward to the first sailor to sight land – a grant of ten thousand silver pieces a year for the rest of his life. With every man aboard the three tiny ships presumably fantasizing that 'it could be me', greed and optimism held out for weeks after they had left their final stepping-off point, the Canaries. But after many false sightings and with supplies running low, the mood changed.

Columbus, the Italian commander, begged and cajoled his Spanish crew to carry on. Some sailors pointed out that he was a mad foreigner, and that they were risking their lives to make him rich – which was an entirely fair charge. Others talked of throwing him overboard if he persisted. After five weeks at sea Columbus called a meeting with the captains of the other two ships, the *Pinta* and the *Niña*, who agreed, grudgingly, to carry on, but only for another four days. Two days later, on 12 October 1492, one of the sailors, Rodrigo de Triana, finally saw land ahead – part of the island chain of what are now called the Bahamas. If Rodrigo had a pleasurable vision of a life of ease now ahead, he had mistaken his captain. Columbus claimed he had seen landfall already, and took the reward for himself. How he avoided being thrown overboard on the return voyage by his disappointed crew is yet another mystery. When they landed, Columbus claimed the island for the Spanish Crown, as San Salvador (its original native name was Guanahani).

The people there were related to the Taíno of the Caribbean, whose deadly enemies were the hunter-cannibals, the Caribs. There were probably no more than two hundred thousand people living in the Caribbean at the time, doing some basic farming, fishing and weaving – and greatly enjoying smoking the dried leaves of tobacco plants, rolled into cigars. Columbus described the Taíno (he called them 'Indians') as peace-loving, gentle people, and told King Ferdinand they could be forced to work, farm, build and wear clothes. Moving on to claim larger islands too, he also kidnapped some natives to show off back in Spain. Within eighteen years of the first Spanish colonizers arriving – on Columbus's second, much longer, visit a year after his first – 99 per cent of the locals would be dead. Most of these deaths were caused by disease.

On the first visit, because his largest ship had been wrecked, Columbus had had to leave thirty-nine men behind to build a settlement and shake some more gold out of the locals. But the Spanish lust for gold and conquest drove even the Taíno to fight back. When he returned, the thirty-nine were all dead. There would always be more settlers, but the Taíno and other peoples of the area were doomed. They passed syphilis on to Columbus's sailors, and thus by stages to all fornicating Europeans; but they virtually disappeared from history, leaving behind only a few of their words, including 'hammock', 'canoe' and 'barbecue'.[4] That second expedition brought with it around twelve hundred people, including some women, along with some of those terrifying newcomers, horses, with mounted soldiers and plenty of guns. To native Americans the odd combination of a gleaming half-man with four long legs, able to spit fire, must have seemed like some monstrous dragon. The second voyage also brought mules, chickens and pigs: this was the moment at which exploration slid into takeover.

The 'Indians', often (in self-justification) libelled as 'cannibals' when some particularly harsh treatment was to be dealt out to them, were considered the property of the new Spanish empire. Their land was to be its land. Did the Spanish Catholic propensity for seeing all non-Catholics as heretics, who either could be converted or would burn for ever, lead them to disregard any notion of native rights? Northern Protestants would behave very similarly; religion was probably simply the excuse. For the new Spanish monarchy the real threat, anyway, was not in the New World, but in the Old.

It came from the rival Portuguese, with whom the Spanish were in competition all over the western ocean. In 1494 the two nations had come to an extraordinary agreement, ratified as the Treaty of Tordesillas, which divided half the world longitudinally between them. The line ran through the two poles and west of the Cape Verde islands off Africa, which were already Portuguese, giving the islands of Cuba and Hispaniola, claimed by Columbus, to Spain. A revision of the first agreement would give the Portuguese most of Brazil; later, in 1529, the Iberian carve-up was extended to the other side of the world, with another line being drawn through the Far East in the Treaty of Zaragoza.

Columbus's third and fourth voyages culminated in landfall in South America proper, and in the discovery of pearls. By then the colonists were squabbling amongst themselves and falling out badly with the tolerant Taíno. Ferdinand and Isabella would trim the too generous deal Columbus had got for himself and begin the long project of turning what had been in effect a private gamble into a state- and Church-sponsored imperium.

The Christian Frontier

To understand why Columbus did what he did, and the apparent absurdity of two countries dividing up between them much of the world (with papal blessing), we have to look more closely at the Iberian politics of his time. If Christian Europe was cut off from the East by the long and expensive Silk Road, then Spain and Portugal must have felt more isolated still. These were states on the edge of Europe, just cleared of Muslims, littered with castles, lines of defence and encampments. Ferdinand and Isabella were frontier monarchs, passionate in their belief in Catholic Christendom. The experience of their subjects had been that, to feel secure, they had to keep pressing on, expanding their land. This was a restless frontier, policed by sailing-boats, a frontier familiar with war.

During the centuries of al-Andalus, only a narrow band in the mountainous north of Spain, the kingdom of Asturias, had remained Christian. As we have seen, Christian kings exploited Muslim division to slowly fight their way south. Under the austere Almoravid dynasty which arrived from North Africa to impose a more repressive form of Islam, many Jews and others found that the squabbling Christian states made them welcome, and there had been a major emigration north. Most of the 'reconquest' had been achieved centuries before the reign of Isabel and Ferdinand. The crucial victory had been at Las Navas de Tolosa in 1212, when the kings of Castile, Navarre, Aragón and Portugal broke the habit of their lifetimes and fought on the same side, crushing the Almohads, a Berber dynasty whose troops came from as far inside Africa as Senegal, as well as from today's North Africa.

By the 1490s all that was left to mop up was the small kingdom of Granada. Muslim forces put up a long and brave resistance, but were eventually starved into surrendering Granada itself, lured by a generous-seeming treaty. The Christians promised that anyone who wished to do so could leave and return to Africa, but that Muslim law would be retained for the Muslims who stayed. Hundreds of thousands chose to stay and live under Christian rule. Some found this intolerable because the original treaty was soon torn up; but many Muslims converted to Christianity. The Jews, perhaps 200,000-strong, were also offered the choice of converting to Catholicism or leaving Spain. It is now reckoned that only around forty thousand went, initially mostly to Portugal, though later to Amsterdam, Constantinople, Venice and even Rome.[5]

The wealth of those who did not convert was seized by the state, and indeed helped fund Columbus's missions. But these were probably the minority. The Bishop of Burgos was a former rabbi; St Teresa of Avila, one of the great mystics of the Counter-Reformation, came from a family of Jewish converts; so, probably, did Bartolomé de Las Casas, the friar and historian who revealed the dark underside of Spanish colonialism in America. Though the Spanish Inquisition was just as brutal and remorseless as its popular image suggests, constantly testing the sincerity of Marranos, or crypto-Jews, and handing over as many as four thousand for execution, Jews and Muslims killed apostates too. For Ferdinand and Isabella, the Inquisition and the forced Christianizing of all Spain was basic to the political union of their kingdoms, Castile and Aragón; an absolute ideological rock on which the new country with its single people would be built.

They were a curious pair, these Catholic monarchs so readily admired in Rome. Isabella, of the royal house of Castile, had had a rocky childhood, including times of real poverty while living with her mentally disturbed mother. The problem was probably genetic: Isabella's daughter was known as Joanna the Mad. Her dynastically ambitious father had touted Isabella around the courts of half the crowned heads of Europe. She had found none of them appealing, and had learned how to nimbly dodge much older men. On one occasion she prayed to God to let her escape betrothal to a titled forty-three-year-old. He died from a ruptured appendix on his way to woo her. (This may explain Isabella's famous piety in later life.) Instead, with the special blessing of the pope – needed because their grandfathers were cousins – in 1469 she absconded in order to marry Ferdinand, of the royal house of Aragón, apparently against everyone's wishes.

Ferdinand seems from his portraits to be a doughy, melancholy-looking man. He became a formidably ambitious ruler, engaged in the endless wars and treaties of the age as he extended the power of the two kingdoms. He was a ferociously hard worker, too, sometimes apparently tying a bandage across his face to help him concentrate. When it came to Moors, heretics and Jews, he was tougher even than Isabella, who liked to be with her troops at the kill. He was genuinely egalitarian in his attitude to his wife (though not to anybody else). *'Tanto monta, monta tanto, Isabel como Fernando'* was their joint motto – 'Isabella, Ferdinand, it's all the same thing' – about as good a recipe for marital happiness as history offers. Sadly for both, he outlived her by a dozen years.

All of this matters because Ferdinand and Isabella established the most powerful dynasty in the West, and probably in the world, at the time. Joanna the Mad married Philip the Handsome, a Habsburg and son of the Holy Roman Emperor: their son, as Charles V, would link the Spanish monarchy to that of Austria, as well as inheriting swathes of Burgundy and the Low Countries, southern Germany, Naples, Sicily and Sardinia. With his election in 1519 as Holy Roman Emperor (buttressed by the fact that his brother ruled Bohemia and Hungary too), Charles would become the first man since classical times to have a chance of uniting Europe. It was a chance that seemed all the greater because of the huge quantity of silver soon pouring into his coffers from the new American empire – to which we now return.

Choked on Silver

It was one of the most one-sided and momentous ambushes of all time, but it did not seem like that to the waiting Spanish as they shivered out of sight behind whitewashed walls. 'Many of us urinated without knowing it, in sheer terror,' confessed one later. Their leader, an illiterate, illegitimate and grizzled fighter called Francisco Pizarro from a dirt-poor town in Spain, had with him just 168 men, sixty-two of them with horses. On that morning, Saturday 16 November 1532, he was facing the ruler of Tahuantinsuyo – we call it Peru – and his army of eighty thousand troops. It is true that the Spanish had guns while the Inca army had weaponry more suitable to a Bronze Age battle – slingshots, bows and arrows, clubs and truncheons, and helmets of wood. But the Spanish arquebuses were slow and unwieldy and Pizarro had only about ten or twelve of them.

The odds still seemed hugely against the impertinent invaders, who had invited the Inca emperor Atahualpa to meet them in the huge square of the town of Cajamarca in the lush green Peruvian highlands. Cajamarca had temples and military buildings, constructed according to a monumental stone jigsaw technique, which still seems far cleverer than any European masonry. At its centre was a large open space surrounded by low-lying buildings used to house worshippers and travellers. Inside these the Spanish were hiding.

Atahualpa had no notion of a trap. He was on his way to be

crowned at the Inca capital Cuzco after defeating the army of his half-brother in a civil war. Though the Spanish had been causing mayhem further north for years, he had never heard of the conquistadors. Pizarro's arrival on the coast had been reported to him by messengers and there was worrying news of looting, but it probably seemed a sideshow compared with the epic Inca civil war. An envoy had told Atahualpa that these were people of little account – unwarlike, disorganized creatures with pale skins, wearing shiny metal shells and sitting on big llamas. These 'horses' were not to be worried about; they did not eat people. One of the new arrivals, a priest called Friar Vicente de Valaverde, wore 'crossed sticks', said the Inca envoy. Atahualpa, therefore, was merely curious. He later told Pizarro he had designs on the horses, which he thought could be useful. As to the Spanish men, he was thinking of taking them as interesting oddities to guard his harem. When he arrived on his litter, decorated with parrot feathers, silver and gold and carried by eighty of his lords dressed in bright blue, six thousand crack soldiers were running jauntily alongside, singing songs, while other troops brushed the road ahead of him. They were largely unarmed and in their ceremonial costumes.

Because they would succumb so easily to Spanish weapons, it is sometimes assumed that the Inca army was a poor one. It was not. These were men trained with ferocious severity, who had beaten every rival force they had ever faced, warriors who expected to fight hand to hand, to the death. When they arrived at the square, it was empty. Eventually the priest appeared and told the emperor he had been instructed to bring him the Christian faith. Friar Vicente held out a Bible, an object Atahualpa had never seen before. Taking it, the Inca struggled to open it. The friar tried to help, but Atahualpa knocked him aside. When he opened the book, he stared at the squiggly black lines and threw it to the ground in disappointment. What a boring reception. What a useless gift!

The priest, outraged at this blasphemy. summoned the ambush. 'Come out, come out, Christians!' he yelled. 'Come at these enemy dogs!' Pizarro, in a prearranged signal, then dropped a cloth he had been holding. Two of his four small cannon fired (the other two failed). The Spanish, forgetting their fear and their uncomfortably wet boots, charged out on horseback and on foot. The noise and surprise caused utter panic among the Inca. They had never faced guns, steel weapons or horses. Men fled in all directions. During the two hours left before sunset at least seven thousand Incas were killed, either trying to protect their sun-god emperor in his litter, or fleeing over a mud wall and rushing away into the fields. The Spanish speared and stabbed and hacked until they were exhausted. Atahualpa's litter was eventually sent flying by mounted horsemen and Pizarro captured him, dragging him inside.

Still stunned by what had happened, the Inca emperor was offered a deal by Pizarro. The Spanish were already amazed by the quantities of gold and silver dishes, jugs, goblets and jewellery they had seized from the enemy. Atahualpa admitted to Pizarro that there was much more where that had come from. For the Inca, gold was associated with the sun, and thus the sun-god. The real value of the objects was in their workmanship and elegance, but for the Spanish the value was merely the metal, the commodity value. Soon they started to melt the crafted objects into ingots. Atahualpa, already aware of the Spaniards' strange obsession, offered, as the price of his freedom, to fill the room he was being held in with gold. It was 22 feet long by 17 feet wide – it still exists – and would be filled to a depth of eight feet. It would then, he promised, in the same way be filled twice over with silver objects. All this would be done within two months. Astonished, Pizarro agreed and promised Atahualpa his freedom – a promise he had no intention of keeping.

At the end of the metal-searching and gathering, which in fact lasted until the following June, the greatest works of the Inca gold- and silversmiths were melted down to make more than 13,000 pounds of sullen yellow ingots and 26,000 of dull silver blocks.

By now the Spanish were thrusting further into the Inca empire, fighting and double-crossing and dividing their enemies. Atahualpa had been useful throughout because of the absolute authority he claimed over his people, even in captivity. This allowed the Spanish to move around largely unhampered while the Inca planned for the eventual recovery of his freedom and his empire.

It was not to be. Charged with trying to raise an army to free himself, Atahualpa was offered a choice of being burned to death or converting to Christianity and being strangled. Since the Inca believed in the preservation of the body through mummification, he chose conversion, and was duly garrotted. Pizarro then had his body burned anyway.

It is easy to see this as a classic confrontation between wicked early imperialists and noble locals. Easy, but wrong: if any leaders were self-consciously imperial it was the Inca, whose empire had erupted out of its base at Cuzco, far to the south, then started seriously to spread just ninety years earlier. Cajamarca had fallen under their control sixty years before Pizarro got there, and the greatest period of Inca advance had come only three decades before the Spanish invasion. Skilled, militaristic engineers rather like the Romans, they had built ten thousand or so miles of roads, taking over cultures throughout the Andes and the Pacific coastal plain by a combination of military prowess and the bribery and intimidation of rival elites.

The Inca had no wheeled transport or writing, and hardly any metal weapons; their communications and bureaucracy were managed by means of an ingenious system of coloured, knotted strings called *quipu*, with runners to carry them from place to place. But Inca overlordship was harsh. All land belonged to the empire, and the people were organized in units of families owing service to the emperor and were not allowed to move. Atahualpa was hardly a saint: he expected slavish obedience to his every whim, casually ordered executions, and liked to drink out of the mummified head of an enemy general.

The weakness of the Inca empire, going well beyond its lack of horses and guns, was its extreme centralism, which would greatly help the Spanish. This system gave them, as long as they controlled Atahualpa, the brain-stem of the entire Inca administration. After killing Atahualpa, they made his brother Yupanqui emperor, and managed to continue to exert some control through him while waging war against the Inca resistance – a war that would go on for another forty years. This was already the Spanish pattern. As in their defeat of the Aztec empire further north under Hernando Cortés during 1519–21, the invaders found that many of the peoples conquered by that recently arisen empire were happy to ally themselves against the local oppressor, having little idea of the deal that they were making. Again, once they had captured the Aztec ruler, Montezuma, the Spanish were able to use his residual authority to control his people – and loot his gold.

Once the local Spanish commanders were in position in Mexico and Peru, they used native control systems and others imported from

Spain – notably the *encomienda*, a system of grants to noble Spaniards which imposed on the indigenous people conditions not far removed from slavery and which had first been deployed against the Muslims at home. In Peru, they simply appropriated the Inca custom of forced labour and applied it to their own needs, particularly to silver-mining at Potosí. One imperial system, after all, was merely replacing two others, so there was nothing of the transformation in relations between peasant and ruler that would happen in North America a little later.

The Spanish had not started out to build a new world in the sense of a new social start, a beginning-again. Far from it. They were adventurers after portable plunder and owing fealty to the Spanish court. Plenty of building went on – of schools, hospitals and barracks as well as churches – but reforms suggested from Madrid happened slowly or not at all. Antonio de Mendoza, an important early Spanish viceroy and marquis in New Spain, advised his successor to do little, and to do it slowly. Many of the key figures of the conquest, and of the decades after it, chose to end their days at home in Spain – Cortés among them.

Again and again the writings of Pizarro's followers harp on the gold and silver, obsessively weighing it, rather than on the people or the landscape. The Spanish in the New World, for all the beauty of their architecture and the brilliance of their music, would not prove especially creative or enlightened empire-builders. They took over a world that had already long been at war with itself, and whose cultural offerings to Eurasia would be limited. The Aztec capital of Tenochtitlán may at the time have been the biggest city on the planet apart from Constantinople, and with its canals, palaces and religious art (not to mention its ruthless domination of subject peoples, and its dark obsession with death and the afterlife) it bore a striking resemblance to Venice; but Aztec religion horrified Europeans, and Aztec art was disregarded. The Maya, who in Yucatán took longer to subdue, were already long past their peak; but their intricate architecture and astrology were equally uninteresting to Europeans of the 1500s.

In North America, very soon, other European settlements would lure a different kind of adventurer – religiously dissident, hardy farmers who really did want a new world, a begin-again society. There, despite attempts to recreate a European-style aristocracy in Virginia and Carolina, the demand for rough democracy (for male Europeans, at least) proved irresistible.

To Mesoamerica the Spanish brought aristocrats, soldiers and priests. Their immense mouldering terrain of churches, convents, haciendas, indentured peasants and slaves produced few new ideas or exports, and eventually proved vulnerable to the North Americans and to Enlightenment-influenced rebellions at home. And once the Spanish monarchy had lost its authority to Napoleon's regiments and effectively collapsed, Mexico declared independence – not in order to create a new, more democratic society but for quite the opposite reason: to maintain the position of the local aristocrats against worryingly radical moves in Spain.[6] The careers of José de San Martín of Argentina and Simón Bolívar from Venezuela are stirring local epics, but they, in turn, were unable to found nations that could challenge the United States, the British or the European empires.

The speed of the Spanish advance during the early stages of the Conquest had been made possible as much by the diseases they carried in and on their bodies as by the weapons in their hands, bold and risk-taking as the Spaniards were. Spanish microbes had reached the Inca capital Cuzco well before Pizarro got there. Smallpox had a devastating effect in the Andes, as elsewhere in South America. It had provoked the civil war, which was raging just as Pizarro landed, by killing the Inca emperor and setting rival sons against one another. From Mexico to the Pacific islands, epidemics had the same effect.

It was the length of the Americans' immunity-destroying quarantine from the germs current in Eurasia, which lasted for some thirteen thousand years at least, that made the impact so great, particularly in the densely populated centre of the American continent. It has been estimated that around 95 per cent of the people living there before the Europeans arrived were killed by the diseases brought across the ocean – measles, smallpox, malaria, diphtheria, typhus and tuberculosis. One may doubt the accuracy of detailed percentages, but it seems a scale of death unmatched at any time in European history.

What did the Spanish, and the rest of Europe, get in return? Oddly few diseases: only syphilis, and that not certainly from Mesoamerican contact. The main thing Spain got was a huge, sudden influx of specie. Gold-fever infected the Spanish, as the Inca empire collapsed. Pizarro's secretary Pedro Sancho began his self-justifying account with the words: 'Concerning the great quantity of silver and gold which was brought from Cuzco . . .' Those first piles of ingots were only the beginning. Once Inca culture had been stripped bare, within twenty years new mining and extractive techniques allowed the full-scale exploitation of the fabled mountain of silver at Potosí, now in Bolivia. At the cost, it is said, of ten native American lives for every *peso* minted there, Potosí would provide two-thirds of the fifty thousand tons of silver that passed from America to Europe during the century and a half to come.

Plunder, however, is a very different thing from prosperity. The gold and silver were carried on Spanish galleons to the Spanish court, but ended up almost anywhere else. A lot went to decorate churches. Charles V spent so much of it on his desperate wars to maintain Habsburg control of the Netherlands, and against the rival French in Italy, that it enriched Flemish victuallers, German armourers and all kinds of mercenaries. He spent more of the loot on paying off his debts to Genoese and Venetian creditors; and they in turn sent it flying further east to China to buy silk, porcelain and other luxuries. There, the Ming empire had by now replaced the Mongol Yuan rulers and established another golden age. Except that it was at times too golden, or rather too silver-addicted, for the plunder from America, having moved through Spain and the eastern Mediterranean, then caused a monetary crisis for the Ming.

If this global whirl of Inca metal were not enough, we must also remember the pirates. The French and English, cut out of the grisly bonanza, used their ships to intercept galleons and carry their booty home. England's Queen Elizabeth turned a blind eye to the piracy, and when the heroic Devon rascal Francis Drake made the journey around South America and into Peruvian waters to steal gold and silver from the Spanish (who had, after all, stolen it from the Incas), Elizabeth's own share was enough to pay off England's entire foreign debt.[7] The pirates had a significance that goes far beyond the romance of individual stories: by luring more Englishmen and Frenchmen across the Atlantic in search of plunder, piracy both improved Northern seamanship and established beachheads in the Caribbean, which would later ease the spread of empire.

As for the homeland of the Spanish conquerors themselves, in the words of the economic historian David Landes, Spain 'became (or stayed) poor because it had too much money'.[8] The Spanish bought all manner of fabrics, foods and exotic goods from their rivals. They exulted in the good fortune that allowed them to enjoy a consumer, or consumption, economy without increased productivity – very much as the West wallowed in its credit-fuelled consumer boom during the early part of the twenty-first century. This was spotted at the time. Landes quotes the Moroccan ambassador to Madrid towards the end of this long splurge, in 1690, who noted that the Spanish had the largest income of all the Christians:

> But the love of luxury and the comforts of civilisation have over-come them, and you will rarely find one of this nation who engages in trade or travels abroad for commerce, as do the other Christian nations such as the Dutch, the English, the Genoese and their like. Similarly, the handicrafts practised by the lower classes and common people are despised by this nation.

It is hard to imagine a more complete programme for national decline than that. In the New World, Spain would build a dozy, already decaying empire of aristocrats, priests and large landowners, and would never experience the jolt into modernity that animated her rivals. Atahualpa was not the only emperor who had failed to spot what was coming.

Man in Black

The look of things, the outward style, can be profound – not trivial at all. During the Reformation one kind of Christian worship, conducted by gorgeously dressed men chanting Latin in their rich, multicoloured churches, was assaulted by another kind. The Germany of Martin Luther was a land of black and white, The stark, black German prose of his preaching, with its urgent choices, strides purposefully over the snow-white of the paper. The spiny black letters impressed with the soot-and-egg mix of early printers' ink carried tens of thousands of ser-mons once delivered by his voice into people's hands across northern Europe. For those who couldn't read, crude black-and-white woodcuts – as different as it is possible to imagine from the richly coloured altar-pieces that had preceded them – would convey the reformers' messages.

Their clothes were plain white, dark, black. Their language was the gut-
tural jab-jab of common German. Their faces glare back from early
portraits, severe and uncompromising.

The north was in revolt against the south. There, all the Italianate
glitter and gleam of the papacy, with its polychrome churches and
gilded Madonnas, represented a Church that had grown worldly. No
wonder that Martin Luther, sturdy and bullish and a great self-drama-
tizer, became the German hero, confronting popes and emperors,
standing, as he put it, 'in the mouth of the great Behemoth, between
his great teeth'. German history before Luther is the history of rulers
and knights, of emperors, archbishops and fables. In many ways he
seems the first modern German, arms akimbo, unfrightened, staring
back at us in the well known portrait. He was a plain man, but no
peasant. His father had worked in the coalmines of Saxony and had
done well enough to become a burgher, with a rich wife and an
impressive stone-built house. He had sent Martin to a good, if brutal,
school, and like so many upwardly mobile parents wanted his son to
become a lawyer. But from early on, Martin Luther showed a darkly
questioning side to his personality, an itchy restlessness.

We must imagine a world in which Hell is real and close; where
the woods and lanes are haunted by fiends and witches; and where the
only possible way out of all this is to secure Christ's help. Germany in
Luther's time was not a comfortable or safe place to be. Apart from
suffering plague and the threat of famine in bad years, it was politically
weak. In the east, the Teutonic knights had bowed to the Poles. In the
north, the Danes had taken Holstein. In the west, the Swiss confeder-
ation was winning its independence. More important – and this was
the case throughout Luther's life – the Muslim armies of the
Ottomans were threatening all of Europe. These early years of the
Reformation coincide with sensational Ottoman challenges such as the
fall of Belgrade in 1521, the capture of Rhodes in 1522, the crushing of
the Hungarians in 1526, the siege of Vienna three years later, and then
further drives into Poland, across the Mediterranean to Malta, and the
long fight with Venice. Though the Southern Catholic powers would
eventually beat the Ottoman fleet at the Battle of Lepanto in 1571, and
though both Malta and Vienna held out, many Christians believed they
were living through the end of Christendom, the last people of a
doomed civilization.

Germany existed as a territory and language area claimed by that 'religious and pseudo-classical myth', the Holy Roman Empire.[9] It did not exist as a nation. Amongst the political minestrone of duchies, princedoms, archbishoprics and free cities there were three hundred or so semi-autonomous principalities, many with their own laws, currencies and family feuds. War and the plague had cut Germany's population. A new and terrible disease, syphilis, was spreading across Europe. 'Ghost villages', which had simply been abandoned, were a common sight. A series of savage peasant rebellions had erupted in southern and western Germany, though not on the scale of the 'Peasant War' of Luther's adulthood, which would claim at least a hundred thousand lives.

So Luther's world felt rickety and impermanent. Death lurked behind every tree. When he was a twenty-one-year-old student, he tells us, one day in 1505 during a summer thunderstorm he had a revelation while walking along a country road. As the lightning crashed down, he promised that if he survived he would enter a monastery. Luther promptly gave up his studies and became a monk in a notably tough, though not extreme, order. For more than a dozen years he was a model monk, hard-driven at his lessons and duties by his ambitious superiors, and studying the conventional texts of Catholicism almost to the point of nervous breakdown. He did well enough to be sent to Rome by his monastery on a diplomatic mission, albeit an unsuccessful one. He was then sent to the new university of Wittenberg to teach.

Universities were starting up across Germany at this time. They offered a way for principalities and ambitious towns to mark themselves out and attract new talent. Wittenberg was one of twenty or so, and known for being forward-looking and experimental. The small town, scarcely more than a walled village, was ruled by Friedrich the Wise, the Elector of Saxony. A shrewd and independent-minded character, Friedrich was one of the seven German 'electors' whose status allowed them to choose the Holy Roman Emperor (not, at this point, a hereditary title), and he had considerable political clout in northern Germany. Later, at the time of his great religious rebellion, Luther would depend on Friedrich for his very survival.

At Wittenberg, Luther's thinking about sin and redemption challenged much of the traditional teaching. Scholars argue still about just how radical his theology really was – it was certainly not unique. The essence of the problem was this. The earlier medieval scholastic tradition insisted that the God of love condemned sinful mankind to Hell on the basis of laws so strict and fierce that they could not be kept to the letter. Luther's view was that mankind was entirely sinful, corrupt, fallen, and could not be transformed into a creature deserving of Heaven simply by repeating prayers or doing good works.

So how could anyone be saved? In a world so intensely religious, this was an urgent question.

Luther solved it when he concluded that God simply brushed aside the sinfulness of those who had true faith – those who were saved, the elect. Sin was too powerful to be defeated by human action. Only a miracle of divine love could overcome it. Christ's sacrifice, taking on himself mankind's sinfulness, was the means by which that miracle happened. To be saved, all you needed was true faith in this. The obvious problem with Luther's view is that it implied that sinful behaviour did not necessarily matter. Trying to overcome sin in a day-to-day way was pointless. Faith was all that counted. Luther's response to such an objection was that the saved would be so grateful, they would not *want* to sin. (This, as many later generations of Protestants would realize, was a little too easy: the Scottish writer James Hogg's satire, *Confessions of a Justified Sinner*, skewered the ease with which hypocrites could have their sinful cake and eat it.)

Luther's thinking was that of a Christian intellectual who had come to loathe the cerebral, sophisticated classical Greek thought of Plato and Aristotle, on which traditional Church theology rested. His main impulse, when he had reached his conclusion about sin, was emotional and personal, an urgent sense of release and joy that demanded to be communicated – and which had nothing to do with the Church hierarchy or liturgies. He described himself as feeling 'born again', an experience still at the heart of modern evangelical Protestantism.

This would always have driven a man like Luther, an odd mix of bruiser and dreamer, into a fight with the Church authorities. But it was the practice of selling indulgences that tipped him over the edge. What was an indulgence? In its most literal sense, it was the transfer of a little of the goodness of Christ and the saints (the 'treasury of merit') to a human sinner. The receiver of the indulgence then had less time to spend in Purgatory – today sometimes seen as the dull air-port lounge of the system, minus the duty-free shops, but then portrayed as a place of purging and agonizing fires, even of torture – before arriving in Heaven. It was not quite a get-out-of-jail-free card, but it was certainly a get-to-Heaven-quicker card.

How did you obtain an indulgence? Prayers and good works could win you one. Travelling to see and touch the relics of saints would, too – and this also brought useful revenue to whichever church or town had the relics (Wittenberg itself had a world-class collection of frag-ments of wood, bones, thorns and hair). But apart from prayers, good works and relics there was a more reliable route: hard cash. Priests had long suggested that recipients of indulgences might want to make a 'charitable offering', to say thank you, as it were. In time, this became a plain cash transaction. As Christ's vicar on earth, the pope could simply sell indulgences. They became his money supply, notes that came in different denominations. He could not only sell them to buy the purchaser time off Purgatory, he could also sell them for the pur-chaser's already-dead parents, who might be crying out to their children for the coins to be paid. Reform-minded clerics from Italy and Holland, France and Switzerland, had spoken out against the crass commercialization of indulgences before now: Luther's blast would be altogether angrier.

The papacy has given history an impressive number of decadent villains, and Leo X, Luther's adversary, was one of them. He was a Medici, the son of the great Florentine ruler Lorenzo the Magnificent, and brought up in an atmosphere of war, artistic exhibitionism and political intrigue. Made a cardinal when he was thirteen, he had little interest in religion as such. When Italian politics landed him the role of pope at the age of thirty-seven, Leo is reported to have said that since God had given him the papacy, 'then let us enjoy it'. A fat, sweaty and hospitable man, he turned Vatican life into a perpetual Roman carnival of indecent plays, bull-fights, dances, banquets and races. Gold poured from his hands in a glittering stream of favours, patronage and personal retail therapy.

Leo's most expensive problem was St Peter's Basilica. The original church had been built under St Constantine in the 330s, over St Peter's supposed burial site. It had fallen into disrepair and was being replaced by a gargantuan new church, intended to awe the world with its scale and beauty. But in 1517 the church was a giant embarrassment, little more than a mucky building site. The huge expense was crippling the papacy. Leo's solution was to declare a fund-raising drive through ever more, and more expensive, indulgences. In Germany a hyper-ambitious archbishop who was raising funds for his own purposes, would act as Leo's agent. The German people would have to be squeezed, and then squeezed again.

In Luther's Saxony, the squeezer-in-chief was a remarkable sales-man called Johann Tetzel. Tetzel was a blow-hard televangelist from the age of pulpit oratory. He would arrive in town trailing a long pro-cession of solemn, berobed priests and followers, and carrying the papal insignia and Leo X's bull (a papal declaration, with the round seal, or *bulla*, hanging from it, showing its authenticity). Oak and iron coffers to receive the loot would be opened, a grand stall set up, and Tetzel would begin. His message was straightforward. If you wanted to avoid hundreds or even thousands of years suffering in Purgatory – pay up. If you wanted to release your dear mother or father from the torments – pay up. According to your wealth and ability – pay up. If this sounds like a satire on his style, the jingle for which he is remem-bered gives the authentic Tetzel style:

> When the coin in the coffer rings
> A soul from Purgatory springs.

For Luther, this was more than the robbing of honest Germans to build a swanky new church in Italy. It was a terrible sin, which would condemn the innocent buyers of indulgences to hellfire, because it meant they would not properly repent or confront their sinfulness, or seek Christ's forgiveness. The most profound matters of faith and pun-ishment had been turned into a cash transaction. It was this that finally exhausted his patience. Protestant Christians the world over know that on 31 October 1517, Martin Luther strode to the oaken doors of Wittenberg's Castle Church and nailed to them a list of ninety-five 'theses', or arguments for debate – an act of defiance aimed at the papacy. It may be so. The original doors are long gone and have been replaced by metal 'heritage' replicas.

Not a man crippled by personal modesty, Luther himself never mentioned the nailing of the theses. It was probably a later story. In Luther's day the church doors were certainly used as a notice-board, a place for announcements of all kinds. So for this locally famous academic monk to nail up some religious arguments would have been possible, though hardly necessary. Nor did Luther intend to start a revolution, or even directly challenge the institution of the papacy. These were points for discussion, in Church Latin, albeit made in his usual punchy style. His students at Wittenberg University would have heard it all before. Luther was still a Catholic, and much of what he said was still official doctrine.

To appreciate why Luther's arguments spread so fast, we need to turn to another small town in Germany, this time in the north-west, Mainz-on-the-Rhine. Here, fifteen years before Luther was born, Johannes Gutenberg had died after inventing Europe's first real printing press. The Chinese and Koreans had long used wood-block printing, and even ceramic printing. Woodcuts had been made in Europe too, long before Gutenberg. What he did was to bring together a system of casting individual metal letters, and groups of letters, so they could be arranged in lines of words, then inked and pressed into dampened paper or animal-skin vellum.

We know relatively little about Gutenberg himself, except that he was skilled in metalwork – we might describe him as a jobbing engineer – and at cutting precious stones; and he was an ambitious entrepreneur, eager to borrow money to build his business. Urban Germany, with its coalmines and stocks of iron ore, and its long-established tradition of making armour, arms and clocks, was not going through an industrial revolution – quite. But it was experiencing an industrious boom, a rise in the status and ambition of craftworkers who would pass on their skills.

Gutenberg bought paper from Italy, experimented with metal alloys and ink mixtures, and hired at least eighteen helpers for his six presses. He intended to produce a printed Bible and wanted it to look as reassuringly like a handwritten one as possible – rather in the way TV drama at first mimicked theatre, or early bloggers tried to mimic newspaper pages online. His planned first run of 180 Bibles of 1,282 pages each was a huge gamble, and in 1454 he had to raise money from all across Europe. His Bible took six months for the casting of the metal type, and two years to set and print. Then it was hand-coloured and illustrated, to make it look 'real'. The effect was similar to contemporary handwriting, compared at the time to woven black-and-white cloth, or textile – hence our word 'text'. The whole process took about three years, as long as it took a scribe to write out a Bible by hand.[10] The scribe, however, produced one, Gutenberg 180.

Printing was an almost overnight craze. The Bibles were admired across Germany, the Low Countries, Italy and Spain. Gutenberg's presses were turned over to other printed work, including grammars for schoolboys, savage tracts attacking the Turks, calendars; and above all, indulgences, made out like huge cheques, with only the time, date and signature to be filled in by hand.

Germany was soon awash with print. Some of the tens of thousands of pamphlets were medical and scientific; others were downright rude. Luther himself, in a sermon on marriage, complained that booksellers were peddling material 'which treats of nothing but the depravity of women'.

So Luther's theses too, nailed up or not, were quickly printed and distributed. He combined them into a single sermon, reprinted twenty-five times in two years. (At the same time, he also changed his pen-name from the Greek for 'the free one', Eleutherius, to the homely German Luter, and then Luther.) His arguments aroused intense interest among a clergy and laity already debating the question of indulgences, the correct notion of sin, and papal authority. During his heyday, Luther is reckoned to have produced, on average, a pamphlet about once a fortnight; his followers, such as the simple shoemaker-writer 'Hans Sachs', and his Catholic foes, contributed many more. Wittenberg had once depended on its ruler's interesting collection of saintly body parts as a revenue-earner. Now it became a boom town because so much printing work was brought to it for the simple reason that Luther lived there.[11]

It could not be long before his arguments were heard in Rome. Set-piece confrontations were arranged. First, he took on fellow Augustinian monks in Heidelberg – and rather effectively; next, at Augsburg, one of Leo X's brightest cardinals; then a brilliant rival theologian in Leipzig, where he was tricked into supporting the Czech reformer Jan Hus, who had been burned at the stake for heresy. Luther was himself condemned as a heretic in a papal bull, which he promptly burned in Wittenberg. Now his relish for a fight really took over. In three famous broadsides, *The Christian Nobility of the German Nation* (addressing those very members of society), *Babylonian*

Captivity, addressing the clergy, and *The Freedom of a Christian*, aimed at all readers, Luther demolished many of the arguments the Church's authority had rested on. These included the special function of priests, their organization as clergy, and the supremacy of the pope.

He had taken the bull – and the *bulla* – by the horns. Again, this would have been impossible without printing presses: the last of these three books was published in thirty-six editions within two years, and translated into Dutch, English, Spanish, Czech and Latin. All Europe was blazing with argument. In faraway England, Henry VIII told his bishops to think up rebuttals to present against Luther. In April 1521 the newly appointed Holy Roman Emperor, the teenage Habsburg Charles V, confronted Luther in person at Worms, where the empire's ruling council, or 'diet', was meeting. Confronted by his own books and told to recant, Luther famously refused. There is no evidence that he actually said: 'Here I stand, I can do no other.' The words were written into his speech later, by an editor after Luther's death. But they are too good, too resonantly right, to scrub out. For it was a potentially perilous confrontation. Luther might have expected to be burned at the stake despite the offer of safe passage to Worms.

After Worms, Luther was spirited away for his own safety by his ruler Friedrich, who kept him in the fabulously Germanic Wartburg Castle. There, disguised with a beard and a false name, Luther again did something amazing – he began translating the Bible into sharp, pungent popular German. He produced a New Testament quickly and then, over several years, a complete Bible. He boasted that he took his style not from the Latin, but from the street: 'Ask the mother in the home, the children in the alleys, the common man in the market, about it and watch what comes out of their mouths.' Many of his coinages, such as *Herzenslust* for 'heart's content' and *Morgenland* for 'the east', remain in modern German. Luther said he wanted 'to make Moses so German that nobody would suspect he was a Jew', and his translation has been called 'the central document in the evolution of the German language'.[12]

The Bibles were soon on sale at the already famous Leipzig book fair, priced at roughly the cost of a calf, or two weeks' wages for a schoolmaster, and by Luther's death it is reckoned half a million were in circulation. Other Bibles in local European languages and dialects had a big effect too – Britain's King James Bible is an obvious example

– but in some ways Luther's impact on German is better compared to
Shakespeare's on English. The historian C.V. Wedgwood put it well
when she said that German phrasing came to him almost too easily,
'bursting forth in plentiful homely images, gross, earthy, graphic . . .
his Bible was perhaps the most astonishing and highly personal translation ever compassed'.

So Luther had a nationalistic effect as well as a religious one.
Slowly, one by one, northern German aristocrats and free towns came
over to his side. Something similar was happening in Switzerland, Holland and Denmark too, where other reformers were busy. But it was
obvious quite soon that Luther's religious reformation and the beginnings of a new Church could not be neatly separated from social
challenge, and even revolution. Pro-Luther crowds started destroying
religious art. Strikes by miners and peasants against tax-gathering clerics used Luther-like arguments. Rebel clerics took the lead in mocking
their old leaders and the old orders. Luther, who depended on the protection of an aristocrat and was himself from a prosperous family,
began to seem nervous, insisting on the importance of temporal
authority.

Then, during 1524–5, a huge peasant rebellion started up across
Europe, from the lands of the Teutonic knights and Hungary, to
Switzerland and then central Germany itself. It was uncoordinated and
desperate. To the established order of late medieval Europe it was terrifying. One of Luther's early followers, the charismatic priest Thomas
Müntzer, led the most extreme movement, predicting the wiping-out
of all earthly authority in an imminent apocalypse. He and his supporters briefly created a semi-communistic 'League of God' in the city
of Mülhausen, until like the other rebellions it was shattered by the
military power of the princes. Across Germany, the battle-hardened
forces of the emperor, who had just returned from victories against
the French in Italy, crushed the peasant armies, exacting terrible
revenge. Luther egged them on. In his April 1525 pamphlet originally
called *An Admonition to Peace* (surely the worst piece of headlining in
German journalism) he wrote: 'Let everyone who can, smite, slay and
stab, secretly or openly, remembering that nothing can be more poisonous, hurtful or devilish than a rebel.'[13]

The original 'rebel' was now firmly on the side of the German
princes who would, in turn, shift their allegiance to Lutheran Chris-

tianity. In Saxony, Hesse, Schleswig, Brunswick and Brandenburg they came over. So did most of the northern towns and cities. Though Charles V tried hard for conciliation, and planned ways to reunite his empire, there were simply too many rulers and influential soldiers now with Luther's cause to make that practicable. Luther told his ally and fellow reformer Philipp Melanchthon that 'agreement in doctrine is plainly impossible, unless the pope will abolish his papacy'. Luther's theology had become more conservative in its social effects; he was a fierce advocate of a husband's rights over his wife, and hostile to easy marriages. Against suitors he wrote: 'If I raised a daughter with so much expense and effort, care and trouble, diligence and work and had bet all my life, body and property on her for so many years, should she not be better protected than a cow who had wandered into the forest?' He also became a bitter anti-Semite.

In 1531 a treaty between Lutheran princes, known as the Schmalkaldic League, made the political split irrevocable. There was then a golden pause. The Peace of Augsburg of 1555 allowed a time of rebuilding and economic growth, during which German culture flourished and German universities became famous – a time when even Elizabethan English plays and actors travelled to Germany to find fame. Yet the great divide that Luther had wrenched open would poison the future of Europe. The Thirty Years War was looming. This would be a catastrophe driven by spear and flintlock, rape and famine, and would bring down on German soil a hell every bit as terrible as the punishment Luther had spent his life so dreading, and that the cheerful monks had sold indulgences to escape from.

Pagans and Pirates

Luther's revolution, amplified and hardened by John Calvin in Geneva and by other reformers, such as Scotland's forbidding John Knox, had come about partly because of a common sense that history *must* soon end. Christ's awesome second coming was surely due, not least because Christendom was so threatened. Christian Europe, which would soon dominate much of the rest of the world, still felt hemmed in, divided, on the retreat. We cannot understand the ferocity of the reformers with their bleak warnings, or the paranoid excesses of the

Catholic Counter-Reformation, led by fanatical Jesuits and by the Inquisition, unless we understand how frightened Christians were. The Ottoman Empire now controlled more of the Mediterranean coastline and waters than did the Christians. Fear of 'the Turk' haunted the imaginations of Christian children, scolded at bedtime. It took Shakespeare to portray the 'Moor' as fully human.

Nor was the threat of 'the Moor' or 'the Turk' limited to the capture of Mediterranean islands, the defeat of Christian fleets or the taking of Christian lands and walled towns. For many Christians, travelling by sea, or even just living near the sea, became perilous. Some of the raids were spectacular. In 1544 Muslim corsairs attacked the Bay of Naples and seized seven thousand men, women and children; ten years later they took six thousand from the 'toe' of Italy, then in 1566 four thousand from Granada in southern Spain, after which it was said to be 'raining Christians' in Algiers.[14] Around most of the Christian coasts of the Mediterranean, life became more dangerous. In Corsica and Sardinia, and around much of Italy, seaside villages were deserted and rebuilt further inland. At sea, the enemy's culling rate of Christian ships was extraordinary. In one short period, between 1609 and 1616, the Royal Navy admitted that 466 English and Scottish ships – though many of these were relatively small – had been seized by Algerian corsairs. A similar rate of attrition was suffered by Dutch, French, German and Spanish shipping, all feeding the hungry need for slaves felt by the Muslim rulers of North Africa, who used the men as labourers and the women as domestic or sexual servants.

As Christian villagers retreated from the shoreline and Christian ships became more cautious, the raiders went further afield. They turned up in the Thames estuary again and again, and took English fishermen from just off Essex and Kent. With the help of a renegade Dutch seaman, Jan Janszoon of Haarlem, who converted to Islam and called himself Murat Reis, they raided Iceland in 1627, burning the church on the island of Heimaey and taking 242 people, as well as more from the mainland near Reykjavik. Janszoon was also on the scene in 1631, when 327 people were taken from the village of Baltimore in West Cork. (He was captured himself later on, by the Knights of Malta, but later escaped and lived to a grand old age. His claimed descendants include John F. Kennedy, Humphrey Bogart and many

Spencers and Churchills, one of them a lady-in-waiting to Queen Elizabeth II.)

Though the high point of Muslim coastal slave-taking was between 1530 and 1640, it continued until the 1780s; and for every major raid, it is believed, there were scores of smaller ones when boats would suddenly appear in coves – villagers would run from their fields, and the corsairs would seize those they could. It is reckoned that, overall, one and a quarter million Christians were enslaved, far more than the numbers of black Africans that were taken across the Atlantic by whites during most of this time. Many would die of plague or ill-treatment in desperate circumstances in Africa. A few converted, and some were rescued or bought out by priests and wealthy families.

All this was a major source of European terror and of a certain strand of storytelling, dimly reflected in Christmas pantomimes and winter tales into modern times. Until recently it has been largely written out of mainstream history, reflecting, in part, white guilt about the Atlantic slave trade, which later became far greater, by a factor of nine or ten. In part, it surely reflects sheer embarrassment. But for Europeans of Luther's time, the gnawing-away at the coasts caused much fear and insecurity.

The more spectacular attacks, though, came from the eastern edge of the European world, as the mighty Ottoman Empire spread ever further. After the rule of the first conqueror-sultan (who had taken Constantinople), his successors spread Islam deep into the Christian world. They faced fierce resistance. The battle of Kosovo, or more poetically, the 'Battle of the Field of Blackbirds', in 1389, was a devastating slaughter of Serbs by Ottomans. But it was decades before the Ottomans finally took Bosnia and Serbia. In Wallachia a man who signed himself Wladislaus Dragwlya was cheered on by the pope and half of Christendom for his victories against Mehmet II in 1459 and 1462. This Christian leader had lived as a boy in the Ottoman court, a hostage sent by his father along with his younger brother. The brother converted to Islam and served the Ottomans; the older boy learned the Koran and Turkish, but turned against Islam.

Better known today as Dracula, or Vlad the Impaler, he proved a formidable guerrilla fighter and rallied Transylvania against the invaders, surviving imprisonment in Hungary before dying in battle in Romania in 1476. His relish for executing prisoners, criminals and rivals by impalement undermined his popularity, however. At one point Dracula had twenty thousand dying and dead enemies hanging from sharpened poles, speared through their rears, around his capital. The boyars, the local princes, began to feel that relatively humane Muslim occupation might be preferable to paranoid and sadistic Christian freedom.

One of the great losers in all this was the extraordinary Jagiellon dynasty of Lithuania-Poland.

In the late 1300s Lithuania was much bigger than today's small state. Indeed, it was the biggest single nation in Europe, stretching through today's Ukraine, Belarus and parts of Russia. Officially it stayed as a pagan country, repulsing the bloody crusading incursions of the Teutonic knights in favour of a family of ancient gods and goddesses. These were mostly divinities of the usual things (fire, the moon, fate, death, evening stars), though, rather appealingly, they also had a god of good grooming. This pantheon met its end only in 1386, when the ruler Jogaila married Queen Jadwiga of Poland and converted to Christianity. His knights and courtiers, seeing which way the wind was blowing, now engaged in mass baptisms in the local rivers.

To the effective union of Lithuania and Poland, Hungary was later added, making the Jagiellon dynasty one of the most powerful in Europe. They, with the Habsburgs to their south, were the effective guardians of the Christian world against Eastern and later Ottoman attack. The battle of Mohacs, still remembered in Hungary today as a moment of national catastrophe, finished off the Jagiellons too. Buda, then Hungary's capital and the place where Vlad had been imprisoned, fell to the Ottomans in 1541.

So far, we have seen a fairly straightforward picture of aggressive Muslim conquest on the one hand, and anxious Christian defence on the other. The true picture was not so straightforward. For in the middle of Europe stood the great Catholic ruler and Holy Roman Emperor Charles V, who to many Christians, the followers of Luther and other reformers, was seen as a greater threat than any Ottoman. His rule was less tolerant of religious difference than Muslim authority was. His grand designs for a renewed, huger empire based firmly on his family authority scared Venetians, Dutch and Frenchmen even more than the advancing armies of Ottoman janissaries. So perhaps it is not so surprising that the best-known (and best) portrait we have of Mehmet II, conqueror of Constantinople, is by Gentile Bellini, who was sent there only twenty-five years after the city's fall by the Doge of Venice to record that scourge of all Christians. Or that in the 1460s there was already a large colony of Florentines in Galata, the town just over the water from Constantinople, running fifty businesses. Galata had churches – the only thing forbidden them was the noisy ringing of bells, which might disturb Islamic tranquillity – taverns, and Lenten carnivals.

Nor should we be surprised that Jews, French Protestants, Lutherans and Orthodox Christians mingled safely under Muslim rule on the shores of the Bosporus. Or that François I of France, fighting the Habsburgs, looked for help in 1525 from Suleiman the Magnificent. Or even that dialogues were constantly going on between Protestant rulers and the Muslims, ranging from letters between Queen Elizabeth I and Sultan Murad III discussing an Anglo-Ottoman military pact, to an offer by Suleiman to provide troops to help Lutherans in Flanders. Many Protestants and Ottomans thought that the simplicity of their devotions and their shared dislike of statues and icons made them natural allies against the Catholics – a division based not on Christ against Muhammad but on 'men of faith' against 'idolators'. This goes a long way towards explaining why it was impossible for Charles V or the popes to rally 'Christendom' as a single force against its enemies.

Ivan, Yermak and the Making of Russia

Why is Russia so big? Why is it the shape it is? These may seem naive questions. But there was no obvious reason why the vast sweep of forest, tundra and mountains of Siberia should be ruled by riverine Slavs living to the west, rather than by Chinese and Mongols to the east. A map of the post-Genghis world would lead one to expect a smaller Russia. And Vladimir Putin's Russia today is one of the world's largest countries, with its huge oil, gas and mineral wealth, its vast hinterland and its claim on the Arctic, because of battles and explorations that took place in the 1580s.

Russia is so big, above all, because of the personal ambition of one Moscow Czar, Ivan IV, known to history as Ivan the Terrible (though non-Russian speakers should note he translates just as well as 'Ivan the Mighty').

The Russians did not start by striving to create an empire, however, any more than the English intended to create Canada, or the United States. In all such cases Europeans were simply exploiting a small technological advantage to win themselves goods which to them felt (or were) essential. Among them are products that have already featured in this history, and will do again, such as salt, timber, iron and (before plastics) ivory, but also one that has not – fur. Before the modern age of synthetic materials, animal skins and furs were among the few ways people could keep themselves warm; and this was particularly important during the cold climatic spell, or 'little ice age', running from the 1550s right through to the early nineteenth century, with particular freezes in the 1650s and late 1700s.

It is from this time that we get some of the loveliest Dutch landscapes of frozen canals and peasant revelries, the great London frost fairs on the iron-hard Thames, and recordings of huge snowfalls in Spain and Portugal. From time to time Iceland found herself completely cut off by sea ice, and famines ravaged North America, France and Scandinavia. For anyone who could afford them, the pelts of bears, foxes, squirrels, beaver, mink and marten were an essential protection. The fur-trimmed ceremonial robes of some of today's judges, lord mayors and guild officials, for instance, date back to this period, when anyone who could pay for it wanted to be able to snug up on a bench, on a civic throne, or anywhere they fancied, in rich furs. The poorer made do with the pelts of rabbits or foxes, but the real warmth came from the thicker, glossier skins of animals that lived in the great northern forests, from Alaska to Newfoundland in one direction, and to European Russia in the other.

This is an age when trappers mattered as much as coalminers, and the rise of Moscow as a rich trading centre depended heavily on the fur trade. As early as 1486 a Greek diplomat, George Trakhaniot, working in Muscovy, reported: 'Many merchants from Germany and Poland gather in the city throughout the winter. They buy furs exclusively – sables, foxes, ermines, squirrels, and sometimes wolves. And although the furs are procured at places many days' journey from the city of Moscow . . . all are brought to this place and the merchants buy the furs here.'[15]

North of Moscow the city of Novgorod (or 'New Town'), founded
by Vikings, had been a pioneer in the fur trade, pushing its influence
into the dense forests of the north-east, then linking up with the
German trading cities of the Hanseatic League, and through them
with the Dutch. For around three centuries – from 1136, when the
burghers of Novgorod dismissed their prince – this was a civic republic whose government was more like that of republican Venice,
Florence or the later Dutch state than anywhere in the Russian world.
Novgorod was ruled in theory by *veches*, or public assemblies, though
wealthy merchant or boyar families and a succession of archbishops
held much of the power. When they wanted princes or princely warriors, they summoned them in. The fur, honey, wax and walrus-ivory
trades allowed Novgorod to create a large, sprawling state of its own,
spreading towards the Urals and the White Sea, and north to the
Baltic. At one end of a Silk Road stretching back to China, it was far
enough north to avoid the ravages of the Mongol horde, though to
keep its independence the Novgorod army had to fight native forest
peoples, invading Swedes and the German crusading knights.

Famous as a centre of religion and culture, Novgorod began to
lose out to the rising power of Moscow with its darker rival tradition
of autocrats, who had themselves emerged from family feuding. Like
the late Roman republic, Novgorod had produced a rich ruling class
whose conspicuous consumption caused resentment among the ordinary citizens. An early historian describes life in the house of one of its
cosmopolitan financiers: 'The conversation went on in German, interspersed with Latin flowers of speech, as later Russian aristocrats used
French. Precious wine from Burgundy was drunk there, poured from
Bohemian decanters into Venetian bowls, to wash down gingerbread
from Nuremberg.'[16]

We last discussed Russia after the Kiev princes had converted to
Orthodox Christianity, then fallen to the Mongol hordes, who smashed
that first Slavic civilization. Moscow was just one of the princely Russian cities that had paid tribute to the Mongols and had begun to slowly
recover during the 1300s. After a bitter war between rival claimants
during 1433–45, its ruling family established a clear system of single,
'vertical succession' which allowed a consolidation of power. Under its
grand princes the state of Muscovy was ready to expand. Lacking the
fertile agriculture of Western European states, however (it had a short

growing season and thin soil), or obvious sources of natural wealth, Muscovy's rulers looked north to the river-trade network dominated by Novgorod, and west to the endless fur-rich forests of Siberia. This could only mean expansion by war. After failing to get help from its neighbouring kingdoms of Lithuania and Poland, Novgorod fell to Moscow's Prince Kholmsky in 1471–2. Had bourgeois, republican Novgorod, not autocratic Moscow, emerged as the dominant power, the political history of Russia might have been intriguingly different – and happier.

By now the Russian trappers had killed so much of the wildlife near Moscow and Novgorod that the lure of Siberia was irresistible. But it would be a family of rich Novgorod merchants who gave the Czar in Moscow, Ivan III, the chance to strike deep into the east. The Stroganovs had helped fund the Dukes of Muscovy while they built up their family wealth with salt-works. Like sub-Saharan Africa, central Russia had too little salt of its own and had imported it from Western Europe. Now the Stroganovs found supplies nearer to hand, in the forests and lakes. This brought them into conflict with Muslim warlords. It is even claimed that the family name, which means 'strips of flesh', derived from the unpleasant punishment meted out to an early family member who was cut to pieces (hence the strips of meat in 'beef Stroganov').

Apparently undeterred, the Stroganovs expanded the family business into fish, wax, hides and timber. Its most influential patriarch, Anika Stroganov, moved south to Moscow and became both the Czar's favourite supplier of furs and other luxuries and a regular source of funds. Both Ivan III and Ivan IV, 'the Terrible', granted large land settlements to favoured aristocratic families, but the Stroganovs wanted to go much further. In 1558, Ivan the Terrible awarded these private-enterprise rulers charters giving them sovereignty over vast areas of untamed land for twenty years, free from taxes and laws, and from intervention from any other authorities. What the Hudson's Bay Company would be to Canada, the Stroganovs were to Russia.

The Czars called themselves 'commanders of all Siberia', but this was an expression of hope rather than signifying the settled conquest of lands inhabited by native peoples – the same was claimed by Mongol rulers too. Ivan would be different. His father had died when he was three, and his mother (possibly poisoned) when he was eight.

The first Muscovite prince (at the age of sixteen) to have himself crowned Czar of all the Russias in 1547 at a Byzantine-style ceremony in the gorgeously painted Cathedral of the Dormition in the Kremlin, Ivan proved a dangerous ruler from the start. He may have been bipolar – he certainly had terrible rages. Many of his opponents just disappeared or died, and later in life he accidentally killed his own son and heir in a drunken fight. But Ivan was also shrewd, and more restlessly ambitious than any previous ruler of Muscovy. He tried to find himself a cultured foreign bride, sending embassies to the courts of Western Europe. He welcomed English traders and wanted to conclude a political union, and even a personal one, with England's Queen Elizabeth. He built up a large library and imported German craftsmen; and he was responsible for some of the grandest churches and palace buildings that still adorn Moscow.

Surrounded by the sea of troubles familiar to most rulers of the time – insurrections, long wars with neighbouring powers, and court intrigue – Ivan nonetheless greatly expanded Muscovy. He conquered the Muslim khanates of Kazan and Astrakhan in the 1550s, finally ending Russia's long spell in the shadow cast by the descendants of the Mongol 'Golden Horde'. But he found himself unable to push west, despite seemingly endless conflicts with Danes, Swedes and German knights in the Baltic. Most dramatically, he created a kind of early totalitarian state, a personal realm known as the *oprichnina*, which, with bleak irony, occupied much of the territory of once-republican Novgorod. Ivan's personal police-come-army, the *oprichniki*, were used to inflict savage repressions, and in 1570 sacked the city of Novgorod, reducing it to a sad and servile ghost of its former self. The territories the Novgorodians had developed across the Urals, reaching toward Siberia, were taken over by Muscovy.

So this was the restless, dangerous and ambitious ruler whom the Stroganov family persuaded to hand over privatized hegemony in huge territories on either side of the Urals, including permission to build forts along the rivers. They became the first Russian oligarchs, fabulously rich, exploiting natural resources, protected by monopolies; and both dependent on, and vital to, Moscow's authoritarian ruler. With their own forts, a huge wooden family palace far from Moscow, and a private army of traders and trappers exploring ever further, the Stroganovs were something new in history, a huge capitalist enterprise and family dynasty all in one. They could be compared to the great Italian merchant-to-prince families such as the Medici and the Borgias, except that the Italians never had the Stroganovs' almost imperial zeal for expansion.

Why would a ruler as obsessed by personal power as Ivan IV have not only tolerated, but encouraged, such an energetic potential rival inside his kingdom? Because his Russia, with its vast and porous borders and enemies on every side, needed the wealth that the Stroganovs' constant supplies of fresh fur, never mind salt and timber, brought to Moscow. He knew, too, that their time-limited charters to lands that the Muscovites themselves had never visited could always be revoked. Not much changes. Oligarchs and tycoons depend on political rulers – so long as those political rulers are decisive – even more than the politicians need them.

The flaw in the deal was that the Stroganovs' trappers and explorers were moving into territory others thought belonged to them. There were the various native tribes who had hunted and fished in the taiga, those vast swampy forests, since the Bronze Age, and perhaps before. These people were not too much of a military threat. But there were also the Muslim khans, who descended from the Mongol invasion and claimed overlordship; they were fiercer, and came into regular conflict with the Russians. The most threatening of these was the rising khanate of Sibir, between the Tobol and Irtysh Rivers, led by Kuchum Khan. In 1571 he stopped paying tribute to Moscow. Ivan, struggling with his wars against Poland, the Livonian knights and the Scandinavians, and threatened as always by Tatars from the Caucasus, could not afford another army to help the Stroganov fur barons subdue Kuchum. In desperation, they turned to a freebooter, a Cossack fighter called Yermak Timofeyevich.

In Russian culture Yermak has something of the status of a Daniel Boone or even a Robin Hood – a romantic hero whose exploits have been retold and embroidered for centuries. He probably fought in Ivan's unsuccessful wars against the battle-hardened Germanic Livonian knights to the west. He was a talented military leader, able to lead some five hundred mercenaries – Cossacks, Russians, Germans and Swedes – into the Siberian khanate. These were not the Cossack cavalry of later times. For one thing, the forest, mountain and river terrain made horses an impractical proposition. Nor did they bring

cannon, but only some muskets and powder. Yermak's tiny force travelled on river rafts, and on foot.

Part of the traditional story has it that Yermak's Tatar enemies had
no knowledge of gunpowder and were as amazed by guns as the
native Americans were at much the same time. Historians have
recently challenged this – the Tatars were more connected to the
human mainstream[17] – but the invaders certainly outgunned the
Muslim defenders, who depended more on bows and arrows. In
1581–2, Yermak arrived in Kuchum's home territory and shortly afterwards seized his capital, Isker. It was a punitive and exploratory
gamble, meant to teach the Muslims a lesson; it would in fact be
Russia's first thrust into a vast territory all of which it would ultimately engulf. The Cossack force did, it seems, manage to defeat an
army five to ten times its size, and for two or three years Yermak was
able to maintain a garrison deep in Siberian territory while sending
increasingly desperate messages back to Moscow for reinforcements.

Ivan, who had previously regarded Yermak as a bandit, was
impressed. He responded by sending him gifts and a pardon. Among
the gifts was a suit of armour. If the story is true, the gift was an
unfortunate one. Lacking both powder and men, Yermak's position
grew increasingly difficult, and he eventually died in a minor battle on
the River Irtysh. He had tried to swim to safety, but had been sunk by
the Czar's armour. True or not, it is a good metaphor for the fate of
successive agents of Russian autocracy, who themselves ended up
unhappily while the state they served grew only stronger.

Soon after Yermak's death, the Russians would again be pressing
on eastwards. Within two generations they had reached the far coast
where Siberia touches Alaska, and the Sea of Okhotsk, north of Japan.

If the Rus were the originators of Russia, Ivan the Terrible was the
true founding father of modern Russia. After his death, Muscovy's
power and coherence would slither and struggle, beginning with a
chaotic 'time of troubles'; but Ivan's achievement in pushing Russian
influence south, east and north created the essential shape of the
country, and thus it would remain. The Russians would continue to be
hemmed in by Poles, Germans and Scandinavians to the north and
west, but they found themselves able to expand over a huge area eastwards. After the defeat of the Muslim rulers of Kazan and Astrakhan,
Russian forces would push further south too, eventually reaching the

Black Sea and the Caspian during the time of Catherine the Great and her extraordinary lover and general, Prince Potemkin. Like the successive waves of an incoming tide, Russian expeditions washed relentlessly across Siberia, bringing the state not only hides, salt and wood, but a perpetual penal colony for its enemies.

Indeed, what had started as a hunt for furs brought the Russians a landmass one and a half times larger than the USA, and a region containing up to 80 per cent of modern Russia's oil reserves and 90 per cent of its gas and coal – vast supplies upon which its modern wealth and global power heavily depend. Siberia is also a rich source of iron, tin, gold and other metals, and possesses the world's deepest lake, Baikal. Without Siberia, our notion of Russia falls apart. It was to the huge expanses behind Moscow and western Russia that the country could retreat and gather itself when confronted by Napoleon, then Hitler. That combined 'ice-box and El Dorado' was where the Czar's enemies and the victims of the Communist gulag perished; and it was the site of space centres and mysterious military bases.

Russia without Siberia would be a large but ordinary Eastern European state. But if Ivan the Terrible can take some of the credit for Russia's later importance on the world stage, he must also take some of the blame for the fear-driven and personalized tradition of Russian political power ever since. Yermak may have been a dashing, romantic freebooter, but he was also the advance army of autocracy.

Two Rulers, One Problem

In the year 1604, King James had many problems. For a start, which James was he? As a Scottish king, he was James VI, 'Jamie Saxt', latest in a long line of Stuarts. But now he was down in London, in England, where he was James I. So what exactly was his kingdom?

He proposed the name of Britain, which the English did not like, and was working on a new flag, an eye-ache of lines and colours, which, to start with, nobody liked. He wanted peace with England's traditional Catholic enemy, Spain. Like so many monarchs, he was also short of cash. But James, intellectually assertive, was particularly worked up about one social problem, a craze sweeping his new kingdom, which he thought utterly disgusting. He took quill to paper and wrote a pamphlet that he called, simply, 'A Counterblaste to Tobacco'.

Across his country, men were imitating the 'wilde, godlesse and slavish Indians' by smoking leaves, 'this stinking smoake being sucked up by the nose and imprisoned in the cold and moyst braines'. The king was particularly outraged by people who smoked over their food: 'As for the vanities committed in this filthie custome, is it not both great vanitie and uncleannesse that at table men should not be ashamed, to sit tossing of Tobacco Pipes, and puffing the smoke of tobacco on to one another, making the filthy smoke and stinke thereof to exhale athwart the dishes?' By now this drooling, red-bearded monarch was getting well into his stride. He concluded with a magnificent eruption: tobacco was a 'custome loathsome to the eye, hatefull to the Nose, harmful to the braine, dangerous to the lungs, and in the blacke stinking fume thereof, nearest resembling the horrible Stigian Smoake of the the the pit that is bottomlesse'.[18]

On the other side of the world, another ruler was having exactly the same trouble. Tobacco had also reached Japan, probably through Portuguese Jesuit influence. The man who was theoretically ruler, the emperor, was a cipher figure: but the country's real ruler, the generalissimo, or shogun, loathed tobacco just as much as James did. He too decided to try to ban it. In far-off England tobacco was regarded as a freebooting and unruly habit, associated with wild gatherings in taverns and the audience for plays. In Japan, bands of unruly males, who sound like seventeenth-century punks, the Kabukimono, had adopted tobacco too.

The Kabukimono formed street gangs who dressed in outrageous clothes, using women's kimonos as cloaks; they wore weird hairstyles and behaved aggressively in the street, attacking passers-by, wrestling and dancing, and flaunting their long fuming pipes. So in 1612 and again in 1615, the Japanese court went further than James and banned smoking. It caused a great stir. Sitting in his office in Osaka, an English merchant called William Eaton wrote on 1 March 1613 to his colleague Richard Wickham in the Japanese capital of Edo (now Tokyo), informing him that at least 150 people had been arrested 'for buying and selling of tobacco contrary to the Emperor's commandment, and they are in jeopardy of their life's, besides great store of tobacco which they have heare burnte'.[19]

At the beginning of the seventeenth century, the similarities between Britain and Japan extended beyond the social threat of the new-fangled drug. They were similarly sized island archipelagos off a much bigger mainland, with whom they had had an uneasy relationship. Like the Scots and English, the Japanese had imported religious ideas, technologies and luxuries across a narrow sea, but had managed to keep themselves a little apart. Like Britain, Japan had only recently been united under a single ruler. In 1582, after a long period of conflict, the humbly born soldier Hideyoshi, of the Tokugawa clan, had made himself shogun. Soon, the two countries would go in diametrically opposite directions during one of the most fascinating experiments early-modern history has to offer. To start with, though, the similarities were more striking.

Hideyoshi's years in power had shown him a ruler with the energy of England's Queen Elizabeth. Like her, he was instinctively tolerant on the subject of religion, and for a while allowed Portuguese Jesuits to convert to Christianity any citizen who was willing. Elizabeth's armies had fought in Holland and France against the Jesuit-influenced Spanish, with notable lack of success. Hideyoshi had organized a major attack on the Chinese empire, via Korea, which his troops devastated, but without any greater long-term success. Hideyoshi had no Japanese Shakespeare to boast of, but his reign was notable for superb castles and paintings.[20] He was also famously determined to restore order and in 1588, as Elizabeth awaited the Spanish Armada, he organized a 'sword hunt', a mass confiscation of daggers, swords and spears from everyone except the samurai military class.

At sea, Japan's ocean-going pirate raiders were Asia's equivalent to Drake, Hawkins and Raleigh. The Englishmen were raiding Spanish ports and ships for gold, other luxuries and (in Hawkins's case) slaves. From Japan's ports famous figures like Captain Wu-Feng were submitting the Chinese to just the same kind of treatment. Both of these rising nations behaved brutally to anyone who got in their way. The Elizabethan English oppressed the indigenous Irish, while Hideyoshi's compatriots did the same to the Ainu people of the northern islands. In economic terms, both Britain and Japan were struggling to deal with the consequences of massive deforestation and the rise of urban society: both London and Edo would soon smell very similar, choked by the fumes of coal-burning fires.[21]

There were many differences, of course – differences in political structure, in religion, and in the fortunes of war. Korea's formidable fleet of cannon-toting warships had done rather better against Japan than the Spanish had against the English. There was a big difference in population, as well. Japan, with around eighteen million people, had perhaps three times as many inhabitants as Britain. She felt herself to be more self-sufficient. That English trader writing about the tobacco ban was a member of the so-called English Factory (really, a trading post) based at Hirado on the island of Kyushu, near Nagasaki. There were no Japanese traders in the West, and the European outposts in Japan would soon be gone. The Jesuits and the Dutch held on longest. The English, who had arrived in 1613, had gone within a decade, unable to make enough money out of trading.

This puzzled King James, who wrote to the Japanese emperor offering 'amitie and friendship'. All he wanted was 'the settling and establishing of an entercourse of commerce and trade for the mutuall good of each others' subjects'. Though hurt at getting no reply to his first letter, James was even prepared to grovel a little: 'Wee have not received any answere from you, which we attribute to the remoteness and distance of the places of our dominions, and not to any back-wardnesse in you.'[22] It was a rare and refreshing example of an early-modern European trying to see things from another point of view.

James's Britain and the shogun of Japan, now Tokugawa Ieyasu, the next in line, faced the same crucial strategic question: how does a small island-nation thrive in a world of ever greater empires?

Britain responded by flinging outwards, building up her fleets and scattering them across the oceans, to America and the Far East. Englishmen and Scots were impelled by religious fervour, but also by the hope of profit. England's first joint-stock company was a trading syndicate, the Muscovy Company, formed in 1555. The English East India Company got its charter from Elizabeth in 1600. Seven years later, the 'London Company' established the colony of Virginia. Explorers became popular heroes, and the appetite to hear all about the rest of the world, which can be tracked through plays, pamphlets and books, seems to have been insatiable. Elizabeth's fleet had been comparatively tiny, but a reorganized Admiralty, plus industrial-scale dockyards – first at Deptford, then at Chatham and Portsmouth – were soon turning out many more ships, and larger ones too. By 1637 when the *Sovereign of the Seas*, with 102 guns, was launched for James's son Charles, Britain could claim to be the possessor of the most formidable ship afloat.

The Japanese could have taken the same approach, and nearly did. From the 1580s they had been trading successfully in their armed 'red seal' ships around Thailand, Vietnam and the Philippines. In 1600 an English sailor called William Adams, who had served with Drake and fought the Spanish Armada, had arrived in Japan. The Dutch ship he was on, drifting and desperate with its crew starving, had dropped anchor. Adams was rescued by Japanese fishermen and taken to the nearest authority, the future shogun, Ieyasu. For the Portuguese, who were on the way towards converting an astonishing half-million Japanese to Roman Catholicism, the arrival of a bedraggled English heretic was not welcome. With true Christian thoughtfulness, the Jesuits suggested to Ieyasu that they crucify Adams.

Instead, the open-minded ruler cross-questioned the Englishman about ships, God and mathematics, and appointed him his adviser. Ieyasu was intrigued by the idea of building up a powerful ocean fleet of his own, and in 1605 Adams oversaw the construction of two excellent European-style ocean-going ships at a new dockyard at Ito. Will Adams, from Gillingham in Kent, became Anjin-Sama, a figure well respected in Japan and remembered to this day, and a close aide to Ieyasu, the warlord who in his way was as influential in forging Japan as a single nation as James was in forging Britain. There is no reason why the seafaring and technically advanced Japanese could not soon have built fleets of galleons, just as they had already copied and improved on European muskets and cannon.

A vigorous debate was going on in Japan about which way to turn. The foreigners brought some interesting goods to trade – their gunpowder was considered good, but their cloth was terrible – and certainly had some fascinating skills. They were also, however, a source of instability, and a large part of the problem was the fast-spreading success of the Christian missionaries. It is estimated that in the early seventeenth century they converted around five hundred thousand Japanese, including ordinary peasants, samurai and landowners, mostly in the south. To begin with, the shoguns were relaxed about it, but the mood changed as the Christian Japanese became troublesome. The siege of Osaka castle in 1614–15 was an epic of its kind, which set the seal on the victory of the Tokugawa as rulers of all Japan. But confronting them behind the massive walls of the fortress, alongside its owner, were thousands of determined samurai – many of them Christians, waving Christian saints' flags.

Thanks to Adams, Ieyasu had been able to distinguish between Protestant Europeans and those rebellious Roman Catholics. Replying affably to James, he had even sent him a rather fine suit of samurai armour. But Ieyasu died suddenly, not long after the siege, possibly of syphilis or cancer, and the new shogun, his son Hidetada, was more ruthless. A purge of foreigners began, initially focused on the Jesuits but freezing all European trade. Twenty years later, in 1637, a major uprising of around thirty thousand peasants, most of them Christian, took place on the island of Kyushu. The revolt was as much about taxation and hunger as about religion, and ended after another epic siege, during which the peasants and rebel samurai held off an army vastly greater than their own. The Tokugawa were only able to suppress them with the help of ships belonging to those other (though Protestant) Christians, the Dutch.

All this was more than embarrassing, and it determined the Japanese view about how best to balance opportunity and risk when it came to foreign influence. Two years later came the dramatic measures known as the *sakoku*, or 'locked-country' policy. The size of Japanese ships was to be restricted by law. They could be big enough only for coastal fishing. Ocean-going ships were dismantled, and it became a capital offence to build them. Just to make sure, ships from now on had to be constructed with a large hole in the hull, making them lethal on the open seas, where a heavy swell would signal their doom – a unique instance of ships being specifically designed to sink. Japanese citizens were forbidden to leave Japan on pain of death, foreigners from entering. Christianity was outlawed, though many Japanese Christians would die rather than renounce their new faith.

Foreigners were finally expelled. When the Portuguese came back in 1640 to protest, their mission was wiped out. Though there were a very few, tightly regulated, trading links left for Korean and Dutch merchants, the country was indeed effectively locked shut. These restrictions stayed in place for more than two centuries. They are widely seen as a classic case of political idiocy. What would have happened had King James, perhaps infuriated beyond endurance by another incident of passive smoking at Westminster Palace, ordered the destruction of the British fleet and a ban on contacts with the continent? The Japanese effectively disinvented modern weaponry, too; so, by the time the US Navy (an institution unthinkable when the policy started) arrived in 1853, the Japanese had no answer to the naked threat offered by its cannon.

Yet there is another side to the story. The more than two centuries of isolation created a more intensely Japanese Japan than would have been possible otherwise. Japan's distinctive buildings, unique traditions of art and theatre, her rituals based on tea, music, courtesans and the seasons, and her original, unusual cuisine, would have been simply 'less so' without the locked doors of the Tokugawa. Even today, Japan is more herself, more distinctive, than other cultures – certainly than the homogenized global culture of the modern British. Cut off from global epidemics spread by shipping and enjoying internal peace, Japan's population grew fast, so that Edo was the world's biggest city by the early 1700s (not that the world would have known). Guns almost disappeared. Internal unity brought an internal trade boom.

The Tokugawa-era Japanese were even able to resolve some of their most pressing environmental problems. They had been as heavily reliant as the English on timber for building – the capital Edo, largely built of wood, was half destroyed by a 'great fire' in 1657, nine years before the same thing happened to London. Wood needed for castles, boats and fuel, and the call for more farmland as the population boomed, had resulted in huge deforestation and erosion. Disaster loomed.

Instead, as Jared Diamond has shown, the Japanese then managed to limit their population, achieving something close to a steady state. They found alternative sources of food, above all at sea, that are still central to the Japanese diet. And they reforested. Thanks to a complicated system of rules about which wood could be used for what, charges for logging, and a growing understanding of silviculture, the Japanese forests returned. Timber was valued, a subject for connoisseurs to debate; better-off peasants knew the long-growing trees would be useful to their grandchildren; and a tough central government imposed the new rules everywhere. As compared with the destruction of forests wrought across much of Britain and then across much of America, there is at least pause for thought about which decision – to spread oneself about or to hunker down – was the wiser one.

Yet that is only half the story. The other point about Tokugawa Japan, which we will return to later, is that it was an intensely conservative and hierarchical society, which never developed the semi-democratic and more open culture of the early-modern West. Conservatism and closure probably went hand in hand. By the time Japan did rejoin the world, it was still run by a hierarchy of aristocrats with medieval views, and its citizens were trained perhaps a little too well to obey orders. This would have implications for twentieth-century history. Japan still has its punks, of course; and despite the edicts of 1612, they remain formidable smokers.

In a Nutshell to New York

The coming British world domination was not yet obvious. The failure to break into the Japanese market was matched by others. The rise of the British as a naval and trading power is now so firmly part of world history that it may come as a shock to find that in the most lucrative contest of all, they were soundly beaten by those rivals who featured in the Japanese story, the Dutch.

Very broadly, the story of European mercantile expansion can be divided into three phases. First, from the late 1400s, came the Portuguese, whose ships explored the African coast. Then, discovering that the Cape could be reached by veering off far west into the Atlantic, allowing the winds to carry them round, they got to India and the Far East. The Portuguese operated as violently monopolistic traders rather than as empire-builders, setting up fortifications to protect their sea routes and repelling all rivals. The Spanish were next to get in on the act, but did not really try to oust the Portuguese from 'their' routes, focusing instead, as we have seen, on the Americas. Portugal's greatest sailor, Ferdinand Magellan, was working for the Spanish when he discovered the route round Cape Horn to South America. He died soon afterwards. One of the ships he had set out with became the first vessel to circumnavigate the world.

The second phase saw two more northerly nations, the English and the Dutch, join the adventure. To begin with they were no more

consciously imperialist than the Portuguese, also being driven by
merchants' hopes of profit. Europe had long had a near-desperate
desire for the spices that grew only in the East. The most delicious and
(it was thought) healthful of these were to be found in the Spice
Islands, wedged in the dangerous seas between Borneo and New
Guinea. Nutmeg, cloves, mace, pepper and cinnamon had been
bought from the islanders there by Muslim seafarers; then taken to
India, thence through the Islamic world to Constantinople, and finally
through Venice to Europe. A profit was made at each stage, so that the
aromatic nuts and seeds were hugely expensive luxuries by the time
they reached Paris or London. Yet before the advent of refrigeration,
in an age of rank meat and dull eating, the appetite for them was as
insatiable as it was for fur. Most spices were also thought to offer protection against illness: nutmeg was supposed to cure syphilis, and even
the plague.

Meanwhile, Portuguese seamanship had found a shorter way
to the Spice Islands. The journey might still take months, even years,
and kill perhaps a third of the sailors who attempted it, but ships
from Europe could now get direct access to the spices. Their owners
would be able, in a single voyage, to make the fabulous profits
that had formerly been shared by traders across half the world. The
losers were the Arab and Indian traders, suddenly and brutally cut out
of the chain; the markets of Constantinople became quieter and the
avaricious palazzo-dwelling merchants of Venice's Grand Canal grum-
bled. The next losers would be the Portuguese themselves, confronted
by better-built ships and bolder adventurers, this time from the lowlands of northern Europe. In particular, the Dutch would mix
seamanship and the arts of commerce that they had learned in Italy, to
produce a world-changing formula.

We human beings remain, in part, quite simple animals: we love
new tastes, pretty, shiny things to look at, soft things against our skins,
pleasurable scents and interesting flavours. This has always been the
case, but for Europe after its centuries of relative isolation it was particularly so. The Dutch were able to impose a virtual monopoly on
what they called, with admirable straight speaking, the 'rich trades' –
not only the spices but also silks and fine Japanese porcelain. The profits were huge. So, however, were the risks. Storms, piracy and spoiled
cargo meant that many investors lost everything. Dividing, sharing out

By taking the Christian message to non-Jews, including in Rome itself, Paul was the real founder of Christianity as a global religion.

The Nazca people of southern Peru were brilliant artists and excellent engineers. But they made one mistake, which proved fatal.

The Byzantine emperor Justinian: he could fight the barbarians but he could not fight famine and plague, nor rebuild the glory that was Rome.

An Emir of Cordoba consults with his advisers: Muslim al-Andalus was a centre of learning and urban sophistication, which put Christendom to shame.

Below left. The Mongol leader Genghis Khan has a good claim to be the single most influential figure in world history; but history would have been happier had he never been born.

Below right. The Catalan Atlas of 1375 shows Mansa Musa, the king of Mali, as a European-style monarch on his throne: in fact he was rather grander than that.

Right. Ivan the Terrible – whose name also translates as Ivan the Great – was the ruler who spread Russia deep into Siberia but also gave her the tradition of ruthless, centralist autocracy she still suffers from today.

Left. Hideyoshi was the great founder of Tokugawa Japan, who ruled at the same time as England's Queen Elizabeth I and is in many ways comparable.

Right. The Inca emperor Atahualpa, murdered by the Spanish: but his gold then helped ruin Spain's economy.

The Dutch tulip mania was a financial bubble which made all Europe laugh. The Dutch learned and prospered again, however – unlike some of their critics.

The arrival of tobacco from the New World and the smoking craze of the 1600s horrified rulers from London to Japan.

Mann sagt su viel sey ungesundt,
Das merck ich ietzt su dieser stundt.

'Yet it moves.' Rough and garrulous Galileo of Pisa, born at the right time to understand the solar system; born in the wrong place to explain how it works.

Timur hands his crown to Babur, 1630: Babur was the real founder of the Mughal empire, which produced radical thinking and glorious buildings, but was eventually brought down by the cost of war driven by religious intolerance.

Louis XIV, the 'Sun King', was the model of the absolutist ruler – a dull theory decorated with fine palaces and flamboyant individuals.

William and Mary, the Dutch king and his wife who turned themselves into British monarchs after invading in 1688 – but only after accepting the supremacy of Parliament.

The Enlightenment was dominated by the French and British: Voltaire and his mistress are bathed in the light of Isaac Newton's Reason.

Jethro Tull's seed drill was one of the gadgets that turned the British into the world's most successful farmers, and so prepared the soil for the industrial revolution.

But what did they drink? Rebel Bostonians, emptying taxed tea into the sea, drank herbal teas and smuggled tea during their protest against the British empire.

Below left. The Australian Aborigine Bennelong, kidnapped by the British to be a translator: he became a kind of time traveller, moving between the Stone Age and the industrial age.

Below right. Toussaint L'Ouverture: the ex-slave idealist whose dream republic was crushed by Napoleon.

THE GUILLOTINE

Promoted, not invented by Dr Guillotin, this was the ultimate democratic killing-machine, treating kings, aristocrats and commoners alike.

Napoleon's 1804 coronation as emperor marked the end of the French revolutionary era: Beethoven was so disgusted that he scratched the Corsican's name off the dedication page of his third symphony.

and selling the risk, as well as guaranteeing the system of dividing profits, led the Dutch to develop the first proper stock market.

Buying and selling paper shares was not *quite* new. Charles V, to raise money for his battles in the Netherlands, had produced a system of annuities, which were transferable and tradable. In Antwerp, foreign bills of exchange were bought and sold in increasingly complex ways, and when the Protestants were expelled from that city in 1585 they ended up carrying on the trade in Amsterdam. There in 1609, the Wisselbank, often seen as the world's first central bank, opened to guarantee the value of different coinages, for a small fee. In a world of clipped and debased currencies, this offered a basic security on which more adventurous trade could stand.[23]

Before the Amsterdam *beurs*, or stock market, opened, just a year after the Wisselbank, the city's speculators had haggled and slapped hands on its New Bridge or in nearby churches. The new building formalized the trading, and its short opening hours added an air of businesslike frenzy so familiar to later traders; soon hundreds of different commodities were being bought and sold. Like the first central bank, the first joint-stock company was founded in Amsterdam, and in a remarkably short time the Dutch had developed all the essentials of a secure and flexible source of funding that individual English aristocrats, British monarchs or the courts of Spain and Portugal simply could not match.

The 'rich trades' involved almost miraculous acts of seamanship and courage. Rival Europeans tried to batter their way through the Arctic ice or penetrate the Canadian wilderness, still looking for a shorter way to the aromatic islands. In London, they tried to mimic the Dutch by founding their own East India Company, but the British discovered, not for the last time, that it is hard to be second into a new market. The Dutch were dug in, determined and utterly ruthless. In a series of vicious battles, heroic sieges, squalid deals and barbarous betrayals they would eventually capture the Spice Islands – and much of the rest of the Far Eastern trade – for themselves. The Dutch businessmen realized that to repel rivals, they would need forts, protected warehouses, secure anchorages and a permanent arrangement with the local rulers whose produce they were after. This meant that the Dutch – even though they were God-fearing republicans – were turning themselves into imperialists. The third phase had arrived. Today's

Indonesia became their Far Eastern base, with a new, Dutch, capital, 'Batavia'.

The under-gunned, under-shipped, under-capitalized British had so far found it impossible to loosen the Dutch stranglehold. In recent years, the heroic story of the British sailor Nathaniel Courthope, who defended the tiny spice island of Run, Britain's first Asian colony, against a long Dutch siege, has made an inspiring bestseller. Thanks to his courageous stance, Britain was eventually able to barter her legal title to Run for another small island then held by the Dutch, called by the natives 'Manhattan'. New Amsterdam would become New York, and the British imperial story would really start in North America, where she was already established in the outposts of Virginia and Carolina.

A yearning for religious freedom rather than spices or simple profit would result in a colonization much more significant than any struggles in the Indian Ocean. British naval power would grow to the point where, during the Napoleonic wars, she would be able briefly to return to the Spice Islands and simply dig up, pot, and transplant the valuable trees to other colonies such as Grenada, thus ending the Dutch monopoly. But that was only after nearly two hundred years of easy profits had poured into the Netherlands. Mostly, the Dutch would make sensible use of their good fortune, producing the world's first stable, consumer-rich middle class. But before that happened, as we are about to see, these sober, business-minded, cold-headed northern Europeans would make half the world gape – and roar with astonished laughter at their expense.

A Very Modern Story

History, in its conventional sense, is made mostly outside the home. Outdoors, generals mount their horses and sailors haul rope. In workshops, inventors hack and twist, and bite their lips and scribble. In the street preachers bawl, and traders are always heaving into sight with something new. But history is not truly made until it is felt *inside* the home. The big changes are the ones experienced around the supper table, or in the sickbed. Sometimes the home is in a new continent, or is burned down or abandoned. The great discontinuities of human life, which taken together we call 'history', are those that have a direct impact on how the mass of us humans live; and where we live, in general, is at home.

Pieter Wynants was a Dutch textile merchant, who also manufactured linen and thread. He had a fine house in Haarlem and on 1 February 1637 had invited some friends for family lunch. It would have been a good spread, placed by the servants before the polite, soberly dressed gathering, on a crisp tablecloth. This is a world we think we know through the great Dutch painters of the golden age – Rembrandt, Rubens, de Hooch and Vermeer – a reassuring world of straight-backed, quizzical people wearing bright white ruffs and surrounded by a softly lit abundance. Yet just beyond the edge of the canvas it was also a world of epidemics, the constant threat of war, fierce religious arguments and financial hysteria. If the Dutch of this period are the first model for today's bourgeois, consumerist society, there was nothing stable or reassuring about it.

At Pieter Wynants's table, everyone knew each other well and all were in the prime of life, their thirties or forties. They were well off and interconnected by their Mennonite faith, members of a Protestant group who were (and are) pacifist, hostile to state interference in religion, and against infant baptism. Among them were no fewer than three women who had been recently widowed by the latest outbreak of bubonic plague. This had taken the lives of around one in eight people in Haarlem, which had run out of places to bury the dead. It had also resulted in these women inheriting money. The host's younger brother Hendrick had a good, if obvious, idea about how they should spend it. He suggested to one of them, Geertruyt Schoudt, whose husband had been a wool merchant, that she should buy some Switzer tulip bulbs; their price was continuing to shoot up, and she would make a hefty profit. Switzers were comparatively dull flowers, not in the same league as the subtly patterned rarities coveted by the most sophisticated tulip connoisseurs. But the great Dutch tulip mania was at its peak. Even Switzers were changing hands at 1,350 guilders a pound, the price of two very fine houses or a pair of fully fitted ships.[24]

We know what happened next, from detailed court records. The widow was dubious about buying the bulbs, and only came round to the idea when another man at the meal, Jacob de Block, offered to

guarantee her the sale for eight days while she raised the money.
Something of the tense, competitive mood at the lunch is captured by
the fact that as soon as Widow Schoudt agreed the deal, she was
offered an instant 100-guilder profit if she sold them again on the spot.
Egged on by Jacob, she refused the offer and decided to hold out for a
far bigger profit. This would be a mistake. For the tulip bulb bubble,
like all financial bubbles, was about to break. Within days the bulbs
would be worth almost nothing.

This tulip mania has been seen as the classic case of financial
hysteria, the precursor to the South Sea Bubble, the 1929 Great Crash,
the 'dot-com bubble' of 1995–2000 and property bubbles before the
most recent banking crash. There is a lot of truth in this. The people
around the Haarlem lunch table were, like so many later investors,
hard-working folk – Mennonites often call themselves 'the plain
people' – who thought they understood the market they were dealing
in. They were doing what had become normal, even 'sensible', in their
milieu. You 'couldn't lose' with tulip bulbs, just as you 'couldn't lose'
with Internet companies or hedge-fund mathematics. Queasy though
it might have made them, the greed-is-good motto of a later investor
had already wormed its way into Protestant Holland.

'Holland' was in fact only one of the territories in a country which
then called itself the United Provinces. This was a better name. Most
of Europe was a province of somewhere, and these particular ones
had banded together as a result of the impact of Luther's Reformation. The Dutch, like their north German neighbours, had mostly
converted to Protestantism. At some point it would have become
absurd for the agricultural and fishing lands on Europe's northern
coast to continue to be ruled from Madrid by the Habsburgs, but the
religious divide gave the Dutch wars of independence a special
urgency and edge. After Philip of Spain intensified the persecution of
'heretics', what had started as protests against high taxes and the quar-
tering of troops turned into a full-scale revolt.

As Europe split itself up into rival religious tribes, Protestant
refugees poured into the Netherlands. Following a heroic defence of
the town of Leiden, the Dutch beat back the first Spanish attempt at
reconquest. The Spaniards' policy of terrorism ruled out the possibility of compromise, and a complicated struggle began, involving
famine, persecution and war by both land and sea. At different points

the desperate Dutch had offered the monarchs of France and Spain the Netherlands crown in return for support, but by 1609 the northern provinces had effectively seceded, leaving the southern Netherlands Catholic and Habsburg. There would be a further Spanish invasion in 1628, and the gathering at Pieter Wynants's house nine years later could not have been sure that more attacks might not be in the offing; the final peace was not signed until a decade after the tulip mania had ended.

By then, as we have seen, the Dutch Republic had established itself as the world's premier sea-going power. A people who had fished and then traded across the North Sea and around Europe's coasts had built up a seafaring tradition second to none – not even their near-neighbours and Protestant rivals, the English. Their merchants could be found in India, China and Japan. Without much in the way of natural wealth, either rich soil or mineral reserves, the Dutch were making themselves rich through a global network. But the same innovations that allowed them to out-finance their rivals carried a risk. Buying and selling shares introduced the thrill of competitive, high-stakes gambling to a once conservative society. The idea of 'futures' – selling not the commodities themselves but their future price, as pure speculation, became commonplace among a people who were already becoming notorious for their lotteries and their addiction to gambling.

Without the huge influx of wealth to the United Provinces brought about by the 'rich trades' and the fact that the most prominent citizens were growing richer still by trading bets, the tulip mania could never have happened. All that was needed now was a mindset change among the vast majority of artisans, inn-keepers, small-time manufacturers and farmers who would never normally have the capital to follow the example of the rich bourgeois. For the first time in history, the little guy could dream of a single, life-changing investment.

The Dutch have been mocked ever since because their speculative boom was focused on something so ridiculous and transient as flower bulbs. To the modern eye, the idea of a tulip being worth a house, or a painting by Rembrandt, is certainly absurd. Should it be? After all, we put apparently disproportionate values on objects whose rarity (real or manufactured) brings the owner status. A painting by Monet is (mostly) better than a masterpiece by one of his followers done twenty years after the heyday of Impressionism. But is it a hundred or a thousand times better? A Chanel bag does the same job as a bag from a high-street store and to the untutored eye does not necessarily look a hundred times nicer. Is the price differential between Beluga caviar and lumpfish roe justified by the difference in the oily globules?

The same point could be made about wine, diamonds, sports cars or brand-label clothes. If anything, the Dutch obsession with tulips was more reasonable than these. Tulips, which had originally grown as wild flowers in the mountains between China and Persia, had been treasured there as being beautiful enough to represent love or even the perfection of God. They had been cultivated and prized by the Ottoman Turks, which is how they arrived in Europe. Difficult to breed to obtain different colours and shapes, they had entranced early botanists and been gifted and swapped by gardeners looking for something especially vivid. Is it any wonder they elicited particular delight under the grey skies of northern France, Holland and Germany?

The mania had begun among learned and specialist connoisseurs who were particularly keen on a small number of bulbs, those that produced flowers with delicate patterns on their petals, complex swirls and dribbles of rich red, yellow or purple on white. In fact, these were tulips suffering from a virus spread by aphids. They were sick. Today they have virtually died out. But in the 1630s, given grand names like 'Semper Augustus' and 'Admirael van der Eijck', they were traded by the super-rich. A single bulb could reach six or seven times the annual wages of a carpenter. (Again, we should think in terms of the competitive frenzy between rich collectors over very rare stamps in today's world.)

The network of growers, traders, publicists and companies that grew from the new commodity then transmitted its enthusiasm to wider Dutch society. Ordinary people could not afford these super-bulbs, but there were plenty of humbler varieties to trade in. Because tulips flower only once a year, for a few weeks in the spring, people found they were necessarily trading a commodity whose performance could be guessed at but not entirely guaranteed. This meant that the trade was carried out in latent tulips, or tulip futures, ahead of the flowering season. Tip-offs, double-dealing, bulb theft and simple ignorance – such as the oft-repeated story of a bulb of fabulous worth being mistaken by a sailor for an onion, and eaten – fuelled the gold-rush atmosphere.

A system of buying and selling now sprang up in inns throughout the Dutch Republic, but particularly in Amsterdam and Haarlem. These mimicked the Amsterdam stock market, but in a beery, winey, smoky atmosphere of misrule. One of the historians of the mania has pointed out that for the people in the taverns, even if they had managed to put aside a little money, both the stock market and the new banks were still out of reach: 'There were no building societies in the seventeenth century, no unit trusts, no personal equity plans, no penny shares, no tax breaks and no tax shelters.'[25] The tavern system, involving bids being chalked on boards and then haggled over by 'friends' of the would-be buyer and seller, was fixed to encourage sales. There were financial penalties for a buyer who refused the finally offered price, and similar ones for sellers who pulled out. Celebratory drinks, rounds of food and singing, greeted deals.

In the peak period of the mania, the four years from 1633, the nominal value of the tulip-bulb trade has been estimated at ten times the value of the mighty Dutch East India Company, on which so much of the real wealth of the Dutch rested. We know exactly when the bubble burst. On the first Tuesday of February 1637, in a Haarlem tavern, a pound of Switzers was offered at 1,250 guilders, and nobody bought them. The auctioneer kept cutting the price, yet still nobody bought them. It must have been a sickening few minutes. The panic took hold, and spread. Within three months, prices had fallen a hundredfold. On paper, at least, hundreds of thousands of people faced ruin, bankruptcy and even starvation. For they had not simply invested spare cash. As with later booms, they had borrowed very heavily against future profits. Others had mortgaged their homes, their land, the tools of their trade. And all for wrinkled, onion-like objects suddenly worth almost as much in a casserole as in a vase.

Yet the really interesting thing about the tulip boom is that it did not end in universal disaster, or even in the widespread bankruptcy of Dutch speculators. The Estates General which ran the republic refused to take special measures, and passed the problem back to the civic authorities. Many towns, in their turn, refused to process or hear any court actions involving the tulip trade, carrying on as if none of it had really happened and allowing the paper losses and the paper gains to wipe each other out. If the dreams of sudden enrichment were snatched away, so were the nightmares of destitution.

The Dutch prided themselves, even then, on their common sense and their ability to talk things through. It was a very Dutch solution and the economy carried on regardless. Tulip-growers were badly hit and there were many individually sad cases, but the republic and its new financial system were hardly shaken.

Indeed, the Dutch went on to make tulips (which grow well in the sandy soil of the Netherlands, as in the sandy uplands of Asia) a normal export trade, just another modest luxury to put on a table in Bristol, Düsseldorf or Lille. Today the Dutch dominate the global flower business, and the system they devised in the early 1600s of stock markets, futures-trading and international dealing dominates the world economy. They provided a fitting answer to the simpler idea of wealth held by the Spanish of the age of Columbus and Pizarro – blocks of gold to be melted down to decorate churches and fight wars, and land to be squatted on for God and for glory. The Dutch way, which is to make the most of meagre land and to use money as a tool, became the modern way. We call it capitalism.

Part Six

DREAMS OF FREEDOM

1609–1796: Enlightenment and Revolution,
from India to the Caribbean

Capitalism worked. But it worked for a few lucky people in a few European towns. For the vast majority of people even in Europe, there was no sense of a revolution. Life went on, dominated by the traditional limitations on how much food could be grown and how much energy could be exploited by burning wood and some coal, by harnessing the muscular help of animals; by means of a little wind and water power, and above all, of the toil of humans themselves. There were some new luxuries, but life remained rural and bounded by old stories and old beliefs.

And for people in Australia, the Pacific Islands, Persia, the Ottoman Empire, Korea, Japan, most of Siberia, India, North America, Indonesia and China, there was no sense of change at all. Their traditions ranged from Stone Age hunting to sophisticated imperial management, but there can have been little sense of anything important having happened, still less of acceleration. Most people everywhere were peasant farmers whose world extended only to the next village or two and who heard little about wider events, except perhaps a year or more after they had happened. In Eastern Europe the farmers were often still serfs, legally tied to their land and treated as property by the landowners. In Gaelic Scotland, Ireland, much of Scandinavia and northern Russia, people lived in their clans or lineage groups, barely linked at all to the outside world. Most Europeans either did not speak the language of whatever nation claimed to rule them, or spoke dialects that would have been incomprehensible in their capital cities.

Just as they had in the Americas, the Spice Islands and a few limited parts of West Africa, a few Europeans were about to disturb and unsettle most of the rest of the world. Many indigenous people were already doomed. They did not have the immunity, the weapons or the level of organization to resist. But in 1600 there was no obvious reason why other parts of the world might not soon catch up with the Britons, the Hollanders and the French. Indeed, the Mughals in India and the Qing dynasty in China seemed further ahead – richer, running vast territories efficiently, and relatively self-sufficient. The victory of Europeans hardly seemed inevitable. So what tilted the balance?

We have already seen how apparently small local changes can have global results. In this period the most important local changes would be in politics, and began in Britain, with no plan. Had the British not been ruled at the time with particular incompetence and pig-headed-ness by one of their worst dynasties, the Stuarts, they might have muddled through the 1700s still obeying monopolistic monarchs. But poor kingship, war and religious argument resulted in a two-stage revolution that gave Britain a new kind of government. First, their rebellious parliamentarians overthrew and killed a king. Next, when one of his successors proved both incompetent and religiously unreli-able, they scared that king enough to make him run away and brought in a husband-and-wife monarchy that was clearly and overtly under the thumb of Parliament.

This was not democracy, but it was a radical spreading of power among wealthier men all over the country. It suggested that people did not necessarily have to put up with whoever ruled them, and posed the possibility of a new kind of nation in which people had rights, were not afraid of their rulers, and could think and act more freely. Something similar had already happened in Holland, but the British experiment had a more profound effect. It made Britain a magnet for persecuted minorities elsewhere in Europe, including the French Protestants, and showed there was one major country where people could publish more or less what they wanted to. It inspired thinkers in France, particularly.

But this experiment was picked up most dramatically by colonists in Britain's thirteen seaboard settlements in North America, who drove the thinking of the British reformers to its logical conclusion by creating a state based on elections, rights and a written-down constitu-tion. It was not simply a change of tack, but a dynamic change of the rules, whose consequences nobody really understood.

Indeed, it started an argument that is still going on between Bei-jing and Washington, Moscow and Brussels: what is the right balance between state authority and individual liberty? No successful state is a steady state. All successful states experience a relentless tug-of-war between conservatism, the wisdom of the tribe, and radicalism, or new thinking. The wisdom of the tribe really matters: it is the accumulated lessons of history, the mistakes as well as the answers, that a polity has gathered up so far. But if this wisdom is not challenged it ossifies. The political revolutions of the British and then the Americans encouraged individuals to alter the balance of powers, without destroying their states. In France, where a conservative monarchy collapsed, revolutionaries tried to wipe out the past entirely and create a new present based only on radical questioning, or 'reason'; it was a bold but bloody failure, copied again and again.

The British-American experiment encouraged new thinkers in natural science to express their ideas more freely than was possible in most of Europe; that in turn would allow experimenters and financial speculators to make the breakthrough in energy use and manufacture that we call 'the industrial revolution'; and that, in turn, gave 'the West' an advantage over the rest of the world that it would keep almost until our own times. This all comes later. What matters in this period is that the British–American experience did not seem the only sensible, or even the most sensible, answer to the question of how to achieve the right balance between wisdom and challenge, between the old and the new. The other fashionable idea was absolutism, the notion that a wise, watchful and energetic leader can safely guide a country between the whirlpools of decline and chaos. In rather different guises, and stripped of its quaint trappings, this idea is still rampantly popular among unelected rulers across much of our world.

And Yet It Moves

A day in August 1609: in one of the most gorgeously decorated rooms in the world, the Hall of the College in the Doge's Palace in Venice, a voluble, red-bearded man caused a sensation. He handed to the Doge, ruler of the Serene Republic, surrounded by his counsellors and naval commanders, a leather-covered tube. After a hubbub of questions and answers, all these men then rushed out of the palace and across the square to Venice's great church, the Basilica of St Mark, and climbed up to the top of the tower. The Doge squinted down the tube. One by one, in turn, so did the rest. On the mainland, miles away, shimmering buildings appeared before their eyes. On nearby islands, the Doge and his men saw people entering their churches; out at sea, galleys still more than two hours' sailing time from Venice could be clearly observed. What they had here was a wonderful military and practical tool. The man who brought it would be richly rewarded.

He was a Pisan mathematician, now lecturing in Venetian territory, called Galileo Galilei. Galileo had stolen the idea from a poor Hollander, who had made his way down from Flanders, where spectacle-makers had invented the telescope, and who had hoped to make a fortune for himself in Italy. But Galileo, working hard on the lenses, improved the gadget hugely. Shrewdly, he had given the telescope to the Doge as a present. Then he went back to his workshop in nearby Padua and made even better ones. It was not long before he turned one of them upwards, to the night sky.

Galileo was already known as a loud-mouthed, exuberant, greedy character who liked to challenge conventional thinking. His work was mostly practical; he advised rulers on ballistics, fortifications and the pumping of water. He had invented a military compass. But he was also known for questioning accepted thinking in the Christian world about nature, then dominated by Aristotle's explanations formulated almost two thousand years earlier. In one of his books, Galileo had a follower of Aristotle ask who could be mankind's guide if the Greek sage were to be abandoned. His interlocutor retorts: 'Only the blind need a guide. Those with eyes and those with a mind must use these faculties to discern for themselves.'[1] These two sentences express perfectly Galileo's enthusiasm for practical, experimental science.

The great breakthrough in challenging the old orthodoxy concerning the Earth's place in Creation had come sixty years earlier when a German–Polish polymath called Nicolaus Copernicus had published *On the Revolutions of the Celestial Spheres*. Many churchmen, Protestants as well as Catholics, had been shocked. Yet the idea of the Earth moving round the sun had not been immediately rejected by the Catholic Church, even though it contradicted the accepted view that God had placed sun, moon and planets on separate shell-like outer spheres to guide and help mankind. To start with, the possibility of the new thinking being accommodated to the Bible was debated. Not for long, though. When the radical roving friar Giordano Bruno, after a lifetime of disobedient speculation, was finally accused of heresy for numerous crimes including arguing that the sun was a star and the universe infinite, he was convicted. With a steel spike through his tongue to stop him talking, he was burned at the stake in Rome in 1600.

The gap between Galileo's optimism about human intelligence and what happened to Bruno goes a long way towards explaining why the renaissance in learning did not lead to a breakthrough in technology and to an industrial revolution in Italy and Spain, in the 1600s, rather than in Britain, in the 1700s. Because we are so used to the order in which things *did* actually happen, we take utterly for granted that the great capitalist leap forward did not occur earlier. It was odd, though. For Italy and other parts of the European south had been immersed in the ideas of the Renaissance and had already developed an expertise in accounting, banking and small-scale engineering that might well have prompted a spurt in development, rather than a sputtering out.

'Renaissance' is not an entirely useful word. Although from the late 1200s through to the 1500s there was indeed a rediscovery and a fresh interest in the classical civilizations, the most interesting breakthroughs were new ones. So this was more birth than rebirth. By the 1400s northern Italy, and parts of northern Europe too, possessed most of the requirements for an enlightenment take-off. Europe's first universities were offering to those who could afford to make use of it a lively education. As soon as printing was more widespread, ideas and arguments travelled fast. In Latin, there was a common language. There was competition, between powerful states such as Florence, Genoa and Venice. At times this overflowed into war, and the sciences of mathematics, ballistics, optics and medicine were advancing fast as rival rulers and armies struggled for advantage. Leonardo da Vinci's enthusiasm for fortifications and novel weaponry is only the most famous example.

Below the level of celebrated inventors existed a powerful base of technical skill, craftsmen and designers able to make the working parts for guns, timepieces, spectacles, and engines for dredging, lifting and pumping. Guilds set professional standards, and common measurements were spreading. A vigorous trading network put the Italians in

touch with the latest ideas and carried news from the Arab world and
the rest of Europe. And trade brought with it a relatively sophisticated
financial system, with long-distance transactions now possible. Italian
thinkers and inventors, as well as artists, had more options than ever
before. Galileo was one of the many who kept moving from town to
town for better deals, like a modern academic for hire. We find even a
very early example of industrial manufacture. At the famous Arsenale
in Venice, rigorously organized and with a workforce of sixteen thousand, the republic could produce one prefabricated, fully equipped
fighting or merchant ship a day (something that took months elsewhere in Europe). This showed that, even if this was an isolated
example, sixteenth-century Italians had something of the organizational capacity of twentieth-century manufacturers.

Casting an eye over Europe, you might have reasonably predicted
that the great advance from agricultural and aristocratic civilizations
to fully urban and industrial ones would begin around the River Po,
rather than the Trent or the Aire, and a century and a half earlier than
it did. Educated Italians had become vigorous, competitive and curious, as well as wealthy. Their curiosity was aimed at the natural world,
and technologies to control it: though when we think of the Renaissance today we think first of 'art' rather than of science or commerce,
as we saw with Leonardo, this was not a division that would have been
understood at the time. In their discoveries about perspective, colour
and distance, lighting and anatomy, other Italian and Dutch painters
had proved themselves intense, steady, analytical lookers. They also
had to be skilled craftsmen and amateur chemists too, collecting the
ingredients, then grinding, mixing, thinning and thickening their
colours, ensuring in the process that they would stay fresh and clear.
Many used ground-glass lenses to help with their looking.

What was Galileo doing, then, other than using his lenses and his
powers of reason to look harder than anyone had before, albeit at
objects rather further away than was then usual? He has been called
the father of 'science', but he would not have understood the word.
His father was a musician and an early experimenter in opera; Galileo
was fascinated by the physics of music, just as he was by the proportions of Dante's Hell. His was a world that feels very close to that of
the Enlightenment and the early industrial revolution.

The difference was that Renaissance Italy, and most of Renaissance

Europe, existed under the authority not just of autocratic local rulers but of a larger power, which by Galileo's time was imposing itself ever more rigorously. The rebirth of classical learning had been used to buttress the Catholic Christian world. Plato was turned into a kind of unwitting early Christian prophet, Aristotle became a pillar of Christian orthodoxy, Ptolemy a champion of the biblical version of the cosmos. Even the Greek and Roman myths were reinterpreted as Christian allegories. Dante, steeped in the pagan Cicero, used the pagan Virgil as his guide to a Christian underworld. The Genoese polymath Leon Battista Alberti studied the Roman architect Vitruvius and ancient Roman ruins (as well as Arab optics); but he was also a devout Christian priest who used his knowledge to build Christian churches, such as the glorious Florentine Santa Maria Novella.

Michelangelo was steeped in the classics. When the great sculpture of the Laocoön – all snakes and muscled writhing – was dug up under a vineyard on Rome's Esquiline Hill in 1506, having been buried since ancient times, he was promptly summoned to view it. (He has even been accused of forging it.) Michelangelo's *David* is a hulking, contemplative Greek giant, except that he is also a Jewish-Christian hero. Again and again, the great trick of the Renaissance was to dress Christian culture in an imperial toga and to make classical philosophy the servant of popes. This has given mankind some of the greatest artefacts ever made, but it put a limit on the scientific advances that could be allowed.

Galileo used his telescope to study first the moon, then Jupiter's moons, then the vast scatter of previously unseen stars. It rammed home to him the impossibility of the Ptolemaic system, with such force that he believed he could win the Vatican over. He was able to have long and serious conversations with leading Vatican thinkers including the cardinal (later made a saint) Robert Bellarmine, who was the main intellectual force behind the Counter-Reformation at the time. But it was not only the fate of Bruno, whose crimes against orthodoxy went rather further than astronomy, that should have made Galileo cautious.

In Venice, one of his great friends was Friar Paolo Sarpi, an eminent scholar and statesman who had led the struggle against the Vatican over the pope's ultimate authority inside that cynical and materialistic republic. Sarpi had also fought hard for Venetian independence in secular matters. Pope Paul V had responded by excommunicating the Doge and all Venetian officials. This was a drastic step for those at the sharp end. In the words of one of Galileo's biographers, 'All of the Venetian republic was cut off from the body of Christ, until the authority of the pope was recognized . . . Baptisms and burials were to cease. Marriages were dissolved and children declared illegitimate. Husbands could desert their wives, and children did not have to obey their parents.'[2] Sarpi responded by having the Jesuits expelled from Venice, and although a compromise was eventually arrived at, Friar Sarpi had paid a high price. Assassins jumped him one night and stabbed him fifteen times, sticking a thin dagger right through his head.

Incredibly, Sarpi survived, while his attackers fled to the Papal States. But this was an eloquent statement of the Vatican's determination to enforce obedience. Threatened by the Protestant Reformation and by new ideas of all kinds, these were the decades of the Pope Militant, the fighting papacy that insisted on absolute deference and, increasingly, on absolute orthodoxy.

Mainly, it seems, out of greed, Galileo then left the relatively secure haven of Venice and returned to work for Florence. Though he was provocative and argumentative, and the religious backlash against him gathered force, he always assumed he could talk his way out of trouble. When Cardinal Bellarmine summoned him on 26 February 1616 and told him that he must abandon any idea that the sun stood still and the Earth revolved around it – and, furthermore, that he must promise not to hold, teach or defend such a notion either in writing or in words – Galileo agreed; but he seems to have come to the hasty conclusion that this was not a 'real' last warning. Meanwhile, all the works of Copernicus were put on the Vatican's list of banned books.

Ill and ageing, Galileo was more or less silent for a while. But then he returned to the attack: his bullish character and love of a good argument with ignorant priests made the final trial almost an inevitability. In 1632, after his book *Dialogue concerning the Two Chief World Systems* had mocked the arguments of the new pope (a one-time friend), Galileo was threatened with torture and being burned alive. After long and menacing interrogations, he eventually recanted, declaring that the Earth did not move round the sun. He was condemned nonetheless as being 'vehemently suspected of heresy'. Legend has it that he defiantly muttered, 'And yet it moves', after publicly abjuring the Copernican system. His punishment was imprisonment, first in Rome, then later at home in Tuscany, where he continued to write.

No enlightenment and no scientific revolution could have emerged from a place where thinkers were forced to 'abjure, curse and detest' ideas they had been driven to by examining the physical world. Renaissance Italy had the makers, the thinkers, the bankers and the competition for take-off, but it also had the Inquisition. The tragedy was that in the north of Europe, although the climate was freer, at the time it mostly lacked the energy of northern Italy. In the north, Galileo was very quickly compared to Christopher Columbus as the discoverer of new worlds – but as an explorer who had spilled no blood and made even more important discoveries. When he was old, under house arrest and on the verge of blindness and death, the Dutch tried to pay him to help them discover the secret of measuring longitude at sea, vital for safer ocean sailing. He was flattered and tempted, but an embarrassed Catholic Church banned him from taking Amsterdam's gold. Some years afterwards the problem was cracked by a Dutchman, Christiaan Huygens, and later more effectively still by the Englishman John Harrison.

Meanwhile, writings advocating the Copernican system stayed on the Vatican's list of banned books until 1835.[3] The power of enlightenment and its revolutionary effect on the human story had moved north.

Absolutism and Its Enemies

The next major idea to dominate Europe was that centralizing and modernizing version of monarchy, 'absolutism'. This could fairly be described as a dull notion exuberantly embellished with stone and scandal. Half the capital cities of Europe still have palaces, arches or other monuments to the rule of some family of absolutists. Some of the most exotic characters in Western history – Russia's Catherine the Great and Peter the Great, Prussia's Frederick the Great – were absolute monarchs from this period. At its most ambitious, the idea was to bulldoze the tangle of local privileges, civic rights, tolls, traditions and charters inherited from the medieval centuries, in the name of the king, who would substitute a single, efficient, properly organized central authority. This authority would improve roads, excavate canals, raise taxes for a standing army and establish reliable laws for all subjects. 'The state? It's me,' said Louis XIV, France's Sun King. He did not mean it entirely as a joke.

Louis and those rulers who copied him worked hard to undermine the old semi-autonomous power of the provincial aristocratic landowners and clerical foundations, creating mesmerizing courts to stun, intimidate and lure. In many ways they provided the basis for the nation-states that followed. Outside France, the most assertive absolutists were the Russian Romanovs, who created a new capital, St Petersburg, and who modelled themselves on Western rulers and especially on the royal house of Prussia, the Hohenzollerns, whom we will meet later. But in this era the greatest rivals of Louis's family, the Bourbons, were the Habsburgs, whose territories were even larger and who we have already come across in Spain.

This noble family was the product of exuberant match-making rather than territorial coherence. Originally from Switzerland, during medieval times they had expanded their power across central Germany and became rulers of Austria. For centuries the Habsburgs were just another of the competing European dynasties, alongside the Luxembourgers, the Jagiellons and many more. But through luck, a little war and a lot of marriage they eventually engulfed Burgundy, the Low Countries and quite a speckle and splatter of central Europe. Above all, from 1438 for almost exactly three hundred years the Habsburgs provided all the Holy Roman Emperors, those would-be Germanic Caesars. In just a few years around the end of the fifteenth century they acquired their Spanish and Hungarian lands and expanded into Italy too, becoming the most important source of power in Europe other than the papacy itself.

Hapsburg rule was not, however, full-blown absolutism. It had grown out of the tangled family politics of the Middle Ages, and had never developed a theory of state power in any modernizing sense. Its imperial headquarters, the vast stone expanses of the Escorial palace in Madrid, and the later grandiose palaces of Vienna, lacked the grip on either the pockets or the imaginations of Germans or Spaniards or Dutchmen that the Bourbons had on the French. The Habsburgs were fighting on too many fronts and across too many territories to establish a single imperial idea. In the sixteenth century the Habsburg line split into the Spanish monarchy, which with its American empire and its control of the Netherlands was the more important, and the Austro-Hungarian line, which sprawled across Eastern Europe.

Consequently, Habsburg rule was never uniform: imperial power in New Spain was a different proposition from its counterpart in Holland. The role of the emperor in Turk-challenged Hungary was more direct than in the German cities and states whose 'electors' and princes selected him. Habsburg rule was a mishmash of political and military power, rarely financially stable, and it came at a terrible genetic cost. The principle of endless interbreeding among the family so as to maintain their possessions demonstrated the sense of the incest taboo – a toll of dead children, and deformed and incapable adults. The physical oddness of the later Habsburgs, pop-eyed, with huge lower jaws and jutting lips, is well recorded by their braver court painters.

The worst of the line was perhaps the wretched Charles II of Spain, who drooled, believed himself possessed of the devil, was unable to chew, liked to observe the exhumed corpses of his relatives, and was – perhaps thankfully – impotent too. His death in 1700, terminating one branch of the family, produced the War of the Spanish Succession, followed in 1740 by the War of the Austrian Succession when that branch died out. This shows just how brittle dynastic politics remained, as late as the eighteenth century; though both wars were in reality less about Spain or Austria than about containing the most vigorous and expansive example of European absolutism, the Bourbon monarchy of France.

The Bourbons had emerged as a cadet, or junior, line of the ancient Capetian dynasty, who traced their roots back to Paris in the 800s. They had emerged out of Navarre (roughly speaking, today's Basque country, on the French–Spanish border) and were on the Protestant, Huguenot, side during the French wars of religion, which ended in 1598. The first Bourbon king of France, Henry IV, was the first to convert back to Catholicism, allegedly remarking that Paris was worth a mass, but he had later been assassinated. The real founder of Bourbon absolutism was Cardinal Richelieu, France's chief minister for two decades from 1624. Richelieu had been a soldier before joining the Church, partly to protect family interests, and had risen to power through the dangerous corridors of a court then in the hands of the young King Louis XIII's mother, Marie de Médicis, before becoming an essential aide and minister to the monarch himself.

Richelieu's strategy was to create a single, forceful authority in France by defeating any internal opposition – he had the aristocrats' castles demolished and crushed the Huguenots – while expanding France's external position against the Habsburgs.

• Under Richelieu the Thirty Years War, which had been essentially one of religion, devastating Germany as Protestant fought Catholic, subtly mutated into a war about France's role in Europe. The Habsburgs, in Spain and Germany, appeared to have France encircled; and the family had ambitions to gain papal approval as a kind of universal European monarchy. So forcing the Habsburgs back until they were virtually broke put a newly unified France into a key position as the major power in Europe. As a result, after Richelieu's death, when the Italian-born Cardinal Mazarin succeeded him as chief minister, the way was clear for Louis XIV, the 'Sun King', to rise above the horizon with a special glow.

Louis reigned from 1643 to 1715, an astonishing seventy-two years, though his personal rule began only in 1661 after Mazarin's death. By that time France had grown – to the south, to the east, to the north. Richelieu had established a new system of tax-collectors, had centralized power at the court, and had promoted early industrial developments, from canals to tapestry-works. Under Richelieu and Mazarin fortresses were built to protect the new France, and ambitious plans were hatched for a French empire in North America. Once Louis was ruling France himself, he continued the policy of relentless hostility towards the Habsburgs, determined to establish himself as the dominant European prince. His court, with its elaborate public rituals, its lavish entertainments and its scandalous gossip, transfixed educated people throughout Europe.

Soon, it seemed that absolute monarchs could come in almost any religious colour – Lutherans and Calvinists in Germany and Scandinavia, Orthodox in Russia, Catholic in Spain and Portugal. Despite Scandinavia's later reputation as a pioneer of democratic thinking, Denmark–Norway (under Frederick III in the 1660s) and Sweden (under the personal rule of Charles XI from 1672) saw early and aggressive forms of absolutism. They had had long traditions of powerful kings and incompetent or divided state councils and were often engaged in bloody wars, which tended to concentrate power in the hands of rulers who were also effective military commanders. This was a time when, after the rampages of its best-known ruler Gustavus Adolphus, Sweden seemed more likely to emerge as the key northern European power than either Prussia or Russia. There, Peter the Great, who came to power in 1682 and ruled for nearly forty-three years, would base his own radical changes on the same mixture of central- ization, anti-feudal modernization and rationalism as had been pioneered in France.

For Louis XIV, the price of the extra fortresses and armies was higher taxation, and in 1649 Paris came close to a first French revolu- tion after the second bout of uprisings known as the Fronde (the name refers to the catapults used by children to hurl stones at the houses of the rich). A system of war based on carefully drilled blocks of soldiers firing muskets, the use of cannon and fortresses, was a powerful bias in favour of a centralized tax authority, but this in turn depended on effectively squeezing town and countryside without at the same time provoking constant revolts. The basic mechanics of taxing, imposing laws and keeping order with quill-pens and mounted messengers were difficult to administer. The absolute monarchs tended to build their dreams in stone – at Versailles, St Petersburg or Potsdam – while fan- tasizing that their writ ran across hundreds of miles of peasant farms, forests and muddy tracks way beyond. For of course, a lot of Europe was still a complicated patchwork of territories well outside the effec- tive rule of the grand monarchs, bleeding away their authority in endless wars against one another.

Monarchical power was never entirely secure, a message soon being heard with uncomfortable volume from the direction of the United Kingdom. Because Britain during this century lurched into civil war and regicide, it is sometimes seen rather separately from the European age of absolutism; in fact, these northern islands were closely knitted into the tensions and dilemmas of the mainland. They had fallen under the control of another dynastic sprawl, this time a Scottish royal house which, in the shape of our tobacco-hating James, had suc- ceeded to the English throne. The Stuarts, like the Bourbons and the Habsburgs, had risen from relative medieval obscurity – in their case during the 1300s – providing nine monarchs, some wise, some foolish, for their small nation. Once in London, the Stuarts were sucked into the maelstrom of the European dynastic rivalries, trying to form marriages and alliances with both Habsburgs and Bourbons, and intervening militarily – though ineffectively – in the continental wars.

The Stuarts soon demonstrated what could happen when a would-be absolutist was unable to raise the money needed for war. Charles I had no Richelieu. His favourites were altogether less effective and less visionary. Unlike Louis XIV's Estates General, Charles's main Parliament, the English one, obstinately refused to be ignored. His system of personal tax-gathering was based not on a network of professional collectors, but on medieval laws that had been half forgotten and were everywhere resented. In France, it was possible to bring an end to the internal religious wars by repressing the Protestants; in Scotland and England, this was impossible. The unintended consequences of this British dynastic failure would be huge, not just for Britain but for the history of Europe and America, because they showed the way forward towards a new kind of government.

In Scotland, where Charles had been born, a Presbyterian revolution was in full flood, displacing a Church of bishops by one of self-governing congregations under church 'elders'. In England, the ancient Parliament had proved increasingly militant during the reign of Charles's father James, and was cussedly difficult about authorizing taxes or supporting Charles's erratic foreign policy. A long, if semi-mythical, tradition of ancient English 'rights', going back to a folk memory of Anglo-Saxon times, was invoked against monarchical tyranny. In 1629 Charles suspended Parliament and ruled for eleven years through his own ministers. But again, lacking any system of direct taxation he struggled with money, and struggled to impose his will on religious matters; for any king a severe humiliation.

When Scotland rebelled against his policies under its National Covenant during 1638–9, Charles was quite unable to control his angry subjects. When he finally summoned the English Parliament again in 1640, needing to raise money, MPs proved doggedly hostile and insisted on establishing their rights anew. Charles dismissed them, but then faced another successful Scottish rebellion, which this time reached into northern England. Being defeated by his own subjects, and facing another uprising in Ireland, Charles was forced to try yet again with the English Parliament.

But by now Parliament was determined on political reform. The Commons insisted that in future only MPs, not the king, could dismiss it. Charles, losing face – along with almost every shred of authority – then failed to arrest the leading MPs and withdrew from the capital, which was now enemy territory. From Nottingham, he raised his standard against the Parliamentarians, and civil war broke out at last in the summer of 1642.

Over the next three years, Charles's armies were comprehensively defeated by the better disciplined and better led troops of Oliver Cromwell's New Model Army. There was a pause, then the fighting resumed. A complex series of campaigns, involving Protestant Scots, Catholic Irish, the English nobility, armies of townsmen and the increasingly professional Cromwellian regiments, as well as the town bands of English volunteers, ended in total victory for Parliament's armies. Despite the protests of his brother monarchs, Charles was tried and beheaded in 1649 – the same year that Louis XIV faced the Fronde in Paris. Charles had been as intense a believer in the Divine Right of Kings as any Bourbon or Habsburg. This was not how the Divine Right, or modern absolutism, was supposed to work.

A British Commonwealth had by now been declared, and it managed to govern capably enough for some years, rebuilding a powerful navy and restoring order, before it degenerated into the personal quasi-monarchy of Cromwell himself. The Lord Protector's Roundhead army plunged into democratic and land-reform arguments far more radical than anything envisaged by Cromwell himself, or by the landowners and generals who formed the core of the republic. Revolutionary libertarians, who seized and ploughed up private land and set up idealistic communities, calling themselves 'Diggers', suggested that the political revolution might be followed by a social one. This was all too much for Britain's new military junta – as it might fairly be styled, after Cromwell too dismissed Parliament – and the radicals were suppressed.

This would hardly be the last time an optimistic revolution, brimming with hope and radicalism, ended up as a military dictatorship. Cromwell's government lost the affection of both radicals and many of the middling people, who felt their liberties were even more curtailed than they had been by the Stuarts. Puritan edicts banning traditional holidays, including Christmas, as well as popular entertainments such as the theatre, pleased the godly and disgusted the rest. After Cromwell's death, and after a very short interval when his son tried to inherit his authority, the Commonwealth was ended when regiments marched on London and invited Charles's son, Charles II, to return from exile in Holland. Sensibly, the new king limited retribution to all but the obvious regicides, and soon British life seemed to have returned to a version of the European political model. But this is not quite true. Parliament would never be truly quiescent again, and Charles realized that he was going to have to court popularity and public approval in a way French and Habsburg monarchs would have scorned. His modest-sized palace was squeezed into the streets and riverside of London, filled with petitioners and idlers, and he showed himself regularly to the people – a stark contrast to Louis' glorious isolation well outside Paris at Versailles.

On the continent, the British revolution had been regarded as a bizarre aberration, caused by the odd circumstance of the coming together of a half-breed religion and an incompetent dynasty. Mazarin and Louis XIV, by now growing confidently into his role, thought the Stuarts of London a poor lot. They had been prepared to strike deals with Cromwell's republic, and had dropped their support for the restoration of Charles II when it suited France to strike other deals. Many British radicals, bitterly disappointed by the Cromwellian junta and then the restoration of the Stuarts, emigrated to the American colonies, where they hoped to form exclusive and 'pure' communities of free and God-fearing farmers.

But the British revolution was not over. It would take only one more incompetent Stuart to finish off untrammelled monarchy there for ever.

Britain Invaded

Was she or wasn't she? The gossip about the queen, a dark-eyed Italian who had suffered many miscarriages, was poisonous. The king's own daughter Princess Anne wrote to her older sister in Holland: 'I can't help thinking the wife's great belly is a little suspicious. It is true indeed she is very big, but she looks better than ever she did, which is not usual.' A week later, she wrote again that with all the gossip and jokes about a fake pregnancy, the queen 'should, to convince the world, make either me or some of my friends feel her belly; but quite contrary, whenever one talks of her being with child, she looks as if she was afraid one should touch her. And whenever I happen to be in the room as she has been undressing, she has always gone into the next room to put on her smock.'[4] This was the tittle-tattle that would take Britain on an altogether different course.

The pregnant Queen was Mary of Modena, wife of James II of Great Britain, a Catholic Stuart who wanted Catholics to be tolerated, and perhaps rather more than tolerated, in his Protestant country. His daughters by his first marriage to an Englishwoman, Princess Anne and her older sister Mary, were Protestants. This second, Italian, wife had failed to provide a son – until now. On 10 June 1688 the queen was delivered of a boy, James Francis Edward Stuart. Fireworks and bon-fires were lit. Commemorative cups and dishes were commissioned, pictures painted, just as happens for a British royal birth to this day. Except that this time the national gossip continued, and spread. The so-called heir, it was said, was not the queen's child at all but a changeling, smuggled into the birth chamber in a warming-pan to ensure a Catholic inherited the throne. In fact the birth had been attended by a small horde of witnesses, cramming the room and the surrounding corridors. But this did nothing to quell the rumour.

Just six months later the Coldstream Guards, one of Britain's proudest regiments, were ordered to leave their posts guarding the king at his palace in Whitehall. Indeed, all the English soldiers in London were told to leave, the Life Guards to decamp to St Albans, and others to Sussex. Into their places marched an invading army, the crack infantry of the Dutch Blue Guard, in their blue and orange-yellow uniforms. These were the spearhead of a huge invading force, twice as big as the Spanish Armada. The Dutch fleet of fifty-three war-ships and about four hundred supply ships had outwitted the Royal Navy, sailing first towards the east coast of England and then using a change in the wind – 'the Protestant wind', people said – to sail west, landing at Torbay in Devon.

The Dutch had caught the British and French fleets napping. Many miles from the nearest English defenders, nearly forty thousand troops had disembarked along with fifty cannon, volunteers and extra horses. They were well equipped with everything a modern army needed, from newly made muskets and pistols to supply wagons, bombs and even wheelbarrows. And this was a truly international invading force. The Dutch monarch William of Orange was leading, along with some Scottish and English renegades, a force of Germans, Swiss, Swedes and even Laplanders. It included, partly just to show that William was a world-conquering fellow, two hundred blacks from the sugar plantations of America, wearing turbans and feathers. The army had marched first to Exeter and then to the Thames, reaching Henley, then Windsor, site of the ancient royal castle. Finally, just as King James was getting into bed at 11 p.m. on 17 December, they arrived in St James's Park in the middle of London. He could not believe his eyes.

Though James had a bigger army and the support of most of the southern landowners, he had been in a state of abject funk for weeks. His daughter, the chatty Princess Anne, was among those who now abandoned him for William and her sister Mary. So too had Anne's closest friend Sarah Churchill, wife of the Duke of Marlborough (the two were so close they used nicknames for one another – Mrs Morley and Mrs Freeman). The regime was crumbling from within. James had already made one attempt to flee to France six days earlier, deliberately dropping the Great Seal in the Thames from his rowing-boat. He had done this because no Parliament was lawful without it, and he hoped thereby to create a constitutional crisis. He did, but the Lords, pragmatic as ever, formed a provisional government anyway, until James was finally packed off by the Dutch to Rochester. A few days later he left for France, his guards having been quietly instructed to let him go. For the next few months all British regiments were ordered not to go within twenty miles of London while the Dutch and Germans set up their camps inside the capital, at Kensington, Chelsea and Paddington.

The British do not, in general, make much of this invasion. Even quite well educated people believe that England has not been invaded since the Normans arrived in 1066. The impression has been left that William was more or less invited in, to sort out some small constitutional issues. This was not so. William had taken a massive military and personal gamble because the Dutch Protestants were desperate. Had James not panicked and fled, or had the wind veered a little, William might have lost everything. Instead, with his wife, Princess Anne's confidante and older sister Mary, he became part of the only joint monarchy in modern British history. But the reign of William and Mary was not yet secure. A major attempt to win back the crown for the Stuarts and Catholicism erupted in Ireland (and to a lesser extent Scotland), and was only thwarted in battle. So this was not even, quite, a 'bloodless revolution'. But 1688 was truly a turning-point in European history because it established a different way of ruling.

William of Orange had assembled his army and navy, and had taken that gamble, because he felt he had no alternative. When his sister-in-law fed him the gossip about Queen Mary's pregnancy, it seemed obvious that the British succession had been settled and the London court would stay Catholic. This was terrible news for Protestant Holland, with her north German allies, leaving them exposed to the most dangerous enemy they had, Louis XIV. The Sun King was squeezing them. He had dramatically increased taxes on Dutch exports to France, and banned the import of the pickled herrings so many Dutch fishermen and traders depended on for their livelihood. He had impounded three hundred Dutch trading vessels. His armies seemed unbeatable.

The Dutch had despaired, years earlier, at the failure of Charles II to come to their aid. But the succession of James II, a Catholic like Louis, made their plight worse. The arrival of his son, whether the boy had been smuggled into the birth chamber or not, was the final blow. William of Orange either had to invade Britain and neutralize the threat of a British–French alliance, or watch his Protestant trading nation, brimming with enterprise, science and middle-class prosperity, be choked to death. So he launched an invasion, one that has been described as 'mounted in defiance of all common sense and professional experience'.[5] As the historian Lisa Jardine has conclusively shown, what happened in 1688 happened because the Dutch decided it must, not because the British asked for it to happen.

Yet its consequences went far beyond anything William could have imagined. Once James had gone, and despite his Dutch Blue Guard, William's position in London was not entirely safe. Strictly speaking, he was only fourth in line to the throne. Most of the big landowners had sat on the fence and waited to see who would win before committing themselves. The army and navy were unhappy, to say the least. Having marched through London, how would he actually establish his authority?

Meeting as a Convention, since in the absence of the Great Seal they could not be a Parliament, the Commons and Lords debated what to do. They would simply declare new constitutional principles as they went along. James had not been ousted, but had deserted his country, thus breaking his contract. ('Contract'? What contract? a traditionalist would have asked.) James and his son were then cut out of the succession on the novel principle that they were Catholics, and that they had been found 'by experience' to be impossible rulers.[6] Next, the peers and MPs offered the crown to Mary alone, a Stuart by blood. This, said William, was not acceptable. He would rather return home with his wife and leave the British to squabble amongst themselves. At which, the MPs backed down and announced a joint monarchy in which William, now William III, would exercise the real authority.

This was a great victory for the Dutchman – or would have been, except that the Commons insisted on something in return. They drew up a Bill of Rights. Agreeing to this meant that William also agreed that in future no British monarch could raise taxes, or have a standing army, without the agreement of Parliament; that he had to allow free and frequent elections; and that he could not be a Roman Catholic. As compared with the absolutist pretensions of continental monarchy, this was the real, the permanent, British revolution. A monarch who controlled neither money nor troops, and whose people dictated his religious views, was no proper monarch at all.

The British parliamentarians had rejected the monarchical tyranny of Charles I and the dictatorship of Oliver Cromwell. They had little time for James's Catholic-absolutist dreams, but nor were they prepared to allow themselves to be squashed under the heel of a Protestant Dutchman. They would have monarchy, but on their own terms only; and for a major power this was something entirely new. The 'Glorious Revolution' would be the cornerstone of British politics and power for more than three centuries to come. The rights and liberties secured by Parliament gave freedom to publish, argue, probe and experiment. This was the unequivocal, world-changing answer to Rome.

Out of it would come the great thinkers of the British Enlightenment and a flourishing inquiry into nature – what would later be called 'science'. Isaac Newton, who published his *Principia Mathematica* the year before William's fleet sailed to Devon, enjoyed his greatest years as a public figure under the new monarchy. Like Galileo, he was firmly convinced that the heliocentric principle was correct, and like Galileo he combined mathematics and practical experiments in a wide range of fields. He produced the first reflecting telescope, for instance, for which he ground his own lenses. Like his colleagues the chemist Robert Boyle, the polymath Robert Hooke – who invented the word 'cell' for the basic building-block of life – and Christopher Wren, he never had to worry about religious orthodoxy or the attentions of the Inquisition.

Under the leadership of the Royal Society, formed during Charles II's reign, these thinkers argued and disputed constantly, but over the meaning of their discoveries, over who invented what first, and over patents – not over divine authority. They were part of what for a time became more of an Anglo-Dutch milieu than a purely British one. Among the Dutchmen who soon made the trip to London was the same Christiaan Huygens who had picked up and partially solved the problem of measuring longitude with an accurate clock, the man that Galileo had been kept away from by the Catholic Church.

Galileo had been fascinated by microscopes as well as by telescopes, and in Rome in 1624 had shown off the multitude of giant insects revealed by his own compound microscope.[7] In London and Leiden, an even greater sense of tiny new worlds being uncovered was experienced when Hooke, Huygens and the renowned Antonie van Leeuwenhoek squinted through their lenses and published some extraordinary pictures of lice, mould and other wriggly, nightmarish tiddlers. If, despite the anxieties aroused by the Inquisition, Galileo did finally arrive in a Christian Paradise, he must have looked down and shaken his head in frustration at being born too far south and a little too early.

What, meanwhile, of that terrible gossip Princess Anne, whose letters had triggered rather more than she bargained for. She became, in good time, plump and stately Queen Anne. Like the Habsburgs, this last of the Stuart monarchs became an unhappy symbol of dynastic weakness: of her eighteen or nineteen pregnancies, all but three produced dead babies – stillborn, miscarried or died very soon after birth. This horrible toll, compounded as a personal tragedy by the death in childhood of the three survivors (two from smallpox) suggests some profound genetic problem. Yet if Anne did not give birth to a successor, her reign does mark the true birth of a modern nation.

In 1707 she became the first monarch to rule over the constitutionally united realms of England, Wales and Scotland – or as it became known, Great Britain. The Scottish Parliament, after a ruinous attempt at creating an empire in central America, had bankrupted the country. It accepted London's bail-out terms and dissolved itself, thereby creating a single British Parliament. Queen Anne's friend Sarah Churchill became one of the most influential women in the land, and it was her husband, the Duke of Marlborough, who would lead British armies across Europe, finally freeing the Netherlands from the French and beating back the Catholic threat.

After this, Britain would begin the process of acquiring the greatest empire in the world and, on the back of her original contribution to politics, royal 'moderatism' rather than 'absolutism', achieve the first industrial revolution too.

The Bourbons of India: From Babur to Bust

The history of India can seem a tangled blur of confusing, romantic names, hidden in thickets of unreliable source materials. We last left her in the political confusion that followed the empires of the Buddhist Mauryans and then of the Hindu Gupta dynasty, which was a golden age for Indian art, architecture and writing. But Hindu India would not be able to maintain its political dominance. The same violent disturbances that shook Eastern Europe, central Asia, Russia and China erupted into India too. The Mongol invaders, coming on the heels of Muslim Turkic armies, would stamp Islam across the northern territories and would dominate the subcontinent until the arrival of the British.

This need not confuse us too much. There are useful parallels between the history of Europe from the 1200s to the 1600s, and of India at the same time. After all, the huge peninsula of Europe and the giant wedge of India are two similarly sized tongues jabbing out from the Eurasian landmass. During this half-millennium both suffered a long conflict between a would-be centre and local or regional identities; and then a long struggle between rival religions which prevented either of these subcontinents achieving political unity.

Europe's would-be centre was the papacy in Rome, working

alongside the Holy Roman Empire and other Catholic monarchies. In India, the would-be centre was Delhi under the Muslim Turkish Khalji and Tughluq dynasties, whose dominance was challenged just as vigorously as Rome's. Rome faced heretics and Protestant revolt: the Delhi Muslim dynasties were confronted by Hindu kings and rebel peoples of the west, centre and south. The Muslims wrecked many of the glories of Hindu civilization, smashing old temples and art, just as the Protestants destroyed monasteries and Catholic religious art. If the one contained countries as diverse as Scotland, Lithuania, England, Poland and Hungary, the other had Malwa, Orissa, Vijayanagara, Jaunpur and the Rajput states.

In some lights they even looked a little the same: one can certainly compare the elaborate carved stone architecture of India during this period with the cathedrals and castles of European rulers. And India can offer up individuals as idiosyncratic as England's Henry VIII or a Borgia pope, and just as well remembered. There was the great Muslim ruler from Delhi, Ala-ud-din, with his regiments of elephant-mounted soldiers and his Turkish cavalry, who drove deep into the south, extracting glittering tribute – almost an Aladdin's cave of the stuff – and who repulsed even the Mongols. There was the poet, intellectual, patron of the arts and mathematician Muhammad Bin Tughluq, sultan of Delhi, whose ferocious treatment of rebels and of those who displeased him became legendary. One such was flayed alive, then his skin was stuffed with rice mixed with his minced flesh and served to his family – behaviour to rival that of the Christian Prince, and warrior, Vlad.

Indian history from the Middle Ages to early-modern times is therefore no more outlandish than European. We find a comparable procession of sieges, marches, dynastic cat-fights and regional rebellions, below which an impoverished peasantry and heavily taxed city traders struggled. What we do not find is any popular breakaway from the rule of kings and princes; there was much Indian philosophy and natural science, but there was no Indian enlightenment, nor (in this period) much political experimentation. Or so we believe. Unfortunately, Indian history outside the Muslim courts is relatively poorly recorded. One modern historian laments: 'Unenlivened by the gossipy narratives beloved of Muslim writers, the contemporary history of Hindu India has still to be laboriously extrapolated from

the sterile phrasing and optimistic listings favoured by royal pane-
gyrists.'8

Yet Hinduism could not be stamped out, any more by Muslim
imams than later by Christian missionaries. Muslim rulers defeated
Hindu rulers, but rarely tried to oppress Hinduism itself or any of the
other religions. There were individual atrocities galore, but not the
cruel mass burnings, forced conversions, torture of heretics or wars of
extermination that Europe knew. And unlike its European equivalent,
Indian seamanship was largely coastal and based on trade, not war or
exploration. There had been warlike fleets, particularly under the
Chola dynasty of southern India during the medieval period, when
Indian fleets reached China; but not for centuries. On land, too, Indian
rulers occasionally mustered armies to push north through Afghanistan towards Persia, or east towards China, but never developed the
global ambitions of Portugal, France or Britain, all of whom established early footholds in India.

Indian history really coheres with the rise of the great Mughal
empire, at around the same time as the Reformation in Europe and
the Spanish arrival in Peru. That starts as an astonishing adventure
story in the wilds of central Asia, and ends as a lesson in the dangers
of absolute monarchy.

Properly called Zahir-ud-Din Muhammad, but generally known by his
nickname 'Tiger', or Babur, the founder of the Mughal dynasty was a
descendant of both Genghis Khan and Tamerlane. Babur had been
born in Uzbekistan in 1483, the same year as Raphael and Martin
Luther. The son of a modest local ruler, he won his first major military victory, the capture of Samarkand, when he was just fourteen.
Struggling against desertions, revolts and the threat posed by much
larger enemies, Babur slowly built up a power base in Afghanistan
before descending on northern India with the new weapon of the age,
the musket. His armies defeated the Muslim Lodi dynasty, capturing
Delhi in 1526, and then overwhelmed the proudly independent Hindu
Rajput rulers too. Dying in 1531, he left behind exquisite gardens (not
least, the one in Kabul, where he is buried), the first Muslim ruler's
autobiography, a reputation for building pillars out of the heads of his
decapitated enemies, and a remarkable dynasty.

The trouble with dynasties, however, is that they produce weaker members as well as stronger ones. Babur's son lost the empire and then regained it, but it was his grandson, Akbar the Great, who really expanded Mughal rule. Akbar, roughly contemporaneous with Elizabeth I, the first Tokugawas and Ivan the Terrible, would rule for half a century. His military victories, featuring mass elephant attacks and cannon, increased the size of his empire to about a hundred million souls, compared with around five million English and the forty million Europeans of the time.

These victories were often hideously bloody, as bad as anything Ashoka had perpetrated. At the siege of Chittor, a Hindu Rajput fortress, in 1567–8, the soldiers chose the traditional death of a suicide charge, while their women and children burned themselves to death rather than be captured alive. Yet thirty thousand civilians survived for long enough for Akbar's forces to massacre them. Akbar, though, is like Ashoka in that he has been remembered more for his peaceful qualities than for his military savagery.

Akbar was a less extreme case than Ashoka. He maintained a vast army, sustained by heavy taxes on the peasantry, but he also created an efficient and relatively fair imperial bureaucracy and was notably open-minded about religion. After founding a new capital city, Fatehpur Sikri, combining gorgeous Islamic, Indian and Persian architectural styles, Akbar had religious rivals take part in open debates with one another, as he sat and listened. The mingling of columns and arches of different styles was echoed by a mingling of world views, as Muslim Sunnis and Shia, Sufis and Hindus, Jains and Sikhs, and even Portuguese Christians, exchanged their ideas about the nature of God. Akbar seems not to have intended himself to convert to any new faith, but instead wanted to bind the faiths together into something fresh, and suitable for his multi-faith empire. In the end this 'something' may have amounted to little more than loyal and pious admiration for Akbar himself. Like the new capital city – short of water, too near to rebel kingdoms – it did not survive, except as the long-remembered possibility of a more tolerant Indian politics.

Akbar was succeeded by his son, Jahangir. This short statement must be followed by an admission: the Mughal habit of sons revolting against fathers and sons fighting sons creates a story too complicated to be related here. The Mughals were as bad as Plantagenets or Ottomans. Suffice it to say that Jahangir, another religiously tolerant man and a great patron of art and architecture, was also an alcoholic, and he ruled jointly with his far sharper wife, who had coins minted in her name. Jahangir was, in due course, ousted by one of his sons, who also disposed of his brothers; he then reigned from 1628 to 1658 as Shah Jahan.

Shah Jahan will always be remembered. He left behind him the most successful architectural emblem in world history. His wife, Mumtaz Mahal, died giving birth to their fourteenth child. Her death drove him in his grief to commission the greatest building India has ever seen, the Taj Mahal. Floating in the dawn, or at dusk, outside the city of Agra, its luminous beauty checkmates the clichéd reproductions in restaurants and advertisements around the world, trumping even the smoky, sprawling industrial town that now encircles it. This fundamentally simple monument to married love is also evidence of the extravagance of scale the Mughal dynasty could then deploy. Shah Jahan's marblemania materialized in the form of beautiful buildings across much of Delhi, Agra and other cities, astonishing contemporary observers.

This was one of the things eighteenth-century absolutism was good at, too. But is it reasonable to bracket together the Mughals in India and the contemporary European rulers under that word 'absolutism'? Mughal rule had very different religious and philosophical roots from the European or Russian monarchies; nor was there a parallel Indian Enlightenment, despite the religious experimentation of Akbar. Yet the Mughals saw themselves as centralizers and modernizers, bringing a new coherence to the subcontinent. The earlier Mughals were intellectually open and curious. Furthermore, educated Europeans of the time, particularly French observers, were keenly aware of the Mughals as a parallel dynasty from whom lessons might usefully be learned. As at St Petersburg or Versailles, Mughal power mobilized huge manpower and resources to create epics in stone, designed to awe.

The Mughals were, however, symbols – even in Europe – for monarchical extravagance. And despite the steady spread of their imperial domains, the power of their armies and the opulence of their court, they were beginning to show that dynasties must also age. The insolent exuberance of Babur had been followed by the youthful intellectual curiosity of Akbar, then the decline of Jahangir and now Shah

Jahan's expensive addiction to huge construction projects. Just as modern corporations who build spectacular new headquarters with fountains and statues outside them are often said to be heading for failure, for all its beauty, was the Taj Mahal the beginning of a decline? And was there something built into the structure of absolutism that made such decline inevitable?

People wondered, even at the time. Comparisons sprang readily to mind because the Mughal dynasty peaked just as Europe's age of absolutism started. The Taj Mahal was completed in 1648. Louis XIV's architects began the great expansion of Versailles a dozen years later. Peter the Great became sole ruler of Russia at the moment the Mughal empire reached its greatest extent. And the reign of the last really substantial Mughal emperor, Aurangzeb, coincided with the arrival of Frederick I as king of Prussia and with the beginning of Spain's Bourbon dynasty. François Bernier, who became Aurangzeb's personal doctor, wrote to Louis's minister Jean-Baptiste Colbert about the astonishing wealth and luxury of the Mughal court, but warned that the system of never-ending taxes and imposts on the Indian peasantry reduced them to effective slavery, and made it hard to improve the land: people who had no stake in the future had no motivation to repair ditches or work harder.[9]

Aurangzeb had started in the usual way, with the murder of a brother after a war of succession and the incarceration of his father. Europeans were agog: the English poet John Dryden wrote a play about 'Aureng-zebe' in 1675, making a hero of the pious Muslim. But the real Aurangzeb would ruin the Mughals. His empire would reach almost all of the Indian subcontinent. It had some of the virtues of absolutist rule – a single legal system, well maintained roads and strong fortresses, standard weights and measures, relatively efficient tax collection, growing trade (not least with the Europeans) and a big standing army, and it kept records. But it became increasingly oppressive.

Aurangzeb had turned his back on the tolerant attitude of earlier Mughals, including his father and his butchered brother. He instituted Islamic bans on alcohol, on dancing and on the writing of history. He sacked the court artists whose delicate miniatures were one of the glories of Indian culture. He created a system of censors and allowed his troops to desecrate or destroy Hindu temples. In a famous though disputed scene, his court musicians, wailing and weeping, conducted a huge burial service with twenty biers: when Aurangzeb asked what was happening, they replied that since he had killed music, they were 'burying music'. He hoped they buried her deep, he replied.

Like other autocrats, he needed ever greater resources to supply his armies and his bureaucracy, but he failed to achieve the economic growth of more open and outward-looking states. He set out to conquer new territories in the Deccan plain and the Indian south: his most famous conquest was of the world's greatest diamond mine at Golkonda, which produced the Koh-i-Noor, the 'French Blue' sported by Louis XIV himself (it reappeared in modern times as the Hope Diamond), and many others. The mine was protected by an eight-mile wall around a granite hill. The attack, in 1687, was long and bloody, but eventually made Aurangzeb the world's richest ruler. He was also one of the world's healthiest rulers, perhaps due to his austere religious ways. He would reign until 1707, dying at eighty-eight while still leading his apparently perennial campaign to subdue all of India.

Eventually, he ruled almost a quarter of the world's people. Yet this long war now seems a great folly, costing far more than Shah Jahan's building mania had. By bleeding the Mughal state dry it would lead to the rise of British India, a consequence Aurangzeb could not have begun to imagine. His greatest enemy was the Hindu Maratha state based in the hilly Western Ghats and along the coast, which at the time was ferociously led by a military genius called Shivaji, who became a hero to Hindus, and the subject of many tall tales as he led his irregular forces in bold raids. From 1681 to 1707, the Marathas and the Mughals fought a war whose only equivalent in Europe was the long wars of the This, That and the Other Succession. Throughout that twenty-six-year campaign the aged Aurangzeb travelled with a movable capital, a tent city allegedly thirty miles around, with half a million followers and thirty thousand elephants, stripping the land of its produce as they went and helping to spread disease.

Like later generals, he discovered that conventional armies find it a struggle to defeat guerrillas, and the fight against the Marathas began to feel like a war without end. It was spreading a hatred of Islam, rather than affection for it. The conflict brought his empire close to financial collapse, and as taxes rose, revolts spread far beyond the south.

This is about as good an illustration as you could get of the dangers of absolutism. An empire driven by the obsession of a single man, religious in this case, relying on repression and territorial expansion, cannot last long. The parallels with Europe are strong: there too the wars were about succession and religious differences, and would go on almost as long; though, thanks to ocean-going fleets, they would spread much further, including to India itself. As to Aurangzeb, as he was dying he apparently told his son: 'I came along and I go as a stranger. I do not know who I am, nor what I have been doing.'

The Mughals would stagger on into the nineteenth century; but they were by now exhausted. When the first adventurers of the British East India Company began to build coastal forts and defeat local armies – along with their French rivals – they would find Mughal India had a rotten door, easy to kick down. Under a pushy upstart called Robert Clive, the British not only barged in with bayonets and cannon, but managed to slip themselves into the Mughal system as tax-collectors for the Agra court. This gave them an instant authority in a strange land, allowing them to steal the Mughal hegemony until they were able to shake them off altogether. Under the Mughal cloak, the East India Company grew into a substitute government. And hidden under the Company's entrepreneurial activities – and almost equally surprised by the turn of events – was the British Crown.

The British Empire would need to start afresh; for on the other side of the world, its first empire, won in the forests of America, was about to fall apart. Nor would it be long before absolutism in Europe, too, began to disintegrate.

Zozo and Fred

On 20 June 1753 there was a hubbub in the streets of Frankfurt. A skeletal Frenchman, famous throughout the Europeanized world, was trying to escape Prussian agents. They had ransacked his luggage and had orders to shoot him if he should try to flee.

His was a bungled escape; his carriage got caught in a traffic jam of hay-carts. At the city gate he was recognized, stopped and taken back by soldiers to be searched. Strip-searching is rarely dignified. The nicotine-addicted François-Marie Arouet, known to his parents as Zozo but to the world by his pen-name Voltaire, pleaded that he could not live without snuff, but his snuffbox was seized. He was escorted to a local inn, the Goat's Horn, where his niece, who was also his lover, was nearly raped by a Prussian soldier, while his clothes, cash, silver buckles and gold scissors were stolen.

Voltaire had already been relieved of his prized Order of Merit and the gold key that was his badge of office as Court Chamberlain to Frederick the Great of Prussia. It was Frederick's agents who had ambushed the philosopher: the king was desperate to get hold of a book of poems and other writings he himself had composed, and of which Voltaire had a rare copy. The writings were too compromising, too radical, for a military monarch. Eventually, the shaken and humiliated Voltaire was allowed to leave for exile in Switzerland. One of the great experiments in enlightened despotism – ideals of freedom and inquiry pursued under the protection of a philosopher-king – had not gone according to plan.

Voltaire had fallen out many times with the rulers of his native France. As a younger man, he had been imprisoned in the Bastille for his insolent compositions. But he had known Frederick for much of his writing life and had seen him as a beacon of hope. Eventually, lured to Berlin to work for Prussia's ruler, Voltaire had become disillusioned, complaining that despite the good conversation and the parties and the music, 'there are prodigious quantities of bayonets but very few books'.[10] Frederick had replied in kind, telling a courtier who complained about his generous treatment of Voltaire, 'I shall have need of him for another year at most, no longer. One squeezes an orange and one throws away the peel.'[11]

Frederick became infuriated when Voltaire attacked in print his French minister for science, Pierre-Louis Maupertuis, a mathematician with a drink problem who had once seduced one of Voltaire's mistresses. Voltaire's diatribe was brilliantly funny, clever and popular, ripping into Maupertuis as a fraud. When he turned on an enemy, Voltaire wielded one of the most lethal pens in Europe. Frederick, however, was also a master of gunnery, and all those bayonets. He ordered the satire to be seized, torn up and burned by the public executioner and told Voltaire he ought to be clapped in irons for his behaviour. Voltaire skedaddled.

Voltaire was undoubtedly one of the most important Europeans of the eighteenth century. His campaigns against Catholic intolerance set the thinking continent alight, just as his tragedies and comedies delighted Paris. His *Lettres Philosophiques*, a combination of essays on the English and a savage attack on the Catholic thinker Pascal, have rightly been called the first bomb thrown at the *ancien régime* of absolute monarchs. From a wealthy Paris family of lawyers and court appointees, he became famous as a poet, a playwright, a philosopher, a polemicist, and as a scientist of sorts – forever dangerous, and always, from the viewpoint of those in power, twinklingly unreliable.

The Great Britain that had emerged from its Glorious Revolution was exceedingly important to him. He had fled there after being beaten up by toughs employed by a nobleman he had offended, then finding that his hopes of justice were blocked by the court and the nobility. Britain seemed different – as did Holland, another country of relative freedom and middle-class prosperity. Voltaire put this down, in part, to parliamentary politics, but also to habits of tolerance: 'If there were only one religion in England, there might be a risk of despotism; if there were two, they would cut each other's throats; but there are thirty, and they live together in peace and happiness.'

Voltaire was a student of Newton's, and when he visited England he paid court to her poets, playwrights and politicians, and to the cream of Hanoverian society. There he met Sarah, Duchess of Marlborough, who had been Princess Anne's girlish companion so long before; the current Queen Caroline, Swift (who had just written *Gulliver's Travels*), Pope, whose *Essay on Man* he adored, and John Gay, of *The Beggar's Opera*. He met Lady Mary Wortley Montagu, who had been to Turkey and brought back the idea of inoculation against smallpox.

Voltaire admired the freedom of English public life and the way the English honoured artists: Newton was buried in Westminster Abbey alongside monarchs, which would never have happened in France, while a famous English actress, Mrs Oldfield, was also buried with honours. Back in Paris, when she died young, the greatest actress of her day, Adrienne Lecouvreur, was denied a Christian burial – actors were 'excommunicate'. She was thrown into a pauper's grave in wasteland at the edges of the city, and sprinkled with quicklime. She too had been one of Voltaire's lovers, and the contrast shook him.[12]

For much of his life Voltaire managed to dodge around the restrictions placed on free thought by the French monarchy, darting into the public spotlight with a brilliant new play or a briefly grovelling poem, while publishing his most provocative works anonymously or abroad. For long periods he retreated into internal exile, at a beautiful provincial château where he wrote, performed amateur dramatics and did Newtonian experiments with his almost equally brilliant lover, Émilie du Châtelet; later, he had to retreat further from the reach of the French court, to Switzerland. He could count on the support of the Parisian public, and had some powerful defenders. He was a shrewd investor to the point of sharpness, trading in military supplies and grain, and it is said that he may well have had to leave England early after forging banknotes. In quarrels he was fearless, but he never knew when to call it a day; and he was no saint.

His situation seems strikingly like that of the greatest composers and writers in Soviet Russia, popular with the public but playing a dangerous game of cat-and-mouse with the regime. In Voltaire's world, of course, the normal form of government was some kind of absolutism. Looking at the great continental powers, a betting man would have assumed the future would continue to revolve around courts and all-powerful rulers. An actual, political, revolution was unthinkable. So when Prince Frederick of Prussia had started to write Voltaire fan letters, the future monarch seemed to present some kind of answer. As Mme du Châtelet put it, 'since it seems that we have to have princes, although no one knows quite why, then at least it would help if they were all like him'.

Frederick too had yearned for English freedom. As a young man he had suffered terribly at the hands of his tyrannical father, Frederick William, who had first established Prussia as a centralized absolutist state. The father believed in absolute duty, military-style discipline and an iron routine. The son, like so many boys and teenagers, was dozy, dreamy, romantic and bookish. He took refuge in music, becoming a virtuoso performer on the French flute, and an addict of French books. Outwardly, he obeyed his father, attended parades and meetings, and accepted the beatings and public humiliation visited on him; but he deployed a form of dumb insolence which further infuriated his father. Frederick was probably homosexual and he certainly showed no interest in women, including his later wife, whom he banished from his court.

Aged eighteen, he plotted to run away from Prussia with a twenty-six-year-old Guards officer called Hans Hermann von Katte, his closest friend, who was said to carry on with the prince 'like a lover with his mistress'.[13] Two years after Voltaire left London, the duo had decided to make for that beacon of relative freedom. But the king had probably been tipped off, and the absconding pair went about their planned flight in a rather lackadaisical way, so that when Frederick sneaked out of the military camp he was quickly captured and brought back. His father ordered him to be imprisoned in a grim military fortress where he was dressed as a convict and cross-questioned with great menace. He was told that he might well be executed on his father's orders. Von Katte, meanwhile, was sentenced to life imprisonment by a military tribunal. Frederick William decided this was not adequate punishment, and suggested the young man have his limbs torn off with hot pincers before being hanged. He graciously commuted this to death by decapitation, but insisted the sentence be carried out in front of his son's eyes.

On 6 November 1730 von Katte was taken from a cell in the same prison where Frederick was being held, to a pile of sand in the courtyard. The prince's face was held up to the bars of his cell by two warders, to force him to watch. In an account written by the preacher afterwards, Katte looked around and saw Frederick at his window, saying goodbye to him with 'some courteous and friendly words spoken in French'. He then removed his wig, jacket and scarf, kneeled on the sand, called upon Christ, and had his head removed with a single sword blow. Frederick, however, missed the last moment: he had fainted.

As he read his way through the works of Voltaire and other radical French writers, Frederick began to imagine a different way of ruling. One could see this as the traumatized reaction to his father's cruelty, combined with the radical idealism of youth, but Frederick was serious in his desire to be an enlightened monarch. He himself was a copious writer and, like Voltaire, a compulsive historian of his own times. He regarded German as a barbaric language and always preferred French, just as he liked French music; he even called his pleasure-palace at Potsdam, outside Berlin, Sans-Souci ('Without a Care'). When he became king, he built on the Prussian tradition of good schools and universities, assembling a court of thinkers and scientists, and began to renovate his cities.

Frederick the Great's Prussia was not simply the militaristic warrior-state of legend, with its bone-headed Junker landowners flogging their peasants and its young men all in uniform. It saw forward-looking experiments in agriculture, early industrial projects (particularly in the iron and steel industries), reading societies, bookshops, newspapers, philosophical clubs and the growth of a relatively sophisticated civic society. Frederick remained interested all his life in promoting advances in farming, road-building, drainage, the building of factories and the education of the young, just as enlightened autocrats were supposed to. He practised religious toleration. Asked whether this extended to Roman Catholics, he replied that he would build mosques and temples if Turks and heathens wanted to come to Prussia. He banned torture. Visitors to Berlin were struck by the relative freedom of speech enjoyed in cafés and bookshops there.

The problem was that this was only one half of Frederick's personality. He might have recoiled from his father's Germanic simplicities, but he idolized the army his father had bequeathed him. His resentment at being forced to marry a woman he did not love was directed not only at his father, but also at the overweening power in the Germanic world that had lobbied for that marriage – the Austrian Habsburg empire. And so when he became king ten years after the traumatic decapitation of his officer friend, Frederick's first act had been to march his armies into neighbouring Austrian-controlled Silesia, a huge territory with considerable manufacturing wealth, and seize it. Frederick's armies almost brushed aside the Austrians rather than merely defeating them, but in doing so he upset the balance of European power-politics and triggered further wars.

In his second act upon becoming king, he again took on the role of aggressor, seizing Saxony. As a result, in his third and biggest conflict, part of the global Seven Years War, Frederick faced a daunting coalition comprising France, Austria, Russia and Sweden, encircling him and threatening to carve up Prussia for ever. He had a small British–Hanoverian force on his side, but he faced overwhelming odds. At this point the philosopher-king was seriously considering a suicidal 'soldier's death' on the battlefield. But Frederick became 'the Great' not because he had cultivated Enlightenment thinkers or because he played the flute well, but because he proved to be a brilliant soldier.

Expert at dividing and confusing his enemies, he won most of his battles, often against great odds.

Just as Alexander the Great could not have achieved his brilliant successes without the army created by his father Philip II, so Frederick could not have achieved what he did without the formidable army created by his father. The Prussian army could move faster and more efficiently in parade-ground formation than any other. In the eighteenth century, parade-ground drill and discipline were essential. Being able to wheel your forces round and rain down fire from unexpected angles, and to hold perfect formation under a hail of musket balls and cannon-fire, was what turned men and muskets into mass weaponry. Frederick's army was composed of harshly drilled young men under the command of aristocrats, themselves trained in the new military academies to see war as a science. These aristocratic Junker families would lose vast numbers of their sons to Frederick's wars, but won for themselves a status in his fast-growing Prussian state that they would lose only in Nazi times.

These wars were perhaps not as socially destructive as those of the earlier Protestant–Catholic conflict, but they were bloody enough, with raping, pillaging, burning of towns and villages and the slaughter of civilians, as well as the carnage of the set-piece battles. It has been estimated that Prussia alone lost around 10 per cent of its population, some four hundred thousand people. (In the First World War, by comparison, Germany lost 2.47 million people, but that was less than 4 per cent of the total population; so Frederick's wars were proportionally more than twice as bloody.)

The consequences were momentous. In Prussia, Frederick had to repair the damage by moving populations into underexploited areas, a kind of internal colonization, and by introducing cheap-food and welfare policies. This in turn resulted in a more powerful and intrusive state. Austria suddenly found that she had lost her traditional position of dominance over the jigsaw of statelets known as the Holy Roman Empire. France, distracted from her key strategic struggle against the rising power of Britain, became entangled in a close alliance with Habsburg Austria, which seemed to many French people – used to Bourbons fighting Habsburgs – unnatural and wrong. The arrival of the Habsburg princess Marie Antoinette to marry the future Louis XVI was only one aspect of the unpopular policy, which would cost the French monarchy dear.

In all of this, Frederick remained an enigma. Who was he, really? One historian of the Prussian state says: 'To the injunction of his brutish father: "be an honest fellow, just be honest", the teenage Frederick had responded with a sly, foppish civility striking the pose of the wry dissembling, morally agnostic outsider.' This slippery, devious and ruthless man had been made, but also ruined, by his father. He was left rereading the classics, despairing of mankind and practising the flute until his teeth fell out, 'devouring the latest works of philosophy and recruiting new conversation partners to fill the places vacated by friends who had died or betrayed him by taking wives'.[14]

Voltaire by now had learned to put not his trust in princes, however much they claimed to like his books. As war ravaged Europe, he responded to the problem of living under absolute monarchs by becoming one himself, albeit in a modest way. At the village of Ferney, on the Swiss–French border, he bought himself an estate that would allow him to dodge French attempts to seize him. He could flee by coach or boat in any one of several directions if the alarm was raised. In 1758 he bought a large house and plenty of land, with walls around it, and took on responsibility for the farmers who lived there. Inside his tiny kingdom he could write his masterpiece, the satirical novel *Candide*, which attacked almost every aspect of old Europe, and contribute to the great encyclopaedia – the *Encyclopédie* – of the new generation of enlightened philosophers, stirring up hornets' nests without himself being stung.

Voltaire was not an atheist, but a deist, believing in a supreme being. But after the catastrophic Lisbon earthquake, which hit the city on 1 November 1755, he had become increasingly hostile to the 'all is for the best' or 'whatever is, is right' thinking of the early Enlightenment. The earthquake had not only killed thirty thousand people in Lisbon, it had overwhelmed Cadiz with a tsunami and shaken neighbouring countries. It hit during a religious holiday, and among those killed were Jesuits about to burn some Portuguese Jews as heretics. All over Europe a great debate ensued about what this disaster signified for the idea of a beneficent God. From Ferney, Voltaire lashed out in all directions – at the Jesuits, at Frederick's militarism, at intolerance of all kinds.

At home, Voltaire turned to farming and to cultivating his tiny patch of borderland France, developing the house into a miniature version of Sans-Souci, rebuilding the church (tolerance, even there), turning the barn into a theatre and welcoming intellectually curious visitors from across Europe to his tiny fortress of liberty. They came from America too, but particularly from England – and Scotland, where the next phase of the Enlightenment was roaring ahead. Among them were the father of modern economics, Adam Smith, and the friend of Dr Johnson and David Hume, the irrepressible James Boswell. By the time of Voltaire's death Ferney had a watchmaking industry that he had promoted, some eighty houses and a thousand inhabitants, whose absolute monarch called himself 'all Europe's innkeeper' and performed nightly for guests.

Voltaire still had plenty of fire left in him. After the torture and hideous public execution of an elderly Protestant in a cooked-up murder case in Toulouse, he ran a furious campaign, which ended in the quashing of the conviction in Paris. '*Écrasez l'infâme!*' – 'Crush the infamy!' – was his battlecry, one he had coined while talking with Frederick in the old days in Prussia. Voltaire lived long, fighting more campaigns for justice – models that would be imitated by journalists and politicians from the Dreyfus case to our own days. He made himself a champion of Protestants, a dangerous thing in France, and he also made something of a fool of himself by denouncing some recently translated Shakespeare as no good. At the end he returned to Paris, where he was treated virtually as a living god himself, cheered and celebrated and crowned with laurels at the theatre. He died on 30 May 1778 after refusing confession and telling two priests, 'Let me die in peace.'

Absolutist France, too, which had seemed such a formidable enemy, was on her last legs. She had been weakened by both Zozo and Frederick, by the new thinking at home and by the devastating costs of war, not least against Britain. The old certainties tottered. How else could the mocking Voltaire have become a hero to Catholic Paris? But the rot had begun on the battlefields of Germany. Going to war is what absolute monarchs do. It means they can never be truly enlightened – for what is the point of banning torture if you leave hundreds of thousands to die slow and agonizing deaths on the battle-field?

But by now the conundrums that had briefly united Frederick and Voltaire when they were younger – how is it possible to combine authority and liberty? can one really legislate for human happiness? – were getting a new kind of answer. Among those who had come to pay tribute to Voltaire in his final weeks was a man from a free coun-try rather bigger than Ferney. He was Benjamin Franklin, sent to France by the new American Congress.

Cold Tea and Mohawks

It remains the most famous protest against a tax in world history. The night of 16 December 1773 was cold and misty in the crowded port of Boston, Massachusetts. More than two hundred men, some disguised as Mohawk warriors, boarded three ships tied up at Griffin's Wharf – the *Dartmouth*, the *Eleanor* and the *Beaver*. All were carrying heavy lead-lined chests of the most sought-after luxury of the day, tea (then pronounced 'tay'). The 340 chests were hauled onto the decks, smashed open with axes and then emptied into the cold black water. It was a long, hard job. Over three hours, the men disposed of some ninety thousand pounds of the tea, originally grown in China and dis-tributed around the world by Britain's East India Company.

This was a protest against the tea tax imposed by the far-off London government, but more fundamentally, against the principle of London rule over colonies whose people had no seats in the Westminster Parliament. As the slogan had it, 'No taxation without representation.' There were many oddities about the 'Boston Tea Party' (though it was not known as this until far later in the next cen-tury). One was that the Americans were at that point actually winning their argument against the British ministers, who were being far more flexible and less determined than history remembers. In 1756 the Stamp Act, an attempt to tax American newspapers, magazines and legal documents, had been repealed in just a year, after boycotts and demonstrations.

Hot tea and cold print added up to the same issue: representation. The Stamp Act had rubbed American noses in their second-class status within the British Empire. Most Americans inside the thirteen sea-board colonies thought of themselves as English, with the birthright of freedom won in the civil wars of the previous century. But they could not obtain the highest offices or negotiate their own trade rules, never mind vote for Parliament. A self-taught Virginia lawyer called Patrick Henry demanded the rights of freeborn Englishmen; and his state passed a motion that taxes could only be levied by the people themselves or by those chosen to represent them. Among those taken aback by the violent rebellion that followed was Benjamin Franklin himself. After a long career as one of the geniuses of Philadelphia, and a classic Enlightenment polymath, Franklin was then in London argu-ing the case for Pennsylvania becoming a royal colony, perhaps with himself as King George's representative there. Franklin, suspected at home of favouring the Stamp Act, heard that his house had been tar-geted by the mob and that he was lucky not to have had it burned down.

After the government backed down over the Stamp Act, it had tried to win back some revenue by introducing various other duties, this time on humdrum but essential commodities such as paint, paper, lead, glass – and tea. In London, Franklin was all for this. But again, the colonists had reacted with marches, boycotts and protests. The boycotts did not stop the Americans drinking tea: some turned to local herbal teas and many others to cheaper, smuggled tea from Dutch ships. And again, after some hesitation, the 'tyrannical' British govern-ment had caved in, repealing all the duties except that on tea, which was retained only so as to assert the shredding principle of Crown sovereignty.

There was a pause in the smouldering crisis, which then ended in bizarre circumstances. In London, the prime minister Lord North's government was over-taxing tea generally, and by doing so was push-ing the East India Company towards bankruptcy. Ministers responded by allowing the Company to sell directly to the colonists, rather than bringing it home and taxing it through London first. This would dra-matically cut the price of American tea, and help the Company. It was a liberal act. Lord North did, however, keep the original modest tax on American tea because this paid for colonial governors and judges, keeping them loyal to King George. Even then, the Bostonians and others were now being offered tea costing less than the smuggled tea they had been drinking. The 'Boston Tea Party' was a tax revolt against a commodity that was getting cheaper, not more expensive. How could that be?

Ministers might have reflected that the only thing worse than losing a war is winning it. For in 1763, a decade before the tea was so nastily brewed in cold saltwater, Britain had ended her Seven Years War against France and Spain in triumph, with church bells ringing across the land. The war had sprawled across much of Europe, where Britain had been helping Frederick. Beyond Europe, Britain had won Bengal in India, islands in the Caribbean, and Minorca in the Mediterranean. But it was in America that the most dramatic shift had occurred. In 1759, the 'year of victories', British forces (including a young George Washington) and their native American allies trounced the French, seizing Canada and Florida. 'New France' vanished from the map. As a result, Britain controlled the whole eastern American seaboard, as well as having the putative 'right' to push west beyond the Appalachians. It was a famous victory, which seemed to establish Britain securely as ruler of America. When the new King, George III, was proclaimed, Americans loyally rejoiced.

This, however, turned out to be the classic example of unintended consequences turning victor into vanquished. First, because of the removal of the French threat, the colonists no longer needed British troops to keep them safe. Second, the American colonists lost the right to expand as they had hoped, because to placate the British Empire's new French-speaking subjects, control over native American lands (in today's Ontario, Illinois, Michigan, Ohio and Wisconsin) went to Canada. Pioneers from Britain's thirteen North American colonies were forbidden to drive further west. In Massachusetts and Virginia, fear of French invasion was replaced by anger about the new carve-up. All this was ominous enough. But, third, the huge cost of the global war had doubled the British national debt, which now took about half the government's revenue to service.[15] New taxes were inevitable.

A later British prime minister, son of the great William Pitt who had presided over Britain's first run of imperial victories, would eventually have to introduce an income tax, so he could prosecute the war against Napoleon. Before that, new taxes mostly meant new duties on goods, and the goods that were most wanted and most valuable (like tea) were the obvious targets. To sum up: in the decade after London's victory, her American colonists needed Britain less, were being boxed in by British diplomacy, and yet had to pay Britain more. The reason the colonists did not want to pay even the lower tea taxes was because they suspected they would be giving up a principle. If they agreed the right of the British to tax them, those taxes would, sooner or later, rise to intolerable levels. They had a point: it would always be easier to tax far-off colonials than loud-voiced landowners and grand merchants represented in Parliament and vocal at home.

Some believed a rupture was inevitable, though in the early 1770s they were a minority. Benjamin Franklin, on an intellectual journey that was distancing him from loyalty to the Crown, put his finger on a looming problem: one day the population of British America was bound to be larger and wealthier than that of the home islands. What would happen then? Would the capital of the British Empire have to shift from London to Philadelphia? Others wanted to remain loyal to the Crown but also to enjoy the maximum freedom to trade without levies, to agree local laws without reference to London, and to take native land without worrying about global treaties.

There is little doubt that, had the king's ministers trodden even more warily, not only repealing unpopular taxes but accepting limits to their power in the new colonies, then the rebellion could have been postponed for a long time to come.

Meanwhile, plenty of smaller mistakes were made. Had British soldiers not responded to humiliating taunts and goading by opening fire and killing protesters in the 'Boston massacre', then that city would not have been the cauldron of anti-British feeling that it became. Had Lord North's government not responded by passing the so-called Intolerable Acts to repress Massachusetts in general and Boston in particular, the colonies would not have retaliated with their own congresses or combined in the first Continental Congress. Had Britain not then sent more and more troops, provoking the creation of militias, and had King George not arrogantly rejected the 'olive branch petition' from the Continental Congress in 1775 affirming American loyalty, full-scale war might have been averted. And indeed, had the British commanders in the 1776–81 War of Independence been better, and luckier, soldiers, then the British forces might have won, at least for a time.

Yet such 'what if?'s are not convincing. To return to Franklin's point, by the 1770s the thirteen colonies had a population of around 2.4 million, mostly British by origin, but Dutch and German too. This was still around four million fewer than Britain herself, but the population was growing fast and was far too substantial to be forever kept out of imperial politics. And 'substantial' means more than numbers. These were people with high levels of literacy, networks of political societies, their own lawyers, newspapers and pamphlets, and their own colonial level of politics. For the many British supporters of the American cause, these were British people no different from any others, and therefore with the same rights. British political philosophy was based on stories of resistance to tyrannical power, going back to medieval times. The argument about the right of representation, which thrummed through the coffee houses and drawing rooms of Philadelphia, Boston and New York, was understood just as clearly by many observers in London's Cheapside, Bristol or Edinburgh.

How could colonies be properly represented in a Parliament that was six to eight weeks' dangerous sailing away? They could not. Yet they knew their rights, and would have them. What was the alternative to independence? Even if the colonists had been given MPs at Westminster, the increase in their numbers in that vastly larger country would eventually have led to American MPs outnumbering British MPs, so that Essex or Hampshire would have been governed by the voting patterns of Pennsylvania and New York. Would that have been more acceptable to George III and his successors? The other possibility, that the Americans could have been encouraged to combine and form their own parliament, retaining loyalty only to the king – in effect, the Canadian or Australian option – is more plausible. But not much.

Instead, the outbreak of rebellion and war in 1775–6 was the best thing that could have happened, both for the colonists and their enemies. It was a relatively short, decisive and (for Britain) humiliating conflict rather than a long-drawn-out and very bloody one, as a later war would probably have been. It became a wider war when Spain, France and the Dutch combined with the Americans against Britain, sparking fears of invasion from London to Scotland. But this never happened. Driving the colonists together, beginning to loosen the individual states and shake them into a nation, the war inspired and energized what would become the world's most successful political system. By forcing Britain to turn her imperial ambitions elsewhere, the loss of the 'first British Empire' led to the acquisition of the far larger second one, centred on India. That, plus the bankruptcy of the French monarchy, caused partly by its financial support for the American rebels, led to Britain becoming a worldwide naval and imperial power and remaining so for the next 150 years.

Yet there were obvious losers, beyond the fifth or so of Americans who had supported the Crown, many of whom lost their property and some their lives. There were the African-Americans who fought with the British against the colonists because they feared that American independence would simply entrench slavery, and hoped that the British might abolish it. When the British Parliament did abolish the slave trade in its territory little more than thirty years after the American Declaration of Independence, their hopes were fulfilled. British observers made much of the oddness of Americans such as Thomas Jefferson, who both fought for liberty and kept slaves themselves. The great English writer and curmudgeon Samuel Johnson famously asked, 'How is it that we hear the loudest *yelps* for liberty amongst the drivers of negroes?'

In 1750 there were about 236,000 blacks in the colonies; by 1810, there were more than a million slaves in the US.[16] But in a further strange historical twist, the French revolt in favour of liberty extended slavery in America: the 'Louisiana Purchase', which passed over from France to the US a vast stretch of the American hinterland, was agreed by Napoleon as a wartime necessity; and as we shall see later, it was in those lands that slavery would really flourish.

The most immediate historical injustice, however, leads us back to the men emptying tea-chests into the waters of Boston harbour – or rather, not to the men but to their chosen 'disguises'. Some of them, as mentioned earlier, were dressed up as 'Mohawks', presumably with painted faces and feathers. We do not know for sure whether it *was* to disguise themselves, or to intimidate the sailors. What we do know is that the real Mohawks in fact mostly took the British side against the colonists – and were amongst the greatest losers from the war. Like the pro-British black Americans, they had sided with the imperial power out of desperate self-interest. It was, after all, the British Canadian treaty that had kept the colonists from pouring into yet more of their territory.

So who were they?

The Mohawks, who called themselves *Kanien'keha:ka*, or 'people of the place of flint', for they were great flint-cutters, using the material for their arrows and spears, were one of the most important Iroquois people of coastal America. Their lands ranged from today's Upper New York State, through Vermont to southern Canada, and they had been trading in furs with the Dutch since the early 1600s. By the later part of the century they were British allies against the French, and when war broke out they almost all sided with the Crown again. This was not because of a strong affection for George III but because they knew very well what the colonists wanted – their traditional hunting land.

It was an old story. The first English colonists had barely survived wintering in the new land, Virginia. Depleted by disease and starvation and at times reduced to cannibalism, they had been saved by native help. But as soon as the numbers of colonists grew and they became better established, attacks on native people increased. It has been persuasively argued that the savage war waged by Elizabethan English armies against the Irish prepared them to view the native Americans as equally barbarous, even subhuman. In English eyes, there was not so much to choose between the cloak-wearing, bothy-dwelling Irish clans and the leather capes and wooden villages of the Americans.[17] These were people who rarely seemed to farm (though in fact the Massachusetts natives did farm), so did they not deserve to lose their land? By 1608, just a year after the first settlers arrived, 'Indian' leaders were protesting: 'We hear you are come from under the World to take our World from us.'

By the 1620s open warfare had broken out, the colonists being able to use firepower to destroy native villages. Tribe after tribe was driven back, killed by new diseases, starved and attacked.

The success of the thirteen colonies was built on the back of the destruction of native peoples, who were culturally quite unready for an economy based on private property and settled farming. Earlier in this book, we saw how counter-intuitive and difficult the shift from hunter-gathering to farming had been in Eurasia. There, it took many thousands of years. In America, native people were expected to make that shift in years or even months. In 1789, in a heart-breaking petition to Connecticut, the Mohegan people said that in times past their forefathers had lived in great plenty: 'When they wanted Meat they would just run into the Bush a little ways with their Weapons and would Soon bring home good venison, Racoon, Bear and Fowl . . . and they planted but little Corn and Beans and they kept no Cattle or Horses for they needed none.' Now, however, they were forced to work the land, keep animals and build fences because the hunting grounds had gone. Only the strongest prospered, 'and poor Widows and Orphans Must be pushed to one side and there they Must Set a Crying, Starving and die'.[18]

In their shifting alliances and in their wars, the Mohawks like many other native Americans were merely trying to preserve enough hunting and fishing land to keep their traditional way of life. They knew they were giving ground, even if the Quebec treaty had bought them time. After being on the losing side in the War of Independence, they were forced to flee further west and north, into Canada. Inside the new United States, no less a figure than Thomas Jefferson wrote in the climactic year of 1776 that he favoured pushing the war into the heart of the Indian lands: 'But I would not stop there. I would never cease pursuing them while one of them remained on this side of the Mississippi. We would never cease pursuing them with war while one remained on the face of the earth.'[19]

This was the true voice of the land-hungry young republic. Within a few decades of independence from Britain, the Creeks, the Choctaws, the Chickasaws and the Cherokees were being ambushed, threatened, massacred, driven out and presented with meaningless treaties by settlers and their leaders, who demonized them as savages. The same fate would befall the people of the plains beyond the Mississippi, just as Jefferson had foretold – the Cheyenne, Arapaho, Sioux and Pawnee. There had been a brief period when native Americans were romanticized or taken to European capitals to be gawped at. But once the logic of colonization and landgrab had begun, they had to be cleared out.

The fake Mohawks of Boston were rebelling for a combination of reasons. They had good reason to resent being taxed without being represented in London, and 'liberty' was more than a cant word. But as they looked forward to a more spacious, richer world of their own, free from the hierarchies and religious bigotries of Europe, they knew it would be available only because another free people, the native Americans, were doomed. And they were not the only ones.

Noble Savages

The kidnap had been successful. It had been meanly carried out. A young British naval lieutenant leading a couple of boats filled with sailors, soldiers and convicts had come across some natives on the beach. They had held up some fat fresh fish, tempting the natives into the shallows. Two men eagerly took the fish and danced together, at which point they were seized and shackled. Others ran up to watch. The lieutenant later wrote that the noise of the men, the screaming of women and children on the beach and the situation of the 'miserable wretches' he had seized made it a most distressing scene, 'by far the most unpleasant service I was ever ordered to execute'.[20]

One of those seized would escape relatively quickly. The other, Woolawarre Bennelong, would learn English, be taught to dress in thick cloth and leather, with buttons and buckles, and would even visit English spa resorts and London itself, attending theatre and concert performances and the House of Commons before returning home. He remains a famous, if ambiguous, figure in Australia to this day.

The kidnapping of Bennelong was part of one of the most bizarre collisions of peoples caused by the age of empire. On the one side were the English, Scots and Irish, a mélange of sailors, soldiers and criminals – men, women and children – who had survived a nightmarish sea voyage so they could be dumped as far away from Britain as it was possible to get. Apart from a few officers they were all, in their way, the victims of a revolution in the economy of the small northern island. In the English and Scottish countryside, the ancient life of the peasants, tending common land and able to gather firewood, kill game and feed their own animals, was finally ending. A more efficient way of farming would help feed the new factory communities. But it also drove huge numbers of the poor to the crowded cities, where many were driven to petty crime to survive. Some were hanged, some festered in small, filthy prisons; and some were expelled, 'transported' to a new world.

In that new world on the other side were somewhere between

750,000 and a million humans who had arrived in Australia as one of the earliest migrations from Africa, perhaps some fifty thousand years earlier, perhaps even earlier than that. They had made their way south along the coastlines of Asia, using land bridges that no longer exist, and had also made formidable sea crossings. They had found a continent with its own unique plants, and animals including marsupial lions, wombat-like creatures the size of hippopotamuses, and giant carnivorous kangaroos (which promptly disappeared).

Before the arrival of the European ships, native Australians lived in some two hundred and fifty nations, each with its own subtly different language, and composed of subsidiary tribes; they had a political system similar to that of native Americans and, presumably, to the Europeans and the Chinese in their hunter-gatherer phase. Australian hunter-gathering had not developed into farming, the soil being mostly thin and lacking the necessary grasses and vegetables to develop. Instead, they used fire-stick cultivation, burning back undergrowth to allow new growth; and had begun systems of canals, fishing-traps and winter settlement villages – and all this before the British invasion.

Jared Diamond argues that, had the European colonization not happened in 1788, aboriginal Australians 'might within a few thousand years have become food producers, tending ponds of domesticated fish and growing domesticated Australian yams and small-seeded grasses'.[21] In other words, within several thousand years of today, they might have advanced as far as the people of Catalhoyuk had, 7,500 years ago. Those apparently tiny differences of flora, fauna and climate have produced human divergences of an awesome kind. Cut off from the rest of human history, the Australians had their own ways of understanding the world, their own entirely different stories, rituals, art and mental maps.

When the first European ships arrived off their coast, they thought them floating islands inhabited by the white-skinned ghosts of their ancestors. The wigs and long hair of the sailors made them assume they were women. When the British sailors dropped their trousers to show they were male, the aboriginals offered them women in the hope that, satisfied, they would leave. The mutual incomprehension was vaster than the oceans separating these people.

So Bennelong became a time-traveller, moving between prehistoric times and the industrial world. He had been kidnapped because the British colony in what is now Sydney was struggling to understand this new world. Its governor, Arthur Phillip, hoped to communicate with the natives, to learn how to stop them attacking his people and stealing things. He needed to explain that the British had arrived peacefully, but for good. There would have to be a translator. 'Baneelon', as one of the soldiers called him, would be the go-between. When he arrived at the British stockade, this soldier reported, he was 'of good stature and stoutly made'.[22] He was also amazingly scarred. He had had smallpox, a scourge brought to Australia by earlier convicts and sailors; but he also had scars on his head, and the marks of spears that had passed through his arm and a leg. Half a thumb was missing and he had a strange scar on the back of his hand. 'Love and war seemed his favourite pursuits; in both of which he had suffered severely.' Bennelong sang, danced and capered, but seemed oddly unwilling to explain the wound on his hand. Eventually he confessed: it came from the teeth of a woman of another tribe whom he was carrying away by force.

Bennelong's story shows also how European attitudes to 'savages' would veer from one extreme to the other in a remarkably short time. Fewer than twenty years before the colonization of Australia by convicts and their guards began, the natives had been admired by Captain Cook and his famous naturalist-helper, Sir Joseph Banks, when Cook 'discovered' the coast of New South Wales. This was the age of the 'noble savage', a term first used in the 1670s but a key idea in the later Enlightenment. 'Savage' simply meant 'wild', and thinkers such as the Earl of Shaftesbury had argued that mankind was naturally moral – the primitive people being discovered by explorers might look different, and wear no clothes, but they could be as good, or better, than any civilized Christian. Bennelong's lust for women of rival tribes and his readiness to use violence against them were a warning against idealizing such people: yet before long, far from that being the danger, Europeans were seeing natives as subhuman, and even hunting them for sport.

To understand other people and places; or to possess them?

For the eighteenth-century European explorers, the noble instinct and the greedy one became inextricably tangled. New animals, new plants and new societies caught the imagination. Naturalists, botanists, surveyors set out aboard armed ships whose flags would later be planted on beaches and headlands, territory being claimed as the property of distant kings – a George or a Louis. Yet to start with, many of these explorers were more open-minded than the later history of empire might lead us to expect. Thus Captain James Cook, when he first encountered the aboriginal people of Australia in 1770, was carrying warnings from the president of the Royal Society in London to be patient with any natives and remember that 'shedding one drop of the blood of these people is a crime of the highest nature . . . they are the natural, and in the strictest sense of the word, the legal possessors of the several regions they inhabit'. Such people had the right to repel invaders.[23] Yet Cook also had secret orders to claim new lands in the name of King George – a glaring inconsistency.

Cook's first impression of the Australians would have pleased the most idealistic European philosophers. He was much struck by their vigour, their health and their clean, lice-free hair; and by their lack of interest in material objects, not simply clothes: 'The same indifference which prevented them from buying what we had, prevented them also from attempting to steal.'[24] He thought they were happy in not knowing 'the superfluous but necessary' conveniences of Europe. Cook, who had struggled his way to his position from a poor Yorkshire family, also liked the equality of their society: 'They covet not magnificent houses, household stuff, etc, they live in a warm and fine climate, and enjoy a very wholesome air, so that they have very little need of clothing.'[25] It seemed a kind of paradise.

Cook and his sailors had arrived across the Pacific from Tahiti, where his ship the *Endeavour* had stopped for three months and where they had found an even more stunning paradise, a land which seemed to them a place of sexual freedom and innocence. With Cook was the aristocratic Banks, then just twenty-six. Banks had indulged himself with the local women and also learned some of the Tahitian language, studied the customs, and ended up identifying himself so closely with native life on the island that he danced ritual mourning dances stark-naked, his body coated with charcoal and white wood-ash, alongside a witch-doctor, two naked women and a boy. The Tahitians seemed to the British, and to French explorers who had preceded them, to be an almost ideally savage people – savage in a good way.

Banks was a radically open-minded product of the Enlightenment, ready to enjoy Tahitian roast dog, to admire their strange water sport, surfing, and to admit that their bodies were plucked and clean, and even that their favoured coconut oil improved with familiarity: 'Surely rancid as their oil is, it must be preferred to the odoriferous perfume of toes and armpits so frequent in Europe.'[26]

So the first British contact with the aboriginal people of the eastern coast of Australia was cautiously friendly. Cook, Banks and the ship's officers found it hard to make themselves understood and impossible to trade with the good-looking men and boys on the beaches, who were scarred from fights but appeared free of any disease. The land seemed balmy and relatively empty, as well as rich in unknown plants and strange animals, many of them the sort that hop. The word 'Australia' was not then generally used – it refers to the Latin for 'southern' and had appeared on early maps as a possible unknown landmass, or had perhaps originated from a Spanish explorer, who named a place he believed to exist after his then monarch, Philip III, whose family was Austrian.

But the coastline that Cook called New Wales, and New South Wales, would stay vividly clear in Banks's imagination when he came home. He was a farmer as well as a botanist, and he believed the soil and water of the rim of Australia would be easily cultivable by European farmers, to support oxen, sheep and wheat. And as wealthy landowner and scientist, Banks became an influential figure in Georgian London. He was a member of the King's Privy Council, of the Royal Society and of a mass of other learned bodies. The nude cavorter of Tahiti grew into the potato-shaped potentate of Piccadilly; the tousle-headed adventurer and collector became the spider at the centre of a web of botanical and learned debates; and he was appointed George III's adviser on his Royal Botanic Gardens at Kew. So it was hardly a surprise that Parliament turned to him when looking for a place to send convicts.

This had become an urgent problem. With a fast-growing urban population and a criminal 'bloody code' which at one point listed 220 crimes punishable by hanging, Britain needed an alternative way of dealing with her convicts. Public opinion was becoming queasier about the practice of killing the poorest, including hanging children, even for small thefts. During the sixty years from 1770, around 35,000 people were sentenced to death but only 7,000 or so were actually hanged.[27] British prisons were few and foul. To many, transporting the convicted by boat somewhere else seemed the humanitarian alternative. Before the loss of Britain's American colonies, some sixty thousand felons had been sent there to work on the land for a few years, until they had earned their freedom. Once the United States' independence closed off that option, felons were instead held in disgusting dismasted old hulks off the Thames. This was a dangerous and impractical long-term answer, however, and ministers were forced to look for another penal colony.

Banks suggested Australia. Here, as in America, British felons could make a new land flower, and then enjoy their freedom. 'Botany Bay', named by Cook after Banks's enthusiasm for plant-hunting, was chosen as the site. In May 1787 the 'First Fleet' of eleven ships, carrying 775 convicts – 192 of them women – plus 645 soldiers, officials and family members, set out for a gruelling thirty-six-week journey. The convicts had been sentenced for a range of small crimes, almost all involving theft – from clothes, watches and food to repeated burglary. (Transportation for political crimes, particularly Fenian rebellion, would come later.) Thus the first of 165,000 convicts arrived in Australia on 20 January 1788. The practice was finally abolished in the 1850s, just ahead of the far greater migration that was the Australian gold rush.

In charge of the First Fleet was an admirer and correspondent of Banks's, the professional seaman Arthur Phillip. He quickly realized that Botany Bay was considerably less inviting than its name suggested, and transferred the new colony to nearby Port Jackson (naming the cove where they first stayed 'Sydney', after Lord Sydney, the home secretary under whose orders he was acting). The natives, however, were not friendly. They had greeted the first settlers with cries of 'Warra, warra, warra!', meaning 'Go away, go away, go away!'.[28] When, instead, the colonists started to build huts, they faced periodic attacks and harassment by some of the fifteen hundred people already living in the area, clans of the Eora people.

Phillip was an ambitious multilingual sailor from a poor family who saw himself as a modern Enlightenment man. He had been in correspondence with Banks, and had no intention of merely running a vast prison. He insisted on the rule of law and the eventual emancipation of the convict settlers, promising that in New South Wales there would be 'no slavery'. It was a tough beginning, however, which at times brought the new colony close to starvation. Lashed and harangued, and very occasionally hanged after all, the unwilling farmers survived on the rations brought out with them and occasionally replenished by British supply ships, while they learned to cultivate the land and tend herds of those other shipboard migrants, cows.

London, rather more worried about the wars with the French, seemed to have forgotten about them, but eventually further fleets and more convicts arrived, and the colony grew.

As to the aboriginal people, furious and puzzled by the invaders, Phillip wanted them well treated. Kill them, he told the soldiers and settlers, and you will hang. His orders from the king were that he reach out to the native people – that he 'endeavour, by every possible means, to open an intercourse with the natives, and to conciliate their affections, enjoining all subjects to live in amity and kindness with them'.[29]

This would have been all very well, had the clans of the area been willing simply to give up their excellent harbour and fishing grounds. They were not willing. One of Phillip's officers, a marine captain called Watkin Tench, wrote that they 'seemed studiously to avoid us, either from fear, jealousy, or hatred. When they met with unarmed stragglers, they sometimes killed, and sometimes wounded them.' Tench came to think that the aboriginals were in fact people of 'humanity and generosity' who were only responding to 'unprovoked outrages' by the whites.[30] Some kind of communication had to be opened up; hence the capture of Bennelong, a married man in his mid-twenties from the Wangal clan.

Bennelong stayed for six months and developed a close relationship with Phillip, calling him 'father' and giving him a native name, before disappearing back into the bush.

Once free, he persuaded Phillip to come to meet him while his people were celebrating the grounding of a whale. Probably as a matter of honour, he then had the governor speared in the shoulder by a 'wise man'. Thomas Keneally, the Australian historian, argues that this was the natural consequence of the aboriginal custom of punishment by spear-throwing, and in Bennelong's mind Phillip was being punished 'for all of it: the fish and game stolen; the presumption of the Britons in camping permanently without permission; the stolen weaponry and nets . . . the random shooting of natives; the curse of smallpox; the mysterious genital infections of women and then of men'. Showing remarkable understanding, however, Phillip ordered there to be no retaliation, and when he eventually recovered from the serious wound, repaired his friendship with Bennelong and oversaw a period of better relations between colonizers and natives. But it would not last.

In 1792 when Phillip returned home, Bennelong and an aboriginal youth came too, rather as native Americans such as the princess Pocahontas had been brought over in earlier times. When Bennelong was paraded around London and taken to the theatre, to court and to provincial towns, he does not seem to have attracted anything like the attention earlier 'savages' had, perhaps because the novelty value was wearing off. Or perhaps it was because New South Wales was already being seen as a grimly practical dumping-ground for unwanted Britons, rather than as an exotic paradise.

It used to be thought that Bennelong returned home to live a sad life, rejected by his own people and drinking himself to death in Sydney; rejected too by colonists who had abandoned any notion of the noble savage for racist contempt. The true story seems to be less extreme, though no less poignant. Bennelong continued as an adviser to the British, and learned English well enough to write to the Phillips family in Britain. He also maintained a powerful aboriginal position and became the clan leader of some hundred people. 'Honour fights', involving spears being thrown at men who had to hold their ground with shields, were an important part of aboriginal life and Bennelong often took part. He remarried and had a son, and ended up a respected elder. But as the colonists took more land and relations with the native people deteriorated, the notion of some kind of peaceful coexistence or friendship collapsed.

Bennelong died, aged fifty, perhaps partly from too much alcohol, but admired by his own people. The *Sydney Gazette*, however, speaking for the colonists, called him in its obituary not a 'noble savage' as Captain Phillips or the young Joseph Banks might have put it, but rather 'a thorough savage, not to be warped from the form and character that nature gave him'. The Enlightenment's admiration for hunter-gatherer people living without clothes or hypocrisy had not taken long to warp itself into colonialist contempt.

Colonization was in the end about force, not friendship. The naked people so admired by Cook for their honesty had been forced off their land because Britain needed somewhere to put her thieves, many of whose families had also been ousted from the land they had lived in for generations. Industrialization and colonization involved multiple migrations and expulsions. In Australia, some aboriginals turned to open revolt. One of them, Pemulwuy, had made a final stand in 1797: he was shot seven times and captured. He escaped, with a manacle on his leg, and was killed in 1802. His severed head was sent to the collection of that great lover of Australia, Sir Joseph Banks.

Australia is only one of the more dramatic instances of a story that was being repeated in the Americas, in Africa and in the Far East as well. Among its victims would be Enlightenment optimism.

The Revolution

They gathered, a citizen army of patriots, declaring themselves for liberty – 'an inalienable right . . . derived truly from the people' – and using a fresh word in European politics. Remembering Athens, they called themselves 'democrats', and announced that the land belonged not to the hated aristocrats or the monarch but to the people.

Wearing ribbons and carrying muskets, they called on the ordinary folk to 'arm yourselves, assemble together and take charge of the affairs of the land'. First one city, then another, fell to this revolutionary uprising. This, however, was not Paris in 1789 but the Netherlands four years earlier, where rebels had declared a new written constitution, and their 'Free Corps' had seized Utrecht, then Amsterdam itself. Just as would soon happen in France, symbols became all-important: the then rulers were the House of Orange, so the colour orange was banned; even carrots had to be displayed with their green leaves, or not at all. The Dutch, however, were a small people, and when they annoyed the Prussian king by arresting a relative, his army invaded and easily snuffed out this unsettling display of democratic idealism.

Snuffing out the French Revolution would be a little harder. When the Bourbon monarchy finally collapsed, embroiled in debt and politically hamstrung, France was the greatest nation in Europe. She was the centre of ideas and fashion. French was the international language of diplomacy and polite society. Her armies were huge and her navy, not yet humiliated by Nelson, seemed awesome. Paris claimed to be the capital of civilization; and to many, still barely aware of China or Japan, this seemed a statement of the obvious. So the impact of the French Revolution – the biggest event in European politics since the fall of the Western Roman Empire – was always going to be felt by the rest of the continent. It proved to be even more important than that. Along with the industrial revolution, it was one of two concurrent changes on the European stage that unquestionably altered the history of humankind.

The revolution in Paris left a legacy that is even harder to weigh. It gave the world the notions of 'left' and 'right'. It introduced 'human rights' in the modern sense into political talk, and influenced the constitutions of countries all over the globe. Even at the time those who were enraptured by it, and those who were terrified by it, understood it as a turning-point in history, the beginning of a new age. It also demonstrated how short is the route from abstract ideals to bloody repression, for this was the first revolution to eat its children – hungrily, publicly and quickly. Its initial impact on the rest of Europe was not to bring the freedom that the likes of Beethoven and Wordsworth hoped for, but to plunge the continent yet again into war, starvation and repression. In 1972, the Chinese Communist leader Zhou Enlai is said to have replied to the American diplomat Henry Kissinger, who had asked about the impact of the French Revolution, simply, 'Too early to say.' Perhaps, forty years on, that is no longer quite true.

Almost everything about the French Revolution is argued about, except when it started. It began when Louis XVI summoned an archaic body called 'the Estates General' on Sunday, 5 May 1789. This body was intended to represent the three different interest groups in France – nobility and clergy, and the 'third estate', which represented everyone else, from wealthy businessmen to peasants. As we have seen, the absolutist Bourbons had managed without it. Louis hoped this proto-Parliament would help him raise taxes, particularly from the aristocracy. France was suffering a now familiar crisis in which soaring debt and a too-narrow tax base meant the old way of ruling had become unsustainable – something that happened with the Chinese Ming and Qing dynasties and the British Stuart one too.

In France, despite the theory of royal absolutism, the great landowners, the clergy and the most powerful commercial concerns enjoyed immunity from most taxes and, indeed, from other legal constraints. There was a thick web of hallowed agreements which someone, somehow, had to cut through, if the French crown was not to become bankrupt. The position had been dramatically worsened by the decision to aid and fund the American rebels against Britain's George III. This had helped soothe France's hurt pride for the loss of her Indian and Canadian territories to the British, but it had turned the long-running debt problem from a malady into a mortal crisis. At the same time, a series of bad summers and rising inflation were making life for the rural poor, which had never been easy, almost intolerable. Louis and his ministers had to find a dramatic answer. But summoning the Estates General, which had been dormant for 175 years, would prove a little too dramatic. Louis ought to have remembered his English history, and the parallel gamble of Charles I when he needed money from the London parliament.

On 17 June, the 'third estate' of non-aristocratic and non-clerical representatives (mostly lawyers, officials, merchants and journalists) overwhelmed the other two estates by insisting the body met as one, and declared itself the National Assembly. Unable or unwilling to suppress this insurgent new institution, Louis found public order was beginning to break down in the capital. On 13 July the revolutionaries tore down the customs posts around Paris, which represented royal authority. The following day, the 14th, they stormed another (though mostly empty) symbol of the *ancien régime*, the fortress and prison of the Bastille. A tide of violence tore through the french crown, as abbeys were attacked, rich aristocrats assaulted and nuns and priests murdered. Some cities declared themselves self-governing.

But power had decisively shifted. The Convention, making up new rules as it went along, now rewrote the constitution of France. To start with, it seemed as if the king could be accommodated in the new order. The revolutionaries destroyed the old system of French provinces and turned them into modern departments; took over Church lands for the state; declared all men equal before the law; ended censorship and torture; cancelled noble privileges and the legal apparatus of serfdom; and began to build a properly representative government system. This was a cascade of change never seen before in history. On 26 August the Assembly issued a 'Declaration of the Rights of Man' whose promises of freedom, liberty and due process rang out across Europe, delighting the young and optimistic and causing courtiers everywhere to fret. The cowed Louis XVI was obliged to attend a mass with the leaders of this revolution, to celebrate its remarkable achievements. The world marvelled.

At each successive stage, however, the pressures of war, hunger and fear drove the different bodies riding the revolution to more extreme positions. The Legislative Assembly, which replaced the National Constituent Assembly after elections in September 1791, was further to the left, but was then itself swamped by the declaration of a republican National Convention. During 1792–5, this fell under the control of an extremist group calling themselves 'Jacobins'. The revolution seemed in peril, hemmed in as it was by Prussian and Austrian enemies; and abroad, at war with the British. The Paris mob, the *sans-culottes* or ragged-legged poor, both intimidated and were manipulated by a new phenomenon – popular demagogues, cousins of the radical leaders of the late Roman republic.

German threats to exact bloody revenge if the king was threatened had the opposite effect to that intended, sparking further extreme violence. In September 1792, priests, aristocrats and others merely suspected of being against the revolution, were murdered in Paris's prisons, and Louis was finally deposed. He was already a captive in the old Tuileries palace in the centre of the capital, after very nearly escaping from France the previous June. He had been spotted and arrested at Varennes, not far from the eastern border. His trial in the winter of 1792 was a passionately argued and public affair. On 33 charges, the deputies voted overwhelmingly for his guilt, with only a few dozen abstentions and no votes against. The vote to put him to death was, however, very close. But close was enough: on 21 January 1793 Louis was executed, having pardoned his enemies, his voice drowned out by drums. His Austrian Habsburg wife Marie Antoinette, who had been a particular hate figure of the Paris mob, was guillotined in October; and their child, aged ten, briefly and only theoretically Louis XVII, died in the hands of unsympathetic foster-parents.

Though the fate of the royal family shocked foreign observers, the greater drama was the bloody fate of the revolution itself. The Convention, which had clustered the Jacobins on the left and the moderate Girondists on the right, continued to be a theatrical arena for speeches, but real power moved to the smaller Committee of Public Safety, run first by Georges Danton and later by Maximilien Robespierre. This, in turn, then fell mostly under the control of the Jacobin Club. The club was perhaps only around 3,000-strong at its height, and far fewer than that had real influence. An inner clique controlled a slightly larger committee, which in turn controlled the front organization. This was very like the way in which Communist revolutionaries in the twentieth century, behind the charade of Party Congresses and parliaments, would set up small inner groups inside 'politburos'– dolls within dolls within dolls. And as with later revolutions in Russia, China, Vietnam and Cambodia, the ruling clique became obsessed by security, treachery and the need for ideological 'purity' – the latter a particular obsession of the green-eyed, chilly and mesmeric former lawyer, Robespierre.

Again, as with later revolutions, great faith was placed in the power of symbols. The French revolutionaries declared a new religion, the worship of a Supreme Being, and set up altars to 'Reason' in vandalized churches. They also ended the old system of counting money in twenties, tens and dozens (which survived in Britain until the 1970s) and created a decimal replacement. The same 'rational' reform was introduced for measurements of distance and, most radically, for a changed calendar. This had twelve months of thirty days each, named after the harvest, mist, frost, snow, rain, wind, seeds, flowers, haymaking, reaping, heat and fruits, and started a new count for the years: year one was 1792. Not only was the familiar world of kings, priests and landowners gone; so too were all the familiar landmarks in money, time and space. Not even Lenin went so far.

This guillotine blade, having severed past from present, ensured there could be no reconciliation. The Jacobins killed nothing like as many people as did later revolutionaries. It has been estimated that forty-five thousand people died in 'the Terror', by public execution or in mob violence; regional fighting beyond Paris saw roadside executions, summary hangings and mass drownings in hulks. The death toll runs into hundreds of thousands if civil war and famine are included right across France; but this was not the liquidation of an entire class,

at least physically. At the time, France had around 250,000 male aristocrats: the carnage barely starts to compare to the millions killed by the
Bolsheviks and the Chinese Communists.

Yet in the smaller world of eighteenth-century France the Terror
was terrifying enough. Numbers are never the whole story; the details
that stick in the imagination matter, too. Paris was by modern standards a small place, and the new killing-machine stood very publicly at
its centre. More humane than botched hangings or hacking with an
axe it may have been, but it offered a spectacularly bloody and public
form of popular vengeance. Dr Joseph-Ignace Guillotin popularized
and propagandized for the head-severing device; he did not actually
invent it. Indeed, he was against capital punishment, and particularly
against it being used as a public spectacle. (Nor, as many people suppose, did he die by means of the device himself; he lived on long after
the revolution, and died of natural causes in 1814.)

Guillotin had wanted the device, versions of which had been used
before in Scotland, England and Germany, to be seen as a modern and
egalitarian way of dispatching serious criminals and the irreconcilable
enemies of change. During the Terror, it became the symbol of the
dictatorship's paranoid determination to kill possible enemies with the
least amount of due process, and provided a suitable reckoning for the
once rich and powerful. Brochures were sold containing lists of those
scheduled for execution, and mobs would gather to crow and mock.
By the end, the slaughter had become routine enough to seem boring,
and the crowds apparently thinned out. (It must have been especially
galling to be transported on a tumbril for your final journey, only to
find nobody was very much interested.)

Of all the tales of the Terror, the one that perhaps best reveals its
ironies is that of Jean-Paul Marat, assassinated in his bath by Charlotte
Corday in 1793. Marat was in flashes a brilliant man. From relatively
humble origins he rose to be regarded as a serious scientist. He had
worked in London's Soho – where he seems to have formed an addiction to strong coffee – Newcastle and Switzerland before becoming a
doctor famous for his cures in Paris, where he ministered to the court
and aristocrats, charging high fees and affecting semi-aristocratic status
himself. He had written political tracts too, including a shrewd analysis of the faults of the British constitution, which he nevertheless
admired. He had argued for a more humane and fairer justice system,

and while inveighing against tyranny during the early stages of the revolution he had insisted that Louis was essentially a good king, assisted
by good ministers.

Yet Marat seems always to have been vain and had a thin skin,
bringing out something close to paranoia in him. His writings on electricity, heat and optics were widely read. He was admired by Goethe
and by Benjamin Franklin, yet he failed to be admitted to the (Royal)
French Academy – and seethed with resentment. He was a man who
picked arguments and had few friends. Once the revolution began and
Marat turned to journalism and politics full time, he found that his
real talent was for aggressive and provocative prose. Lashing out at
moderates such as Lafayette, he called his newspaper *L'Ami du Peuple*
and increasingly saw himself as the ultimate People's Friend, the
uncorrupted man of no party, roughly dressed, inspiring the poor to
demand their economic rights as well as their political voice. Elected
to the National Assembly, he became the voice of extremists and even
faced trial for his violent incitements – a show trial in which the prime
showman was the accused, Marat himself, triumphantly acquitted.
Still, he had to escape briefly to exile in London, and when he returned
he was often on the run, sometimes resorting to the Paris sewers.

Marat always insisted on his squeamishness and his dislike of violence. He hated even to see an insect hurt, he would say. Yet when he
picked up his pen on behalf of a revolution beset by rural royalist
rebellion and foreign armies, the demon of extremism took over. Early
on, in December 1790 before the Terror had really begun, he wrote in
L'Ami du Peuple that it was not on the battlefields but in the capital that
the enemy must be attacked. There must be popular executions: 'Six
months ago, five or six hundred heads would have been enough to pull
you back from the abyss. Today because you have stupidly let your
implacable enemies conspire among themselves . . . perhaps we will
have to cut off five or six thousand; but even if we must cut off 20,000,
there can be no time for hesitation.'

Later, he casually upped the figure by ten times, then to half a million – the thinking of an embryonic Stalin or Mao. Vitriol poured from
his pen, as he led the attacks on the more moderate Girondin faction
who would soon be defeated by the Jacobins. Where did his anger
come from? Physically ugly, suffering from a painful and unsightly skin
disease, and coming from a family of religious and political exiles, he

must have possessed elements of personal vengeance in his makeup. But he seems to have been genuinely terrified of a return of the royalists, who, he kept warning the revolutionaries, would slit their throats, rape their wives and disembowel their children in front of their eyes.

Marat was killed rather more briskly than that by a Girondin sympathizer, a woman from Normandy called Charlotte Corday. She bore some similarities to Marat. She too had had a tough early life – her mother had died young and she had been sent to a convent – and she too had been greatly influenced by Enlightenment thinking, particularly Rousseau and Voltaire. (The story of the female thinkers and agitators of the revolution is one that has begun to be addressed by historians only in the past decade or two.) She too was terrified of the prospect of France falling into civil war and had been especially horrified by the prison massacres of the previous September.

In July 1793 she arrived in Paris, bought a kitchen knife and talked her way into Marat's house. By then his political power was on the wane, but he continued to work while sitting in a copper-lined bath, to soothe his diseased skin. There, Corday talked to him about the Girondin refugees and he promised that they would soon lose their heads. As soon as his wife had left, she stabbed him through the chest, severing his carotid artery, killing him quickly as he cried for help. Corday was of course guillotined herself, but before she died she explained that she blamed Marat for the wave of killings, and had killed one man to save a hundred thousand – just as Robespierre had justified the execution of the king.

Marat lived on as a symbol of the revolution, a martyr whose bust was placed in churches and schools, and whose death was memorialized by the greatest French revolutionary artist, Jacques-Louis David. The painting shows Marat, prone, his skin flawless, a letter still clutched in one hand. The pose strongly echoes paintings of Christ's deposition, minus the angels or grieving Marys, and indeed Marat was compared to Christ in the purity of his love for the common man. The individual who made the comparison, in his eulogy of Marat, was his friend the Marquis de Sade. Something similar happened to those other gore-tainted extremists, Lenin and Trotsky, after their deaths. Anger and pitilessness morphed into love and pity, and a cult was erected. Meanwhile, the revolution degenerated into a slither of accusation and counter-accusation; group fell on group, and the streets ran with blood. Even Robespierre fell to the guillotine, screaming with pain and fear and horribly wounded after trying to shoot himself in the face.

Within a year of Marat's death, the frenzy of revolutionary killing and idealistic extremism seemed to be burning itself out. Wars abroad took up more of the time and energy of the next phase's rulers, those of the so-called Thermidorian Reaction. They in turn had to ask for military help against royalist rebellion, and so, from 1799 to 1802, the young Corsican general Napoleon Bonaparte took control first as consul and then, in 1804, as emperor. He would cement some of the key reforms of the revolution, at least in principle, while instituting a military dictatorship that would drown half of Europe in blood while choking the other half with gunpowder smoke. Marat's hatred of tyrants had helped elevate a new one.

The 'Bolsheviks' of the revolution had given way to a personality cult with secret police and wars to fight. Yet the original principles of the early stages of the revolution – liberty, equality and fraternity or, more prosaically, legal fairness and an end to the special privileges of monarchs and aristocrats – hugely influenced reform movements from Holland to Germany, England to Italy.

To start with, Napoleon's apparently unbeatable armies seemed to be carrying revolutionary freedom with them. Napoleon's greatest civil achievement was the French legal code, or Code Napoléon, a radical simplification and rationalization of old laws, producing a single coherent system; it reshaped France and was influential across the continent. At its height the Napoleonic Empire would reach as far as the Duchy of Warsaw, the tip of Italy and the Balkans, stripping away old aristocratic rights, ending religious discrimination – including against the Jews – and spreading its new laws and the metric system. Ludwig van Beethoven had originally called his third symphony *The Bonaparte*.

Beethoven is said, however, to have torn out the title page in protest when Napoleon crowned himself emperor, and retitled it the *Eroica*, dedicating it 'to the memory of a great man' – with the emphasis on memory. For although in Italy, Spain, Germany and the Netherlands, the Napoleonic armies swept away old rulers and substituted new ones, they often turned out to be from amongst Napoleon's own family or from his closest supporters. As the tottering Habsburgs and Hohenzollerns watched in horror, he seemed to be building something closer to a new family empire than a new political order; this was closer to the Sun King's vision of a Europe dominated by French royalty than it was to the republicanism of Robespierre or Danton. Napoleon would eventually fall a victim to overreach, most famously in his attempt to subdue Russia, ending in a death march back through the snow; but also in his long and ineffective campaign against Spanish partisans, aided by the British under Wellington.

After the battle of Trafalgar in 1805, when Nelson's fleet destroyed both the French and Spanish fleets after a spectacularly dangerous manoeuvre, costing the life of the famous admiral among many others, Napoleon had no hope of invading Britain itself. This led to a long stand-off between sea power and land power, during which the British blockaded continental ports but could not grapple effectively with 'the Corsican tyrant' himself, whose greatest victory came at the end of the same year, at Austerlitz, where he shattered the combined armies of the Austrians and Russians.

Until his Russian failure, Napoleon's military genius had awed and confounded all other major European armies; it was only in 1813, at the battle of Leipzig – or 'the Battle of the Nations' – that they combined in big enough numbers to finally defeat him. Russians, Prussians, Austrians and Swedes, together hugely outnumbering the French, plus some Italian and Polish allies, fought what was, to that date, the largest land battle in European history, involving some six hundred thousand troops. Napoleon's defeat led to the coalition armies seizing Paris and to a mutiny by his own senior generals; then his abdication, followed by exile on the island of Elba.

Napoleon's return from Elba, and the immediate rallying of his soldiers to him, constitute one of the great adventures of nineteenth-century history. But it *was* only an adventure. The 'hundred days' of his final rule, when the fat Bourbon Louis XVIII fled Paris, ended at the battle of Waterloo, where the Duke of Wellington's combined army, aided by the Prussians arriving at the last minute, defeated the French. Napoleon's last exile, to St Helena in the South Atlantic, put him far from reach, and he died there in 1821.

Napoleon had forced the other European powers to mobilize their troops and to learn to fight on a scale that would not be repeated until the First World War. And for a while he had threatened the rule of the monarchies that had dominated Europe for a thousand years. But wars of conquest and republicanism are mutually inimical, and his political legacy was surprisingly small.

This was not true of the revolution, whose final disarray had allowed him to rise in the first place. Europe would return to the old order, for a while; to a system of reactionary alliances dominated by the Austro-Hungarian Empire, the final glimmer of Bourbon France, and the grim shadow of Russian Czarist authority as 'the policeman of Europe'. But France never quite healed. She remained radically divided between her old royalist, Catholic identity and her new republican, revolutionary ones, a division that would erupt in two further revolutions, tear French society apart in the Dreyfus affair, and continue to shake the country through the 1930s, culminating in the collaboration of the Vichy regime with Nazi Germany. Across the rest of Europe, the memory of the 'Rights of Man', of republican government and of just, modern law would animate radicals throughout the nineteenth century. The continent-wide revolts of 1848 showed that the new thinking, which had started in Paris two generations earlier, could not be forgotten.

The real conundrum is whether it is ever possible for a full-scale revolutionary upheaval not to progress to mass murder and eventually to military dictatorship. Does it make sense to compare the English Levellers, say, to French Jacobins, or to Russian Bolsheviks? Is it utterly unhistorical to compare Cromwell, Napoleon and Stalin? The situations were very different, and the main players thought of themselves in very different terms. But this much can be said. Once old authority – however intolerable, deaf to change, sclerotic and contemptible – has been toppled, there is rarely a new order waiting politely in the wings, more rational, more humane, more forward-looking.

Power maddens. *Our enemies circle. Traitors are all around us. Emergency powers are needed. Severity now will lead to gentleness later. This is no time for squeamishness.* And the caving-in of authority goes on, until so much misery has been caused that there is an exhausted acceptance of the mailed fist and the dictator's first promise – which is law and order. Everyone claims to speak for the people, but of course the people – the actual majority of living adults – are voiceless. Monarchies and empires have their succession problems, as we have seen. These

include palace coups, idiot children, war between siblings and the overthrow of one family by another. But the problems of moving from
one system of government to an entirely different one seem bloodier
still.

Black Jacobin

Today, Haiti is of one of the poorest, most desperate, blighted, cor-
ruptly run, environmentally degraded places on earth. Three hundred
and fifty years ago, it was one of the richest. Then called Saint-
Domingue, it was the lush, rich-soiled western half of one of the
Caribbean's largest islands, whose mountains were clad in forests of
hardwood, whose hills were planted with coffee, cocoa, mangoes and
oranges, and whose plains glittered with the light from banana,
tobacco and sugar plantations. A French colony, its wealth had built
some of the grandest squares and mansions in Bordeaux, Nantes and
Marseille. It was considered the single most important island colony in
the world. By the time of the French Revolution its ports welcomed
more than 1,500 ships a year: France employed 750 huge vessels and
24,000 sailors just for the Saint-Domingue trade.

So why did such a lush, successful place become the nightmarish
demonstration of all that can go worst in human public life? The
answer is slavery, and what happened when slavery collided with the
high ideals of French democracy. Saint-Domingue saw the first and
only successful revolt by black slaves against their white oppressors.
And though the eventual outcome was bleak for the people of Haiti,
quickly forgotten when the white northern nations had moved beyond
sugar plantations and slave ships, the uprising has at its heart one of
the most inspiring leaders of the eighteenth century.

His name was Toussaint L'Ouverture. His father was an African
chief who had been captured in war, sold as a slave and bought by a
French planter. His son Toussaint, one of eight children born to the
displaced chieftain and his Catholic wife, had a privileged upbringing
compared with most slaves, learning a little French and Latin, and
rising to become overseer of livestock on his master's estate. Though
he never suffered the tortures and regular whippings of most of the
wretched sugar-plantation workers, he was nevertheless a slave until

freed, aged thirty-three. By the time of the French Revolution, he was already in his forties and grey-haired, and known as 'Old Toussaint'. His surname 'L'Ouverture' was a nickname referring either to his later ability as a military commander to find 'openings' in enemy ranks, or possibly to the gaps between his teeth.[31] He was small, a superb horseman, and a man of charisma.

Toussaint's world was part of the Atlantic slave trade, which lasted for nearly four centuries until it ended in the late nineteenth century. It is estimated that 12.4 million people were captured in Africa, loaded onto slave ships and taken to the Caribbean, South America and North America, nearly two million of them dying on the crossing, even before they reached the plantations.[32] Add to that the huge death rate caused by the African wars, after Ashanti, Dahomey, Kongo and other kings, realizing how lucrative captives could be, slaughtered both old and young, then took the healthy adults to the coast in death marches. Then add the mortality rate in the holding-pens for slaves on the coast and the number who died in the first year or two of plantation 'seasoning', and the total death rate was probably higher than the number of slaves crossing the Atlantic – some sixteen million.[33]

The systematic capture of African slaves to work in the labour-intensive open-air factories of the sugar plantations had been pioneered by Arab Muslims, who had faced slave rebellions themselves in Mesopotamia. But this was pushed to its logical extreme by the combination of Atlantic navigation, the conquest of fertile new lands, and by Europe's insatiable desire for cheaper sugar, tobacco and cotton. It was the Portuguese who began the business on their early acquisitions, the Cape Verde islands and Madeira, in the late 1400s. Their large colony in Brazil explains why Portuguese slavers would eventually account for 40 per cent of the trade; but soon most other European seafaring nations were involved too, from the Spanish and French to the Dutch and the Danes. In the eighteenth century, however, it was the British who had become dominant.

There are few darker (or better-known) stories in history than that of the 'Middle Passage', the stage in the triangular trade in which crammed slave-ships took the human muscle from Africa to the Americas. The sugar and other raw materials their labour produced were then imported back to Europe, European manufactured goods having been sent to the colonies in the first stage of this traffic. In effect, before the full flood of the industrial revolution, the more advanced European economies were using foreign human labour as the machines to drive their own prosperity. Today, the stories of the anti-slavery movement of outraged Christian reformers are particularly celebrated. But brave men and women though they were, they do not wipe away the two centuries of trade.

All this is simple, and not so remote. The sweet taste of sugared tea in the mouth – the satisfying smack of rum on the lips – the soft feeling of a fresh cotton shirt – the calming exhalation of good tobacco smoke – these were the intense physical pleasures that allowed generations of Europeans to avert their eyes from the slave economy on which they depended. Even with television and the other modern communication media, it remains very easy to enjoy a slickly designed computer tablet, a line of cocaine or bright throwaway clothing without thinking too hard about how they come to be so cheaply available. From the 1600s on, huge fortunes were made from Glasgow to Lisbon, fine terraces erected in Bristol and Nantes, powerful politicians funded in London, Paris and Amsterdam, by the slave trade. The cruelty of the trade, from the brandings and whippings on the plantations to the feeding of slaves to sharks and the use of cannibalism as a punishment, was so nauseating that it makes a mockery of much of the style and intellectual swagger of Enlightenment Europe. The slave ships, packed with shackled men and women, stank so badly that their arrival could be smelt when they were well offshore. Sharks followed them across the Atlantic for the bodies regularly tossed overboard.

Saint-Domingue was one of the hungriest markets for slaves during the heyday of British and French slave-shipping because the disease-ridden tropical climate and the rigours of cutting and boiling sugar-cane killed them off so quickly that the landowners always wanted more. In the century running up to the French Revolution around 850,000 slaves had been brought there; but far from the black population increasing, as one might have expected, by the time the revolution broke out there were only 435,000 blacks in the colony. There was nothing specifically French about this. The figures for British-run Jamaica were similar. It is a loss of life so huge that it goes a long way towards explaining what happened when those slaves finally did rise up.

The colony, ruled by Louis XIV's 1685 Slave Code, had developed a complex and volatile population. There were the rich white planters, often the second, or the disgraced, sons of French aristocrats. There was a larger class of poorer whites – shopkeepers, artisans, plantation overseers and some farmers. Then there was a yet larger class of part-white, part-black people, the abundant fruit of a century or more of white men taking black women. These 'mulattos' were in turn divided into a hierarchy, depending on how black or white their parentage was. Some had become relatively rich themselves and were deeply resented by the poorer whites, though they had no political rights. Finally, in the huge majority, came the blacks – mostly, but not all, slaves. Groups of escaped blacks had found refuge in Saint-Domingue's highlands, where they practised voodoo cults and occasionally plotted to attack the plantations.

Into this explosive mix, arriving like a firecracker, came news of the French Revolution. The rich whites were, unsurprisingly, mostly royalists, as were the local officials and army officers. But many of the other whites were enthusiastic republicans, as were many mulattos. Then, hovering across the border and hoping to take advantage of the chaos were the Spanish in their colony, which was the other half of the island, Santo Domingo; and not far across the sea, the British, with their colony of Jamaica and their awesome navy.

The story of the Haitian Revolution was therefore bound to be a complicated one. Rebel slaves sometimes joined with the Spanish against the French revolutionaries; the French fought on each side; the mulattos might take the royalists' side, or even that of the invading British. Everyone was struggling for position, while the news from Paris kept changing. In the early part of the revolution, middle-class Parisian democrats, many of whom had made good money from the sugar trade, were keen to preserve slavery. Anti-slavery campaigners, including Englishmen, hoped the revolution would be a turning-point, but in this they were frustrated. Debates in the Convention about Saint-Domingue were conducted in mumbled, embarrassed code, avoiding the very word 'slave'.

Later, as the revolution became more democratic, black rights were proclaimed. In January 1794 a former slave, Jean-Baptiste Belley, speaking in the Convention, demanded the abolition of slavery and was acclaimed with great emotion. The twentieth-century Marxist historian C.L.R. James, who wrote the pioneering account of the Haiti uprising, said: 'It was fitting that a Negro and an ex-slave should make the speech which introduced one of the most important legislative acts ever passed by any political assembly.'[34] Yet all too soon, as the anti-Jacobin reaction set in, the mood in Paris swung violently against the slaves and in favour of the old order.

The man trying to hold a course that would lead to the complete freeing of all the blacks of Saint-Domingue was Toussaint L'Ouverture. To start, with the French Revolution brought conflict between the rival royalist and republican French, and between the poor whites and the mulattos, who wanted their rights too. There were uprisings by slaves on other French islands, Martinique and Guadeloupe, too.

Toussaint, a Catholic and a herbal physician, began as a cautious and moderate leader of the rebel slaves, looking for compromises and ready to do deals for an amnesty for the leaders – which, treacherously, would have left most of the rebels returned to slavery. For a time he fought with the Spanish royalists against the revolution, so suspicious was he of the poorer white radicals. But as he became a more experienced and successful military leader – he had carefully studied Julius Caesar's *Gallic Wars* and seems to have had as much natural aptitude for war as Napoleon himself – Toussaint adopted the all-or-nothing Rights of Man approach of the Jacobin leaders in Paris. He turned a ragtag mob of angry slaves into a disciplined, clever and determined army that won victory after victory.

Their greatest was against the British, who tried to take over the colony, pretending to side with the blacks and mulattos and the cause of liberty but really intent on exploiting France's weakness. British ministers were all too aware that slaves on their island, Jamaica, had revolted in 1760. Toussaint toyed with British offers, but was becoming ever more enthusiastic about the ideals of the French Revolution, if not about the agents sent by France to keep him in check. He inflicted on the British army one of the most embarrassing defeats in its history. This has been quietly ignored by patriotic historians, but it cost so many British casualties that it rivalled the toll in the Peninsular War against Napoleon.

Toussaint was a complicated leader. He genuinely seems to have revered France but decided that, in practice, this colony had better be run almost independently by himself, just to make sure no attempt was made to bring back slavery. As the revolution stumbled and more conservative leaders took power in Paris, he warned them that if they were to try it, they would be attempting the impossible: 'We have known how to face dangers to obtain our liberty – we shall know how to brave death to maintain it.'[35] By this time, for all the bloodshed and suspicion, the slave revolt had radically changed racial attitudes on the island. When a mulatto rival of Toussaint's called Rigaud was accused of refusing to obey him because his leader was a full-blown negro, he erupted: 'Is it a tint of colour, more or less dark, which instills principles of philosophy or gives merit to an individual?' He went on: 'I am too much a believer in the Rights of Man to think that there is one colour in nature superior to another. I know a man only as a man.'

After expelling the British and taking over Santo Domingo, Toussaint became for several years the virtual dictator of the colony. He seems to have done an extraordinary job in restoring a land devastated by war, making the workers go back to the plantations to prevent famine, beginning to establish schools and a system of local government, creating lawcourts, building a fine hotel, introducing simple taxes and tackling smugglers. Surrounded by other former slaves and liberal whites, he held open soirées where he could be petitioned, and criss-crossed the island on horseback to check every administrative detail. He introduced a printed constitution, with a general assembly subordinate to himself as governor. Gleaming there in the Caribbean was the chance of a genuinely multiracial commonwealth ruled by blacks.

It was gleaming far too brightly, however, for the liking of that other self-appointed ruler, Napoleon Bonaparte, who had no time for blacks and fully understood that the permanent loss of Saint-Domingue, which had once accounted for two-thirds of France's overseas wealth, would be a terrible blow. He played cat-and-mouse with Toussaint, until a brief interlude of peace with Britain and his other enemies allowed Napoleon to send twenty thousand troops – the largest army that had ever left France by ship – to crush the black revolution.

Toussaint had by now fallen out with some of his ablest lieutenants and more radical black supporters, who thought he was too lenient to the whites and too hard on his own people. He dithered about whether he wanted a complete break with France, and about how radical his new free island should be. But when Napoleon's generals landed, they found him almost as difficult to defeat as the British had. A savage new war broke out, and the black regiments, singing their revolutionary songs back at the French, came close to winning. Had a few of Toussaint's senior commanders not switched sides, he could have held on until the season of rain and disease arrived to finish off the invaders. As it was, he parleyed for an armistice, was betrayed, arrested and packed off to France, where Napoleon had him confined in an icy prison until he died.

This was not the end of the story, however. Toussaint's capture did not crush the spirit of the freed slaves. The French commanders began a brutal attempt to exterminate the mulattos and to kill so many blacks that they would be cowed back into slavery. But the mass drownings, burnings and attacks with specially trained dogs had the opposite effect, and a new guerrilla war began. For the first time, it became something close to a full race war, the black forces now led by a whip-mark-scarred former slave called Jean-Jacques Dessalines. He had been a brilliant general under Toussaint, but possessed none of his moderation or modesty. Terrible atrocities were committed by both sides. As local revolts erupted all around them, French willpower gave out and the remnants of Napoleon's grand invasion force fled from the island, to be captured by waiting British naval ships.

Dessalines, in another echo of Napoleon, had himself crowned emperor in 1804, parading into town wearing an American crown, and transported in a British-made ceremonial carriage. The following year, perhaps egged on by the traditional enemies of France who wanted the colony finished off once and for all, Dessalines ordered a massacre of the whites left on what was now called 'Haiti'. Two years later the British Parliament at last outlawed the Atlantic slave trade, and the Royal Navy began seizing slavers' ships and freeing around 150,000 slaves. The plantation system was starting to collapse. That, plus the devastation of Haiti caused by years of war and the international isolation created by Dessalines's massacre of whites, condemned the island to pariah status.

Its natural wealth had been greatly augmented by the colonists' planting of sugar-cane, coffee, tobacco and the other goods that sucked it into the centre of an international trading system. But all this depended on systematized brutality. So far, people had managed to look the other way, but by the late eighteenth century Britain, at least, was able to prosper mightily at home, with her steam-based industries, and had no need of the disgusting business. Yet had it not been for the slaves of Saint-Domingue taking the promises of the French Revolution at face value and showing the world that blacks could fight as well (or better) than their supposed masters, then the abolitionists might have had a harder time. The saddest thing of all, though, is that had Toussaint survived and built his little republic, a more substantial legacy might have been left behind; and Haiti today might have avoided its fate as a land of dictators and poverty.

Cowpox

In Boston in the 1720s, there lived a witch-hunting reverend called Cotton Mather, who did his best to find the hand of God in the appalling toll of children he and his wife had lost to the great scourge of the age, smallpox. 'A dead child,' he reflected, 'is a sign no more surprising than a broken pitcher or a blasted flower.' But Mather noticed a strange thing about his slave Onesimus, who had been born in far-off Libya. Onesimus, who did not catch the disease, had scratches on his arms which he had been given as a child in Africa. Like other African slaves, he had been inoculated according to tribal customs. Mather was intrigued. He began to wonder. He was not intrigued enough to spare his slave when he committed some minor misdemeanour and so had to be sold, but the germ – of an idea, for once – had been planted.[36]

On the other side of the Atlantic at the same time, a brilliant and well connected lady was on the same track. Mary Wortley Montagu had contracted a bad dose of smallpox in 1715, which destroyed her facial beauty and nearly killed her. When she went with her husband as ambassador to Turkey, she learned about the Ottoman habit of inoculation, or 'variolation' as it was called – a small nick in the skin, a little diseased matter inserted, and just a very mild dose resulted. The Turks used the trick to protect the beauty of women on their way to the harem. Lady Mary used it to protect her six-year-old son. Back in England a couple of years later, she did the same to her daughter and then persuaded her friend Princess Caroline to try it on the royal children.

In England as in America, a great argument then erupted. Smallpox was a hideous and deadly disease. It had been known in ancient China, India and Africa and may have reached Greece and Rome in classical times. It certainly affected the Crusaders, who brought it home to Europe in the 1100s, where it became endemic. It produced rashes and then horrible seeping pustules across the face and body, dreadful cramps, blindness and often death. Survivors were generally scarred, often mutilated and blinded. Children were especially affected, and smallpox spread most effectively in the crowded conditions of European villages and towns. It has been estimated that by the eighteenth century one in ten of the deaths in England was from smallpox. In Glasgow between 1783 and 1802 it accounted for a third of child deaths. The situation was at least as bad in Russia, and across the century in Europe alone it may well have accounted for sixty million deaths.[37]

When we see recreations of the villages of Jane Austen's England, or Enlightenment Edinburgh, or the American towns of the Revolutionary era, the film-makers will generally have left out one thing that would have stood out a mile – the crowds of pustule- and scar-covered people, their eyes squeezed shut by the mutilations of smallpox, wretched beyond description. One study concluded that 'in terms of sheer numbers of people killed, blinded, crippled, pitted and scarred by smallpox over two thousand years of written and oral history, this disease was probably the worst pestilence ever to afflict mankind'.[38]

Yet people had known from ancient times that giving someone a small dose of smallpox could bring on a mild attack, which would stop them getting the full-blown disease later. Ancient Chinese doctors had gathered the scabs of smallpox sufferers, dried them, ground them up, and then blown them up the noses of patients, using special bone tubes. They also deliberately placed the pus in children's clothing. In India and parts of Africa, people had it pushed into their veins with thorns, or they swallowed it, or smeared it into open wounds. This was the tradition that Rev Mather came across amongst Boston slaves and that Lady Mary had met with in the wooden houses of Constantinople. It was no secret.

But it was not really an answer, either. European doctors tended to shun the practice, and not for ridiculous reasons. A person infected with a small dose could still go on to develop a full attack, and die or find themselves maimed. A death rate of around 3–5 per cent was expected, which made 'variolation' a real risk. Others were scarred or blinded. In London one of Lady Mary's distinguished friends, the Earl of Sutherland, lost his son after inoculating him. In crowded conditions, introducing 'variolation' could actually spread the disease faster than it would naturally do. Finally, the dirty knives used by European apothecaries often spread other infections. English doctors, eagerly followed by cartoonists, had mocked Lady Mary and even suggested that inoculation was part of a foreign plot to kill off English babies.

So great was the smallpox scourge, however, that variolation slowly became more popular. As practised in England, it was a horrible experience. The boy or girl to be inoculated would be starved for several weeks so as to weaken the constitution, then bled so as to thin the blood, while being kept on a sparse vegetable diet. Then the cut would be made and smallpox inserted by tying bandages with dried scabs around the wound. To keep the disease from spreading, the child would then be tied down and kept in a 'pest-house' or barn with other sufferers, for ten days until the new scabs fell off. The conditions were foul and the experience scarred many people mentally as well as physically. One eight-year-old child who went through the ordeal in smallpox-ravaged Gloucestershire later complained that he had been reduced to a skeleton and never slept well afterwards. His name was Edward Jenner.

Jenner had lost most of his family early on and was brought up by a kindly and much older brother, a moderately well-to-do vicar. From an early age he was fascinated by botany and soon became determined to become a doctor, a job that then meant apprenticeship rather than university. In London he became a favourite of the greatest surgeon of the age, John Hunter, and was offered the chance to go on Captain Cook's second voyage to Australia. He preferred, however, to return to Gloucestershire for the quieter pleasures of country doctoring. There he regularly came across the ravages of smallpox. In between practising medicine, growing cucumbers, experimenting with balloons and caring for an ill wife, he kept his ears open; and found himself pondering on a local folk-tale.

Apparently, milkmaids sometimes caught a bovine version of smallpox, called cowpox. Once they had been infected with this much milder disease, it was said, they were immune for life from the great scourge. It has even been suggested that the long tradition of songs and poems describing the creamy beauty of milkmaids started because they had unpoxed complexions. At least one farmer, Benjamin Jesty, had been sure enough of the truth of the story to infect his wife with cowpox pus, in 1756. All sorts of strange things happened in the countryside.

But it was forty years later that the now middle-aged doctor did his famous experiment. Hearing that a farmer's daughter, a milkmaid called Sarah Nelmes, had contracted cowpox in the village of Berkeley in Gloucestershire, on 14 May 1796 Jenner persuaded her to let him take some matter from her sores, and keep it. He then cut the arm of a boy called James Phipps, the son of a local labourer, and infected him. Young Phipps duly went down with the milder disease. Once he had recovered, on 1 July Jenner cut him again and tried to infect him with the smallpox material. (The ethics of using animals for medical experiment are hotly debated today; in eighteenth-century England, using a working-class boy seems to have caused little comment.) James failed to catch the disease. Jenner, who by then had been a doctor for twenty-four years, was certain enough of the result not to bother with many more tests, and quickly wrote up his idea in a pamphlet. It was an almost instant bestseller.

The story of how, and why, the news spread so fast is almost as interesting as the discovery itself. First, Jenner was a member of the local scientific debating club, and he presented his breakthrough as proven science, not simply as a country remedy. Though much of his argument was wrong, it took hold because there was a large and open-minded audience ready and waiting for it. Second, though a mere country doctor, he was well connected. Thanks to the fashionable spa town of Cheltenham – one of the resorts that grew up when the French wars made it impossible for wealthy Britons to travel abroad – he was in touch with influential aristocrats and writers, who spread the word.

Soon the cowpox treatment became all the rage in Britain, then quickly travelled abroad. In 1799 Princess Louisa of Prussia wrote to Jenner asking for 'vaccine' matter (the word comes from the Latin for 'cow'), and in the same year this new medical star was presented to George III. Where royalty and aristocracy led, the middle classes followed. The next year, the host and hostess of a dinner party that Jane Austen was attending insisted on reading out Jenner's pamphlet to the assembled company. By 1801 the Royal Navy was inoculating its sailors, while at his country home, Monticello in Virginia, the US President Thomas Jefferson inoculated thirty people himself. That year the empress of Russia named the first child vaccinated in her country, 'Vaccinof', and it was estimated that a hundred thousand people in Europe were treated. The great discovery even leapt across the barriers thrown up by the interminable European war: in 1804 Napoleon had a medal cast to honour Jenner, then had his armies inoculated. In fact, Napoleon so revered Jenner that when the country doctor wrote to him on the subject, the French emperor agreed to free some British prisoners of war. One of Jenner's greatest supporters in Paris was our famous do-gooder Dr Guillotin.

But the discovery was attacked, too. Ignorant cartoonists mocked the notion of infecting people with stuff from cows. Doctors warned that nothing good would come of it. More seriously, another famous intellectual of the age, Thomas Malthus, included a blast against Jenner in the second, 1806, edition of his famous book warning against overpopulation. For Malthus, the death-toll caused by smallpox was a good thing, keeping the population numbers down naturally. If the vaccine worked, then other diseases would simply pop up to take the place of smallpox and make the necessary cull. 'Nature will not, nor cannot be, defeated in her purposes,' wrote Malthus. 'The necessary mortality must come, in some form or another.'

In fact, the vaccination system would make smallpox the first great scourge to be eradicated. Arguments delayed the necessary legislation in many countries, including Britain, till later in the nineteenth century. Smallpox continued to kill, blind and maim people across the world well into the twentieth. But, thanks to Jenner's discovery, the United Nations was able to announce in 1980 that the disease had been completely eradicated. The country doctor, using the new belief in experimentation and the power of publication, had done infinitely more for the happiness of humanity than any of the political revolutionaries of his age so loudly declaring the rights of man.

Part Seven

CAPITALISM AND
ITS ENEMIES

*1800–1918: The Industrial Revolution Upends Life
around the Planet – and Then Attacks Itself*

The Industrial Revolution

Between the mid-1700s and the end of the 1900s, the world would change more than at any time since the invention of farming. The term 'industrial revolution' technically makes no sense, since 'revolution' implies a return to something previous, while this was all new. But it has stuck. This mega-change, based on machines that used the earth's stored energy (in coal and oil) to produce everything from cheap clothes to tinned food – and, not least, to build other machines – reshaped mankind's relationship with nature. It allowed people to travel far more quickly across the sea, by steamship, and across the land, by train. It allowed them to light their homes and workplaces cheaply and effectively, greatly extending their useful hours, particularly in northern latitudes. It brought well made clothes, household goods and entertainments to millions of people in Europe and America who could never before have dreamt of enjoying such things.

But it came at a price so high that many thinkers hated this revolution, and questioned whether it was worth while. For it forced millions into repetitive, grindingly hard indoor jobs and into crammed, insanitary urban housing. Its environmental effects, in densely populated towns or valleys, could be terrible. Victorian Britons died in huge numbers from lung diseases caused by air pollution – almost a quarter of deaths were caused by bad air.[1] In 1866, government inspectors found one river, the Calder, so polluted that its water made effective ink, while the Bradford Canal, teeming with the chemical by-products of industry, was regularly set on fire by local boys, the flames rising six feet along it.[2]

As the revolution spread to the United States and continental Europe, then Japan, the same thing happened to the huge rivers and lake systems there. This revolution also made wars far more destructive. It made it easy for the industrially advanced countries to bully, take over and exploit the less advanced ones, destroying in the blink of an eye cultures that had existed for centuries. Indeed, this was the most significant period of 'creative destruction' that human societies had ever experienced. And although the countries leading it included some that would dominate the story of the twentieth century, above all the United States and Germany (with France and Russia following not far behind), this transformation began in the damp islands of Britain.

There, the harnessing of coal, chemicals, ores and electricity was slow, compared with any political revolution. It took place in Britain over the course of a century or so, from the mid-1700s to about 1850, beginning in relatively remote areas such as Coalbrookdale in the Ironbridge Gorge, Shropshire, where coal and iron were traditionally found near the surface, and in the Cornish tin-mining areas; and around the then modest town of Birmingham. Its pioneers were men of business and gentleman-scientists, rather than visionary change-makers; their ceramics and their metal trinkets were deliberately made to mimic old, familiar handmade objects, and the use of machines was all about immediate profit. There was no master plan, no revolutionary cell. The profits were big enough to inspire rapid, even desperate, copying and competition. By the time the industrial revolution spread to Germany and the United States, as well as to smaller countries such as Belgium, the cascade of changes was gathering speed, and on the back of early British breakthroughs.

So why Britain? And why then?

Industrialization was more about politics than about geographical chance, even though Britain did have large deposits of coal and iron. It could not have happened without capitalism – the capital-intensive, market-based, relentlessly disruptive, creative/destructive system of funding, buying and selling that the world still lives under today. Industrialization can also happen without capitalism. The Soviet Union and Communist China showed that. But in both cases it required extreme violence, huge waste and above all, the theft or purchase of capitalist-created technology. We cannot run control experiments with history, but it seems that industrialization could not have been brought about and sustained outside a market system. And that, in turn, to get going properly, needed a special set of circumstances.

Such circumstances occurred first in Britain in the eighteenth century, not because the British were specially gifted by nature – think of the Chinese and Greek inventors, the French and Spanish explorers, the Italian and German craftsmen – but because happy coincidences collided to make something entirely new, rather as a chance mixture of chemicals can produce a chain reaction.

The coincidences occurred in what had seemed a pretty poor country. Britain had nothing like the gold and silver wealth of the Spanish colonies, nor the huge army and glittering court of France. It had decapitated one monarch, had had to beg his exiled son to return, and had then imported a foreign dynasty. Any overseas conquests it had at the beginning of its capitalist period were still marginal and, with the notable exceptions of tobacco and some sugar plantations, still unprofitable. Nor was this a time of peace when Britons could concentrate on affairs at home. Having just staggered through destructive civil wars, Britain was now entering a period, from 1689 to 1815, when almost one year in two would be spent at war with her European rivals. The country was still thinly populated but already mostly denuded of timber. In 1696 a civil servant called Gregory King had reckoned the population of England and Wales to be just five and a half million, of whom about a tenth lived in London. Many of the more independent-minded and ambitious, particularly religious dissenters, were desperate to emigrate and start again.

Yet behind this somewhat desolate picture, huge changes were afoot. The first was happening away from the cities, on flat and rolling agricultural land where improving landowners, making use of shorter leases, plus some new, professional, farmers, were greatly increasing the yield of their fields. The key effect would be on people, both on their numbers and on where they lived. It has been estimated that before the seventeenth century, no developed country had been able to feed its population without four-fifths of its people being employed as farmers.[3] From China to France, from the new USA to Russia, this left an absolute maximum of a fifth of the population to do everything else – to be the soldiers, sailors, priests, rulers, bureaucrats, craftsmen and traders. These had surplus wealth, but they did not add up to nearly enough consumers for a capitalist take-off.

In England, however, the enclosure of common land, drainage, and new systems of crop rotation changed those proportions radically.

You cannot much improve agricultural yields on the traditional small strips of land; nor is there an incentive to invest in new techniques, hedges or drainage if the leases are short. But from the late 1500s and accelerating through the following century, the takeover and enclosure of what had been common land was changing the shape of the English countryside. Larger fields, where more food could be grown, were being carved out, protected by longer hedges and longer leases. This was a controversial procedure, ripping up by the roots ancient traditions of ownership and husbandry. To modern eyes the English countryside can look cosy, even dozy, but to country people of the seventeenth and eighteenth centuries much of it would have looked bleakly new, raw and unfamiliar, with its great, stark squares of tillage. The Church and many writers protested at the devastating effect of all this on the new rural poor. The pain being caused to Old England echoes through plays by Shakespeare and from the angry rural poetry of John Clare.

But the consequence was that by 1700 England's agriculture was the most productive in Europe, probably twice as productive as that of her nearest rivals. A year later, Jethro Tull introduced his famous horse-drawn seed drill. Soon after that, four-field crop rotation, using clover and turnips to keep fields rich and abundant, was brought in from Flanders. Lacking any scientific knowledge, farmers nevertheless successfully bred new, much larger varieties of sheep and cattle: within a century, at London's Smithfield market the average weight of a sheep rose from twenty-eight pounds to eighty.[4] The changes happened raggedly, with Essex, Hertfordshire, Norfolk, Suffolk and Leicestershire leading the way, but by the 1750s or thereabouts they were reaching more of the Midlands and the north too, driven by enthusiastic reforming propaganda in the newspapers, themselves the product of new and faster printing presses. Far fewer people were producing much more food, allowing far more people to do . . . something else. Soon the labour force in the English fields was not 80 per cent of the population, but around 32–33 per cent, an astonishing change.[5] Other countries were also learning to feed themselves with fewer farmers, but not to the same extent.

For Britain this meant two things, both important for the leap into capitalism. First, the ancient fear of famine was receding. There would still be times of hunger after wet, cold springs, but surplus grain was being stored and new foods imported. People are less likely to take risks when they are scared of being hungry, so the spirit of adventure thrived. Second, there were now far more people available to become shopkeepers, artisans, traders and the like, paid with coins rather than, in the old days, with food. The new town-dwellers would be the new consumers. Thanks to the accelerated international trade already described, bringing spices, Indian fabrics, wines, tobacco, sugar, silks and ceramics to Britain's shores, these people now had things to consume – new wants they had not known before. Supplied and protected by her ships, both merchant and military, Britain became a market economy long before she was an industrial one.

A better-fed market economy meant more people. By 1700 life expectancy in England was around thirty-seven years, which sounds very low but was better than France's twenty-eight. It requires only a very slight improvement in the rate of reproduction and survival to produce a very fast growth in population. By 1850, at the zenith of the British industrial revolution, the population had tripled.[6] Without the changes in the fields and villages, this could not have happened. But without the right political system, the same is true. As we have seen, the wars and the political revolution of the previous century had hacked away much of the independent power of the British monarchy, which now found itself embedded in Parliament. This set-up represented not 'the people', but the well-off people such as landowners (who included owners of mines), wealthy merchants and investors in trade, as well as the ruling cliques of towns and cities.

Put like this, Britain might seem to have simply swapped a monarchy for an oligarchy. But the wars of religion had shaken Britain up quite a lot more than that. The overthrow of royal supremacy resulted in a genuinely independent judiciary, while Parliament had sole authority for setting taxation. Britain still had her great landowners, but her tradition of primogeniture kept the numbers of the aristocracy limited, while the trauma of the Civil War led the earls, the barons and the viscounts to tread more carefully. France, by contrast, had an ever-growing aristocracy entitled to many perks and rights and weighing more heavily on their food-producing peasants.

In Britain, one consequence of the relative weakness of the old order was that the bad habit of raising money by selling such perks and monopolies began to wither. Under James I, it has been said, the typical Englishman had a house built with monopoly bricks and heated by monopoly coal. 'His clothes are held up by monopoly belts, monopoly buttons, monopoly pins', and he ate 'monopoly butter, monopoly currants, monopoly red herrings, monopoly salmon, monopoly lobsters'.[7] The countless trade tariffs and barriers continued across France, Germany and Italy, but were disappearing in Britain. The British developed a national bank using the government's authority to back its loans, thereby stabilizing the national debt and bringing some sense of security to the capital markets. London was nothing like as important a financial centre as Amsterdam, but it was getting there. After the Bank of England was founded, in 1694, local banks began to spring up all across the country.

If it is hard for us today to be sure about the meaning of the changes happening around us, it was just as hard for the Britons of this fast-changing age of markets. Many did not feel particularly free. Gamekeepers with their man-traps, punitive local magistrates, the threat of the naval press-gang, tight religious restrictions constraining ambitious young men – petty tyranny was everywhere. But absolute tyranny had vanished. The law relied on barbarous punishments, but it could also be used by many who were not rich to protect their interests. Parliament could be lobbied, in response to the rising interest in changing laws that stymied change. When inventors and the first capitalists challenged the old order, patent law and parliamentary debate would be the cornerstones of their success.

There was another key difference from most of the European continent. Alongside better farming, more secure laws and less oppressive government, the British now had a freer press than anywhere else. This had started with the cranking-out of pamphlets and broadsheets full of libels, and the vituperative arguments over religion that plagued the 1600s, but had developed into the nearest thing yet seen to a free market in ideas. Scientists, or 'natural philosophers' as they still called themselves, could publish their speculations without fear of the censor. Newspapers carried a mass of information about new systems of farming and newfangled gadgets, as well as the doings of princelings and generals and the prices of commodities. In Britain, arguments about trade policy and finance could be fought out openly.

Importantly, even though Britain was hobbled by many trade

restrictions and poor transport, industry was already in place. It was simply not yet organized into factories. Rich men funded families working with spinning and weaving machines in their Yorkshire cottage homes; in the growing Midland towns and villages, makers of nails, buckles, screws and buttons operated in their family workshops. In the traditional coalmining areas, above all around Newcastle, owners were experimenting with machines as they struggled with the ancient problem of how to keep the deeper mines free of water. As with the tin industry, they had used waterwheels and pulleys as far back as anyone could remember, but were now trying out primitive steam engines.

In 1679 the French inventor Denis Papin exhibited his 'steam digester' at the Royal Society and eight years later had developed a better pressure-cooker and steam pump. Two Devon engineers appropriated his idea, and improved on it. Thomas Savery had made some primitive but ingenious devices including an early steam engine, which was being used by Cornish miners during 1708–14; then, about 1712, a Baptist preacher and engineer called Thomas Newcomen produced his more efficient version. It was slow to take on in the West Country tin-mines, but after he persuaded colliery owners in Warwickshire and Newcastle to give his engines a try, their use rapidly increased in the mining areas of Yorkshire, Lancashire and Staffordshire too. But they seemed to be for just one thing, as suggested in the description that Newcomen gave of his company: 'Proprietors of the Invention for Raising Water by Fire'. The engines were for clearing mines of water, but they used so much coal they could only be sited right beside coalmines.

Even at this point, Britain had things other countries had not – inventors, plentiful raw materials, a food surplus; and there were small local outbreaks of ingenuity. But nobody would have predicted the almost volcanic eruption of inventiveness about to take place here, such as had not happened in Italy, Germany, China, France or Japan.

To look a little more closely at this development, it may be helpful to follow the career of the man who took Newcomen's invention and changed it into something that would bring power from the coalmines into thousands of factories, onto railway tracks and aboard ships.

James Watt

The career of the engineer and engine-inventor James Watt is a classic example both of the limitations of the age and of how those limits could be suddenly and brilliantly breached. Watt's father was a crafts-man, merchant and small-time capitalist. He was based at the Scottish port of Greenock, gateway to Glasgow, where ships arrived laden with tobacco, timber, herring, linens and sugar. Watt senior sold the essen-tials of shipbuilding, designed a crane for use in the docks, invested in ships and mended the sailors' instruments. His boy James was bright, if sickly. He was good with his hands, and particularly adept at mathe-matics.

The Scotland he grew up in was already known for its high level of literacy and the practical zeal of its universities. It had become for-mally linked to England only when Great Britain had come into being, three decades before James Watt's birth, and was still a somewhat awk-ward and uncertain junior partner in the new nation. When James was nine, North Britons (as Scots sometimes called themselves), as well as Englishmen, had experienced the 1745 Jacobite rebellion. This last throw by the Catholic Stuarts had united Gaelic clans, French and Irish adventurers and Scottish and English Catholics alike. Though 'Bonnie Prince Charlie' and his supporters talked of a Stuart restoration, behind this was something more radical: a restoration of the pre-capitalist, aristocratic, feudal order, a true revolution against the New Times. The rebellion reached Derby before the clansmen, worried about the harvest and their families, headed north again. Finally defeated in 1746 by the discipline of a hardened modern army – the Battle of Culloden Moor was more like a nineteenth-century con-frontation in the colonies than a fight between well matched opponents – the revolt collapsed. It shattered not New Times but the old ways, the Gaelic and clan world of the north and west.

For a long time, at least among novelists and romantic poets, the cruelty of the victors and the poignancy of a pre-modern way of life expiring in the heather overshadowed the truth, which was that Cullo-den was good news not only for England, but for Scotland too. As one Scottish historian has put it, the 1707 Union of the two countries 'implied a Scotland with expanding horizons and possibilities; growing

commerce and trade; the good things in life';[8] success for Prince Charlie would have closed this off. Watt's life would straddle the best of
Scotland and the best of England, exemplifying the new Britain of
expanding horizons and possibilities.

After the uprising, Scottish politics was virtually cancelled. The
country was ruled from London by proxies. In Edinburgh there was
no royal court to siphon off ambition, as there was across the rest of
Europe. So two or three generations of Scots had to look elsewhere
for work and excitement. Thanks to its Presbyterian Bible-based religion, Scotland was unusually literate and its four universities were free
of the dead hand of the English Anglican establishment. At Edinburgh, Glasgow and Aberdeen students were encouraged to think
things out from first principles, to challenge received wisdom. The
result was a remarkable flowering of new thinking – the famous Scottish Enlightenment.

Watt, lacking the Greek- and Latin-based education of the English
gentleman, was prime material for this development, eagerly sucking
in the new ideas being promoted by men who would become friends,
such as the pioneering chemist Joseph Black and the philosopher of
capitalism, Adam Smith. Before that, though, he had to find himself a
living. It was no big leap for him to want to learn how to make mathematical instruments, essential accompaniments to the new scientific
learning. And in 1755 it was natural enough for him to make the long,
jolting journey south from Scotland to London, to the great stinking
metropolis, for his training. But at once Watt came up against an
ancient barrier to bright boys in a hurry. The medieval guilds, which
still controlled London's trades, tried to keep out non-locals, and
insisted all apprentices serve for seven years. Watt was an incomer anxious to get ahead fast. He wanted his training to be completed in a
year, and eventually bought it, but this dodge left him dangerously
open to the naval press-gang; writing to his father he complained that
they 'now press anyone they can get . . . unless one be either a Pren-
tice or a creditable tradesman, there is scarce any getting off again'.[9] If
Watt had been seized for the Navy, he could not have appealed to the
Lord Mayor for a reprieve, since he was already evading the apprenticeship system.

He was lucky, and got back safely to Glasgow, keen to open his
own workshop. But Glasgow, like London, was an old town ruled by

royal charter, whose guilds were trying to hang on to their stranglehold. And because Watt had no entrée with the burgesses of Glasgow,
the relevant guild, the 'Hammermen', refused him permission to open
his shop, even though there were no other mathematical instrument-
makers in Scotland at the time. Had this been a representative picture
of Britain, of a land of marauding press-gangs seizing men from the
streets to serve in the Navy, and trade guilds hanging on to their
ancient rights to the exclusion of all but their chosen few, then Watt
would have had to resign himself to a lifetime of piecework, and
nobody would have heard of him today. Or, had the Jacobites succeeded, he would have ended his days in frustration in a backstreet
workshop in Glasgow.

Instead he was saved by the Scottish Enlightenment. Specifically,
he was given a job repairing astronomical instruments that had just
arrived from Jamaica for Glasgow University. There he built up a workshop, making his own instruments and becoming indispensable to the
professors. As a practical man with no classical learning, he would
have been merely a hired hand at Oxford or Cambridge. In Glasgow,
he was soon regarded by the scientists as their social equal. He opened
his own shop in the town and began to study the latest gadgets, including steam engines. In 1763, aged twenty-seven, he was asked to repair
a model of a Newcomen engine belonging to the university. Watt
mended it, but found it infuriatingly badly made and inefficient.

The principle was easy enough: the steam went into the cylinder,
pushing up a piston. Then the steam condensed back to water, creating a vacuum, which brought the piston down again. It was the
up–down motion that drove the pump for the coalmines. The trouble
was, most of the steam escaped. How could it be made to work
better? Two years on, still puzzling over the idea of 'latent heat', a
phrase coined by his friend Black – that is, the heat taken in or thrown
out during a change of form, as when water boils or ice melts – he
suddenly found the solution. It was, at least as he recalled it, a classic
Eureka! moment.

One sunny Sunday morning in Glasgow, Watt was passing an old
wash-house (presumably a steamy sort of place) when it suddenly
came to him that since steam would rush into a vacuum wherever it
was located, he could put a separate tube or cylinder alongside the
main cylinder to take the steam and condense it back to water again. So

the main cylinder would stay hot, and far less energy would be wasted. The engine would use less coal and make more power. This doubling-up, the separate condenser, may seem a simple idea. But would it have occurred to anyone who was not both interested in scientific theory (as explained by Watt's university friends) and also a practical instrument-maker with leisure to think and room to tinker? There was a long way to go, and many frustrations, failures, wrong turnings and experimental mistakes to be met with, but Watt's understanding would transform the industrial scene, first in Britain, then around the world. He took a simple coalmine pump and made it into an engine with universal applications. Watt recalled: 'I had not walked farther than the golf-house when the whole thing was arranged in my mind.'[10]

But he could not advance without money, support and the help of other engineers. What he needed next was capital, the backing to allow him to produce prototypes, then engines for sale. Though there was a growing number of private banks in Britain, it was still too early for an inventor to go to his bank manager and hope to be loaned sufficient cash. Most entrepreneurs borrowed from friends, wives or other relatives. Watt's first backers were his physicist friend Joseph Black and, more substantially, an eager English entrepreneur, one John Roebuck.

Roebuck, like Watt, was a product of the new Britain. He was a Sheffield and Birmingham chemist who had established a successful ironworks at Carron in Stirlingshire. Its short-range cannon, known as the 'carronade', would be used by everyone from the Duke of Wellington to the Imperial Russian army, and later by the new United States. In the past, manufacturing had happened simply where it had sprung up, quite by chance. Roebuck had done things differently. He had started from first principles, asking where there was good water-power, supplies of ore, limestone and coal and good transport links, and had then built his operation from scratch. It happened to be in Scotland, but he imported his key workers from England. His action has been referred to as 'a decisive change in the structure of industry'.[11] Roebuck needed coal for his ironworks, so he had bought a coalfield near by, but found that it suffered from the perennial pre-Watt problem of too much underground water. Hearing of the Watt design, he helped fund an early version, but that one was not strong enough.

Though he went into partnership with the young engineer, Roebuck himself went bust – an early bank crash was partly responsible – and sold his share of Watt's invention to another eager Englishman, Matthew Boulton of Birmingham. That city now becomes a crucial part of the story.

Birmingham had long been a centre for blacksmiths and metalworkers. It had supplied huge numbers of swords for Cromwell's armies during the Civil War, guns for both sides during the Jacobite rebellion, and buckles and buttons for half the world. But as a town it was a late developer and enjoyed the wonderful bonus of *not* having a royal charter, so the guilds and craft companies had no hold there, which kept it open to entrepreneurs and commercial adventurers. Dissenters had gathered there, and the city already had a thriving intellectual life. Soon, members of the famous Lunar Society, experimenters such as Erasmus Darwin, Charles's brilliant grandfather, and the chemist and dissenting radical Joseph Priestley, would assemble on the Sunday nearest the full moon (so that they could get home more safely) to debate chemistry, physics, evolution, the new canals and factories, and much else.[12] Birmingham was a long way from London – and all the better for that.

Among these Lunar Men was Boulton. He was one of those eighteenth-century figures whose energy and breadth of interests compare well with any Renaissance man. His father, another Matthew, had been a successful Birmingham metalworker. Matthew the younger invented new kinds of steel buckles, which rapidly became so fashionable that they had to be exported to France, then imported back again, since clearly nothing so chic could possibly have come from Birmingham. He had gained capital by marrying an heiress, then inherited the family business in 1759 and expanded it hugely to Soho, just north of Birmingham, where he gambled everything on a huge new manufacturing centre, driven by water-power. There he arranged his workmen in designated rooms, depending on which goods were being made there – buckles, watch-chains, sword handles or metal boxes. These items were soon being sold all over Europe, but the factory – for that is what it was – depended still on specialized but manual skills, with a little help from flowing water. What Boulton needed was a more reliable source of power.

Boulton and Watt lived far apart, but moved in similar circles; both promoted the new canals, the great transport breakthrough of the pre-railway age, and both were in touch with the same natural philosophers and other enthusiasts. Boulton had met Watt in 1767 and shown off Soho to him, trying to encourage the Scot to come to Birmingham. But Watt, constantly setting his steam engine aside for other projects, was slow to respond. It was all of seven years later, after the traumatic death of his wife, that he finally decided to leave Scotland and move south. Had she lived, and had his civil engineering projects in Scotland been more successful, he would have been remembered, probably, as a designer of Highland canals.

Instead, in 1774 James Watt came south to Birmingham, and one of his coalmine engines – what he called a 'fire-engine' – was set up at Soho. It worked, not brilliantly, but well enough. Watt soon went into full partnership with Boulton, whose main business continued to be metalworking. Watt would now divide his time between two equally important tasks. He tinkered and experimented, worked away incessantly at honing his machine, introduced a series of small but crucial improvements. Having the large and experienced Soho workforce of mechanics helped considerably, but one can equally well imagine the same scene being played out on the outskirts of Paris or Hamburg.

At the same time, however, Watt and Boulton were conducting a long and ferocious legal battle in the British courts and in Parliament itself to protect their intellectual copyright against the ideas-thieves already at work. The notion that an inventor deserved a large share of the profit from his idea, that mechanical devices could make men rich, was a new one. Earlier inventors had often behaved like philanthropists, scattering their thoughts before the press and hoping, mainly, for fame. But patents, and therefore profits, were essential for stimulating the horde of bright and ambitious people who would turn industrial Britain into a kitchen garden of invention. Watt's struggles with politics and the law were wearisome, and must have seemed fruitless at times, but they were as important to the history of industrialization as was his engine. and these struggles would have achieved nothing in other European countries at the time.

Boulton, despite having received a second marital windfall (new wife, new fortune), struggled desperately for capital. Many of the new machines were sold to Cornish tin companies, who derived the money to pay for them partly from what they had saved on coal. But sharp practice and protests about monopolies, as well as slow payment for other products sold abroad, caused him serious difficulties.

Watt's engines were first employed in mines, but soon also in mills grinding flour, in breweries and then in other factories. Altogether, between 1775 and the end of the century the firm produced about 450 steam engines. Boulton was now expanding into coin production. At this time Britain was experiencing a plague of fake coinage, so crippling that the Royal Mint had stopped minting. Boulton at his 'Soho Mint' had already produced free-market coins as well as coins for foreign governments, for the British in India, and then for the British at home. Coins depended for their high quality on fixed amounts of metal, accurate shaping and industrial-scale manufacture: accuracy and reliability Boulton's new system, with its Watt engines, could deliver.

Looking back at their story, it becomes easier to see why industrialization took off first in Britain. The state was still old-fashioned. What we today call 'infrastructure' was primitive. There were some good roads and some new, useful canals, but muddy and dangerous travel was the norm. The banks were shaky, commercial law was full of holes, Parliament was a cockpit where vested interests fought the newcomers, and the country as a whole was obsessed with its overseas wars. But in both Scotland and England a vigorous, free exchange of new ideas was taking place. Far from London, and outside the ancient guild restrictions, men were able to build, trade and experiment freely, lobby the politicians and take pride in the new philosophy of capitalism explained by Watt's friend Adam Smith in his *Wealth of Nations*, published in 1776. They could also get rich. Watt and Boulton represent pioneers of railways and iron bridges, of new types of ship, gas lighting, electricity; initiators of revolutions in pottery, glass, fabrics and machine-tools, men of genius as varied as Humphry Davy, Michael Faraday and Abraham Darby. They were all remarkable. They were also all lucky: that time, that place.

Dark, Satanic and Infectious

But the industrialization of parts of Britain came at a terrible price. Wrenched from the old seasonal rhythms and religious holidays, people were being forced to work differently. During the 1700s, it has been calculated, the average number of work days in a year in Britain rose from 250 to 300. Those were lost days for living and loving, for storytelling and teaching. People who had risen with the sun found themselves stumbling to work in the dark, to artificially lit factories and workshops where they would spend twelve hours on their feet, their time regulated by large mechanical clocks. The famous coal-black factories with their huge chimneys were rare enough at first, mainly in the Lancashire cotton towns, but the packed, cheap housing and the ubiquitous coal smoke soon presented a convincing image of hell to writers as various as Charles Dickens, Friedrich Engels and Queen Victoria.

Although children had always worked in the fields, doing the lighter jobs, they were now pressed into an industrial labour force where they would be so ill-treated that even in these tough times a movement to limit their hours arose. Driven by the same Christian outrage as fuelled the anti-slavery movement, it resulted in a series of Factory Acts limiting hours and setting out health and safety require-ments. But the lives of early-nineteenth-century child workers are grimly apparent from the clauses of the first of these Acts, in 1802, which specified that children could work up to eight hours a day from the age of nine, and twelve hours from the age of fourteen; that they should not begin work until after six in the morning; and that they should sleep no more than two to a bed and get an hour's instruction in Christianity on Sundays. Even with light fines, these laws were much ignored. Further reports, scandals and laws followed; Dickens and his novelist friend Elizabeth Gaskell highlighted factory conditions in their books, and pioneering journalists explored the northern cities as if they were alien jungles – which, for middle-class southerners, they were.

Industrialization also changed the politics of the British, in many unexpected ways. During 1811–16 in Nottinghamshire, Yorkshire and Lancashire, the old artisan, cottage-based handloom weavers revolted violently against the new mechanized factory looms that were destroying their livelihoods. Taking their battle name from a fictitious woodland freedom fighter called King Lud, these 'Luddites' smashed machines, attacked employers and magistrates and, having practised night manoeuvres outside industrial cities, ended up clashing with the army. Many were hanged or sent to Australia. In 1830, agricultural workers in Kent began the 'Swing Riots' – another attack on the new job-destroying technology, in this case mechanized threshing machines.

The New Poor Law of 1834, which replaced the Elizabethan system of parish relief with a national network of grim workhouses designed to force the poorest out of the countryside and into towns to find work, or to live in deliberately harsh conditions, segregated by sex, in prison-like buildings, provoked violent protests in cities such as Bradford, Oldham and Huddersfield. In 1834, too, the 'Tolpuddle Martyrs', six agricultural labourers from Dorset who had formed a union against low wages, were transported to Australia. The popular protest that ensued resulted in a campaign that became seminal in the development of trade unionism. For many visiting continentals, from the German capitalist Engels to the French artist Gustave Doré, Britain was both an amazing example of new ways of making things and a vision of human inequality pressed too far.

Before the advent of industrialization, British politics had been a balance between the influence of the old elites – landowners and gentry – the city merchants and the clergy, plus the new entrepreneurs. Now that balance ended. From 1780 to 1830 the population of England doubled. Industrial output leapt threefold. Much of the increased wealth accrued to the towns, and governments found themselves forced to defend the property rights of mill-owners, to send soldiers to put down workers' protests, and to tilt both the law and the political system to reflect the new wealth and the new power. The House of Commons had originally been elected from constituencies whose origins were now half lost in time, many of them tiny 'rotten boroughs' bearing no relation to the growth of industrial cities. The most important tariff system, the Corn Laws, taxed imported food to protect the income of British farmers and landowners, so keeping the price of bread artificially high. In an orgy of reform, both of these imbalances would be swept aside.

The food issue had been sharpened by Britain's long war with France and her continental allies. We have seen how huge advances in British farming made the industrial revolution possible; but the further leaps in population then outpaced the farming revolution, so that by the late 1790s Britain had stopped exporting grain. 'Food security', which would be such an issue for the British during the two world wars, was a prime national concern during the Napoleonic era too. Tariffs were seen as a way of protecting and promoting home-grown food. Yet industrialization was feeding – literally – on what now had to be imported.

Though clouded by the high-flown rhetoric of free trade and the advance of civilization, this was really a fight between the more southerly Britain of the fields and the northerly Britain of the factories. In 1846 the factories, and the north, emerged as the winners, when a Tory prime minister, Robert Peel, abolished the Corn Laws at the cost of his own position. By then, the political change was under way too. The Great Reform Act of 1832 swept away the most corrupt boroughs and increased the franchise by around 60 per cent, but it failed to extend the vote to enough poorer citizens to satisfy the growing working- and middle-class movement for democracy. Much of the story of later-nineteenth-century politics would be about the constant pressure for reform, and the series of further Acts that would extend voting rights and begin to give cities like Birmingham the political clout they had lacked in the lifetimes of Watt and Boulton.

So the British state shifted from a position of essentially supporting the power of land, of the ancient city guilds and of the chartered merchant companies, to one of essentially supporting capitalism and industry. Religious controversies, always important, were gradually crowded out by class struggles, as trade unions and political reformists such as the Chartists demanded new rights. British industry had emerged victorious in the competition stakes. Having overwhelmed foreign competitors, the British began to adopt free trade as a national religion. This may have been unfair to other countries, struggling to catch up, who would require a period of protection to develop their own industries; it certainly gave the British a reputation for stinking hypocrisy, as well as for skill and hard work.

It also became clear that the optimistic theories of Adam Smith and his free-trade followers underplayed the role of war. Many of Britain's early technical skills related to her mighty fleet (think of Watt's father, and nautical instruments, and those devastating carronades). Her young consumer economy was fed by the success of British bayonets and cannon in India, America and the Caribbean. Britain would probably have been the first to industrialize anyway, but had France not been preoccupied by the revolutionary and Napoleonic wars during the crucial decades she might have run her old adversary close. (Gas-lighting, so important to making early-industrial city life safer and the days longer, got a major boost in Britain because of the massive accumulation of unwanted musket barrels after Napoleon's defeat in 1815, which were turned into gas pipes.[13])

Both of the major nations that were the next to pick up industrialization protected their own industries and used them to promote nationalism. The United States had great advantages as a rising industrial power. It had a young people, seemingly unlimited land, long rivers for transportation, large natural resources and a new, enlightened political system that positively encouraged people to challenge European orthodoxy. Germany had different advantages. After Napoleon had abolished the Holy Roman Empire, those who spoke German were still divided into around three hundred separate countries, mini-countries, micro-countries, free cities and other political flecks and speckles. But they had huge coal and iron reserves, a long and excellent tradition in metalworking and, in Prussia, a rising national leader. The Prussians drew other smaller German states into their customs union, or *Zollverein*, which encouraged free trade and began to wear away some of the maze of different measuring systems, currencies and related laws. After defeating first the Austrians and then the French, the united Germany led by Prussia was able to forge ahead at a remarkable pace.

It seemed obvious that industrial growth needed a liberal political order to thrive in. Yet most of Europe had been under the hegemony of the illiberal Habsburgs of Austro-Hungary and other, lesser monarchies, with the Russian Czar still acting as a policeman of last resort. During the nineteenth century the struggle to build liberal political states, in which capitalism and therefore modernization could thrive, was the main internal European cause. By and large liberalism and nationalism marched together. The unification of Italy, a long and complex struggle against Austrian occupiers, local monarchies with medieval origins, such as the Kingdom of the Two Sicilies and the Duchy of Modena, and against Papal conservatism, was driven by a sense that Italy needed a modern, united democratic state to pull her into the modern world. (In fact the absolute monarchs had not always done badly; the Naples-based Kingdom of the Two Sicilies had some highly effective shipyards and railway engineering companies.)

Nowhere was the tension between traditionalism and modernization sharper than in France. The post-Napoleonic monarchy curdled into a fully reactionary one under Charles X. Ousted by a revolt in July 1830, he was replaced by the more liberal Louis-Philippe, the 'bourgeois monarch'; but France lagged far behind Britain in its franchise and a formidable reform movement began to grow. The problem for middle-class liberals was that change was likely to be provoked by the poorer and angrier masses, who they themselves also feared. Poor crops and widespread hunger in turn provoked the ripple of uprisings that made 1848 the year of revolutions in Poland, across the Habsburg empire, and in smaller countries such as Denmark, Belgium and Switzerland. In France, the ancient monarchy was finally overthrown and a Second Republic declared, which would become, within four years under Louis-Bonaparte, the Second Empire. This two steps forward, one back pattern was widespread. Most of the uprisings failed, and few produced clear political advances. Perhaps their most important side-effect was the biggest new political idea of the mid-century: the messianic socialist creed of Marxism.

Karl Marx had come from a wealthy Rhineland family but spent his early adult years as a philosopher-rebel, finally finding safety in liberal Britain. With his co-author and financial supporter Friedrich Engels, he argued for a purely material vision of historical advance, in which the struggle between the rich owners of capital and industry and the workers who produced the real wealth would eventually result in a Communist world, where the working class owned the full value of their work, and the state – monarchical, bourgeois, parliamentary or republican – withered away. In *The Communist Manifesto* of 1848, addressed to rebelling German workers, he expressed himself in clear, biting and exciting imagery. His huge later work of 1867–94, *Capital*, attempted to use statistics to demonstrate the scientific truth underlying his vision. It became the secular bible of twentieth-century revolutionaries, even though Marx assumed the revolution must start in advanced Germany or Britain, rather than backward Russia. Marx's work spread among the extreme socialists of Europe but was at that time a minority taste compared with Christianity-tinged and more moderate, parliamentary visions of socialist politics. His analysis lacked the subtleties of traditional political and moral philosophers, but he had a vivid understanding of the ruthless competition hiding below the dimpled smile of bourgeois capitalism. The future would be nothing like his prediction; but the world around him in the mid-nineteenth century was very much as he described it.

Both the United States and Germany exploited technologies first developed in Britain. They stole patents, copied machines, debriefed British workers and set up their own technical colleges. This was inevitable. In an interconnected world, good ideas cannot be hidden. Anyway, key breakthroughs exploited in the British industrial revolution had themselves come from overseas – that early steam engine from France, but also the wet-spinning of flax and the Jacquard loom, and four-field crop rotation from Holland. The Japanese did the same after 1945; the Chinese are doing it now to Japan and the US. One day, with any luck, Africans will steal Chinese systems. Copying happens far more quickly than inventing.

For both the US and Germany the most important early technological innovation was the railway (though both also followed the British in digging new canals). In Britain, 1830 is often given as the year when the railway system really came of age; but it was also the year when the first US railway opened. By the 1860s, the Americans had nearly 30,000 miles of track and by 1870, 50,000 miles, compared with the 6,000 miles built in Britain during 1830–50 at the height of the 'railway mania'. By 1875 Germany too had overtaken Britain in railway miles. A similar overleaping would happen with iron and steel; but both the US and Germany would soon move on to new technologies of their own, from the telegraph to more advanced chemicals and engines. In both cases industrialization drove, and was driven by, nationalism. In the US the railways knitted together a new, huge country. Whereas in Britain they had been built by private money and labour, which often had to fight politicians trying to obstruct new lines, in the US the government loaned army engineers to help. In Germany, though the first railways were designed to link the industrial towns, unification made the railways a key agent in binding the new nation into one.

Capitalist-industrialist theory emphasized openness and free markets, and argued that the more trade, the less national conflict. In practice, nationalism and capitalist industrialization marched in lock-step. The American experience involved cartels, bribery scandals, political corruption and the brutal suppression of workers' organizations, as well as the racist exclusion of some would-be industrial workers, such as the Chinese, by others, such as the Irish. Industrialization was a far more violent and less pure process than early writers on capitalism had hoped and expected. The theory, nice though it was, had emerged from the unique experience of the British as the first, unchallenged seedbed of this momentous change in human life. And there were many places where it would completely fail to take root.

From Card-player to Saint: Russia's Lost Opportunity

The scene was a small but fashionable Russian resort town in the foothills of the Caucasus mountains, Pyatigorsk, in the summer of 1853. An artillery officer, a keen but disorganized soldier who had been fighting Chechen rebels on behalf of the Czar, was in a bad way. He was in many respects a typical young aristocrat of his time. He had gambled away huge sums at gaming tables in St Petersburg, as well as here with army colleagues. His career was in the doldrums. He dreamt of a more modern Russia, less under the thumb of the Czar and his censors, while he wrote war stories. He had chased many women, not least using his position as a landowner to jump on serf girls, and constantly made plans to reform his life, then forgot them again. With his large brow and huge fringe, he was a striking figure – glaring, almost wolf-like.

Now his gambling debts were getting on top of him. A few months before, he had had to get his brother-in-law to sell a second village on his estate, along with its twenty-six serfs and their families – people were disposed of like so many coins. Now he realized he would have to sell the main house itself, the place built by his grandfather, where he had been born. He signed the chit. The grand house was duly bought by a rival landowner, who had it taken apart, loaded it all onto wagons and rebuilt it on his own land. Left behind were two much smaller wings of the house, a gaping hole between them.

Neither the casual selling of serfs to pay card debts nor the exploitation of serf women was unusual behaviour among Russia's bored, pampered, discontented noble sons. But this man was Leo

Tolstoy, in his late twenties. The world's greatest-ever novelist, he would become a figure of moral authority not only in Russia, where he would be idolized, but around the world. In later life, with his flowing patriarchal beard and dressed in a peasant smock, he would call for Russians to recover their peasant roots, immerse themselves in country life, educate their former serfs and pursue the highest Christian ideals. Returning to live in one of the wings of the formerly grand country house he had sold, Yasnaya Polyana, near Tula, about 120 miles from Moscow, Tolstoy would spend much of the rest of his life trying to atone for his youthful sins. Part of the power of his writing in *War and Peace* and *Anna Karenina* derives from his ruthlessly honest exposure of his own addictions and selfishness, and the delight and zest with which he embraced rural Russia.

Three years after that last gambling disaster in the Caucasus, Tolstoy was back at his estate, learning to live in the diminished house – the hole where the central section stood is now covered by trees but must then have been a daily embarrassment.

Tolstoy had taken part in the Russian defence of Sebastopol during the eleven-month siege in 1854/5 that would decide the outcome of the Crimean war. The conflict between Czarist Russia on the one side, and Britain, France and Turkey on the other, was really about Russia's ambitions to drive ever further south through Asia, threatening other imperial powers. It had been a shock for all the armies involved. Great bravery on each side had failed to disguise the incompetence, poor equipment and outdated tactics of the British cavalry, the French infantry and the Russian forces too – but it was the Russians who eventually lost and the Czar's prestige that fell furthest.

Russia had a new Czar, Alexander II, brought up by comparatively liberal intellectuals. He realized that from now on it was impossible to argue that Russia, having lost a war on her very doorstep, had successfully modernized. The Russian soldiers who had fought and died to defend their motherland were, for the most part, also serfs. That is, they were tied to the land and could be treated as chattels by their owners. The same had been true of the Russian armies that had defied Napoleon in 1812 and then defeated him in 1813. Then, some of the officers felt they had earned their freedom in battle. They were ignored; but the same feeling resurfaced with greater force after the Crimea.

Wars often radicalize, and defeats do so more than do victories. In

March 1856, Alexander gave a speech in which he warned the landowners that he intended to abolish serfdom from above, by law, rather than wait for it to abolish itself from below in some kind of uprising. Alexander and his advisers knew it would be difficult. Many landowners would be outraged. There were practical problems, such as creating a new system of law and local government in the countryside to replace the serf system. Then there was the embarrassing fact that many landowners were already broke: their lands and their serfs were mortgaged and technically owned by banks in Moscow and St Petersburg. Most land was useless and valueless without the serf labour that kept it fertile. The serfs would starve without land of their own, and they had no money. So this was a huge and convoluted project, and would be one of the most dramatic attempts at reform from above ever made. It was also awesome in scale. A census of 1857, four years before the serfs were freed, showed that more than a third of Russians, some twenty-three million people, were serfs. That compares with some four million black American slaves at the time.

Serfdom went back to feudal, even classical, times and originally meant simply agricultural labour that was tied to land, with a surplus to be handed over to the owner – church, baron or city. As we have seen, it had slowly died out in Western Europe, getting a hefty shove from the labour shortages caused by the Black Death. Even there, a few forms of serfdom remained until quite late – Scottish coalminers were serfs until 1799. To the east, serfdom was far more widespread. It had arrived later but was successfully imposed by landowners and monarchs for far longer. In the eighteenth century and well into the nineteenth, serfs could be found in Poland, Prussia, Austria, Hungary and many of the smaller German states. Russian serfdom, however, was of a different scale and order.

The Russian serfs were not quite slaves (though the word 'serf' comes from the Latin for 'slave'). Their owners could not kill them, or sell them abroad. Outright slavery, which mainly existed for house servants, had been abolished by Peter the Great in 1723. But from the 1550s onwards, the laws of Muscovy had given landowners ever greater powers over their peasants. A century later, full serfdom became general in the agricultural 'black soil' regions of central Russia. Serfs were tied to their landowners' fields and villages, and harsh penalties were imposed for trying to escape. Often they were forbidden to marry anyone from outside their estate. As Tolstoy had demonstrated, they could be bought and sold along with the land; those needed to farm the land were kept, while 'surplus' serfs could be sent to work for others. They could be freely punished by their owners: this included beating. Serf girls and women were often raped by their owners. Very few serfs were literate.

The gap between the grander Russian landowners, who spoke French and enjoyed frequent trips to St Petersburg, or abroad, and their serfs was as large as that between English rulers of the Raj and ordinary Indians, or Caribbean sugar plantation owners and African slaves. The closest parallel is with the American plantations where, just as on the Russian estates, entire communities lived cut off from city life, with their own bakeries, orchards, accommodation, stables, granaries and justice system. So Russian serfdom was hardly unique in the oppressive atmosphere it generated. For near-subsistence farmworkers, in any part of the world, who had to send some of their crop and livestock to owners, degrees of freedom were largely theoretical. The rise of Russian serfdom coincided, after all, with that of full-blown absolutism in France. Peasants led lives not much freer under the Bourbons than those of Russian serfs under the Romanovs.

Yet Russian serfdom had unique aspects that made Russia feel fundamentally different from Western European societies. For a start, there was no ethnic divide in Russia between owner and serf. They were all the same mix, mostly Slav with some Tatar and sometimes some German. Master, mistress and servants looked alike and had similar names. Serfs, living for generations on the same dark soil, sharing the old stories and the old music, devoutly adhering to the Orthodox religion, seemed to many liberal Russian landowners more 'real', more authentically Russian than they were themselves. To numerous writers and intellectuals Russia seemed uniquely cursed, but when at times radicals tried to 'go towards' the serfs and befriend them, these sceptical, conservative-minded peasants regarded them with bafflement or hostility.

For tens of thousands of poorer landowners there was not even a big cultural divide between them and their human 'property'. Serfs cooked in the master's kitchen, suckled and brought up his children, told stories around the fire and taught the lore of the countryside to the little nobles growing up amongst them. They shared hunting trips.

Serfs could be the talented craftworkers, musicians, decorators and builders that their owners relied on for goods and services, as better-off Western Europeans relied on free, waged workers. Landowners could be asked by the patriarchs of serf families to resolve family disputes. So there was an intimacy in Russian serfdom as experienced in houses and villages remote from the cities, that some Russian landowners felt to be both more embarrassing and more emotionally touching than rural servitude in some other places.

Russian serfdom was not in any sense a form of early capitalism. The slavery of the sugar and cotton plantations came about because humans were used as field machinery in a new system of trade and capital accumulation. Russian agriculture was actually held back by serfdom, since nobody – not the landlord, worried about revolt, nor the serf, who did not own the land he worked on – had an urgent interest in investment for agricultural improvement. Above all, serfdom in Russia cannot be understood without bearing in mind that the Russian autocratic system, which we saw beginning to harden as far back as the reign of Ivan the Terrible, felt dangerously unstable.

The Czars were at the top of the pile, but they were regularly murdered in palace coups, often led by senior officers; or later, assassinated. The nobility, which had been organized in strict order of rank – according to the Table of Ranks of 1722 – were formally the servants, even the slaves, of the Czar; and for much of this period they owed him service, to be conducted in state offices – the army, the law and local government. They often depended on the Czar for their incomes, since the Russian agricultural output was so low; and ultimately, on the Czar's authority to keep them above the serfs. Protests and peasant rebellions were frequent enough – nearly eighteen hundred outbreaks of 'disorder' were recorded between 1826 and 1856 – to keep them on their toes.[14] Yet the Czar could not possibly rule Russia without the nobility. Even after Czar Peter III freed them from their obligation to serve him, in 1762, the formal system of serfs-serve-nobles-then-nobles-serve-Czar remained the idea behind the Russian state. At times it seems to have felt more like a three-way stand-off.

The great rebellion against this state of affairs had happened after the Russians' war with Napoleon, which during 1812–14 brought many young Russian aristocrats deep into Western Europe. In Paris they imbibed the new spirit of the Enlightened age. It tasted better than vodka. When they marched home again, they felt newly ashamed and embarrassed by the archaic, fossilized nature of the Czarist state.

In December 1825 rebel officers, later known as the 'Decembrists', launched a revolt in St Petersburg against a new Czar, Nicholas I, after his brother Constantine had refused to accept the throne. After a five-hour confrontation between rebel and loyalist troops in the centre of the city, the Czar ordered his men to begin firing, and the rebellion collapsed. Five conspirators were hanged, and 121 were stripped of their titles and sent into exile in Siberia. There, many were joined by their wives and families and lived not as landowners but as simple farmers. The sons of one were described by their mother as playing with the local peasants, fishing for trout, trapping rabbits, hunting for birds' nests and 'camping in the woods with the wild boys'. Their father also went native, growing a long beard, ceasing to wash and working in the fields. His name was Sergei Volkonsky and he was a cousin of Tolstoy's, who met him when he finally returned from exile; he based one of his central characters in *War and Peace* on the admirable older man.[15]

These 'Decembrists' were in general a great inspiration to the younger generation of Tolstoy's time. Remorse for his gambling, shame about his position as an owner of serfs, and admiration for the liberal exiles of 1825, all fused in Tolstoy's mind. It was the same, or similar, for many other liberal landowners and writers. Among the less likely liberals in 1856 was the new Czar Alexander II himself. After the failure in the Crimea he began to work on widespread reforms, including reform of the army, the civil service and the criminal code, and a loosening of censorship. But his most dramatic move related to serfdom. It would go, outright. Even the serfs were suspicious about that. How much land would they get for themselves? Would it really be something for nothing?

Tolstoy got an early glimpse of what might happen when, in 1856, after Alexander's announcement of forthcoming reform but before the emancipation law had been agreed, he decided to give all his serfs their personal freedom, and to sell them land cheaply over the next thirty years. He called a meeting at Yasnaya Polyana (which translates, roughly, as 'Bright Meadow'), but found them highly suspicious. A recent biographer of Tolstoy says: 'The peasants were convinced they would be given their freedom when the new czar was crowned, and so believed Tolstoy's offer of a contract was just a cunning ruse to swindle them. After several more meetings they refused all his revised offers.'[16] Tolstoy travelled abroad, meeting the former exile Volkonsky, before settling down at Yasnaya Polyana again to write and enjoy a spot of domestic bliss. (Though his wife, producing thirteen children and spending her spare time copying out his near-illegible manuscripts, found life rather less blissful.)

He did eventually manage to free all his serfs to till their own land. He built a school at his own expense for the peasants' children (a rather high proportion of them, his own illegitimate sons) and taught them himself, by now dressing in peasant clothes. He wrote children's books to help spread literacy throughout Russia. As a local magistrate he would help the peasantry against his own class, and he told the local children he was determined to become a peasant himself. He was, however, a rotten farmer, managing to starve his pigs to death. After he had dismissed his stewards, the historian Orlando Figes writes, 'The experiment was a complete failure . . . He did not know how to cure hams, how to make butter, when to plough or hoe the fields, and he soon became fed up and ran away to Moscow.'[17]

While Tolstoy was struggling with his pigs and his conscience, Alexander's ministers were struggling with hostile landowners and foot-dragging committees, as the Czar tried to find a way of freeing Russia's serfs without making the nobles rebel against him. The result was the Emancipation of Serfdom manifesto of March 1861. It was a noble-sounding document, published two years before Abraham Lincoln's Emancipation Proclamation freeing US slaves, but it would satisfy almost nobody. Tolstoy heard about it while he was abroad, during his only visit to London, where he had just heard Charles Dickens give a public reading, visited some schools, and made use of the library at the new Victoria and Albert Museum. He realized at once that the manifesto's high-flown language and tone would not be understood by the peasantry.

What he did not know was just how limited emancipation would be. The landowners fought doggedly to keep as much as possible of their status, with the result that for nearly half a century to come, the freed serfs would have to make huge payments to the government for land they regarded as their own. The government, in turn, compensated the landowners. These payments were based on inflated estimates of the value of the land, while to further compensate the nobility the peasants' share overall was cut, by up to a quarter. Though freed to marry who they liked, to trade and own property, they would stay under the control of their own local courts, would need passports to travel, and would continue to be subject to corporal punishment.

This was so far from what the Russian peasantry had hoped for, such a bitter disappointment that there were nearly nineteen hundred outbreaks of disorder in 1861, some involving bloody repression by troops. Landowners bemoaned their new relative poverty, and the loss of their ability to directly punish 'their' peasants in the old way. Over time, many peasants left the land and migrated to the cities, where they would become the new factory workers and where their children would one day become the raw proletarian material for Lenin's Bolshevik revolution.

The Czar continued to try to reform the censorship laws, education, the law, the military and local government. A well informed newspaper reader in Paris or London in the early 1860s might well have compared the terrible civil war tearing the United States apart with the comparatively orderly reform programme being run from St Petersburg, and assumed that Russia would become the stronger power. Czarist Russia had started far behind the USA in its industrial development, but was growing fast by the 1880s. In truth, Russian autocracy had no answer to the growing demands of people who were freed, but freed to be poor, or to those of intellectuals who wanted full democracy. During the later years of Alexander II's reign, revolutionary and terrorist groups spread. Terrible famines underlined the continuing backwardness and weakness of Russian agriculture and society. When the Czar was blown up by a terrorist bomb in 1881, his successor Alexander III abruptly ended the period of reforms and restored the censors and the secret police.

Tolstoy watched the condition of Russia with mounting despair. He was no enthusiast for urbanization or industrialization. Moscow he found a place of 'stench, stones, luxury, poverty, debauchery', in which the displaced peasants 'wax our floors, rub our bodies in the bath and ply as cabmen'.[18] After the huge success of his novels he buried himself in country pursuits – beekeeping, growing orchards, hunting – as well as fathering his huge family and looking after his school, and all interspersed with more writing and some satisfyingly vicious literary quarrels. By the later 1870s he was talking of becoming a monk. Artists and writers came to pay homage to this apparent secular saint, who advocated Christian rural simplicity and seemed to offer a third way between Czarist repression and socialist revolution.

By the beginning of the twentieth century, Tolstoy was a globally famous guru, a lifetime's journey away from the brash young artillery officer who had lost his home, his villages and his serfs at the card table. He may also have become something of an egomaniac and a bore (gurus mostly are), but his life story still shows a satisfying arc of learning and redemption, which his Russia never managed. His home remains a monument to a lost Eden, with its plain rooms, its library of elevating books, orchards, schoolhouse, granaries and woodland, where Tolstoy lies buried in a simple earth mound. Around the estate, however, the impoverished, ugly Russia of a century of war and political failure is all too close at hand. Had the 1860s seen a convulsion there as dramatic as the American Civil War – to which we now turn – then perhaps the old Russia could have evolved into a country of middle-class business, prosperous cities and democracy. We cannot know.

Liberty's Victory, by the Skin of Her Teeth

They were days of exhaustion and relief, of sadness and delight. On 4 April 1865, a steamer called the *Malvern* was making her way upriver from Washington, capital of the United States of America, to Richmond, Virginia, former capital of the Confederacy. Jefferson Davis, the President of the Confederate, or rebel, states, had been attending church when a cavalry officer arrived with a note from his top general, Robert E. Lee, telling him to flee. As Richmond resounded to the explosions of powder magazines and the noise of hungry crowds looting food stores and slurping whisky – which was also running in the gutters – the town's bridges were blown up and its governing body, huddled in carts and carriages, disappeared in a haze of dust. The *Malvern* chugged on up the James River, past dead horses, wrecked boats and flotsam, until she ran aground. A twelve-oared boat was lowered and into it clambered a leathery, whiskery man with a buzzard's nose and a beard like a hearth-brush. Abraham Lincoln had come to see for himself the capital of the rebellion that had come so close to destroying America's republican dream.

Lincoln strode ashore at a place called Rockett's Landing and found a crowd waiting for him, without a white face to be seen. He had not intended the Civil War to be a liberation struggle for America's slaves; but as it had worsened and his position had grown more desperate, he had issued his famous Declaration of Emancipation. Now he was greeted by shouting black Americans calling him 'the great Messiah' and 'Jesus Christ'. As a sixty-year-old man went down on his knees in front of him, Lincoln said: 'Don't kneel to me. You must kneel only to God and thank him for your freedom.' The man replied that after so many years in the desert without water, he was looking 'on our spring of life'. Surrounded by former slaves, Lincoln shook their hands and, with just a dozen sailors as protection, began the two-mile walk to the centre of the hungry, burning city.

Lincoln was soon at the middle of a larger, mixed crowd. The Southern whites, his recent enemies, simply stared. One of those walking with Lincoln remembered: 'Every window was crowded with heads. Men were hanging from tree-boxes and telegraph-poles. But it was a silent crowd. There was something oppressive in those thousands of watchers without a sound, either of welcome or hatred. I think we would have welcomed a yell of defiance. I stole a look sideways at Mr Lincoln. His face was set.'[19] But nobody fired.

In this Holy Week, on 9 April, an immaculately dressed Lee would surrender his famous Army of Northern Virginia to the grimy figure of General Ulysses Grant. Lee had calculated that further bloodshed, whether on the battlefield or by guerrilla bands, would be futile. The war was over. The North went wild with joy and the beaten Confederacy mourned. Five days later, on 14 April, Good Friday 1865, Lincoln, back in Washington, was receiving congratulations from a seemingly endless stream of well-wishers who told him they had never doubted he would win. Less than a year earlier he had thought he was finished, that he would lose both presidency and war. Still, this was a good day.

Lincoln enjoyed the theatre, a rare relaxation. He had been warned by friends in Washington that showing himself, with no guards, in public, was dangerous. Seated in his box, he and his friends would be unable – in the words of one protesting friend a year earlier

– to defend themselves 'from any able-bodied woman in this city'.[20] But Lincoln had just walked right through the rebel capital. He was not inclined to heed warnings in his own.

He was not much inclined to go to the particular play being offered, either. Called *Our American Cousin* and playing at Ford's Theater, it was a weak comic offering spattered with puns, by an English dramatist called Tom Taylor, though it did have a popular actress, Laura Keene, as its star. Lincoln's wife begged him to come. He agreed. General Grant and his wife were supposed to accompany them, but cried off – Grant detested social occasions – and the President's intention to attend was advertised in that afternoon's papers. He spent the intervening time working on his cabinet papers and meeting an aggrieved black woman whose husband had been refused his army pay. He promised to take up her case. He told his wife he had never felt happier. Yet Lincoln may have had some presentiment of disaster. For the first time he raised the possibility that sometime he would be assassinated, and said he did not really want to go to the theatre – he would go, but only so as not to disappoint the public.

Sitting in his flag-bedecked presidential box, hidden from most of the audience, Lincoln was being guarded – just not very well. His assassin had bored a peep-hole from the neighbouring box and, having barred the door, was able to slip in behind him. Carrying a dagger in one hand and a single-shot Derringer pistol in the other, he shot the President from less than five feet away. The bullet passed diagonally from the left side of his skull through his brain, lodging behind his right eye. A young major who was sitting with the Lincolns was stabbed but tried to grab the assassin, who leapt onto the stage, becoming entangled with the Stars and Stripes. Despite breaking his ankle, he managed to get away before the audience had any idea of what was happening. Lincoln's unconscious body was carried to a house opposite the theatre. There he died at 7.22 the following morning, surrounded by weeping members of his family and cabinet. There had also been an attempt to kill William Seward, Lincoln's secretary of state, and plans to kill the vice-President too.

The presidential killer was John Wilkes Booth, one of the ten children of an actor who had been named after Brutus, the assassin of Caesar, and who had named his John Wilkes after the radical English writer. The boy grew up bookish and wanting to act. A fervent defender of the Confederate cause, he had watched the public hanging of the violently anti-slavery rebel John Brown. Booth's father had been a good actor, though an alcoholic prone to bouts of insanity (which is very common among actors). The son was a less good actor who had once nearly killed himself on stage in an accident with his dagger. In fact, he was something of a buffoon. He loathed Lincoln, but was also consumed with guilt for not taking up arms in the Confederate army himself. He wanted to strike a blow for the doomed South. But the motives of assassins are rarely surprising or even interesting.

Though Lincoln's death shocked the world and turned him into America's greatest democratic martyr, whose giant memorial statue in Washington makes him seem more the nation's father than Washington himself, it is as well to remember that, at the time, this assassination delighted many Americans. One Texan newspaper, for instance, the Houston *Telegraph*, said that until God's judgement day,

> the minds of men will not cease to thrill at the killing of Abraham Lincoln . . . It goes upon that high judgment roll for nations and for universal man, with the slaying of Tarquin, of Caesar, of Charles I, of Louis XVI, of Marat . . . Not a soldier, nor a woman, an old man nor a lisping child with true heart to this Southern land but feels the thrill, electric, divine, at this sudden fall in his own blood of the chief of our oppressors.[21]

Lincoln's war was the most important conflict of the nineteenth century, more significant than the imperial wars fought by the British or the wars of liberation in South America, or the war Russia lost in the Crimea. It can be plausibly argued that it was more important than the wars fought and finally lost by Napoleon at the beginning of the century, too. French hegemony over the rest of the European mainland would never have lasted, given the limitations of armies and communications at the time; but the American Civil War locked together a huge nation which otherwise would have fragmented, and probably into more than two parts. By doing this, the war created the superpower of the following century. Had the United States broken up in the 1860s, then there would probably have been no Atlantic aid in 1917 or 1941 for the embattled European democracies, nor a single power so great that it could later confront the Soviet empire. It was also a turning-point for the concept of republican government, which was still rare. Quiet supporters of the Confederate cause included most of the Conservative and aristocratic right in Great Britain, Napoleon III in France, and the monarchical party in Spain. Lincoln's war changed America; and therefore changed the modern world.

Its bare statistics measure up to the scale. The American Civil War of 1861–5 was the most lethal war fought by any country in the West between 1815, Napoleon's final defeat at Waterloo, and the German advance into Belgium which started the First World War. It was easily the most lethal war in US history. Some 620,000 soldiers died, only 60,000 short of the deaths of US servicemen in every other war put together. Four times as many Americans died in a single Civil War battle, Antietam, as died on D-day in 1944. A quarter of all the white males of serving age in the Confederacy were killed.[22]

But what was the war about?

It had not started as an attempt to end slavery in America. Lincoln was a consistent and loud opponent of slavery. For many Americans, particularly in the South, his election as President made the war inevitable. But he had been very clear that he did not mean to abolish slavery in the states that already practised it. He only meant to ensure that slavery did not spread into the new states being carved out of the US landmass, and to maintain the authority of the federal government over all states existing up to then. In a letter written at the start of the war he declared: 'My paramount object in this struggle is to save the Union, and is not either to save or destroy slavery. If I could save the Union without freeing any slave I would do it.' He believed that slavery would eventually die out, even if it took until the following century, and he took seriously the idea that America's blacks might all be sent to Africa. Yet in an address to the newly formed Republican Party in 1858 he acknowledged that the slavery argument could not be avoided: 'A house divided against itself cannot stand. I believe this government cannot endure permanently half slave, and half free . . . It will become all the one thing or all the other.'

Now that slavery is almost universally regarded with abhorrence, the rise of anti-slavery opinion in the North, driven by Protestant clergy and others influenced by the European Enlightenment, seems inevitable. The more interesting question is why slavery was such a powerful force across the southern United States, and why it provoked so many people who felt themselves to be honourable, religious and decent, to die and kill in order to defend their 'peculiar institution'. It was not because most were themselves slave-holders. Of the eight million whites in the fifteen slave states at the beginning of the war, just 383,000 had slaves, of whom half had fewer than five. A small minority of whites, some three thousand out of those eight million, had more than a hundred slaves, and so were very roughly equivalent to the popular image of grandees in big houses with slave plantations.[23] The majority even of the slave-holders were relatively small-time farmers working alongside their slaves; in fact, most people in the South were just farmers, often struggling on poor land.

American slavery, though it long pre-dated the Declaration of Independence, had been an intimate vice of the founding fathers of the United States. Both George Washington and Thomas Jefferson were slave-owners, as were most of the grandees of Virginia and the other southern states. They might have felt the odd tweak of conscience, but they could not run their complex agricultural businesses without it. At the time of independence, slavery was legal in all the thirteen states. In the South, tobacco, sugar, rice and cotton required grindingly hard work in the fields, and without mass immigration or the willingness of native Americans to do this work, slavery seemed the only option. In the northern states, where the climate and soil necessitated a different kind of farming, it was far less widespread. The enforced discipline of the field-work, often for fourteen hours a day, did produce an agriculture that has been calculated as 35–50 per cent more efficient than that of the free northern states, making the South, at the beginning of the war, richer than any European country except Britain. Far from being a basket-case economy, as later northern propaganda suggested, it has been argued that 'Only Sweden and Japan have been able to sustain long-term growth rates substantially in excess of that achieved by the ante-bellum South between 1840 and 1860.'[24]

So this was a boom economy which urgently wanted to spread into new US states such as Kansas and Texas. To understand what was at stake, we have to remember the extraordinary, westward-leaping expansion of the new republic. Jefferson, the third US President, had prepared a grid of new lands, mapping out fourteen new states. During the Napoleonic wars, his government had vastly increased the size of the US in a single deal, perhaps the most significant real-estate deal of all time, the 'Louisiana Purchase', mentioned earlier. In April 1803 Napoleon, who like most conquerors was short of money, and was fixing his sights on an invasion of his last remaining serious foe, Britain, had sold the sprawl of French-claimed territories west of the US to Washington, announcing that irresolution was no longer in season: 'I renounce Louisiana.' For $15 million, arranged by Barings Bank of London, the Americans got land more than twice the size of what King George had surrendered, taking the borders of the country to the Rocky Mountains. In 1812 they fought and lost a war against the British which they had hoped would bring them Canada as well, yet had only resulted in the burning and occupation of Washington.

But this barely halted the story of expansion. In 1819 the Spanish gave up Florida too. The old barrier of the Appalachians was breached, and within thirty years half of the citizens of the US were living beyond them, reaching deep into the continent's heartland. The spread continued at breakneck speed. Texas, seized from the Mexican Spanish and starting out as an independent state (which briefly toyed with the idea of joining the British Empire), became part of the US in 1845. Three years later, after a vicious war with Mexico, the US purchased all of California and New Mexico for another paltry sum.

The great question was: what kind of society would this new America be once its original inhabitants had been defeated, killed or shoved into reservations? For the time being, most of the new territories were wild and lawless: 'mountain men', trappers, explorers, fevered gold-prospectors and adventurers were pushing hard westward against the divided native people. But already two different versions of the US were apparent. To the south was a slave and plantation economy, which hoped and expected to expand, perhaps even into the Caribbean and Latin America. To the north was first the small-farmer economy, then quickly the industrial economy driven by European immigrants – Germans, Irish, Scandinavians, as well as English and Scots. This was essentially an urban-capitalist America, with strong Christian-Protestant influences echoing the hostility to slavery by now so vehement in Britain.

One by one those northern states had abolished slavery on their own territory, beginning with Vermont in 1777. By 1804 all the northern states were at least in the process of doing so, and in 1808

Congress, following the British lead a year earlier, voted to end American involvement in the Atlantic slave trade. But this only led to a programme of internal slave-trading and slave-breeding developing in the cotton and sugar-growing South. The founders of the Union understood very well that this was a dangerous division. John Adams, one of the original Boston rebels and the second US President, feared that it might 'produce as many Nations in North America as there are in Europe'.[25] In 1820 a rough deal had been struck, the Missouri Compromise, dividing the continent laterally along a line south of which slavery was allowed, and north of which it was not. But nobody thought this could hold, once the great expansion began. There was too much land and money in play.

The South had been accustomed to dominate Washington politics, providing a disproportionate number of Presidents, judges, leading Congressmen and senators. It was affronted by the growing power of the anti-slavery campaigners of the North. In 1850 things nearly came to a head when California was admitted to the Union. Southern threats to secede were only halted by a last-minute compromise that it should be admitted as a non-slavery state, but that fugitive slaves who escaped to the North must be returned. Yet the pressure piled up again. We saw earlier how the railway was transforming America, but the real prize was a line connecting the Pacific to the Atlantic. The promise of such a huge investment was partly what kept California in the Union. But to make the connection with the new industrial hub of Chicago, the line would have to run through Kansas and Nebraska. This would bring statehood for Kansas, a territory north of the Missouri line, which ought therefore to have been free. But Kansas also had land suitable for tobacco and hemp, which attracted the slave-owning plantation lobby.

Pro-slavery politicians argued that it was the right of new states like Kansas to decide their own destiny. Owners, with their slaves, poured in from one direction. Abolitionists and northern farmers poured in from another. A spectacularly vicious guerrilla war began, with atrocities committed by both sides. John Brown, the militant abolitionist, whose hanging was watched by Booth and whose corpse featured in a famous Union war song, led a raid of blacks and whites on Harpers Ferry, a small town in West Virginia with an arsenal. He had hoped to start a general slave insurrection, and failed. Caught and hanged, he became a martyr for the North and a terrorist in the eyes of the South.

So by the time the war began there was already a trail of blood, and huge unresolved arguments about the limitations of slavery in America. There had also been passionate warnings from the southern states that they would leave the Union rather than submit.

The final key factor was the growing economic and demographic power of the industrial North. Immigrants went there for the jobs; in the plantations of the South, there was little that poor whites from Europe wanted to do. The raw figures on industrial development at the time tell the tale. Of the money invested in manufacturing in America, just 18 per cent came from the South. The North had nine times the South's industrial capacity, two and a half times as many people, the vast majority of the new European immigrants, and far higher rates of literacy. The new America growing to the north-west, with cities like Chicago and Detroit, was on the urbanizing, capitalist side. The South had three times as many illiterate whites as the North. So the plantations may have been more efficient than the northern farms, and in their own way plugged into a global economy, but this was a fight between entire societies, and one side had started off as clearly more developed than the other.

These are the economic and geographical facts. Layered on top of them were cultural differences which may have felt, to those involved, more important. In the South many regarded slavery as a natural human system, with honourable origins in biblical and classical times, and actually kinder than the industrial 'wage-slavery' of the northern cities, with their 'factory niggers'. This had a germ of truth. By 1850, children born as slaves in the South lived on average a dozen years longer than children born in the industrial heart of England, in Manchester. The slave population was growing fast, no longer needing to be topped up by Atlantic-plying ships, which suggested a certain level of health. For the pro-slavery Americans, slaves were also property, and property rights were fundamental to their constitutional rights, something the federal government had no authority to tamper with. Had not slavery existed *throughout* the US at the time of the thirteen colonies' rebellion? Confederates would put the face of the slave-owners Jefferson and Washington on their banknotes.

Most Southerners were poor whites or slaves, but the Confederacy presented itself not just as a hierarchical, romantic and conservative society, but as finer-grained and more humanly authentic than the seething, turbulent Yankee North. There are links between the aristocratic values of the English royalists of that earlier Civil War, the Jacobite romantics of the following century, and the southern US planters' attitudes. They shared a distaste for the merchant values of the city, which would develop into deep loathing for the values of urban, industrial capitalism. We have already seen how the defeat of absolute monarchy in England, and then of the Jacobite cause in Scotland, pushed forward enlightenment, science and then industry. To the south, all this was anathema. At the beginning of the war, William Howard Russell, the London *Times*'s fine reporter, remarked that the South was ferociously hostile to 'trade, commerce, the pursuit of gain, manufacture and the base mechanical arts'.[26] One American historian of slavery writes of a ruling elite in the slave states, with their aristocratic spirit, 'emphasizing family and status, a strong code of honour, and aspirations to luxury, ease and accomplishment'.[27]

This is the South of *Gone with the Wind* and romantic cavalier-generals, tresses waving and moustaches bristling, charging the Union infantry, as if Prince Rupert of the Rhine had been born again to ride through Virginia, or Bonnie Prince Charlie were fighting for Kentucky. This is also, of course, the South of Lost Causes, but it cannot be stated too strongly that nothing about this war, despite the industrial imbalance, was inevitable.

One of the best and least partisan historians of the conflict, James McPherson, points out that to win the war as it had developed by 1863, the North had to conquer vast territories, cripple the southern economy and destroy its armies; a tough task – so that 'Northern superiority in manpower and resources was a *necessary* but not *sufficient* cause of victory.' The South only had to hang on and survive. McPherson argues that there is a plausible parallel world in which, with a few twists of fate, the rebel states could have won the war – in which case history would have careered off in a very different direction.

Had Lincoln, the steely Kentucky lawyer and political genius, not been elected in the first place – or had he lost the presidency, as he very nearly did, halfway through the war – the North might have had to come to terms with slavery. Had the brilliant southern generals

'Stonewall' Jackson and Robert E. Lee had a little more luck, they might have defeated the northern armies so decisively, before the arrival of better northern generals such as Sherman, that the Union side's will to fight could have collapsed. It came close to doing so in any case. There were moments when incompetent Union generalship and rising discontent about Lincoln and the war – including the worst riots in US history in New York, killing 120 people during protests against the draft – came close to winning political victory for the Confederacy.

Eventually the sheer force of the more populous, industrial, better organized North, which avoided the food shortages and the rampant inflation plaguing the South, brought devastation to its cities along with Lee's surrender. But it was a close-run thing – as close-run as the near-German victory in the Great War just as US forces began arriving in Europe. That really was a war whose outcome revolved on particular battles and personalities, one reason why it continues to exert such a grip on historians' imaginations.

So why did they fight, that majority of southern manhood who were neither slave-owners nor wealthy, but a quarter of whom perished, leaving many of the rest mutilated? In the end, their letters suggest that it was loyalty to home, family, local traditions that mattered most. They were fighting against what they saw as the arrogant assumptions of alien cities, against a threatening and colder future of wages, factory bosses and hypocritical Yankee preachers. Some of the Confederate soldiers were themselves opposed to slavery. Robert E. Lee thought it a pernicious institution and owned no slaves of his own. He resigned his Union commission and fought on the Confederate side only because he could not desert his home, Virginia, and his family. Many felt similarly. They were fighting for Georgia or Tennessee or South Carolina, for their drinking friends and their cousins and parents. They were fighting for locality against nationhood.

Their defeat not only soldered the South and North together under the rule of a federal government that had become far more powerful as a consequence of the war; it also allowed the last big surge west, as the US we know today finally took shape. The railroad whose Kansas track had helped provoke the war would bring settlements right across the central plains and deserts of America. Demobbed soldiers from both armies headed west, looking for a fresh start. The native Americans of the Plains – people including the Sioux, the Cheyenne and the Arapaho, who when they embraced the horse in the early 1700s had changed their culture, becoming superb hunters – would be pressed ever further back until they were finally torn apart by US soldiers. Unfortunately for them, the war had hardened and brutalized European-American attitudes: in 1864 a particularly horrific massacre of native women and children was perpetrated at Sand Creek, Colorado.

Once the war was over, the destruction of native culture accelerated, particularly once gold had been discovered in the Black Hills of Dakota. The 1870s saw relentless attacks on the Plains Indians and their attempts to fight back, which culminated in Crazy Horse's superb defeat of that Civil War hero General George Custer at the battle of the Little Big Horn in 1876. Yet even the Sioux, the boldest and most aggressive of the tribes – it could almost be said, the Zulu of America – had no chance against the much larger, better armed and disciplined soldiers sent against them. And these were merely the advance party of a teeming migration of farmers, hunters, cattle-ranchers, bartenders and shopkeepers. Had the Confederacy survived intact, then no doubt the Native American peoples would still have succumbed to the guns and sheer numbers of the incomers; but it would not perhaps have happened quite so quickly.

The war also greatly advanced American industrial capitalism. Among the men who dodged service with the Union armies by buying themselves stand-ins were the oil-refining mogul John D. Rockefeller, the uberbanker J.P. Morgan and the steel giant Andrew Carnegie. The war economy had created a bottomless need for steel for armaments, for oil as a source of lighting and lubricants, for coal to power the Union's trains and ships; it also allowed clever speculators to make fortunes manipulating commodity prices, and bankers to form close new relationships with Washington politicians. The concentration of power in relatively few hands that was characteristic of American capitalism in its 'heroic' era, and the brutal treatment of strikers and trade-unionists, can largely be traced back to wartime attitudes.

There is a final, essential, point to be made about the Civil War. Although it soldered the Union together and paved the way for American hegemony, it did not provide the salvation for black Americans that those people greeting Lincoln at the Richmond riverside had hoped for. Some 180,000 blacks had left the South and enlisted in the Union armies during the war, many fighting heroically. But Lincoln had moved towards ending slavery only cautiously, in stages, driven by the demands of an increasingly desperate conflict. In the North, the fear that the war might be lost increased the influence of hardline abolitionists. At the front line, slave escapees became steadily more significant. Lincoln told his cabinet in 1862 that emancipation had become 'a military necessity . . . We must free the slaves or be ourselves subdued.' (The Confederate army, by the end, was using black soldiers too.) His 1863 Declaration of Emancipation applied to the slaves in the ten rebel states, and was designed in part to undermine the southern economy and its ability to fight; only towards the end of the conflict was slavery made illegal throughout the US, in the Thirteenth Amendment to the constitution.

Yet legally freeing the four million slaves of the South, and thus ending America's ignominious status as the world's largest slave nation, was a long way from giving those blacks security or prosperity. During the 'Reconstruction' which followed the war, the defeated southern states were put under direct military control before being allowed back into the Union. Towns and plantations destroyed, white soldiers imprisoned and the northern influence of the 'carpetbagger' suggested for a while that the old order really had gone for good. Many former slaves quickly left for other parts of the US, ignoring their old owners' pleas to stay and work for cash. After his estate-burning, town-torching, crop-trampling march through the South, the Union general William Sherman had begun a policy of handing land directly to ex-slaves, the 'forty acres and a mule' policy. In some states, blacks began to advance in politics.

All this was, however, largely illusory. 'Reconstruction' also meant corruption. Northern politicians had neither appetite nor capital to actually run the southern states. Nor were they happy about tearing up the constitutional right to property involved in land redistribution. There is an interesting parallel with the Russian emancipation of the serfs. In both places, the land without the serfs or the slaves to work it was almost valueless; but both serfs and former slaves found there was very little work available except the old, hard field-work. So how real was their freedom?

A delegation of freed slaves from South Carolina complained to
the Union authorities: 'We are left in a more unpleasant condition
than our former . . . We have property in homes, cattle, carriages, and
articles of furniture but we are landless and homeless . . . This is not
the condition of really free men.'[28] Disillusioned Russian peasants,
back on their land, back making payments in grain and chickens to
landowners, could not have put it better.

Many American blacks would eventually settle in northern and
north-western industrial cities, becoming the 'factory niggers' their
former masters had mocked. In the South, many others became subject to a form of extortion known as share-cropping. They got land, a
shack and tools to work the land from a landowner or shopkeeper –
sometimes the same person – advanced on credit. The terms were
such that they had little chance of working their way to profit, and a
poor harvest or two could make them economic slaves, if not legal
ones.

Yet this was only the start. Southern states would bring in segrega-
tionist 'Jim Crow' measures, which humiliated the black population
and relegated them to second-class status, a shrill echo of slavery itself.
Given, also, the emergence of white-terrorist movements such as the
Ku Klux Klan, for decades after the war to free them the life of black
Americans was almost as bleak as before the conflict started – and, as
we have seen, some thought bleaker. Relations between black and
white Americans would simmer unhappily for a century, until they
confronted each other again in the 1960s: many would say the old
wound is not healed today.

All that said, the war changed the United States irrevocably, and for
the better. The republic had not begun as anything resembling a
democracy, or even as a conventionally centralized state. The postal
service was the only federal institution most Americans came into
contact with. But now that huge westwards expansion introduced a
new, rawly democratic tone, and the influx of millions of poor European migrants turned the new nation's cities into energetic melting-
pots. As well as empowering capitalist moguls, the war had required a
national army in the North, conscription, direct taxation, more powerful federal courts and the start of social welfare.

The defeat of the South enabled the original constitution to be
reinterpreted as a democratic document, giving citizenship rights to all

men (though women remained excluded from politics). Abraham Lincoln started to use the word 'nation' rather than 'union', and in his Gettysburg Address his promise of 'government of the people, by the people, for the people' became something of a new founding declaration for American republicanism.

American capitalism ensured that the power of the rich elites continued to chafe, angering farmers, factory workers and those who lost everything in periodic crises and crashes. By the late 1860s, America was neither culturally united, nor a true democracy. But she was on the way to becoming the Titan that would emerge in the twentieth century.

Samurai Agony

The last stand of Saigo Takamori and his samurai fighters against the modern army of Japan, on 24 September 1877, took place at the moment when, on the other side of the Pacific, the Plains Indians were being shot down by the US army.

Like the battles of Crazy Horse, this was one of the great set-pieces of romantic military futility. The sword-wielding, sake-drinking, poem-writing, ancestor-worshipping and essentially medieval warriors of Takamori's rebellion charged a conscript army whose ranks were filled with the sons of peasants, but which possessed modern rifles, cannon and mines. After terrible slaughter in the early hours of the morning, Saigo had no more than about forty men left. They had already celebrated their coming deaths, and flung themselves one last time at the bullets. Saigo himself, hit in the right hip, fell, then called on his comrade Beppu Shinsuke to help him to an honourable death – to commit hara-kiri. In fact, it seems that Saigo was too badly injured and shocked to disembowel himself, but Beppu sliced his master's head off, as custom demanded. After the battle, it took some time to locate the missing head, so that it could be laid with Saigo's bodies for the victorious Japanese officers to contemplate.[29]

This is a very Japanese story, from the sight of the archaic samurai warriors charging down the hillside to its emphasis on the honour of ritual suicide. After his death, Saigo Takamori became a kind of saint for many Japanese, a symbol of tradition and honour, who had ascended to the heavens; or, alternatively, he had not died but had been exiled in Russia – or perhaps India – whence he would return in victory. Twelve years after his death, his popularity was such that he was posthumously pardoned by the Japanese emperor for his rebellion, and became an enduring national hero. Yet the Japaneseness of these events should not be overdone. The true story is more complicated than just aristocratic sword-fighters versus the modern world; this was indeed a confrontation between old ways and the mercantile and industrial world that has parallels elsewhere.

It is reminiscent of the charge of the Scottish Gaelic clans at the muskets and cannon of the Hanoverian army at Culloden in 1746. Bonnie Prince Charlie, who really did go into exile, was also for some a symbol of a lost and somehow finer world. In different ways, the more recent defeat of the American Confederacy was also comparable, a contemporary civil war about modernization and the power of capitalism. Though slavery was never involved, Saigo's 'Satsuma rebellion' was an attempt to restore traditional values and defy the new times. In the Japanese case, the modernizing government had come about because of a dramatic overseas intervention – the arrival of European warships, and in particular of Commodore Matthew Perry's US fleet in 1853–4.

There had been other Western jabs at Japan through the first half of the nineteenth century, provoking growing Japanese worry and anger. But before their own war broke out, the Americans already had a special interest in the Pacific. Their 'mountain men' crossing the Rockies, and their whalers cruising the coast, had begun to colonize California. There was now a voracious appetite for whale oil, and the Yankee whalers had already depleted the whales around the American coasts, so were pushing ever further across the Pacific (an ironic reflection on today's whale politics, which pits conservationist Americans against plundering Japanese).

We last left the Japanese in the early 1600s, self-isolated and about to experience their more than two centuries of enclosed development under the Tokugawa shoguns. This conservative rule had brought order and stability, but only slow economic development. It allowed the intensity and otherworldiness of Japanese culture, a society of strict hierarchies and exquisite art to flourish; but meant there was

little of the industrial and commercial development that was revolu-
tionizing Europe and America.

This 'Japaneseness' did not translate directly into a strong national
political feeling. Here was a land divided by its mountainous spine, by
the gaps between its many islands and its long coastlines, where most
people felt only local allegiances. For hundreds of years the emperor,
though revered for religious reasons, had been politically insignificant.
At the top of the Tokugawa system, under the shogun himself, was his
bakufu, or military government (the word means 'tent government').
Around that, on their lands – the most loyal nearest – almost in con-
centric circles, were the great landlords or barons, the *daimyo*, who in
turn depended on the far larger class of privileged warriors, the
famous samurai.

Hundreds of thousands of fighters, some 6–7 per cent of the population, boasted of their ancestry and told tales going back to the fierce
civil wars of the 1400s and 1500s and beyond. The samurai enjoyed
special privileges, such as wearing two swords in public, and received
payments (in rice) which roughly accorded to the landholdings most of
them had given up. Many still lived in all-male barracks or in towns
clustered around the castles of the *daimyo*. The life of a samurai was
supposed to be dominated by military training, the contemplation of
death, and the higher arts.[30] In practice, the long peace of the Tokugawa period had given most of these men little or no experience of
battle. There were plenty of popular complaints that these so-called
warriors had never seen a fight in earnest except for quarrels around
brothels or drinking-dens. In practice, the more ambitious had evolved
into an administrative class, running the territories of the rulers in a
country still organized into around 280 different *daimyo* estates, or
domains, rather like a version of pre-unity Germany, in which local
dialects were often mutually incomprehensible.

The *daimyo*, whom most Samurai served, were themselves organized into categories, depending on their historic family loyalty, or
absence of loyalty, to the Tokugawa clan. A system of one-year-in,
one-year-out enforced residence in the capital Edo (today's Tokyo)
made the *daimyo* families effectively hostages of the shogun and of his
government, and they posed little threat. In a country that had spent
so much of its history engaged in complex civil and clan warfare, the
peace that resulted was a major political achievement.

Tokugawa Japan was no paradise, particularly for the farmers at the bottom of the social pile and the outcast families who (as in India) did the dirtiest jobs. There were periodic famines, peasant revolts, volcanic eruptions and serious crime problems in the cities. But these were centuries without civil war or imported epidemics, during which the population grew faster than in Europe. The production of rice wine, paper luxuries, expensive cloth, lacquered and wooden items, grew, and the roads between the towns, generally larger than those in Europe, were crowded with traders. But this period also brought a complacent, even arrogant, attitude to the outside world. As Western ships began to arrive off the coast again, one Japanese critic complained: 'Recently, the loathsome Western barbarians, unmindful of their base position as the lower extremities of the world, have been scurrying impudently across the Four Seas, trampling other nations under foot. Now they are audacious enough to challenge our exalted position . . . What manner of insolence is this?'[31]

The Tokugawa-era Japanese had no real answer to the insistent demands of the Americans for trade. Following Adam Smith and theorists such as David Ricardo, nineteenth-century economics saw trade as a great beneficent power in the world. As noted earlier, countries which were mutually enriching one another were thought less likely to go to war. What this happy liberal belief ignored was that so much of the really profitable trade brought huge riches because it was unequal and – from India to China to Japan – imposed down the muzzles of cannon: 'Peaceful free trade – or we shoot.' Once trade was fully opened up, the West found much in Japan that it wanted, from fine lacquered furniture and silks to the vivid prints that so influenced the Impressionist painters. The Japanese would take a radically different route from the Chinese, building a modern industrial economy and army. But the price for Japan was the destruction of its earlier self, and this was a painful and paradoxical process, which a century on would enmesh America in further war.

The paradox had started with those samurai. With some of the leading landowners they began to agitate against the Tokugawa shogun. As he and his advisers reluctantly accepted that they had to sign the unequal trading treaties being demanded by the Westerners, which included such humiliations as foreigners being immune to Japanese laws, there had been a fierce backlash. The Tokugawa *bakufu*, the military government, was doing its best to reform the old system, but gently. The rebels wanted the foreign devils simply expelled. They appealed to that symbol of ancient Japan, so long out of politics, the emperor at his court in Kyoto. Which way should Japan turn? In a revealing story of this confusing time, one samurai, Sakamoto Ryoma, broke into the home of a *bakufu* official involved in modernizing the navy, intending to assassinate him. But the official, Katsu Kaishu, asked the samurai to listen to his explanations before he killed him: after an afternoon of discussion about the importance of a strong navy, the would-be assassin was convinced and changed sides.

Yet increasing unrest caused by opening up to the West, revolts, inflation and the desertion of *daimyo* supporters weakened the Tokugawa regime, creating a crisis into which more rebel samurai flung themselves. A national argument was taking place, about the need to shift from an essentially feudal and traditionalist society to a modern one, in essence not so different from the struggles in Russia and America. Japan would achieve her modernization with far less bloodshed than the United States had – though it would be a less democratic transformation – and far more successfully than Russia. Eventually, after more than two centuries of relative stability, the shogunate collapsed, and in 1867–8 the young emperor Meiji returned as the supreme ruler of Japan. This period is remembered as the 'Meiji restoration'.

Traditionalists now got a horrible shock, which led directly to the confrontation between Saigo's samurai and the Japanese army; for the new regime promptly did exactly what the conservative and anti-foreigner samurai had hoped to prevent. It modernized, and very fast. The 280-plus *daimyo* landholdings were abolished and turned into seventy-two Western-style prefectures, effectively creating a single national territory for the first time. Samurai lost their privileges, from the right to carry swords to their untaxed stipends. Who, in the 1870s, needed poetry-crazed, sword-fighting (and somewhat rusty) warriors? Old rules about dress, haircuts and where people could live were torn up. Japanese town-dwellers started to experiment with Western clothing.

A modern conscript army, based on Western military thinking, was created. Compulsory education was brought in. The capital moved from old Kyoto to Edo. A new land tax swept away complex feudal arrangements, and in 1872 railways arrived. After a rocky start, the Japanese turned to the German experience of state-directed capitalism to create their industries, and to the British to help build a modern navy. By 1889 a new constitution, creating a house of peers and a house of representatives, the latter elected but on a tiny franchise (about 1 per cent of men had enough property to vote), had been unveiled. Japanese citizens were granted civil rights and there was a flowering of popular democratic movements.

This added up to the most dramatic, fastest (non-revolutionary) reform programme in modern history. It was almost a revolution – but not quite, because it was driven by samurai and landowners, albeit mostly middle-ranking ones, and occurred under the authority of an ancient imperial system. It made Czar Alexander II look lazy. Yet it produced turbulence and reactions almost as extreme as many another revolution. There were revolts by peasants and samurai who could not accept the loss of their old powers – and who were still supported by many conservative-minded Japanese in the cities and villages. Saigo Takamori was only the boldest of the rebels, and he, like so many other samurai, had started on the side of the Meiji restoration. He broke with the new regime only in 1873, when it failed to take his advice to invade Korea – a plan he hoped would restore the glamour and authority of the warrior class.

Saigo had been born in the domain of Satsuma, or Kagoshima, on the island of Kyushu, the southernmost of the main Japanese islands. It was famous not only for its small oranges but for being backward, traditionalist and having an unusually high number of samurai – about a quarter of the male population.[32] It was also famously independent-minded, and headed by an ancient *daimyo* family who represented themselves as the independent kingdom of Satsuma at the 1867 Paris International Exhibition. Saigo's family were poor samurai, but he was bright and scholarly and worked his way up from clerking jobs to a role at the centre of Japanese political life in Edo. His political career had its ups and downs, including two banishments, but by the mid-1860s he was representing the interests of Satsuma at the imperial court in Kyoto. There he emerged as an opponent of the Tokugawa regime but, though conservative in much of his thinking, he became a political reformer.

After the Meiji restoration he even emerged as a hardliner, enthusiastic about the creation of the modern conscript army that would later finish him off, keen on destroying the old samurai stipend system, and ruthless in destroying the power of the old regime and its supporters. He was about the least likely rebel against the Meiji emperor, whom he revered, that it is possible to imagine. Indeed, Saigo's own Satsuma lord, Shimazu Hisamitsu, thought he was a destructive reformer bent on turning proud old Japan into a colony of the barbarian nations. The Korean crisis provoked his resignation from the government, but Saigo's internal conflict as between the old samurai culture he had been brought up in and the demands of modernization may have made his life feel intolerable.

As soon as he left the government and returned to Satsuma, he began an almost Tolstoyan life of hunting, farming and setting up children's schools to teach Confucian values. He did not write novels, but he did write poems:

I moor my skiff in the creek of flowering reeds
With a fishing-pole in hand, I sit on a stepping-stone
Does anyone know of this high-minded man's other world?[33]

Saigo was also, by now, an iconic national figure in Japan whose every move was watched.

Precisely what turned him from visionary in voluntary exile, warning of decadence in government, into the leader of a full-scale military rebellion is hard to pin down. But the revolt was provoked by the Tokyo administration, who sent spies – and possibly assassins – after Saigo, and tried to seize arms stored in Satsuma. It began as an uprising of private military school students in Kagoshima. Saigo put himself at their head and announced that he was setting off for the capital with this local army, to challenge the government. Beginning with more than twelve thousand men, armed with rifles, carbines, howitzers and mortars as well as their swords, they collected supporters as they marched north through the snow. But they then halted for an unsuccessful fifty-four-day siege of the huge seventeenth-century Kumamoto Castle, which allowed the opposition to land a much larger and far better-equipped army of sixty thousand loyal samurai and conscript soldiers. In ferocious battles, the rebels were forced back through a long retreat, fighting and losing men all the way, until their final downhill charge and Saigo's death.[34]

So this is not quite the simple story of traditionalist samurai fighting hopelessly against a modernizing government that it first seems. Had it been, Saigo Takamori would not be the tragic hero he remains for many Japanese. His tale is more interesting, and sadder, than that. He was a modernizer, too, for much of his life (and fought more often in a French-influenced modern uniform than in samurai clothes). He was torn between his country's past and its future, and it was only when he found himself with his back to the wall that he chose to fight for its past. Even then he had no coherent project beyond the very vague notion of wanting a more 'virtuous' government. The ambiguous nature of his revolt is shown by his declaration in the course of it that he was not fighting to win, but for 'the chance to die for principle' – in other words, to turn himself into a symbol. That he certainly did.

Japan's success as a modernizing power would soon astonish the world when she defeated the Imperial Russian Navy at the battle of Tsushima in 1905. But though clad in modern steel and European uniforms, in its heart twentieth-century Japan retained many of the medieval instincts of the samurai class, with its emphasis on death, honour and family lineage and its contempt for outsiders – at least until the disastrous 1940s. Saigo represented both Japans, which was one too many for a single life.

The Mystery of Imperialism

That the age of modern imperialism should start in Europe is no surprise. Europeans had been in deadly competition with one another for centuries. Their domestic sea, the Mediterranean, had fostered seamanship, piracy and trading rivalries, so that as soon as their craft were able, they were bound to go further afield, round Africa and across the Atlantic. When they first took, or bought, a piece of land, then built a fort and stayed, it was generally to protect their new trade against other European enemies: the Portuguese fortified against the Dutch, the Dutch built forts to keep out the British; the British and French built settlements against each another. Though the obvious and primary story of empire is that of Europe's colonizing nations imposing themselves on less powerful non-European peoples, it began because of internal European competition.

This explains the speed, rapacity and aggression of the continent's imperial expansion. Local enmities and rivalries, simmering for centuries, were exploding afresh in new lands. In thinking of empire we must remember mutual Dutch and Spanish loathing, born of Habsburg Spain's brutal attempt to hold on to and suppress the young Protestant republic; the very longstanding Spanish–Portuguese rivalry; the mutual contempt of English and Dutch sailors, nurtured in sea battles up and down the Channel and the Thames. Often, these were religious feuds as well as national ones. We have to recall how envious the British court had been of the dominance of Catholic Bourbon France; and how furious French merchants, Jesuit missionaries and aristocrats were when the British seemed to be stealing a march on them in the forests of America. Had the boot been on the other foot, it would have been as if Africans had not only colonized Europe, but had been playing out an ancient and bitter competition among themselves at the same time – Kongo against Mali, Zimbabwean against Bantu, as they hacked and surged their way through the valleys of the Thames, the Rhine and the Rhône.

Had this been all, it would have been a simple, if unpleasant, tale. We would have been able to define Europe's age of empire as the predictable result of one part of the world developing better technologies and organization than most of the rest of it, and then for a short period taking what they could. There is nothing specifically European about this – no original sin. Muslim Arabs, Mongol herders, Chinese border-people and Maori seafarers all behaved just as murderously when they had the chance. Whenever you get all-male warrior bands unleashed on normal settled family based people, there is a high risk that they will behave abominably. Untethered from the bonds of mutual need, nurtured empathy and the possibility of shame inside their own society, they are likely to kill randomly and even rape and torture. Whether the men concerned are British, American, Spanish, German – or Hindu, Aztec or Zulu – makes little difference.

Yet European imperialism did not simply let loose bands of greedy, lonely men, itchy with national rivalries, on other parts of the world. It also thrust upon them European national and religious cultures, which were well developed and had a strong sense of their own special history and cultural value. So the story of the British in America could not be just the story of military conquest, traders and trappers, but also had to be about law, Christian dissenters, moral arguments and political rebellion. When the Spanish arrived in Mexico and Peru, they brought microbes and mayhem, but they also brought monasteries and the mass. Nineteenth-century French colonies struggled to reconcile republican citizenship with ownership of the new lands and people. The Dutch settlement in South Africa (not strictly an imperial moment) was a republican-Christian exodus from the homeland, deeply rooted in a Calvinist sense of mission, the Dutch as a people chosen during the Reformation in Europe. German imperialism in Africa was an extension of that court's belief in Germany's destiny as the new European superpower, more disciplined and less raggedly democratic than its decadent liberal rivals.

All this came with a huge dollop of humbug and self-seeking propaganda. It had to. How could Catholic Portuguese explain themselves in Brazil or the Congo, without insisting they were bringing eternal Christian light to the darkness – as well as slave-trading? When the British in India blew mutineers from the barrels of cannon, or gunned down protest movements, they had to tell themselves they were bringing the rule of law, education and proper administration which would, in the long run, benefit their Muslim and Hindu subjects. When the 'scramble for Africa' began, French, Belgian and British newspapers inveighed against the evil of the Arab slave-traders: for it was to free the African that their soldiers were shackling their tribal lands.

Yet European societies had become more open and more self-critical at just the same time as they were acquiring empires. They had advanced beyond the point where they could live on a diet of humbug without feeling ill. The missionaries included many men who enjoyed lording it in steaming backwaters, ordering servants around and taking their sexual pleasure from the conquered, thousands of miles from their families and fellow citizens. But they also included genuine Christians aghast at the moral consequences of imperialism – men like Bartolomé de Las Casas, the Dominican friar who campaigned against the worst excesses of 'New Spain' and insisted on the full humanity of the native people; or, in Africa, Scotland's David Livingstone.

At home, almost from the beginning, European societies were divided on the subject of imperialism. The nonconformist, Baptist and free-trade strain in British political life fought vigorously against the slavers and other empire enthusiasts. A large, vocal group of pro-Americans existed in London well before the Boston Tea Party. In France, there was a long tradition of writing that mocked European pretensions of being more advanced than the people they were enslaving and conquering. The victory of the anti-slave-trade lobby in early-nineteenth-century Britain was a battle won, not the end of a war, but it was nonetheless hugely significant.

Every European society that acquired an empire was affected, often for the worse. We have seen the effect of American gold and silver on Spain. Though Portuguese wealth was based for centuries on its African and Brazilian conquests, by the mid-twentieth century the country had become a backwater, snoring under dictatorship. Britain became socially and politically divided between the free-traders and liberal nonconformists on the one hand, and on the other the empire-lovers clustered around the court, the military and London. Had the imperialists lost much earlier, then perhaps Britain today would not be a post-manufacturing, post-industrial nation overdependent on the financial services that are the last vestige of imperial stretch. She would certainly have experienced far less mass immigration and would have a shorter record of involvement in overseas wars.

So it is important to remember that imperialism was never simply about one country invading or occupying others. It was two-way. It always involved internal choices and the victory of one lobby or economic interest over others. Outside the Dutch Republic, where capital was raised from the growing middle class, this generally meant the victory of the court, and the military associated with the court.

Societies that were divided into many little courts, such as Germany or Italy, could only join in the imperial game when they had come together and formed a single military and financial hub. And as soon as they did, almost their first act was to try to acquire overseas territories. They seemed among the most brutal of the imperialists, but this was because they were late. Britain had fought her way to dominance in India, and massacred Tasmanians, and helped wipe out native American peoples, before the full glare of modern communications made it all too embarrassing. The Dutch had behaved savagely to the Javanese before anyone in Europe knew or cared. The Germans with their machine-guns in East Africa, and Mussolini with his aircraft and gas in Ethiopia, were easier targets for outrage.

The only European countries that were virtually non-participant in empire-building at this point were the ones that already had empires inside Europe, such as the Austro-Hungarians (and to a lesser extent the Russians), or that were too small or landlocked to hope to compete, such as the Swedes, Norwegians, Swiss and Poles. These have often built the more equal, more successful societies today, which may not be a coincidence. There is, however, one glaring example of a small country that did acquire a vast empire. Though an odd story, it is one that tells us a lot about how imperialism actually worked.

Leopold the Nasty

The personal empire carved out of the guts of the African continent by the Belgian King Leopold II was the most extreme, almost ridiculous, example of European imperialism. Belgium was a small also-ran in nineteenth-century Europe, a nation of two languages, which had only become independent in 1830 (and is now again barely a nation). The Belgians had gone shopping for a king in the monarchical bazaar of Germany. They had opted for Prince Leopold of Saxe-Coburg-Saalfeld, who had been a swashbuckling officer with the Russian army fighting Napoleon. He had married the second-in-line to the British throne, who had died before she could become queen; and he was Queen Victoria's uncle. Indeed, he had helped arrange her famously happy marriage to his nephew, Prince Albert. After accepting Belgium's invitation – he had earlier turned down the chance of becoming King of Greece – Leopold proved in many ways a good king, supporting social reforms and behaving with the circumspection of a constitutional monarch.

He was, significantly, King of the Belgians, not King of Belgium – the head of a people, not the owner of a fiefdom. As the age of empire matured, this chafed on Leopold. His relatives, notably his niece Victoria, possessed fine empires. Belgium had nothing. It was a crammed and relatively poor country, where emigration was discussed as a way to avoid social revolution. Leopold asked the Turks if they would sell him Crete. He tried for Cuba, and even Texas, before it joined the USA. He wondered about the Faroe Islands. He covetously eyed parts of South America too. Nothing was available. Leopold died disappointed; but he passed this colony mania on to his son, the sly, gangling, large-nosed Leopold II. This son was more of a mess than his father. He was struggling in an unhappy marriage, and roamed the world. An unappealing figure and a world-class hypocrite, he disliked the minor role offered by constitutional monarchy in Europe and was unimpressed by Belgium in general. '*Petit pays, petits gens,*' he moaned.

As heir, he travelled around observing British imperialism in Egypt, studying in Seville the financial inflows of the Spanish empire, and reading about the treasure that had streamed into Holland from the Dutch colony of Java. As an importuning would-by buyer outdoing his father, young Leopold asked if he could buy part of Borneo. He fantasized about purchasing something in Abyssinia, or maybe on the Nile. Perhaps the Argentines could find him something? Or maybe he could snaffle a morsel of China? Fiji? Vietnam? The Philippines? An island off Uruguay? Or in the Pacific? Like his father, he was on the verge of becoming a comic-opera figure: 'Trainee emperor in need of empire. Will consider all offers.' Yet he had already received a grim warning about the dangers of Europeans parachuting themselves onto foreign thrones. His sister had married the ill-fated Austrian Archduke Maximilian, whom the French had packed off to Mexico as their puppet-emperor. Unimpressed, the Mexicans had executed him, providing the inspiration for a very fine painting by Manet. The bereaved wife, Leopold's sister, went mad, and he kept her hidden away in a palace for the rest of her life.

What transformed all of this from byway in European dynastic history into world-class tragedy was the penetration of central Africa by European explorers. From the late 1840s, Britons such as the flamboyant multilinguist Richard Burton and his comrade (later enemy) John Speke began to chart the African interior, starting with their search for the origins of the Nile. The heroes of London's Royal Geographical Society were not motivated by a desire to extend the British Empire – though fame, and the wealth accruing from successful bookpublishing certainly were lures. Nor was the British government much interested. When Verney Lovett Cameron tried to rescue the great David Livingstone, the Scottish Congregationalist missionary and explorer, he failed, but he returned to London having crossed the continent and brimming with tales of its rivers, lakes and rich soil. Ministers could not have cared less.

Livingstone had crossed the continent himself, in the opposite direction, travelling light and managing not to offend most of the African chieftains he met. He believed strongly in Western, Christian civilization, and he wanted to save souls as well as to chart rivers and lakes, but he came from a religious tradition that was suspicious of earthly, militaristic power. Like Cameron, he was a genuinely outraged critic of African slavery. The same could not be said of Henry Morton Stanley, a Welsh boy who had suffered a horrible upbringing in a poorhouse before getting to America, where he managed to fight on both sides during the Civil War until he emerged as a brilliantly self-publicizing and unreliable journalist.

Employed by a New York press tycoon, he was sent to find Livingstone. Cruelly misusing his native bearers and driven by a reckless hunger for fame, he was able to ask, 'Dr Livingstone, I presume?' and make himself a global celebrity. Stanley too returned to London and, though now an American, wanted the British to claim the huge new land. But like Cameron, Stanley found no enthusiasm in London for annexing the Congo. Leopold II, reading the explorers' reports in his daily copy of *The Times*, delivered freshly ironed to his breakfast table at his palace outside Brussels, thought differently.

Leopold wanted, as he said, a slice of 'this magnificent African cake', and he began a cunning campaign to help himself. He decided to pose as a philanthropist. As we have seen, Muslim slavers had long preyed on African kingdoms, and after the anti-slavery movement had ended British involvement in the Atlantic trade, African slavery had become a fashionable moral cause. So Leopold set himself up as a Crusader, telling Queen Victoria he wanted 'to bring civilization to Africa' and in 1876 convening a lavish conference in Belgium, where explorers, politicians and do-gooders from all over Europe and Russia were honoured, given medals, listened to and served superb banquets. Free drink and flattery go a long way, as Brussels knows well. Leopold told everyone he merely wanted to shine the light of civilization on the natives, and suggested a network of European stations in the Congo, staffed by doctors, scientists and others, to help abolish slavery, establish 'harmony among the chiefs' and 'pacify' the region. Impressed, the grandees of the Brussels conference agreed to form the International Association of Africa with King Leopold as president. His cake knife was poised.

Burton, Speke and Livingstone would have been aghast at the consequences of their heroic and lonely voyages. They might have thought it unlikely this land would soon be taken over by Europeans. Malaria, yellow fever, thick forests, wild beasts, hostile natives and ferocious heat had so far kept most outsiders at bay. This was the interior of what was called, without any European self-consciousness, the 'Dark Continent'. But Stanley, who was in Africa when the Brussels conference was held, was a very different cast of man. He was ambitious for worldly success and, spurned by the British, was easily wooed by Leopold II. Within five years of the conference Stanley and his Belgian team had carved a river through the rock and jungle to reach the huge and navigable waterway of the Upper Congo. Soon riverboats would be using it to trade, to create small settlements and to reach one-sided, bogus 'treaties' with local chieftains.

Even in the 1880s, the legality of simply taking a vast slice of Africa for one's personal empire (the parliament of Belgium had made it clear it had no wish to be involved) was controversial. But Leopold's serpentine diplomacy won him the support of the US President. France and Portugal, who both had interests in the area, were furious, but Leopold played off the European powers against each other. It helped that nobody felt threatened by Belgium. So Leopold won the backing of Bismarck's Germany and then of the British. The 'International Association of the Congo', flying an old Congo king's flag, became in effect a shell company for Leopold's new empire. In 1885 the Belgian parliament backed his scheme and he began to call himself 'King-Sovereign of the Congo Free State'. Shares were sold and funds raised, though Leopold retained personal control. Soon, at terrible human cost, a railway was being blasted from the coast to the safe waters beyond the huge rapids and falls that divided the mighty Congo River from the sea.

Armed traders poured into the belly of Africa, first buying up all the ivory they could find. Chiefs were fooled into signing over their lands. Villagers were cajoled, bullied and threatened so they would hand over their supplies of food and ivory. Elephants were hunted to near-extinction in all the areas the whites could reach. The rule of the rope and the whip reached deep into the Congo; the supposed humanitarian crusade had become a new form of slavery.

Ivory was hugely valuable because it was used for everything from false teeth to piano keys, but once the pneumatic bicycle tyre had been invented, rubber – which grew wild, the sap of creepers, across the Congo – was even more so. Native Africans were forced to deliver ever greater amounts of the sticky, unpleasant gum. If they seemed reluctant, their wives and children would be held as hostages. Those who protested – and there were rebellions – were mowed down with the new fast-action rifles and machine-guns, or strung from trees, or whipped to death. A brutal native army, officered by Belgians, cut the hands off those it had killed so as to claim a financial bounty. Often, to make up the numbers or out of pure sadism, hands and ears were cut off the living.

Away from their families, their priests and their neighbours, out of reach of newspaper reporters, ordinary Belgian men turned into the perpetrators of massacres. It was a story not so different from the transformation of quiet Lutheran shopkeepers and Swabian farm-hands into SS killers in Nazi extermination camps. Congolese were like Jews, not quite human. Society's restraints had been stripped away. 'Nobody' was watching. From Antwerp off went adventurers, guns and ammunition, along with shackles and manacles, to the Congo. What came back were cargoes of ivory and rubber, and huge profits, including for Leopold, who began splurge-spending, not just on mistresses and luxuries but on expanding his royal palace and on new buildings to impress his Belgian subjects.

The apparent success of Leopold's audacious gamble caused worry and jealousy elsewhere in Europe, and the 'scramble for Africa' began. The British had been mainly settled in the far south of the continent, a much easier climatic and geographical area for Europeans, living uneasily alongside Dutch Boers and native people. In the far north, the French had begun to seize Algeria in 1830, and the Suez Canal was being built with French and British money during 1859–69.

But it was Leopold's rubber bonanza, and the discovery of diamonds around the Orange River in South Africa, followed in the 1880s by a gold rush, that turned expansion into a frenzy. The French pushed into West Africa, into countries such as Chad, Senegal and Mali that had been at the core of earlier African civilizations, as they tried to link the river basin of the Niger with their North African possessions across the Sahara. The British proceeded north from South Africa, through today's Zambia, Zimbabwe, Kenya and Malawi, trying to link the

Cape with Egypt in a huge north–south stripe of control. Germany, late into the game, seized chunks of the remaining carcass – Tanganyika, Togoland, Namibia. From the 1890s until 1914, the frenzy caused snarling and squabbling between the European powers. Germany's unsatisfied hunger was one of the causes of the First World War.

From the ravaged rainforests of the Congo Basin, stripped of rubber and elephants, then depopulated by the Belgian slaughter, to the brutal regimes that emerged from the humiliation of conquest and exploitation, the 'scramble for Africa' was late imperialism with almost no redeeming aspects. Some of the worst behaviour seen in modern Africa, from the use of child soldiers (a Belgian idea) to the amputation of rebels' arms, feet or hands, originated at this time. The lines on the map drawn back home in Europe, dividing tribes and language groups, are at least partly responsible for the sequence of failed states, unable to command loyalty, that litter contemporary Africa. True, European doctors brought drugs and medicines that began to turn the tables on ancient African diseases; but these same drugs allowed Europeans to enter parts of the continent, and exploit them, for the first time. Africa was less populous, and as soon as medically protected and industrially armed people arrived, almost completely helpless. To give him a kind of cold credit, Leopold realized this early and instinctively.

His Congolese empire was so barbaric that word got out, and European protests grew. The story of the writers and campaigners who publicized the horrors of the Belgian Congo is an impressive one. A former shipping clerk called Edmund Morel, who had spotted the disparity between the cargoes leaving and arriving in Antwerp – only guns and ammunition going out, lucrative ivory and rubber coming back – was a key leader in the agitation, setting up the Congo Reform Association. Morel was a 'good European' pendant to hang against Leopold. Other famous men, including the British–Polish novelist Joseph Conrad and the later Irish nationalist Roger Casement, were also influential, though the Christian nonconformist tradition was more important than any one individual. This became the first humanitarian campaign of the modern age, an Edwardian equivalent of Live Aid or Amnesty International.

The steady rain of horror stories in European and American newspapers infuriated Leopold. He reacted by bullying, bribing and hiring his own propagandists, but none of it worked. When a commission of inquiry he set up himself failed to whitewash the story, he eventually gave up and sold his private empire to the Belgian state, after which reforms began. Adam Hochschild, the American writer who has written a careful modern history of Leopold's empire, quotes calculations suggesting that between 1880 and 1920 murder, starvation, disease and a falling birthrate cut the human population of the Congo by about half: 'That would mean . . . that during the Leopold period and its immediate aftermath the population of the territory dropped by approximately ten million people.'[35]

Stuffed animals, uniforms, chains and native loot are on show at one of Leopold's tasteless, rather grotesque buildings on the outskirts of Brussels. The people of Belgium, quite understandably, have done their level best to forget this clever and remarkably unpleasant monarch. But the most dramatic act of imperial chaos was performed not by a latecomer, but by the originator of modern imperialism.

Opium, War and Tragedy

The story started, however, with a Chinese victory over the British, masterminded by one of the most intriguing and tragic figures of the nineteenth century, Lin Zexu, or 'Commissioner Lin', as he is mostly remembered. The scene was a small village downriver from the great city of Canton, a world of water, grey-green, hot, misty, vibrating with mosquitoes, smelling of mud. Lin, a large man with a loud laugh and a substantial moustache, was overseeing the destruction of a huge drugs haul. On the orders of the Chinese emperor, he was meticulously disposing of twenty thousand chests of opium, worth many fortunes.

Getting rid of so much of the sticky, strong-smelling dark drug was very difficult. Lin had a team of five hundred digging huge pits, lined with stones and timber. The wooden chests were upended. The balls of opium, bound in poppy leaves, were then crushed underfoot and thrown into the pits, where they were dissolved in water with salt and lime, stirred into a foul-smelling porridge, before being allowed to trickle into a stream, then into the sea. There was so much opium that the job took three weeks to complete. Lin, who was an amateur poet as well as a popular and successful government official, had already composed a prayer to the sea, apologizing for the pollution and advising fishes and other sea creatures to go and hide somewhere safe until the opium was dissolved.[36]

This was the finale of Commissioner Lin's dogged campaign against foreign merchants in Canton, mainly but not entirely British, as he tried to bring an end to the opium trade. The Chinese were not the first users of opium, or even early adopters. The bitter, gritty powder that comes from white poppy seeds had been used in classical times and around the Arab world. It had been grown in India under the Mughals and shipped across Asia by Indian and Dutch merchants. Even as Lin's men were emptying their wooden chests into the Pearl River, it was being used in Britain too. Writers such as Thomas de Quincey and poets such as Coleridge and Crabbe were addicts. The British conqueror of India, Robert Clive, died of an overdose. Opium had been prescribed as laudanum, a liquid 'medicine' that was also very popular among working-class men and women struggling to adapt to the industrial revolution. It was even being given to babies to stop them crying. But only the Chinese had moved in large numbers to a new way of taking the drug – smoking it, mixed with tobacco. This produced a stronger, more addictive and therefore much more dangerous high – the difference has been compared to snorting cocaine and smoking 'crack'.

No one knows for sure how many Chinese men (for it was mostly a male preoccupation) had become addicted by the 1830s. Estimates at the time varied between four and twelve million. Whatever the true figure, everyone thought the rate of addiction was growing fast, despite a ferocious edict against the trade issued by the emperor in 1799. As a boy, Lin had seen the effects of the drug in his home province of Fujian, where it turned hardworking men into dazed zombies. He became a passionate anti-drugs campaigner. He was also a rising star of Chinese bureaucracy who had put down a peasant revolt by persuasion, and was known as 'Blue Sky' because of his reputation as a rare uncorrupted official. Appointed to confront the problem in Canton by the emperor, Lin had arrived with a sophisticated mix of carrots and sticks. The carrots included an eighteen-month amnesty for drug addicts and a refuge for smokers trying to kick the habit. The sticks included the death penalty for pushers – slow strangulation for

Chinese, decapitation for foreigners.

But the most important sticks were for beating foreign traders with. For opium was pouring in from British India, where the new colonial power had taken over the Mughal poppy fields. To start with, it was an unofficial and surreptitious trade, which the officially sanctioned British East India Company deplored. There was a modest amount of smuggling, mostly through the one gateway for foreign merchants into imperial China, the so-called factories, a small quarter of trading sheds, houses and courtyards, just outside Canton. But then global economics kicked in.

The biggest British addiction was not opium but tea, which was then grown only in China. This benign national obsession, which continues to this day and had played such a strange role in the loss of the American colonies, was both expensive and very lucrative for the British government. During the early nineteenth century it taxed tea at 100 per cent of its value, at times bringing in enough to cover half the cost of its global war machine, the Royal Navy. The Chinese, however, had long refused to buy manufactured British goods to balance the value of the imported tea, so a huge and potentially ruinous outpouring of British silver and gold was happening instead. That was what really worried London. To begin with, compared with tea and silver, opium was a sideshow.

Then those laudanum-addicted factory workers became part of the story. The British cotton mills, producing cheap clothing, had a ready market in India. If Indian opium brought silver back from China, then India could buy cotton – and other goods – from Britain, and Britain could pay for her tea. It was the kind of multiple trade suddenly opened up by industrialism. Silver for tea – bad for the British – became a four-way minuet of tea, opium, cotton and silver – which was very good for the British. The British East India Company sold opium in India to 'country merchants', independent traders whose ships then took it to feed the growing Chinese market. When the Company's monopoly was finally abolished, this still surreptitious drug trade became a flood.

This was what had caused the crisis that brought Lin to Canton in the first place. The poor Commissioner thought he was merely stamping out an evil addiction. In fact, he was about to set two empires at war.

★

The Opium Wars are remembered as the worst the British Empire engaged in, a ruthless attack on the territory, morality and sovereignty of a dozing, decaying and incompetent China. In China to this day, the 1842 Treaty of Nanking, which ended the first Opium War, humiliated the emperor and kicked open the ocean-front doors of his empire to British trade, is remembered as a national humiliation. The Communist rulers from 1949 onwards used the one-sided treaty as a prime example of how the country's final Qing dynasty had failed the Chinese people. In the West, including Britain, the evil of the trade in opium, cynically peddled alongside missionary tracts, is regarded as one of the imperial exploits for which there can be no excuse.

The true story is just a little different.

For a start, the Qing empire was not tottering. It had a weak emperor and was facing internal revolts, but that was hardly exceptional in Chinese history. The dynasty had ruled China only since 1644, when Britain herself had been in the throes of revolution. Just as Charles I faced his final defeat, the last Ming emperor Chongzhen had hanged himself in his palace as an upstart rival burned the outskirts of Beijing. The capital soon fell to the Manchu coming in from the steppes, northern nomads originally, whose army contained Mongols proud of their forebear Genghis Khan. The Ming empire, though one of the greatest dynasties in China's long history, had suffered a debilitating financial crisis. After the failure of the old system of money based on strings of copper coins, and then of printed paper money, it had relied on silver, mostly imported. (Money had been at the root of King Charles's troubles too.) When silver imports dried up, the Ming court had to turn to ever more oppressive taxes.

Since the most powerful and richest groups in China had won exemption, or otherwise dodged payment of their taxes (shades of Louis XVI's France), the burden fell on the poorer, particularly in the towns. A run of bad harvests and plague epidemics provoked revolts and some major rebellions. The most serious of these was led by Li Zicheng, who called himself 'the dashing prince', destroyed some great cities and ended up ousting the last of the Qing before himself being defeated by the Manchu.

Nobody would have bet bad money, never mind good, on the Manchu successfully ruling China. They were ethnically distinct, from beyond the edges of the empire proper. Their heartland was to the north-west of Korea, but they had built up such a powerful network of alliances and clients – Mongol, Tibetan and some Han Chinese – that they were able to set up in northern China and declare themselves the northern dynasty. After 1644 they appropriated the 'Mandate of Heaven' from the Ming and eventually conquered the south, ruling an area very similar in size and shape to modern China. Yet they remained incomers. The Ming, who had sent the famous fleet of war-junks to India and Africa, and then recalled them, and had been responsible for one of the finest flowerings of Chinese art and culture, had been a native dynasty who had defeated the earlier 'outsider' dynasty of the Mongol Yuan. How could a band of semi-barbarians seize and run the greatest empire on the planet?

Yet this is what the Manchu did. They did it first by war, displaying terrifying ruthlessness when they took their first major city, and using cannon and cavalry in battles that would have looked quite like those being fought in Europe at the time. They then imposed Manchu dress codes on the conquered Han, plus shaved foreheads and long queues – the caricature 'Chinese' look that would soon become famous in Europe. Han and Ming resistance continued for a long time, as did Muslim and other regional revolts; and the Manchu were never fully accepted. But they did reform and improve the Ming system of administration; and under a series of great emperors – Kangxi, Yongzheng and Qianlong – they successfully ruled an increasingly populous and wealthy empire from the 1660s until the opium crisis, through the age of the French and American revolutions and the coming of industrial capitalism. This was a major achievement.

China's eighteen provinces were ruled by a hierarchy of officials, selected via the savagely competitive system of learning and reciting classic texts. The millions lured to study them would mostly fail their exams, and though the system hardly promoted original thinking, it did produce accomplished and dedicated bureaucrats. Inside the empire, a complex network of state postal routes kept the capital closely informed about what was happening thousands of miles away. The Chinese military forces had fallen behind those of Europe in technical skill, but not very far behind. They had had cannon for far longer than the Europeans, their junk-warships had long experience of defeating the local pirates; and, having put down numerous revolts, the emperor's armies were battle-hardened. Manchu China was not, in short, a basket-case. Had the dynasty not been faced with the effects of that far-off industrial revolution, there is no reason to think it would not have continued to grow stronger. It was only doomed because of what had happened in Manchester and Birmingham.

Immediately before the opium crisis, China had had a long-ruling, tough and diligent emperor, one Daoguang, sixth in the Manchu line. He ruled around four hundred million people, the overwhelming majority of them peasants, but including a number of powerful trading cities sending grain, salt, silk and luxuries up and down the country. It was the world's richest and most populated country, and conducted its business in five languages. In that respect, it was more like the Austro-Hungarian Empire of the Habsburgs than any other. But China under the Qing had no local rivals. There was just China, centre of the world, and weak, supplicant states somewhere out there on the fringe.

This explains the dismissive attitude to the huge British diplomatic mission to Beijing in 1793, led by Lord George Macartney. Gorgeously attired and bringing British woollens, guns, clocks, paintings and musical instruments, and even a hot-air balloon (with keen balloonist attached), Macartney had arrived on a large warship with ninety-five attendants. His expedition had required 2,495 porters to carry it overland. His lordship was shrewd and had negotiated the difficulties of approaching the emperor, including how to dodge the humiliating 'kowtow'. But his proposal for a permanent British embassy in Beijing and a Chinese one in London, as a prelude to wider trade, was contemptuously rejected. Qianlong accepted George III's greeting of 'humility and obedience', but explained he did not want the gadgets, 'nor do we have the slightest need of your country's manufactures'.[37] For the Chinese, the British were just another minor tribe over the horizon.

Thus, when Commissioner Lin arrived in 1839 to deal with the serious, but local, difficulty of British merchants flooding southern China with highly addictive drugs, he felt he was in a position of strength. He was well aware that the tea trade was good for Chinese growers and merchants, and he was not trying to close his country off entirely.

His brusque way was well captured in a thoughtful but stern letter he wrote to Queen Victoria. He had no idea that opium was legally available in Britain – what a bizarre thought! – and patiently explained that 'this poisonous article is manufactured by certain devilish persons in places subject to your rule. It is not of course either made or sold at your bidding.' He told her to stop the trade and report back to him, promising that if she did so, 'you will be acting in accordance with decent feeling, which may also influence the course of nature in your favour'. Queen Victoria never got the letter, though it was later published by *The Times*, leading to much ignorant laughter about ignorant foreigners. In fact, a vigorous argument about the iniquity of the opium trade was going on in London; but the complex trade involving tea, silver and cotton too was just too lucrative to give up.

Lin's great mistake was to threaten force against the foreign merchants in Canton. He began by intimidating the super-rich Chinese merchants who worked with them. Peremptorily, he ordered the British, the Americans and others to stop trading in opium and to hand over all their stock for destruction. When they refused, he had the doors of the 'factories' nailed shut, and barred the supply of food. The foreigners found themselves quickly deserted by their servants, some of whom turned up later as part of an intimidating array of Chinese soldiers, to be drilled in front of the merchants' windows. Gongs were banged all night to keep them awake. This amounted to something between a siege and a hostage crisis, in the wake of which Lin would enjoy an immediate and total success. The British official in charge eventually promised the merchants that the British government would refund their losses, so long as they handed over all the opium Lin demanded. Faced with ruin and fearing for their lives, they agreed. Lin got his opium and destroyed it publicly, with none of the 'leakage' of so many modern drugs busts. And the British departed, many of them gathering on ships off Hong Kong.

The problem for Lin was that by involving the British government official who had promised a British refund, he had made this a political challenge, not simply one concerning traders. This made it very easy for the opium lobby in London to whip up the case for war. It is perfectly clear from newspaper and parliamentary debates of the time that many people understood exactly the nature of the opium trade, and why the trade was almost as addictive as the drug itself. The British were tea addicts; their government was addicted to taxes; drug addicts in China were too far away to count. But this hard, unpalatable and amoral argument was now sugared with synthetic indignation about the outrageous treatment of British subjects – servants of the Crown, no less – and Lin's impudent threats. Profits? No, this was a matter of pride. Lin did not help his case by demanding that Britain promise to hand over to the Chinese authorities anyone aboard an opium-smuggling ship, which meant death. Lin was undeniably smug about his success, and aggressive towards what he saw as craven British weakness. The Chinese were famously proud.

But so were the British, and the difference was this. The Chinese had an army which, while brave, still used muskets as well as spears and bows and arrows; plus a navy of wooden junks whose cannon were fixed and thus could not be aimed. The British had disciplined modern troops and a navy based on steam-powered gunboats. In the *Nemesis*, a formidable iron paddle-steamer that was almost unsinkable, they had the latest military vessel too.

The war began with complicated provocations, counter-demands, insults and murders, but once the Royal Navy arrived in force off the Chinese coast, it was a one-way affair. Canton's Pearl River was block-aded. Key ports up the coast, including Shanghai and Nanking, were bombarded and seized. Chinese troops were mown down. Manchu soldiers, who did not believe in being captured alive, killed their wives and children before committing suicide; and peasant militias were torn to pieces by British muskets. By then Lin had been publicly derided by the emperor as 'no better than a wooden image', and sacked. The humiliating Treaty of Nanking that eventually followed included a massive indemnity awarded by China to Britain, the opening of five Chinese ports to international trade, the handing over of Hong Kong as a British colony and – yes – the legal continuation of the opium trade. Within two years, a quarter of the boats arriving in Hong Kong were carrying opium.

This was a disaster for the Manchu dynasty, but it was also a disaster for China. The loss of imperial authority was soon challenged by a bizarre cult led by a southern Chinese man who, unlike Lin, had failed his examinations, and who later announced that he was the younger brother of Jesus, and thus the son of God. Hong Xiuquan's movement, known as the God Worshippers, was particularly aimed at opium addicts. By now, drug addiction had swept China, and addicts who wanted to come off opium were encouraged to commit themselves to a rigorous regime of abstinence. Part proto-Communists, part religious fanatics, in 1853 Hong's followers rose in rebellion and seized Nanking, inflicting immense butchery. Hong established a kind of court there that lasted for more than a decade. The long struggles of the Taiping Rebellion, as the God Worshippers' revolt was called, ravaged central China and are estimated to have caused the deaths of twenty million people, in the single most devastating civil war in human history.

In the midst of this came a second war between Britain, this time joined by other Western forces, and the Manchu empire.

This 'Second Opium War' is remembered particularly for the burning of the emperor's Summer Palace outside Beijing by British troops, in revenge for the grisly deaths of captives in Chinese hands. The Summer Palace was a lot more than a building. It was a vast area of beautiful palaces, pagodas, pavilions, libraries, temples and gardens containing a storehouse of Chinese art, whose devastation was one of the severest cultural wounds inflicted on China by any outsider. This would be the equivalent of an army destroying all of central London's churches, cathedrals, palaces and museums, or razing the heart of Paris. Lin, who had thought he was bringing a cleaner, brighter future to the Chinese by tackling the scourge of drug addiction, heard nothing of this. He had been pardoned by the emperor and ordered to take on the Taiping Rebellion, but luckily for him he died before the full horror of what he had unwittingly unleashed was known. Modernization has never looked as foul.

Familiar, and Strange

By the 1880s capitalism had drawn in countries all around the world in a dash for modernisation. The imminent First World War would be not only the war of empires, but the first war between well matched capitalist enemies – which is why it would be so horrific. In many ways, the world at the end of the nineteenth century was a reverse image of today's. Almost all countries except the US and France were still monarchies, not yet republics, while the European powers dominated and Asia lay prone. There were no international institutions of relevance. Racism was almost universal, and considered natural. But in other ways, there were strong parallels with today: the world was opening up, with much faster communications, major migrations of people and an explosion of inventiveness, producing a new consumer economy which spread between continents.

The most important new fact, following on from faster travel, the introduction of telegraph cables and mass publishing, was simply that ideas spread almost immediately. There were particular centres of inventiveness. Germany, united under Prussian leadership after winning a short, decisive war against France, had a special reputation for engineers, technical schools and ambitious businessmen, and came up with an astonishing range of inventions in a very short period. Nikolaus Otto, who worked mainly in Frankfurt and Cologne, has a claim to be the most influential individual of the nineteenth century for his invention of the four-stroke internal-combustion engine, but he would be driven close by Karl Friedrich Benz from Karlsruhe, whose gas-powered, three-wheeled car, the Motorwagen, was patented in 1885, and who followed it with a stream of bigger, more powerful vehicles; and by Rudolf Diesel, the Bavarian inventor of the diesel engine.

There ensued a tumult of inventiveness from the United States to Italy, Austria to France, Britain to Switzerland, as individuals and small companies competed to improve both the fuel and the engineering, with new camshafts, cooling and steering systems, brakes and bodywork. The Clément-Panhard four-wheeler, launched in 1894, was perhaps the first to look more like a modern car – well, a little – but it was quickly overtaken.

The development of the car was a triumph of the capitalist system, which had evolved first in Britain, then had quickly spread. Part of the Germans' secret was their excellent technical and engineering education and their long tradition of craftsmanship; and Germany, like the US and France, now had an effective patent system, enabling inventors like Benz and Otto to become rich. (Poor Diesel was less good at business, and having run out of money, probably committed suicide in the English Channel.) Technical journals and the robust exporting of different models accelerated the race to improve automobiles, which soon outpaced earlier industrial breakthroughs like steam-powered trains and shipping. To start with, cars were for rich show-offs and regarded with widespread suspicion and derision, particularly when exported far from their place of origin, to Australia or Japan.

America's single greatest inventor, Thomas Edison, whose cre-
ations included the light bulb, the phonograph and the movie camera
(among more than a thousand patents in his name), was a fanatical
enthusiast for mass production. He is certainly a rival to Benz as one
of the shapers of the coming century. One of his protégés, an engineer from an Anglo-Irish immigrant family called Henry Ford, was
encouraged by Edison to set up an automobile manufacturing company. After various setbacks and downright failures, in 1908 Ford
introduced his Model T, a cheap, easy-to-maintain and easy-to-drive
car for the masses. The spread of newspapers was fundamental to the
new publicity machine used by Ford and other motor manufacturers –
they advertised local and national car races, featuring famous drivers
and gimmicks of all kinds. More important still, in 1913 Ford and a
group of his employees evolved the moving assembly line, which
enormously speeded up production. This, along with Ford's paternal-
istic attitude to his employees – he was a relatively high payer, but
bitterly hostile to trade unions – led to 'Fordism' becoming shorthand
for the next phase of industrial capitalism.

We have already seen the effects of the hunger for rubber (first
bicycle tyres, soon car tyres) on Africa, but Ford-era capitalism needed
a lot more – gas, oil, minerals and steel. Its products sold to Europe
and her colonies, the US and parts of South America, but its hunger
for raw materials reached even further afield. These developments
would release mankind from a heavy dependence on horses and
human portering, while creating a world where far more people had
far more liberty of movement, freeing them up to do more business.
Such innovation would also, of course, produce serious atmospheric
pollution and expand oil-drilling, with particular political consequences for the Middle East.

But feeding people matters more than allowing them the freedom
of mobility. So, more important even than the car were the late-
nineteenth and early-twentieth-century breakthroughs in fertilizing
soils. The depletion of phosphorus and nitrogen is an inevitable by-
product of intensive farming, which slowly but surely reduces crops.
Birdlime, or guano, collected from the cliffs of Chile and Peru, was
brought to Europe and the US to help replace nitrogen; the invention
of an artificial phosphate-based fertilizer by an English farmer also
kept up yields. However, it was only in 1908 when a German scientist,

Fritz Haber, worked out how to extract nitrogen from the air using ammonia, that the huge expansion in agricultural productivity followed. Haber was a fervent nationalist who later made poison gas for the German army during the First World War, but as a Jew he had to flee to Britain when the Nazis took power – so, an ambiguous figure. But it has been claimed that artificial fertilizers have allowed an extra two billion people to live, and eat, today, making Haber one of the most influential figures of all time. In the short term, however, there were other Germans whose effect on the world would rival his.

The Cheerful Fellow from Berlin

What sort of person best defined the first part of the twentieth century? Not a soldier, despite the wars. Not a professional revolutionary, or a scientist. Not even Ford or Edison. No, from the British in India to the colonial administrators of France, through to the terror state of Lenin and the capitalist economy of the United States, the characteristic noises of this time are the scratch of pen on paper and the clack of the typewriter. So the answer to our question is: the bureaucrat. This is the age of the professional administrator taking a trolleybus to work, where his files are waiting. In his office, he will hang up his coat, light a cigarette, then settle down at his desk to tally tax receipts or numbers of counter-revolutionaries arrested, or write a report about typhoid cases. And what he wants above all things, whether he is working behind mosquito screens in Calcutta or ice-rimed windows in Moscow, is promotion.

Chinese officialdom had once been famous for its meticulous records and impartial, if ruthless, administration. By the late nineteenth century, the advanced economies of the West had caught up. The power of the state was growing fast. In Britain, David Lloyd George and Winston Churchill planned to create state pensions and state insurance. In Japan, the ministers of the Meiji restoration were pushing ahead with their crash course in modernization and education. But nowhere was the advance of bureaucracy in the service of modernization more thoroughgoing and professional than in Berlin. The German Chancellor Bismarck had unified Germany by means of war and by the extension of a trade-friendly customs union, and then further knitted the nation together with the world's most impressive welfare state. German officialdom was famous. It had an almost military atmosphere. But the difference was that in the wood-panelled offices of the German state, unlike in the crack regiments of the Prussian army, non-aristocrats could rise to the top.

Arthur Zimmermann was one of the most perfect examples of the new man. He was genial, a 'good fellow', modest, efficient and tireless. In 1916, the American ambassador in Berlin described him as 'a very jolly large sort of German', and the *New York Times* celebrated his rise towards the top of the Kaiser's foreign service as a victory for 'a man of the people' who had worked his way into a world previously dominated by Prussian Junkers, aristocrats with their 'von' titles. Zimmermann was middle-class, 'a big, ruddy, good-humoured, square-headed bachelor of fifty-eight with blue eyes, reddish blond hair and bushy moustache'.[38] Born in a part of Prussia now in Poland, he had trained as a lawyer before joining the consular service in Berlin. On his adventures he had seen the suppression of the rebels in China. By dint of hard work, efficiency and obedience he had risen through the ranks and still seemed bluff, direct and unstuffy; and he sported a duelling scar, then almost mandatory for an ambitious German male. He had moved to the foreign service in 1902, and had continued to rise. His pen never stopped. His advice was always sound.

Yet there is a case to be made that Zimmermann was the most destructive man of his generation. He was responsible for drawing America into the First World War, and thus for the ruinous postwar peace treaties dominated by President Woodrow Wilson. He fomented the Irish Easter Rising, with its tragically bloody consequences. He tried to have Islamic jihad against the British declared across the Middle East (but luckily failed). And he was also a key player in the German decision to send the revolutionary leader Lenin in a sealed train to Russia in order to make things worse there. That was undoubtedly a kind of success. Without the arrival of Lenin it is far less likely that his minority Bolsheviks would have been able to hijack the anti-Czarist revolution and create the Soviet state. It is quite a charge list.

The American historian Barbara Tuchman surely got it right when she said that being 'a self-made man in the aristocratic ranks of the Foreign Office' had the effect 'of making Zimmermann more Hohen-

The young Tolstoy would turn from being a wastrel, gambling landowner into a passionate friend to Russia's serfs . . . while writing some books on the side.

A Russian Revolution in 1825; but the Decembrists, who wanted to make Russia more European, failed and were executed or sent to Siberia.

The bombardment of Fort Henry, Tennessee: the American Civil War, creating the colossus of the modern US, was the most important conflict of the nineteenth century.

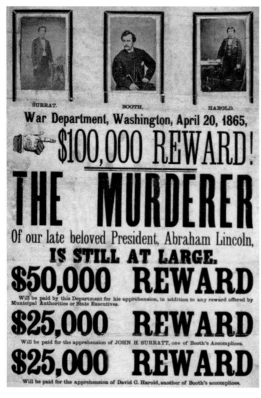

SURRAT. BOOTH. HAROLD.

War Department, Washington, April 20, 1865,

$100,000 REWARD!

THE MURDERER

Of our late beloved President, Abraham Lincoln,

IS STILL AT LARGE.

$50,000 REWARD

Will be paid by this Department for his apprehension, in addition to any reward offered by Municipal Authorities or State Executives.

$25,000 REWARD

Will be paid for the apprehension of JOHN H. SURRATT, one of Booth's Accomplices.

$25,000 REWARD

Will be paid for the apprehension of David C. Harold, another of Booth's accomplices.

John Wilkes Booth, assassin of Abraham Lincoln, was soon caught: but in the South this failed actor became a hero for killing 'the tyrant'.

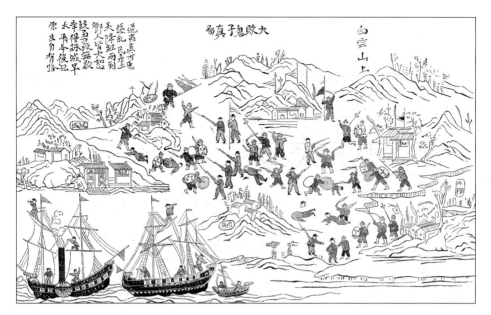

Above. The Chinese view: during the Second Opium War of 1856–8, the Chinese had no chance against British gunboats and infantry.

Left. King Leopold II had nothing but contempt for the Belgians – 'small people, small country' – and built a personal empire in Africa, with tragic results.

Right. No nation drove the second industrial revolution with quite the verve of the Germans: Karl Benz demonstrates his 1886 motorized tricycle.

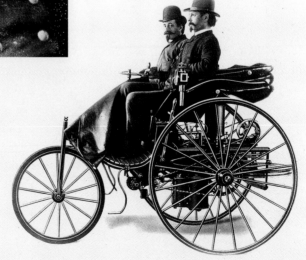

Above left. The founder of Soviet power; but Lenin was brought to power, quite literally, by the Germans who sent him by sealed train to Russia.

Above right. Hitler told the world just what he intended to do: the world refused to believe him.

Mao, five years before he became the most lethal leader China – and the world – has ever seen.

Arm in arm: but
Muhammad Ali Jinnah's
rejection of a single
successor state to the
British Raj meant his
Pakistan and Gandhi's
India would become
sworn enemies.

Robert Oppenheimer,
the cultured liberal scientist
who ended up calculating
the exact height at which his
bomb would burn to death
the maximum number of
civilian men, women
and children.

Above left. Margaret Sanger: the working-class radical who did more for twentieth-century women than any politician, male or female.

Above right. Castro's successful crushing of the US-backed Bay of Pigs invasion of Cuba was part of the prelude to the missile crisis which brought the world to the edge of annihilation.

Protestors in Boston, 1970: 'Ho, Ho, Ho Chi Minh'. American and European students who turned against their parents' generation found new heroes in the Marxist revolutionaries of the East.

The blithe Western assumption that history would lead inevitably to liberalism was given a rough jolt when Iran turned to a militant Islamic theocracy in 1979.

Prague, 1989: the collapse of the Soviet empire was remarkably fast and mostly remarkably peaceful too.

A statue of the Iraqi dictator Saddam Hussein being torn down after the US-led invasion: but what followed this liberation was also horrific.

In 1997 Garry Kasparov, perhaps the world's greatest ever chess-player, played an IBM supercomputer in a match billed as 'the brain's last stand'.

zollern than the Kaiser. Because he wanted to be "one of them" he was the more anxious to be orthodox, the more easily taken into camp by the ruling elite.'³⁹ The zeal of the outsider to belong, and so to be pliable, is a story often encountered in institutions, from governments to international banks. In this case, the rise of Zimmermann to the very top of the German foreign service came at a crucial point in the First World War, when there was huge political pressure for a giant gamble. Zimmermann was there because he would force the pace inside what had become a kind of royal-military dictatorship, not because he was a democratic or modern kind of man.

The issue was simple. Imperial Germany's first gamble had failed. The lightning-fast strike against France in 1914 had failed to reach Paris and end the war there and then – though they had got within a tantalizing forty-three miles of their target. Instead, the small British Expeditionary Force, alongside desperate French and Belgian armies, had held the German attack. By 1915 both sides were literally bogged down along a line of trenches running from the North Sea to Switzerland. It was clear that the new technology of warfare, a combination of huge artillery pieces, machine-guns, gas and barbed wire, was far more effective defensively than in attack. Nobody could break through. Although the German army had inflicted huge defeats on Czar Nicholas II's Russian armies in the east, Germany was now blockaded by sea; she could not hold out for ever.

There was, though, one way for Germany to achieve victory, even over the manpower and industrial muscle of the British Empire, and that was to starve Britain of fuel, food and raw materials. This was entirely possible. Though the war at sea between battleships was no more decisive than the war on land, Germany's awesomely effective U-boat fleet had a real chance of sinking so many merchant ships that Britain would be forced to sue for peace. At this point, the Royal Navy had no effective answer to submarine warfare, and the Atlantic was becoming a shipping graveyard. The problem for Germany was that, to be wholly effective, their U-boats had to be allowed to sink any ship making for a British or French port, including neutral ships, and above all American ones. 'Unrestricted' U-boat warfare would enrage the US public, which had so far avoided involvement, and might lead to the strongly anti-war President Wilson declaring against Germany. Yet if German U-boats sank enough ships quickly enough, Britain might collapse before the United States could arrive to help, and the war would end. That race was the essence of the gamble.

Zimmermann had a cunning plan. If the Americans did declare war on Germany, why not persuade Mexico to invade them from the south? And it would be even more worrying for Washington, if Japan could be brought into the anti-American plot. Though Japan had plumped for joining the Allies against Germany, she might be persuaded to switch sides. Decades before Pearl Harbor, Imperial Japan and the US were rivals across the Pacific, and American public opinion was regularly shaken by fear of 'the Yellow Peril'. By 1915–16 the US was worried that Germany and Japan were indeed 'getting together' in a new pact to squeeze out the democracies. In 1913 Japan had sold arms to Mexico's dictator, General Huerta. In April 1914 just before the First World War, the US and Mexico had fought in the Mexican port of Veracruz over a German arms cargo, killing nearly two hundred. Mexico, though riven by its own political conflicts, was united in patriotic anger over the huge territories the United States had taken from them in the past century, and was increasingly anti-American in mood. Viewed from Berlin, this was dry tinder.

Zimmermann went to work. In January 1917 he sent secret messages to the German ambassador in Washington, Count von Bernstorff, informing him that unrestricted U-boat warfare would begin on 1 February and asking him to send on a still more dramatic message to the Mexicans via the German ambassador in Mexico City, Heinrich von Eckhardt. This read, in part: 'Make war together, make peace together, generous financial support and an understanding on our part that Mexico is to reconquer the lost territory in Texas, New Mexico and Arizona.' It further suggested that Japan would join in against the US and that the German submarines offered the prospect of 'compelling England to make peace within a few months'.

What Berlin did not know was that, long before, British Naval Intelligence had cracked their diplomatic codes, and the sensational news was read in London before it was read by the German ambassador himself. President Wilson was still desperate to avoid joining the war, but once he and the US public knew the Germans' intentions, the pressure to go to war would be unstoppable. In a complicated manoeuvre to prove its authenticity, British Intelligence showed the

'Zimmermann telegram' to a US embassy official in London, who passed it to the White House.

In America, all hell broke loose. Wilson released the news first to senators and Congressmen and then to the press. German-Americans and the anti-war party were aghast, but promptly suggested that a German–Mexican–Japanese plot to invade the US was so outlandish it must be a British forgery. Many senior US politicians and writers harbouring no love for the British Empire loudly proclaimed it a fake, a cynical London ruse. Even at this late stage it was just possible that the Americans would be sufficiently suspicious to avoid the rush to war. But they had not reckoned on Zimmermann. Two days later, at a press conference in Berlin, he was called upon, by an American journalist secretly in the pay of Germany, to limit the damage. 'Of course, Your Excellency will deny this story,' said the reporter. 'I cannot deny it,' replied Zimmermann. 'It is true.'

So, fuelled by fears of the Prussian Invasion Plot and with US newspapers warning their readers of 'hordes of Mexicans under German officers sweeping into Texas, New Mexico and Arizona' while Japan would seize and 'Orientalize' California, in April 1917 America went to war.[40] Germany's unrestricted submarine warfare worked with deadly effectiveness and did indeed bring Britain very close to the edge, within weeks of running out of oil and other vital supplies, including many foods. Only the late realization that the convoy system could be made to work saved the day. By then, the US was sending boatloads of soldiers over to Europe. Germany would make a last attempt to break the deadlock on the Western Front, but she had lost her great gamble. And for that, the friendly middle-class bureaucrat Arthur Zimmermann must take much of the blame. Barbara Tuchman concluded that the US would have probably entered the war eventually, 'But the time was already late and, had we delayed much longer, the Allies might have been forced to negotiate. To that extent, the Zimmermann telegram altered the course of history . . . In world affairs it was a German Minister's minor plot. In the lives of the American people it was the end of innocence.'[41]

Had this been all, Zimmermann's impact on his century would already have been remarkable. But this was not all. As foreign secretary, he was also privy to secret German plans to bring Czarist Russia, already reeling from military defeat, to total collapse. Once Russia sued for peace, the German armies in the east would be free to reinforce their comrades on the Western Front: this was another side of the 'one last throw' of German policy that Zimmermann lived for. Yet its outcome was perhaps even more disastrous than the botched Mexican plot against America.

During the early spring of 1917 the Swiss town of Zurich was seething with people displaced by war – Italians, French, Germans, Irish, Russians. They included famous composers like Busoni, writers such as James Joyce, Stefan Zweig and Romain Rolland, and a modest platoon of professional agitators and revolutionaries. One of these, from a family of minor nobility, was a quiet-looking man who lived with his wife and a female assistant and spent much of his time reading in public libraries or going for long walks in the Swiss forests and mountains. He had never had a job and, apart from a few months in 1905, had been living outside Russia for seventeen years. During that time he had spent most of his energy on ferocious political arguments with a wide range of left-wing and liberal thinkers. He avoided classical music because it made him feel soft and sentimental; he had little use for literature; and his writing style was leaden. He had adopted the revolutionary name Vladimir Ilich Lenin.

Like the other Communist leaders, Lenin was taken by surprise when the February Revolution erupted in St Petersburg (then known as Petrograd). The war had been disastrous for the Czar and his regime. German armies had made mincemeat of the under-equipped, if huge, Russian forces. Terrible suffering by ordinary soldiers was matched by increasingly dangerous shortages of food, including bread, in the cities. Nicholas II had sacked most of his competent ministers, lost the loyalty of many of his officers, and had rejected out of hand any suggestions for reform. Lenin, though he had thought that with the war would come some kind of crisis, had worried that he would not see an actual revolution in his lifetime. So when the news was brought to him by a young Polish neighbour that four regiments of the Petrograd garrison had joined striking workers and protesting women and provoked a full-scale uprising, Lenin was delighted – but astonished and anxious too.

He had to get back. This was the moment he had spent his life waiting for, and here he was, stuck, thousands of miles away and with a war going on in between. Lenin had strengthened his grip on the 'majority', or Bolshevik, group of the Russian Communists by insisting that good Marxists must not take sides in a capitalists' war. Other socialists, in Germany, France, Britain, and indeed Russia, had put aside their hostility to their governments and had been swept along by patriotic feeling. For Lenin, a war in which the rich sent the poor to fight one another was disgusting. A plague on all their houses – as a Russian, he would be pleased to see Russia lose.

The only advantage of war, he thought, was that it might so shake the 'bourgeois' countries and Czarist Russia that they would come tumbling down, leading to a real war, an uprising of workers against owners. Now that seemed to be happening. But as the revolution swept ahead in Russia, it was not Lenin who was leading it, but unknown voices in the Petrograd workers' soviet along with a broad coalition of liberal reformers and moderate socialists who had formed a provisional government. Despite the chaos and a breakdown of law and order in parts of Petrograd, the two groups seemed to be working relatively harmoniously together. In London, Paris and Washington there was widespread pleasure that the Czar had abdicated and a feeling that a new government would strengthen, not weaken, the Russians' appetite to keep fighting.

Zimmermann, the Kaiser and the German high command were worried about exactly that. They wanted a fast and preferably complete collapse in Russia. So, for rather different reasons, did Lenin. Would it not suit Berlin to help get Lenin back to Petrograd? The Russian revolutionary Maxim Litvinov and the British Conservative Winston Churchill spoke in similar terms. Litvinov said the Germans needed to eliminate the Russian army from the scene before the Americans arrived: 'Objectively we played the part of a bacillus introduced in the East,' he said later. Churchill commented that the Germans (with friend Zimmermann to the fore) had with a sense of awe 'turned upon Russia the most grisly of all weapons. They transported Lenin in a sealed truck like a plague bacillus from Switzerland into Russia.' James Joyce, when he heard the news about his Zurich neighbour, compared it to a German Trojan Horse. Everyone involved understood what was going on; one German general compared Lenin to poison gas.[42]

The 'sealed truck' was in fact an ordinary German train whose carriages were marked on the outside in such a way as to avoid customs and keep up the pretence that the dangerous Russian revolutionary had never set foot on German soil. With the revolutionaries ensconced in their second-class carriages enjoying good German food, and having insisted smoking could only be done in the lavatories, Lenin and his helpers rattled and wrote their way across Germany and through neutral Sweden to Petrograd's Finland railway station. Zimmermann's foreign office and Ludendorff's high command were so keen to get Lenin into Russia that, had Sweden blocked him, they would have sent him through the German front lines.

He did not disappoint them. On the train he had written down his essential arguments. They included no cooperation with the Provisional Government, an immediate demand for peace with Germany on any terms, and power to be taken by the soviets, the committees of workers and soldiers – led, of course, by himself and the Bolsheviks. Meanwhile, the Germans had helped fund Lenin's revolutionaries as well as transporting them, something the cheering crowd at the station could not have known. The bacillus had been delivered.

Up to then, the Communist faction in the Russian capital had been seriously divided. Many orthodox Marxists believed, following the philosopher, that proper revolution could only come about after a bourgeois, liberal era – that you could not simply leap from an underdeveloped peasant economy into a socialist one. So their job would be to wait, educate and agitate, while the moderates got on with the job of holding Russia together. They were aghast at Lenin's uncompromising message, laced as it was with torrents of satire and abuse.

Russia was certainly at boiling point, and Lenin's readiness to provoke civil war in no way alarmed the desperate workers and soldiers to whom he appealed. As the arguments raged, alongside demonstrations, marches and late-night meetings, the Provisional Government pledged to carry on the war with Germany. Alexander Kerensky, a moderate socialist leader (whose father had been Lenin's schoolteacher), emerged as the man who could meld the Petrograd soviet and the government together. He became prime minister, tried to rally the troops, and declared Russia a republic with himself as president. But Kerensky, for all his rhetoric and energy, was no more able to direct the Russian armies to victory than the Czar had been. For the troops had given up. They would fight no longer. The Bolsheviks, now fully under Lenin's direction, and his spell, chose their moment and struck. The October Revolution, promising bread and peace, was swiftly followed by the peace treaty the Germans had required; and by something close to a group dictatorship directed by Lenin; and then by civil war, famine and catastrophe.

In a fair court of history, Arthur Zimmermann would be acquitted of responsibility for these terrible events. Of direct responsibility, anyway. Though a key player, he was only one of the German clique that sent Lenin to Russia – Kaiser Wilhelm signed off the idea, and the military leader Ludendorff was also involved. Nor can we be sure that Lenin would not have found another way home, though it is hard to see how; or know what would have happened in Petrograd had Lenin never arrived, or had he been delayed during those crucial months of mid-1917. It is possible that others would have orchestrated the over-throw of the Provisional Government, and that Russia would have anyway fallen into dictatorship and civil war. On these grounds, the Scottish legal verdict of 'not proven' would surely have been handed down.

And yet . . . Lenin was a very rare, self-certain, charismatic, fright-ening and narrowly focused leader, much more impressive than his rivals. He scared, out-argued, bullied, out-organized and out-thought lesser revolutionaries, always pushing things towards the extreme, always knocking compromise aside; and never flinching at the terrible cost in blood and suffering that his politics inflicted. He was another Robespierre, a man with ice in his blood; utterly convinced that some kind of human paradise was in the offing, and that any means justified getting there. With his tight little system he called 'the dictatorship of the proletariat', his secret police and his purging of those who dared disagree, Lenin started what Stalin finished. Both, of course, employed many hard-working, zealous state bureaucrats with an eye to the next promotion, affable men who liked a drink and just wanted to belong. Arthur Zimmermann, one suspects, would have fitted in rather well.

Part Eight

1918–2012: OUR TIMES

The Best and Worst of Centuries

Two men are sitting in a Russian prison during the Stalin Terror. One has just been tortured. The other is awaiting his turn. They are arguing about history. Aleksey holds out no hope for humanity. He says: 'Man is simply man, and there's nothing that can be done with him. There is no evolution. There is one very simple law, the law of the conservation of violence. It's as simple as the law of the conservation of energy. Violence is eternal, no matter what is done to destroy it. It does not disappear or diminish; it can only change shape.'

The other man, Ivan, disagrees. For him, 'human history is the history of freedom, of the movement from less freedom to more freedom'. Aleksey, who will soon be dead, mocks Ivan. There is no history. It is just 'grinding water with a pestle and mortar . . . the humanity in humanity does not increase. What history of humanity can there be if man's goodness always stands still?'[1] The argument takes place towards the end of an angry novel, *Everything Flows*, by the Russian writer Vasily Grossman. He was writing it in the early 1960s, looking back at life under Stalin, the second most lethal mass killer of modern times. (The first is Mao, the third, Hitler.) His argument, however, was about mankind, not simply Russia. The twentieth century made it the most important argument of all. Do we learn? Do we become better? Does the violence stop or does it get greater, the more of us there are?

It was a century of a great apparent paradox. The killing *was* greater than ever. In raw numbers it outstripped even the Mongols, all the plague-armed catastrophes of the European invasion of the Americas, and all earlier wars. This killing happened because leaders arose promising to radically improve humankind, or part of humankind, and were able to exercise near-total power. The 'bloodiest century in history' has become a cliché of history. Yet it is challenged by, among others, the scientist Steven Pinker, who points out that the terrifyingly large numbers of deaths are partly accounted for by the vastly greater number of people alive: you can't kill people who are not there. If the blood-count is adjusted for population, then modern times do not look quite as bad. The Mongol Conquests (already described), the very violent revolt in eighth-century China, the conquests of Tamerlane, the fall of ancient Rome and the final fall of the Ming dynasty – all killed proportionally more than did the Second World War.[2]

Furthermore, our knowledge of recent violence, photographed, totted up, filmed and kept for us in diaries, memoirs and speeches, is more detailed and more vivid than our knowledge of the violence of, say, sixteenth-century Africa or medieval French villages, or the empires of early Korea. This 'historical myopia', Pinker argues, encourages us to view the past far too leniently and our recent history too bleakly. For specific historical reasons, unlikely to be repeated, the twentieth century saw a war of annihilation between Hitler's Germany and Stalin's Russia which, having spread to much of the rest of the world, was ended by the use of nuclear weapons.

Of itself that hardly means that people have become more violent or more wicked. In fact, Pinker claims, when one includes small wars, domestic violence, violence against children and the old, cruelty to animals, religious sacrifices, slavery and violent crime, people are actually becoming less violent and 'better'. This is so even in Africa, which has been particularly plagued by wars in recent times. Societies with a rule of law, in which women have more authority, and which are bound together by international treaties (and kept from huge wars by nuclear weaponry), are producing gentler ways of living. Backing up Pinker, the US researcher Matthew White, who introduced the word 'atrocitology' to explain his ranking of lethal events, points out that during the twentieth century more than 95 per cent of all deaths were from natural causes.

This is a crucial point, which should be underlined from the start. The vast majority of us live most of our lives in what I have called 'the lulls', those long periods of quiet social stability. Then we die of diseases of old age. Better medicine and food, cleaner water and more effective policing have brought a huge rise in lifespans, as well as a huge (and unsustainable) rise in human numbers; so the lulls have gone on for longer. To take just one example: without that discovery by Fritz Haber in 1919 of how to fix nitrogen to produce man-made fertilizer, it is said, two billion people now alive would not be alive.[3] And in some countries that have suffered hideous famine – China being the clearest example – the twenty-first century has seen an explosion of material wealth and opportunity. Far more people have lived better, more peaceful lives in the past century than ever before. Alongside the slaughter of twentieth-century industrial wars and the threat of nuclear war, we have to remember the good times brought to hundreds of millions of people who have experienced peace and plenty on a scale that has no historical precedent, not even during the 'Roman Peace' of the early empire. So, the best of times, too.

The Problem of Politics

A key theme in this history has been the mismatch between mankind's ability to understand the world and so reshape it, and on the other hand the lack of progress in how we are ruled. Science strides ahead; politics stumbles around like a drunk. We saw it in the age of discovery and the age of empire, but it was particularly glaring in the twentieth century – and, I would add (so far), the twenty-first too.

Our two Russian convict-philosophers were having their argument because of the greatest failure of twentieth-century politics: namely, the belief, tested to destruction, that mankind was on an inevitable journey from hierarchies and classes to a paradise of ungoverned equality. Communists felt that the means – cruelty and tyranny – were justifiable because of the grandeur of their ends. They were not the first to make this mistake. Catholic Inquisitors, for instance, felt the same way. But by the 1930s, with the apparatus of a huge state in their hands, the Soviet Communists had the power to go further, and to try to annihilate whole classes, nationalities and categories of humanity who, they felt, were getting in the way. (Marxists never resolved the conundrum that though their victory was inevitable it had to be struggled for with maximum guile, discipline and ruthlessness. If it was inevitable, why the need for struggle?)

Did Stalin and his coterie really believe it? He lived the high life himself, travelling between luxurious private apartments, a 'Red Czar' whose smallest flickers of irritation terrified his minions. Stalin had started as a gangster and behaved like a gangster boss – wily, cold-hearted and cynical about human motives. But it would be wrong to conclude that Communism was itself a purely cynical coating for a system essentially not so different from that of Ivan the Terrible. Without vast numbers of true believers, leather-coated killers, simple workers, chairmen and bureaucrats who genuinely thought they were on the side of history and working to make the world anew, Stalinism could never have happened. The problem was not Communism's cynicism, though it produced cynicism; the problem was its sincerity.

Something similar can be said of Communism's mutant rival sister, Fascism. Neither Benito Mussolini in Italy, nor Adolf Hitler in Germany, thought of the inevitable march of history in quite the way that Communists did. Nor were they trying to abolish whole classes. But they did have a sincere belief, communicated to millions of sincere believers, that their part of the human race was special, that it had been shaped to dominate others and had a right to glory. Not historical inevitability; but *destiny*. Letters and diaries from the Nazi commando groups who systematically butchered Jewish women, old men and children show that they believed this was the right thing to do, however unpleasant. The bogus science of race, laced with scientific-sounding language about hygiene, helped them distance themselves from what they were actually doing.

Marxism was a bogusly 'scientific' version of history; Nazism was a bogusly 'racial' version of evolutionary biology. Just as species were in endless competition, so were the races. For the stronger to fail to struggle against, and destroy, the weak, was a moral failure: it meant humanity would decline, rather than advance. In Hitler's world, this amounted to an Aryan duty to advance at the expense of Slavs, Jews and other, lower forms of humanity. It would lead not to a Communist Utopia, but to a golden age. Both regimes had to kill their way to paradise – kill rebellious, selfish peasants, kill rival socialists, kill class enemies, kill Jews. Attacking better-off peasants, or 'kulaks', or attacking Jews, they used similar language, labelling their enemies bestial and subhuman, vermin or bacilli. Interestingly, neither seemed able to imagine the coming paradise except in the most banal and old-fashioned terms: Communist and Nazi propaganda alike beckoned followers towards a world of apple-cheeked mothers in semi-rural sunlit landscapes, overseen by a mustachioed father figure – a schmaltzy, timid Eden.

If this were the story of modern times it would be bleak. But the twentieth century also brought an expansion of democracy that had seemed impossible during its darkest decades. The 'American Century' brought liberty and choice to millions around the world. This was the triumph of the market economy, defended by science, which had produced weapons so destructive that the great powers of the planet no longer dared to go to war against each other. Russians still do not have the freedoms of Americans, Europeans or many others. But they have more freedom than Grossman could have dared hope when he invented the argument in the prison cell.

We could argue, therefore, that this is an overwhelmingly positive story. The follies of politics in the twentieth century were only the logical conclusion of ideas that had developed in Europe much earlier. Racism, Utopianism, a belief in national destiny, anti-Semitism, a weakness for strong leaders . . . these are hardly new. Surely, after the experiences of Marxist dictatorship and of the Nazis, they are lessons learned for all time? Have we not broken through into a politically chastened and better world, with our United Nations, our declarations of human rights, our international criminal courts? There is a lot to that argument. The fact that wars still go on, in Afghanistan, Africa and the Middle East, does not disprove the theory of general advance; it just reminds us that progress is bumpy.

Yet there are two bumps so large they cannot be steered smoothly around. The first is that, in fact, democracy has not spread effectively. The highly intelligent political scientist Francis Fukuyama proclaimed in *The End of History and the Last Man* that the big arguments about politics were over. They had finished with the triumph of liberal, free-market democracy. Some countries and cultures would take longer than others to get there, but eventually everyone would. In a world where undemocratic but booming China, and oil- and gas-based autocracies (Russia, Iran, Saudi Arabia) loom so large, this no longer feels likely. Fukuyama was wrong, because democracy, it turns out, is not a system. It is a culture. It is based on habits, attitudes, long-established divisions of power, ingrained belief in law and absence of systemic corruption and cynicism. You can import a system and set it up, and get it working. You cannot import a culture. This does not mean most of the world is doomed to live under tyrannies or kleptocracies. It just means that it is a little early for democrats to declare the game over.

The second bump concerns the nature of democracy itself. Recently, democracies have mostly based themselves on the ability of competing political parties to offer voters a better material future (more stuff) year by year, and generation by generation. But because science and peace have boosted the planet's population beyond what its natural resources can bear, this is not a plausible long-term proposition.

To feed, clothe and entertain ourselves, we humans have dug deep into Earth's reserves of oil and water, and have (probably) irreversibly changed the climate by the quantity of carbon dioxide our activities have released. If all Chinese people, all Indian people, all the peoples of South-East Asia and Africa, expect the material goods of today's Western middle class, they are going to be badly disappointed. In the West, we now have the first generations of adults who expect their children to be worse off, materially, than they are. Democracies have survived trade recessions, and have managed to hold together during dangerous wars; but they have not yet dealt with a long period of lowered expectations and less prosperity. Until we see how they do so, we cannot assume that liberal, market democracy is secure. We have learned some of the lessons from what follows in this part of the book; but not all of them.

The Man in Landsberg

July 1924, and a bizarre scene was being witnessed in spacious, well lit rooms on the first floor of the Landsberg Prison near Munich. The prisoner, convicted of high treason after a cock-eyed attempt to overthrow the German government, was dressed in leather shorts and a short mountain tunic. He had put on weight and his rooms were crammed with gifts from well-wishers – cakes, chocolate, bouquets of flowers. Visitors thronged. According to one friend, 'The place looked like a delicatessen store. You could have opened up a flower and fruit and wine shop with all the stuff stacked there.' Hitler looked visibly fatter.[4]

Indeed, the flabby thirty-five-year-old beer-hall agitator eventually had to declare a new regime and order visitors away, so that he could have some quiet time to settle down at his desk and slowly start to dictate a book. Its original snappy title had been 'Four and a Half Years of Struggle against Lies, Stupidity and Cowardice',[5] which was shortened by his editor to *My Struggle*, or in German, *Mein Kampf*. Hitler would do more than any other human being to unleash hell into the twentieth century, but nobody who bothers to read *Mein Kampf*, which had sold six million copies by 1940, could claim that he tried to disguise his plan. Far from it. He too was sincere.

Hitler is of course best known for his determination to rid Germany, and later Europe, of the Jewish people. Some historians have questioned his personal involvement in the Holocaust. Others have argued that the industrial mass murder began almost by accident, once Germany had invaded Poland, Baltic Russia and the Ukraine. As he sat composing *Mein Kampf*, surrounded by his flowers and his boxes of chocolates, Hitler put the Jewish question like this. Was there, he asked, any 'form of filth or profligacy . . . without at least one Jew involved in it? If you cut even cautiously into such an abscess you found, like a maggot in a rotting body, often dazzled by the sudden light – a kike!'[6] He compares the Jews to 'pestilence, spiritual pestilence, worse than the Black Death', and to blood-sucking spiders.

Some have said that, despite this, Hitler only wanted the Jews moved elsewhere and bore them no personal ill-will. In *Mein Kampf* (the second volume, written after his release from prison) he says: 'If at the beginning of the War and during the War, twelve or fifteen thousand of these Hebrew corrupters of the people had been held under poison gas . . . the sacrifice of millions at the front would not have been in vain.'[7] Hitler equates Bolshevik Communism and Jewry, but also finds the Jews pulling the strings of its apparent enemy, international capitalism. The Jews are weak, yet also everywhere in control; they are tiny in numbers but dominate Germany. They control the press, the left-wing parties, the banks, everything. They have to be destroyed.

Hitler was a rare human. Biographers and historians believe he had almost no capacity for empathy, perhaps because of a cold and violent childhood. He was a fantasist who happened to live at a time and in a place already so disrupted that he could make his fantasies come true, though only for a few years, before they collapsed in on themselves. Poorly educated, lazy, physically unappealing, he was nevertheless able to mesmerize audiences, hypnotize individuals who met his dark stare, and whip a nation into a frenzy of adulation. Yet without Germany's defeat in the First World War, without Lenin's triumph in Russia or the long history of European anti-Semitism, he would have been a nobody.

Almost nowhere in Europe had been immune from anti-Semitism. The first Jewish ghetto had been created in Venice. English kings had burned, persecuted and expelled Jews. During the crusading period, French monarchs had confiscated Jewish wealth and expelled them. The Catholic Inquisition had offered them a choice of conversion or death. The history of the Russian empire is littered with murderous anti-Jewish pogroms. And in the early twentieth century, few places were as passionate in their anti-Semitism as Austria and Germany. Vienna, where the struggling would-be artist Hitler had spent some of his hardest formative years, had a particularly vicious anti-Jewish political and newspaper culture, epitomized by its populist mayor Karl Lueger. As Hitler's biographer Ian Kershaw says, 'It was a city where, at the turn of the century, radical anti-Semites advocated punishing sexual relations between Jews and non-Jews as sodomy, and placing Jews under surveillance around Easter to prevent ritual child-murder.'[8]

Hitler must have imbibed some of this, but he knew Jews and indeed used Jewish acquaintances to help market his not very good paintings of the city at a time when he was living in a home for destitute men. Though a 'pan-German' who wanted all Germans to unite in a single *Reich*, and an early lover of Richard Wagner's art which is shot through with anti-Semitism, there is no reliable evidence that he was a notable anti-Semite during his early years, and there are even suggestions that he sympathized with the left-wing Social Democrats.

Much was written later, when he was Germany's ruler, claiming a consistent line, but that turns out difficult to prove. Hitler says in *Mein Kampf* that he was shocked during the Great War, when he was home on leave, by how many Jews were not fighting. The book seethes, too, with claims about Jewish involvement in prostitution. Hitler may have been impotent, and he certainly expressed feelings of repulsion, even horror, about sexual licence; which may have become somehow mixed up with stories about Jews going back to medieval times. It is likely, however, that Hitler's loathing of the Jews really began shortly after Germany's defeat in 1918, when he returned with his regiment, as a highly decorated corporal, to Munich.

As a native Austrian he had been lucky to be accepted by a Bavarian regiment, and had fought in the trenches as a message-carrying runner with considerable bravery. The defeat of the Imperial German Army was something he found hard to accept. Almost worse was that when he returned, with few prospects, Munich was a hotbed of revolution. Over the winter and early spring of 1918–19, anarchists and Communists established a revolutionary 'Red Republic' in Bavaria, mimicking the Bolshevik seizure of power in Russia. There followed a time of food shortages, assassination, seizure of property, violence and left-wing censorship. It fell far short of the 'red terror' experienced to the east, and it was soon ended by a right-wing military counter-attack, but it left deep scars.

Many of its leaders had been Jewish. Hitler, who had been an elected military representative during the Red Republic, understood early on the advantage to an agitator of having a single easily definable enemy. In that milieu of small, angry meetings and small, angry parties, he made a name for himself for the extremism of his language and his one-culprit rhetoric. In the bars and cafés of Munich, German army 'handlers' used him to promote their campaign against the left and against the moderate republican government in far-off Berlin. Jews, Bolsheviks, swindling capitalists and the traitors who had allowed Germany to be beaten were all, for Hitler, essentially parts of the same nest of enemies.

Apart from his time in the army, it could be said that up to then Hitler had really done nothing with his life except talk. He had made bad paintings, loafed around, lived off small amounts of family money . . . and talked. His rants about art, music, Germany, history and politics had echoed around the cheap boarding houses, cafés and bars of Linz, Vienna and Munich. Now, talking became his job.

Young Hitler is so buried under the leprous grime of his reputation, the Holocaust and our image of his pallid white face with its ridiculous moustache, that it is hard to imagine back to a time when he seemed charismatic. He clearly was, though. The small right-wing party he joined and which eventually evolved into the Nazi party quickly came to depend on him as their most popular speaker. He could hold a room for two hours of sarcasm, shouting, joking, smearing and preaching, interrupted by cheers, boos and laughter. In between denouncing the German government and the victorious

Allies, he was calling for Jews to be sent to concentration camps to keep them away from good Germans, and for them to be expelled from Germany. He was soon being compared to Luther and even to Napoleon. His audience, which seems to have been made up of small-time businessmen, shopkeepers, clerks, demobilized soldiers and a surprisingly high proportion of women, found him the best entertainment, as well as the best teacher, to be had.

By the early 1920s Germany seemed to many to be on the edge of Communist revolution. Right-wing 'folkish' thinkers and military men were constantly debating about how to respond. They discussed the need to depose the government in Berlin, so keen to appease the French; to win back a larger German homeland; and to rebuild the German fighting forces. Paramilitary groups stockpiled guns. Funding was available from business tycoons terrified of socialist revolution. Parties formed, quarrelled, split and reformed. General Ludendorff, who had helped lead Germany in the war, re-emerged as a hero of the right. And Munich, after its brief experience of revolution, had become a centre of reactionary thinking. Hitler was in the right place. He had formed alliances with paramilitary organizers, notably Ernst Röhm. He had won powerful admirers in the army, including Ludendorff. He had the backing of extremist newspapers and gangs of organized thugs.

He had even personally designed the flag that would soon be known globally, the black swastika on a white circle against a red background. The swastika had long been a symbol of German anti-Semitic thinking. An ancient and common symbol of happiness, used by Hindus, Buddhists and animists, it had become popular after the German archaeologist Heinrich Schliemann uncovered examples from ancient Troy and proposed them as signs of Aryan identity. The swastika was used by German nationalists before Hitler: what he did was to refine a design and colour combination for the tense, rotated broken cross to make it, in the words of a recent art critic, 'perhaps the most potent graphic emblem ever devised'.[9]

Hitler may have been a bad painter but he was a brilliant propagandist, obsessively careful about image. He had hundreds of photographs of himself taken in different poses and different clothes, hats and coats, rejecting almost all of them until he got the right image of the lonely, driven leader. He pored over the uniforms of his storm-trooper guards and his party followers, as well as later architectural visions, with an attention he never gave to policy or bureaucracy. In an age of political brands, Hitler was an evil genius of a brand-manager.

How had he come, then, to find himself in prison in 1924? He had led a ludicrously bungled attempt at a coup, initially against the regional government in Bavaria but directed ultimately against Berlin. His party, the German Workers' Party, which became the National Socialist German Workers' Party, or NSDAP, 'Nazi' for short, was still relatively small. But the general movement of 'patriotic organizations' and similar parties was big. German army generals and even the local political rulers in Munich seemed broadly sympathetic. By the autumn of 1923 there had been long discussions about overthrowing the government, a putsch to be led either by the army or by the paramilitary groups, or perhaps following a Mussolini-style march on the capital. Hitler, by now described as 'the German Mussolini', believed that, given the right impetus, Ludendorff, with the army in Bavaria, would join in a general uprising against Berlin. It wasn't an entirely unreasonable hope. All that was needed was the spark.

This came from the barrel of Hitler's Browning revolver at around 8.40 p.m. on 8 November 1923, in a huge beer-hall, Munich's Bürgerbräukeller. Beer-halls were, and are, where Munichers did their politics – large, cavernous spaces well suited for speeches and high emotion. That night, most of the leading men of the city had gathered for a long-advertised anti-Communist meeting – there were about three thousand people in the hall. Gustav Ritter von Kahr, a right-wing politician now installed as Bavaria's leader, was in full flow when storm-troopers led by Hermann Goering, the former fighter ace, burst into the room.

Immediately, Hitler jumped onto a chair, fired his pistol at the ceiling and declared that the Bavarian government was deposed and a national revolution had begun. He shepherded the political leaders and a general into a neighbouring room, and told them they would join him in a new German government. If things went wrong, he had a bullet in his gun for all of them, including himself, and he later declared to the crowd: 'Either the German revolution begins tonight or we will all be dead by dawn!'[10] Ludendorff was fetched and, though taken aback, joined in. Hitler announced that in order to 'save the

German people', there would be a march 'on that sinful Babel, Berlin'.[11]

He had assumed that the army and Bavaria's political elite would be marching behind him. Faced by his storm-troopers and his threats, they had briefly agreed, but given neither proper preparation nor plan, they had no intention of starting a civil war. So as soon as they could they defected, and Hitler's putsch began to sputter. While his restless mob was wondering what to do, the army and police were closing in. What the historian Alan Bullock called Hitler's 'revolution by sheer bluff' had failed. The following morning, he and Ludendorff led about two thousand Nazis on a march through Munich towards the war ministry, though it was unclear just what they meant to do next. In face of a police cordon, shooting broke out, killing four policemen and sixteen Hitler supporters. Hitler either threw himself to the ground, or was pushed; the man standing next to him was killed. Ludendorff, the old soldier, had simply kept on marching towards the police. They stood aside. But nobody followed him.

Though some of the other putschists escaped, Ludendorff turned himself in and Hitler was arrested at a friend's house. The trial of nine men accused of high treason began on 24 February 1924 in the former Munich infantry school. Hitler, perhaps embarrassed that he had ducked down so quickly at the first gunshots, then proved himself again a master propagandist. He took full responsibility, denied nothing, and spent much of the trial delivering long and defiant political speeches. The judges seem to have been largely sympathetic, and for the crime of treason, which had led to the deaths of police, hostage-taking and robbery, Hitler was given a sentence of only five years. He would in fact be let out much more quickly, serving just thirteen months. Had he been standing a foot to one side during the coup and been shot, or had he received a more serious sentence, or had he served the sentence he was given, then undoubtedly mankind would have been luckier. Hitler's closing speech at his trial made him famous around Germany. One of the many adulatory letters sent to him in prison was from a young PhD student in Heidelberg called Josef Goebbels. Even his jailers saluted him with 'Heil Hitler' and, partly through *Mein Kampf*, he had ample time to further develop his personality cult – though he never developed his ideas. There was still a long way to go before Hitler would finally be installed as German Chancellor, in 1933, able to dismantle the legal state and build his regime of expansionist terror. That journey depended upon a new world economic crisis that would snuff out Germany's slow and steady postwar return to economic health; and upon bad leadership by other countries as well as a series of disastrous mistakes by rival German politicians.

For his part, Hitler had learned the hard way that, in order to seize power, he could not simply co-opt the German army, however bitter and resentful many of its officers might be. He would have to win politically.

In many ways this suited his talents better. By 1924 he had already assembled his armoury of uniformed intimidation, quiet business backing and extreme rhetorical provocation, which would take him nine years later to power in Berlin. The leader cult was growing. Inside the party, which had been banned but which he would refound in 1925, he had established the principle of personal leadership untrammelled by democracy or voting, which he would later impose on all of Germany. His chaotic working patterns, which forced those around him to second-guess what he might want, thereby allowing him to distance himself from any mistakes, were also becoming familiar. Above all, the ideology was clear: a single worldwide enemy, the Jewish people, were behind all the misfortunes Germany had suffered. They must be eradicated.

By the time of the Munich putsch, Hitler had also decided that Germany could not be content with regaining her old imperial borders and uniting herself with Austria, nor simply with wreaking revenge on France. Germany needed more land. It could be found only in the east, including Russia, which was now under Jewish control and therefore a lesser civilization. In *Mein Kampf* we read that 'the new Reich must again set itself on the march of the Teutonic knights of old, to obtain by the German sword sod for the German plough'.[12] Later, Hitler says, 'State boundaries are made by man and changed by man.' The German nation is 'penned into an impossible area', and a reckoning with France is only useful 'if it offers the rear cover for an enlargement of our people's living space in Europe'.[13] No clearer warning of the attacks to be launched on Poland, the Ukraine and Russia herself could have been given. It was all there, in black and white, from the day *Mein Kampf* was first published.

For Germans of the 1920s, the trauma of near-starvation in the latter part of the Great War was a recent memory. Britain's Royal Navy had imposed a blockade on Germany that had reduced middle-class Germans to chewing unripe potatoes – Germany's attempt in turn to starve Britain through her U-boat campaign was, as we have seen, a close-run failure. But though Germany had been defeated on the Western Front, she had triumphed in the east against the Russian empire. During the Great War, Germans had ruled their own mini-empire in Poland, the Ukraine and Belarus. In Hitler's view, to stop Germany being starved again, she had once more to seize the rich agricultural lands to her east. One recent historian of the mass killings in the 'bloodlands' of central Europe puts it like this: 'The true Nazi agricultural policy was the creation of an eastern frontier empire . . . by taking fertile land from Polish and Soviet peasants – who would be starved, assimilated, deported or enslaved. Rather than importing grain from the east, Germany would export its farmers to the east.'[14]

Naive credulity, too, is part of the recurring pattern of human history. Had so many people who thought themselves worldly-wise, from Stalin to the British government, American ambassadors to French statesmen, not preferred to believe that Hitler didn't really mean it, some of the greatest disasters of the twentieth century could have been avoided. There seems to be a deep desire to look at our enemies and believe we are looking in a mirror – that, deep down, we are all the same – so that we flinch from the rare reality of outspoken, frank evil. In this case it was all there, in cold print, unequivocal, from the beginning. Whatever one might say of Hitler, nobody could accuse him of not giving fair warning.

Hitler and the Rest of Us

Now all the cards fell badly. Whole library shelves have been filled with meticulous accounts of German politics in the years after Hitler's brief imprisonment, when he was able to rapidly rebuild the Nazi party and take it via elections to power in 1933. Had Germany had a stronger political hub, able to withstand the buffeting of the Communist left and the Fascist right, things could have been different. Had the German constitution not already put effective power into the hands of a Chancellor legitimately able to bypass the German parliament, the Reichstag, Hitler's ascent would have been far harder. Had the other European powers acted to punish his early aggressive acts, in the Rhineland, over the Austrian *Anschluss* and the taking of the German-speaking Czech lands, the putscher himself might have been putsched well before the fatal year, 1939. There were generals waiting and willing; but the politicians of democratic Britain and France failed them.

For it is wrong to see the rise of the Nazis as a purely German phenomenon, or even as a purely European failure. There is an American view that in 1941/2 the US had to come to rescue Europe, for a second time, from a great evil that had really nothing to do with the New World. This is hardly the full tale. The Hitler story could not have happened without a worldwide failure of leadership, including by the United States. In the 1920s and 1930s the world was already inextricably interconnected. The First World War had left a badly divided-up Europe and Middle East. This was the fault of the US President Woodrow Wilson, as well as of the British and French leaders Lloyd George and Clemenceau. But the ineffectual League of Nations, partly designed by Americans, was then abandoned by the US, to dither and witter during America's age of isolationism. Europe was left to deal by herself with the consequences of American state-making – a patchwork Yugoslavia, a swollen Poland, the German minorities in Czechoslovakia and Danzig. The sense of grievance in Germany and Austria was not conjured up by the Nazis. They were immersed in grievance. It was what they swam in.

Even then, Germany might have escaped political extremism and strengthened her democracy through the later 1920s and beyond, had it not been for the Great Crash of 1929, which happened first in America's runaway consumer economy. This could have been followed by a local correction, except that weak leadership in the democracies, including under Ramsay MacDonald in Britain and President Herbert Hoover in the US, took the world towards a general trade depression and mass unemployment. This greatly raised the prestige of dictatorship as an alternative route to growth: protectionist tariffs and the freezing-up of world business seemed to be bringing capitalist democracy to its knees. The yearning for a patriotic strongman to take charge and suspend the normal rules of the market was not confined to Munich.

Many European nations had had only a short experience of democratic politics, anyway. Spain, after a century of authoritarian monarchy, dictatorships, coups, rebellions and restorations, had fallen under the sway of a new dictator, Primo de Rivera, before the Second Republic was declared in 1931 – this was the left-wing government that would in turn be destroyed by civil war after the military rebellion of General Francisco Franco. With its intense religiosity and its peasant economy on the one hand, and its industrial cities and republican traditions on the other, Spain had been divided long before Franco's rebellion. Italy was a new nation, still learning the culture of democracy, when the former journalist and left-winger Benito Mussolini seized power in 1922 in an audacious coup, later mythologized as 'the march on Rome'. Like Spain, Italy had been divided by increasing industrial militancy. Poland had only five years of parliamentary government between her victory over the Bolshevik Russians in 1919–21 and the seizure of power by General Jozef Pilsudski in 1926. As in Germany, anti-Semitism and nationalism would be powerful currents in Polish politics as the Great Depression neared.

The central European countries that had emerged from the 1919 carve-up of the ruined Austro-Hungarian Empire were newer still. Dictatorial monarchs held sway in Yugoslavia and Albania; the dictators General Metaxas in Greece and Kimon Georgiev in Bulgaria; there was Admiral Miklos Horthy's regime in Hungary, a military government in Portugal and a form of monarchical authoritarianism in Romania. So although Germany became the most extreme example of European Fascism, this was a fashion, not a German invention. Because the democracies would eventually triumph in Western Europe it is easy to forget that, from an interwar perspective, the democracies seemed the odd ones out.

The relationship between democracy and prosperity seemed far less obvious than it had been. Italy, not Germany, had been the test case. There, Mussolini's boasted corporatism, involving the reclaiming of marshland, subsidies to increase grain production and eventually the takeover and amalgamation of banks and industrial businesses, appeared successful. True, Il Duce was behaving badly abroad, but after all, his desire for some kind of African empire to provide raw materials and cheap labour was no different from what other European countries had aspired to, and achieved. It turns out that Fascism did not much help the Italian economy. In the decade between the Great Crash and the start of the Second World War it was growing at around half the rate of pre-war times, and nearly half of Italians were still employed on the land. The total rate of investment actually fell during Mussolini's pre-war rule. But none of this was obvious to outsiders at the time.

Hitler himself found economics dull and secondary. His chaotic personal way of running Germany more or less excluded him from economic planning. One of his biographers says bluntly: 'The extraordinary economic recovery that rapidly formed an essential component of the Führer myth was not of Hitler's making.'[15] Fascinated by cars, Hitler authorized huge detachments of workers, paid very little and organized in militaristic camps, to build the new autobahns as well as labouring on other drainage and forestry projects. Unemployment crashed from around six million at the beginning of his time as Chancellor to negligible levels by 1938–9. The exclusion from the unemployment figures of women, who Nazis thought should be at home looking after their families, and of Jews, was part of the statistical story. Another part of it was the banning of independent trade unions and strikes.

Still, those huge public sector projects and the even larger project of rearmament soaked up many of the previously workless. Under Hjalmar Schacht, the central banker and economics minister, the Nazis ran a semi-military version of Keynesian economics, keeping prices low and building up huge government deficits during the later 1930s, when military investment was running well ahead of ordinary industrial spending. An unsustainable sprint towards war was taking place. Imports were limited to essential raw materials and food; everything that could be replaced or substituted inside Germany, was. Goebbels talked about 'fantastic sums' being spent on armaments, while Hitler repeatedly urged that 'money' – by which he meant economics – was meaningless compared to the need for military readiness. 'The economy' did not really exist in Nazi thinking as a separate entity from the nation, armed and ready.

Germany had a superb scientific and industrial infrastructure, however, which had survived the defeat of 1918, and a powerful network of business leaders who were left mostly alone by Hitler in return for backing the Nazis. It would take a long time for the expulsion of the Jews and the imposition of Nazi ideology to cripple German ingenuity and industrial flair. Even late into the war, despite shortages of power and raw materials the big German combines were still producing new weaponry of outstanding quality.

Yet the huge deficits and the short-term planning for a war economy told their own story. By the time he was planning the invasion of Poland, Hitler was using the unsustainable nature of the German economic boom, created to prepare for war, as a reason for the *necessity* of war. The real nature of this gamble was not widely understood at the time. Hitler's economic miracle was trumpeted at home and abroad. In America, even Franklin Delano Roosevelt, with his 'New Deal' public works programme, seemed to be finding it harder to get the US economy moving.

The democracies would recover their confidence. Before rearmament became the priority, growth was returning both in Britain under Stanley Baldwin and in the US under Roosevelt. But the biggest political difference between nations struggling with recession in the interwar period and nations struggling with it today, after the 2008 banking crash, is that, the first time round, there seemed to be effective alternatives to capitalist democracy. Mussolini, who seems a buffoon today, was widely regarded as a Roman genius. At the other end of the spectrum, ignorance about the true state of affairs in the Soviet Union made it possible for Stalin's propagandists to dupe the West into believing he too was making a successful leap into a triumphantly powerful industrial economy.

Katharine and Margaret

In New York in the summer of 1921, while Adolf Hitler was ranting in Munich drinking-dens, two women in their forties one day sat down and eyed one another. One was a red-haired agitator, born of working-class Irish stock in upstate New York. The other was an elegant daughter of America's industrial aristocracy, who spent much of her time looking after her schizophrenic husband at their Californian hideaway. Margaret Sanger and Katharine Dexter McCormick were very different kinds of American, who together would do more to change women's lives by the later part of the century than any politician, in the US or Europe. Their cause, however, was undeniably political. It was to give women control over their own fertility or, to put it more bluntly, to help them stop having babies they did not want, while continuing to have the sex they did want.

Margaret Sanger is a feminist heroine but not an easy woman to warm to. She was self-promoting, often disloyal, and an unreliable witness. Even her own highly sympathetic biographer admits: 'In her memoir, Margaret was not always completely honest about her life.'[16] She savagely attacked Marie Stopes, the British birth-control pioneer, merely for being a rival, and cast off her first husband and (for a while) her children with shocking coolness. Later she would be attacked for racist and eugenicist views. But there is no reason to think that courageous campaigners need be consistent or easy to get on with; it is more often the other way about.

Sanger's determination to give women control over their reproduction was deeply rooted in the experiences of her early life. Her father was a free-thinking Irish radical, but a ferocious patriarch at home, in a small town in New York state. Her mother, a devout Catholic, had no fewer than eighteen pregnancies in twenty-two years, and died aged fifty of cervical cancer. Margaret trained as a nurse, and watched young working-class women die of botched abortions in the slums of Manhattan, where people lived seven or eight to a room. She spent the years before the First World War with an anarchist and socialist crowd, helping organize strikes, talking of revolution, of the morality of assassination and of the joy of sex. Slowly, however, she turned her focus onto the simpler, more practical issue of how to help women desperate for contraceptive help. As the world went to war in 1914 Sanger launched a magazine, *The Woman Rebel*, advocating something she had found a new phrase for, 'birth control'. But she came immediately into conflict with another powerful current in American public life – puritanism.

Anthony Comstock was a mutton-chop-moustached postal inspector and former soldier, who had formed the New York Society for the Suppression of Vice. He boasted of having had fifteen tons of books and four million pictures destroyed, as well as thousands of people arrested. Comstock found vice everywhere. He had a special nose for it. He found vice in medical textbooks, in the display of wax dummies in tailors' shops, in postcards, novels and the plays of George Bernard Shaw.

His greatest achievement was the 1873 US federal Comstock Act, which prohibited the sending of obscene or lewd material by post. This included items used for, and any information about, birth control. In the words of the Act, any item or article 'for the prevention of conception, or for causing unlawful abortion' would attract a large fine, or between six months and five years in prison, with hard labour. Comstock would trap doctors into giving advice on contraception by sending pitiful-sounding letters, apparently from desperate women, and then pursuing any doctor compassionate enough to write back, often achieving long prison sentences for them.

Sanger, meanwhile, wanted to publish a book giving contraceptive options. In 1914 Comstock and his law came after her. Under an assumed name, fearing prison, Sanger fled to Britain. There she met the sex campaigner Havelock Ellis and had a brief affair with H.G. Wells, which was mandatory for left-wing women in Britain during this period. But the most important outcome of her European exile was a visit to a Dutch contraceptive clinic in 1915.

For as far back as we have written records, we know that women have tried all sorts of devices and techniques to avoid pregnancy, from lint tampons soaked in honey, which were used in ancient Egypt, to wet tea-leaves, pieces of oiled paper, sponges dipped in vinegar, home-made glycerine suppositories, and condoms made from everything from leaves and bark to sheep's gut. (Some of the more outlandish remedies, such as crocodile dung, turn out to have a scientific justification, since crocodiles often eat a weed that contains a contraceptive-enhancing drug.) The invention of latex and new forms of rubber had produced better condoms, and also caps and diaphragms for women; and it was only when Sanger got to Holland and was shown the published pamphlets about their use and the latest diaphragms that she became aware of what was possible. This was really at the heart of her meeting with Katharine McCormick.

For Sanger had returned to the United States and started to publish contraceptive advice, opening the first clinic offering help in Brooklyn in 1916. She had swiftly fallen foul of the law again, and in 1917 was sent to a workhouse for thirty days. But the tide of opinion was slowly turning, and using her court appearances to promote the cause, Sanger was becoming a heroine to American women's rights campaigners. Using a loophole in the law which allowed contraception on medical advice, she was able to successfully publish pamphlets and books. By the early 1920s she had set up a fund-raising and campaigning organization, an all-women birth control clinic, and was speaking across America – and, indeed, in Japan and China too. What she needed for her clinic, however, were actual contraceptives. That meant diaphragms, which were not easily legally available in the US. And that led her to McCormick.

Katharine Dexter McCormick's world had been very different. She was as near as the US had to aristocracy. She came from a proud and wealthy family that had arrived in America in the 1640s, taken a prominent part in the rebellion against the British Crown, and had become pioneers in Michigan, where the town of Dexter was named after them. By the late nineteenth century they were part of the super-rich Chicago elite, mingling with famous family names like Pullman, Kellogg and Otis. Katharine's father, a philanthropic lawyer, had died when she was quite young, and her mother had progressive views, including supporting votes for women.

Showing great determination, Katharine had worked her way through the Massachusetts Institute of Technology, one of the first women to get a science degree there. She became a keen suffragist and had married another wealthy young radical, the scion of the McCormick industrial empire, whose agricultural machines had helped open up the mid-West to farmers. Unfortunately, her husband Stanley quickly fell ill with schizophrenia and would spend the rest of his life needing virtually full-time care. She threw herself into a double life, overseeing his psychiatric treatment and campaigning for women's suffrage – which was how she had heard of Sanger.

The United States had come comparatively late to voting equality. Before the First World War, only a few nations had experimented with such a radical step, notably the Finns, the Norwegians and the Australians. Individual US states, such as Oregon, Washington and California, had given women the vote too. But it took the war and its immediate aftermath to produce a landslide of change, in places such as Britain, Germany, Austria, most of Eastern Europe and Russia, New Zealand and Holland. The battle in the US had been long and tough but, just as in Britain, it threw up a new generation of women campaigners who learned to speak in public, to organize successfully and to disrupt their opponents' meetings. Earlier in this book we saw how war can drive change, from political systems to new technologies; a transformation in the public rights of women can be added to the list.

The need for women to do war work had certainly transformed their situation in America, where Katharine became chair of the women's committee of the National Council of Defense, which was in charge of Red Cross supplies, child welfare, looking after the rights of women in factories and much else. By 1920, when the US Congress finally passed the Nineteenth Amendment to the constitution, imposing women's suffrage throughout the country, Katharine was looking for new challenges. The following year, when she received a flyer from Sanger announcing the first American Birth Control Conference at New York's Plaza Hotel, she wrote back and suggested a meeting. Two tough women; and they clicked.[17]

Katharine McCormick had money, connections and influence. Margaret Sanger needed all of these, but she also needed contraceptive devices for her 'Clinical Research Bureau'. In her admittedly unreliable autobiography she describes the day her clinic opened and was mobbed by women: 'Halfway to the corner they stood in line, shawled, hatless, their red hands clasping the chapped smaller ones of their children. All day long, in ever increasing numbers they came . . . Jews and Christians, Protestants and Roman Catholics alike made their confessions to us.' One told her that she had had fifteen children of whom only six were living: she was thirty-seven but looked fifty. Another told Sanger: 'If you don't help me, I'm going to chop up a glass and swallow it tonight!'

By help, these women meant contraceptives, not more advice, but at this stage this was still difficult. Comstock himself was long gone, but the American political mood remained puritanical: the sale of alcohol was banned from 1920 to 1933 – the first and greatest failure in the war on drugs. The 'prohibition era', though, actually helped the birth-control campaigners because bootleggers were willing to smuggle diaphragms with the booze, if only in small quantities. Where were the diaphrams? In Europe.

So, one day in 1922, Mrs McCormick went shopping. She headed off on a liner for a four-month trip with three large trunks and five suitcases, apparently intent on snapping up rather large amounts of the latest European fashions. Her family owned a château in Switzerland, overlooking Lake Geneva. It had been a famous gathering-point for Enlightenment intellectuals. Posing as a doctor, Katharine now ordered large quantities of diaphragms from French and Italian manufacturers to be sent to the château, while she bought a lot of dresses and coats. Next, she hired local Swiss women to sew more than a thousand diaphragms into the clothes, which were then tightly packed into her luggage, now comprising eight trunks. She then imperiously marched her contraband past French and US customs officials, delivering them by truck to the Sanger clinic.

Were that all, it would have been a significant contribution to the birth-control movement, which McCormick continued to quietly fund, though soon Sanger also married a rich man, an oil baron, and would have no further money troubles. But it was far from all.

In 1947, Stanley McCormick died. Nobody could have asked for a better wife: Katharine had looked after him devotedly, lavishing his family money on gardeners, servants, doctors and musicians to make his self-torturing life a little easier. Given the belief that insanity was hereditary, his illness may well have contributed to Katharine's decision to have no children of her own; and that in turn would have sharpened her interest in contraception. Now he was gone, his family wanted some control over the huge fortune, but Katharine was still rich almost beyond imagining. What could she do with the money? She wrote to Sanger. Both women were now in their seventies; but their reconnection would be even more significant than their original meeting.

On 27 October 1950, Sanger replied to the letter from McCormick in which she had offered Margaret financial help: 'I consider that the world, and almost our civilization for the next twenty-five years is going to depend upon a simple, cheap, safe contraceptive to be used in poverty-stricken slums, jungles and amongst the most ignorant people.' The eugenic note was not a slip of the pen. She went on to add that 'now, immediately, there should be national sterilization for certain dysgenic types of our population who are being encouraged to breed and would die out were the government not feeding them'.[18] McCormick and others would get her off that hobby-horse, but for both of them the key thing was to find that 'simple, cheap, safe' answer.

A few months after receiving Margaret's letter, Katharine McCormick arranged a dinner in New York with a research scientist from

Massachusetts who looked strikingly like Einstein, but who was actually a world expert in mammalian eggs. If anyone could find that answer quickly, Gregory Pincus was the man. How much would it cost? $25,000, he thought. In fact McCormick would spend nearly $2 million. Soon both Sanger and McCormick, those formidable elderly ladies, were hovering over Pincus in his Massachusetts lab.

Pincus was not working alone. A gynaecologist called John Rock had been studying progesterone, a key hormone in fertilization which helps ensure the body does not produce multiple pregnancies. So had two other scientists, a young Jewish refugee from Vienna called Carl Djerassi, and Frank Colton. None of these had it in mind to produce a contraceptive pill; synthetic hormones were the big new thing at the time, in great demand by the drug companies. But Djerassi, while working in Mexico, synthesized a drug that was much stronger than natural progesterone and could be taken orally. It was initially intended to combat severe menstrual bleeding, but it would be key to the success of what would soon be called simply 'the Pill'.

Pincus was already famous, or notorious, as the man who had fertilized rabbit eggs in a test-tube, earning himself the 'Dr Frankenstein' label in newspapers and causing waves in the scientific world. Before the war, Harvard had denied him tenure – Pincus thought, because he was 'a self-advertising Jew who published too soon and talked too much'.[19] He set to work on his new task, then in 1952 bumped into one of the men who had been studying progesterone, again not in order to prevent pregnancy, but this time in order to help infertile women. Though he was a devout Catholic this man agreed to work with Pincus, helping him towards the breakthroughs that would lead to an oral drug which Colton and Djerassi would refine. Plenty of hurdles had to be cleared en route, but after a successful clinical trial, at a conference in Tokyo in 1953 Pincus announced what they had achieved. And . . . nobody took any notice.

The commercial struggle to test and produce a saleable product took years, but the Pill was finally unveiled on 11 May 1960 as a contraceptive. Few innovations have made as big an impact on as many people. How much more effective was it than other methods of contraception? A detailed study in 1961 found the failure rate from condoms was high, 28 per cent; from diaphragms even higher, nearly 34 per cent, and from vaginal suppositories, 42 per cent. With the Pill, it was less than 2 per cent.[20] Women voted yes: in its first year, four hundred thousand Americans took it. By 1965, it was estimated that a quarter of all married women under the age of forty-five in the US were taking it; by 1984 the worldwide estimate was up to eighty million.[21] It is important to remember that modern science is all about collaboration, shared achievement and serendipity, rather than about a single genius leaping naked from his bath, yelling 'I've got it!'

This is also a story about capitalism. Had poor Stanley McCormick's father not made a fortune from harvesting-machines, Katharine would not have had the money to go over to Europe and smuggle diaphragms home, or to bankroll Pincus in his search for the Pill. Had the US drug companies not been so keen on the profits to be made, they would have struggled less hard to develop synthetic hormones. Had America not become a rich consumer economy whose women expected greater freedom and were already experiencing the liberating effect of new machines in the home, the take-up of the new Pill would have been slower. Given the rapid advance of biochemistry at the time, it would certainly have happened eventually; though at another time, when Christian moralism was less influential in American life. In the 1930s, say, or indeed today, the Pill might not have been licensed so easily.

Certainly, without those two determined septuagenarians, it would not have happened when it did. One had started out as an anarchist and political radical, hoping for the downfall of American capitalism; the other was married to American capitalism. The Pill needed them both, the political agitator who challenged conventional thinking, and the quietly resolute financial backer. This unlikely partnership goes some way to explaining the underlying strength of American culture, its radicalism and its energy.

The Pill was morally controversial. It probably always will be. Many religious people, notably Roman Catholics, oppose contraception in any event, while others blame it for a radical loosening of traditional sexual morality in the 1960s and afterwards. It can have serious side-effects; add to that the fact that many women feel angered that less effort has been made to find an oral contraceptive focusing on the other sex, one that would stop men being able to fertilize eggs. All the same, this was a democratic technology, which people voted for by buying it. Because of it, women were for the first time easily and reliably able to distance sexual pleasure from the likelihood of pregnancy. A different relationship, between the body as a zone of pleasure and delight, and reproduction, became possible – something the young Sanger and her anarchist friends had talked about nearly sixty years before. The argument that the market can be as destabilizing for some as it is liberating for others, and as revolutionary as any state action, is perhaps nowhere better demonstrated than in the Pill.

A War of the Empires

The First World War had been a European tribal war, which drew in other continents and peoples mainly on account of Europe's empires. Canadians, Australians, New Zealanders, Indians and South Africans rallied to the British Empire's summons. Germany's attempt to conjure up jihad against the British in the Middle East helped bring the crumbling Ottoman Empire, and the Arabs, into the conflict. America joined in, as we have seen, because her own security seemed threatened by both German submarines and Mexican intrigues. The countries of Europe were still so world-dominant that when they collided, the alarm was sounded almost everywhere around the planet.

The Second World War followed the same pattern – some historians have depicted it as the second half of a single conflict. It too began in Europe and sucked in much of the globe. But there was a key difference. Early German victory on the European continent humiliated the other European powers, weakened their empires and spread the war to Asia. It made it easier for a new empire, the Japanese, to rip through old colonies around the Pacific; it also meant the Japanese, already at war in China, were bound to come into conflict with America. Early German victories had another effect: they convinced Hitler that he was indeed a military genius and encouraged him to carry through his original dream and invade the USSR. This had the perverse effect of ranging the United States and the old European imperial powers, above all Britain, alongside their bitterest political enemy.

So though the Second World War is sometimes seen as the last great ideological war, a battle to 'save democracy', the inconvenient fact is that it was won partly by Stalin's totalitarian regime, and could not have been won without it.

It would be more accurate to see this as the last great imperial war. Japan was trying to build an empire in China and Manchuria and on the relics of the British and Dutch Far Eastern empires (and hoped to include British India). The German plan was for the creation of a German empire in what had been central Europe and western Russia. Even Stalin, constantly attacking 'imperialism', had been in on the act. After abandoning world revolution for 'socialism in one country', he had updated Russia's traditional imperial attitude. We have seen how in Ivan the Terrible's time Russia engulfed Kazan and began to devour Siberia. This was followed by the invasion and seizure of the Caucasus and by the establishment of Russian hegemony over the Ukraine, Georgia, Chechnya and Mongolia. The Russians regarded Finland, the Baltic states and much of Poland as naturally 'theirs' too; the Second World War began when the Russians were already fighting the Finns. Stalin's vision of the Union of Soviet Socialist Republics really signified Russian control over as much of this vast area as was militarily possible. He was even prepared to order the mass migration of entire peoples in order to subdue dissent. The national minorities had lower status, barely disguised by a folkloric veil of harmony; it was later said that in the USSR 'the minorities dance'.

Finally, the forced engagement of the US after Pearl Harbor on 7 December 1941 led to America dominating half the world through a virtual empire, not of guardhouses and governors, but of nuclear firepower, proxy wars, commodities and finance. They ended up with a permanent military presence stretching from Japan to Western Europe; deeply involved in the politics of South America; and with large fleets that swiftly replaced Britain's Royal Navy as guardians of Western influence. Still strongly hostile to the 'old empires' of Europe, American success in the war would be followed by a dramatic spread of American business, and by the emergence of the dollar as the world's most important currency. All this was good news for those who breathed freely under the US shield, saved from the Communist-imperial vision. But others saw it as the moment of lost innocence when an American republic became the American empire.

*

From the first, it was clear that ideology would take second place to national self-interest. The Nazi–Soviet Pact of August 1939 settled the fate of Poland, which was invaded and divided up the following month. From then until the end of 1941, a period of nearly two and a half years, the United States managed to stay out of the war. But for about two years, until the surprise (to Stalin) invasion of the USSR in Operation Barbarossa in June 1941, the Soviets and Nazis were working uneasily together. As the military historian Max Hastings reminds us, this enabled Hitler's armies to receive huge material help from the Soviet Union: 'Supply trains continued to roll west until the very moment of the invasion; the Luftwaffe's aircraft were largely fuelled by Soviet oil; the Kriegsmarine's U-boats had access to Russian port facilities.'[22]

So from 1939 to 1941 the war was confined to a relatively limited area. It was essentially a duel between those old Great War enemies, the British and French on one side and the Germans on the other; but this time the French had been knocked out. Had Hitler been able to invade Britain in 1940, or found some other way to force the British to sue for peace, the war might have ended there.

If that had happened, we would today be less dominated by America, and Soviet Russia would have stayed essentially behind her earlier borders. The entire continent of Europe would not have been under direct German control. Spain's General Franco had spurned a full-scale military alliance with Hitler, which, given the help he had received during the Spanish Civil War, seemed wary to the point of ingratitude. Mussolini's Italy was an ally, but not a carbon-copy. Sweden, Switzerland and Ireland stayed neutral. Greece, Romania, Hungary and Yugoslavia might have remained altogether untouched by the fighting. Would so many Jews have died? Would cities like London, Hamburg, Dresden and Coventry have stayed untouched? Outside Europe, had the British sued for peace it would probably have led to the swift collapse of her empire. Churchill thought so. India might well have come under Japanese control. The US, isolationist, would presumably not have acquired the atomic bomb so early, since to do so relied on British and emigrant Jewish scientists as well as on a huge industrial effort to beat Hitler's scientists.

Such musings belong to speculative novelists, however, because the British leader refused to sue for peace; because Britain prevented a

German invasion; and because Hitler's thinking, the way he had constructed Nazi Germany, and his personality in the end rendered his
attack on the Soviet Union inevitable. His rhetorical universe was
founded on a conflict between Germanism and Jewish Bolshevism,
and his offer to the German people was of a great new empire that
would make them rich and secure, and that could only come about via
the collapse of the Soviet Union. It would have been better for him to
have humbled Churchill first; but eventually he had to turn towards
Moscow. In *Mein Kampf*, Operation Barbarossa was already visible on
the horizon.

Britain's defeat of the Luftwaffe in the late summer and autumn of
1940, which has become an almost Arthurian or Shakespearean myth-
story for the modern British, meant more than just frustrating the
invasion. It meant that when the US joined the war it could pose a
direct threat to Germany, not just to Japan. Roosevelt had dodged and
prevaricated as he tried to help Britain with aid and old destroyers,
while soothing an American public still hostile to war. However much
Americans warmed to the plucky Londoners during the Blitz, the
thought of plunging into a new world war to save the British Empire
was not a popular one.

In any case, Germany was not the most obvious enemy. Japan's
war against China had made the Tokyo militarists the most hated figures in Washington. And Japan had tried to briefly attack Siberia but
had been pushed back by the Russians; her high command now
believed the American oil embargo necessitated her driving south,
with a view to winning a big enough Pacific empire to give her security against the US. The notion that Japan might actually conquer the
continent-sized United States was of course always absurd, but her
rulers still thought that sufficiently dramatic military successes would
intimidate Washington into an early peace. Tokyo assumed – as did
most observers – that Hitler was bound to be victorious in Europe.

It is reasonable, therefore, to suppose that something like the Pearl
Harbor attack was bound to happen. The devastatingly successful
torpedo-bomber assault on the US Pacific Fleet, which sank four battleships and many other vessels, was, at a technical and operational
level, a feat of military genius. It certainly kept the Americans at bay
while the Japanese armies swept through South-East Asia. It was
also, however, an act of strategic idiocy. It showed how little Tokyo's

politicians and military chiefs understood America. It brought the
world war to the Pacific and made the eventual defeat of Japan
inevitable. And because Britain was still holding out, still connected to
the US by the lifeline of the Atlantic and still supported by the formidable resources of her empire, it made US entry into the war against
Hitler plausible in a way it had not been the day before the Japanese
warplanes struck.

Some leaders instantly understood all this. Churchill telephoned
Roosevelt for confirmation of the attack. The US President told him
that 'we are all in the same boat now' and Churchill later recorded his
visceral, emotional reaction: 'So we had won, after all.' Interestingly,
Hitler completely misread the event, delighting that Japan was now on
Germany's side: 'We can't lose the war at all. We now have an ally that
has not been conquered in 3,000 years.'[23] As for the Americans, her
entry into the conflict merely confirmed Hitler's belief that Germany
faced a worldwide Jewish threat.

The history of the Second World War is, of course, the history of
battles, of leaders and their strategies, of planes and tanks and armies.
It can be recounted in a series of place names that resound and will
continue to rumble for a long time to come – Warsaw, Dunkirk,
Alamein, Stalingrad, Kursk, Singapore, Midway, Okinawa, Nagasaki. It
is composed of 'battles' which in earlier times would have comprised
entire wars – the Battle of Britain, the Battle of the Atlantic, the Battle
of the Pacific. The first generations of postwar historians and mem-
oirists emphasized the titanic role of leaders such as Churchill, Hitler,
Roosevelt, Eisenhower, Rommel, Tojo and Zhukov, and focused
strongly on the equipment used, the fighters and bombers, the battleships and tanks, the rockets and radar. They were followed by
historians who put more emphasis on the slaughter of civilians and
cities, and the failures of judgement.

The morals drawn from this conflict, which killed perhaps around
seventy million people (twice as many of them civilians as soldiers),
were varied. For the Russians, who lost more both in total and as a
percentage of the population of the Soviet Union, it is the Great Patriotic War. At the time it seemed a vindication of Stalin (despite his
wobbles early in the war) and of the Red Army, whose victory over the
ultimate evil, Nazism, involved few others. For the Americans, it was
the war to save democracy, which established the moral and physical

hegemony of their nation. For Jews (and many Gentiles) it was the Shoah, or Holocaust, the ultimate ethical failure of European civilization, whose consequence was modern Israel. For many Arabs it was the war that persuaded Europeans to steal their land for the Jews, making the Arabs pay for European guilt. For Germans it was the consequence of their time of madness and for the British their 'stand alone' moment, which outshines any of the more dubious episodes of empire, or military reverses.

And so on. Most people have drawn simple lessons, as we mostly need to. Yet as we gain distance and perspective, many of the first lessons are being revised. The huge 'Russian' death-toll also involved the deaths of massive numbers of Ukrainians, Poles and others who were not ethnically Russian; and indeed many of them were killed by Russians. The postwar Stalinist determination to play down the special horror of what happened to European Jewry – 'Do not divide the dead' – reduced a dreadful truth to patriotic self-congratulation. Furthermore, the deliberately inflicted famines and mass deportations inside the USSR before 1939 had ravaged vast territories, which were then more vulnerable to German depredation.

Hitler intended simply to empty vast areas between the Black Sea and the Baltic for German settlers, but Stalin's treatment of the same area – a 'breadbasket' emptied to feed Soviet cities – paved the way. One superb recent study, *Bloodlands* by Timothy Snyder, begins simply: 'In the middle of Europe in the middle of the twentieth century, the Nazi and Soviet regimes murdered some fourteen million people. The place where all of the victims died, the bloodlands, extends from central Poland to western Russia, through Ukraine, Belarus, and the Baltic States.' They died between 1933 and 1945, and though about half of all the soldiers who died in the Second World War died in this same area, 'not a single one of the fourteen million murdered was a soldier on active duty. Most were women, children and the aged; none were bearing weapons; many had been stripped of their possessions, including their clothes.' Of the fourteen million, roughly two-thirds were killed by the Nazis, and one-third by the Stalinists.

Add to the account the long period when the Soviet Union and Nazi Germany worked together, slicing up Poland and fuelling war, and the huge material help given to the Red Army by the British and Americans once Hitler had invaded, and the story of the Great

Patriotic War starts to look rather more complicated. The greatest moral failing of pre-war Nazi Germany was not the collapse of democracy but the campaign to dehumanize Jews, to warp and shrivel empathy so drastically in the minds of the German people that Jewish people became very easy to kill. But if one looks at the campaign run by Lenin and then Stalin to reduce the better-off farmers, the kulaks, to the status of loathsome enemies of the people, was this not similar?

Kulaks, like Jews, were depicted as coarse, bloated, ridiculous beings. Like the German soldiers, Bolshevik commissars found it very easy to kill kulaks, and incite others to join them. This had started with Bolshevik hatred of the ignorant peasantry. In its emphasis on a 'merciless war' to 'crush' the enemy and on the celebration of terror, the language of Lenin and his cronies was not dissimilar in tone to Hitler's at the same time. By the early 1930s under Stalin, hatred of kulaks had been disseminated through posters and campaigns. The behaviour of the Red Brigades ravaging the countryside looking for grain and those who stored it, is strongly reminiscent of German soldiers' later behaviour: 'They would urinate in barrels of pickles, or order hungry peasants to box each other for sport or make them crawl and bark like dogs, or force them to kneel in the mud and pray.'[24] Mass rape and then starvation followed. Cannibalism was rife. The same ritual humiliations and dehumanizing of Jews and peasants would be practised by the Germans when they arrived a decade later.

Germany's own Jews were comparatively few by 1939, and the vast majority of them died not in Germany but in the violated territories to the east. Though six million would die, Hitler's 'hunger plan' for the region meant another thirty to forty million non-Jews were expected to die from starvation, to free their soil for the invaders. Before the Shoah, the Russians had killed much of the intelligentsia and professional leadership of Poland and many of the brighter and more ambitious Ukrainian peasants.

Once the war started, both the Russian and German armies conducted themselves with astonishing ferocity, mass-raping and murdering civilians in enemy territory and killing prisoners of war. During the first phase of Barbarossa, as many Soviet PoWs were dying as British and US PoWs died during the whole war.[25] The Russians would repay the Germans in kind, with mass rapes and shootings as they headed back towards Berlin. Nor was the violence limited to nation against nation. It is thought that more Russian soldiers were killed by their own officers for cowardice or desertion – some three hundred thousand of them – than all the British troops killed during the Second World War.[26]

The Great Patriotic War was also a triumph of human willpower, notable for the heroic sieges of Leningrad and Stalingrad, and the determined suffering of millions of soldiers. In the end Stalin's Russia had more military factories, situated far to the east, beyond the German advance and able to churn out far more fighting equipment; and more men; and more land. The Red Army vastly outnumbered the Germans, and overwhelmed them with tanks and aircraft. But the 'Great Patriotic War' also left its victor a grey, fearful, stunted and fundamentally pessimistic society. The Soviets would end the war ruling their own enslaved European empire and threaten worldwide nuclear annihilation; but unable to build a decent society.

The American experience of the war was much easier. It produced the huge industrial boom at home, which raised living standards and set the United States on a firm route to global market domination, which is only now ending. Far fewer Americans died, proportionally and absolutely: around 417,000 in total, against 5.7 million Soviet casualties, or 2.5 per cent of the US's population in 1939 as compared to around 25 per cent in the case of the USSR (or Japan). Hastings points out that 17,000 Americans lost limbs while fighting – but 100,000 became amputees as a result of industrial accidents at home.[27] The US fought the war with growing skill, tenacity and awesome technical advances, but fought it in other people's countries. This war that never seriously reached US civilians has been remembered for its moral simplicity as 'the good war'. Yet America could not have won the good war without its ally, Soviet Russia, nor without the survival of another bête noire of US politicians, the British Empire.

America's war was dominated by three events. The first was the remorseless destruction of the Japanese in the Pacific, most crucially at the battle of Midway in June 1942, as the US fleets and airpower began to destroy at sea the advances won by Japanese bayonets and infantry on land. This ended with the dropping of the atomic bomb and the occupation of Japan itself. The second, with the British, was the slow and bloody victory of convoys and long-range aircraft against the U-boats in the Atlantic, which allowed the reinforcement of Britain herself and the supplying of the USSR. This in turn led to the third great event, the 1944 invasion of France by US, British and Canadian forces. By then the Americans had turned much of southern England into a vast encampment for US firepower, whence British and American bombers were annihilating German cities. America would end the war unstained by war crimes, optimistic about the future of democracy, and stronger than ever before.

Inside the US, Japanese citizens were interned, but for many life continued almost normally. There was a huge military-driven industrial boom, which set the seal on Roosevelt's New Deal expansion of federal government, and a vast expansion of Washington bureaucracy. American women were recruited to work in the factories, giving them opportunities and self-confidence they might not have had in peacetime.

The British experience of the war was deeply ambiguous. No thoughtful Briton could have missed the message contained in a series of early defeats. Britain and France had gone to war on the basis of the fantasy that they could somehow – nobody knew how – come to Poland's aid. After an initial quiet spell, the British were humiliated in Norway and then comprehensively defeated by the German blitzkrieg through France. The Battle of Britain saved the islands from the threat of invasion, and the Luftwaffe blitz on British cities produced a remarkable outpouring of solidarity and defiance. But these events could not dispel the poor performance of the British army in Greece and initially in North Africa, nor the humiliation of the Japanese advance almost to the borders of India, after the surrender of Singapore. The defeat of German armies at El Alamein and the increasingly savage bombardment of Germany by RAF Bomber Command, who lost a huge proportion of their aircrew, began to restore national self-confidence, as did the successful invasion of Sicily, then Italy.

But it was obvious even after D-Day that British power was shrivelling. In the Far Eastern empire, the defeat of white European armies by the Japanese would never be forgotten, while India would go almost as soon as the war was over. By then Britain was virtually bankrupt, deeply in hock to the United States for its war-fighting equipment and even for food. As with defeated France and Holland, the British grip on other parts of the world was fatally weakened. France would lose her empire in Indo-China and North Africa; but for

France, the humiliation of that surrender did have a silver lining. Ever since the revolution, France had been struggling between her monarchical history and her more recent secular and republican personality. After the fall of conservative France's client Nazi state, headquartered at Vichy, this argument effectively ended.

The Melting of Nations

Europe had given the world modern nationhood. It had been an ambiguous gift. We have seen how Europeans advanced from living in territories ruled by families to developing a stronger sense of themselves as rival and thoroughly coherent language groups. Monarchies had slowly and painfully given way to representative democracies; mythic pasts had been concocted for the new nations, along with striped flags, wedding-cake parliament buildings and unified legal systems. This way of doing things had been exported first to North America. Then Latin America had taken it up, and Japan too. In Africa, colonial frontier lines from the nineteenth century became national boundaries in the twentieth, as tribal societies reorganized themselves into liberated nations. In the Middle East, Europeans carved nation-states out of the rotting corpse of the Ottoman Empire. Though there were many people around the world who did not think of themselves as members of nations, the European system was so far advanced that it became impossible to imagine it reversed. A world of national identities and passports came together, apparently quite logically, in the United Nations, founded in San Francisco in 1945.

But just at this moment, when Europeans might have celebrated the global domination of their local political invention, this next world of flags, boundaries, constitutions and presidents, they instead began to try to melt the nation-state away again. The reason was obvious: nationalism had just torn Europe apart.

In particular, after four modern wars between Frenchmen and Germans – the Napoleonic, the Franco-Prussian, and the two world wars – these countries had to come to a new understanding. In a now divided Germany, nationalism had virtually collapsed. Under Charles de Gaulle, France was rebuilt politically: French presidents would achieve more personal power than politicians anywhere else in

modern Europe. France soon cast aside the autocratic and self-intoxi-
cated de Gaulle, but France's always formidable political class would
find in the embryonic European Union a new national purpose. West
Germany became the key French ally.

Committed to very tough financial policies so as to ensure no
return to the inflation of the Weimar years, lacking substantive military of their own, and doggedly determined to work their way up
from the ashes of 1945, the West Germans, now with their capital in
the small town of Bonn, created a success story for which 'economic
miracle' was a fair description. Other smaller European countries such
as Belgium, the Netherlands and Luxembourg formed a customs
union, as did France and Italy. All were beneficiaries of the huge postwar American aid package, the Marshall Plan, which poured food and
industrial essentials into the ravaged continent – or rather, into that
part of it on the western side of the 'Iron Curtain'. US motives
included the need to stave off Communism and keep the loyalty of
Western Europe, but it was a programme of great generosity and
wisdom that allowed Europe to recover from the war remarkably
quickly.

The first crucial anti-national step was the formation of the European Iron and Steel Community in 1952 which, though it included
Belgium, Italy, Luxembourg and the Netherlands too, was essentially a
way of integrating French and West German heavy industry so closely
that they simply could not go to war again. It was followed by the
same six members joining together as a trading union, the European
Economic Community, in 1958. Driven by a commission of civil servants from the member states, regular summits of national leaders
and later including a parliament, the EEC evolved by stages into
today's European Union of twenty-seven nations. Always the drive
was towards supranationalism, a persistent, gentle downward pressure
on national independence. It was touted as bringing greater trading
efficiency and therefore prosperity, and when the Soviet Union collapsed, Eastern European states rushed to join it as a guarantor of
market freedom and enrichment. But the EU's real aim was to melt
the nations down, abolishing national customs posts, using not an
army but harmonized laws, common standards and eventually a single
currency too, the euro – aimed for since 1969 but not fully launched
until 2002.

This was highly political, but not politics as Europeans had ever known it before. It was the deliberately bland alternative to Europe's vivid interwar years with their short-lived socialist governments, the Soviet-funded Communist fronts, and the strange glamour of Fascism. 'Europe', with its own flag, anthem, aid and foreign policies and central bank, is neither country nor empire. Counted as a single economy, it is the world's largest, a little ahead of the US, but has no military forces nor any real leader – no visible president in world affairs. Rich, nervous, herbivorous, feared by nobody except nationalists, it is also admired enough to be copied, in a more dilute form, by South Americans and Africans. Yet it has not managed to convince its own people it is really democratic, either. Nor is it. A democracy has always depended on a common sense of belonging, mostly based on a language and shared history; Europe's nation-states still enjoy too much local support for their citizens to think of themselves as European first, and French – or Greek – or British – second. The economic crisis which hit members of the Euro currency in 2010–12 exposed the tensions dramatically.

Politics continued, of course, inside the European states. Left-wing Germans in the West abandoned Marxism for a soft social democracy, which also became popular in Scandinavia. In some countries, notably France and Italy, Moscow-backed Communists struggled seriously to gain power, but were pushed back by capitalist parties, generally social democratic or Catholic. In Italy, the Communists later broke with Moscow and developed their own form of 'Euro-communism', but never defeated the American-backed centrist parties, who delivered growth and good times, despite being corrupt. Franco's Spain, and Portugal after the dictatorships of Salazar and Caetano, managed to shed their quasi-Fascist identities and embrace mainstream politics. In Britain, a socialist government ousted Churchill's Conservatives and went further in the creation of a welfare state than ever before; but it had gone by 1951, after which Britain too experienced a long period of centre-right government. France, Britain, Belgium and Portugal all expended much political energy struggling with the problems of decolonization – often a barely dignified scuttle.

The war, which had opened in a Europe dominated by dictators and had become a war of empires, produced a Europe of committees, self-consciously managing to get by without political heroes; and shorn of empire. British critics of the European project, referring to its political capital in Brussels, spoke of the 'Belgian empire', but this was at least partly a joke. If it was an empire, it was one whose colonies had come voluntarily, even eagerly, under its embrace, and whose impact on the rest of the world was minimal. World influence was anyway something that postwar Europeans mostly shrank from. Culturally, and in her business attitudes, Europe became a follower of America. In other circumstances the US would surely have also risen to dominate Europe. But the war hastened this dramatically. America, which had grown a mighty state apparatus first in response to the Depression, and then in war, was handed a global role that many Americans would have regarded with incredulity and alarm just seven years earlier. But this was the inevitable consequence of America's new weapon.

The Missing City

In the auditorium of a small hastily built town for some six thousand people in the desert high country of New Mexico, a tall, gangling man in his early forties pushed his way through the crowd. It was the afternoon of 6 August 1945. The man climbed onto the stage, then turned and looked down. He paused. Then he put his hands together over his head in the traditional boxer's fist-pump of triumph. A ragged cheer went up. He told the crowd he was proud of what they'd achieved together. Later on, people would disperse for parties; but some did not feel like partying. Some just hung around and talked about what they had done.

The man was Robert Oppenheimer. The town was Los Alamos. The crowd were the people, scientists, soldiers and helpers who had made the world's first atom bomb. And what they had achieved a few hours previously was the death by burning, radiation and debris of seventy thousand Japanese civilians in the city of Hiroshima. The total death-toll would rise fast through cancers and other effects to as many as two hundred thousand.

Oppenheimer, the director of the 'Manhattan Project' which produced the bomb, was a cultivated mongrel – an excellent example of the intertwining of European and US twentieth-century history. He was an early opponent of Fascism who had gone so far as to hand money over to Communists to help the anti-Fascist cause in the Spanish Civil War. He would later be accused of having been a paid-up member of the Communist Party himself, something he denied. He was fixated by Hitler. He told the crowd that day in Los Alamos that he was only sorry America hadn't developed the bomb early enough to use it against the Germans. (Hitler had killed himself three months earlier, on 30 April, and the German surrender had been signed on 9 May.) Oppenheimer's team was full of Europeans, refugees from Nazi Europe or simply dedicated scientists determined that it would be the democracies, not the dictatorships, that first got 'the bomb'.

J. Robert Oppenheimer was German-Jewish himself, at least by origins, though his wealthy New York family were uninterested in traditional Jewish traditions or religion. He was brought up in an intensely highbrow, liberal family who had paintings by Van Gogh, Renoir and Picasso on their walls, who loved the music of Beethoven, learned Latin and Greek, and travelled to Europe. They were members of the Ethical Cultural Society, a secular Jewish organization which stressed good works and humanitarianism. As a young man, entranced by science, Oppenheimer would idolize the young physicist Niels Bohr and then go to Cambridge to study physics and maths. In Europe he would mingle with some of the greatest minds of theoretical physics at its most exciting period – the Danish Bohr, the Englishman Paul Dirac, the German Werner Heisenberg, the Austrian Wolfgang Pauli, the Italian Enrico Fermi and the Jewish-German Max Born. He would study at Göttingen, the Saxon university, and in Zurich.

Yet Oppenheimer was also intensely American, and his story exemplifies the shift of power from Europe to the US. Delighting in the countryside of New Mexico and California, by the mid-1930s he was settled at Berkeley, California, teaching at the California Institute of Technology. It may have been on the West Coast, but it was certainly not cut off from events in Europe. Jewish refugees from Germany, socialists and pro-Moscow Communists were part of his social circle. Arguments about the nature of Stalinism, what could be done about Hitler and the failure of the democracies to intervene in the Spanish war bubbled away on terraces overlooking San Franciscan gardens and continued during horse-rides. The Depression, followed by

Roosevelt's New Deal, had radicalized many in California, and Oppenheimer was not especially unusual in flirting with Communist thinking and the various 'front' organizations. He read Sidney and Beatrice Webb's propagandistic account of the glories of life under Stalinism, *Soviet Communism: A New Civilisation?*

This was the political side of Oppenheimer's world, which would get him into trouble after the war when US anxiety about 'red' infiltrators was at its height. But it was only a part of his life, and rather smaller than the part that led him to run the Manhattan Project. An intellectual gannet who gobbled up information in many fields, Oppenheimer worked on everything from the positron to the neutron star and black holes. He did key work on quantum mechanics and gravitational collapse, and was unlucky to miss a Nobel Prize.

It had been clear well before the war, from research on the structure of atoms, that in theory it would be possible to release vast amounts of energy – a huge explosion – by splitting atoms and creating a nuclear chain reaction. Albert Einstein had signed a letter to Roosevelt warning him of the danger of such a novel weapon. He had suggested that the American President order the stockpiling of uranium (the likeliest raw material for such an explosion because of its weak atomic structure) and press ahead urgently with research. After two émigré German scientists in Birmingham made a mathematical breakthrough showing it would be possible to produce the reaction in a quantity of uranium or plutonium small enough to be carried in an aircraft, the US started to take the idea seriously.

The secret project to be first with an atomic bomb was approved by Roosevelt in October 1941, and accelerated after the attack on Pearl Harbor that December. In the summer of 1942 a team including Oppenheimer concluded that a nuclear-fission bomb was possible. But the science was still little understood; at one point there was a real worry that such a bomb might ignite the earth's hydrogen-based atmosphere and end all life on the planet. Though the project was under the firm control of the US military, the charismatic Oppenheimer was eventually put in charge of the scientific and technical side. It was an inspired choice. He suggested the Los Alamos site, a remote and beautiful part of New Mexico he knew well from his hiking and horse-riding. Uranium ore was bought from the Belgian Congo and scientists were assembled from all across America, and Britain.

Among US intelligence officers there were severe worries about Oppenheimer's alleged Communist sympathies, which were not soothed when he suggested sharing their knowledge with Stalin. But there was no doubt that Oppenheimer and most of his team were obsessed with the need for speed, and a real fear that the Germans, led by Oppenheimer's old friend Heisenberg, might get there first. Huge amounts of money, infrastructure, testing and competitive argument produced exactly the surge in creativity that Oppenheimer had hoped for. It became increasingly clear that Nazi Germany would not be able to respond with a usable weapon. But with Bohr alongside – the Dane had escaped via Sweden to Britain just ahead of the Gestapo – Oppenheimer argued, the American bomb must be used anyway. It might well end all wars, but it would have to be seen around the world to have that effect.[28]

With Germany on the edge of final collapse, the target would have to be Japan. Some scientists, such as the Hungarian Leo Szilard, who had been the first in the 1930s to properly investigate nuclear chain reactions, warned frantically against using the bomb on Japanese civilians, saying it would start a deadly arms race with Russia. Roosevelt had recently died, and the new President, Harry Truman, ignored the argument. It is possible that Truman and his team wanted the bomb to be used before Japan had a chance to sue for peace, perhaps using Stalin as an intermediary. The USSR was now just coming into focus as America's new world enemy, and it would be convenient for Stalin to see just what the US was capable of.

Oppenheimer agreed with Truman on this and took part in detailed discussions about the 'tremendous' visual impact of the bomb, the need for it to kill large numbers of people, and the precise height for the explosion to have the maximum impact. It must not be detonated too high, or through clouds, or in rain or fog, 'or the target won't get as much damage'.[29] These words have to measured against Oppenheimer's famous reaction when the test bomb was successfully detonated at a desert site codenamed 'Trinity', on 16 July 1945. Much later, he said that he remembered Vishnu's words from the Hindu scripture the Bhagavad-Gita (which he had studied): 'Now I am become death, the destroyer of worlds.' Others dispute whether he actually said this at the time, though just ahead of the Hiroshima attack he did say, thinking of the victims, 'Those poor little people, those poor little people.'[30]

Oppenheimer was caught in one of the greatest moral challenges a scientist has ever faced. On the one hand, he was well aware of the awesome power of the weapon he was in charge of making. It could be a force for good, if it stopped conventional war. But as an admirer of the Soviets, he was well aware that they would struggle to acquire the bomb as quickly as possible; and that the future politics of the nuclear age were unpredictable. This intensely cultivated humanitarian, rather spiritual man had given his all to a machine intended to burn to death hundreds of thousands of innocent people. He had done it first of all because of the dreadful possibility that Hitler would soon have his own ultimate 'wonder weapon' and defeat the democracies; but now, because it simply had to be used.

Apart from anything else, Oppenheimer wanted to know if it worked. Like any theoretical physicist, he had lived his intellectual life on a plane of exciting abstraction that only rarely intersected with the ordinary world. Without world war, and the industrial and financial might of the United States, who would have spent the money and effort trying to test a theory like this? Here was a very rare chance to see whether he and the rest of his community of physicists had got it right. There is a sense in the arguments he used, and in his ambivalent language, that he did not want to argue through the consequences with quite the toughness that he argued the science. Perhaps inextinguishable curiosity overcame any political scruple; both are equally strong parts of the human spirit.

Today Hiroshima, where the first bomb was detonated, is a bright, modern regional city with beautiful tea-gardens, clean shopping malls and a reputation for excellent seafood. Immaculately dressed children learn and play at the primary school near the city centre where, in 1945, every child – except one – and every teacher was burned to death, along with most of the rest of the population. Hiroshima simply disappeared. A busy, old-fashioned city, with European-style buildings, numerous rivers and bridges and crowded housing, became a flat, charred space. Only a few shards of buildings remained vertical, and a few black-blasted trees. Nagasaki was next; and the Japanese surrender, which had been delayed by ferocious cabinet arguments, came almost immediately after that.

Oppenheimer became a celebrity in the US, though he warned that the time might come when people would curse the names of Los Alamos and Hiroshima. He told the American Philosophical Society that he had made 'a most terrible weapon . . . a thing that by all the standards of the world we grew up in is an evil thing'.[31] Was science, he asked, actually good for mankind? Today, for the whole of a human lifespan, the greatest countries of the world have not gone to war with one another, thanks to the threat of nuclear war. But with Pakistan, India, North Korea, Israel and soon perhaps Iran all now possessors of nuclear weapons, the danger of some coming nuclear conflict has grown rather than lessened. Oppenheimer's worries, like his 'most terrible weapon', have become universal.

Gandhi and the Empire

In 1930, it has been said, there existed three people who had achieved instant global recognition, not only for themselves but for what they stood for.[32] One was Charlie Chaplin. One was Adolf Hitler. And the third was a sixty-year-old troublemaker, dressed in rough cloth. On 12 March at six in the morning, he set off carrying a bedroll and a shoulder-bag, a spindle so that he could do some spinning at night, his diary, a watch and a mug. Accompanied by seventy-eight supporters, he was embarking on a 240-mile walk through villages in western India, and would arrive at the coast twenty-five days later. There, he proposed simply to gather up some salt and get himself arrested.

Mohandas Gandhi did exactly what he said he would do. Trailed by journalists and film crews from around the world, he walked, bent, scooped . . . and was arrested. The pictures were perfect. He had created an instantly recognizable symbolic image, salt in his hand, the salt flats behind him. The image was a trick. The pictures were taken days after he had arrived at the coast, and in a more photogenic spot. But Gandhi got the worldwide notice he wanted. The greatest exponent of a new kind of politics was taking on the world's largest empire, and winning hands-down.

Indian salt was taxed, not very heavily, by the British authorities, as it had been by the Mughals before them. Gandhi had considered, and tried, many ways to embarrass the British authorities in India. He had called for the prohibition of the sale of alcohol. He had called for a boycott of education. He had loudly backed striking workers. He had had moral successes, but without any political breakthrough. Salt was, however, an inspired target. Everyone ate salt. (Well, everyone except Gandhi, who was actually trying to exclude it from his diet as unhealthy.) The salt tax earned the government little but it was disproportionately hard on the poorest. Gandhi said that apart from water it was the only thing whereby, by taxing it, 'the state can reach even the starving millions, the sick, the maimed and the utterly helpless. The tax constitutes therefore the most inhuman poll tax the ingenuity of man can devise.'[33]

By collecting salt himself and refusing to pay the tax on it, he was challenging the British to charge and imprison him – a polite, comparatively elderly and skeletal man – and make themselves look ridiculous. They duly did so. But to put maximum pressure on the British, Gandhi needed a world audience. The US was particularly influential. To Americans, the salt-tax revolt conjured up an immediate historical parallel, their own rebellion against the British tax on tea. The stunt was classic Gandhi: it looked simple and he seemed almost clownish, yet this was a carefully, even coldly thought-through gambit.

Gandhi was already regarded by millions around the world as a living saint. He had been dubbed 'Mahatma Gandhi', or 'great-souled Gandhi', by Rabindranath Tagore, India's Nobel Prize-winning poet. He was famous for his ascetic lifestyle and ferociously uncompromising moralism. 'If I need only one shirt to cover myself with but use two, I am guilty of stealing one from another . . . If five bananas are enough to keep me going, my eating a sixth one is a form of theft.'[34] Eight years earlier, when he was being tried yet again for his campaign of civil disobedience, the British judge sentencing him confessed: 'You are in a different category from any person I have ever tried or am likely to have to try . . . Even those who differ from you in politics look upon you as a man of high ideals and of a noble and even saintly life. It is my duty to judge you as a man subject to the law.'

Gandhi's trick was like a martial arts move in which the individual uses seeming weakness to defeat an apparently mightier opponent. First in South Africa, campaigning for the rights of Indian workers (not black Africans), he had developed his theory of *satyagraha*, or 'firmness in the truth'. In practice this comprised campaigns of non-cooperation, of civil disobedience and of aggressive fasting so as 'to make the opponent think and understand'. Gandhi always tried to be extremely polite and to smile while he was leading protests, and he spoke admiringly of many aspects of British life, which only made him harder to deal with. He actively sought out imprisonment and led his followers, based in his ashrams, to do the same.

This form of moral blackmail, when raised to the level of global politics, can have a striking effect. Gandhi has inspired fighters against injustice around the world, including the civil rights campaigners under Martin Luther King in the United States in the 1960s, the Polish shipyard workers of 'Solidarity' in 1980, who confronted the Communist regime there; and the later anti-Soviet rebels in Hungary and Czechoslovakia, right up to the protesters who brought down Egypt's Hosni Mubarak. The force of ordinary people, well organized and peaceful, confronting power and using the international spotlight to help them, has been one of the few potent and cheering political ideas of the twentieth and twenty-first centuries.

In his domestic life, Gandhi's willingness to court confrontation was less attractive. He used his readiness to fast or to deprive himself of something to exert iron control on those around him. If he had a row with his wife, he fasted. If two people slept together in the ashram, he fasted. If his son let him down, he fasted. The more people wept and begged him to reconsider, the happier he was. And while moral blackmail as a political tactic has its uses, it should not become a way of life. Combined with Gandhi's strange determination to sleep with young women beside him without touching them, in order to prove he could be celibate, and his almost manic enthusiasm for enemas, this reminds us that saints are in general more to be admired from afar than to live with.

Gandhi's moral authority, however, roused all India. Albeit briefly, he was able to unite Muslim and Hindu campaigners; and to bring untouchables and other low-caste Indians into the same movement as educated businessmen and British-trained Indian lawyers. Early on, he had understood the power of the image, and thus of what one wore. As a young law student in London he had dressed in a three-piece suit and bow-tie. As a radical lawyer in India, he had dressed in formal English clothes, but topped them with a turban. Fighting for indentured labourers, he dressed himself in the same kind of cotton tunic as they wore. And as the campaigns against expensive British-manufactured cloth gathered pace, he chose to wear only rough Indian cloth. As his global reputation grew, he insisted on being photographed clad only in a loincloth, having spun the cotton for it himself.

Gandhi turned himself into a brand. Charlie Chaplin with his cane and baggy trousers, and Hitler with his military cap and moustache, were both worlds away from Gandhi. But they had all hit on the importance, in a world of photographs, of being recognizable.

And Gandhi, who roused a subcontinent, was also lucky in his chosen opponent. The trouble with the British was that they wanted to be liked and admired, as well as to wield power; and Gandhi knew them well. His own influences included British thinkers such as Ruskin and Edward Carpenter, the radical former match-girl and spiritualist Annie Besant, and the British suffragists. He wrote excellent English, and could not have operated successfully without English as a language which both united Indian campaigners and allowed him to reach a global audience.

Above all, the British were susceptible, at least at times, to Gandhi's kind of blackmail. They were embarrassable. They repressed and imprisoned, but they did not like it. Hitler, for one, simply could not understand this. (Gandhi completely misunderstood Hitler, seeing him as similar to the British. Hitler was not as bad as he was depicted, he said, and suggested German Jews should insist on staying in Germany and simply challenge the Nazis to shoot or imprison them – which rather missed the point.) Hitler, for his part, had told the British viceroy before the war, 'All you have to do is to shoot Gandhi . . . You will be surprised how quickly the trouble will die down.'[35]

Gandhi against Hitler would have been a rather shorter tale than Gandhi against the British Empire. But almost from the time of their original takeover of India, the British had dreamed of being good rulers. After the early decades of private looting by officials of the East India Company, Westminster had struggled to create a system of government that would be seen as fair and, in the long run, good for the subcontinent. Thereafter, the history of the British in India had been a see-saw, lurching between repression and reform.

The story had started in the 1750s with Robert Clive, a pudgy clerk who mysteriously evolved into a military genius, beat French and local armies and established the East India Company's dominance under the Mughal throne. But when he came home he was accused of having grabbed too much personal wealth, and committed suicide, aged forty-nine. After him, Warren Hastings arrived as governor-general, and over fourteen years built up a far more effective administrative system. His reward was to be impeached during a spectacular seven-year political trial at Westminster, again for corruption. He was acquitted, but left the stage a broken man. During that trial one of his tormentors, the Irish philosopher-politician Edmund Burke, complained that so far the British had simply taken from India, behaving no better than orang-utans or tigers: 'England has erected [in India] no churches, no hospitals, no palaces, no schools; England has built no bridges, made no high roads, cut no navigations, dug no reservoirs.'[36]

Later administrators took his strictures to heart. Apart from banning some of the crueller Hindu traditions, such as suttee, when widows proved their devotion (or had it proved for them, by relatives) by flinging themselves alive on funeral pyres, cities were built and British-style laws were introduced; along with an army in which Indian regiments were formed on British lines and under British command. English education was promoted, and administrators such as the historian Thomas Babington Macaulay looked forward to eventual self-government. This was still a patchwork India, which some of the new British arrivals found hard to understand. Others would admiringly study the ancient cultures they had so easily subdued. Yet it is not possible to possess another culture and to look up to it; or not for long, anyway.

Colonialism would bring benefits to India, including the archaeological rediscovery of Hindu cultures all but forgotten by Muslim-ruled India, which had, after all, arrived through another once alien invader, the Mughals. But as Gandhi well understood, colonialism corrupts both sides. It brutalizes the colonial power, making it unable to live up to its own highest ideals; and it humiliates the colonized people, making it hard for them to respect either their rules or themselves. British India's age of comparative imperial innocence was ended in 1857 in what British schoolchildren were told was the Indian Mutiny, and what Indian schoolchildren call the National Uprising, or the First War of Independence. It was bloody and desperate. It started over rumours about cow and pork fat being used to grease (Hindu and

Muslim) soldiers' cartridges, but soon became a more general revolt against British rule. On paper, the British were lucky to hold on, given their tiny numbers. Many Indians, from princes to whole regiments, stood aside, while the rebels were divided and badly led. After massacres and heroic sieges, the mutineers were abominably treated, many being blown to pieces from the mouths of British cannon. Great Mughal monuments were despoiled and vandalized.

India now became a British possession in the full meaning of the word, and several generations of very clever, dedicated professionals were sent across the sea to run the Indian Civil Service. It is still remembered as one of the least corrupt and most efficient bureaucracies in human history.

Boys from the new public schools of England, drilled in classical literature and notions of fair play, arrived to collect taxes and administer justice to tens of thousands of people – whose unfamiliar languages they struggled to learn – and across vast areas. The high noon of the British Indian adventure brought the subcontinent not only churches and canals, but nearly thirty thousand miles of railway and a single common language – English replaced Persian, which had never been widely understood south of the Mughal heartland. They brought a system of common law. The British, who dominated for rather longer than the Mughals, left no Taj Mahal, but they did leave teeming modern cities and in New Delhi a magnificent capital. They oversaw the growth of a population that by 1901 was second only to China's, and a rising, politically conscious if rather small middle class.[37] They left cricket, too.

The classically educated civil servants could not, however, administer away the fundamental unfairness of imperialism. At times their lack of understanding of India, and the dogmatism of Christian evangelicalism and moralistic liberalism, made them intolerable. Many claimed Indians were naturally slothful, sly, treacherous, superstitious and, in general, no damn good. This meant that, as in Ireland, when famines came, the British rulers were too quick to stand aside, blaming the victims for their misfortune. So millions died. Even outside the famine years, India's economy was unable to grow properly. First, her exports were sold to Britain, at low prices; then her industries were exposed without protection to the impossible competition of the British industrial revolution; and later still, when Indian businesses were beginning to grow, they were hamstrung by tariffs and regulations.

On top of all this, the cost of administering and protecting the British Empire in India was ultimately met by the Indians themselves – British salaries, pensions, debts, interest and military adventures accounted for a quarter of the taxes levied in India.[38] (Later, as Britain's industrial might waned and her economy struggled, many British came to believe that they had not only civilized India but paid to do so. Not at all. Even empires that consider themselves high-minded rarely pillage the home country to aid the conquered.) Had India not fought in the First World War, or spent her capital buying British steam engines and manufactured goods, but reinvested her wealth in her own development, might she not have overtaken China long ago? It is impossible to say. But economic complaints, plus the growing humiliation of educated Indians excluded from a say in running their own country, made eventual revolt inevitable.

There were slow, cautious political reforms, from the introduction of indirect elections to Legislative Councils in 1892, to more elected members in 1910, and a vague promise of what sounded like Home Rule, made during the First World War when two million Indians volunteered. But none of this stilled the agitation and occasional bomb attacks, which were met with savage reprisals. The worst moment of later British rule in India was the 'Amritsar Massacre' of April 1919, when General Reginald Dyer ordered his troops to fire, continuously and without warning, on a crowd in the Punjabi town. Some in the crowd were protesters, others were villagers celebrating a spring festival. The soldiers, with easy targets, fired 1,650 rounds and killed between 379 and 530 people (the figures are disputed), and seriously wounded more than 1,200 men, women and children. Dyer, who said he was taking revenge for an earlier riot which had left five Europeans dead, followed this up by forcing Indians to crawl on their bellies at the spot where a missionary had been attacked. He was relieved of his command but was entirely unrepentant, and treated as an imperial hero by Conservative newspapers when he returned home.[39]

If Dyer represents the brutal worst of the British in India, we have to set against him men like Allan Octavian Hume, who as an official had been infamous for taking the side of Indians and who in retirement founded the Indian National Congress in 1885. At first a campaigning organization wanting self-government, it would evolve under Indian leadership into the prime political force leading the campaign for independence.

After Amritsar, Indian opinion hardened. Motilal Nehru, a moderate, strongly pro-British lawyer who had been active in Congress and had sent his son Jawaharlal to Harrow and Cambridge, took his homburg hats, his expensive London suits and ties, his wife's dresses and the rest, and burned them in a bonfire. He got rid of his British furniture and dressed himself in Gandhi-style cotton. His son would go on to announce India's independence in 1947, become its first and longest-serving prime minister and the only man to rival Gandhi in modern Indian history. In a sense, his trajectory was sparked by Amritsar, the moment when British reform and appeasement of Indian opinion was drowned out by gunfire.

After Amritsar, Gandhi's campaigns of non-cooperation, as well as violent strikes, riots and attacks, made India increasingly hard for the British to govern. Gandhi's global authority grew to the point where, much to Winston Churchill's disgust, he was leading discussions with successive viceroys. When he came to London for round-table talks on India's future in 1931, he was invited to Buckingham Palace by King George V and mobbed by workers. Yet Gandhi was unable to placate either the Muslim politicians or the more extreme Hindu nationalists at home. British reform plans were real and substantial. After elections, Indian provinces were run by Congress politicians, with British civil servants taking orders from them. But because of the opposition of the princes, who feared – rightly – that they would lose their authority in their semi-autonomous states, and because of political skulduggery in London, plans for a new, Indian-dominated regime in New Delhi were never fulfilled.

During the Second World War, when India was threatened by Japan, some Indian nationalists went over to the enemy. Congress had a policy of non-cooperation with the British authorities. Nehru was interned and Gandhi was jailed, though both were later released. At times the British authorities struggled to keep control. The British Labour politician Stafford Cripps was sent out to offer terms for postwar self-government, but these were considered insufficiently democratic and were rejected by both Gandhi and Nehru. Gandhi wanted Britain to win the struggle, but remained bizarrely convinced that non-violence was a better way of defeating Nazism. During the Battle of Britain he suggested the British should invite Hitler and Mussolini to invade: 'Let them take possession of your beautiful island, with your many beautiful buildings. You will give all these, but neither your souls nor your minds.' The idea was politely rejected in favour of anti-aircraft batteries and Spitfires.[40]

By the middle of the war it was clear that India would be independent, one way or another. Britain's loss of prestige after the Japanese assault, and her bankruptcy after six years of fighting, left only the details of the separation to be agreed. With the election of a Labour government in 1945, the royally connected Lord Mountbatten was sent out to conclude the final arrangements, to a tight schedule set from London. However, despite Gandhi's best efforts, the Muslim–Hindu divide had widened during the years when Congress had led the independence struggle.

Snubbed by the Hindu leaders, the fastidious lawyer Mohammad Ali Jinnah led his Muslim League in a different direction, campaigning for their own statehood in the north-west, the Punjab and Bengal. Based on an acronym derived from the first letters of the Muslim-majority provinces, this would be called Pakistan There would be no single successor-state to the British Raj. Gandhi himself had campaigned hard for unity. As brutal intercommunal killing broke out, he went on another of his walks, preparing to fast, and pleaded with Hindus and Muslims to regard one another as brothers. But once the line of demarcation had been drawn between India and Pakistan (then including faraway Bangladesh in the east), a huge migration began, in both directions, accompanied by frenzied killing.

Mutual suspicions and dislike going back to the Mughal period, and which the British over two centuries had been unable or unwilling to smooth over, now erupted. In the Punjab in particular, Muslims, Hindus and Sikhs declared war and it may be that a million people died, hacked to death, shot, bludgeoned, burned, or simply from lack of food and water. Around ten million people moved north or south of the new border, the biggest such forced removal in history, even bigger than those in Germany and Russia a few years before. It was a hideous conclusion to Gandhi's peaceful lifelong campaign. He was grief-stricken, and began another fast in protest against the violence, refusing to celebrate India's independence day. Hindu extremists now regarded him as a traitor. On 30 January 1948, one of them assassinated him.

Playing the lead part in the drama that ended British rule in India, and creating a new model for protest against injustice, Gandhi can be seen as one of the most successful politicians of the twentieth century. But the country that emerged was utterly alien to his original vision for it. A lifelong follower of Tolstoy and his vision of the simple peasant life, Gandhi had looked forward to a spiritual India, one that would turn its back on railways, factories and great cities and return to the self-sufficient life of the village. He was a radical conservative, a peaceful version of those Communists who wanted to reject all Western civilization. Many of his English friends had also been idealist vegetarian-ruralists who looked forward to mankind returning to hamlets, orchards and hand ploughs. He also wanted, of course, a single India of Muslims, Christians and Hindus living together in harmony.

What happened instead was partition, capitalism, urbanization and two mutually hostile states, still arguing today over Kashmir and both of them nuclear-armed. The pantomime of military hatred enacted at border ceremonies is about as far removed from Gandhi's dream as it is possible to imagine. India herself is now one of the most powerful economies in the world, with bustling cities, factories, a well educated middle class and a democracy which, despite corruption, occasional assassinations and resurgent Hindu extremism, has been more successful than most postcolonial nations. With a population of 1.2 billion people and a GDP roughly twice that of Britain, it is one of the countries that are likely to dominate the next century. It is not, however, the country that Great-Souled Gandhi wanted.

A Cold War with Tropical Interruptions

For many countries, and many brave people, the Cold War was not cold. It was hot enough in Korea and Vietnam, in Angola and Somalia, on the borders of China, across swathes of Latin America and in the Middle East. For rebels in Hungary, Czechoslovakia, Poland and Afghanistan, it was a pulse-racing, lethal fight. It underpinned the deadly politics of the postwar Middle East, where America's ally Israel fought Arabs backed by the Russians, and Iranians fought Iraqis. It might have started as a struggle between two models of civilization, two leaderships, two capitals, but it sprawled so far and wide that for forty years there was hardly anywhere on earth unaffected. Because the central drama of nuclear bluff and escalation, a game of poker with the planet, was played out between small groups of men in offices in the United States and the USSR, it is easy to forget that the actual blood was being spilled almost everywhere else.

It had begun as a competition between two recent allies who were confused about just what they were doing. How great were their territorial claims to be? Was this an existential conflict about mankind's future, and if so how far would each side go? Because of this confusion, the fifteen years from 1948 to 1963 were the Cold War's most dangerous phase. After that, though America's bloody and embarrassing Vietnam War was still to come, the fundamental military stalemate underlying the 'balance of terror' was clearly understood in Washington and Moscow, and the initial cautious steps towards nuclear treaties began. After the first explosions of thermonuclear devices – by the US in 1952, by the USSR nine months later, then again far more lethally by the Americans in 1954 – it was obvious that war between the two powers would probably end the human race. Their confrontation, therefore, had to be carried on by proxies, as well as in the slower, but ultimately decisive, field of economics.

This pattern became apparent even before the USSR, at least, had any real ability to launch nuclear attacks on its capitalist enemies. The Marshall Plan, under which the Americans funded Western European postwar reconstruction, had started in 1947 with help for Greece, where Communists and monarchists were fighting a civil war, and for Turkey, threatened by Stalin, who wanted Soviet bases for a Mediterranean fleet. The US deepened its involvement in Europe far beyond aid, when its Central Intelligence Agency, authorized afresh to engage in a huge range of subversion, sabotage and propaganda, intervened in the Italian elections of 1948 to frustrate a Communist victory there. In the same year, Stalin's men showed themselves even more determined to hang onto their territorial gains of 1945 by authorizing a violent putsch against Czechoslovak democrats.

Both sides were forming wider alliances against the other. In April 1949 the North Atlantic Treaty Organization (NATO) formalized US military protection for Western Europe, a huge relief for Europeans becoming fixated by the aggressive rhetoric and the tank divisions to the east of what Churchill called 'the iron curtain'. The sheer size of Red Army forces meant no immediate response was needed, but the Warsaw Pact followed in 1955. Yet neither side was ready to contemplate direction military action against the other. This was less the residual sentiment between wartime allies than fear of the US atom bomb and exhaustion on the Russian side – they had lost something like ninety times as many people as the Americans – together with a brief period of optimism in Washington that a new United Nations might make war something for historians alone to study.

The first great test of this mutual wariness came with Stalin's attempt to provoke a change in divided Germany. He tried to throttle the small enclave of West Berlin, deep inside the Communist 'German Democratic Republic', by blockading it of all supplies. His aim was probably to reopen the division of Germany and perhaps create a neutral buffer country, though he remained oddly convinced that Germans would eventually choose to come over to the Communist side. It did not work, however, thanks to a massive and long-sustained airlift. This brought the one-time allies nose to nose, but the USSR backed down in the spring of 1949 and West Berlin continued open for business, a magnet for democratic values, to which embarrassingly large numbers of people from the East fled.

It was on the other side of the world that the real fighting began. Europe was, for once, saved from being the front line and the zone of maximum danger. At the end of the war Korea, however, had both Red Army forces in the north and US forces, part of the anti-Japanese push, in the south. Though both superpowers pulled their troops out and agreed a division of the peninsula halfway down it, this left a right-wing regime in the south and an aggressive Communist one, led by Kim Il Sung, in the north. In 1950 he persuaded Stalin that he could seize the whole country very quickly. He nearly succeeded, and it was only thanks to a US-led landing behind the Communist front line that the tide of battle turned.

Now, however, Mao – whose story we shall come to later – intervened and three hundred thousand Chinese 'volunteers' poured over the border and shoved the Americans back, into a humiliating retreat. Fighting under the new, unfamiliar flag of the United Nations, US,

British and Australian troops eventually repulsed the Maoist forces. Washington could, of course, have used atomic bombs, but chose not to, and suffered a bloody and prolonged period of trench warfare instead.

Why? It could hardly have been the threat of a swift Soviet reprisal. We know now that Russian pilots were present over the skies of Korea; and the Russians had had a bomb of their own (thanks to their spies in the West) since the previous year, though they were not yet in a position to effectively challenge in a nuclear exchange. It was rather because the US did not want to set a precedent; the bomb was not to be used lightly, or merely to even the score in a conflict that did not touch America's future. If it *were* to be used in this way, the Russians would eventually do the same. So the Korean War, bloody enough, ended in a stalemate close to the line where it had begun, and in the establishment of two regimes that would become caricatures of their sponsors – one, dourly and violently Stalinist, the other rampagingly capitalist.

From now on, the US and the USSR competed in a frantic arms race, involving not just nuclear warheads but submarines, intercontinental ballistic missiles, satellites, spy planes and hidden silos. But at the same time they searched restlessly around the world for allies to prop up and countries to bring over to their side, fomenting and supporting wars and dictatorships across Africa, Asia and South America. The United States intervened aggressively in Latin and South America, and supported the Shah of Iran and the southern part of former French Indochina, by now called Vietnam, as well as trying – mostly unsuccessfully – to court Arab countries. The USSR concentrated on her European satellites and two increasingly difficult relationships. The more important one was with her impetuous Communist ally, China; and the other was with the most independent-minded Communist country in Europe, Josip Broz Tito's Yugoslavia, which had liberated itself from the Nazis without Soviet help and considered it had no need to kowtow to Moscow.

Both these countries became part of a wider movement which showed that, despite the appearance of world-threatening, globe-encircling superpower dominance, neither the United States nor the USSR was quite as strong as it looked. Countries whose leaders had sufficient self-confidence could dodge quite successfully between the

Bear and the Eagle; and even play them off against each other. In Indonesia in 1955, Yugoslavia and China had been among the countries meeting to form the Non-Aligned Group. There was India too, now a socialist republic but still within the British Commonwealth, determined to have good relations with Russia as well as with the West; and Egypt, whose nationalist leader Nasser would soon humiliate the old imperial powers, France and Britain, but would also spurn US aid in favour of Russian. When France left the military command structure of NATO in 1966, having recognized Maoist China, she too became more like a non-aligned power than a full part of the Western bloc.

In Africa, a long and often tragic struggle began for the fealty of former colonies. Would these new republics retain fond links with their European colonizers or declare themselves people's republics and send their brightest and best to study Marxism-Leninism in Moscow?

Among the anticolonial parties across the continent, Africanists fought Marxists, while Western governments chose to turn a blind eye to one-party despotism, corruption and worse – the local dictator might be a bastard, but he was 'our' bastard. This allowed the rule of dictators such as Idi Amin in Uganda, Mobuto Sese Seko in Zaire – the former Belgian Congo – Hastings Banda in Malawi and Daniel arap Moi in Kenya. On the Soviet side, the monstrous Mengistu Haile Mariam of Ethiopia and the weird, incompetent Marxists of Angola's MPLA and of Mozambique's Frelimo were backed by Moscow – without any great enthusiasm, but merely because the Cold War had to be fought everywhere, for every slab of baked soil and every hungry, wary child. In Angola, the United States had backed a rival nationalist guerrilla force, Unita, but as the African observer Richard Dowden mordantly put it, 'It was hard to see what Angola gave the Soviet Union apart from bad debts and sun in winter for its generals.'[41]

The speed of decolonization, which catapulted into power across Africa groups and individuals who had not had the time or support to prepare for it, was also part of the Cold War story. This was not simply about European governments, from Lisbon to Brussels and London to Paris, scuttling because they no longer had the will to hold their old colonies against black liberation movements. It was as much because, focusing on the Communist threat, they had no stomach for wars against Soviet proxies and preferred to cut a deal early on with 'pro-

Western' new rulers, in the hope that trade would continue, while the politics of the new country took second place.

The East–West confrontation allowed apartheid South Africa to keep both Britain and the US for a long time as unhappy 'neutral friends' because of its vehement anti-Communism. The Cold War permitted Robert Mugabe, the destroyer of Zimbabwe, to be tutored in Marxism even though he first thrust aside his overtly pro-Moscow rival Joshua Nkomo. As we tot up the sad history of misrule, corruption, racism, torture and waste in Africa's twentieth century, many of the uncountable millions of African lives blighted during this period must also be added to the real cost of the Cold War.

Both sides, by the mid-1950s, had new leaderships struggling to find ways to cope with the balance of terror. In the US, Harry Truman, a tough-minded President who had nevertheless been heavily influenced by Roosevelt's idealism, was replaced by Roosevelt's old military commander, 'Ike' Eisenhower. To start with, at least, he held a more aggressive view of the possible use of nuclear weapons. And after Eisenhower, in 1961, would come a young Democrat, John F. Kennedy, who used soaring rhetoric about America's global destiny as the champion of free people, and who would be pitched almost immediately into confrontation with Moscow.

Both these leaders faced in Nikita Khrushchev a bullfrog-like new Soviet leader, a genuine worker who had risen under Stalin and who acted with impetuosity (and some personal coarseness). At the beginning of Khrushchev's rule, the USSR was still behind the West in missiles but was starting to catch up. The launch into space of Russia's first intercontinental ballistic missile, and its Sputnik earth-orbiter, in 1957, was a terrible shock to Western politicians. Khrushchev believed that Soviet methods in science and economics could lead to the USSR overtaking the United States; meanwhile, he wanted a less terror-drenched atmosphere at home, denouncing the crimes and personality cult of Stalin in a secret speech to the ruling Communist Congress – though it didn't stay secret for long.

But anyone who thought a slightly more liberal atmosphere implied any lessening of Moscow's determination to hang onto its 'socialist' satellites was brutally disabused in 1956, when Soviet tanks crushed rebellion, and some twenty thousand people died.

In 1962, it was Khrushchev and Kennedy who brought the world closer to nuclear annihilation than ever before – or, so far, since. The cause was Cuba, whose Marxist revolution under Fidel Castro the Americans had tried, and failed, to overthrow in a botched invasion at the Bay of Pigs. Khrushchev thought that shipping and installing Russian missiles on the island would be a good way to both protect his new Caribbean ally and to threaten America, which also had medium-range missiles aimed at the USSR, mostly in Turkey. This was a very 'hot' time in the Cold War; the Russians had tested a bigger bomb, had sent Yuri Gagarin aloft as the first man in space, while their East German allies had sealed off West Berlin with the notorious Wall, designed to stop a flood of emigrants. (The East German state had shrunk by two million citizens.)

These acts suggested that Communism was better-armed than ever, and more determined. The determination was real enough, but in fact the USSR was still far behind the Americans in missile capability; in Cuba, Khrushchev hoped to bolster Soviet prestige and encourage Latin American revolutionaries. Kennedy, too, expected this effect. He warned the Russians that if their supply ships carrying extra rockets to Cuba strayed beyond a certain line, he would attack them. He also insisted that the current sites be demolished. Torpedoing Russian ships would mean full-scale war. After Kennedy's ultimatum, the world held its breath.

In the nick of time, Khrushchev backed down and the missile bases were dismantled, which seemed a great victory for the US President. It was – but his opposite number in the Kremlin ended up getting a lot of what he wanted, notably the removal of US missiles in Turkey and the acceptance that Castro's Marxist regime was there to stay. A 'hotline' to connect the US and Soviet leaders was installed. There were still some very dangerous moments to come. They included the outbreak of fighting in 1969 between Chinese and Russian troops on their border, and the bloodiest, most painful US Cold War failure, the war to repel Communism in Vietnam. The conflict spread to Laos and Cambodia too, lasted from 1965 until 1975, and demonstrated conclusively that aerial bombardment cannot destroy guerrilla forces.

But after the Cuban crisis, both Washington and Moscow accepted that they had to edge back from a situation in which a tiny miscalculation could end human history. The Nuclear Test-Ban Treaty was followed by a Nuclear Non-Proliferation Treaty in 1968, then the first strategic arms-limitation talks, or SALT 1, in 1972, limiting the number of ballistic missiles. Another treaty, banning defence against nuclear missiles, showed that the doctrine of 'mutually assured destruction', or MAD – what Oppenheimer had hoped for in his less grim moments – was official policy. The period of agreed coexistence, named 'détente', arrived, during which both systems attempted to live with each other, in a divided world. At the time it seemed an endless stasis, the Cold War now, finally, a Frozen Peace; or, to change the metaphor, it was as if two heavy-weight wrestlers had ended in an exhausted clinch, bear-hugging one another, unable either to break free or to topple the opponent.

Though apparently safer than the earlier phase of aggressive competition, the Frozen Peace proved an illusion too, but more because of what happened inside the two camps than between them. No political systems are really static. Behind the Iron Curtain, though the Soviet system did match – indeed, heavily outspent – NATO in armaments, the Soviet economy was failing to produce the growth in wealth that could have persuaded its people that it was truly a better society, and that the political repression and sheer dreariness of life were worth while. Khrushchev had been blamed, and paid the price, for Cuba as well as for domestic failings, when he was removed from power in 1964; but the new regime of old men, led by Leonid Brezhnev, lolled over a society beginning visibly to stagnate. The crushing of the Czechoslovak uprising of 1968, which had been greeted as the 'Prague Spring', showed the world just how popular Communism really was among its own people.

But it was first in the West that the new mood of mutiny and rebellion against old leaders shook things up. America's bloody Vietnam War, which required a draft of young men into the army, provoked increasing protests at home. Both the Democrat Lyndon B. Johnson and the Republican Richard Nixon struggled to figure out how to combine their military strategy with the demands of a younger nation, swollen by the 'baby boomers', products of a postwar rise in the birth rate. An historian of the Cold War, John Lewis Gaddis, points out that enrolments in US colleges and universities had risen threefold between 1955 and 1970: 'What governments had failed to foresee was that more young people plus more education, when com-

bined with a stalemated Cold War, could be a prescription for insurrection . . . This was something never before seen: a revolution
transcending nationality, directed against establishments whatever
their ideology.'[42]

Anti-Vietnam protests rocked Berlin, Paris and London, but it was
in the United States itself that the political prestige of the Cold Warriors was most badly damaged. At around this time, more damning
evidence was coming into the public arena of the covert operations of
the CIA, in Guatemala and in Chile, where they helped topple a freely
elected leftist government. Its leader, Salvador Allende, along with
thousands of others, died, and many were horribly tortured. This
seemed entirely counter to the vaunted moral superiority of the
democracies. Young radicals adopted as icons and heroes the enemies
their leaders were fighting – Castro, Che Guevara, Ho Chi Minh and
Mao – and a wave of leftism swept through the campuses. Nowhere
did this radicalism break through to change Western leadership –
not even in France, where the 'events' of 1968 were at their most spectacular. But it showed that 'détente' did not mean stability.

In the end, it would be the Soviet side that collapsed, far more quickly
and dramatically than Western analysts had expected. Under Nixon,
before his illegal wire-tapping and his lies brought down his presidency, the United States had ended its old enmity with Mao's China,
thus adding to the sense of paranoia and encirclement in Moscow. An
ever-older leadership, ever clearer evidence of economic failure and
ever more embarrassing evidence of Western plenty stirred discontent. Russian agreement to a world declaration on human rights
encouraged dissidents at home, who spread news to the rest of the
world about the repression and brutality of the Soviet system; Alexander Solzhenitsyn's writing was particularly influential. In Poland,
shipyard workers protested, and the election of a Pole, Karol Wojtyla,
as Pope John Paul II, in 1978, was followed by scenes of mass enthusiasm when he visited his homeland, to the horror of its atheist rulers.
When the USSR invaded Afghanistan the following year, to protect a
client Marxist ruler, it became embroiled in a costly, bloody war. The
US responded cleverly by backing Islamist guerrillas; or at least, it
seemed clever at the time.

The fall of the Soviet Union was not brought about by guns, quite;

but it was by the cost of guns, or rather missiles. A new US president, the sunny-natured and apparently rather simplistic former actor, Ronald Reagan, ordered the beginning of a system of defence against Russian missiles – his 'strategic defence initiative', which because it involved satellite-tracking, and in deference to a popular film, was immediately dubbed 'Star Wars'. The USSR and NATO had been engaged in a new round of nuclear competition since 1977, when the new Russian SS20 missiles threatened Western Europe and the US had responded by basing their own Pershing and Cruise missiles there. For the Russians, trying to match this proposed new system was economically ruinous – impossible. Reagan's increasingly contemptuous and hawkish rhetoric about 'the evil empire' showed the US had a leader who no longer feared the Russian threat. Many thought this foolish, but it coincided with a series of embarrassingly elderly and short-lived leaders of that empire, first the terminally ill Yuri Andropov from 1982 to early 1984, then Konstantin Chernenko, who seemed barely alive to start with.

There were dangerous moments to come, as the Soviet system tottered on its feet. But with the arrival of Mikhail Gorbachev the USSR finally had a leader with the vigour and self-confidence to discuss proper disarmament with Reagan. Their three key summits during 1986–7 prepared for a radically new relationship; even Britain's super-hawkish prime minister Margaret Thatcher warmed to Gorbachev as 'a man I can do business with'. Internally, though, Gorbachev seems to have had no master-plan. He knew things had to change and that the Soviet system was doomed, but he somehow hoped that freshly moderate Communists could retain power while these vast territories became more politically open and economically liberal. His policies of openness and rebuilding (*glasnost* and *perestroika*) flinched from a real lurch towards market economics and capitalism of the kind the Chinese Communist Party was then embracing. What Gorbachev intended was a move away from global confrontation, perhaps even the end of the Cold War. What he intended for the USSR was less clear.

The momentous year 1989 provided the answer. Beginning in Hungary, which refused to keep its Iron Curtain with Austria in good repair, the Eastern Europeans simply broke away – and Gorbachev would not act to stop them. Poland, where the independent Solidarity

movement led by the former shipyard worker Lech Walesa had led the
way for others, now had elections for the lower house – which saw
Solidarity swept to power. East Germans began voting with their
wheels, packing their belongings into their boxy little Trabant cars and
heading through Hungary to Austria, and freedom. After days of confusion in East Berlin, and no backing for any kind of crackdown
coming from Moscow, the Wall itself was opened, and ecstatic Germans began to pour through – and then to dance on it, and then to
knock it down. The Bulgarian Communists caved in and announced
free elections; in Prague, vast demonstrations broke the Czech Communists' spirit, and a 'velvet revolution' installed the former dissident
and playwright Vaclav Havel as president. In Romania, one of the cru-
ellest and most idiosyncratic of the Soviet satellites, things did not end
so peacefully. Its dictator Nicolae Ceauşescu ordered troops to shoot
on the crowds, but failed to quash the uprising; he and his wife were
quickly caught, tried and shot.

The following year saw the reunification of Germany and the start
of the collapse of the USSR itself, as the Baltic republics broke away.
Gorbachev was the victim of a coup by outraged hardliners, but they
soon found that the collapse he had (by his wise inaction) overseen
was impossible to reverse. The army would not support them, and a
new leader emerged – the alcoholic showman Boris Yeltsin, who publicly defied the plotters, standing on a tank in front of the Russian
parliament building. Yeltsin in effect dissolved the Soviet Union, looking on benignly as vast countries such as the Ukraine announced their
independence.

The Cold War ended because one philosophy of government and economics, Marxism as practised by the Soviet Union, had tested itself to
destruction. The USSR had – Russia has – great natural resources,
including oil, gas, timber and massive expanses of excellent agricultural land. Despite starting late, it once looked an excellent candidate
for successful industrialization, of a kind that would have greatly
improved the material life of its people, who were by global standards
well educated. But its system of monopolistic state enterprises,
directed from the centre and caught in the web of fear, corruption and
laziness created by Communist rule, resulted in waste, shortages, cynicism and hopelessness.

In the end, there was little to hold people's loyalty beyond the memory of the heroism of the Great Patriotic War, which young Russians found less impressive than had their parents. Released from the same system, the Eastern European states, which lost no time in applying to join the European Union, showed that after a couple of generations of repression, enterprise and energy can revive remarkably fast.

Russia herself would suffer a worse fate. She had never enjoyed a democratic culture, having moved almost immediately from Czarist autocracy to Marxist dictatorship. As Western consultants were flown in to advocate, for fat fees, the fast privatization of enterprises and free-market shock therapy, as well as to advise on the creation of new parties, Russia experienced a terrible time of rocketing prices, unemployment and asset-stripping by a new class of 'oligarchs', some of them no better than robber barons. When the old Communist elite rebranded itself and returned as born-again nationalists, ready to do deals with the swaggering new super-rich of Moscow and (newly renamed) St Petersburg, ordinary Russians found themselves with the worst of both worlds – cynical, autocratic and repressive politics alongside a twisted idea of capitalism at its rawest. Who lost the Cold War? They did.

Deng & Son – Chinese Rebirth

Nations have often been too big, as well as too small. The story of China in the nineteenth century and through the first half of the twentieth is the most obvious case. To a Westerner it can seem an incomprehensible and endless muddle of wars, rebellions, coups and collapses. There were attempts at modernization, including the introduction of railways, telegraph systems and steamships in the last decades of the imperial Qing dynasty, and the establishment of modern constitutions and apparently modern parliaments when that dynasty collapsed shortly before the First World War. China's modern history presents a series of larger-than-life reformers, trying to drag a vast empire of peasants and landlords into the age of industrial urban mankind. But it seemed too big a job. The land was too large, its constituent parts too disparate and too weakly linked.

Those who struggled include some hugely impressive figures who deserve to be better-known today. One was Li Hongzhang, the great shaker-up of late imperial China, who developed its industry and plotted to return it to independence and real power. Another was Yuan Shikai, a tough farmer's son who rose up through the army to become a king-maker, and president of the Chinese Republic. Then, of course, there are the more famous figures such as Sun Yat-sen, Yuan's sometime collaborator and rival and another farmer's son, who is generally recognized as the founder of modern Chinese Nationalism. Finally there is Chiang Kai-shek, leader of the Nationalist Kuomintang, reformer of Chinese banking, language, education and communications; but also a corrupt and ultimately ineffective military dictator. Each of these were leaders every bit as potent and ambitious for their countries as a Roosevelt, a Churchill or a Mussolini.

The trouble, however, is that all of them were destroyed by the scale of the job and by the circling wolf-pack of China's enemies. Li Hongzhang died defeated in 1901, after negotiating a humiliating and ruinous peace treaty with Russia, France, Britain and Japan in the wake of the Boxer Rebellion and the seizure of Beijing. Yuan Shikai became increasingly dictatorial and declared himself emperor in 1912, as the country was once more being humiliated by Japan. Forced out, he left China tearing herself apart under competing warlords. Sun Yat-sen, whose reputation remains very high in both China and Taiwan to this day, nevertheless became an increasingly militaristic and dictatorial leader; he died of cancer in 1925 while China was still ravaged by the warlords and his Kuomintang government controlled only the south. Chiang Kai-shek, despite alliances with Russia's Communists as well as with the United States, was never able to rule mainland China effectively – again during a time of military catastrophe at the hands of the Japanese, and while the Chinese Communist insurgency was becoming unstoppable.

These regimes had all failed to impose effective central authority. What this produced was not a China of quiet, harmonious self-governing villages and towns freed of an arrogant Beijing but a China of lawlessness, fear, terror and insecurity. In the huge rural hinterlands, millions of Chinese continued to plant and eat their rice, tend their animals, worship traditionally, gossip, bicker, live and die without knowing much about the nearest large town, never mind national politics. The same could be said of peasants everywhere during the first half of the twentieth century, from Corsica to Iceland, Turkey to Chile.

But the failure to build a single effective modern system of money, taxation or communications, or military power, left the people of China at the mercy of local landlords and bandits, foreign invaders, religious extremists; and with little or no support when famines came or warlords rampaged. The death-tolls during the last years of the Qing dynasty and in China's forty years of non-Communist republican government are impossible to be precise about, but the figures are estimated to be very large. In one of the few villages that survived the annihilation of custom and tradition at the hands of Mao's Red Guards, there stands a watchtower used by the villagers to scour the countryside for bandits. It was built in 1918.

None of this was new to the Chinese. The Taiping Rebellion of 1850–64, launched by quasi-Christian zealots who seized much of southern and central China, had resulted in an estimated twenty million deaths, making it one of the most catastrophic episodes in world history. The Boxer Rising of 1898–1901 was a military disaster that showed the world just how weak Qing China really was. Japan's seizure of Manchuria and its invasions of northern and coastal China resulted in massacre after massacre, among which the Rape of Nanking in 1938, when around 200,000 civilians were murdered and up to 80,000 women were raped, is only the most notorious. The Chinese death-toll in the chaotic fighting of the Second World War has been estimated at around twenty million, outstripping by far every other nation except the Soviet Union.

Around these grim statistical peaks are the jagged mountains of innumerable local rebellions by religious and secret societies, Muslim generals and regional warlords; add to this decades during which the notion of a single China was only cultural and linguistic (and that, only just) rather than political. The first-hand accounts of starvation resulting in cannibalism, of villages empty of children and animals, and the remorseless trail of grainy photographs showing the beheadings of wretched rebels or of captured government troops – never mind the vengeance wreaked by outsiders in the shape of burned-down temples and shattered city centres – add more unpleasant detail than most readers will want to dwell on.

So while the rule of Mao Zedong and the Chinese Communist Party after 1949 produced the greatest human catastrophe of the twentieth century, it cannot be understood without remembering what had come first. The Chinese yearning for unity and order is not an obscure political shibboleth. The greater the population, the more sprawling and varied the terrain, the harder unity and order are to impose. Since the Manchu had overturned the Ming dynasty in 1644, China's rulers not only had the huge heartland of the country to think about, with its immensely long coastline, but vast northern and eastern territories occupied by Mongols, Tibetans and Muslims. Currencies, languages, swamps and mountains produced internal divisions that even a modest-sized country would have struggled to overcome.

Though Japan eventually came to a sticky end too, having confronted, unsuccessfully, the rising superpower of the United States, her rapid advance in the late nineteenth and early twentieth centuries under the Meiji emperors showed what could be done in a comparatively small and united nation with strong central authority. Like the Japanese, the Chinese had tried to import Western military techniques, to build or buy new iron-clad warships, modernize their bureaucracy and open up their education system. But the Chinese leaders – whether imperial or republican – simply did not have the grip or the authority to make things happen. Again and again they were shamed by outside leaders who did.

This produced a manic impatience among Chinese intellectuals, particularly on the left, which was finally expressed in the rule of Mao, with his lurching directives for breakneck industrialization. China's rulers had never been in touch with the people. There were, and are, too many of them, spread across too wide a terrain. Both emperors and Marxists, having locked themselves away behind high walls in Beijing, would have had to work very hard to see the consequences of their policies on the real China. In 1901 the dowager empress Cixi, an extraordinary woman who was the real power in the country for nearly half a century, came face to face with real China when she was fleeing Beijing, about to be invaded by Western armies. How were they doing, her people? She found famine victims who had eaten everything, dogs, cats, leaves and bark, and were now eating each other.[43] The difference was that when Mao eventually saw the results of his famines, more widespread by far than the one that killed around two million in Cixi's time, he was delighted.

Mao's China has obvious parallels with the story of the early Soviet Union, also embracing a vast and divided area with a weak centre. Mao, like Stalin, arrived in power armed with a doctrine, Marxism-Leninism, which promised a classless heaven-on-earth once enough bourgeois enemies had been killed. This was a philosophical weapon without a moral safety-catch.

During the 1920s Moscow was trying to foment world revolution, and saw the chaos of China as very promising territory. The Nationalist Kuomintang (in power during 1927–45) were sufficiently left-wing in their rhetoric and large enough in support to be the Russians' favoured partner; so for many years the still-tiny Chinese Communist Party was ordered to cooperate with, and infiltrate, the Nationalists. Kuomintang leaders went to listen and learn in Moscow. When, however, Chiang Kai-shek turned to the right in the late 1920s and began to go after the Communists, they were forced to retreat north-west, to the wild country near the Russian border. The Kuomintang forced them further and further back until, in 1934, a key Communist army was hemmed in and on the edge of annihilation.

The desperate retreat across inhospitable terrain, to link up with other Red forces, became known as the 'Long March'. It was really a series of marches, a retreat from the Nationalist army. Its biggest political impact was to elevate Mao, who had fallen from favour, as the de facto leader of China's Communists. It has been used ever since as a Maoist foundation myth, a story of hillside hideouts, heroic river crossings and desperate mountain battles, one whose details are probably buried for ever under an avalanche of posters, films and wishful thinking. China's National Museum at Beijing's Tiananmen Square, just opposite Mao's mausoleum, has at its centre a room of epic paintings about the Long March. Technically at least, some of them are rather good.

Stalin had had his eye on Mao from his early days as a Communist guerrilla leader in Shanghai, but for a long time hedged his bets. He not only backed Chiang Kai-shek, but kept Chiang's son in Moscow as a hostage. When Chiang was kidnapped by a rival and Mao wanted him killed, Stalin intervened to save him. Once the Japanese attacked

China in 1937, it was strongly in Stalin's interest that both Communists and Nationalists forget their differences and unite against the invaders. Mao, however, playing a ruthlessly cold game, kept his distance. With a smaller and worse-trained army than his rivals and ruling by terror and purge, Mao carefully built up his position, strengthening his base in the north-west of China, while the invaders and the Nationalists fought across the coastline and plains.

Though nearly destroyed in the immediate aftermath of the Second World War, the Chinese Communist armies had survived to win Stalin's support. Their involvement in the anti-Japanese struggle came late; Mao had always intended to finish off Chiang Kai-shek, only once he had been sufficiently weakened by the Japanese. Now hundreds of aircraft, tanks and artillery pieces, and hundreds of thousands of machine-guns and rifles, all from captured Japanese and German stocks, were handed over to Mao by the Russians. Military training – some of it, apparently, by former Japanese soldiers – came as part of the package, as did Korean troops and Chinese soldiers who had been on the Japanese side in Manchuria. The Russians also helped repair Chinese railways and bridges.

In return, Mao sent food to Russia. In an eerie echo of Stalin's decision in the 1930s to export grain to the West to buy industrial plant, thereby contributing to the terrible Russian famines, Mao's food-for-industry deal triggered famine in his own territories. When the full-scale war was joined with Chiang's forces in 1947–8, the Communists owed a huge amount to the Russians, something Mao never publicly acknowledged.[44] The Nationalists eventually fell because of bad generalship, widespread corruption, and the exhaustion of a movement that had been fighting the Japanese for ten long years. Mao's men used terror tactics, including the deliberate starvation of the people of the city of Changchun, where around three hundred thousand are thought to have died, to force surrender. Chiang Kai-shek retreated to the island of Taiwan, where his successors continue, at least in theory, to regard themselves as the rightful government of all China.

The proclamation of the People's Republic of China by Mao Zedong on 1 October 1949 made him the ruler of around 550 million people. While the West was well on the way to recovery from the war, and Europe and America luxuriated in a material plenty and a personal freedom that humankind had never before known, the Chinese were enduring terror and hunger. This state of affairs ended not in a new cataclysm, but instead in a swerve towards compromise, which eventually created the economic giant of today's China. Why this happened is a complicated and tragic story, with glints of heroism.

The man more responsible for China's escape from Maoism than any other was Mao's diminutive and gritty one-time follower, Deng Xiaoping. Considering the impact of the country that he created, Deng has a good case to be considered the most influential single human being of the latter part of the twentieth century. But before we discuss where he led China to, and how he made the great switch, we need to understand where he led China from.

Mao's land seizures and political purges in the early 1950s killed up to three million people. Many were driven to suicide – in the city of Shanghai so many flung themselves from the roofs of tall buildings they were known locally as 'parachutes'.[45] But this was only the start. Two authors, Jung Chang and Jon Halliday, argue that the system of prisons and work-to-death camps that Mao established, in imitation of the Soviet gulag system, may well have killed twenty-seven million. Unlike in the Soviet Union, however, Mao's killers liked the terror to be seen and heard. Many of the executions were carried out in public in front of crowds dragooned to watch: the psychological effect of Mao on the Chinese was surely even greater than that of Stalin on the Russian psyche.

Mao's greater ambition was to make China a world superpower, indeed *the* world superpower. To do this he would have to turn a nation of peasant farmers into an industrial giant. He intended to do this within just a few years by taking ever larger amounts of food away from the peasantry and swapping it for Soviet know-how; and by creating grandiose industrial and irrigation systems. None of this was original; it too was borrowed from Stalin. But by 1950 Stalin had the atomic bomb, as well as the status of a Soviet emperor and world-war victor. Mao decided that to overtake Stalin, he had to copy him on a larger scale and at an even more breakneck speed.

The results were on a larger scale, certainly. The so-called Great Leap Forward, which partly created and partly coincided with four years of famine, from 1958 to 1961, killed an estimated thirty-eight million people, the worst cull in history. Mao showed absolutely no pity or even much interest. He certainly knew what was going on, because even subservient party officials reported back. The peasant landholdings were collectivized so the state could keep more of the food. Again and again, he mocked the peasants as greedy and idle and suggested cutting their rations further. He said the corpses would be useful for fertilizing the ground.

The people were told to melt down all their metal so as to make, then feed, back-yard furnaces. Giant canals, dams and reservoirs were constructed without planning, and so badly built that many later collapsed, causing human and environmental disasters. One of Mao's madder ideas was to cut down on food waste by destroying all the sparrows in China. This was to be done by getting everyone to make so much noise that the birds would not be able to land and would die of exhaustion in the sky. It worked well enough to cause a plague of some of the pests that the sparrows fed on.

These spasms of frenzied mass activity were being ordered because Mao always had his eye on making China all-powerful. First, he said, she would control the Pacific with a huge new navy, and then eventually the world. He had planetary ambitions. Mao spoke of setting up an 'earth control committee' with a single uniform Maoist plan for all humanity; what this would imply for the Chinese themselves was irrelevant. Chang and Halliday quote him saying in Moscow in 1957 that he was prepared to sacrifice three hundred million Chinese – about half the population at the time – for the victory of world revolution. His keenness to help the North Koreans in the war against the West in that country, when he threw tens of thousands of Chinese soldiers into battle, and his enthusiasm for using nuclear weapons both suggest this was no joke.

May 1968 was a month of turbulence. Across the West the hippy revolution, the era of 'peace and love' and 'flower power', was being challenged by student revolts. In Beijing lived Deng Pufang, twenty-five years old, a brilliant physics student. His life had been unusually blessed. As the older son of one of Communist China's leaders, he had been brought up in the beautiful, exclusive area of Zhongnanhai in the centre of the capital, next door to the Forbidden City. This was where Mao Zedong and the other top Communists lived, in what has been described as 'a hidden fairyland of lakes, parks and palaces where

Marco Polo strolled and Kublai Khan built his pleasure dome; where emperors and empresses, concubines and eunuchs, took their leisure'.[46]

But Deng Pufang was in a terrible state. He had been beaten to a bloody pulp by self-declared 'Red Guards'. His father was now denounced as a 'capitalist roader', and his children had already been forced to denounce him publicly. The young man was lying in pools of blood on the concrete floor of a stripped-out former university dormitory, four floors up. The window had been torn out. Deng Pufang was told he would never leave the room alive – the only way out for him was through the window.

He has said that, in despair, he jumped. This was not unusual. One of the tactics used by the Red Guards was 'suiciding', a word neatly balanced between killing yourself and being killed. Either way, he was found mangled on the pavement below, his spine smashed. He might have been healed, had he been given medical treatment, but when he was taken to hospital by passers-by he was refused admittance – the son of a capitalist-roader had no right to health care. Deng Pufang was left to cope as best he could on a damp floor with other crippled patients. Amazingly, he lived. Paraplegic, he learned to weave wire baskets to earn money for food. For a year, his parents had no idea what had happened to him.

His father was Deng Xiaoping. A wiry man who had led Communist armies in their final victory over the Nationalists in 1948–9, he had been one of Mao's comrades on the Long March. Indeed, Deng had been a favourite – Mao called him 'the little man'. Like Mao, Deng came from a relatively well-off farming family in a remote corner of rural China, and had been brought up in a large thatched house many miles from the nearest road. The China of the early twentieth century was, as we have seen, a politically complicated and dangerous place. Deng's father was a respected political reformer and was also allied with the local warlord, which, then and there, was not entirely a paradox. His bright son, remembered by playmates as being particularly good at somersaults, was sent off to the nearest town to study under a radical teacher who prepared pupils to travel abroad on a Chinese–French study programme.

In 1920 Deng sailed to France, where the money for study soon ran out. In Paris, he worked on the shopfloor of the Schneider and Renault

factories and in restaurants, living off milk and croissants. Mingling
with other poor immigrant workers, he began picking up the revolutionary ideas coursing through Europe at the time, and in 1925 became
a Communist, meeting Zhou Enlai, later Mao's number two, who was
also in Paris. After a visit to Moscow, Deng returned to China as a fully
fledged revolutionary, and was soon plunged into the underworld of
Shanghai politics and guerrilla revolt. After this blooding, he joined
Mao's fighting forces during the Long March. After Mao's victory he
proved himself a loyal and ruthless follower, first in Sichuan, his home
province, and after 1952 in Beijing as a member of the ruling clique.

Deng had supported the murderous purges of 'rightists' and the
folly of the Great Leap Forward. He was becoming known as Mao's
golden boy, and by 1955 was a member of the ruling politburo, and
the fourth most powerful man in China. So Deng was no liberal. But
these were desperate times. By the time the Cultural Revolution was
under way, Mao's policies had already made him the greatest killer in
human history. By the early 1960s the economic and human destruction caused by the Great Leap Forward was so massive that even Mao's
inner clique realized that things had to change. At a huge conference
in 1962 of seven thousand Communist Party delegates, the policies of
seizing food and other essentials for export, and spending everything
on factories and weaponry, were drastically scaled back – in direct con-
tradiction of everything Mao had stood for.

Peasants were allowed to start farming their own land again. The
famine began to recede. In the new liberal atmosphere Deng, one of
the prime movers of the policy change, quoted a peasant as saying that
it did not matter whether the cat was black or white; if it caught mice,
it was a good cat. This expression of economic pragmatism was something Mao had long held against him. Deng seemed to be saying that
the choice of capitalism or Marxism was less important than growth.
The handbrake turn in policy had, in truth, been forced on Mao by
those around him – Zhou Enlai, the Chinese president Liu Shaoqi, and
Deng himself. Maoism seemed on the retreat.

The Cultural Revolution, unleashed in 1966, was Mao's response.
Though it started over what seemed a tiny issue – a historical play
put on in Shanghai which Mao considered a satirical attack on himself – it was intended to upend Chinese society. Not for the first time,
Mao would use creative destruction to strengthen himself against his

enemies. Four extremist supporters, including his terrifying wife Jiang Qing, a former actress from Shanghai, led the assault on all forms of authority below that of Chairman Mao himself. The young – schoolchildren, students, factory workers – and anyone in a basic job or a clerical position, could be recruited as 'Red Guards'. Whipped up by violent and scabrously abusive posters, and self-organized into detachments, wearing their distinctive red armbands, they smashed classrooms and offices, terrorized teachers and bureaucrats, and in an orgy of gang violence often turned on one another.

Writers, artists, and sometimes people merely wearing spectacles, were seized, had their heads shaved and were denounced by screaming crowds. Old men and women had dunce's caps put on them, wooden placards hung round their necks, and then were beaten, sometimes to death. Many killed themselves. Children denounced their parents; students their teachers. In the first phase around half a million people are reckoned to have died, but some writers put the overall death-toll during the decade when the Cultural Revolution raged, from 1966 to 1976, at up to three million – and this from deliberate, often public, killing, rather than the effects of famine and failed policies. One study claims far more deaths, around twenty million.

The Gang of Four declared they would defeat the 'four Olds'. These were 'Old Thought, Old Culture, Old Customs, Old Habits'. In practice this meant that anything or anyone associated with Chinese tradition was to be destroyed – temples, religious practice of all kinds, traditional weddings and festivals, irreplaceable books, paintings, sculptures and ancient buildings were all attacked. Today's voracious enthusiasm for buying back ancient Chinese art in Western salerooms derives partly from the lack of Chinese cultural objects left after the Cultural Revolution. Not even the most extreme French revolutionaries, trying to wipe out the calendar and religion of the *ancien régime*, nor the Moscow Leninists, had attempted to draw such a deep line between past and present.

This was the storm that broke on the family of Deng Xiaoping and on President Liu Shaoqi. Mao – well out of it himself, on an estate far from Beijing – had called on the Red Guards to 'bombard the centre'. At a party for his seventy-third birthday, he toasted 'nationwide all-round civil war'. As a result, the leadership compound of Zhongnanhai was soon surrounded by a vast camp of rebels with loudhailers and protest banners. On 1 January 1967 people who had been working for the Communist leaders' telephone exchange, now calling themselves a 'combat team', broke in and denounced Liu and Deng. They were followed by clerical staff, now 'the Red Flag Regiment'. A vicious game of cat-and-mouse began, featuring public humiliation of the leaders who were forced into the 'aeroplane position', with their arms reaching above and behind their heads, and numerous 'self-criticism' meetings. Liu proved a tough nut: when he was beaten particularly badly his young children were brought in to watch the president and his wife suffer. Aged seventy, ill with diabetes and pneumonia, he endured three years of agony and humiliation, refusing to abase himself to Mao, before he finally died.

Deng, perhaps because of his closeness to Mao during the years of the Long March, was not treated quite as badly. Mao announced that he 'should not be finished off with one blow'. But after being arrested he was stripped of all his posts. In October 1969 he and his wife were exiled from Beijing – where unknown to them, their son Pufang was still lying untreated in a concrete cell – and sent south to Jianxi. There they lived simply, chopped wood for fuel, grew vegetables to eat and were taken to work at a tractor-repair plant. Deng was apparently still a good worker, popular with his colleagues, and spent much of his time walking to keep fit, and reading widely.

He and his wife were desperate to be reunited with Pufang, who finally rejoined them in the summer of 1971, still in a terrible state. Deng, who had not been very active as a father during his long years as soldier and leader, massaged his son daily to try to bring some life back into his legs, and turned him every two hours to avoid bed sores.

Back in Beijing, the Cultural Revolution was careering into chaos. Just as the revolutionary violence of France had ended in the guillotining of most of its leaders, and just as Russia's old Bolsheviks had ended up with bullets in the back of the head, so the Chinese leaders began to fall out. Lin Biao, who had been nominated as Mao's successor, plotted a coup and was discovered. He and his family died in a mysterious plane crash. Deng, who had been an enemy of Lin's, was allowed back to Beijing and slowly rehabilitated. He refused, however, to engage in very convincing self-criticism, pretending to be deaf at party meetings and larding his self-analysis with sarcasm.

Mao had decided the correct line to take about the Cultural Revolution (and about the Great Leap Forward) was that it had been '70 per cent positive, 30 per cent negative'. Deng, despite the urgings of the Gang of Four, begged to disagree. By this time Mao was very ill, with a rare disorder of the nerve cells. Zhou Enlai, much loved in China, died before him, in January 1976. Zhou, Deng's old comrade, had protected him during his disgrace and may have saved his life. But now the Gang of Four were again attacking Deng as their number one enemy. In death Zhou would protect him again – and accomplish his most remarkable feat. For after dying, Zhou killed off the Cultural Revolution and buried Maoism.

It happened like this. The Gang of Four did not want too much mourning for Zhou. He had been pliable, but he was a moderate, not one of them. The people of China seemed to feel very differently. There were already signs of rebellion against the Cultural Revolution, in Sichuan, which had had to be closed to foreign visitors, and in Shanghai. In Nanking memorial marches took place in Zhou Enlai's memory, and in Wuhu posters went up denouncing the Gang of Four as 'farting rumour-mongers' and calling Jiang Qing 'poisonous snake, devil woman!' But the most extraordinary event took place that year in Tiananmen Square in the heart of Beijing, the vast space carved out on Mao's orders from the old city, and scene of the massacre of 1989.

The month of April saw an old Chinese festival for the souls of the departed. With the advent of Communism this had been rebranded as a time to remember revolutionary martyrs. Zhou might be being officially 'forgotten', but the pupils of Cow Lane Primary School were not put off. They arrived in the square and laid a wreath for him. It was quickly removed, but pupils from a middle school followed suit. And then factory workers, office workers, other school and university students, even soldiers. These wreaths were not removed. Slogans appeared on many of them, denouncing the Gang of Four in the rudest terms. Of Jiang Qing one said:

> You must be mad
> To want to be an empress
> Here's a mirror to look at yourself
> And see what you really are![47]

The Gang were indeed looking on, in mounting horror. On the day of the festival itself, 5 April, it is reckoned that some two million people arrived in the square – the biggest protest since the Communists had come to power in 1949. Was this to be the beginning of a general uprising? The crowd and the placards were cleared away and the Gang continued to rant against Deng, even responding to an earthquake, which had killed a quarter of a million people, by calling on the stricken city, Tangshan – as if it were to blame for the event – to redeem itself by intensifying its attack on Deng Xiaoping's 'counter-revolutionary revisionist line'.[48]

But what the crowd in Tiananmen Square had demonstrated was that the orchestrated anarchy of the Cultural Revolution now sickened China; and when Mao died in September 1976 the Gang were soon arrested in what was, in effect, a coup by the moderates. Jiang Qing, who showed admirable defiance in court, eventually killed herself.

Deng was still in official disgrace, but by the following year had been rehabilitated again and was well on his way to real power. He outmanoeuvred Hua Guofeng, Mao's chosen successor, and encouraged criticism of the Cultural Revolution in the 'Beijing Spring' of 1976. Deng was never a liberal figure. The later Tiananmen Square protest and massacre showed how ruthless he could be when caught between students demanding civil rights and the forbiddingly leftist Maoists still in the party. But he opened up China to outside influence, tore up the extreme policies that had caused so much misery, and set his country in the direction of emulating the 'Asian Tiger' economies all around it.

His was a kind of bravery that perhaps we make too little of, the bravery of the gritted-teeth survivor, the man who bows his head and keeps going without ever quite grovelling, always keeping his eye on what he believes to be essential. His is the victory of the tortoise. Deng made modern China out of the ruins of Maoism, waiting through the dramas and disasters until his moment came – never giving in, never capitulating, but always avoiding that last, lethal confrontation. Today's China, Deng's China, remains in some ways a coldly unsentimental place. For all the superlatives that can be applied to its growth, its industrial might, its vast new cities and its rampant consumerism, it is still a nation where the poorest workers are very badly treated, where children can be knocked down by drivers who then reverse over them to ensure they don't have to pay for hospital treatment, and where the kindness of strangers is more rarely encountered than elsewhere.

Except that there is a coda to the story. Deng Pufang, the son who was thrown from a window and crippled, who nearly died and was later lovingly tended in exile by his father, survived. He became a passionate humanitarian and campaigner, establishing the China Welfare Fund for the Disabled. He was among the organizers of China's triumphantly successful 2008 Beijing Olympics. Now a revered, wheelchair-bound figure and a leader of a different kind, he too carries a message from the darkest days of the 1960s. The father led China to prosperity; in today's China of economic miracle and breakneck growth, the son's message of kindness and care will matter just as much.

Jihad

If American leaders had been told during the 1970s that they would win the Cold War only to find their next big problem overseas would be wars of religion, they would probably have laughed in nervous disbelief. Some might have guessed this was a reference to Israel. After the Nazi murder of the six million, US backing for a Jewish homeland state in Palestine had been decisive – but also provocative. The outrage of dispossessed Muslim Arabs after 1948, and their supporters in the Middle East, had failed to prevent a strong Israeli state develop, a kind of fortress-state with American backing. But this, plus the West's reliance on Middle Eastern oil, and therefore on undemocratic but pro-Western regimes, made America hated by many Muslims. During the long fight with the Soviets, this barely seemed to matter. The Islamic world was militarily and economically weak – and still is. Whenever Israel was attacked, it easily repulsed its foes. Terrorist hijackings were pinpricks. Weren't they?

Looking back, the first ominous sign had come as early as January 1979 in Iran, when a coup against the repressive, Western-backed Shah Muhammad Reza Pahlavi ushered in an Islamic revolution. The Americans were humiliated. It soon became clear that after so long concentrating on the Soviet threat, Western governments had proved spectacularly inept at dealing with resurgent Islamism. In the eight-year conflict between the two rivals that began in 1980 and resulted in around a million deaths, the US and her allies decided that, on balance,

they preferred the sordid dictatorship of Iraq's Saddam Hussein to
Iran's Ayatollah Khomeini. The doctrine of 'my enemy's enemy is my
friend' has rarely been so dramatically disproven. Two years after the
end of his war with Iran, and heavily in debt, Saddam invaded the
small oil-rich state of Kuwait. Americans, British troops and others
were forced to go to war to turf him out again – but, foolishly respect-
ing UN resolutions, did not carry on to his capital Baghdad and
remove him from power.

Yet this embarrassment was topped by the Western mistakes in
Afghanistan. As we have seen, the US responded to the Russian invasion of 1978–9 by backing extreme Islamist groups, including from
Saudi Arabia, in their decade-long guerrilla campaign against the Russian army. By doing so America bolstered and fomented wider Islamist
militancy, represented by the severely repressive Taliban in Afghanistan
and by the worldwide jihadists of al Qaeda. This terror organization
was formed in 1988 and led by Osama bin Laden, the son of a Saudi
construction tycoon with a burning hatred of Westerners. Bin Laden
had wanted the Saudi government to use his guerrillas against the
Iraqi invasion of Kuwait, and was furious that a Muslim country
should have preferred the help of infidel Americans. Bin Laden moved
to Sudan and then Afghanistan, making little secret of his hopes for a
general anti-American campaign.

It was as if Washington could not take quite seriously a threat
posed by religiously inspired enemies. This was particularly odd given
that US support for Israel was itself a religious cause, passionately
promoted not only by American Jews but very many evangelical
American Christians. The contempt for American materialism shown
by Muslim radicals was answered by Christian contempt for backward
Islam. Meanwhile, Israel's border wars made her enemies throughout
Iran, Iraq, Syria and Egypt. One of bin Laden's key rallying points for
Muslim extremists was the liberation of Palestine and the destruction
of the Jewish state of Israel, an ambition also of Iran's. In the Islamist
mind, the US and Israel were inextricably linked, while the West was
fundamentally hostile to Muslims. Part of the evidence for this had
come from the breakup of Yugoslavia into smaller states, including
predominantly Muslim Bosnia and Herzegovina, and insisting on their
ancient differences. This led to horrible scenes that reminded many
Americans, and Europeans too, of Nazi genocide.

The look on President George W. Bush's face when he was told of the al Qaeda attacks on the 'twin towers' of the New York World Trade Center on 11 September 2001 was a defining image: the world's last superpower hearing that history had not ended, after all. The terrorist attacks in New York and Washington, which killed nearly three thousand people there and in Virginia and Pennsylvania, had been meticulously planned and carried out. They provoked a surge of patriotic anger and defiance in the United States. A swift military campaign by the US and her allies in Afghanistan, where bin Laden and his organization were based, toppled the Taliban regime which had been harbouring them. This began a long war, still not over, in which the West and its local allies tried, and failed, to subdue Afghani resistance and create a democratic state. The corruption and unpopularity of the Kabul regime and the ability of Taliban fighters to withdraw across the border to Pakistan have made this an impossible war for the Americans and Europeans to win, even though bin Laden himself was finally hunted down inside Pakistan, and killed, in 2011.

Significant, too, was the decision by President Bush and allies led by Britain's Tony Blair to invade Iraq for failing to abide by UN resolutions on disarmament. Blair had faced large anti-war protests, while allies such as France protested hotly against invasion. It later became clear that Saddam Hussein did not have the weapons of mass destruction that Bush and Blair had said he did; and that he may have miscalculated in deciding that he would be safer if they thought he did have them. At all events, a huge bombardment of Baghdad began in March 2003, leading to a swift military victory against Saddam's army. Saddam, once Washington's least-bad friend, was eventually tracked down and hanged. Rarely has success on the battlefield, however, led to such a difficult aftermath. Widespread disorder, followed by a vicious civil war, kept US, British and other troops in Iraq in large numbers until 2011. Appalling abuse of prisoners, the inability of the Coalition to damp down sectarian violence, and a chaotic refugee crisis, undermined much of the moral authority Western forces had claimed at the start of the conflict. Estimates of Iraqi civilian deaths have ranged widely, from more than 600,000 to around 150,000.

The Afghan and Iraq wars had been battlefield successes but strategic failures. They reminded the world that not even the most apparently dominant superpower can do whatever it wants; and that invading somebody else's culture (as well as their land) to impose democracy is a risky idea. It had worked with West Germany and Japan after the Second World War, but that was in countries that had had some prior democratic experience and had been militarily devastated after global conflict. They were also more worried about the threat of Soviet hegemony than American. More generally, the Afghan and Iraq experiences challenged the idea that the whole world was converging on a single political-economic system, or could do.

Instead of the end of history, more was heard about culture wars, or clashes of 'civilization', including religion. In parts of the West with large Muslim populations, such as England, Holland and France, a new edge of suspicion was detectable. In parts of the Muslim world such as Iraq, Pakistan and Egypt (even after the overthrow of its dictator Mubarak) that had Christian populations, these minorities felt more threatened. With the US opening a large and secretive detention centre for terror suspects at Guantanamo Bay in Cuba, deploying torture and introducing fiercer security legislation, it became clear how badly the 'war on terror' had damaged open societies – and their highest ideals, too. Dilemmas about how to deal with dangerous Islamist critics returned the West to problems raised, but never solved, by the trial of Socrates in ancient Athens.

Splurge

Had the West at least continued to dominate economically, that would have been something. But by 2009, the People's Republic of China was contributing more than half of the world's economic growth. China today is doing nothing new. It is going through the shift from country to city, into basic manufacturing and thence to more sophisticated manufacturing, that happened to Britain and the eastern US in the first industrial revolution, and to Japan, Korea and Taiwan after the Second World War. The grim working conditions in the factories, the raucous enjoyment of material plenty by the winners in the cities, and a certain recklessness about pollution as the country goes for growth at all costs, have all been seen before. This is a familiar trading-up. Only three things are different. First, China is run by men who call themselves Communists. Second, China is very big. Third, all this is happening at warp speed.

By the year 2025, China is expected to have 219 cities of more than a million, compared with thirty-five in Europe.[49] Its growth has affected almost every part of the globe. China is gorging on minerals and land in Africa, Mongolia, Latin America and Australia. Its low-cost manufacturing has given the West a glut of cheap goods, helping destroy manufacturing businesses here. As a consequence, it has a vast chest of foreign exchange which, the writer Jonathan Fenby points out, 'could buy the whole of Italy, or all the sovereign debt of Portugal, Ireland, Greece and Spain as of 2011, plus Google, Apple, IBM and Microsoft plus all the real estate in Manhattan and Washington DC, plus the world's fifty most valuable sports franchises'.[50]

In 2010 China ran a $273 billion trade surplus with the US. There has never been a significant instance in history of an underlying economic power not mutating into political, and generally military, power. Countries can maintain a previous dominance with a swollen and technically advanced military for quite some time after their economic advantage has slipped. Britain did it in the early twentieth century. America is doing so now. But it comes at a high cost: energy and treasure that could have been used to recharge an economy are being spent on overseas commitments. The American economy is still four times larger than China's, but Chinese growth rates are shrinking the gap at an impressive pace. Recent studies suggest China may overtake the US by 2020, and thirty years later might have an economy twice the size of America's.[51]

So China's power will change the world hugely. Chinese leaders still claim sovereignty over Taiwan, as well as small islands in the South China Sea, and refuse to acknowledge protests about human rights abuses at home, or in Tibet. The growing size of the Chinese navy has produced a ripple of unease around the region, from Australia and the Philippines to Vietnam and India. China's Communist rulers, no longer presenting quite such a united front as they once did, face their biggest problems at home, dealing with the need for constant high growth to keep a more assertive and consumer-minded population content, with challenges to official censorship, with pollution threats, and with the difficulties of diversifying their economy. They proclaim their peaceful intentions. But economic power brings political power. It always has; and as the Chinese sovereign wealth funds probe deeper into Western corporate life, Americans and Europeans are uneasily aware of how little they know about where the Chinese government ends and Chinese business begins.

China is also a key part of the great capitalist imbalance that followed the Cold War. The West relaxed. It makes too little and spends too much, a process greatly aided by China's deliberate undervaluing of its currency. The fragility of Western capitalism today was first shown up by a banking crisis in 2008, in essence not much different from that of 1929. Then, as before, bankers had been using novel and little-understood ways of lending more money, including to house-buyers who were gambling on prices rising so they could pay off their debts. Complex algorithms used to measure risk meant that only a very small number of people, even in the relevant banks, understood what they were doing. This might have carried on for a long time in periods of ever-upward growth, but despite important new revenue-producing electronic products, the boom did not reflect underlying economic strength. America was buying cheap goods from China and living, in effect, on Chinese credit.

When in 2007 the US housing bubble burst, many banks found they were sitting on assets such as collateralized debt obligations (CDOs) worth nothing like their assumed value. Some big companies went bust, and a wave of failure swept the US and Europe, leading to costly bail-outs of banks by Britain, Ireland and the US. Only fast action by leading governments staved off a sharp and general recession, though the West was plunged into a period of low, or no, growth, and political leaders lost much authority.

So they should have done; for behind the crisis was a failure of political gumption. In the United States and in European countries, notably Britain, the tycoons of a deregulated financial world had intimidated everyone else. Old safeguards separating traditional banking from riskier forms of investment banking had gone. Regulation was 'light-touch'. Bankers were paid astronomical salaries and bonuses, without much comment. Politicians seemed content to take the taxes a rampant financial sector offered, spend them on things electorates wanted, and not ask too many questions. Meanwhile, Western economies were looking unbalanced. There was much less manufacturing.

Both governments and private individuals had learned to ramp up debt, to spend now and pay later. Economic policy had virtually vanished from political debate. So once the good times ended, there came a period of reckoning and anguish. In the US, among Republicans, this led to a revival of aggressively anti-state free-market rhetoric. In Europe, entire countries tottered on the edge of bankruptcy, and of falling out of the euro. There were riots in Athens, London and Madrid; there were protests on Wall Street. None of it felt like the victory of the West.

Thus Cold War triumph, which had had Washington cavorting with delight at the new 'unipolar' world (a concept not known to geometry, never mind politics), was followed by a stinging political hangover. The West's economic dominance was slipping away to China. The fashionable form of Wall Street capitalism was having a nervous breakdown. And far from there being no new enemies, the US and her allies were confronted around the world by adherents of an ancient religion who seemed to reject the entire project of modernity as it had developed in the twentieth century, but who could not be destroyed on the battlefield.

Was any of this surprising? Financial capitalism has always evolved through bubbles and crashes. Wherever wealthy companies or individuals are able to huddle together, improperly regulated, they will conspire against the public. Adam Smith told us that. The failures were to be located inside the same democratic-representative structures that were supposed to be the trump card of the West: politicians who spent too much money campaigning to really get tough on the bankers, and too much time worrying about geopolitics to attend to the health of their own economies. Their voters wanted cheap goods and easy credit, and it was comfortable to give them what they wanted. Finally, the philosophy of modern market capitalism, while greatly superior to that of state socialism, was narrow and unhistorical. It put consumerism on a pedestal while underestimating long-term human instincts such as spiritual questing, tribalism and fear. But they hadn't gone away.

The Thinking Machine[52]

On 11 May 1997 an event happened in New York that deserves to be
remembered far into the future. Someone who had a good claim to be
the world's sharpest man was defeated by a computer. Garry Kasparov
is held by many to be the greatest chess-player of all time, a grand-
master so good he is in a category all of his own. It would be lazy to
say that Kasparov played like a machine. He had an astonishing
memory and a great sense of strategy, but he was also courageous and
emotional. A reflective, pugnacious Jewish Armenian who had grown
up in the high-pressure world of Soviet chess, he became the world's
number one player aged just twenty-two and kept the title for most of
the following two decades until he retired in 2005.

Kasparov had taken on machines before. In Hamburg in 1985 he
played simultaneous matches against thirty-two chess programs, and
beat them all. Four years later at a match in New York, IBM challenged
him with their 'Deep Thought' computer. Kasparov had warned that
if he lost, it would be 'unpleasant' for the human race. He wanted 'to
be the man who saved human pride'. He won the game in two and a
half hours. Seven years on, the IBM team had a new machine, 'Deep
Blue'. In Philadelphia in 1996 Kasparov lost a game to it, but had come
back to win the match. Now came the much-hyped, much-touted
rematch. At a tower block in Manhattan, the Equitable Center, the
world's media were watching for what both sides suggested would be
an epic struggle between the human brain and the new power of computing. Posters around the city showed Kasparov staring intently into
the middle distance, with the caption: 'How do you make a computer
blink?' *Newsweek* magazine carried a cover shouting: 'The Brain's Last
Stand'.

Was all this mere commercial hyperbole? Not entirely. Ever
since chess spread from its origins in India in the 500s, first through
Persia and the Muslim world and then into Europe, it has been recognized as a special game that tests human memory and planning to
the maximum. It is often, and naturally, compared to mathematics;
the brains that are good at chess are also often good at maths. Yet
it also requires a kind of genius that cannot be reduced to rules. It is
a severe test of logic, but it has always had a mystique that neither

card games nor other board games, even chess's Chinese rival, Go, possess.

Feng-Hsiung Hsu, one of the scientists behind Deep Blue, says that since the 1940s computer theorists had dreamed of a machine that could play chess. One of the pioneers of Artificial Intelligence said in the 1950s: 'If one could devise a successful chess machine, one would seem to have penetrated to the core of human intellectual endeavor.'[53] Kasparov agreed: but he was determined to prove that a machine could only play like a machine, and that at some important level it was stupid, emanating no creative energy.

The first game seemed to confirm Kasparov's confidence – he won easily. The second game was the turning-point. For non-chess-players its importance can be hard to understand; but it *was* important. Kasparov decided to sacrifice a pawn to give himself a better position later. Computer chess programmes are designed to grab short-term advantage, and therefore Deep Blue ought to have told its non-human player to take Kasparov's pawn. He assumed it would. Computers play chess not by intuition but by giving a score or number to all possible moves, then scoring the possible counter-moves of its opponent, then scoring its own next possible moves, and so on.

Easy? The number of possible combinations of moves in a game of chess is greater than the number of atoms in the universe. Just to look a few stages ahead requires extraordinary computing power; human chess-players use their sense of patterns and psychology instead. But now Deep Blue behaved like a (very good) human player. After some time in what its creators called 'panic mode', the fridge-sized metal box refused to take Kasparov's pawn. It made another, long-term, tactical move instead. It was not playing like a machine.

Kasparov seemed to have been spooked by the computer's apparent intuition. Shortly afterwards, he conceded the game and stalked off, shaking his head. In fact, the computer had made a mistake in a later move and Kasparov could still have managed a draw rather than losing – something he was shocked by when told later. He has argued that, on this basis, he did not really lose. In the following games he drew three and lost the last, playing so badly that it was hardly considered a contest at all.

In the post-match press conference, Kasparov was asked whether the IBM team had cheated – whether there had been 'some kind of human intervention during this game'. He replied that it reminded him of the goal that the Argentinian footballer Maradona had scored against England in 1986, when he had knocked the ball into the net with his hand but had not been caught by the referee, and had claimed: 'It was the hand of God.' The IBM team of scientists, lined up beside him on the platform, were furious at the slur. From their point of view, many years of hard work were being denigrated by a bad loser. The controversies about this episode will never subside. Kasparov had repeatedly asked for printouts of what the computer was doing, and never got them, because the IBM team thought that would have given him an unfair advantage, including in any future match. After the match was over, Deep Blue was disassembled and put into storage; it has never been used since.

There is another point about the kind of contest that was going on here. Was it really man against machine? Kasparov suffered from exhaustion, worry, anger and suspicion, which the computer, using vastly more computational power than any Kasparov had encountered before, did not. So to that extent, it was. He had an ego. It had none. Yet Deep Blue was itself the creation of human brains, who described its chess struggle with fatherly concern. Feng-Hsiung Hsu has written that the contest 'was really between men in two different roles: man as a performer and man as a toolmaker . . . Deep Blue is not intelligent. It is only a finely crafted tool that exhibits intelligent behaviour in a limited domain.' Though Kasparov lost the match, he added with a feline twist, only he had real intelligence: 'Deep Blue would never have been able to come up with the imaginative accusations.'[54]

Later Kasparov himself came close to agreeing: Deep Blue was a great achievement, he said, but it was 'a *human* achievement by the members of the IBM team . . . Deep Blue was only intelligent the way your programmable alarm clock is intelligent. Not that losing to a $10 million alarm clock made me feel any better.'[55] Alongside the computer scientists, no fewer than six chess grandmasters had been working on the programmes: Kasparov was taking on not simply a corporation (and IBM did massively well from the publicity, gaining kudos it had been losing to the new kids of Silicon Valley), but also a lot of accumulated human knowledge and preparation.

All that said, the possibility of machines matching and outpacing human intelligence in many fields is clearly a real one, taking place all around us today. The interweaving of billions of people's imaginative lives through the Internet is the most obvious way technology has changed our lives recently; but Artificial Intelligence, or AI, may soon prove itself much more significant. Major advances in enabling machines to 'see' (one of the hardest problems) and respond to natural human language are occurring now. New insights into the way the chemical-biological human brain processes information, and how this can be mimicked by later generations of computer, are lively subjects in the universities and labs. So Kasparov's look of astonishment when Deep Blue made its crucial move ought to be remembered as a special moment in human history.

The dream of machines able to match human intelligence is an ancient one, but it only became a serious scientific subject in the 1950s, thanks to advances in computer science and, to a lesser extent, in the understanding of the brain. Alan Turing, the brilliant scientist and pioneer in computing who was critical to Britain's wartime organization at Bletchley Park (which broke secret German codes), became fascinated with it. He had worked before the war on computer theory; in 1936 he had proposed what became known as a 'Turing machine', which would read symbols on a long tape, to make mathematical calculations. At this time, punched cards and vacuum tubes were the best technology available, but war tends to accelerate invention and the 'Colossus' machines at Bletchley Park used to break Nazi codes are generally regarded as the world's first proper computers, in the sense of being programmable and digital, as well as electrical.

In 1950, Turing proposed his famous 'Turing test'. This posited that if a judge was having a conversation with a human being and a computer (the identities of each being disguised through a keyboard) and was not able to tell which was which, the computer had passed the test. This, he suggested, was the sensible, measurable answer to the question about whether machines could ever think, or achieve consciousness. He did not live to see the advances that would follow. Turing was gay, and in 1952 was convicted for 'gross indecency' with another man and obliged to accept chemical castration as part of his punishment, as well as losing his clearance to work on government projects. He died of cyanide poisoning, probably an act of suicide, in 1954.

Two years later a conference took place at Dartmouth College,

New Hampshire, where Marvin Minsky, one of the fathers of AI, and John McCarthy, the computer scientist who coined the term, led discussions on natural language, computer programming and mathematical logic. It was a breakthrough moment for the new discipline. Back then, the optimism of people like Minsky and McCarthy ran far ahead of what was possible. Urged on by fiction writers like Arthur C. Clarke, predictions were made in the late 1950s and 60s that artificial intelligence would have arrived by the 1970s or 80s. Turing himself had focused on chess as a useful test-system for AI because of its complex logic and patterning; in 1958 two key scientists at Carnegie Mellon University, Pittsburgh, had predicted that by 1968 a digital computer would be the world's chess champion.[56] All that had held them back was lack of computing power – the physical slowness of the machines available.

But they were working on it. After transistors replaced the old vacuum tubes, the problem was packing together and powering enough of them. Transistors are basic semiconductors switching electronic signals, and thus the essential components of digital computing. The first generation used copper wires and were relatively slow. Many people worked on the problem, but it was an employee of Texas Instruments called Jack Kilby who was generally credited with this advance. In 1958 he etched transistor elements onto slices of germanium, a carbon-based semi-metal, and connected them with fine gold wires to an oscillator and amplifier. Silicon would soon prove to work better, but the 'chip' had been born – in essence, pieces of cooked, sliced sand that are engraved using ultraviolet light and gas to turn them into electrical switches. In 1965 Gordon Moore, a co-founder of Intel Corporation, said mankind would now see a repeated annual doubling of the number of transistors that could be fitted onto a circuit, and though widely criticized for this explosive exponential prediction, he has been proved largely correct. By the late 1970s, entire microprocessors were being put on a single chip. For the IBM team this was essential to their chess-playing machine, which began with a circuit board of six thousand transistors.

What can we expect next? The enthusiasts rest heavily on the idea of acceleration, or exponential growth – the notion that technological progress multiplies by a constant figure, rather than simply adding a constant (as in linear growth). The difference is between a very slowly rising stable line and one that starts slowly and then suddenly erupts upwards to a near-vertical line of 'take-off'. A graph of human population increase during the timespan described in this book shows something like this. Moore's law on computing power does the same. More generally and unscientifically, much of the underlying shape of the story told here is of exponential growth – the millennia of hunter-gathering, followed by the relative speed of the farming revolution, then the ever-faster hurtle through towns, cities, empires and industrial technology.

The scientist and writer Ray Kurzweil has popularized the phrase 'the Singularity' – dignified, like God, with a capital letter – which he defines as the time when the pace of change is so rapid and profound that human life is transformed. The idea came from a mathematician and science-fiction writer called Vernor Vinge, who boldly plumped for the year 2030 when 'computer super-intelligence' would give birth to the Singularity, leading to a time when large computer networks might wake up as a superhuman intelligence. The language is close to religious, and may yet provoke a new religion or cult. Kurzweil proclaims 'a transforming event looming in the first half of the twenty-first century'. Like a black hole changing the patterns of matter and energy, 'this impending Singularity in our future is increasingly transforming every institution and aspect of human life, from sexuality to spirituality'.

Popular culture has been quick to seize on the darker possibilities of this phenomenon for human freedom. If Shakespeare wrote his history plays partly as a warning to Tudor audiences about the future, the Hollywood creators of *The Terminator*, *Blade Runner*, *Matrix* and many other films are warning their twenty-first-century audiences about the possible outcomes of exponential growth in computer intelligence. The merger of the human and the human-built would mean that people could go beyond their frail, biological bodies – in terms not just of how long they live but of how well they think. 'Our thinking,' Kurzweil writes, 'is extremely slow: the basic neural transactions are several million times slower than contemporary electronic circuits. That makes our physiological bandwidth extremely limited compared to the exponential growth of the overall human knowledge base . . . The Singularity will allow us to transcend these limitations of our biological bodies and brains.'[57]

There are plenty of sceptics, who argue that machines will continue to be useful tools for mankind, perhaps soon driving our cars and trains, cleaning our homes, as well as today's machines standing in for factory workers or researchers; but they will not achieve consciousness, or threaten our human control of the planet. Jack Schwartz, an American mathematician, forcibly argued that computers cannot, like brains, take 'relatively disorganized information' and use internally organized structures to generate actions and thinking in the real world. But he also warns that if AI really is happening, 'Since man's near-monopoly of all higher forms of intelligence has been one of the most basic facts of human existence throughout the past history of this planet, such developments would clearly create a new economics, a new sociology, and a new history.'[58]

Though scientists vigorously debate the meaning of 'consciousness' – is it anything more than very integrated and sophisticated neural networks dealing with information? – the proposed Singularity touches the depths of human self-understanding. Technologies are never neutral in their effects, nor predictable. Early telephones were proposed as devices for listening at home to concerts of classical music, while early enthusiasts for the Internet saw it as a worldwide academic library rather than as a place for social networking, politics or porn. Some scientists are starting to turn their attention to whether artificial or machine intelligence can be programmed to be wise, as well as to learn and self-replicate.

The key underlying theme of this history has been the mismatch between growth in mankind's technical ability to shape the world (in which AI follows on from the growing of fatter carrots, the invention of gunpowder and steam engines) and the lack of development in mankind's political ability to govern itself successfully. Good government generally leads to technical advance, since free speech, reliable patent law, the ability to make profits and the guarantee of personal security generally encourage inventors. But it does not necessarily work the other way: technical advance does not produce political virtue. Bad government, whether that means oppression, or a heedless enthusiasm for consumption today with no thought for later generations, or merely corruption, is more widespread; and the technological fruits of good government tend to fall into bad hands.

Garry Kasparov played, thought and lost that game in 1997 as a mercurial, flawed human being. Feng-Hsiung Hsu was right: Kasparov lost not to a machine but to tool-making humans, as human as him, as passionate as him. Later they were able to dismantle the computer they had created with the sole intention of beating him, and put it away. But like nuclear weapons, or the Internet, the biggest technological advances cannot be easily dismantled and set aside. They are handed over to the dangerous and uncertain arena of politics. So it is good to report that Kasparov, having retired from chess, then threw himself into the cause of political reform in his Russian homeland, where he has become a vocal, and apparently fearless, critic of President Putin's authoritarian government.

A Fair Field Full of Folk

In the late 1300s a clerk from rural England, William Langland, had a vision of the world's crowded humanity, or as he put it in his Christian poem *Piers Plowman*, 'a fair field full of folk'. He could never have envisioned just how full the field would get. In his day, there were perhaps twice as many people alive as there had been when Jesus Christ was born. Since 1950, the population has grown at up to a hundred times the speed it grew after the invention of agriculture, and ten thousand times as fast as it did before that. It is now about seven billion, or seven times what it was as the industrial revolution got going.

This is a great human achievement. Those who say there are simply too many of us, too many individual life experiences, have got to imagine wiping out many billions of other human beings (rarely themselves, or their families) – a genocidal vision outdoing any of the maniac rulers described in this book. The huge increase in population in the last century, and continuing in this, is a problem caused by success – by the success of vaccination and clean-water programmes, and of the 'green revolution' in agriculture. Without the latter, involving mechanization, new crop varieties, irrigation and fertilizers (after 1940), it has been estimated that mankind would have needed extra farmland the size of North America to feed itself. To put it another way, some two billion people are alive because of it. Yet most observers believe so many billions of humans are too many for the planet to sustain indefinitely; we need too much water, we consume too much carbon-based energy, and we take over too much land to feed ourselves, for the biosphere to cope.

By far the best-known problem is climate change, the effect of a sharp rise in the amount of carbon dioxide in the atmosphere. This is mainly caused by the burning of fossil fuels, and as a greenhouse gas, it stops the planet cooling itself as efficiently as it needs to, thereby raising temperatures. By how much, and with exactly what effect, are unknown. An increase in 'wild' or unpredictable weather patterns may be one of the consequences. Looking at possible projections, this is either a problem rather overstated today and which can be dealt with by greener ways of generating energy; or it is an imminent catastrophe that could make this the last human century. But the scientific consensus tilts towards the alarming end of the spectrum. Another English visionary, the scientist James Lovelock, who pioneered a way of thinking about the Earth as a living entity (it was always a metaphor), speaks for many who are terrified about the possible effects. Unlike Langland, Lovelock talks of the planet suffering 'a fever brought on by a plague of people'.[59]

Climate change is only the most discussed of the effects of the vast leap in human numbers. Though the planet is girdled by water, relatively little of it is fresh water and readily available for humans to use for growing food, for drinking and in industry. There are now severe water shortages in many parts of the world, particularly Asia and Africa, as more and more people suck from rivers that grow no larger – or, because of the construction of huge dams, have grown smaller.

The quality of soil is another looming problem. Soil is where the world's eighty-mile crust of rock meets the atmosphere – where geology meets biology. It is both very thin and utterly precious. The historian J.R. McNeill describes it beautifully: 'It consists of mineral particles, organic matter, gases, and a swarm of tiny living things. It is a thin skin, rarely more than hip deep, and usually much less. Soil takes centuries or millennia to form. Eventually it all ends up in the sea through erosion. In the interval between formation and erosion, it is basic to human survival.'[60] After the breakthroughs of Haber and others (mentioned earlier) across much of the world, the degradation of soils has reached a point where even the intensive use of fertilizer is not improving crop yields. In Africa, food production per head has actually fallen since 1960; in China, about a third of arable land has been abandoned because of erosion.

Then there are the problems of deforestation and the extinction of species. Humans have always destroyed forests, both because they wanted the wood (a problem for the ancient Greeks, the Nazca and the Japanese, as we have seen) and to expand their farmland. Northern Europe was once covered in trees. But the deforestation of the twentieth century was particularly dramatic, removing perhaps half of the remaining total; and was concentrated in tropical areas, notably the South American rainforests of the Amazon and Orinoco, and in West Africa and Indonesia. The importance of forests for maintaining the health of the atmosphere, and coping with the carbon problem, is now well understood; but these rainforests contain a very high proportion of endangered plant, insect and animal species, which may in turn harbour many useful secrets for human survival. If, as many scientists predict, around 30 per cent of current species become extinct over the next century, then that would be a huge planetary event, another mistake by the clever ape.

Two last problems must be added to this rather woeful litany. Overfishing and the acidification of the oceans are causing an environmental disaster that would be a worldwide scandal if we were able to see clearly below the waves; and it is a disaster affecting an important source of food. Add to this the atmospheric pollution in the megacities that increasingly dominate as human habitations (more than half of us now live in cities), which has caused a huge loss of life, albeit generally in the older and weaker. McNeill estimates a twentieth-century toll from air pollution of up to forty million people, equivalent to the combined casualties of both world wars, or about the same as the 1918–19 flu pandemic.

Like other problems, this was a 'failure of success', in this case caused by the arrival of cars, air travel and a lifestyle more materially rich; many of those most affected by pollution have migrated from villages and small towns to the cities, prepared to live in slums, favelas or shanty towns simply to have the chance to exploit the greater opportunities of urban life. Across the globe, the move from the countryside to cities (most dramatic in China and India) is the single biggest migration in human history.

★

In finishing this history I was greatly tempted to find another subject than 'the environment'. Warnings of global catastrophe hang over us everywhere, darkening our imaginations. Yet the fourfold increase in humanity during the past century is surely the biggest single piece of news. The fresh problems it throws up cannot be smuggled into other stories, or relegated. It is the final evidence for one of the major themes of this book, mankind's extraordinary technical intelligence. It is the higher end of the curve that began with fire and hand-axes, moved through the selection of grasses and the domestication of animals, advanced to steam engines and vaccination, and further.

But it also confronts us with the second obvious theme, which is the long lag in our advancing political and social intelligence. Only by doing better here can we solve the failures of success.

The news is not all bad, by any means. Let us return to Steven Pinker, who in *The Better Angels of Our Nature* pointed out that we are far less likely to die violently today than ever before. Overall, early societies had much higher rates of killing than later ones. Some criticized his arguments about the death-rates in hunter-gatherer societies (dealt with earlier in this book), but his statistical evidence from medieval times onward has been generally accepted. The decrease in killings has come about partly because, as states grew larger in size and smaller in number, there were fewer wars between them. Partly it reflects the increase in law and order, especially in cities. Partly, too, it reflects the humanitarian movements of modern times, from the Enlightenment campaigns against slavery and torture to the growing intolerance of domestic violence today. As we get to know more about each other's lives and live in more heavily managed, crowded societies, we seem to be becoming less violent, and kinder.

Or, to put it briefly, civilization works.

Anyone who has read at all carefully accounts of city life in earlier centuries, or noted the frequency of murders and assaults in so many of the books we have come to call 'classics of literature', will feel the force of this. Western-style democracy has not spread in the way post-1989 optimists predicted, but most of the world is more ordered, more curbed and regulated, than ever before. (Smokers, adventurers and others often say, too much so.) If we hold that the first job of government is to protect the lives of its citizens, then surely politics has advanced, rather impressively.

We can add to this some notable successes at the global scale, in disarmament, in bringing war criminals to justice; and in dealing with specific problems such as the outlawing of CFC gases (which thin the ozone layer. Through international agreements from the late 1970s to 1995 these were reduced by 80 per cent, and abolished in the major countries. The United Nations is a slow-moving, pompous and often infuriating organization, but its Universal Declaration of Human Rights still sets a basic standard around which most of the world rallies, at least in theory; and few would really like to see it gone. As individual countries compete for water resources, argue about deforestation, the ice caps and the oceans, and struggle to change to greener forms of energy, international agreements are becoming the essential politics of the new century. Some fail, as did the 2009 UN Copenhagen summit on climate change. Some supranational systems, such as the European Union, have failed to bind themselves into a democratic culture. But we are part of a much more interconnected and mutually aware human family than at any time since the migration from Africa.

We also have some, at least, of the skills we need to deal with the problems caused by our success. Global warming is a profound worry but it is not – probably – our doom. It can be checked. Lovelock is not alone in being a leading 'green' thinker who champions nuclear power as a vital way to reduce carbon emissions. It remains to be seen whether the current fashion for wind-farms is passing folly, but there is an increasing range of alternatives to coal and oil. Solar energy holds great promise. Nuclear fusion, though not yet a workable technology, also has great potential. Equally far ahead, though certainly thinkable, are the technologies known as 'geo-engineering', including putting reflecting aerosols or shades into space to cool the planet. These would require major new international agreements, since different countries would be differently affected. But history suggests that, with so much of our resources and brainpower concentrated on alternative forms of energy, breakthroughs will come. Any aliens looking down and betting on human ingenuity will not have lost much money so far.

There is another reason for moderate optimism: wherever societies have grown wealthier and female education has advanced, the birth rate has fallen. In agricultural societies, where human muscle was wealth but infant mortality was high – that is, through most of our social history – the shrewd thing to do was to have as many children as possible. But we are fast learners; and as infant mortality has fallen, contraception has become more available and women have had more opportunities, that 'instinct' has rapidly reversed. So the very fast spike in population, which probably has another forty years to go simply because of the youth of many people currently alive, ought to gently reverse.

Here, however, is the problem. Today's population is growing in the wrong places. When we read about a famine in Ethiopia, it is worth knowing that Ethiopia's population has grown from around five million people at the beginning of the twentieth century to some eighty million today, and is estimated to double by the middle of this century – by when the number of people in Africa is expected to have risen by another billion. The likelihood of human populations falling not benignly by choice, but through war, disease and famine remains high. The countries with the youngest populations – tens of millions of young men, many of them unemployed – are the countries at most danger of a violent future.

The truth is that to cope with the failures of success we will need to utilize everything we can muster: the scientific and technical fixes, the international agreements – *and* changes to our own behaviour and expectations. Martin Rees, Britain's Astronomer Royal, believes mankind will now find itself braving the rapids for two generations, a make-or-break hurtle during which we will have a fifty-fifty chance of survival. But he has also argued, in his 2010 Reith Lectures for the BBC, that talk of an optimum world population is senseless because

> we can't confidently conceive what people's lifestyles, diet, travel patterns and energy needs will be beyond 2050. The world couldn't sustain anywhere near its present population if everyone lived like present-day Americans . . . [but] more than ten billion people could live sustainably, with a high quality of life, if all adopted a vegetarian diet, travelling little but interacting via super-internet and virtual reality.

This may be unlikely and unappetizing, but today's parents in the West are the first generation to worry that their children will live more meagre, if less wasteful, lives than they have. A world population of around today's size, or bigger, is plausible; and a wide range of scientific fixes, such as those mentioned for tackling global warming, and genetically modified food, would help the planet cope. What is not plausible is the notion of a bigger population enjoying the new freedoms of car use, air travel and foods flown in from around the globe that many of us enjoy now.

But apart from the bleak precedent of the interwar years, the democracies have not had to cope with any period when material life got significantly poorer. Their party systems, electoral cycles and political rhetoric are so fixed on the offer of better times ahead that it is hard to imagine the alternative. There are other ways of living usefully and happily, as people have demonstrated throughout history. Greater concentration on family and community life, on spiritual life, on education and the arts – the ways we have lived through the lulls – are all part of the story. Unfortunately, our willingness to believe the promises of rabble-rousers and our greed, our capacity for anger and violence, are part of the story too. *Homo sapiens* is sometimes translated as 'clever man'. We are a clever ape, a very clever ape, albeit in a spot of bother. But a better translation is 'wise man'. We have a little way to go.

Notes

Introduction

1 David Gilmour, *The Pursuit of Italy* (Allen Lane 2011), p. 33.
2 Niall Fergusson, *Civilization* (Allen Lane 2010), p. 43.
3 J.R. McNeill and William H. McNeill, *The Human Web* (W.W. Norton 2003), p. 4.
4 McNeill and McNeill, op. cit., p. 7.

Part One: Out of the Heat, towards the Ice

1 Tim Flannery, *Here on Earth* (Text Publishing Company 2010), ch. 4.
2 Stephen Oppenheimer, *Out of Eden*, pp. 343–6.
3 Mark Pagel, *Wired for Culture: Origins of the Human Social Mind* (Allen Lane 2012), pp. 216–17.
4 Chris Stringer, *The Origin of Our Species* (Allen Lane 2011), p. 245.
5 Brian Fagan, *Cro-Magnon* (Bloomsbury Press 2010).
6 Stringer, op. cit., p. 242.
7 Cynthia Stokes Brown, *Big History* (W.W. Norton & Company 2007), p. 52.
8 Flannery, op. cit., quoting C.P. Groves, *Perspectives in Human Biology* (1999), 'The Advantages and Disadvantages of being Domesticated', and M. Henneberg, 'Decrease of Human Skull Size in the Holocene', *Human Biology* 60, pp. 395–405.
9 The theory of Steven Mithen, quoted in Brian Fagan, op. cit.
10 See, for example, Lawrence H. Keeley, *War before Civilization* (Oxford University Press 1990).
11 Steven A. LeBlanc with Katherine Register, *Constant Battles: Why We Fight* (St Martin's Griffin/Macmillan 2004).
12 See Jared Diamond, *Guns, Germs and Steel* (W.W. Norton 1997), ch. 5,

and Spencer Wells, *Pandora's Seed: The Unforeseen Cost of Civilization* (Allen Lane 2010).

13 Diamond, op. cit., p. 139.

14 Spencer Wells, op. cit., pp. 37–41

15 Ian Hodder, *Catalhoyuk: The Leopard's Tale* (Thames & Hudson 2006).

16 Rodney Castleden, *Stonehenge People* (Routledge 1987)

17 Castleden, op. cit.

18 Gwendolyn Leick, *Mesopotamia: The Invention of the City* (Penguin Books 2001), p. 163.

19 Leick, op. cit., p. 59.

20 Ian Morris, *Why the West Rules – For Now* (Profile Books 2010), p. 206.

21 J.A.G. Roberts, *A History of China*, 2nd edition (Palgrave Macmillan 2006), p. 3.

22 Wen Fong (ed.), *The Great Bronze Age of China* (Thames & Hudson 1980), p. 70.

23 David P. Silverman (ed.), *Ancient Egypt* (Duncan Baird 2003).

24 See Dr William Murnane in David Silverman, op. cit.

25 The best book on Deir el-Medina is Morris Bierbrier, *The Tomb-Builders of the Pharaohs* (American University in Cairo Press/British Museum 1982).

26 Cathy Gere, *Knossos and the Prophets of Modernism* (University of Chicago Press 2009), opening pages.

27 Evelyn Waugh, *Labels* (1930), quoted by Mary Beard in her review of Cathy Gere, op. cit., at www.martinfrost.ws

Part Two: The Case for War

1 My information here relies on many secondary sources, including most obviously Herodotus and Thucydides, but also Robin Lane Fox, *The Classical World* (Penguin 2005); Raphael Sealey, *A History of the Greek City States, 700–338 BC* (University of California Press 1976); and J.K. Davies, *Democracy and Classical Greece* (Fontana 1978), plus J.M. Roberts, *History of the World* (Penguin 2007) and William McNeill, *World History* (Oxford University Press 1998).

2 Caroline Alexander, *The War That Killed Achilles* (Faber 2009), has much influenced this thought.

3 Alexander, op. cit., p. 5.

4 See Michael Wood, *In Search of the Trojan War* (BBC Books 2005), p. 182.

5 Alexander, op. cit., p. 13.

6 Jonathan Sacks, *The Great Partnership: God, Science and the Search for Meaning* (Hodder & Stoughton 2011), ch. 4, 7.

7 See Mark S. Smith, *The Early History of God: Yahweh and the Other Deities in Ancient Israel* (HarperCollins 2002), ch. 1.

8 Karen Armstrong, *The Bible: The Biography* (Atlantic Books 2007), p. 24.

9 See Simon Sebag Montefiore, *Jerusalem* (Weidenfeld & Nicolson 2011), pp. 40–6.

10 See Ilya Gershevitch, *The Cambridge History of Iran*, vol. 2 (1985), ch. 7, pp. 392ff

11 All Herodotus quotations are taken from the Penguin edition, translated by Aubrey de Sélincourt in 1954.

12 Robin Lane Fox, *The Classical World* (Allen Lane 2005), p. 61.

13 J.K. Davies, *Democracy and Classical Greece* (Fontana 1978), p. 88.

14 Ramachandra Guha, *India after Gandhi* (Macmillan 2007), pp. 115–16.

15 The story is told in John Keay, *India Discovered* (HarperCollins 2001), ch. 1.

16 John Keay, *India: A History* (HarperCollins 2002), pp. 24ff.

17 Keay, *India*, op. cit., p. 35.

18 See Romila Thapar, *The Penguin History of Early India* (Penguin Press 2002), ch. 5, and Trevor Ling, *The Buddha* (Temple Smith 1973), pp. 66ff.

19 Keay, *India*, p. 64.

20 See Jacques Gernet, *A History of Chinese Civilisation* (Cambridge University Press 1992), pp. 41ff.

21 John Keay, *China: A History* (HarperPress 2008), p. 53.

22 Karen Armstrong, *The Great Transformation* (Atlantic Books 2006), p. 35.

23 Benjamin Schwartz, *The World of Thought in Ancient China* (Belknap Press 1985), p. 56.

24 Lionel M. Jensen, 'The Genesis of Kongzi in Ancient Narrative', in *On Sacred Grounds . . . the Formation of the Cult of Confucius*, ed. Thomas A. Wilson, Harvard East Asian Monographs 217 (2002).

25 Annping Chin, *Confucius: A Life of Thought and Politics* (Yale 2008).

26 Arthur Waley (tr.), *The Analects of Confucius* (Allen & Unwin 1938).

27 Armstrong,*The Great Transformation*, op. cit., p. 206.

28 Plato, *Phaedo*, in the 1892 Benjamin Jowett translation, usefully republished by Sphere Books in 1970.

29 I.F. Stone, *The Trial of Socrates* (Cape 1988), p. 66.
30 Stone, op. cit., p. 146.
31 William H. McNeill, *A World History* (Oxford University Press 1998), p. 148.
32 See Robin Lane Fox, *Alexander the Great* (2006).
33 Arrian, *Anabasis Alexandri* (Life of Alexander), Book VII, part 4.

Part Three: The Sword and the Word

1 *Rome and China: Comparative Perspectives*, ed. Walter Scheidel (Stanford/Oxford University Press 2009).
2 See S.A.M. Adshead, 'Dragon and Eagle', *Journal of South-East Asian History*, vol. 2, October 1961.
3 John Hill, *The Peoples of the West* (2004), translation from the *Weilüe* of Yu Huan: see Washington.edu/silkroad/texts.
4 Romila Thapar, *The Penguin History of Early India* (Penguin Books 2002), p. 321.
5 Ramachandra Guha, *India after Gandhi* (Macmillan 2007), pp. 378–9. I am also indebted to Toby and Saurabh Sinclair for their help in this passage.
6 Sima Qian, quoted in John Keay, *China: A History* (HarperPress 2008), p. 89, and in sundry other places.
7 See for example the competing views of Derk Bodde and new evidence quoted in John Man, *The Terracotta Army* (Bantam 2007), pp. 118–19; and John Keay, *China: A History*, pp. 75–6. They are differences of emphasis rather than fact.
8 Diarmaid MacCulloch, *A History of Christianity* (Allen Lane 2009), pp. 70–1.
9 Norman Cantor, *The Sacred Chain: A History of the Jews* (HarperCollins 1995), p. 61.
10 Shlomo Sand, *The Invention of the Jewish People* (Verso 2009), pp. 166–9.
11 Sand, op. cit. p. 151.
12 I am indebted to Mary Beard for putting me right on some of this, though she bears no responsibility for my anti-Roman-religion prejudices!
13 Robin Lane Fox, *The Classical World* (Allen Lane 2005), p. 306.
14 Mary Beard describes this, however, as 'sheer Greek fantasy'.

15 Nigel Bagnall, *The Punic Wars* (Pimlico 1990), ch. 1.

16 See Barry Cunliffe, *The Ancient Celts* (Oxford University Press 1997), and Terry Jones and Alan Ereira, *Barbarians* (BBC Books 2006).

17 Robin Lane Fox, *The Classical World*, op. cit., p. 379.

18 Ian Morris, *Why the West Rules – For Now* (Profile Books 2010), pp. 296–7.

19 Morris, op. cit., p. 306.

20 Karen Armstrong, *The First Christian: St Paul's Impact on Christianity* (Pan Books 1984), p. 45.

21 Acts 9: 3–5.

22 Charles Freeman, *A New History of Early Christianity* (Yale 2009), p. 210.

23 For more on this see Peter Watson, *The Great Divide* (Weidenfeld & Nicolson 2012).

24 My information is drawn from Helaine Silverman and Donald Proulx, *The Nasca* (Wiley-Blackwell 2002), and Michael Mosley, *The Incas and Their Ancestors: The Archaeology of Peru* (Thames & Hudson 1992).

25 Joe Nickell, *Unsolved Mysteries* (Kentucky University Press 2005).

26 See the work of David Beresford-Jones of the McDonald Institute for Archaeological Research, Cambridge University.

27 J. Armitage Robinson, *The Passion of St Perpetua* (Cambridge University Press 1891), and Freeman, op. cit., p. 205.

28 David Woods, 'On the Death of the Empress Fausta', *Greece & Rome*, vol. xlv, pp. 70–83.

29 Freeman, op. cit., p. 237, quoting Eusebius.

30 Tom Holland, *In the Shadow of the Sword* (Little, Brown 2012), pp. 40–1.

31 See Hugh Kennedy, *The Great Arab Conquests* (Weidenfeld & Nicolson 2007), p. 56.

Part Four: Beyond the Muddy Melting Pot

1 John Julius Norwich, *The Popes: A History* (Chatto & Windus 2011), ch. V.

2 John Keay, *China: A History*, p. 231.

3 Ian Morris, *Why the West Rules – For Now* (Profile Books 2010), p. 337.

4 Norman Davies, *Europe: A History* (Oxford University Press 1996), pp. 222ff.

5 Quoted by Jonathan Lyons, *The House of Wisdom* (Bloomsbury 2010), p. 15.

6 Lyons, op. cit., ch. 3.

7 Lyons, op. cit. My account of al-Khwarizmi and Averroës rests heavily on his book.

8 Jonathan Clements, *The Vikings* (Robinson 2005), p. 103.

9 Geoffrey Hosking, *Russia and the Russians* (Allen Lane 2001), p. 31.

10 Clements, op. cit., pp. 12–13.

11 Jonathan Shepard in Maureen Perrie (ed.), *The Cambridge History of Russia*, vol. 1, pp. 54–6.

12 Diarmaid MacCulloch, *A History of Christianity* (Allen Lane 2009), p. 507.

13 A.J.H. Goodwin, 'The Medieval Empire of Ghana', *The South African Archaeological Bulletin*, vol. 12, no. 47, pp. 108–12.

14 Nehemia Levtzion, *Ancient Ghana and Mali* (Holmes & Meier 1980), pp. 125–6.

15 See Felix Chami and Paul Msemwa, 'A New Look at Culture and Trade on the Azanian Coast', *Current Anthropology*, vol. 38, no. 4, pp. 673ff.

16 Al-Umari, quoted in *Corpus of Early Arabic Sources for West African History*, ed. and tr. J.F.P. Hopkins (Cambridge University Press 1981), pp. 266–8.

17 Ibn Battuta, quoted in Hopkins (ed.), *Corpus*, pp. 283ff.

18 J.D. Fage, *A History of West Africa* (Cambridge University Press 1969), p. 24.

19 See for instance, John Reader, *Africa: A Biography of the Continent* (Penguin 1997), who also provided my source for the difficulty of arousing camels.

20 Ibn Khaldun, quoted in Roland Oliver (ed.), *The Cambridge History of Africa*, vol. 3 (Cambridge University Press 1977), p. 379.

21 Oliver (ed.), *The Cambridge History of Africa*, vol. 3, p. 391.

22 Felipe Fernandez-Armesto, *Civilisations* (Pan Books 2000), p. 98.

23 Ivan Hrbek in Oliver (ed.), *The Cambridge History of Africa*, vol. 3, p. 90.

24 Charles Hercules Read, quoted in Neil MacGregor, *A History of the World in 100 Objects* (Allen Lane 2010), p. 501.

25 See John Man, *Genghis Khan: Life, Death, and Resurrection* (Bantam 2004), p. 34.

26 Man, op. cit., pp. 15–17.

27 John Keay, *China: A History*, p. 357.

28 See Orlando Figes, *Natasha's Dance* (Penguin 2002), ch. 6.

29 Morris, op. cit., p. 392.

30 Man, op. cit., p. 137.

31 Richard Humble, *Marco Polo* (Weidenfeld & Nicolson 1975), p. 209.

32 Frances Wood, *Did Marco Polo Go to China?* (Secker & Warburg 1995).

33 Bamber Gascoigne, *The Dynasties of China* (Robinson 2003), p. 128.

34 William J. Bernstein, *A Splendid Exchange* (Grove Press 2008), p. 75.

35 Wood, op. cit., p. 104.

36 Wood, op. cit., p. 43.

37 See John Julius Norwich, *A History of Venice* (Penguin Books 1983), pp. 215–16.

38 See Morris, op. cit., pp. 396–8.

39 See Daron Acemoglu and James A. Robinson, *Why Nations Fail: The Origins of Power, Prosperity and Poverty* (Profile Books 2012), pp. 100–10.

40 See John Julius Norwich, *Byzantium: The Decline and Fall* (Viking Books 1995), p. 171, and Judith Herrin, *Byzantium* (Penguin Books 2007), p. 250.

41 John Julius Norwich, *Byzantium: The Early Centuries* (Penguin Books 1990), p. 25.

42 John Julius Norwich, *Byzantium: Decline and Fall* (Viking 1995), p. 182; and the previous quotation is from Nicetas Choniates, in Norwich, *Decline and Fall*, p. 179.

43 Zhou Jiahua, 'Gunpowder and Firearms', in *Ancient China's Technology and Science* (Chinese Academy of Sciences, Foreign Language Press 2009), pp. 185–9.

44 See Judith Herrin, *Byzantium* (Allen Lane 2007), p. 142.

45 See Norwich, *Byzantium: The Apogee*, p. 323, and Norwich, *Byzantium: Decline and Fall*, p. 420.

46 Norwich, *Byzantium: Decline and Fall*, p. 429.

47 *The Notebooks of Leonardo da Vinci* (Oxford World Classics, 2008).

48 See David Gilmour, *The Pursuit of Italy* (Penguin 2011), ch. 3.

49 For a good explanation of this, and the workshop system, see Patricia Lee Rubin and Alison Wright, *Renaissance Florence: The Art of the 1470s* (National Gallery Publications 1999).

50 Giorgio Vasari, *Lives of the Artists* (Penguin 1965), p. 233.

51 See the essays by Martin Kemp and Jane Roberts in *Leonardo da Vinci* (South Bank Publications/Hayward Gallery 1989).

Part Five: The World Blows Open

1 James Wilson, *The Earth Shall Weep* (Grove Press 1998), p. 20, working from Russell Thornton's figures.

2 Wilson, op. cit., p. 21.

3 Hugh Thomas, *Rivers of Gold* (Weidenfeld & Nicolson 2003), p. 63 and notes on Toscanelli.

4 Thomas, op. cit., p. 124.

5 See Norman Cantor, *The Sacred Chain* (HarperCollins 1995), p. 190.

6 See the opening chapters of Daron Acemoglu and James A. Robinson, *Why Nations Fail* (Profile 2012), which follow this argument in greater detail.

7 Ian Morris, *Why the West Rules – For Now* (Profile Books 2010), pp. 460–3.

8 David Landes, *The Wealth and Poverty of Nations* (Harvard 1998), ch. 12.

9 Gerhard Benecke, *Society and Politics in Germany, 1500–1750* (Routledge & Kegan Paul 1974).

10 For Gutenberg, see Stephan Fussel, *Gutenberg and the Impact of Printing* (Ashgate 2005), tr. Douglas Martin; for Luther and printing, see Thomas Robisheaux, *Rural Society and the Search for Order in Early Modern Germany* (Duke University Press 1989).

11 Diarmaid MacCulloch, *Reformation* (Allen Lane 2003), p. 152.

12 Malcolm Pasley, *Germany: A Companion Guide to Social Studies* (Methuen 1972).

13 MacCulloch, *Reformation*, p. 160.

14 These figures come from Robert C. Davis, 'Counting Slaves on the Barbary Coast', *Past and Present*, vol. 172, August 2001, and from his *Christian Slaves, Muslim Masters* (Palgrave Macmillan 2003).

15 Quoted in Donald Ostrowski, 'The Growth of Muscovy', in Maureen Perrie (ed.), *The Cambridge History of Russia*, vol. 1 (2006), p. 227.

16 Yuri Semyonov, *The Conquest of Siberia*, tr. E.W. Dickes (George Routledge & Sons 1944), p. 11.

17 R.G. Skrynnikov, quoted in Alan Wood, *Russia's Frozen Frontier* (Bloomsbury Academic 2011), p. 28.

18 Neil Rhodes (ed.) and others, *King James VI and I: Selected Writings* (Ashgate 2003).

19 Antony Farrington (ed.), *The English Factory in Japan*, vol. 1 (British Library 1991), p. 296.

20 See R.H.P. Mason and J.G. Caiger, *A History of Japan* (Tuttle Publishing 1997), and John Whitney Hall (ed.), *The Cambridge History of Japan*, vol. 4 (1991).

21 Morris, op. cit., p. 451.

22 Quoted in Farrington, op. cit., p. 75.

23 Larry Neal, *The Rise of Financial Capitalism* (Cambridge University Press 1990), ch. 1.

24 For comparative prices, see Mike Dash, *Tulipomania* (Victor Gollancz 1999), pp. 123, 183. In this section I have relied heavily on his book and that of Anne Goldgar, *Tulipmania* (University of Chicago Press 2007). For a general view of the Dutch Republic at the time, no book has bettered Simon Schama's *The Embarrassment of Riches* (Knopf 1987).

25 Dash, op. cit., p. 134.

Part Six: Dreams of Freedom

1 James Reston Jr, *Galileo: A Life* (Cassell 1994), p. 69.

2 Reston, op. cit., p. 74.

3 J.L. Heilbron, *Galileo* (Oxford University Press 2010), p. 358.

4 Quoted in Lisa Jardine, *Going Dutch* (HarperPress 2008), pp. 56–7.

5 N.A.M. Rodger, *The Command of the Ocean* (Allen Lane 2004), p. 151.

6 See David Starkey, *Crown and Country* (HarperPress 2010), p. 394.

7 Heilbron, op. cit., p. 258.

8 John Keay, *India: A History*, p. 251.

9 Keay, op. cit., p. 322.

10 See Roger Pearson, *Voltaire Almighty* (Bloomsbury 2007), ch. 13.

11 Pearson, op. cit.

12 These stories can all be found in Roger Pearson, op. cit. – a splendid introduction to Voltaire's world as well as his life.

13 Christopher Clark, *Iron Kingdom: The Rise and Downfall of Prussia* (Penguin Books 2006), ch. 7; the description of Katte's execution comes from the same source.

14 Clark, op. cit., ch. 8.

15 John Ferling, *Independence: The Struggle to Set America Free* (Bloomsbury Press 2011), ch. 2.

16 Figures from the Economic History Association/ Jenny B. Wahl.

17 Ronald Takaki, *A Different Mirror* (Little, Brown 1993), p. 31.

18 Takaki, op. cit., p. 45.

19 Takaki, op. cit., p. 45.

20 See Thomas Keneally, *Australians: Origins to Eureka* (Allen & Unwin 2010), p. 127.

21 Jared Diamond, *Guns, Germs and Steel* (Vintage Books 2005), p. 155.

22 Watkin Tench, *A Complete Account of the Settlement at Port Jackson* (published on the Internet by Project Gutenberg).

23 Keneally, op. cit., p. 18.

24 *Captain Cook's Voyages*, ed. Glyndwr Williams (Folio Society 1997), p. 125.

25 See Richard Gott, *Britain's Empire: Resistance, Repression and Revolt* (Verso 2011), p. 84.

26 Richard Holmes, *The Age of Wonder* (HarperPress 2008), p. 37.

27 V. Gatrell, *The Hanging Tree* (Oxford University Press 1994).

28 Gott, op. cit., p. 85.

29 See Keith Smith, 'Bennelong among His People', *Aboriginal History*, 33, p. 10.

30 Tench, op. cit.

31 C.L.R. James, *The Black Jacobins* (Vintage Books 1989), ch. IV. Though this was written by the West Indian Marxist in 1938 and contains some now outdated material about the brilliance of Lenin and the coming African revolution, it remains the essential and superbly researched account of the Haiti revolt.

32 Marcus Rediker, *The Slave Ship* (John Murray 2007), p. 5.

33 Matthew White, *Atrocitology* (Canongate 2011), p. 161.

34 James, op. cit., p. 140.

35 James, op. cit., p. 197.

36 Arthur Allen, *Vaccine* (W.W. Norton 2007), pp. 36–49.

37 For these and other figures see Allan Chase, *Magic Shots* (W. Morrow, New York 1983), pp. 42–9.

38 Chase, op. cit.

Part Seven: Capitalism and Its Enemies

1 J.R. McNeill, *Something New Under the Sun: An Environmental History of the Twentieth-Century World* (W.W. Norton 2000), ch. 3.

2 McNeill, op. cit., ch. 5.

3 Joyce Appleby, *The Relentless Revolution* (W.W. Norton 2011), p. 60.

4 J. Steven Watson, *The Reign of George III* (Oxford University Press 1960), p. 33.

5 Appleby, op. cit., pp. 80–3, and Joel Mokyr, *The Enlightened Economy: Britain and the Industrial Revolution 1700–1850* (Yale University Press 2009), ch. 1.

6 Mokyr, op. cit., ch. 1.

7 Christopher Hill, *The Century of Revolution, 1602–1715* (Edinburgh University Press 1961), p. 32; also quoted in Appleby, p. 40.

8 Arthur Herman, *The Scottish Enlightenment* (Fourth Estate 2001), p. 142.

9 John Lord, *Capital and Steam Power* (London 1923), ch. IV.

10 See Herman, op. cit., p. 306.

11 By Lord, op. cit.

12 See Jenny Uglow's brilliant book about them, *The Lunar Men* (Faber and Faber 2002).

13 Mokyr, op. cit., ch. 7.

14 See Gregory L. Freeze, *Russia: A History* (Oxford University Press 1997), p. 201.

15 This story is brilliantly told in Orlando Figes, *Natasha's Dance* (Allen Lane 2002), pp. 96ff. It is an indispensable guide to the time, and unlike so many books of Russian history, very well written.

16 Rosamund Bartlett, *Tolstoy: A Russian Life* (Profile Books 2010), ch. 6.

17 Figes, op. cit., p. 238.

18 See A.N. Wilson, *Tolstoy* (Hamish Hamilton 1988), p. 334.

19 Carl Sandburg, *Abraham Lincoln: The War Years*, vol. IV (Harcourt, Brace, New York 1939), pp. 176–7.

20 Sandburg, op. cit., vol. III, p. 441.

21 Herbert Mitgang, *Abraham Lincoln: A Press Portrait* (Quadrangle 1971), pp. 476–8.

22 See James M. McPherson, *Drawn with the Sword: Reflections on the American Civil War* (Oxford University Press 1996), part II, ch. 5.

23 Esmond Wright, *An Empire for Liberty* (Blackwell 1995), pp. 472–3.

24 Wright, op. cit., p. 466.

25 David Reynolds, *America: Empire of Liberty* (Allen Lane 2009), ch. 6.

26 Quoted in McPherson, op. cit., ch. 1.

27 Eugene D. Genovese, *The Political Economy of Slavery* (New York 1965), quoted in McPherson, op. cit., ch. 1.

28 H.W. Brands, *American Colossus* (Random House 2010), pp. 145–6.

29 These details are taken from Mark Ravina, *The Last Samurai: The Life and Battles of Saigo Takamori* (John Wiley 2004), the first and last chapters.

30 A good account of Samurai history can be found in Charles J. Dunn, *Everyday Life in Traditional Japan* (Tuttle Publishing 1969), ch. 2.

31 Aizawa Yashushi, quoted by Andrew Gordon, *A Modern History of Japan* (Oxford University Press 2009), pp. 20–1.

32 Ravina, op. cit., ch. 1.

33 Ravina, op. cit., p. 196.

34 See Stephen Turnbull, *Samurai: The World of the Warrior* (Osprey Publishing 2003), ch. 9.

35 Adam Hochschild, *King Leopold's Ghost* (Macmillan 1999), p. 233. My account relies both on this book and on John Reader's *Africa: A Biography of the Continent* (Penguin Books 1998).

36 The accounts of Lin and the early stages of the First Opium War are taken from W. Travis Hanes III and Frank Sanello, *The Opium Wars* (Sourcebooks 2002); and Jack Beeching, *The Chinese Opium Wars* (Harvest/HBJ 1975).

37 See John Keay, *China: A History* (HarperPress 2009), pp. 446–9.

38 Barbara Tuchman, *The Zimmermann Telegram* (Viking Press 1958), p. 107.

39 Tuchman, op. cit., p. 108.

40 Tuchman, op. cit., pp. 183–7.

41 Tuchman, op. cit., p. 200.

42 See Ronald W. Clark, *Lenin: The Man behind the Mask* (Faber and Faber 1998), pp. 196–210.

Part Eight: 1918–2012: Our Times

1 Vasily Grossman, *Everything Flows* (Vintage Classics 2011), p. 220.

2 Steven Pinker, *The Better Angels of Our Nature* (Allen Lane 2011), p. 195.

3 See T. Hager, *The Alchemy of Air* (Harmony Books 2008), quoted by Andrew Charlton, *Man-Made World*, his essay on the aftermath of the Copenhagen climate change summit, 2010.

4 Charles Bracelen Flood, *Hitler: The Path to Power* (Hamish Hamilton 1989), p. 589.

5 Alan Bullock, *Hitler: A Study in Tyranny* (Hamlyn 1952/1973), ch. 3.

6 Adolf Hitler, *Mein Kampf*, tr. Ralph Manheim (Pimlico 1992), pp. 53–4.

7 Hitler, op. cit., p. 620.

8 Ian Kershaw, *Hitler* (1-vol. edition; Penguin 2009), p. 42.

9 Martin Kemp, *Christ to Coke* (Oxford University Press 2011), p. 74.

10 Kershaw, op. cit., pp. 127–9.

11 Bullock, op. cit., ch. 3.

12 Hitler, *Mein Kampf*, p. 128.

13 Hitler, op. cit., pp. 596–7.

14 Timothy Snyder, *Bloodlands: Europe between Hitler and Stalin* (The Bodley Head 2010), p. 19.

15 Kershaw, op. cit., p. 270.

16 Madeline Gray, *Margaret Sanger: A Biography of the Champion of Birth Control* (Richard Marek, New York 1979), p. 37.

17 See Armond Fields, *Katharine Dexter McCormick* (Praeger 2003), ch. 20.

18 *The Selected Papers of Margaret Sanger*, vol. 3, ed. Esther Katz (Illinois Press 2010), p. 265.

19 Bernard Absell, *The Pill* (Random House 1995), p. 121.

20 Robert Jutte, *Contraception: A History* (Polity 2008), p. 210.

21 Absell, op. cit., p. 169.

22 Max Hastings, *All Hell Let Loose* (HarperPress 2011), p. 143.

23 Kershaw, op. cit., p. 656.

24 Snyder, op. cit., p. 39.

25 Snyder, op. cit., p. 182.

26 Hastings, op. cit., p. 150.

27 Hastings, op. cit., p. xviii.

28 Kai Bird and Martin J. Sherwin, *American Prometheus: The Triumph and Tragedy of J. Robert Oppenheimer* (Alfred Knopf/Atlantic Books, 2009), pp. 287–9. Much of my account of Oppenheimer is taken from this excellent biography.

29 Bird and Sherwin, op. cit., pp. 296, 314.

30 Bird and Sherwin, op. cit., p. 314.

31 Bird and Sherwin, op. cit., p. 323.

32 Jad Adams, *Gandhi: Naked Ambition* (Quercus 2011), p. 2.

33 John Keay, *India: A History* (HarperPress 2000), p. 486.

34 Adams, op. cit., p. 136.

35 Adams, op. cit., pp. 220–1.

36 See Brian Lapping, *End of Empire* (Granada 1985), pp. 24ff.

37 See Andrew Roberts, *A History of the English-Speaking Peoples Since 1900* (Weidenfeld & Nicolson 2006), p. 12.

38 Keay, *India: A History*, pp. 450–1.

39 Keay, op. cit., pp. 475–6.

40 Adams, op. cit., p. 229.

41 Richard Dowden, *Africa: Altered States, Ordinary Miracles* (Portobello Books 2008), p. 84.

42 John Lewis Gaddis, *The Cold War* (Penguin 2011), p. 184.

43 See Jonathan Fenby, *The Penguin History of Modern China* (2009), p. 92.

44 See Jung Chang and Jon Halliday, *Mao: The Unknown Story* (Jonathan Cape 2005).

45 See Jung Chang and Halliday, op. cit., p. 342.

46 Harrison E. Salisbury, *The New Emperors: China in the Era of Mao and Deng* (Little, Brown 1992), pp. 3–4.

47 From Roderick MacFarquhar and Michael Schoenhals, *Mao's Last Revolution* (Harvard University Press 2006).

48 Richard Evans, *Deng Xiaoping and the Making of Modern China* (Hamish Hamilton 1993).

49 Jonathan Fenby, *Tiger Head, Snake Tails* (Simon & Schuster 2012), ch. 1.

50 Fenby, *Tiger Head, Snake Tails*, ch. 1.

51 Martin Jacques, *When China Rules the World*, 2nd edition (Penguin Books 2012), p. 518.

52 This section was suggested by, and bears a heavy debt to, one of the BBC researchers and assistant producers for *History of the World*, Chris O'Donnell.

53 Feng-Hsiung Hsu, *Behind Deep Blue* (Princeton University Press 2002), p. 4.

54 Feng-Hsiung Hsu, op. cit., pp. ix–x.

55 Garry Kasparov, *New York Review of Books*, 11 February 2010.

56 See Daniel Crevier, *AI: The Tumultuous Search for Artificial Intelligence* (Basic Books 1993).

57 Ray Kurzweil, *The Singularity Is Near* (Duckworth 2009), ch. 1.

58 Quoted in Nils J. Nilsson, *The Quest for Artificial Intelligence* (Stanford University Press 2010), Web version, p. 647.

59 James Lovelock, *The Revenge of Gaia* (Penguin Books 2006), p. 3.

60 J.R. McNeill, *Something New Under the Sun* (W.W. Norton 2000), ch. 2.

Bibliography

General Histories

Of the general histories I read, two by British historians stand out as exceptional: J.M. Roberts's huge and magisterial *History of the World*, published by Penguin – I used the 2007 version – and Richard Overy's *The Times Complete History of the World*, first published in 1978. Felipe Fernandez-Armesto's *Civilisations* (Pan Books 2000) is as vivid and inspiring as ever. Neil MacGregor's *A History of the World in 100 Objects* (Allen Lane 2010) hung over me all the way through the later stages of this project as a terrifying example of how to write with wit and erudition across a vast field. The American historian William Hardy McNeill, whose *World History* I used in the Oxford University Press 1998 edition, is a Titan of global history-telling. I hugely recommend *The Human Web* which he co-authored with J.R. McNeill (W.W. Norton 2003). The latter, John R. NcNeill, is also the author of a superb environmental history of twentieth-century humanity, *Something New Under the Sun*, in the Global Century Series in 2001. And for a very big-picture view, I thoroughly recommend Cynthia Stokes Brown's *Big History* (W.W. Norton & co, 2007).

Almost everybody, whether they agree with everything he says or not, has been influenced by the work of Jared Diamond, whose *Guns, Germs and Steel, Collapse: How Societies Choose to Fail or Succeed* and *The Third Chimpanzee* are all essential reading. Of the recent big-history proponents, Ian Morris's *Why the West Rules – For Now* (Profile 2010) is now essential too. I was also heavily influenced by Steven Pinker's *The Better Angels of Our Nature* (Allen Lane 2011) and Matthew White's *Atrocitology* (Canongate 2011). Other recommended general books include Daron Acemoglu and James A. Robinson, *Why Nations Fail* (Profile 2012), and Francis Fukuyama's *The Origins of Political Order* (Profile 2011).

Books Used and Cited

What follows is not a complete list of books read in whole or part for this volume – others can be found in the notes - but comprises those I found were particularly useful. In a project of this size it is probably inevitable that many seminal and mighty works have been ignored or missed: if any of their authors happen to be reviewers, then I am particularly apologetic.

Absell, Bernard, *The Pill* (Random House 1995)

Adams, Jad, *Gandhi: Naked Ambition* (Quercus 2010)

Adshead, S.A.M., 'Dragon and Eagle', in *Journal of South-East Asian History*, vol. 2, October 1961

Alexander, Caroline, *The War That Killed Achilles* (Viking 2009)

Allen, Arthur, *Vaccine* (W.W. Norton 2007)

Applebaum, Anne, *Gulag: A History* (Random House 2003)

Appleby, Joyce, *The Relentless Revolution: A History of Capitalism* (W.W. Norton 2011)

Armstrong, Karen, *The First Christian: St Paul's Impact on Christianity* (Pan Books 1984)

—— *The Great Transformation* (Atlantic Books 2006)

—— *The Bible: The Biography* (Atlantic Books 2007)

Axworthy, Michael, *Iran: Empire of the Mind* (Penguin 2008)

Bagnall, Nigel, *The Punic Wars* (Pimlico 1990)

Bainton, Roland H., *Here I Stand: A Life of Martin Luther* (Pierce & Smith 1950)

Bartlett, Rosamund, *Tolstoy: A Russian Life* (Profile 2010)

Beeching, Jack, *The Chinese Opium Wars* (Harvest 1975)

Beevor, Anthony, *Berlin: The Downfall 1945* (Viking 2002)

Benecke, Gerhard, *Society and Politics in Germany, 1500–1750* (Routledge & Kegan Paul 1974)

Bernstein, William J., *A Splendid Exchange* (Grove Press, New York 2008)

Bickers, Robert, *The Scramble for China* (Allen Lane 2011)

Bierbrier, Morris, *The Tomb-Builders of the Pharaohs* (The American University in Cairo Press 1992)

Bird, Kai and Martin J. Sherwin, *American Prometheus – the Triumph and Tragedy of J. Robert Oppenheimer* (Alfred Knopf/ Atlantic Books, paperback edition 2009)

Blackburn, Robin, *The American Crucible* (Verso 2011)

Brands, H.W., *American Colossus* (Random House 2010)

Buchan, James, *Adam Smith and the Pursuit of Perfect Liberty* (Profile 2006)

Bullock, Alan, *Hitler: A Study in Tyranny* (Hamlyn 1952)

Cantor, Norman, *The Sacred Chain: A History of the Jews* (HarperCollins 1995)

Cartledge, Paul, *The Spartans* (Macmillan 2009)

Chami, Felix and Paul Msemwa, 'A New Look at Culture and Trade on the Azanian Coast', *Current Anthropology*, vol. 38, no. 4

Chang, Jung and Jon Halliday, *Mao: The Unknown Story* (Jonathan Cape 2005)

Chase, Allan, *Magic Shots* (W. Morrow, New York 1983)

Chin, Annping, *Confucius: A Life of Thought and Politics* (Yale 2008)

Clark, Christopher, *Iron Kingdom: The Rise and Downfall of Prussia* (Penguin 2006)

Clark, Ronald W., *Lenin: The Man behind the Mask* (Faber and Faber 1998)

Clements, Jonathan, *The Vikings* (Robinson 2005)

Crevier, Daniel, *AI: The Tumultuous Search for Artificial Intelligence* (Basic Books 1993)

Cunliffe, Barry, *The Ancient Celts* (Oxford University Press 1997)

Dash, Mike, *Tulipomania* (Gollancz 1999)

Davies, J.K., *Democracy and Classical Greece* (Fontana 1978)

Davies, Norman, *Europe: A History* (Oxford University Press 1996)

Davis, Robert C., 'Counting Slaves on the Barbary Coast', *Past and Present*, vol. 172, August 2001

—— *Christian Slaves, Muslim Masters* (Palgrave Macmillan 2003)

Diamond, Jared, *The Third Chimpanzee* (Hutchinson 1991)

—— *Guns, Germs and Steel* (W.W. Norton 1997)

—— *Collapse: How Societies Choose to Fail or Survive* (Penguin 2005)

Dowden, Richard, *Africa: Altered States, Ordinary Miracles* (Portobello Books 2008)

Duggan, Christopher, *The Force of Destiny: A History of Italy since 1796* (Allen Lane 2007)

Dunn, Charles J., *Everyday Life in Traditional Japan* (Tuttle Publishing 1969)

Evans, Richard, *Deng Xiaoping and the Making of Modern China* (Hamish Hamilton 1993)

Fage, J.D., *A History of West Africa* (Cambridge University Press 1969)

Fara, Patricia, *Science: A Four-Thousand-Year History* (Oxford University Press 2009)

Farrington, Antony (ed.), *The English Factory in Japan* (British Library 1991)

Fenby, Jonathan, *The Penguin History of Modern China* (2009)

—— *Tiger Head, Snake Tails* (Simon and Schuster 2012)

Fergusson, Niall, *The Cash Nexus: Money and Power in the Modern World* (Allen Lane 2001)

—— *The War of the World* (Penguin 2006)

—— *The Ascent of Money* (Penguin 2008)

Ferling, John, *Independence: The Struggle to Set America Free* (Bloomsbury 2011)

Fields, Armond, *Katharine Dexter McCormick* (Praeger 2003)

Figes, Orlando, *A People's Tragedy* (Cape 1996)

—— *Natasha's Dance: A Cultural History of Russia* (Allen Lane 2002)

Flannery, Tim, *Here on Earth* (Text Publishing Company 2010)

Flood, Charles Bracelen, *Hitler: The Path to Power* (Hamish Hamilton 1989)

Fong, Wen (ed.), *The Great Bronze Age of China* (Thames & Hudson 1980)

Forbes, R.J. and E.J. Dijksterhuis, *A History of Science and Technology* (Penguin 1963)

Freeman, Charles, *A New History of Early Christianity* (Yale University Press 2009)

Freeze, Gregory L., *Russia: A History* (Oxford University Press 1997)

Fussel, Stephan, *Gutenberg and the Impact of Printing*, tr. Douglas Martin (Ashgate 2005)

Gaddis, John Lewis, *The Cold War* (Penguin 2011)

Gandhi, Mohandas, *The Story of My Experiments with Truth* (Penguin 2002)

Gascoigne, Bamber, *The Dynasties of China* (Robinson 2003)

Gatrell, Vic, *The Hanging Tree* (Oxford University Press 1994)

Gay, Peter, *The Enlightenment: An Interpretation: 2: The Science of Freedom* (Weidenfeld & Nicolson 1970)

Genovese, Eugene D., *The Political Economy of Slavery* (New York 1965)

Gere, Cathy, *Knossos and the Prophets of Modernism* (University of Chicago Press 2009)

Gernet, Jacques, *A History of Chinese Civilisation* (Cambridge University Press 1992)

Gershevitch, Ilya (ed.), *The Cambridge History of Iran*, vol. 2 (Cambridge University Press 1985)

Gilmour, David, *The Pursuit of Italy* (Penguin 2011)

Goldgar, Anne, *Tulipmania* (University of Chicago Press 2007)

Goodwin, A.J.H., 'The Medieval Empire of Ghana', *South African Archaeological Bulletin*, vol. 12, no. 47

Gordon, Andrew, *A Modern History of Japan* (Oxford University Press 2009)

Gott, Richard, *Britain's Empire: Resistance, Repression and Revolt* (Verso 2011)

Gray, Madeline, *Margaret Sanger: A Biography of the Champion of Birth Control* (Richard Marek 1979)

Grossman, Vasily, *Everything Flows* (Vintage Classics 2011)

Groves, C.P., 'The Advantages and Disadvantages of being Domesticated', in *Perspectives in Human Biology* (1999)

Guha, Ramachandra, *India after Gandhi* (Macmillan 2007)

Hager, Thomas, *The Alchemy of Air* (Harmony Books 2008)

Hall, John Whitney (ed.), *The Cambridge History of Japan*, vol. 4 (Cambridge University Press 1991)

Hanes III, W. Travis and Frank Sanello, *The Opium Wars* (Sourcebooks 2002)

Hastings, Max, *All Hell Let Loose: The World at War 1939–45* (HarperPress 2007)

Heilbron, J.L., *Galileo* (Oxford University Press 2010)

Henneberg, M., 'Decrease of Human Skull Size in the Holocene', *Human Biology* 60

Herman, Arthur, *The Scottish Enlightenment* (Fourth Estate 2001)

Herodotus, *The Histories* (Penguin 1954)

Herrin, Judith, *Byzantium* (Allen Lane 2007)

Hill, Christopher, *The Century of Revolution, 1602–1715* (Edinburgh University Press 1961)

Hill, John, *The Peoples of the West* (2004), translation from the *Weilüe* of Yu Huan: see Washington.edu/silkroad/texts

Hitler, Adolf, *Mein Kampf* (Hutchinson 1969)

Hochschild, Adam, *King Leopold's Ghost* (Macmillan 1999)

Hodder, Ian, *Catalhoyuk: The Leopard's Tale* (Thames & Hudson 2006)

Holland, Tom, *In the Shadow of the Sword* (Little, Brown 2012)

Holmes, Richard, *The Age of Wonder* (HarperPress 2008)

Hopkins, J.F.P. (ed. and tr.), *Corpus of Early Arabic Sources for West African History* (Cambridge University Press 1981)

Hosking, Geoffrey, *Russia and the Russians* (Allen Lane 2001)

Hsu, Feng-Hsiung, *Behind Deep Blue* (Princeton University Press 2002)

Hughes, Bettany, *Helen of Troy* (Cape 2005)

Humble, Richard, *Marco Polo* (Weidenfeld & Nicolson 1975)

Jacques, Martin, *When China Rules the World*, 2nd edition (Penguin 2012)

James, C.L.R., *The Black Jacobins* (Vintage Books 1989)

Jardine, Lisa, *Going Dutch* (HarperPress 2008)

Jensen, Lionel M., 'The Genesis of Kongzi in Ancient Narrative' in *On Sacred Grounds . . . the Formation of the Cult of Confucius*, ed. Thomas A. Wilson, Harvard East Asian Monographs 217, 2002

Jiahua, Zhou, 'Gunpowder and Firearms', in *Ancient China's Technology and Science* (Chinese Academy of Sciences, Foreign Language Press 2009)

Jones, Terry and Alan Ereira, *Barbarians* (BBC Books 2006)

Jutte, Robert, *Contraception: A History* (Polity 2008)

Katz, Esther (ed.), *The Selected Papers of Margaret Sanger* vol. 3 (Illinois Press 2010)

Keay, John, *India Discovered* (HarperCollins 2001)

—— *India: A History* (HarperCollins 2002)

—— *China: A History* (HarperPress 2008)

Keeley, Lawrence H., *War before Civilization* (Oxford University Press 1990)

Kemp, Martin, *Christ to Coke* (Oxford University Press 2011)

—— and Jane Roberts, *Leonardo da Vinci* (South Bank Publications/Hayward Gallery 1989)

Keneally, Thomas, *Australians: Origins to Eureka* (Allen & Unwin 2010)

Kennedy, Hugh, *The Great Arab Conquests* (Weidenfeld & Nicolson 2007)

Kershaw, Ian, *Hitler 1889–1936: Hubris* (Allen Lane 1998)

—— *Hitler 1936–1945: Nemesis* (Allen Lane 2000)

Kurzweil, Ray, *The Singularity Is Near* (Duckworth 2009)

Landes, David, *The Wealth and Poverty of Nations* (Harvard 1998)

Lane Fox, Robin, *The Classical World* (Allen Lane 2005)

Lapping, Brian, *End of Empire* (Granada 1985)

LeBlanc, Steven A. with Katherine Register, *Constant Battles: Why We Fight* (St Martin's Griffin/Macmillan 2004)

Leick, Gwendolyn, *Mesopotamia: The Invention of the City* (Penguin 2001)

Levtzion, Nehemia, *Ancient Ghana and Mali* (Holmes & Meier 1980)

Lewis-Smith, David and David Pearce, *Inside the Neolithic Mind* (Thames & Hudson 2005)

Ling, Trevor, *The Buddha* (Temple Smith 1973)

Lord, John, *Capital and Steam Power* (London 1923)

Lovelock, James, *The Revenge of Gaia* (Penguin 2006)

Lyons, Jonathan, *The House of Wisdom* (Bloomsbury 2010)

MacCulloch, Diarmaid, *Reformation* (Allen Lane 2003)

—— *A History of Christianity* (Allen Lane 2009)

MacFarquhar, Roderick and Michael Schoenhals, *Mao's Last Revolution* (Harvard University Press 2006)

McPherson, James M., *Drawn with the Sword: Reflections on the American Civil War* (Oxford University Press 1996)

Man, Charles C., *1493: How the Collision of Europe and the Americas Gave Rise to the Modern World* (Granta 2011)

Man, John, *Genghis Khan: Life, Death, and Resurrection* (Bantam 2004)

—— *The Terracotta Army* (Bantam 2007)

Mansel, Philip, *Constantinople* (John Murray 1995)

Mason, R.H.P. and J.G. Caiger, *A History of Japan* (Tuttle Publishing 1997)

Miles, Richard, *Ancient Worlds: The Search for the Origins of Western Civilisation* (HarperCollins 2010)

Mitgang, Herbert, *Abraham Lincoln: A Press Portrait* (Quadrangle 1971)

Mokyr, Joel, *The Enlightened Economy: Britain and the Industrial Revolution 1700–1850* (Yale University Press 2009)

Mosley, Michael, *The Incas and Their Ancestors: The Archaeology of Peru* (Thames & Hudson 1992)

Neal, Larry, *The Rise of Financial Capitalism* (Cambridge University Press 1990)

Nilsson, Nils J., *The Quest for Artificial Intelligence* (Stanford University Press 2010)

Norwich, John Julius, *A History of Venice* (Penguin 1983)

—— *Byzantium: The Early Centuries* (Viking 1988)

—— *Byzantium: The Apogee* (Viking 1991)

—— *Byzantium: Decline and Fall* (Viking 1995)

—— *The Popes: A History* (Chatto 2011)

Oliver, Roland (ed.), *The Cambridge History of Africa*, vol. 3 (Cambridge University Press 1977)

Oppenheimer, Stephen, *Out of Eden* (Constable 2003)

Ostrowski, Donald, 'The Growth of Muscovy', in Maureen Perrie (ed.), *The Cambridge History of Russia*, vol. 1 (Cambridge University Press 2006)

Pagel, Mark, *Wired for Culture: Origins of the Human Social Mind* (Allen Lane 2012)

Pasley, Malcolm, *Germany: A Companion Guide to Social Studies* (Methuen 1972)

Pearson, Roger, *Voltaire Almighty* (Bloomsbury 2007)

Perrie, Maureen (ed.), *The Cambridge History of Russia*, vol. 1 (Cambridge University Press 2006)

Powell, Barry P., *Writing: Theory and History of the Technology of Civilisation* (Wiley–Blackwell 2012)

Ravina, Mark, *The Last Samurai: The Life and Battles of Saigo Takamori* (John Wiley 2004)

Reader, John, *Africa: A Biography of the Continent* (Penguin 1997)

Rediker, Marcus, *The Slave Ship* (John Murray 2007)

Reston, James Jr, *Galileo: A Life* (Cassell 1994)

Reynolds, David, *America, Empire of Liberty* (Allen Lane 2009)

Rhodes, Neil (ed.), *King James VI and I: Selected Writings* (Ashgate 2003)

Roberts, Andrew, *A History of the English-Speaking Peoples Since 1900* (Weidenfeld & Nicolson 2006)

Roberts, J.A.G., *A History of China*, 2nd edition (Palgrave Macmillan 2006)

Robinson, J. Armitage, *The Passion of St Perpetua* (Cambridge University Press 1891)

Robisheaux, Thomas, *Rural Society and the Search for Order in Early Modern Germany* (Duke University Press 1989)

Rodger, N.A.M., *The Command of the Ocean* (Allen Lane 2004)

Rubin, Patricia Lee and Alison Wright, *Renaissance Florence: The Art of the 1470s* (National Gallery Publications 1999)

Sacks, Jonathan, *The Great Partnership: God, Science and the Search for Meaning* (Hodder & Stoughton 2011)

Sale, Kirkpatrick, *The Conquest of Paradise* (Hodder & Stoughton 1991)

Salisbury, Harrison E., *The New Emperors: China in the Era of Mao and Deng* (Little, Brown 1992)

Sand, Shlomo, *The Invention of the Jewish People* (Verso 2009)

Sandburg, Carl, *Abraham Lincoln: The War Years*, vol. IV (Harcourt, Brace, New York 1939)

Schama, Simon, *The Embarrassment of Riches* (Knopf 1987)

—— *Citizens* (Viking 1989)

Scheidel, Walter (ed.), *Rome and China: Comparative Perspectives* (Stanford/Oxford University Press 2009)

Schwartz, Benjamin, *The World of Thought in Ancient China* (Belknap Press 1985)

Sealey, Raphael, *A History of the Greek City States, 700–338 B.C.* (University of California Press 1976)

Sebag Montefiore, Simon, *Stalin: The Court of the Red Tsar* (Weidenfeld & Nicolson 2003)

—— *Jerusalem* (Weidenfeld & Nicolson 2011)

Semyonov, Yuri, *The Conquest of Siberia*, tr. E.W. Dickes (George Routledge & Sons 1944)

Silverman, David P. (ed.), *Ancient Egypt* (Duncan Baird 2003)

Silverman, Helaine and Donald Proulx, *The Nasca* (Wiley–Blackwell 2002)

Smith, Keith, 'Bennelong among His People', *Aboriginal History*, 33

Smith, Mark S., *The Early History of God: Yahweh and the Other Deities in Ancient Israel* (HarperCollins 2002)

Snyder, Timothy, *Bloodlands: Europe between Hitler and Stalin* (The Bodley Head 2010)

Stone, I.F., *The Trial of Socrates* (Cape 1988)

Stringer, Chris, *The Origin of Our Species* (Allen Lane 2011)

Takaki, Ronald, *A Different Mirror* (Little, Brown 1993)

Tench, Watkin, *A Complete Account of the Settlement at Port Jackson* (published on the Internet by Project Gutenberg)

Thapar, Romila, *The Penguin History of Early India* (Penguin 2002)

Thomas, Hugh, *Rivers of Gold* (Weidenfeld & Nicolson 2003)

Tuchman, Barbara, *The Zimmermann Telegram* (Viking Press 1958)

Turnbull, Stephen, *Samurai: The World of the Warrior* (Osprey Publishing 2003)

Uglow, Jenny, *The Lunar Men* (Faber and Faber 2002)

Vasari, Giorgio, *Lives of the Artists* (Penguin 1965)

Waley, Arthur (tr.), *The Analects of Confucius* (Allen & Unwin 1938)

Watson, Peter, *The Great Divide* (Weidenfeld & Nicolson 2012)

Watson, Steven, *The Reign of George III* (Oxford University Press 1960)

Wells, Spencer, *Pandora's Seed: The Unforeseen Cost of Civilization* (Allen Lane 2010)

Williams, Glyndwr (ed.), *Captain Cook's Voyages* (The Folio Society 1997)

Wilson, A.N., *Tolstoy* (Hamish Hamilton 1988)

Wilson, James, *The Earth Shall Weep* (Grove Press, New York 1998)

Wood, Alan, *Russia's Frozen Frontier* (Bloomsbury Academic 2011)

Wood, Frances, *Did Marco Polo go to China?* (Secker & Warburg 1995)

Wood, Michael, *In Search of the Trojan War* (BBC Books 2005)

Woods, David, 'On the Death of the Empress Fausta', *Greece & Rome*, vol. xlv

Wright, Esmond, *An Empire for Liberty* (Blackwell 1995)

Index

Abbasids 195–6, 226
Abd al-Rahman I 198
Abd al-Rahman III 199
aboriginal Australians 10, 13, 77, 354–6
    encountering of by Cook and Banks 356,
        357–8
    and European colonization 355, 360–2
    kidnapping of Bennelong 355–6, 360
absolutism 311, 317–21, 334, 335, 337, 346
Abu Bakr 180
Achilles 54
Actium, battle of (31 BC) 153
Acts of the Apostles 160
Adams, John 422
Adams, William 294
Afghanistan
    invasion of by Soviet Union (1978–9) 528,
        546
Afghanistan war 547–8
Africa 20, 208–17, 503, 524–5
    agriculture 209, 210
    annexation of Congo by Leopold II 442–4,
        445
    art 216
    decolonization 524–5
    desertification of North 24
    development of society 209
    domestication of camels 210–11
    European imperialism in 444–5
    evolvement of hominids in 8, 9
    food production 560–1
    Mali empire 208, 211–14, 215
    migration of early humans from 9–10, 77
    and Muslims 210
    penetration of by European explorers 441–2
    population growth 564
    pre-colonial societies 208–16
    religion 214
    salt trade 211
    'scramble for' 438, 444–6
    slave trade/slavery 215, 442
    succession issue 214
    see also individual countries
agriculture 17–24, 28, 251
    Africa 209, 210
    Britain 389–90
    changes brought about by 23–4
    China (ancient) 40, 88
    and climate change 20, 21–2
    development of new skills 23
    and emergence of early villages 22
    and enclosures 389–90
    and Fertile Crescent 21
    and fertilizers 456–7, 470–1
    health and lifespan of early farmers 18–19
    India (ancient) 80
    Minoan 48
    Native American 253–4
    origins 20–2
    and population growth 18, 19, 22–3, 559
    Russia 411
    slash-and-burn 28
Ahiram, King 59
air pollution 387, 561
Akbar the Great 333–4, 335
Akkadians 34, 36
Aksum 209
al Qaeda 546, 547
al-Andalus 192, 195, 198–200, 202, 247, 260
Ala-ud-din 331
Alans 190
Albania 484
Alberti, Leon Battista 315
Alcibiades 97–8
Alexander II, Czar 408–9, 412, 413
Alexander III, Czar 414
Alexander III, the Great, King of Macedon 101–8,
        116, 126, 143, 176
    adopting of Persian culture 106
    conquests 104–5, 107
    death 107, 142
    education 101, 104

Alexander III, the Great, King of Macedon (*cont.*)
  killing of Cleitus 105
Alexandria (Egypt) 143, 145–7
Alexandria Library 145–6
algebra 197
Algeria
  seizure of by French (1830) 444
Allende, Salvador 528
Almohads 200, 260
Almoravids 211, 260
alphabet
  Greek 61
  Phoenician 60, 61
Ambedkar, B.R. 119
Amenhotep III 44
American Civil War (1861–5) 414, 415–26, 430
  and blacks 426–8
  death toll 419
  economic and cultural factors 423–4
  impact of 418–19, 425–9
  reasons for fighting by Confederate soldiers 425
  Reconstruction following 427
  and slavery 419–20, 421–2
  surrender of Lee's army 416, 425
American colonies 310–11, 324, 348–51, 359, 437–8
American War of Independence (1776–81) 349–51, 352
Americas 100, 251–2
  behind in development compared with Eurasia 164–5
  and Columbus 255–8
  European invasions and colonization 251–2, 253–5, 258–9
  killing of natives by European diseases 253, 254, 258, 267
  native societies 253–4
  and the Nazca 165–9
  Spanish conquest of Incas and Aztecs 262–6, 267–8
  tectonic activity and natural disasters 165
Amin, Idi 524
Amrapali 82, 85
Amritsar Massacre (1919) 517, 518
Analects 90, 92, 94
Anasazi people 17
Anatolia 20, 31, 58
anatomy 146
ancestor worship 26, 31, 40, 132
Andes 20
Andropov, Yuri 529

Anemospilia temple 49
Angel, J. Lawrence 19
Angkor Wat 194
Angola 524
animals
  early domestication of 20, 21, 23, 28
  reverence of in hunter-gatherer societies 13–14
animism 214, 215
Anne, Queen 324, 326, 329–30
anti-Semitism 476
Antigonus the One-eyed 142–3
Antiochus IV, King 126–7
Antiochus XIII, King 128
Antoninus Pius, Emperor 155
Antony, Mark 148, 149, 151–3
Apsu (god) 33
Aquinas, Thomas 201
Arabia 63, 175–7
Arabs
  conquests made by 178–9
  invasion of Spain 194
  sacking of Rome (846) 188
  and Second World War 499
  trade 251
Aramaic 60
Arapaho 353, 426
Archimedes 146
Arian Heresy 174
Arians/Arianism 236
Aristobulus 128
Aristotle 100, 101, 104, 200, 312, 315
  Politics 135
arms race 523
Armstrong, Karen 93
Arrian 106
Arsenale (Venice) 314
art
  ancient Egypt 42–3
  Byzantium 234
  cave 14, 17
  and first Mesopotamian cities 35–6
  Minoan 46–7, 49
  Nazca 168
  pre-Colonial Africa 216
Artificial Intelligence 552–8
Aryans 77, 79–80
Ashoka 115–19, 143, 333
Assyrians 60, 64–5
astrolabes 199, 256
astrology, and Muslims 196
Astyages, King 68

Atahualpa, Emperor 262–5
Athens/Athenians 70, 71, 73–7, 96–9
    democracy 74, 98
    drama 76–7
    and Four Hundred 98
    Parthenon 76
    rule of the Thirty Tyrants 98–9
    slavery 74–5
    Syracuse disaster and defeat of by Sparta
        97–8
    war with Persians 75–6, 96
Atlantis 47
atom bomb 506–9, 510
Augsburg, Peace of (1555) 279
Augustus, Emperor 151, 152, 153, 154
Aurangzeb, Emperor 335–6
Austerlitz, battle of 371
Australia 254–62
    Cook's voyage to 357, 358
    European colonization 354, 355–6
    transportation of British convicts to and first
        settlements 358–60
Australian Aboriginals *see* aboriginal Australians
Austria 343
    anti-Semitism 476
    and Habsburg rulers 318
Austro-Hungarian Empire 319, 372
Averroës (Ibn Rushd) 200, 201
Avicenna 200, 201
'axial age' 84
Aztecs 88–9, 164, 265, 266

Baal (storm-god) 63
Babur (Zahir-ud-Din Muhammad) 220, 332,
    334
Babylon/Babylonians 34, 35, 36, 65, 105
Baghdad 195, 199, 226
Bahamas 258
Baldwin, Stanley 486
Ban Chao, General 112
Banda, Hastings 524
Bank of England 392
banking crisis (2008) 550
Banks, Sir Joseph 356, 357–8, 362
Baron, Salo 129
Basil II, Emperor 207
Battle of Britain 502, 519
Bavaria
    establishment of 'Red Republic' 477
Bay of Pigs 526
Beard, Mary 131
Bedouin 177, 178

Beethoven, Ludwig van 370
Beijing 222, 228
Belgium 440–6, 504
    annexation of Congo by Leopold II 442–4,
        445
Bellarmine, Cardinal Robert 315, 316
Belley, Jean-Baptiste 376
Benedict, St 190
Benin empire 216
Bennelong, Woolawarre 354, 355–6, 360–1
Benz, Karl Friedrich 455
Berbers 194, 198, 211
Berlin Blockade 522
Berlin Wall 526
    fall of 530
Bernier, François 335
Bible
    Luther's translation 277–8
    printing of by Gutenberg 275–6
Big Bang 3
Bimbisara, King 82
bin Laden, Osama 546, 547
Bin Tughluq, Muhammad, sultan of Delhi 331
Birmingham 398
birth control 487–9, 490–4, 564
    invention of the Pill 492–3
birth rate 563–4
Bismarck, Chancellor 457–8
Black Death 141, 230–1, 409
Black, Joseph 395, 397
blacks
    impact of American Civil War on 426–8
    see also slave trade/slavery
Blair, Tony 547
Bletchley Park 555
Bodhgaya 86
Bohr, Niels 507, 509
Bolivar, Simón 267
Bolsheviks 463, 464–5, 500
Bonnie Prince Charlie 394, 430
Booth, John Wilkes 417–18
Boston Tea Party (1773) 346–8, 351
Boswell, James 345
Botany Bay 359
Boudicca, Queen 141
Boulton, Matthew 398–400
Bourbons 318, 319–20, 362
Boxer Rising (1898–1901) 532, 533
Boyle, Robert 329
Brahmi script 118
brain, human 8, 12
Brezhnev, Leonid 527

Britain 321–4, 505
  agriculture 389–90
  American colonies 348–9, 350, 352, 437–8
  and American War of Independence (1776–81)
    349–51, 352
  colonization of Africa 444–5
  comparison with Japan 292–3
  and Corn Laws 402–3
  and Cromwell's republic 323–4
  decline in power 502
  defeat of by Saint-Domingue 377
  and First World War 461
  free press 392
  and Great Reform Act (1832) 403
  and imperialism 437, 439
  in India 337, 438, 514–18
  and industrial revolution 388–404
  invasion of by William of Orange (1688) 325–7
  and Napoleonic Wars 371
  as naval and trading power 293–4, 297, 300,
    351, 453
  Neolithic 27–32
  Norman conquest 203
  opium trade 448, 451–2, 453
  and Opium Wars 449, 452–4
  Parliament 322–3, 324, 328, 391, 392, 400
  politics and industrialization 401–3
  population 389, 391, 402
  railways 406
  and Second World War 496–7, 499, 502
  and Seven Years War 348
  slave trade 374
  tea addiction 448, 452
  and tobacco 291
  wool trade 192
  see also English Civil War
bronze, invention of 34
Bronze Age 31, 55, 56
Brown, John 422–3
Bruno, Giordano 313, 315
Buddha (Siddhartha Gautama) 82–5, 86, 93
Buddhism 85–6, 114, 118, 119
Bulgaria 484, 530
Bulgars 202
bull leaping, Minoan 48–9
Bullock, Alan 480
bureaucracy
  Chinese 156, 457
  German 457–8
burials
  ancient China 88, 125
  Neolithic 26

Burke, Edmund 515
Burton, Richard 441
Bush, George W. 547
Byblos 60
Byzantium 174, 193, 207, 233–41
  art 234
  collapse and fall of Constantinople 113,
    232–3, 240–1
  comparison with China 239–40
  court procedures and rituals 239
  extent of empire 235
  founding 234, 235
  Fourth Crusade against 236–8
  religion and spirituality 235–6
  use of 'Greek fire' 240
  and Vikings 204, 206, 207, 235

Caesar, Julius 139–42, 148–51, 156
  assassination (44 bc) 151
  and calendar 150
  and Cleopatra 149–50
  conquest of Rome 142
  defeat of Pompey 148
  destruction of Gauls 140, 141–2
  growth in cult of 150
  military campaigns 139–40
  political career 139
Caesarion 150, 153
Cairo 220
Cajamarca (Peru) 262, 265
calendar
  Celtic 140
  and French Revolutionaries 366
  Mayan 164
  naming of days of the week 35
  Roman 139, 140, 150
Caligula, Emperor 155
Calvin, John 279
Cambodia 194
camels, domestication of 210–11
Cameron, Verney Lovett 441
Canaan/Canaanites 60, 63, 65
canals
  British 399
  Chinese 188
Canary Islands
  Spanish colonization 256
Cannae, battle of (216 bc) 135
cannibalism
  and Neanderthals 15–16
Cantor, Norman 129
Cape Verde islands 256

capitalism 306, 309, 388, 404, 406, 454, 456, 493, 551
car, development of 455–6
carbon dioxide emissions 560
Caribbean 255, 258, 268, 348, 374
Carnegie, Andrew 426
Carthage 60, 113, 134–7
Casement, Roger 445
Castleden, Rodney 28, 29, 31–2
Castro, Fidel 526
Catalhoyuk 25–7, 29, 32
Catherine the Great 290, 317
Catholics/Catholicism 283, 294, 312, 315, 327, 359, 493
    Counter-Reformation 280
    and Spanish Inquisition 259, 260–1
cave art 14, 17
Ceaușescu, Nicolae 530
Celts 100, 140, 165
Central Intelligence Agency *see* CIA
CFC gasses 563
Chandragupta 116–17
Chang, Jung 537, 538
Chaplin, Charlie 511
chariots 34
    West African 209
Charlemagne 187–8
Charles I, King 322–3
Charles II, King 324
Charles II of Spain 319
Charles V, Emperor 114, 262, 268, 277, 279, 282, 299
Charles X, King of France 405
Chartists 403
Châtelet, Émile du 340
Chernenko, Konstantin 529
chess 552–3
Cheyenne 353, 426
Chiang Kai-shek 532, 535, 536
children
    employment of in factories 401
Chile 528
Ch'in dynasty 121–2, 123–5, 131, 156
China, ancient 20, 22, 36–41, 87–94, 111–15, 188
    agriculture 40, 88
    architecture 88
    attempts to control flooding by first dynasty 37–8
    and Buddhism 86, 114, 122
    burials 88, 125
    canal system 188
    cities 40, 88
    civil war 156
    and Confucius (Kongzi) 82, 86–8, 89, 90–1, 92–3, 123
    and Da Yu 36–8, 39, 40, 41
    dynasties 39
    Han 111–12, 115, 120, 156–9
    human development 38
    internal conflict and semi-anarchy after break-up of Han state 158
    and Legalism 123
    links with Roman Empire 112–13
    mythical emperors 39
    religion and religious rites 41, 122–3
    rituals 91–3
    Shang dynasty 39, 88–9
    and smallpox 381
    Xia dynasty 37, 39–40
    and Zheng 120–2, 123–5, 156, 180
    Zhou dynasty 39, 88, 89–90
China (modern) 531–45, 548–50
    arrest of Gang of Four (1976) 544
    and Boxer Rising (1898–1901) 532, 533
    and bureaucracy 457
    Communist-Nationalist conflict 535–6
    comparison with Byzantium 239–40
    Cultural Revolution 540–1, 542–3, 544
    economic growth 548–9
    and God Worshippers 453–4
    Great Leap Forward 537–8, 540
    gunpowder invention 240
    and industrialization 407
    inventions 227
    Japanese invasions 533, 535–6
    Long March 535, 540
    Manchu conquest and rule 449–51
    Mandate of Heaven 239
    and Mao Zedong's 87, 94, 124, 522, 534 43
    Marco Polo's travels to 225–6, 228, 229
    military forces 450, 453
    Ming dynasty 268, 450
    Mongol conquest of and rule 219, 222, 227, 228–9
    navy 549
    opium trade 446–8
    and Opium Wars 449, 452–4
    Qing dynasty 449, 531, 533
    Rape of Nanking (1938) 533
    relations with Soviet Union 523
    relations with United States 528
    and Second World War 533
    Song dynasty 227, 228, 230
    and Taiping Rebellion (1850–64) 454, 533

China (modern) (*cont.*)
 Tang dynasty 226
 Tiananmen Square protest (1989) 543, 544
 trade with Muslims 226–7
 under Deng Xiaoping 544
 Yuan dynasty 219
China Welfare Fund for the Disabled 545
Chinese, origins of 38
Chinese Communist Party 534, 535
Chittor, siege of (1567–8) 333
Christianity/Christians 66, 85, 129, 130, 146,
  170–5, 180, 189
 advancement of by Constantine 172–3
 conversion of the Rus 207
 and Crusades 192
 growth and spread of 163, 171
 Lutheran 269–79
 and martyrdom 170–1
 missionaries 180, 189, 213, 294, 438
 Muslim coastal slave-taking 280–1
 outlawing of in Japan 295
 and Romans 162, 163, 170–5
 spread of by St Paul 160–1, 162–3
 triumph of 170–5
Chronicle of Past Times 205
Churchill, Sarah (Duchess of Marlborough) 326,
  330, 339
Churchill, Winston 457, 463, 496, 498, 522
CIA (Central Intelligence Agency) 521, 528
Cicero 129, 139
cities
 ancient China 40, 88
 ancient India 78
 birth of first 32–6
city-states, Greek 70–1, 72, 101–2
civil engineering 40
Cixi, dowager empress 534
Claudius, Emperor 129
clay tablets 33
Cleisthenes 73
Cleitus, General 105
Clement IV, Pope 228
Cleopatra 142, 144–5, 147–51, 154, 159
 and Antony 149, 151–2
 and Caesar 149–50
 suicide 153
climate change 169, 560, 563
 and collapse of Roman Empire and Han
   China 158
 and early agriculture 20, 21–2
 and emergence of first cities 33
 and origins of humans 8

Clive, Robert 337, 447, 514–15
Code Napoléon 370
Coeur-de-Lion, Richard 237
coinage
 Britain 400
 Lydian 69
Cold War 520–8
Coligny Calendar 140
Colossi of Memnon 44
Colossus machines 555
Colton, Frank 492
Columbus, Christopher 215, 230, 254, 255–9
Communism 471, 472, 505, 526
 fall of (1989) 529–30
Communist Manifesto, The 405
computers 552–6
Comstock Act (1873) 488
Comstock, Anthony 487–8
Confucianism 93
Confucius (Kongzi) 82, 86–8, 89, 90–1, 92–3, 123
Congo
 annexation of by Leopold II of Belgium
   442–4, 445
Congo Reform Association 445
Conrad, Joseph 445
Constantine the Great 172–5, 192, 234
Constantine VII 240
Constantine XI Palaeologus, Emperor 232, 233
Constantinople 175, 186, 232, 234, 235
 fall of to Turks (1453) 113, 232–3, 240–1
 sacking of by Fourth Crusaders 238
Continental Congress 349
contraception *see* birth control
convicts
 transportation to Australia 358–9
Cook, Captain James 356, 357
Copernicus, Nicolaus 201, 312, 316, 317
Corday, Charlotte 367, 369
Córdoba 186, 198, 199
Corinth 97
Corn Laws 402–3
Cortés, Hernando 265, 266
Cossacks 289
Counter-Reformation 315
Courthope, Nathaniel 300
cowpox 382–3
Crassus 139, 141
Crete 46–8
Crimean War 408
Cripps, Stafford 518
Crispus 173–4
Critias 98

Cro-Magnons 10, 13–14, 15
Croesus, king of Lydia 69, 73
Cromwell, Oliver 323–4
crossbows 156–7
Crusades/Crusaders 192–3, 227, 381
    Fourth (1202–4) 236–8
Cuba 526
Cuban Missile Crisis (1962) 525–6
Culloden Moor, battle of (1746) 394, 430
Cultural Revolution (China) 540–1, 542–3, 544
Custer, General George 426
customs unions 504
Cyprus 147
Cyrus, King 66–70, 73
Czechoslovakia 530
    and Prague Spring (1968) 527

Da Yu ('Great Yu') 36–8, 39, 40, 41
daimyo 431, 433
Damascus 128, 161
Dandolo, Enrico 237
Daniel, Book of 127
Danton, Georges 366
Daoguang, Emperor 451
Daoism 122
Darby, Abraham 400
Darius III, King 105
Darius, King 75
Darwin, Charles 3
Darwin, Erasmus 398
David, Jacques-Louis 369
Davis, Jefferson 415
Davy, Humphry 400
Dawkins, Richard 7
days of the week, naming of 35
de Gaulle, General 503
death rate 562
Decembrists 411–12
Declaration of Emancipation (US) 416, 427
decolonization 524
Deep Blue computer 552, 553–4, 555
Deep Thought computer 552
deforestation 561
Deir el-Medina 44–6
Delian League 96
demes 73–4
democracy 56, 99, 473–4, 562
    Athenian 74, 98
    as a culture 473
    expansion in twentieth century 473
    relationship between prosperity and 484
Deng Pufang 538–9, 542, 545

Deng Xiaoping 537, 539–40, 542
Denisovans 9
Denmark–Norway 320–1
Dessalines, Jean-Jacques 379
détente 527, 528
dhamma 118
Diamond, Jared 21, 296, 355
Dickens, Charles 401
dictatorships 484
Dido of Tyre (Elissa) 60
Diesel, Rudolf 455
Diggers 323
Diocletian 172
Dionysus 103
Djenne 212
Djerassi, Carl 492
DNA 8
dogs, early domestication of 28
Dorians 55, 79
Dowden, Richard 524
Drake, Francis 268
drama, Athenian 76–7
Dreyfus affair 372
Dutch *see* Netherlands
Dutch East India Company 305
Dyer, General Reginald 517

Earth
    early history 3
    moving around the Sun discovery 312–13,
        316
East India Company 293, 299, 337, 346, 347, 448,
    515
Eastern Europe 309, 531
    impact of Black Death on 231
    and second serfdom 231
Eaton, William 291
economic crisis (2010–12) 505
Edict of Toleration (313) 173
Edison, Thomas 456
Edo (Japan) 296
Egypt, ancient 41–6, 58, 105
    and Alexandria 145–7
    art 42–3
    and Cleopatra 142, 144–5, 147–51, 154, 159
    conquest of by Arabs (642) 179
    craftsmen 45
    culture 42
    monuments and temples 44–5
    and Nile 40, 43, 44
    Ptolemaic 143–5, 147–8
    self-sufficiency of 42

Egypt, ancient (*cont.*)
  Upper and Lower 43
  village life 44–6
Egypt (modern) 524, 548
Einstein, Albert 508
Eisenhower, Ike 525
El Cid 199
El (god) 632
El Niño (500) 169
Elamites 66
Elizabeth I, Queen 268, 283, 292
Ellis, Havelock 488
Emancipation Proclamation (US) 413, 416, 427
enclosures 389–90
energy, alternative forms 563
Engels, Friedrich 405
England *see* Britain
English Civil War 310, 323, 391
Enlightenment 329, 345
environment 560–1
Eratosthenes 146
Eridu 32, 33
Erlitou 40
Ethical Cultural Society 507
Ethiopia 216, 524, 564
Etruscans 131
Euclid 146, 196
eunuchs 239
Euphrates river 32
Eurasia 77, 164, 202, 209, 219, 267, 352
Euripides 104
euro 504
Europe 113–14, 185–93, 298, 503–6
  comparison with India 330–1
  enmities and rivalries within 437
  impact of Black Death 231
  and imperialism 436–40
  isolation of early 191–2
  and Peasant Rebellion (1524–5) 278
  secrets of later success 190–3
  tribal migrations 190–1
  see also individual countries
European Economic Community (EEC) 504
European Iron and Steel Community 504
European Union 504–5, 563
Eusebius 173, 174
Evans, Sir Arthur 47–8
Eve, Mitochondrial 6–7
exploration/explorers 357

factories 401
Factory Acts 401

Fagan, Brian 12, 15
Faiyum mummy portraits 146–7
famines 18
Faraday, Michael 400
farming *see* agriculture
Fascism 472, 484–5
Fatehpur Sikri 333
Fausta 173–4
Fenby, Jonathan 549
Feng-Hsiung Hsu 553, 554, 559
Ferdinand and Isabella 255, 256–7, 259, 260, 261–2
Fertile Crescent 20, 21, 32
fertilizers 456–7, 470–1
feudal system 191
Figes, Orlando 413
First World War (1914–18) 343, 454, 458, 459–62,
    483, 494
  causes 445
  German U-boat campaign 459–60, 461, 482
  and Russia 462, 464
  'Zimmerman telegram' and US entry into
    460–1
Five Pecks of Rice movement 159
Flannery, Tim 12
Flood 65
floods/flooding 24, 33, 36, 37, 38, 40
Florence 243
Ford, Henry 456
Fordism 456
Four Hundred 98
Fourth Crusade (1202–4) 236–8
France 311, 437, 503–4, 524
  alliance with Habsburgs 343
  and American War of Independence 64, 351
  aristocracy 391
  and Bourbons 318, 319–20, 362
  Code Napoléon 370
  colonization of Africa 444
  Fronde 321, 323
  and Haitian Revolution 378–9
  and Napoleon 114, 370–2, 378, 384, 408,
    421
  post-Napoleonic monarchy 405
  Second Republic 405
  and Second World War 502, 503
Franco, General Francisco 484, 496
François I, King of France 283
Franklin, Benjamin 346, 347, 349
Franks 192
Frederick I, King of Prussia 335
Frederick II, the Great 318, 338, 340–4
Frederick William, King of Prussia 340

French Revolution 311, 362–70, 372
  and Declaration of the Rights of Man 365
  execution of Louis XVI and Marie Antoinette 365
  and Haitian Revolution 376
  impact and legacy of 363, 372
  and Marat 367–9
  reforms 366
  starting of 363–4
  storming of Bastille 364
  the Terror 366–7
French wars of religion 319, 322
Friedrich the Wise 271
Fronde 321, 323
Fukuyama, Francis
  The End of History and the Last Man 473
Fulani 215
fur trade (Russia) 284 5

Gaddis, Jon Lewis 527
Gagarin, Yuri 526
Galata 283
Galileo 311–12, 313, 314–17, 329
Gan Ying 112
Gandhi, Mohandas 511–14, 518–20
Gang of Four 541, 543–4
gas-lighting 404
Gaskell, Elizabeth 401
Gaugamela, battle of 105
Gauls 134, 140–1
Genghis Khan 217, 219, 220–5, 227, 247
Genoa 192, 220, 229
geo-engineering 563
geometry 146
George III, King 348
Georgia 223
Georgiev, Kimon 484
Gere, Cathy 47
Germany 269–70, 275
  and Berlin Blockade 522
  and bureaucracy 457–8
  colonization of Africa 438, 445
  fall of Berlin Wall 530
  and First World War 459–62, 494
  and imperialism 438, 439
  and industrialization 404, 406
  inventiveness 455
  in Luther's time 270–1
  patent system 455
  Peasant Rebellion (1524–5) 278
  railways 406
  reunification (1990) 530

  and Second World War 494–501
  see also Nazis
Ghana 211
al-Ghazali 200, 201
Gibbon, Edward 154, 158
  The Decline and Fall of the Roman Empire 154
Gilgamesh, King 33
Gilliéron, Émille 48
glasnost 529
global warming 563
Glorious Revolution (1688) 325–8
God Worshippers 453–4
gods 33–4, 62
  Egyptian 144
  India 81
  and Mesopotamian cities 36
Goebbels, Josef 480, 485
Goering, Hermann 479
Golkonda mine (India) 336
Gorbachev, Mikhail 529, 530
Goths 192
Granada 260
Grant, General Ulysses 416, 417
Great Crash (1929) 302, 483
Great Leap Forward (China) 537–8, 540
Great Reform Act (1832) 403
Great Wall of China 124, 240
Greece, ancient 53–62, 70–7, 82
  and Alexander the Great see Alexander the Great
  alphabet 61
  city-states (*polis*) 70–1, 72, 101–2
  conflict with Mauryans 116
  conflict with Romans 134
  disaster causing collapse of first civilization 55, 59, 70
  fall of 113, 137
  fighting methods 71–2
  Hellenistic culture 107, 126
  and Indians 78
  Jewish revolt against Seleucid 126–7
  Mycenaean 58–9
  navy 72
  Olympic Games 72
  and religion 71
  war against Persians 75–6
  war against Romans 134, 136–7
  war elephants 134
  see also Athens/Athenians; Sparta/Spartans
Greece (modern) 486, 521
'Greek fire' 240

Gregory X, Pope 228–9
Grossman, Vasily
    Everything Flows 469
Guantanamo Bay (Cuba) 548
Guatemala 528
guilds 313
    Italian 244
Guillotin, Dr Joseph-Ignace 367, 384
guillotine 366–7
Gulf War 546
Gun 37
gunpowder 240
Gupta dynasty 119, 330
Gustavus Adolphus, King of Sweden 321
Gutenberg, Johannes 275–6

Haber, Fritz 457, 470
Habsburgs 282, 318–19, 320, 344, 404
Hadrian, Emperor 155
Hagia Sophia 233, 235
Haiti (Saint-Domingue) 373–80
Haitian Revolution 373, 375–9
al-Hakam II 199
Halliday, Jon 537, 538
Hamilcar 136
Han dynasty 111–12, 115, 120, 156–9
Hannibal 134, 135, 136
Hanno the Carthaginian 209
Hanseatic League 192, 285
Harrison, John 317
Hastings, Max 496, 501
Hastings, Warren 515
Hatshepsut, Queen 44
Hattusa 58
Hausa 215
Havel, Vaclav 530
Hawaii 12
Hebrews 62–6, 130
Heinrich events 11
Helen of Troy 54, 57, 58, 59
Hellenistic culture 107, 126
henges 31
Henry IV, King of France 319
Henry, Patrick 347
Henry VIII, King 277
Hephaestion 104, 106, 107
Heraclius, Emperor 179
Herod, King 129, 152, 159
Herodotus 68, 69–70, 75, 76, 77
Herophilos 146
Hidetada 295
Hideyoshi 292

Hilkiah (high priest) 65
Hinduism/Hindus 331, 332
Hiroshima 506, 510
Hitler, Adolf 472, 474–82, 485–6, 499, 507, 511
    attack on Soviet Union 496, 497
    character 475–6
    charisma 477–8
    and economics 485
    and Gandhi 514
    hatred of the Jews 475, 476, 478, 481
    ideology 481
    as master propagandist 478, 480
    Mein Kampf 475, 476, 480, 481
    Munich putsch and imprisonment (1923)
            474–5, 479–80, 481
    rise to power 481, 482–3
    and Second World War 494, 498
    and swastika 478
Hittites 58
Hochschild, Adam 446
Hodder, Ian 25–6
Hogg, James 272
Hohenzollerns 318
Holland 302 *see also* Netherlands
Holland, Tom 177
Holocaust 472, 475, 499, 500
Holy Land 179, 192
Holy Roman Empire 189, 271, 331, 343, 404
home 300–1
Homer 56–7, 59, 104
    Iliad 53, 57, 59
    Odyssey 54
Homo erectus 8, 10, 12, 38
Homo heidelbergensis 8, 9
Homo sapiens 8, 9, 10, 11, 12
homosexuality
    Greek 72, 137
    Roman 137–8
Hong Kong, handing over as a British colony
            453
Hong Xiuquan 453–4
Hooke, Robert 329
Hoover, Herbert 483
Horthy, Miklos 484
Horus 41, 144, 150
House of Commons 402
houses, Neolithic 25–6, 29
Hua Guofeng 544
huarango trees 169
human sacrifice
    ancient China 88
    Aztecs 164

human sacrifice (*cont.*)
    Minoans 49
    Nazca 168
humans
    impact of climate on movement of *Homo Sapiens* 11
    migration out of Africa 4–5, 9, 10–11
    origins 8–10
    spreading of 12
Hume, Allan Octavian 517–18
Hungary 282, 484, 529
Huns 190, 202, 218
Hunter, John 382
hunter-gatherer societies 4–6, 12, 13–17, 49, 562
    belief systems 13
    conflict and tribal war 6
    division of labour 5, 16
    and grandmothers 5
    lessons to be drawn from 16–17
    lifespans 19
    reverence for animals 13–14
    tribal bonding 6
Hus, Jan 276
Huygens, Christiaan 317, 329
Hyrcanus 128

IBM 552, 554
Ibn Battuta 213, 214
Ibn Khaldun 214
Ibn Marwan 198
Ibn Rushd *see* Averroës
ice ages 8, 20, 21, 27, 284
Iceland 284
    Muslim raids (1627) 280
Ieyasu, Tokugawa 293, 294, 295
Ife culture 216
Igor 206
imperialism 436–40
    and 'scramble for Africa' 438, 445–6
Inanna (god) 36
Incas 262–5, 267
    conquest of by Spanish 262–5, 267–8
    expansion of empire 265
    society 265
India, ancient 77–86
    agriculture 80
    Brahmin system 81, 83
    caste system 81–2
    cities 78, 83
    clan organisation 82
    culture 79–80

    gods 81
    Gupta dynasty 119, 330
    Mauryan 115–16, 330
    migration of people into 78
India (modern) 119, 330–7, 524
    and Amritsar Massacre (1919) 517, 518
    British in 337, 438, 514–18
    Buddhism 86
    Civil Service 516
    comparison with Europe 331
    Delhi Muslim dynasties 330–1
    and Gandhi 511–14, 518–20
    independence (1947) 518
    independence campaign 518–19
    Mughal empire 332–7
    Muslim-Hindu conflicts 331–2, 519
    partition of 519–20
    salt tax revolt 511–12
    and Second World War 518–19
    war between Mughals and Marathas 336
Indian Mutiny (1857) 515–16
Indian National Congress 517–18, 519
    indigenous peoples 309–10, *see also* aboriginal Australians; native Americans
Indonesia 524
indulgencies 272–3
Indus 40
industrial revolution 251, 311, 387–92
    factory conditions and child labour 401
    Germany 404, 406
    and Luddites 401–2
    and nationalism 406–7
    negative impact of 387–8
    positive impact of 387
    reasons for starting in Britain 388 93, 400
    United States 404, 406
    and Watt's steam engine 396–7, 399–400
infant mortality 563–4
Internet 555
Inuit 15
inventiveness 455
Ionian revolt (499 BC) 73, 75
Ionic 57
Iran 545
    war with Iraq 545–6
Iraq 546
    invasion of Kuwait 546
    post-war 547
    war with Iran 545–6
Iraq war (2003) 547–8

Ireland 309, 327, 496
    Easter Rising 458
    Elizabethan war against 352
    famines 516
Iron Age 56, 67, 80
Isabella *see* Ferdinand and Isabella
Isis 144, 150
Islam 24, 66, 85, 130, 175–81
    and Africa 210
    golden age of 194–202
    origins 178
    splits within 180
    spread of and early military success 178–80,
        189
    see also Muslims
Islamism 545–6, 546
Israel 63, 64, 65, 520–1, 545, 546
Israelites 63, 64, 126
Italy 186, 243
    city-republics 243
    and 'Euro-communism' 505
    and imperialism 439
    and Mussolini 439, 472, 484–5, 486
    Renaissance 242, 313–17
    unification of 404
Ivan III, the Great 286
Ivan IV, the Terrible 283–4, 286–8, 289, 290, 411,
    495
ivory 443–4

Jackson, 'Stonewall' 425
Jacobin Club 366
Jacobins 365, 366
Jacobite rebellion (1745) 394
Jagiellon dynasty 192, 282
Jahan, Shah 334–5
Jahangir 333–4
Jamaica 377
James, C.L.R. 376–7
James I (James VI of Scotland), King 290–1, 293,
    321, 391–2
    'A Counterblaste to Tobacco' 291
James II, King 325, 326, 327, 328
Janszoon, Jan 280
Japan/Japanese 292–6, 495
    ban on smoking 291
    comparison with Britain 292–3
    conversion to Christianity by missionaries 294
    culture 296
    and First World War 460
    Hideyoshi years 292
    invasions of China 533, 535–6

Meiji restoration and reform 433–4, 457, 534
    outlawing of Christianity 295
    Pearl Harbor attack 497–8
    peasant revolt in Kyushu (1637) 295
    resolving of environmental problems 296
    sakoku ('locked-country') policy 295–6
    and samurai 295, 431–2
    samurai rebellion 429–30, 433, 435–6
    ships 294, 295
    and tobacco 291
    Tokugawa 292–7, 430–3
    and trade 294
Jardine, Lisa 327
Jaspers, Karl 84
Java/Javanese 439, 441
Jefferson, Thomas 351, 353, 384, 420
Jenner, Edward 282–4
Jeremiah 65
Jericho 24, 25
Jerusalem 64, 65, 128
    and Crusaders 192
    fall of to Arabs (638) 179
    siege of (70) 162
    siege of (586) 65
Jesuits 87, 280, 292, 293, 295, 316, 437
Jesus Christ 83, 85, 161, 162, 172, 180
Jews 62–3, 65–6, 126–30, 260
    and afterlife 127
    and anti-Semitism 476
    Babylonian exile 65–6, 126, 130
    expansion of communities 127–8, 129
    and Hellenistic culture 126
    and Holocaust 472, 475, 499, 500
    Maccabee revolt against Seleucid Greeks
        126–7
    proselytizing 129
    releasing of from exile by Cyrus 66
    revolt against Rome 161–2
Jiang Qing 541, 543, 544
Jin dynasty 158, 222
Jinnah, Mohammad Ali 519
Joanna the Mad 261, 262
John Paul II, Pope 528
Johnson, Lyndon B. 527
Johnson, Samuel 351
Jones, Sir William 78–9
Jordanes 218
Josiah, King 64–5
Joyce, James 463
Judah 64, 65, 126–7, 128–9, 152
Judaism 41, 62, 66, 129, 163 *see also* Jews
Judas Maccabeus 127

Jupiter 35
Justinian, Emperor 186–7

Kabukimono 291
Kahr, Gustav Ritter von 479
Kalinga 117
Karakorum 224, 228
Kasparov, Garry 552, 553–4, 555, 558–9
Keay, John 79–80
Keneally, Thomas 360
Kennedy, John F. 525
Kenya 524
Kerensky, Alexander 464
Kershaw, Ian 476
Khasakhemwy, King 42
Khazars 202–3, 206
Kholmsky, Prince 286
Khomeini, Ayatollah 546
Khrushchev, Nikita 525–6, 527
Khwarezmid empire 222
al-Khwarmi, Muhammad 197
Kilby, Jack 556
Kim Il Sung 522
King, Gregory 389
King James Bible 277
King, Martin Luther 513
Kissinger, Henry 363
Klu Klux Klan 428
Knossos, palace of 47–8
Knox, John 279
Koh-i-Noor diamond 336
Kongzi *see* Confucius
Koran 178
Korea 292, 293
Korean War 522–3, 538
Kosovo, battle of (1389) 281
Kublai Khan 219, 227, 228–9
Kuchum Khan 288, 289
kulaks 472, 500
Kuomintang 532, 535
Kurzweil, Ray 557
Kush 209
Kuwait 546
Kyushu 434

Lachish 64
Landes, David 268–9
Langland, William
    Piers Plowman 559
language 6, 13
Lao Ali 121
Las Casas, Bartolomé de 261, 438

Las Navas de Tolosa, battle of (1212) 260
Lascaux caves 17
League of Nations 483
Lebanon 63
LeBlanc, Stephen 17
Lecky, W.E.H. 234–5
Lecouvreur, Adrienne 339
Lee, Robert E. 415, 416, 425
Leeuwenhoek, Antonie van 329
Legalism 123
Leipzig, battle of (Battle of the Nations) 371
Lenin, Vladimir Ilich 220, 369, 458, 462–5, 500
Leo III, Pope 188
Leo X, Pope 273–4
Leonardo da Vinci 313, 421–7
    The Last Supper 245–6
Leonidas, King 76
Leopold I, King of the Belgians 440–1
Leopold II, King of the Belgians 441–3, 444, 445–6
Lepanto, battle of (1571) 270
Les Rois (France) 15
Li Hongzhang 532
Li Zicheng 449
Licinius, Emperor 173
life expectancy 391
Lin Biao 542
Lin Zexu 446–8, 451–2, 453
Lincoln, Abraham 415–17, 419, 424, 427, 429
    assassination 417
    Gettysburg Address 429
Linear B script 58
Lisbon earthquake (1755) 344
Lithuania 282
Little Big Horn, battle of (1876) 426
Litvinov, Maxim 463
Liu Shaoqi 541, 542
Livingstone, David 438, 441–2
Lloyd George, David 457, 483
Lombards 192
London 392
Long March (China) 535, 540
longitude 317, 329
Longshan culture 38–9, 40
Lorenzo the Magnificent 243–4, 273
Louis XIV, King of France 318, 320, 321, 324, 327, 335
Louis XVI, King of France 343–4, 363, 364, 365
Louis XVIII, King of France 371
Louis-Philippe, King of France 405
Louisiana Purchase 351, 421
Lovelock, James 560, 563

Lu Buwei 120–1
Luddites 401–2
Ludendorff, General 478, 479, 480
Lueger, Karl 476
Luke 160, 161
Lunar Society 398
Luther, Martin 269–79
    background 270
    confrontations 276–7
    opposition to selling of indulgences 272–4
    theology and arguments of 271–2, 274–5, 276–7, 279
    translation of Bible into German 277–8
Luxembourg 504
Luxor temple 42
Lydians 69
Lyons, Jonathan 201

Macaulay, Thomas Babington 515
Maccabee revolt 126–7
McCarthy, John 556
McCartney, Lord George 451
McCormick, Katharine Dexter 486–7, 488, 489, 490–2, 493
MacCulloch, Diarmaid 163
MacDonald, Ramsay 483
Macedon/Macedonians 101, 102–3, 143
machines
    and human intelligence 552–8
McNeill, J.R. 560, 561
McPherson, James 424
Madeira 256
Magellan, Ferdinand 297
Maimonides, Moses 200, 201
Malawi 524
Mali 208, 211–14, 215
Malthus, Thomas 384
al-Mamun, Caliph 197
Man, John 222
Manchu 449–51
Manhattan Project 506–7, 508–9
al-Mansur, Caliph 196
Manzikert, battle of (1071) 238
Mao Zedong 87, 94, 124, 522, 534–43
Mapungubwe 210
Marat, Jean-Paul 367–9
Marathas 336
Marathon, battle of (490 BC) 75, 79
marathon race 75
Marco Polo see Polo, Marco
Marcus Aurelius, Emperor 112, 155
Marduk (god) 67

Marie Antoinette 343–4, 365
Mark, St 83
Marlborough, Duchess of see Churchill, Sarah
Marlborough, Duke of 326, 330
Mars 35
Marshall Plan 504, 521
martyrdom 170
Marx, Karl 405–6
Marxism-Leninism 535
Marxism/Marxists 405, 471, 472, 530
Mary of Modena 324–5, 327
Mary, Queen 326, 328
al-Masudi 196
mathematics
    Abbasid Muslims 196–7
    Mesopotamia 35
Mather, Cotton 380
matrilineal drift 7
Mattathias 127
Mauryan India 115–16, 330
Maxentius 173
Maximilian, Archduke 441
Maya 164, 193, 266
Mazarin, Cardinal 320, 324
Medicis 244
Medina 178
Mediterranean 436
Megasthenes 116
Mehmet II, Sultan 232–3, 281, 283
Melanchthon, Philipp 279
Mendoza, Antonio de 266
Mengistu, Haille Mariam 524
Mengzi (Mencius) 82–3
Mennonites 301, 302
Mercury 35
Merneptah, Pharaoh 63
Mesoamerica/Mesoamericans 24, 42, 164, 254, 267
Mesopotamia 24, 32–3, 42, 105, 164
    conquest of by Arabs (639) 179
    emergence of first cities 32–4
    and mathematics 35
    and religion 63
    see also Akkadians; Babylon/Babylonians; Sumerians
Metaxas, General 484
Mexico 20, 267, 441, 460
Michelangelo 315
microscopes 329
Middle East 10, 38, 64, 130, 141, 192, 456, 483, 503
Midway, battle of (1942) 501
Milan 242

Minoans 46–9, 58
    art and architecture 46–7, 49
    bull-leaping 48–9
    destruction of 49
    human sacrifice 49
    Knossos palace 47–8
Minos, King 48
Minotaur 48
Minsky, Marvin 556
missionaries
    Christian 180, 189, 213, 294, 438
    Jesuit 87, 437
Missouri Compromise 422
mitochondrial DNA 10
Mitochondrial Eve 6–7
Model T 456
Mohacs, battle of 282
Mohawks 351–2, 353
Mohegan people 352–3
Moi, Daniel arap 524
Mongols 114, 204, 217–25, 330
    break-up of empire 224
    brutality of 222–3
    conquest and rule of China 219, 222, 227,
        228–9
    conquests and expansion of empire 219–20,
        222–3, 224, 226, 285, 470
    and Genghis Khan 217, 219, 220–5, 227, 247
    and Kublai Khan 219, 227, 228–9
monotheism 56, 62, 66, 114, 129–30, 159
Montagu, Lady Mary Wortley 280, 339, 382
Montezuma 265
Monzi 83
Moon 31, 35
Moore, Gordon 556
Moore's law 557
Moors 194–5
Morel, Edmund 445
Morgan, J.P. 426
Moroccans 215
Morris, Ian 38, 157, 159, 220
Moscow 285–6
Moses 62, 64
Mother (of human race) 4, 6–7, 9
Mountbatten, Lord 519
Mozambique 524
Mubarak, Hosni 513
Mugabe, Robert 525
Mughals 332–7
Muhammad 85, 177–8, 179, 180
mulattos 376, 379
Müntzer, Thomas 278

Murad III, Sultan 283
Musa, King 208, 212–13, 215
Muscovy Company 293
Muslim League 519
Muslims 270
    and Abbasid caliphate 195–6, 226
    and Africa 210
    and astrology 196
    coastal raids and slave-taking 280–1
    conquest of Spain 194, 197–8 *see also*
        al-Andalus
    conquests 270, 281, 282
    contempt for Christian Europeans 196
    dialogues with Protestant rulers 283
    hatred of America by many 545
    and mathematics 196–7
    trade with China 226–7
    see also Islam
Mussolini, Benito 439, 472, 484–5, 486
Mycenaeans 58–9

Nagasaki 510
Nanking, Treaty of (1842) 449, 453
Napoleon Bonaparte 114, 370–2, 378, 384, 408,
    421
National Academy of Sciences 18
National Convention 365, 366
nationalism 503–4
    and industrialization 406–7
Native Americans 253–4
    agriculture 253–4
    attacks on by colonists and demonization of
        as savages 352–3
    destruction of after American Civil War 426
    impact of European settlers on 254–5, 258
    tribal systems 254
native Australians *see* aboriginal Australians
NATO (North Atlantic Treaty Organization)
    521–2, 524, 529
Natufians 21–2
navies
    ancient Greece 72
    British 323, 376 *see also* Royal Navy
    Carthage 135
    Chinese 453, 549
Nazarenes 161, 162
Nazca 165–9
Nazi-Soviet Pact (1939) 496
Nazis 372, 472, 479
    economic growth and policy 485–6
    factors explaining rise of 483
    see also Hitler, Adolf

Neanderthals 9, 14–16
Nebuchadnezzar, King 65
Nehru, Jawaharlal 518
Nehru, Motilal 518
Nelmes, Sarah 383
Nemesis (paddle-steamer) 453
Neolithic Britain 27–32
    belief systems 31
    burials 26
    settlements/towns 24–7, 29
    and Stonehenge 29–31
Nero, Emperor 155, 161
Netherlands 298–300, 437, 504
    development of first stock market 299
    and imperialism 439
    invasion of Britain by William of Orange
        325–7
    and Java/Javanese 439, 441
    rebellion (1785) 362
    and 'rich trades' 298–300, 303
    settlements in South Africa 438
    tulip mania and bursting of bubble 301–2,
        303–6
    wars of independence against Spain 302–3
New Guinea 20
New Model Army 323
New York 300
New York Society for the Suppression of Vice 487
New Zealand 12
Newcomen, Thomas 393
newspapers
    and British free press 392
Newton, Isaac 328–9, 339
Nicaea, Council of (325) 174, 236
Nicene creed 174
Nicholas I, Czar 412
Nicholas II, Czar 462
Niger, River 211
Nigeria 212, 213, 216
Nile, River 40, 43, 44
Nineveh 64, 65
Nippur 35
nirvana 84
Nixon, Richard 527, 528
Nkomo, Joshua 525
noble savage 17, 356, 361
nomads 218–19
Non-Aligned Group 524
Norman Conquest (1066) 191
North Atlantic Treaty Organization *see* NATO
North, Lord 347
Norwich, John Julius 234–5, 238

Novgorod 285, 286, 287
Nubians 209
Nuclear Non-Proliferation Treaty (1968) 527
Nuclear Test-Ban Treaty 526
nuclear weapons 511, 521, 523, 525, 529

Octavian *see* Augustus, Emperor
ojos 166, 167
Old Testament 63, 126, 146
Olga 206
Olympias 103–4
Olympic Games 72
Onesimus (slave) 380
opium 446–7
opium trade 451–2
Opium Wars 449, 452–4
Oppenheimer, Robert 506–11
Oppenheimer, Stephen 7
Orkneys 28, 29
Osaka castle, siege of (1614–15) 294–5
Osiris 41, 144
Ostrogoths 190
Otto, Nikolaus 455
Ottoman Empire 47, 241, 270
    Christian fear of 280
    conquest of Constantinople (1453) 113, 232–3,
        234
    conquests and spread of 270, 281
    war with Venice 270

Pagel, Mark 6
Pakistan 20, 519
Palestine 63, 545
papacy 187, 188, 273, 316, 330–1
Papin, Denis 393
Paris, Matthew 223
Parthians 112, 152
Pasargadae 66, 68
pastoralism 217–18
Pataliputra 116, 118
patents 329, 392, 399, 455
Paul, St 160, 162–3, 180
Paul V, Pope 316
Pearl Harbor 497–8
Peasant Rebellion (1524–5) 278
Peel, Robert 403
Pella 102
Pemulwuy 362
perestroika 529
Pericles 76
Perpetua 170
Perry, Commodore Matthew 430

Persepolis 105
Persia/Persians 67–70
    conquest of by Alexander the Great 105
    and Sassanids 178–9
    war with Greeks 75–6, 96
Peru 166
Peter I, the Great, Czar 317, 321, 335, 409
Peter III, Czar 411
Peter, St 83, 163, 174
Pharisees 160
Pheidippides 75
Pheidon of Argos 72–3
Philip II, King of Macedon 101, 103–4
Philistines 64
Phillip, Arthur 356, 359–61
Phipps, James 383
Phoenicians 60–1
Pilsudski, General Jozef 484
Pincus, Gregory 492
Pinker, Steven 469–70
    The Better Angels of Our Nature 562
piracy 268
Pitt the Younger, William 348
Pizarro, Francisco 262–5
plague 186, 232, 301 *see also* Black Death
Plato 77, 95, 97, 100, 315
    Phaedo 96
Pleistocene 8
Pliocene 8
Plutarch 98, 148–9, 152
Poland 484, 496, 528, 529–30
polis (city-state) 70–1, 72, 101–2
pollution 387, 561
Polo, Marco 219, 220, 225–6, 227–8, 229–30
polytheism 62
Pompey (Gnaeus Pompeius Magnus) 128, 138–9, 141, 142, 147, 148
Poor Law (1834) 402
population growth 559–60, 562, 564
    and agriculture 18, 19, 22–3, 559
Portugal/Portuguese 260, 297, 484, 505
    and colonization 256, 259
    and imperialism 437, 438, 439
    rivalry with Spain 259
    and slave trade 374
    and trade 297
Potemkin, Prince 290
Potosí (Bolivia) 268
Prague Spring (1968) 527
press-gangs 395
Priestley, Joseph 398
Prinsep, James 115–16

printing press, invention of 275–6
Protestants 274, 283, 299, 320, 331, 343
    Dutch 302, 326
    expulsion from Antwerp (1585) 299
    in France 322
    see also Reformation
Prussia 340, 343, 404, *see also* Frederick the Great
Ptolemy I, King of Egypt 143
Ptolemy II 143
Ptolemy III 143
Ptolemy XII 147–8
Ptolemy XIII 148
Punic wars 134–5, 136
puritanism 487, 490
Pyrrhus, King of Epirus 134

Qianlong, Emperor 451
Qing dynasty 449, 531, 533

racism 454
railways
    Britain 406
    United States 406, 422, 425
Rameses III 44
Rape of Nanking (1938) 533
Reagan, Ronald 529
Red Brigades 500
Rees, Martin 564
Reformation 269–78, 302, 316
Register, Katherine 17
religion 66
    Africa 214
    ancient China 41, 122–3
    ancient Greece 71
    Byzantium 235–6
    hunter-gatherer societies 14
    Mesopotamia 62
    Minoan 48–9
    Roman 131, 159
    see also Buddhism; Christianity; Islam; Judaism
Renaissance 242, 247, 313–16
revolutions (1848) 372, 405
Ricardo, David 432
Richelieu, Cardinal 319–20
Rig Vedas 79
Rivera, Primo de 484
Robespierre, Maximilien 366, 370
Rock, John 492
Rockefeller, John D. 426
Roebuck, John 397–8
Roger II, King of Sicily 197

Röhm, Ernst 478
Romania 484, 530
Romanovs 318
Romans/Roman Empire 111–15, 131–56, 157
    and Augustus 151, 152, 153, 154
    and Caesar see Caesar, Julius
    and Christianity 162, 163, 170–5
    collapse 113, 158
    conquest of Judah by Pompey 128–9
    corruption and decadence 137–8
    destruction of Gauls by Caesar 140–1
    gladiatorial fights 138
    grandeur and prosperity 157
    Jewish revolt against 161–2
    links with Han China 112–13
    military system and subjugation of foes 133–4
    money and politics 132, 137–8
    origins 131
    and Ptolemaic Egypt 144, 147–53
    Punic Wars and destruction of Carthage
        134–5, 136
    religion and belief system 131, 159
    rise of 113
    rule of by Etruscans 131
    Senate 132–3
    society 132, 155–6
    and Spartacus revolt 138, 139
    taxation 137
    war against Greeks 134, 136–7
Rome 111
    sacking of by Arabs (846) 188
Romulus and Remus 131, 132
Roosevelt, Franklin Delano 486, 497, 498, 502,
    508
Rosetta stone 143
roundhouses 29, 31
Roxana (wife of Alexander the Great) 106
Royal Navy 280, 325, 379, 384, 448, 453, 459, 482
Royal Society 329
rubber 444
ruling class, and first cities 34, 35
Run 300
Rurik 206
Rus (Vikings) 203, 206–7, 219
Russell, William Howard 424
Russia (pre-Soviet) 202–3, 206, 251, 283–90,
    407–15, 461–5
    agriculture 411
    conflict with Muslim khans 288
    conversion to Christianity of early 207
    and Crimean War 408
    Decembrist revolt 411–12

emancipation of serfs 409, 412, 413–14, 427
emergence of Moscow as dominant power
    285–6
expansion of empire 289–90
February Revolution (1917) 462–3
    and First World War 462, 464
fur trade 284–5
industrial development 414
instability of autocratic system 411
invasion of Siberia 288–90
and Ivan the Terrible 283–4, 286–8, 289, 290,
    411, 495
Mongol invasions 219–20, 223, 224, 285
October Revolution (1917) 465
peasant rebellions 411, 414
serfdom 409–11
and Stroganovs 286
and Vikings 206–7
Russia (post Soviet) 531
Ryoma, Sakamoto 433

Saba/Sabaeans 176
Sacks, Jonathan 62
Saddam Hussein 546, 547
Sahara 208
St Peter's Basilica (Rome) 128, 273–4
St Petersburg 318
Saint-Domingue (Haiti) 373–80
sakoku 295–6
Salome, Queen 128
SALT 1 527
salt trade (Africa) 211
Samaria 64
Samaritans 61
Samarkand 222, 223
samurai 295, 429–30, 431, 432–3, 434, 435–6
San Martín, José de 267
San Salvador 258
Sancho, Pedro 267–8
Sand, Shlomo 129
Sanger, Margaret 486–7, 488–9, 490, 491, 493
Sanskrit 78–9, 119
Saracens 189
Sargon of Akkad 36
Sarpi, Friar Paolo 315–16
Sassanids 178–9
Saturn 35
satyagraha 512–13
Saul see Paul, St
Savery, Thomas 393
Scandinavia 320–1
Schacht, Hjalmar 485

Schliemann, Heinrich 47, 57
Schmalkaldic League 279
Schwartz, Jack 558
science 329
Scipio Africanus 136
Scotland 80, 322, 330
    kingship 193
    and Presbyterianism 322, 395
    Union with England (1707) 394–5
Scottish Enlightenment 395, 396
Scotus, Duns 201
'sea peoples' 43, 58, 190
Sebastopol, siege of (1854/5) 408
Second World War (1939–45) 470, 494–503, 518
    Allied invasion of France (1944) 502
    battles and leaders 498
    death toll 498, 499, 501, 533
    defeat of Luftwaffe by Britain 497, 502
    invasion of Soviet Union by Germany 497,
        500
    morals drawn from 498–9
    Pearl Harbor attack and US entry into 497–8
    suing for peace by British speculation 496
    US destruction of Japanese in Pacific 501
Secret History of the Mongols, The 217, 222
Seko, Mobuto Sese 524
Seleucids 126, 143
Seleucus Nicator 116
September 11 (2001) 547
serfs/serfdom 191, 409–11
    emancipation of Russian 409, 412, 413–14, 427
settlements
    emergence of first 22
    Neolithic 4–7
Seven Years War 342, 348
Sforza, Galeazzo Maria 242
Sforza, Ludovico, Duke of Milan 241–2, 246
Shaftesbury, Earl of 356
Shang dynasty 39, 88–9
Shang, Lord 123
Shang-Shu (Book of History) 39
Shangdu (Xanadu) 219, 228
Sheba, Queen of 176–7
Sherman, William 427
Shetland 29
Shia Muslims 180
Shikibu, Murasaki
    The Tale of Genji 193
Shivaji 336
Siberia 288–90
Sibir, khanata of 288
Sicily 97

Siddhartha Gautama *see* Buddha
Silbury 31
Silesia 342
Silk Road 226, 230, 260
Sima Qian 82, 91, 120–2, 123, 124
Singh, Jaipal 78
Singularity, the 557, 558
Sioux 106, 353, 426
Skara Brae (Orkney) 29
slave trade/slavery 442
    Africa 215, 442
    and American Civil War 419–20, 421–2
    and Athens 74–5
    Atlantic 215, 281, 374–5
    cruelty of 375
    enslavement of Christians by Muslims 280–1
    and Haitian Revolt 373
    and Middle Passage 374
    outlawing of by Britain 379
    and United States 351, 421–2, 423
    and US Declaration of Emancipation 413,
        416, 427
Slavs 190, 202
smallpox 267, 380–4
Smith, Adam 345, 395, 400, 403, 432, 551
Snyder, Timothy
    Bloodlines 499
social democracy 505
Socrates 94, 95–6, 97–8, 99–100, 103
soil 24, 560–1
Solidarity 513, 529–30
Solon 69
Solzhenitzyn, Alexander 528
Song dynasty 227, 228, 230
Songhai 214, 215
South Africa
    apartheid 524
    Dutch settlements in 438
South Sea Bubble 302
Sovereign of the Seas 293–4
Soviet Union 525–6
    arms race with United States 523
    and China 523, 535–6
    collapse of 504, 528–9, 530–1
    and Cuban Missile Crisis 526
    and Gorbachev 529, 530
    invasion of Afghanistan (1978–9) 528, 546
    and Khrushchev 525–6, 527
    killing of kulaks 500
    nuclear weapons 525, 529
    and Second World War 494, 495, 498, 500–1
    see also Russia

Spain/Spanish 505
  break-up of Muslim 200, 202
  Christian 'reconquest' of 260
  colonization of Americas 258–9
  colonization of Canary Islands 256
  conquest of Aztec empire 265
  conquest of by Muslims 194, 197–8 *see also* al-Andalus
  conquest of Incas 262–6
  and Dutch wars of independence 302–3
  encomienda 266
  and imperialism 437, 438
  rivalry with Portuguese 259
  Second Republic 484
Spanish Civil War 496
Spanish Inquisition 259, 260–1
Sparta/Spartans 58–9, 73, 75–6, 97, 102, 103
Spartacus war 138, 139
Speke, John 441
Spice Islands 298, 299
spices 298
Spring and Autumn Annals, The 91
Sputnik 525
Stalin, Joseph 465, 469, 471–2, 486, 495, 498, 499, 535–6, 537
Stamp Act (1756) 346–7
stamp-seals 36
Stanley, Henry Morton 442, 443
steam engines 393, 406
    Newcomen 393, 396
    Watt 396–7, 399–400
Stephen 160
stock market
    development of first by Dutch 299
Stone Age 12, 15, 22, 29
Stone, I.F. 98
Stonehenge 29–31
Stopes, Marie 487
Stringer, Chris 9, 11
Stroganovs 286, 287–8
Stuarts 321–2, 324, 394
Suez Canal 444
Suleiman the Magnificent 283
Sulla 138, 139, 156
Sumatra, volcanic eruption 10
Sumerians 24, 34, 35, 36
Summer Palace (China) 454
Sun 31, 35
Sun Yat-sen 532
Sunni Muslims 180
Sutherland, Earl of 382
swastika 478

Sweden 320–1
Sweet Track (Somerset) 30
Swing Riots (1830) 402
syphilis 258, 267, 271, 295, 298
Syracuse 97, 98
Syria 179
Szilard, Leo 509

Taíno 258, 259
Taiping Rebellion (1850–64) 454, 533
Taiwan 549
Taj Mahal 334, 335
Takamori, Saigo 429–30, 434–6
Taliban 546, 547
Tang dynasty 226
Tangut 222
Tarsus 159–60
Tatars 220, 221, 289
taxation, Roman 137
tea 448
telescope, invention of 312
Tenochtitlán 266
Teotihuacán (Mexico) 164
Teresa of Avila, St 261
'terracotta army' 120, 125
Tetzel, Johann 274
Teutonic knights 193, 219, 270, 282
Thatcher, Margaret 529
Thebes 44, 58, 82, 102
Theodora 186
Theodoric 187
Theodosius, Emperor 129
Thermidorian Reaction 370
Theseus 48
Thirty Tyrants 98–9
Thirty Years War 279, 320
Thor (god) 35
Thucydides 77
Tiamat (goddess) 33
Tiananmen Square
    mourning of Zhou Enlai (1976) 543–4
    protest (1989) 543, 544
Tiberius, Emperor 129, 155
Tibet 549
Tigris river 32, 40
Timbuktu 211, 212
tobacco 291
Tokugawa 292–7, 430–3
Toledo 201
Tolpuddle Martyrs 402
Tolstoy, Leo 407–8, 410, 412–13, 414–15
Tomyris 67–8

Tordesillas, Treaty of (1494) 259
Toscanelli, Paolo 256
Toussaint L'Ouverture 373–4, 377–8, 380
Tower of Babel 65
towns, Neolithic 24–7, 29
trade 56, 251–2, 432
trade unions 402, 403
Trafalgar, battle of (1805) 371
Trajan, Emperor 155
Trakhaniot, George 284
Trojan War 54, 55, 58–9
Troy 57–8, 59
Truman, President Harry 509, 525
Tsushima, battle of (1905) 436
Tuareg 210
Tuchman, Barbara 458–9, 461
tulip mania (Netherlands) 301–2, 303–6
Tull, Jethro 390
Turing, Alan 555, 556
Turing test 555
Turkey (modern) 521
Turkey/Turks, Ottoman *see* Ottoman Empire
Tyre 60

U-boat warfare (First World War) 459–60, 461, 482
Uganda 524
Uli, Mansa (King) 212
Uluburun shipwreck 55
al-Umari 212
Umayyad dynasty 194–5, 198
Unita 524
United Nations 503, 563
United Provinces 302
United States 525
    arms race with Soviet Union 523
    capitalism 426, 429
    countries intervened in during Cold War 523
    and Cuban Missile Crisis 526
    expansion of 420–1, 428
    and First World War 460–1, 494
    global market domination 501
    and industrialization 404, 406
    isolationism 483
    and Israel 546
    and Louisiana Purchase 351, 421
    and Marshall Plan 504, 521
    nuclear weapons 529
    and prohibition 490
    railways 406, 422, 425
    relations between blacks and white Americans 428

    relations with China 528
    and Second World War 495, 497–9, 501–2
    and slavery 351, 420, 421–2, 423
    and Vietnam War 521, 526, 527–8
    war with Mexico 421
    and women's suffrage 489–90
    see also American Civil War; American War of Independence
Universal Declaration of Human Rights 563
universities 313
Ur 36, 62
Uruk 33, 36

vaccinations 559, 562
    and smallpox 382–4
Valley of the Kings 41
Vandals 190
Varangian Guard 204, 235
variolation 381–2
Vasari, Giorgio 244
Vatican, list of banned books 316, 317
Venice/Venetians 135, 192, 220, 229–30, 231, 237–8, 243, 311–12
Venus 35
Verrocchio, Andrea del 243, 244, 246
Vespasian, Emperor 155
Vespucci, Amerigo 256
Victoria, Queen 440, 442, 452
Vietnam War 521, 526, 527–8
Vikings 203–8, 251, 254
    and Byzantium 204, 206, 207, 235
    key to expansion of 205
    longships 204
Vinge, Vernor 557
violence, in twentieth century 469–70
Visigoths 190, 194, 202
Vlad the Impaler 252, 281–2
Vladimir 206–7
Volkonsky, Sergei 412, 413
Voltaire 337–40, 344–5
    Candide 344
    Lettres Philosophiques 339
von Katte, Hans Hermann 341
voting equality 489

Walesa, Lech 530
war
    as driver of change 53, 54–5, 56
War of the Austrian Succession 319
war elephants 116, 134, 143
War of the Spanish Succession 319
'war on terror' 548

warrior class, emergence of 34
Warsaw Pact 522
Washington, George 420
water management
    Nazca 166, 167
    Sabaeans 176
water shortages 560
Waterloo, battle of 371
Watson, Peter 164
Watt, James 394–400
Waugh, Evelyn 48
Wedgwood, C.V. 278
Wellington, Duke of 371
Wells, H.G. 488
Wendi, Emperor 188
White, Matthew 470
William III (William of Orange) 326–8
Wilson, President Woodrow 458, 459, 461, 483
Wisselbank 299
Wittenberg 271, 273
Wodin (god) 35
Woman Rebel, The 487
women
    and birth control 486–9
    Gaulish 140–1
    Roman 132
    and voting rights 489
workhouses 402
Wren, Christopher 329
writing
    evolvement of in Mesopotamia 33
    and Phoenician alphabet 60, 61

Wu-Feng, Captain 292
Wynants, Pieter 301

Xanadu *see* Shangdu
Xenophon 7
Xeres 75–6
Xia dynasty 37, 39–40
Xiongnu 158, 218

Yahweh 63, 64, 65, 66, 130
Yeats, W.B. 234
Yellow River 37, 40
Yeltsin, Boris 530
Yermak Timofeyevich 288–9
Younger Dryas 21–2
Yuan dynasty 219
Yuan Shikai 532
Yugoslavia 484, 523, 524
    break-up of 546
Yupanqui, Emperor 265

Zaire 524
Zaragoza, Treaty of 259
Zheng, Emperor 120–2, 123–5, 156, 180
Zhou dynasty 39, 88, 89–90
Zhou Enlai 363, 540, 543
ziggurats 32–3
Zimbabwe 210, 525
Zimmermann, Arthur 458–9, 460, 461–2, 463, 464
Zimmermann telegram 460–1
Zoroastrianism 66
Zozo *see* Voltaire

Picture Acknowledgements

Page 4 – top: © Peter Horree / Alamy; middle: © Lebrecht Music and Arts Photo Library / Alamy; bottom: © Alinari / The Bridgeman Art Library.

Page 5 – top: © Ancient Art & Architecture Collection Ltd / Alamy; bottom left: © Masterpics / Alamy; bottom right: © Victoria & Albert Museum, London / The Bridgeman Art Library.

Page 6 – top: 1738, common domain, Wiki; bottom: © Mary Evans Picture Library / Alamy.

Page 7 – top: © Pictorial Press Ltd / Alamy; bottom left: © Dixson Galleries, State Library of New South Wales / The Bridgeman Art Library; bottom right: © The Art Archive / Alamy.

Page 8 – top: © Mary Evans Picture Library / Alamy; bottom: © World History Archive / Alamy.

Section Three

Page 1 – top: © Pictorial Press Ltd / Alamy; bottom: © Private Collection / Archives Charmet / The Bridgeman Art Library.

Page 2 – top: © Niday Picture Library / Alamy; bottom: © David Cole / Alamy.

Page 3 – top and bottom: © World History Archive / Alamy; middle: © GL Archive / Alamy.

Page 4 – top left and bottom: © Pictorial Press Ltd / Alamy; top right: © David Cole / Alamy.

Page 5 – top: © Dinodia Photos / Alamy; bottom: © Pictorial Press Ltd / Alamy.

Page 6 – top left: © Pictorial Press Ltd / Alamy; top right: © Photos 12 / Alamy; bottom: © Marmaduke St. John / Alamy.

Page 7 – top: © AFP / Getty Images; bottom: © Time & Life Pictures / Getty Images.

Page 8 – top: © Gamma-Rapho / Getty Images; bottom: © AFP / Getty Images.